Third Edition

Delinquency and Juvenile Justice in American Society

Third Edition

Delinquency and Juvenile Justice in American Society

Randall G. Shelden
Emily I. Troshynski
University of Nevada–Las Vegas

WAVELAND

PRESS, INC.

Long Grove, Illinois

For information about this book, contact:
Waveland Press, Inc.
4180 IL Route 83, Suite 101
Long Grove, IL 60047-9580
(847) 634-0081
info@waveland.com
www.waveland.com

Preface

Writers of textbooks, no matter what the subject, never know if there will be another edition. There is no way of predicting how many colleagues will assign the book for a class. The opportunity to create another edition, and in this case with a new coauthor, is gratifying.

Revising a textbook may seem like a simple process—updating some statistics for the tables and graphs and adding a few recent studies on the subjects covered. When teaching our classes on delinquency, we are constantly reminded that trends are no longer "recent" within a year or two. Race and inequality remain central themes in the exploration of juvenile delinquency, but other aspects of the topic have changed significantly since the previous edition.

One continuing trend is the decline in juvenile crime. That background has facilitated the search for alternatives to the traditional processing of juveniles through the juvenile justice system. California, for example, has evolved from an ineffective system mired in violence to working toward eliminating all its congregate facilities. Recently, San Francisco has taken the bold and unprecedented step of voting to close juvenile hall (detention center). Whether or not this will be successful remains to be seen. The Supreme Court continues to rely on neuroscience to determine the constitutionality of punishing juveniles. Research has demonstrated, for example, that zero-tolerance policies are counterproductive. Similarly, school suspensions have abated in some districts, allowing some relief from the school to prison pipeline. These changes have improved disproportionate minority contact, although more progress is needed.

We thank the thousands of researchers and writers who make the writing of a textbook possible. We also thank our colleagues at UNLV for creating a nurturing environment. Finally, Randy thanks his wife Virginia and stepdaughter Marcie for their support in yet another textbook revision. And he gives special thanks to graduate assistant Sheila Carver for her excellent work on this and other projects. Emily also thanks Sheila and another amazing graduate student assistant, Ashley Shank, for their comments and thoughts about helpful discussion questions.

Contents

Introduction

Sensational media stories ("if it bleeds, it leads") prime public opinion to embrace policies with little contemplation of the consequences. In the late 1990s, inaccurate predictions of a wave of superpredators—impulsive, remorseless young people who would commit violent crimes and be unresponsive to any type of intervention—frightened the public. The policies created to address a crisis that never happened changed the landscape of the juvenile justice system.[1] Youths who engaged in behavior including shoplifting were caught in a punitive system that judged them delinquent, housed them in large youth prisons, and separated them from their families, their education, and their communities.

Juvenile superpredators became a repeated theme.[2] The news media, along with politicians from coast to coast, suggested an epidemic of youth violence. Stories of violent crime committed by younger and younger perpetrators proliferated. Media stories about violent youths and random, innocent victims constructed images that continue to perpetuate myths related to juvenile delinquency.[3] A more accurate analysis tells us something else: while a few juveniles do commit horrific crimes, such incidents are the exception rather than the rule. Serious violent crimes are committed predominately by adults. In fact, the most serious forms of violence are committed by adult white males—such as Stephen Paddock shooting from his room in the Mandalay Bay resort at people attending a music festival in Las Vegas in October 2017, killing 58 and injuring more than 500.

THE REALITY OF JUVENILE DELINQUENCY

When we speak of the phenomenon of juvenile delinquency, we are referring to a wide variety of mostly harmless behaviors, often done on the spur of the moment, involving a group of youngsters with no serious harm to victims. The typical delinquent does not make the headlines, and he (most of the offenses are committed by males, although a substantial minority—about 25%—are committed by females) is rarely arrested and rarely makes an appearance in one of the thousands of juvenile courts in the country. Even among those referred to court, at least half never come back on another offense.

This section looks briefly at some of the myths about juveniles and the crimes they commit.

Juvenile justice policies have historically been built on a foundation of myths. From the "dangerous classes" of the nineteenth century to the superpredators of the late twentieth century, government responses to juvenile crime have been dominated by fear of the young, anxiety about immigrants or racial minorities, and hatred of the poor.[4]

By far the most destructive myth about juvenile crime was the creation of the superpredator myth.[5] Images of barbarous children with no conscience dovetailed with another media myth about a generation of babies born with severe neurological problems because their mothers used crack cocaine. The superpredator myth fueled legislation such as The Violent and Repeat Juvenile Offender Act of 1997 at the federal level. Forty-seven states amended laws on juvenile crime to weaken confidentiality protections and to lower the ages at which juveniles could be prosecuted in adult court. A number of other myths, none of which are supported by empirical evidence, swirl around juvenile crime.

Myth 1: Today's youth are more criminal than ever.

As figure 2-1 in chapter 2 makes clear, the overall crime rate for youths has declined dramatically. The juvenile violent crime (murder, rape, robbery, and aggravated assault) arrest rate reached a historic low in 2015: 143.3 versus a peak of 477.8 in 1994 and the previous low of 259.7 in 1984.[6] The rate in 2017 was 144.4. Fewer teens are being locked up than at any time in nearly 20 years.[7] The juvenile arrest rate for all offenses reached 8,476 per 100,000 persons ages 10–17 in 1996; it declined 72% to 2,408 in 2017.[8] That year, 92.3% of all individuals arrested were adults (18 or older)—adults accounted for 89.9% of violent crime arrests, 86.4% of property crimes, and 94.2% of drug abuse arrests.[9]

Myth 2: As the number of teenagers rises, so does the crime rate.

The number of teenagers has little to do with overall crime. For example, one study noted that the young male population in Los Angeles in the late 1980s declined, but homicides increased rapidly. The researchers also found that between 1980 and 2005 the number of juveniles in the population of Los Angeles County rose by 34%, while their overall crime rate declined.[10] In 1990, there were 64.2 million people younger than 18 in the United States, increasing to 72.4 million in 2000, followed by 74.1 million in 2010, and 73.6 million in 2016.[11] Crime rates have fallen since the early 1990s.[12]

The fallacy of this myth played a prominent role in creating the superpredator myth. John DiIulio predicted there would be 270,000 juvenile superpredators by 2010. Franklin Zimring deconstructed the numbers to determine the basis of the estimate. DiIulio based his estimates on studies claiming that 6% of boys in Philadelphia were chronic delinquents.[13] Chronic does not necessarily mean violent, and no study of youth population supported the projection of predatory violence. DiIulio had looked at projections that the number of boys under 18 in the United States would increase by 4.5 million by 2010; 6% of that number is 270,000. Zimring pointed out that the numbers didn't make sense on a number of levels. If 6% of males under 18 were superpredators, there would have been 1.9 million in 1995—twice the number of children referred to juvenile court that year for any reason. In addition, 93% of juvenile arrests for violence occur after age 13. More of the projected increase in the juvenile population would have been under age 6 than over age 13 in 2010.

Myth 3: Youth of today are using more guns and committing more violent crime than ever.

This myth is based on purely anecdotal evidence, especially the headline stories about the rare youth who uses a gun in a killing. As mentioned in myth 1, the juvenile violent crime rate is at historic lows. Youths under the age of 18 comprise approximately 25% of the population in the United States. In 2017, there were 14,384 arrests of people younger than 18 for carrying or possessing a weapon—11% of weapons violation arrests.[14] In 2017, 4.8% of high school students carried a gun at least one day during the 12 months before the survey.[15] Juveniles are far more likely to be killed by their own parents at home than killed by one of their peers at school by a ratio of 15 to 1. A related myth is that the rise of "gangsta rap" has caused a rise in homicides by youth. Quite the opposite is true. Throughout the 1990s the number of rap music albums sold doubled (from 74 million to 125 million), while the number of teenage males arrested for murder decreased by half.[16]

Myth 4: Teenagers are the biggest part of the drug problem.

Adolescent (ages 12 to 17) admissions for substance abuse treatment declined 47% from 2004 to 2014. Marijuana and alcohol accounted for more than 80% of adolescent admissions in each of those years. Opiate admissions represented 2% of the admissions from 2004 to 2008 and 3% the remaining years.[17] In 2016, 7.9% of any illicit drug users in the previous month were ages 12 through 17 compared to 23.2% of current users ages 18 through 25.[18] In 2000 juveniles accounted for almost 13% of all drug arrests versus 6.3% in 2016.[19]

Myth 5: Youths who commit murder and other serious crimes need to be treated as adults.

"Old enough to do the crime, old enough to do the time" might work as a bumper sticker, but it is terrible public policy.[20] Research has found that incarceration of youth for more than a handful of months—even within juvenile incarceration facilities—increases the risk of repeat offenses and of new crimes against persons. Juveniles held in adult facilities are at increased risk of sexual, physical, and psychological abuse. Teenagers are placed in solitary confinement or segregation to protect them from predatory adults; their suicide rates are 36 times higher than the adults in the same facilities. They experience deprivation, violence, exposure to antisocial adults, and limited opportunities for social skill development. The vast majority of youth will eventually be returned to their communities, and the harms of incarceration increase the risks to the public. There has been a movement to raise the age for juvenile court jurisdiction. New York and North Carolina for years used 15 as the upper limit for juvenile court. Both states passed laws in 2017 that raised the age to 18; Missouri did the same in 2018. Four states (Georgia, Michigan, Texas, and Wisconsin) have not changed their upper limit from 16.[21]

Juvenile status includes confidentiality and protections against the loss of civil rights. The life chances of youths processed as adults are greatly reduced compared with those of youths processed in the juvenile justice system.[22] Historically, judicial waiver was the method for transferring cases from the juvenile court to adult court, and there are procedural safeguards that include the right to a hearing, representation by counsel, and a statement of reasons for the waiver. The number of delinquency cases waived to criminal court more than doubled between 1985 and 1994 before declining 75% through 2015. In 2015, there were 3,200 waivers; 50% were for person offenses, 31.2% for property offenses, 9.4% for drug offenses, and 9.4% public order.[23] There are, however, nonjudicial transfer laws where certain crimes, by statute, are excluded from juvenile court (statutory exclusion) and transfer laws in which the prosecutor decides the jurisdiction (direct file). The extent of juveniles tried in adult courts is unknown; 22 states do not report any of their transfers. Of the 28 states and the District of Columbia that do, only 5 list judicial waivers separately from direct filings by prosecutors.[24]

Myth 6: Once juveniles commit a crime, they will not change their criminal behavior.

Neuroscience and social science debunk this myth.[25] Research in neurobiology and developmental psychology has established that the part of the brain needed for impulse control, decision making, and long-term planning is not fully developed until the mid-20s for many people. Young adults are more susceptible to peer pressure; they are less future oriented; and they are more volatile in emotionally charged settings.[26] Most youth who engaged in violent misconduct during adolescence will age out of the behavior.[27] Jay Giedd, a leading neuroscientist who studies adolescent development, said impulsive juveniles commonly progress to adults who weigh the consequences of their actions. "The capacity for change is amazing."[28]

In *Roper v. Simmons*, the Supreme Court barred the execution of juveniles for capital crimes committed when younger than 18. The court cited neuroscience research that shows juveniles have not yet developed the capacity to postpone gratification, to think clearly about consequences, and to resist impulses. The Court used the same reasoning in *Miller v. Alabama* that banned sentences to life without the possibility of parole for capital crimes committed by youth under the age of 18. Neuroscience and fifty years of psychological data on how and why kids differ from adults offer evidence that bad choices made by adolescents need not define a lifetime.

Myth 7: There are options other than crime; juvenile delinquents choose to be bad.

Most adolescents who commit crimes have been exposed to multiple childhood adversities—poverty, family and community violence, parental incarceration, parental substance abuse and mental illness, and neglect or abuse.[29] Participation in sports and other extracurricular activities can help youths avoid harmful behavior. The quantity and quality of community resources vary widely. Even when there are educational and vocational opportunities, gaining access may be problematic for adolescents who lack family guidance and support.

NORMAL ADOLESCENT BEHAVIOR OR DEVIANCE?

These and other myths about juvenile crime will be discussed throughout this book as we survey the various behaviors typically committed by individuals legally classified as juveniles (in most states those under the age of 18). Surveys have consistently shown that virtually all youngsters commit some act that could theoretically result in an arrest by the police and a referral to the local juvenile court. In this sense, there is nothing "deviant" about delinquency—it is very common adolescent behavior. When the offenses involve serious loss of property or serious harms to other human beings and when they are repeatedly committed over an extended period of time, then the behavior extends beyond adolescent misjudgments.

It is important to remember, however, that persistent delinquents—some call them chronic delinquents—do not appear out of nowhere for no apparent reason. With few exceptions, these youths have been victimized repeatedly, often starting as young as infancy. Those who work with these youngsters can corroborate a sad fact: the victimizer of today is the victim of yesterday.

Xavier McElrath-Bey was sentenced to 25 years in prison for murder at the age of 15. At the age of 13, he had lived with his mother, a foster mother, a group home, on the streets, and in abandoned buildings. He had been arrested 19 times and shot in the face. Before the murder conviction, he had 6 convictions ranging from armed robbery to aggravated battery. McElrath-Bey said "When I was growing up in my neighborhood, I saw people getting shot and beaten up. I saw dead bodies. And it gave me a general sense of uneasiness and fear. I was on constant alert. I had to join the gang to have some semblance of safety."[30] He was convicted of murder after luring a 14-year-old rival gang member into an abandoned building where older teens stabbed and beat him to death. He spent most of his 17th year in solitary confinement before resolving to change his life. While in prison, he realized he was responsible for the death of another person. While he knew he could never change what he had done, he could try to compensate by helping other children to keep them from dying or being imprisoned. He earned a bachelor's degree in social science while in prison and was released at age 26. He earned a master's degree in human services, eventually entering the field of restorative justice.

Cultural Influences

What also needs to be pointed out is that the nature of the crime problem in the United States is directly related to our culture. The overall rate of crime—especially violent crime—is much higher in this country than in any other in the world. Any serious effort to reduce the problem must confront this fact and seriously consider some drastic changes in our way of life and our attitudes about children.

Even the most hardened youngsters can be salvaged. The authors of a very unique book, *Reclaiming Youth at Risk*, borrow heavily from Native American culture in exploring positive youth development.[31] Their circle of courage model is based on four universal growth needs of children: belonging, mastery, independence, and generosity. Their innovative approaches to building relationships with youths, fostering their self-esteem, and instilling positive values has been adopted by hundreds of schools and programs. We will discuss positive youth development in more detail in the final chapter of this book.

It is time that we consider that we adults are just as much a part of the problem as are troubled youths, perhaps more so. If we make even a cursory list of the incredible harms adults have committed over the centuries, the misdeeds of our modern adolescents—including the most hardened who sit in our jails, detention centers, and residential facilities—pale by comparison. In short, if we want to know where the answers lie and where to begin to look for solutions, we should start by looking in the mirror. We should ask: Is there anything that *I* can do differently? Is there something wrong with *my* attitudes, *my* beliefs, and *my* actions that contribute to the problem? If we want some answers, we should start the search *within ourselves*.

Fear Colors Reaction

The reaction to the offenses of young people is way out of proportion to the harm caused. One such overreaction occurred in Las Vegas, home of the authors. It was well publicized and involved a nine-year-old boy accused of vandalism. His "crime" consisted of writing his initials, the names of some of his friends, and making some other markings in a cement sidewalk next to a construction site. According to testimony in the case, the child said that one or two workers at this site told him that he could write on the sidewalk, and so he did. The police came to his school and arrested him in front of his classmates—handcuffs and all! One of the district attorneys charged him with a felony, calling his behavior a very serious crime. The child was eventually placed on probation. This was an example of *zero tolerance* mentality, which we will revisit in later chapters.

The crimes that prompt public fears are rare but receive intense media coverage. School shootings or drive-by shootings "stick in your mind forever and break your heart: kids killing kids, lives wasted, and lives lost due to teen violence."[32] The zeal to punish violent, hardened teenagers conflicted with the traditional role of juvenile courts to decide age-appropriate interventions and to rehabilitate.

The crimes committed were considered too serious to be handled by juvenile courts that could only supervise offenders until a specified upper age limit.

In the tough-on-crime climate of 2000, California voters passed Proposition 21 that gave prosecutors the discretion to direct file serious crimes committed by juveniles in adult court. Prosecutors had 48 hours after an arrest to decide whether the juvenile or criminal court would have jurisdiction. From 2006 to 2016, black youth were 8.5 times more likely than white youth to be tried as adults; Latino youth were almost 3 times more likely; 68% of the 10,298 cases were direct filed.[33]

Neurological science mapping how the brain develops and the rehabilitative potential of juveniles paved the way for reform. The US Supreme Court, lawmakers, and criminal justice experts recognized fundamental differences between adolescents and adults. Many states revised some of their punitive statutes. In November 2016, California voters passed Proposition 57, which ended direct file by prosecutors; 64% of voters approved the measure—almost the identical percentage that approved Proposition 21 sixteen years earlier. Proposition 57 explicitly emphasized rehabilitation and made developmental milestones and the capacity for change central to any judicial transfer decision. After Proposition 57 was passed, there was a 31% decline in transferring juvenile cases to adult court over 2015 levels.[34]

Critics of direct transfer and judicial waivers have repeatedly noted that they target mostly the poor and especially racial minorities. The general issue of race will be one of the central themes of this book. Indeed, one cannot realistically examine the problem of delinquency—especially our reaction to it—without considering race. The war on drugs and the war on gangs launched during the 1980s became blatant examples of some of the most racist policies in US history. As will be pointed out in several chapters, these *wars* (why is it that we so often use the war metaphor?) have consistently targeted racial minorities and the poor. Whether categorized as collateral damage, the result of unintended consequences, or the primary intention of those who established the policies, the effects on minorities and the poor have been devastating.

There are many examples of fear of crime spurring the passage of punitive legislation. The state of Oregon, traditionally known as a liberal state, passed Measure 11 in 1994. The Measure conflicts with contemporary understanding of brain science.[35] Other states have revised their statutes in light of such evidence, but Oregon has not. Measure 11 was passed in a climate of fear of crime accompanied with an eroding trust in the criminal justice system It created lengthy, mandatory minimum prison sentences for 16 (adding 6 more crimes in 1997) person-on-person crimes, eliminated early release, and created mandatory waiver for youths 15 years or older. Black youth comprise 1.8% of the general population in Oregon but 15.5% of Measure 11 indictments. Measure 11 offenders require close custody, which can cost almost $96,000 annually per juvenile. Cases involving sex crimes account for one-third of the Measure 11 indictments of youths. If convicted of a class A felony sex offense in juvenile court, the offender is eligible for relief from the sex registry after two years. If tried in adult court, the offender must register for a minimum of 10 years after completing the sentence (6.25 to 8.3 years) and post-prison supervision.

When reforms have been implemented in various states, they have primarily concentrated on nonviolent crimes; the public can sympathize with minor youthful mistakes and recognize the need for less punitive responses. For those who commit serious crimes, however, there are very strong, diverse opinions. How should one address the extraordinary human and social costs of murder? Beliefs about just punishment are contentious. Impassioned advocates for victims decry leniency, while ardent defenders of juveniles say that condemning a child to lifetime imprisonment essentially takes another life. Public opinion shifts between those who believe children who commit serious crimes should be tried and sentenced as adults and those who believe that committing an adult crime does not turn a child into an adult.

The documentary, *They Call Us Monsters*, follows 3 boys taking a 20-week screenwriting class at the Compound, a high-security facility for juveniles awaiting trials on violent crimes in Los Angeles. To their advocates, they are juveniles. In the criminal justice system, they will be tried as adults. To their victims, they are monsters.[36] Jarad Nava was charged with 4 attempted murders in a drive-by shooting when he was 16; one of his victims is 17 and permanently confined to a wheelchair. Juan Gamez was also age 16 when charged with first-degree murder; he has an infant son and faces deportation even if not convicted. Antonio Hernandez, addicted to methamphetamine, was charged with 2 attempted murders at age 14; halfway through the screenwriting class, he was released with time served. Returning to his neighborhood, he resumed the same gang life and drug use that contributed to his incarceration. (Jarad and Juan were both convicted at trial; Jarad was sentenced to 162 years and will be eligible for parole in 2037; Juan was sentenced to 90 years and will be eligible for parole in 2027.[37])

Ben Lear works with InsideOUT Writers, an organization that uses writing programs as rehabilitation for incarcerated inmates. He sat in on the screenwriting class. He found it impossible to reconcile the age and demeanor—kind, inquisitive, thoughtful, and articulate—of the boys with the crimes they were accused of committing. He decided to make the documentary to introduce people to a population that is usually hidden from public view.[38] He found himself repeatedly alternating between finding the boys endearing and being horrified by their crimes. He says the audience may look at the boys as sociopaths but encourages people to go deeper and entertain the idea that they could be temporary sociopaths.[39] The documentary raises issues about the responsibilities of society to the offenders and to their victims—and whether the juveniles have the capacity to change and deserve a second chance.

CONSERVATIVE, LIBERAL AND RADICAL VIEWS OF CRIME

In order to sort through the constructions and solutions discussed in this text, we need to be aware of ideologies that influence various perspectives. The media is one of many sources that present conflicting viewpoints. The reality perceived by various parties is shaped by the lenses through which it is viewed.

Crime has always been and continues to be a hot political topic—the subject of countless commentaries by pundits and almost always an issue in state and local elections. Various perspectives and proposals are offered by both politicians and by scholars. These views fall into three political and ideological perspectives. The two most common are the conservative view and the liberal view. The radical view is rarely expressed among politicians, although certain aspects of this perspective can be found among the various proposals for reducing crime. The concise summary of these views is not an exhaustive overview but rather a primer on these perspectives.[40]

The Conservative View

From a conservative perspective, democracy and the free enterprise system are working well, with most problems caused by individuals or groups of individuals who seem, mainly because of some character flaw(s), unable to succeed within the overall system. In essence, some individuals or groups make bad or irrational choices (it is assumed everyone has free will) that put them in problematic circumstances. The most effective way to address social problems such as crime is through the economic system. For example, cutting taxes on corporations is viewed as an incentive to create jobs, which will offer opportunities to earn money and thus avoid crime. The conservative view generally assumes that less government is better, except for enforcing the laws. The use of tax dollars for social programs to assist the general public is to be avoided whenever possible. Equality can be achieved mainly through hard work.[41] Part of the conservative philosophy is a strong belief in rugged individualism that incorporates the idea that one does not need help from others or the government.

The term conservatism has its roots in the Latin word *conservare*, meaning to save or preserve. Although the perspective has had a variety of meanings over the years (as has liberalism), it generally refers to a philosophy that supports tradition and the status quo. One definition of conservatism is: "Preference for the existing order of society—an opposition to all efforts to bring about rapid or fundamental change."[42]

The linguist George Lakoff compares conservatism to the traditional nuclear family with a strict father model—authoritarian and hierarchical. In order to become a good and moral person, a child must learn to obey the rules and to respect authority. Proper behavior is taught through the use or threat of punishment. Within such a system "the exercise of authority is itself moral; that is, it is moral to reward obedience and punish disobedience."[43] More importantly, rewarding someone who has not developed self-discipline is immoral. As a result, conservatives generally do not endorse welfare, affirmative action, or lenient punishments, all of which are considered rewards for laziness, failure to excel, and deviance. There is often an erroneous assumption that those who are rich and famous became so through their own efforts, with little or no help from others.

Moral strength can be seen as a metaphor.[44] The metaphor suggests that the world is divided into good and evil. In order to stand up to evil, one must be morally strong; one becomes morally strong through a system of rewards and punishments that teach self-discipline. Crime and deviance are the result of moral weakness and indulgence. Teenage sex, drug use, and other deviant behaviors stem from lack of self-control. A person with proper self-discipline should be able to resist temptation. Those who do not must be, and deserve to be, punished.

The conservative view of crime and criminal justice can be summarized very simply. People commit crime because they think they can get away with it, largely because the pleasure they get from committing the crime is greater than the potential pain they would receive if caught and punished.[45] This is the basis of deterrence theory. From this perspective, people refrain from committing crime because of *fear* of getting caught and punished. In order to reduce crime, the pain must be increased so that it is greater than the pleasure received from committing the crime. If we increase the odds of getting caught and the severity of punishment, potential criminals will think twice before committing the crime—"if you can't do the time, don't do the crime." Conservatives see criminals as having defective choice mechanisms. Specifically, they believe obeying rules and going to school are essential elements in eventually earning a living and becoming a productive member of society. Choosing not to participate in these behaviors leads to delinquency, substance abuse, crime, violence, or any number of deviant combinations.

The Liberal View

Liberals view the relationship between democracy and free enterprise as problematic, with most benefits accruing to a small minority that has created a huge gap in both income and wealth. The system does not work for some individuals, who suffer from problems with the social structure rather than problems created by their own choice. They should, therefore, be helped by those more fortunate. Liberals see plenty of flaws in the system and therefore support the use of tax dollars for various social programs for work, housing, health care, and so on. Liberals see the goal of government as providing for the general welfare of society.

In contrast to conservatism's strict father model, Lakoff sees liberalism as centered around a nurturant parent model in which both parents share responsibilities.[46] Nurturing requires empathy for others and helping those who need help. Social responsibility is a core value that stresses concern for the well-being of the community and the entire society. Rather than acting like an *authoritarian* parent, liberals stress the importance of acting like an *authoritative* parent, guiding children based on reasoning. Children develop through positive relationships to others; obedience is the result of respect not out of the fear of punishment.

Liberal responses to crime differ from conservative responses. For example, the liberal viewpoint believes prisons should focus on rehabilitation via education, work, and social skill enhancement. Prison rehabilitation should be followed by help after release for problems related to housing, schools, health clinics, etc. For liberals, this systemic approach, although costly at the outset, is the most effective way to reduce crime and, at the same time, improve society.[47]

The Radical View

Various terms are used to describe a third perspective—*radical, critical,* or *Marxist*. From this viewpoint, the problem of crime stems from the very nature of capitalism. Capitalist societies are characterized by conflict—between classes (e.g., labor vs. management), races (black vs. white), and gender. Inequality is created and perpetuated by the capitalist system, largely because profits are concentrated in the hands of a few. In fact, in recent years there has been the greatest upward shift of wealth and income since the 1920s.[48]

From this perspective, government represents the interests of those in power.. Karl Marx is the best known proponent of the radical view. He saw capitalism as a system that exploits workers for the benefit of the owners. For Marx, true democracy cannot coexist with capitalism. In his words, the state is the instrument of the ruling class. Although Marx was not particularly focused on crime, his analysis can be viewed as tying the plight of the criminal to the plight of the general, exploited society. Crime is the result of living in a system where access to success goals is limited and even restricted. A radical perspective focuses on "those social structures and forces that produce both the greed of the inside trader as well as the brutality of the rapist or the murderer. And it places those structures in their proper context: the material conditions of class struggle under a capitalist mode of production."[49]

Social policy is essentially the management of varying interests. When viewpoints conflict, there is a tendency to dismiss those who do not agree with us as misinformed rather than reflecting on the foundations for the differences of opinion. Rarely is there a single answer to complex social problems. An engaged participant can look at the evidence presented and evaluate the foundation on which it is based. Does the argument present potential for resolving a problem, or does it contribute to myths about issues that create fear and misunderstanding? Misinformation is as readily accessible as reliable information, and the Internet disseminates both at dizzying speeds. Without the necessary background, we may make poor decisions that ignore the long-term implications of policies that address difficult issues. We hope this brief introduction to three perspectives help you navigate the complexities of the nature of juvenile delinquency and potential policies to address problems.

UNDERSTANDING JUVENILE DELINQUENCY

Before we can seriously consider any solutions, we must begin by first trying to develop a general *understanding* of the phenomenon of juvenile delinquency. This is the overall aim of this book. Chapter 1 reviews the historical record of how the problem of delinquency began to be defined and the responses to it during the early years of the nineteenth century. The history of our response to the behaviors committed by children has not been a very glorious one. In fact, adult society has imposed on its youth some of the most egregious harms ever inflicted on one group of people. We find the roots of our somewhat contradictory responses to delinquency in the early days of the nineteenth century: benevolence mixed with loathing and cruelty; a "velvet glove" cloaked in an "iron fist." And the targets of the most repressive policies have consistently been those deemed the most dangerous—starting with Irish immigrants in the early nineteenth century and ending with African Americans and Hispanics in the twenty-first century.

Chapters 2 and 3 explore delinquency in some detail, starting with a general survey of how much delinquency there is, its nature, and the variety of behaviors labeled delinquent. Part II looks at two specific forms of delinquency: gang delinquency and female delinquency.

Part III considers the very important question of why there is delinquency and crime. The most common theories of delinquency are summarized in chapters 6 and 7. Chapter 8 explores one of the most important variables related to crime and delinquency—social class and inequality. As will be noted, U.S. society is highly unequal; in fact, it is the most unequal among all the industrialized democracies. Inequality determines not only rates of juvenile offending but also, and especially, the official response. Chapters 9 and 10 present a detailed look at two of our most important institutions that are strongly correlated with delinquency: the family and the schools.

Part IV of the book explores some of the most common responses to crimes committed by our youth. Chapter 11 describes the processing of cases from the police to the juvenile court. Chapter 12 explores the double standard of juvenile justice with a close look at how girls fare within this system. Chapter 13 takes a critical look at juvenile institutions, with an emphasis on their failure for more than 150 years to adequately deal with the problem.

The book ends with some suggestions in chapter 14 to reduce the number of children labeled delinquent and a discussion of some alternative responses. We hope the reader will come away with a better understanding of the phenomenon of juvenile delinquency. Ideally, if we can combine our understanding and energies to make the world a better place for children, everyone will benefit.

Notes

[1] Krista Larson and Hernan Carvente, "Juvenile Justice Systems Still Grappling with Legacy of the 'Superpredator' Myth," New York: Vera Institute of Justice, January 24, 2017.

[2] Victor Kappeler and Gary Potter, *The Mythology of Crime and Criminal Justice*, 5th ed. (Long Grove, IL: Waveland Press, 2018).

[3] Gayle M. Rhineberger-Dunn. "Myth versus Reality: Comparing the Depiction of Juvenile Delinquency in Metropolitan Newspapers with Arrest Data," *Sociological Inquiry*, 2013, 83(3): 473–497.

4 Barry Krisberg, *Juvenile Justice and Delinquency* (Thousand Oaks: CA, Sage, 2018), 1.

5 Ibid.

6 Statistical Briefing Book, Online, October 22, 2018, http://www.ojjdp.gov/ojstatbb/crime/JAR_Display.asp?ID=qa05218&seloffenses=35

7 Melissa Sickmund and Charles Puzzanchera, "Juvenile Offenders and Victims: 2014 National Report," Pittsburgh, PA: National Center for Juvenile Justice, December 2014.

8 Office of Juvenile Justice and Delinquency Prevention, "Law Enforcement and Juvenile Crime: Juvenile Arrest Rate Trends," Washington, DC: Author, December 6, 2017, http://www.ojjdp.gov/ojstatbb/crime/JAR_Display.asp?ID=qa05200

9 Federal Bureau of Investigation, "Crime in the United States, 2017," Washington, DC: Author, 2018, table 38.

10 Mike Males, Dan Macallair and Megan Doyle Corcoran (2006). "Testing Incapacitation Theory: Youth Crime and Incarceration in California." San Francisco: Center on Juvenile and Criminal Justice; see also an updated version of this paper in: R. G. Shelden and D. Macallair (eds.), *Juvenile Justice in America: Problems and Prospects* (Long Grove, IL: Waveland Press, 2008), 63–81.

11 Charles Puzzanchera, Anthony Sladky, and W. Kang (2017). Easy Access to Juvenile Populations 1990–2016, http://www.ojjdp.gov/ojstatbb/ezapop/

12 John Gramlich, "5 Facts about Crime in the United States," Washington, DC: Pew Research Center, January 30, 2018.

13 Kappeler and Potter, *Mythology*.

14 FBI, "Crime in the United States 2017," table 38.

15 Centers for Disease Control and Prevention, *Youth Risk Behavior Surveillance—United States,* 2017. Atlanta: Author, June 15, 2018, 67(8).

16 Mike Males, M., "Dubious Demography: The Myth that 'More Youth Means More Crime.'" (Unpublished manuscript, 2005).

17 Substance Abuse and Mental Health Services Administration, Center for Behavioral Health Statistics and Quality *Treatment Episode Data Set (TEDS) 2004–2014, National Admissions to Substance Abuse Treatment Services*, BHSIS Series S–84, HHS Publication No. (SMA) 16–4986, Rockville, MD: Author, 2016.

18 Substance Abuse and Mental Health Services Administration, *Key Substance Use and Mental Health Indicators in the United States: Results from the 2016 National Survey on Drug Use and Health*, Rockville, MD: Center for Behavioral Health Statistics and Quality, Substance Abuse and Mental Health Services Administration, 2017.

19 FBI, "Crime in the United States, 2016," table 20.

20 Judith Edersheim, Robert Kinscherff, Gene Beresin, and Steven Schlozman, "Bad to the Bone: Seven Myths about Juveniles in Jail," Boston: MGH Clay Center, August 20, 2015.

21 Anne Teigen, "Juvenile Age of Jurisdiction and Transfer to Adult Court Laws," National Conference of State Legislatures, January 11, 2019.

22 Donna Bishop and Charles Frazier, "Transfer of Juveniles to Criminal Court: A Case Study and Analysis of Prosecutorial Waiver." *Notre Dame Journal of Law, Ethics & Public Policy*, 2012, 5: 281–302.

23 OJJDP Statistical Briefing Book Online, March 27, 2018, https://www.ojjdp.gov/ojstatbb/court/qa06502.asp?qaDate=2015

24 Josh Rovner, "How Tough on Crime Became Tough on Kids: Prosecuting Teenage Drug Charges in Adult Courts," Washington, DC: The Sentencing Project, 2016.

25 Edersham et al. "Bad to the Bone."

26 Vince Schiraldi and Bruce Western, "Time to Raise the Juvenile Age Limit," *Chicago Tribune*, October 6, 2015, 15.

[27] Edersham et al. "Bad to the Bone."

[28] Duaa Eldeib, "Young Killers Who Stay in Juvenile Court Take Vastly Different Paths," *Chicago Tribune*, June 12, 2015, 8.

[29] Ibid.

[30] Dawn Turner, "Former Prisoner Fights for 'Throwaway' Children. *Chicago Tribune*, October 27, 2015, 3.

[31] Larry K. Brendtro, Martin Brokenleg, and Steve Van Bockern, *Reclaiming Youth at Risk: Our Hope for the Future*, Rev. ed. (Bloomington, IN: National Education Service, 2002).

[32] Jennifer Taylor, "California's Proposition 21: A Case of Juvenile Injustice," *Southern California Law Review*, 2002, 75: 983–1019, 983.

[33] Laura Ridolfi, Maureen Washburn, and Frankie Buzman, "Youth Prosecuted as Adults in California," Oakland, CA: W. Haywood Burns Institute and National Center for Youth Law; San Francisco, CA: Center on Juvenile and Criminal Justice, November, 2017.

[34] Ibid.

[35] Oregon Council on Civil Rights, "Youth and Measure 11 in Oregon," Portland: Author, February, 2018.

[36] Ben Lear, "They Call Us Monsters," PBS, May 22, 2017. The documentary was filmed in 2013 and released in 2017. California passed SB260 in January 2014 that allows juveniles to become eligible for parole after serving at least 15 years.

[37] Emily Jordan, "*They Call Us Monsters*: Teenage Boys Facing Life in Prison Become Screenwriters," Salon, July 5, 2017.

[38] Craig Phillips, "Ben Lear Shows Reality and Human Face of Juvenile Justice System," PBS, May 17, 2017.

[39] Matt Smith, "Meet the 'Monsters': Documentary Looks at California Juvenile Debate," *Youth Today*, February 8, 2017.

[40] Jim Palombo was the inspiration for this topic. He discusses the three perspectives in his book *Criminal to Critic: Reflections Amid the American Experiment* (Lanham, MD: Rowan and Littlefield, 2009). Jim's book is an excellent place to begin a more in-depth study, as are the other references in this section.

[41] The *Student News Daily* Web site provides a good chart comparing the conservative and liberal views on a number of current issues. Retrieved from http://www.studentnewsdaily.com/other/conservative-vs-liberal-beliefs/

[42] Retrieved from http://www.information-entertainment.com/Politics/polterms.html

[43] George Lakoff, *Moral Politics: What Conservatives Know that Liberals Don't*, 3rd ed. (Chicago: University of Chicago Press, 2016), 67.

[44] Ibid, 71–76.

[45] The classic statement of this view is found in Cesare Beccaria, *On Crimes and Punishment* (New York: Bobbs-Merrill, 1963); reprinted by Transaction Publishers in 2009 (edited by Graeme Newman and Pietro Maronqui).

[46] Lakoff, *Moral Politics*, 12.

[47] A good summary of this approach to addressing the crime problem is provided by Elliott Currie. *Crime and Punishment in America* (New York: Metropolitan Books, 1998).

[48] Institute for Policy Studies, "Income inequality," Washington, DC: Author, 2017. Retrieved from https://inequality.org/facts/income-inequality/

[49] Richard Quinney and John Wildeman. *The Problem of Crime: A Peace and Social Justice Perspective*, 3rd ed. (Mountain View, CA: Mayfield, 1991), 77.

PART I

The Nature and Extent of Delinquency

Chapter 1

Delinquency and Juvenile Justice in Historical Perspective

This chapter traces the development of the juvenile justice system from colonial times to the present. From our current historical vantage point, this is not a story with a happy ending. Indeed, we have continued to succumb to what many refer to as an *edifice complex*—we have continued to view the solution to many human problems as requiring some form of edifice—a courthouse, an institution, a detention center, etc. Paraphrasing the mantra in the movie, *Field of Dreams*, is chillingly accurate in this context: "If you build them, they will come." As soon as you construct these edifices, they will be filled almost immediately.

Another major theme of the chapter is that each new institution (e.g., reform schools, training schools, etc.) has been established on the heels of the failure of old institutions that had become overcrowded, inhumane, and costly. Each new institution was supposed to alleviate some of the problems created by existing institutions, but the replacement institutions soon became equally harsh and overcrowded.

The third theme of this chapter is that the juvenile justice system has been used mostly to control the behavior of the children of the urban poor, especially racial and ethnic minority groups. More informal—and less repressive—mechanisms have been reserved primarily for the children of the more privileged classes.[1]

THE INVENTION OF CHILDHOOD

Neil Postman notes that the custom of celebrating a child's birthday did not exist until around 1800. Until the late nineteenth century the terms *adolescence* and *teenager* were not part of the language.

> It is quite possible for a culture to exist without a social idea of children. Unlike infancy, childhood is a social artifact, not a biological category. Our genes contain no clear instructions about who is and who is not a child, and the laws of survival do not require that a distinction be made between the world of an adult and the world of a child.[2]

Another way of putting this is to say that puberty is a biological fact, while childhood and adolescence are social facts. There is no biological reason why young people cannot assume most adult roles several years after the onset of puberty. Before the industrial revolution when farming was the dominant way of life, a boy was considered a man as soon as he could fire a weapon or plow the fields or do countless other things men did. Similarly, a girl became a woman soon after puberty, when she was able to get pregnant. A close examination of anyone's family history will show women giving birth starting as young as 13 or 14.

In recent years we have seen what can be described as an extension of childhood and adolescence well beyond what was considered normal 150 years ago. College males aged 20, 21, or 22 may be seen on any college campus acting rather childish, doing all sorts of things that would have been unthinkable a century ago when there was no leisure time for such behavior. Nineteenth-century counterparts would have been married with two or more children and either working on the farm or, in the twentieth century, working in mines and factories. Starting at the age of 10, most youths were working 14 hours a day 150 years ago.[3] As more and more immigrants arrived in this country to fill the jobs previously held by 10- to 15-year-olds, child labor laws were passed. Compulsory schooling came about during the same period of time—something had to be done to occupy the youths displaced by the new immigrant labor force.

Much of the behavior that is brought to the attention of juvenile courts around the country would not be crimes if it were not for the fact that we have set an arbitrary age for dividing childhood from adulthood. Adult legislators in various states determine what acts constitute delinquency if committed by persons under a specified biological age. To give you an idea of the arbitrary nature of setting the age, consider that until recently a few states set the legal age for adulthood at 16, others used 17, and many used 18. Why the difference? Did the states that established 16 or 17 as the legal age know something that the other states did not know? Note also that adults of 18 often cannot purchase alcohol.

Later in the chapter, we discuss status offenses—crimes that are offenses only if committed by someone under the age of adulthood. These behaviors include running away from home, truancy, being unmanageable or incorrigible, curfew violations, liquor or cigarette law violations, etc. These offenses depend on arbitrary designations. In one state you can drink at 16; in another you will be arrested for exactly the same behavior. In one state you can run away from home at age 17, but in another state you will be arrested (even if you had a very good reason for running away, such as fleeing from an abusive parent).

Little Adults

In the Middle Ages (AD 500 to 1400) infancy ended at around seven, and adulthood began immediately; there was no intervening stage. Art in the Middle Ages depicted children as little men and women.[4] People in the Middle Ages were not conscious of children as a distinct social category. Unlike today, the typical child had very limited contact with a biological parent. In most families children were sent to another family for a period of apprenticeship, usually some sort of domestic service that lasted from about age 7 to 14 or 18. The child never developed a heavy dependence on his or her parents, since the typical household included many adults, not just the immediate family—there were visitors, friends, distant relatives, servants, etc.[5]

More crucially, children were never segregated into special quarters, schools, or even activities. There was no separate world of childhood. Children shared the same clothing, the same games, and the same stories with adults. They lived their lives together, never apart. There was no concept of privacy. In the Middle Ages, children witnessed all adult behavior. They were not innocent as we understand the term today, nor did parents worry about protecting children. Paintings by various artists of the time showed how the culture of the period did not hide anything from children.

Literacy

A key reason for the lack of distinction between adults and children was the lack of literacy. Throughout the Middle Ages, communications were primarily oral. Childhood ended at around the age of seven—the age at which children have command over speech and are able to understand others. During the Middle Ages, the Catholic Church determined that the age of seven was when a person knew right from wrong and could reason.

People did what was necessary to survive. Children were valuable sources of labor for communities and families. There was a very high rate of child mortality in the Middle Ages.

> In part because of children's inability to survive, adults did not, and could not, have the emotional commitment to them that we accept as normal. The prevailing view was to have many children in the hope that two or three might survive. On these grounds, people obviously could not allow themselves to become too attached to the young.[6]

One historian notes: "Of all the characteristics in which the medieval age differs from the modern, none is so striking as the comparative absence of interest in children."[7]

Johann Gutenberg is generally attributed with inventing the printing press in 1456 in Mainz, Germany (although the Chinese and Koreans had earlier versions).[8] Gutenberg's invention changed the course of Western history. It created a symbolic world. The printed book affected how humans thought about the world. The emphasis was on logic and clarity. The Renaissance (which began in about 1350, but the most sweeping changes took place after the introduction of the printing press) was a period of learning, commerce, and exploration. The need for binding contracts, deeds to property, and maps required an educated public.

With the coming of books came a sharp distinction between those who could read and those who could not. Adults learned to read first, and eventually it was accepted that the young would have to *become* adults by learning to read. Before literacy, the only line of separation was the ability to communicate orally. Before the technology of the printing press exploded, literacy was restricted to the clergy and those wealthy enough to afford tutors. Books were copied by hand and available only to the most privileged. European society invented schools—and in so doing invented childhood.[9]

Schools

The growth of schools in England highlights the impact of these developments. During the sixteenth century, villages all over England built schools to provide instruction for their children.

> Because the school was designed for the preparation of a literate adult, the young came to be perceived not as miniature adults but as something quite different altogether—unformed adults. School learning became identified with the special nature of childhood. . . . The word *schoolboy* became synonymous with the word *child*.[10]

Childhood began with learning to read and "became a description of a level of symbolic achievement."[11]

As childhood became a distinct social category based on literacy, other stages of childhood became visible. Children were "segregated at schools, receiving special printed materials geared to distinct stages of learning."[12] These stages soon emerged as separate peer groups and created a distinctive youth culture.

Learning in a school setting required the development of self-control. Starting around the sixteenth century, "both schoolmasters and parents began to impose a rather stringent discipline on children. The natural inclinations of children began to be perceived not only as an impediment to book learning but as an expression of an evil character."[13] One of the primary purposes of education was to teach children to overcome possibly evil natures and to control their behavior. The school's emphasis on overcoming unacceptable behavior was an early example of a social control mechanism for a group based on age and a forerunner to the modern juvenile justice system.

The school was one of the key institutions for segregating children from adults and perpetuating the differences. All of this came about simultaneously with the emergence of capitalism and a market society where a new generation of workers needed to be socialized to take their place in the coming industrial order. Merchants, the emerging capitalist class, needed their children to be able to read and write in order to handle the paperwork of their business enterprises.[14] Childhood began as a middle-class idea, in part because the middle class could afford it. It would be another century or so before this idea filtered down to the lower classes.

Remember that the cultural change in society that created childhood was influenced by important economic and political changes. Other significant developments after the printing press were industrial capitalism and the factory system. Although literacy, schooling, and childhood had developed rapidly in England until 1700, the demand for factory and mine workers restricted those developments—especially for the children of the poor.

PUNISHMENT OF CHILDREN IN THE COLONIES

Prior to the nineteenth century, any sort of deviance (however defined) on the part of children was dealt with on a relatively informal basis. For the most part, the behavior and the control of children was largely a responsibility of parents and perhaps other adults in the community. Although there were often strict laws governing the behavior of youth (especially in New England), they were rarely enforced, and the corresponding punishments were rarely administered. The Quakers, for example, followed one of two patterns. "When a child misbehaved, either his family took care of his discipline or the Quaker meeting dispensed a mild and paternalistic correction."[15] In cases where children's misbehavior was especially troublesome, apprenticeship (sending a youth away from home to live with someone who could teach him or her a trade) was often used as a form of punishment.[16]

The *stubborn child law* passed in Massachusetts in 1646 was the first example of involving the state in the lives of youth.

> If a man have a stubborn or rebellious son, of sufficient years and understanding (viz) sixteen years of age, which will not obey the voice of his Father, or the voice of his Mother, and that when they have chastened him will not harken unto them: then shall his Father and Mother being his natural parents, lay hold on him, and bring him to the Magistrates assembled in court and testify unto them, that their son is stubborn and rebellious and will not obey their voice and chastisement, but lives in sundry notorious crimes, such a son shall be put to death.[17]

This law was grounded in the Puritan belief in the innate wickedness of humankind— wickedness that required that children be subjected to strong discipline. This law was unique in several other respects: it specified a particular legal obligation of children; it defined parents as the focus of that obligation; and it established rules for governmental intervention should parental control over children break down.

Parens Patriae

The appearance of adolescence as a social category coincided with an increasing concern for the regulation of the moral behavior of young people.[18] Although entirely separate systems to monitor and control the behavior of young people began to appear during the early part of the nineteenth century, differential treatment based on age did not come about overnight. The roots of the juvenile justice system can be traced to much earlier legal and social perspectives on childhood and youth. One of the most important of these was a legal doctrine known as *parens patriae*.

Parens patriae originated in medieval England's chancery courts. At that time it was essentially a property law—a means for the crown to administer landed orphans' estates.[19] *Parens patriae* established that the king, in his presumed role as the father of his country, had the legal authority to take care of his people, especially those who were unable to take care of themselves. The king or his authorized agents could assume the role of guardian of the child and thus administer the child's property. By the nineteenth century, this legal doctrine had evolved into the practice of the state's assuming wardship over a minor child and, in effect, playing the role of parent if the child had no parents or if the existing parents were declared unfit.

In the American colonies, for example, officials could bind out as apprentices "children of parents who were poor, not providing good breeding, neglecting their formal education, not teaching a trade, or were idle, dissolute, unchristian or incapable."[20] Later, during the nineteenth century, *parens patriae* supplied (as it still does to some extent), the legal basis for court intervention into the relationship between children and their families.[21]

The idea of the state as parent—and especially as father—has important implications. The objects of a patriarch's authority have traditionally included women in addition to children. The idea of patriarchy has also reinforced the sanctity and privacy of the home and the power (in early years, almost absolute power) of the patriarch to discipline his wife and children.[22] The doctrine of *parens patriae* grants legal power to the state to act as a parent with many of the implicit parental powers possessed by fathers. As we shall see, governmental leaders would eventually utilize *parens patriae*, once a rather narrowly construed legal doctrine, to justify extreme governmental intervention in the lives of young people. Arguing that such intervention was for the good of juveniles, the state during the nineteenth century became increasingly involved in the regulation of adolescent behavior.

Defining a Juvenile Delinquent

The term *juvenile delinquent* originated in the early 1800s. Its meaning derives from the combined meanings of the two terms: (1) delinquent means failure to do something that is required (as in a person being delinquent in paying taxes) and (2) juvenile means someone who is malleable, not yet fixed in their ways, subject to change and being molded (i.e., redeemable). By the 1700s, with colleges and private boarding schools developing, various informal methods of social control of more privileged youth emerged (this paralleled the emergence of capitalism and the need to reproduce the next generation of capitalist rulers).[23] Eventually, more formal systems of control emerged to control working- and lower-class delinquents, including the juvenile justice system and uniformed police.

Informal systems of control have always been reserved for the more privileged youths, while the less privileged have been subjected to formal systems of control.

If we examine history closely, it has almost always been the case that minority youth were much more likely to be viewed as hardened criminals rather than juvenile delinquents (i.e., malleable and thus redeemable). Little has changed today; a majority of those certified or waived to adult court in recent years have been minorities. The kinds of behaviors and the people labeled as delinquent have always been subjective decisions—delinquency is in the eye of the beholder.

THE HOUSE OF REFUGE MOVEMENT

During the early nineteenth century, prominent citizens in eastern cities began to notice the poor, especially the children of the poor. The parents were declared unfit because their children wandered about the streets unsupervised, sometimes committing crimes in order to survive. Many believed that the lack of social control over this group could be the source of even greater future problems. Poor and immigrant children, their lifestyles, and their social position soon became synonymous with crime and juvenile delinquency.

The causes of criminality were attributed both to the social conditions of the cities and to family upbringing. One belief was prominent: "parents who sent their children into the society without a rigorous training in discipline and obedience would find them someday in the prison."[24] Reformers, upon examining the life histories of adult convicts, found that early childhood transgressions were the prelude to worse things to come. The concept of pre-delinquency remains popular today.[25]

Observers focusing on the children of the poor discovered another problem. Children, some as young as six or seven, appeared with increasing regularity in criminal courts. Many children were confined in the Bellevue Penitentiary in New York City in close association with adult offenders.[26] Child reformers believed that such practices were inhumane and would inevitably lead to the corruption of the young and perpetuation of youthful deviance, perhaps to a full-time career in more serious criminality.

A number of philanthropic associations emerged to deal with these problems. One of the most notable was the *Society for the Reformation of Juvenile Delinquents* (SRJD), founded in the 1820s.[27] James Gerard, a lawyer and SRJD member, commented that most of the children appearing in the criminal courts of New York were neglected by parents of poor character; as a result, they were being "brought up in perfect ignorance and idleness, and what is worse in street begging and pilfering."[28] The most common solution to the problem of delinquency then and in years to come was to remove the children from the corrupting environments of prisons, jails, unfit homes, slums, and other unhealthy environments and place them in theoretically more humane and healthier environments.

The SRJD, composed primarily of wealthy businessmen and professional people, convinced the New York legislature to pass a bill in 1824 that established the *New York House of Refuge*, the first correctional institution for young offenders in the United States.[29]

> Managers shall have power in their discretion to receive and take into the House
> of Refuge, to be established by them, all such children who shall be taken up or
> committed as vagrants, or convicted of criminal offenses in the said City. . . .
> Managers shall have power to place the said children committed to their care,
> committed during the minority of said children, at such employments, and to
> cause them to be instructed in such branches of useful knowledge, as shall be
> suited to their years and capacities; and they shall have the power in their discre-
> tion to bind out the said children with their consent, as apprentices or servants
> during their minority.[30]

The following excerpt from one of the original documents of the SRJD,
dated July 3, 1823, provides insight into the actual goals of the founders of this
institution.

> The design of the proposed institution is, to furnish, in the first place, an asylum,
> in which boys under a certain age, who become subject to the notice of our Police,
> either as vagrants, or houseless, or charged with petty crimes, may be received, ju-
> diciously classed according to their degrees of depravity or innocence, put to work
> at such employments as will tend to encourage industry and ingenuity, taught
> reading, writing, and arithmetic, and most carefully instructed in the nature of
> their moral and religious obligations, while at the same time, they are subjected
> to a course of treatment, that will afford a prompt and energetic corrective of
> their vicious propensities, and hold out every possible inducement to reformation
> and good conduct. It will undoubtedly happen, that among boys collected from
> such sources, there will be some, whose habits and propensities are of the most
> unpromising description. Such boys, when left to run at large in the city, become
> the pests of society, and spread corruption wherever they go.[31]

How did the founders decide on the design of the house of refuge, and where
did they get the idea that reform could take place within an enclosed institutional
edifice? They may have been influenced by the writings of John Howard, one of the
leading prison reformers of that era. In his famous work on prisons published in
1784 he made reference to St. Michael's Hospice in Rome.[32] When he visited this
institution in 1778, he saw areas designated for manufacturing and the arts, as well
as the prison for young men described below.

> Over the door is this inscription: For the correction and instruction of profligate
> youth: That they who when idle, were injurious, when instructed might be useful
> to the State. In the room is inscribed the following admirable sentence, in which
> the grand purpose of all civil policy relative to criminals is expressed. It is of little
> advantage to restrain the bad by punishment unless you render them good by
> discipline.[33]

The hospital also had a room for women. The inscription stated that this part
of the hospital was "for restraining the licentiousness and punishing the crimes
of women."[34] The founders of SRJD may also have been influenced by Jeremy

Bentham and his *panopticon* design for prisons, factories, hospitals, schools and other structures.[35]

Religion played a key role in the development of the House of Refuge, as it had throughout the history of prisons for both youths and adults.[36] Quakers were among the leaders of the refuge movement. The reformers of the late eighteenth and early nineteenth centuries spent a good deal of time and energy complaining about the moral decline of the country, especially in New York City. Two vices were identified as the leading causes of delinquency: saloons and theatres.[37] Immorality would be a common charge leveled against juveniles throughout the nineteenth century and beyond.[38]

SRJD pushed for the passage of statutes that punished behaviors such as wandering the streets rather than being at school or at work, begging, vagrancy, and coming from an unfit home (as defined from a middle-class viewpoint) with custody in the house of refuge. All of these behaviors coincided with those of the urban poor. The legislation also established specific procedures for identifying the proper subjects for intervention and the means for the legal handling of cases. According to law, the state, or a representative agency or individual, could intervene in the life of a child if it was determined that he or she needed care and treatment—the definition of which was left entirely in the hands of the agency or individual who intervened.

The New York House of Refuge officially opened its doors on January 1, 1825. Immigrants received the brunt of the enforcement of these laws; between 1825 and 1855, 63% of commitments to the refuge were Irish. One house of refuge superintendent said about a delinquent boy "the lad's parents are Irish and intemperate and that tells the whole story."[39] Of the 73 children received at the New York Refuge during its first year of operation, only one had been convicted of a serious offense (grand larceny). Nine were committed for petty larceny, and 63 (88%) were committed for "stealing, vagrancy and absconding" from the almshouse.[40] These numbers indicate that delinquency statutes more often described a way of life or social status (e.g., poverty) than misconduct. The major crime was simply being poor.

The rich and the powerful in New York became increasingly fearful of class differences. One reformer remarked that the "rising generation of the poor" was a threat to society.[41]

> Early nineteenth century philanthropists also undertook charitable work for their own protection. They feared imminent social upheaval resulting from the explosive mixture of crime, disease, and intemperance which they believed characterized the lives of poorer urban residents. Without relieving the poor of responsibility for their conditions, these philanthropists saw in their benevolences, ways of avoiding class warfare and the disintegration of the social order. The French Revolution reminded them, however, that the costs of class struggle were highest to advantaged citizens like themselves.[42]

Changing Conceptions of Delinquency

In the eighteenth century, juvenile delinquency "slowly ceased to mean a form of misbehavior common to all children and instead became a euphemism for the crimes and conditions of poor children."[43] That perception dominated popular thinking by the nineteenth century. Managers of the New York House of Refuge believed that the major causes of delinquency were, in order of importance: ignorance, parental depravity and neglect, intemperance, theatrical amusements, bad associations, pawnbrokers, immigration, and city life in general. Throughout this period, reformers emphasized the necessity to combat the adverse influences of an undesirable environment, including poor family life. The only effective treatment for juvenile crime was to place the youth in wholesome surroundings.[44] A report by a Unitarian minister in 1830 stated that three-fourths of the young picked up by the police were from families that looked to their children to help support them. Instead of citing the inequalities that existed at the time and the exploitation on the part of factory owners (who employed large numbers of children), the report said that this condition was due to the "idleness and intemperance of the parents." The report further noted that these children "are every day at once surrounded by temptation to dishonesty."[45]

While reformers blamed social conditions as the primary cause of delinquency, they also blamed the youngsters themselves. Time and again reformers stressed that it was up to the individual to avoid the temptations that such social conditions produced. A report by the SRJD noted that the youths in the refuge were "in a situation where there is no temptation to vice . . . and where, instead of being left to prey on the public, they will be *fitted* to become valuable members of society."[46] It was as if the evil conditions of the inner cities were a form of bacteria to which some people were immune while others were not. The goal of reformation was to cure individuals afflicted with the disease of delinquency and to immunize them against future criminality. The medical analogy has been with us ever since.[47]

Social reformers, such as the SRJD and the child savers of the late nineteenth century (discussed below), have often been described as humanitarians caring for the unfortunate children of the poor. According to the SRJD: "The young should, if possible, be subdued with kindness. His heart should first be addressed, and the language of confidence, although undeserved, be used toward him." The SRJD also said that the young should be taught that "his keepers were his best friends and that the object of his confinement was his reform and ultimate good."[48]

Beliefs prominent among even the most benevolent reformers of the period influenced what went on inside the New York House of Refuge. A report on the existing penitentiary system in New York (specifically Newgate and Auburn) issued by SRJD when they called themselves the Society for the Prevention of Pauperism helps explain attitudes at the time. The report advocated solitary confinement (practiced at the Eastern State Penitentiary in Philadelphia) and stated that prisons should be "places which are dreaded by convicts" and "generally productive of terror."[49]

The results suggest that the "best interests of the child" were usually not served. Children confined in the houses of refuge were subjected to strict discipline and control. A former army colonel working in the New York House of Refuge said the delinquent should be taught the fundamental military principle of prompt, unquestioning obedience.[50] Strict discipline was believed necessary for self control (to avoid the temptations of evil surroundings) and respect for authority (a basic requirement of a compliant labor force). Corporal punishments, solitary confinement, handcuffs, the ball and chain, the silent system, and other punitive practices were commonly used in houses of refuge.[51]

Superintendent Curtis of the New York House of Refuge was reportedly a kind person who believed in leniency toward the inmates. Even he, however, succumbed to the temptation to deal with any sign of disorder with severe punishment, including locking the inmates up in a small cage known as the "side table" where they ate in isolation. He also lashed boys' feet to one side of a barrel and their hands to the other; their pants were removed, and they were whipped with a cat-o-nine tails.[52]

As would be the case for most other institutions for juveniles and adults throughout the nineteenth and into the twentieth century, houses of refuge contracted the labor of its inmates to local entrepreneurs. The male inmates made brass nails, cane chairs, and shoes; girls performed domestic chores.[53] After being trained, the children were released—boys to farmers and local artisans and girls bound out as maids. The more hardened boys were indentured to ship's captains.[54]

Within a few years there were houses of refuge in Boston, Philadelphia, and Baltimore. It soon became evident, however, that the original plans of the founders were not being fulfilled, for crime and delinquency remained a problem. Many of the confined children found the conditions unbearable; protests, riots, escape attempts, and other disturbances became almost daily occurrences.[55] Originally intended to house first offenders, the institutions eventually confined more hardened offenders (most of whom were hardened by the experiences of confinement) and soon succumbed to the problem of overcrowding. The cycle continued to plague institutions built throughout the nineteenth and twentieth centuries and continues to the present day.

While the early nineteenth-century reforms did not have much of an impact on crime and delinquency, they did succeed in establishing methods of controlling children of the poor (and their parents as well). "The asylum and the refuge were two more bricks in the wall that Americans built to confine and reform the dangerous classes."[56] While the poor and the working classes were usually viewed as lazy, shiftless, and dangerous, the trait that tended to strike the most fear into the hearts and minds of the privileged was idleness. Indeed, an idle mass of underprivileged and deprived people was an obvious threat to the security of the upper class.

The major assumptions about the causes of crime and delinquency included idleness, lack of a work ethic, and lack of respect for authority. Authority generally means those in power—the ruling class and its representatives. Respect for authority legitimizes a particular social order and set of rulers. When one lacks respect for authority, one withholds legitimacy from the existing order and ruling class. It is important to instill such values in the minds of citizens, especially those who violate the law or otherwise behave contrary to role expectations.

The SRJD asked citizens to visit the House of Refuge in New York "and see that idleness has become changed to industry, filth and rags to cleanliness and comfortable appearance, boisterous impudence to quiet submission."[57] The rhetoric of the founders and managers of houses of refuge did not meet the reality experienced by the youth held in these facilities. A look at one of the most significant court challenges to the refuge movement provides additional insight into the origins of the juvenile justice system.

Court Decisions and Effects

Argued in 1838, *Ex Parte Crouse* arose from a petition of habeas corpus filed by the father of Mary Ann Crouse. Without her father's knowledge, Crouse had been committed to the Philadelphia House of Refuge by her mother on the grounds that she was incorrigible. Her father argued that the incarceration was illegal because she had not been given a jury trial. The court noted that Mary had been committed on a complaint stating that the "infant by reason of vicious conduct, has rendered her control beyond the power of the said complainant [her mother], and made it manifestly requisite that from regard to the moral and future welfare of the said infant she should be placed under the guardianship of the managers of the House of Refuge."[58] The court ruled that the institution was not punishment; rather, it was a place to assist families with troubled youth and to reform behavior.[59]

On several occasions, parents tried to remove their children from the House of Refuge—apparently unaware that the SRJD had, in effect, usurped their parental rights and privileges. Many pleaded with the SRJD to give them another chance at providing for their children. There were some cases, however, that were almost identical to what the father of Mary Crouse faced. One father, "on returning from the hinterland, found that his wife had committed his daughter during his absence. He went directly to the Refuge and requested her discharge."[60] They did, but warned him to pay attention to her morals.

The Pennsylvania Supreme Court rejected the appeal of Mary Crouse's father, saying that the Bill of Rights did not apply to juveniles. Based on the *parens patriae* doctrine, the court asked, "May not the natural parents, when unequal to the task of education, or unworthy of it, be superseded by the *parens patriae* or common guardian of the community?" Further, the court observed that: "The infant has been snatched from a course which must have ended in confirmed depravity."[61] The court ignored the fact that Mary's father wanted to care for her—and predicted future behavior based on vague criteria, a practice that became increasingly common over the years.

The ruling assumed that the Philadelphia House of Refuge (and presumably all other houses of refuge) had a beneficial effect on its residents. It "is not a prison, but a school," the court said, and therefore not subject to procedural constraints. Further, the aims of such an institution were to reform the youngsters in their care "by training . . . [them] to industry; by imbuing their minds with the principles of morality and religion; by furnishing them with means to earn a living; and above all, by separating them from the corrupting influences of improper associates."[62]

What evidence did the justices use to support their conclusion that the House of Refuge was not a prison but a school? They solicited testimony only from those who managed the institution. This was probably because the justices of the Pennsylvania Supreme Court came from the same general class background as those who supported the houses of refuge; they believed the rhetoric of the supporters. In short, they believed the promises of the reformers rather than the reality.

A more objective review of the treatment of youths housed in these institutions, however, might have led the justices to a very different conclusion. Subsequent investigations found that there was an enormous amount of abuse within these facilities.[63] Outside companies contracted for cheap inmate labor, exploiting rather than training. Religious instruction was often little more than Protestant indoctrination (many of the youngsters were Catholic). Education, in the conventional meaning of the word, was almost nonexistent.[64] An assistant superintendent for the New York House of Refuge wrote a scathing critique of the institution, charging that it was a place where vagrants learn crime and that it had the features of a penitentiary rather than an asylum from harm.[65]

Thirty-two years later, *People v. Turner* (1870) provided an intriguing addendum to the history of the houses of refuge. Daniel O'Connell was incarcerated in the Chicago House of Refuge because he was "in danger of growing up to become a pauper." His parents, like Mary Crouse's father, filed a writ of habeas corpus, charging that his incarceration was illegal. The facts were almost identical to the *Crouse* case, but the outcome in the Illinois Supreme Court was far different. First, the court concluded that Daniel was being *punished*—not treated or helped by being in this institution. Second, the Illinois court based its ruling on the *actual practices* of the institution, rather than on the claims of managers of the institution. Third, the Illinois court rejected the *parens patriae* doctrine because they concluded that Daniel was being imprisoned.

The Illinois court based its reasoning on traditional legal doctrines of the criminal law and emphasized the importance of *due process* safeguards. In short, while the court in the *Crouse* case viewed the House of Refuge in a very rosy light, praising it uncritically, the court in the O'Connell case viewed the refuge in a much more negative light, addressing its cruelty and harshness of treatment.[66] After the ruling, only children who had committed felonies could be sent to reform schools. Gender could be one reason for the different outcomes of the two cases.[67]

The Pennsylvania courts continued to defend the decision in the *Crouse* case. Sixty-seven years later, the Pennsylvania Supreme Court ruled in *Commonwealth v. Fisher:*

> the legislatures surely may provide for the salvation of such a child, if its parents or guardians be unwilling or unable to do so, by bringing it into one of the courts of the state without any process at all, for the purpose of subjecting it to the state's guardianship and protection.[68]

The reasoning would not be overturned until 1967 in the *Gault* case (see chapter 11).

The United States in the mid-nineteenth century was a nation constantly moving west. The new settlements needed labor, including farm laborers, helpers in retail stores, washerwomen, and kitchen girls. Simultaneously the eastern cities like New York, Boston, and Philadelphia were overpopulated with immigrants from all over Europe. Fleeing economic ruin, political repression, starvation, and religious persecution, they came to the United States by the millions.[69] The capitalist class promised jobs for everyone, but for most the reality was quite different. The immigrants in the overcrowded tenements and slums soon became the dangerous classes, a term applied to them by those in power.[70] Especially troublesome were the children of the urban poor. They, along with their adult counterparts, needed to be controlled in some way.

About the same time, reformers began to complain about the conditions of the houses of refuge. Not satisfied that these institutions were doing an adequate job of reformation, new methods were recommended. In Massachusetts, for instance, the first compulsory school law was passed in 1852, thereby creating a new category of delinquent, the truant, and a new method of controlling youths. New York passed a similar law in 1854.[71] The legislation was a means of placing abandoned and neglected poor children in institutions; the goal was more about control than about education.

In New York, the Association for Improving the Conditions of the Poor established the New York Juvenile Asylum in 1853. The primary aim of this association was to create a house of detention for children exposed to morally corrupt influences. It would remove them from "dangerous and corrupting associates and place them in such circumstances as will be favorable to reform, and tend to make them industrious, virtuous, and useful members of society."[72] Not much changed in the almost three decades since the opening of the first house of refuge.

Placing-out Movement

Houses of refuge were congregate-style institutions confining large numbers of juveniles in highly regimented institutions in urban areas. Reformers sought new innovations for out-of-home placement, believing that family homes were far better places for reform than institutions. The placing-out movement began in Boston in the1830s. Prominent citizens wanted to establish a reform school for boys who had not yet been convicted of a crime but were roaming the streets. In 1849 the Massachusetts State Reform School for Boys, an institution positioned somewhere between the houses of refuge and the public school system, opened. A similar school was opened for girls in Lancaster in 1855, the first of many such institutions based on the family system.[73] The Ohio State Reform Farm was a family system for boys that opened in 1857.[74]

The cottage or family plan was based on a belief in rural purity, a dominant theme at that time.[75] However, the end result was anything but pure.

> Institutionalists and advocates of placing out bickered constantly. Nativist Protestants expressed their preferences, thus hastening the development of Roman Catholic institutions. Delinquent girls did institutional housework and often were sexually abused when placed out. Negro children were initially more fortunate, since few institutions accepted them. Once admitted, they were usually segregated. By the Civil War, several institutions had experienced rioting and incendiarism, which usually began in the workshops where contract labor encouraged exploitation.[76]

New York also used a placing-out system, the most famous of which was operated by the New York Children's Aid Society founded by Charles Loring Brace in 1853. Brace believed that a family-type setting, preferably in the country, would avoid the often brutalizing and impersonal routines in houses of refuge.[77] The Society placed children in family-type institutions (such as the Ohio State Reform Farm) or in actual residences or farms located west of the Allegheny Mountains. Millions of children travelled west on what were commonly referred to as orphan trains.[78] Economic factors played an important role, and many of these children provided landowners with a cheap source of labor:

The Children's Aid Society divided New York City into sections and assigned to each section a visitor (part of the Friendly Visitor program popular throughout the nation; visitors eventually evolved into social workers).

> The visitors would go from house to house, trying to persuade the families to send their children to the public schools or to the industrial schools of the Children's Aid Society. When a visitor found a homeless or neglected child, he took him to the central office of the society, where, after securing the parent's consent—if they could be found—it prepared to send him to a farmer's home in the West.[79]

Usually the parents could not be found because they were away during the day (when the visitors called) either working or seeking work. A few notable cases suggest that parents and their children did not always passively succumb to the benevolences of the reformers.[80]

For example, the Baltimore House of Refuge had a case in which a mother attempted to regain custody of her daughter who had been placed in a home by the refuge. The officials reported:

> After we had found a home for the little girl, the mother made an application for her, which we refused. She succeeded in finding where the child was, and demanded it. The man with whom we had placed her was quite firm, and refused to surrender her, but told the mother that if she conducted herself well, the mother might visit her. She threatened legal proceedings, but our power over the child was superior to hers and thus the injudicious interference of the parents was prevented.[81]

During the last half of the nineteenth century, the number of court cases challenging the state's power over children increased. Most commitments were for begging, poverty, destitution, neglect, and dependency. In some cases, it was difficult to tell why children had been taken away from their parents. Court decisions give evidence that children were not committed to institutions because of any violation of the law or because of failings by parents, "but simply because the parents were poor and behaved as poor people always have. . . . The existence of only the flimsiest procedural protections reveals an unspoken assumption that the state had an equal if not superior interest in the children and the burden was on the parents to show to the contrary."[82]

Toward the end of the nineteenth century it was clear that earlier reforms and the existing institutions were doing little toward the reformation of delinquents and the reduction of crime. The asylums constructed during the early and middle years of the nineteenth century had failed in their original intention to reform. They remained in place, however, with the new goal of custody. The dangerous classes could no longer be banished as they had been during the colonial period. They had to be controlled physically; banishment could result in endangering another community.[83]

Although custody became the order of the day, some reformers continued to agitate for more effective reformation. New theories of crime and delinquency had emerged by this time, heavily influenced by the positivist school of criminology that popularized the medical model of deviance. The Progressive Era ushered in a new series of reforms commonly known as the child-saving movement and resulted in the establishment of new institutions to care for, control, and protect wayward youth. One such institution was the juvenile court.

THE CHILD SAVING MOVEMENT AND THE JUVENILE COURT

Like their earlier nineteenth century counterparts, the *child savers* were a group of upper-middle-/upper-class whites with business and professional backgrounds threatened by the deleterious social conditions in the slums of Chicago and other cities. Surveys by noted reformers Z. R. Brockway and Enoch Wines found that children were still being kept in jails and prisons with adult offenders. The child savers dedicated themselves to saving these children and diverting them from the adult criminal justice system.

The Juvenile Court

The reformers advocated for the establishment of a juvenile court based on the doctrine of *parens patriae*. The child savers argued that only such a court could serve the best interests of the child. The 1899 Illinois Juvenile Court Act removed all cases involving juveniles (at first the upper age was 16; later it was raised to 17) from the jurisdiction of the criminal courts and formally established the juvenile court.[84] The legislation created new categories of offenses and extended the state's power over the lives of children and youth.

The new laws that defined delinquency and pre-delinquent behavior were broad in scope and quite vague, covering: (1) violations of laws also applicable to adults; (2) violations of local ordinances; and (3) truancy and ill-defined behaviors such as vicious, immoral, profane, or indecent conduct, incorrigibility, growing up in idleness, living with any vicious or disreputable person, and many more—these behaviors would eventually be known as *status offenses*.[85]

The charge of immorality was almost always applied to girls. The case files of the first three decades of the Cook County Juvenile Court show that immorality constituted between 20 and 55 percent of all charges made against girls. Most of the remainder of the charges were incorrigibility—a charge that typically masks various kinds of sexual behavior by girls and/or child abuse.[86]

Prior to the passage of the Juvenile Court Act in Chicago in 1899 several states already had laws defining status offenses. For instance, Tennessee passed an act in 1895 to establish county reformatories that could commit those under the age of 16 if

> by reason of incorrigible or vicious conduct, such infant has rendered his control beyond the power of such parent guardian or next friend, and made it manifestly requisite that from regard to the future welfare of such infant, and for the protection of society he should be placed under the guardianship of the trustees of such reformatory institution.

Children could also be committed as vagrants or if they were "without a suitable home and adequate means of obtaining an honest living, and who are in danger of being brought up to lead an idle or immoral life."[87] The Tennessee code reproduced, almost word-for-word, the original act that had created the New York and Philadelphia Houses of Refuge.

Reformers believed that delinquency was the result of a wide variety of social, psychological, and biological factors. They believed that one must look into the life of the child offender in intimate detail in order to know the whole truth about the child.

The judge of the juvenile court was to be like a benevolent, yet stern, father. The proceedings were to be informal without the traditional judicial trappings. There was neither a need for lawyers nor constitutional safeguards because (1) the cases were not criminal in nature and (2) the court would always act in the best interests of the child. The court was to be operated like a clinic, and the child was to be diagnosed in order to determine the extent of his condition and to prescribe the correct treatment plan, preferably as early in life as possible.[88]

Even the terminology of the juvenile justice system was, and to some extent still is, different. Children are referred to the court rather than being arrested; they are detained in a detention center or adjustment center instead of being jailed pending court action; they are petitioned to court not indicted; there is an adjudication rather than a trial; if adjudicated guilty, juveniles can be committed to a training school or reform school rather than sentenced to prison.

Envisioned as a benevolent institution that would emphasize treatment, the juvenile court turned out to be a mixture of two orientations. The social welfare orientation emphasized treatment, while the legal institution orientation emphasized punishment. The confusion can be traced to the mixed legacy of the court that combined a puritanical approach to stubborn children and parental authority with the Progressive Era's belief that children's essential goodness can be corrupted by undesirable elements in their environments. James Finckenauer termed the mixture ambivalent or even schizophrenic.[89] The attention of the juvenile court and its supporters was fixed primarily on the children of the poor, especially immigrants. The court provided an arena "where the dependent status of children was verified and reinforced, and where the incapacities of lower-class immigrant parents were, in a sense, certified."[90]

The juvenile court system extended the role of probation officer, a role originally introduced in the mid-nineteenth century in Boston.[91] This new role was one of the primary innovations in the twentieth-century juvenile justice system, and the role became one of the most crucial in the entire system. The probation officer "was expected to instruct children and parents in reciprocal obligations, preach moral and religious verities, teach techniques of child care and household management."[92] Part of the probation officer's role was likened to that of an exorcist, for he was required to, in a sense, ward off or exorcize the evil temptations of the city. One reformer, Frederic Almy, wrote in 1902: "Loving, patient, personal service" would provide the "*antiseptic* which will make the *contagion* of daily life harmless."[93]

The Child Savers

Many of the child savers suggested a number of social factors as causal forces of delinquency, but few carried their arguments to the logical conclusion of changing the harmful environmental factors. The solution continued to focus on the control, rehabilitation, or treatment of individual offenders or groups of offenders from a particular segment of the population. The existing social structure was accepted as good; it was necessary to lead those who went astray back so that they could fit into the existing social order and class system. Unfortunately, the only place they were permitted to fit was at or near the bottom of that order.

Most of the programs advocated during this period placed primary emphasis on the individual and his or her moral and other personal shortcomings and received justification from psychological, psychiatric, and psychoanalytic theories of delinquency just beginning to emerge during the late nineteenth century. The works of G. Stanley Hall and William Healy, both of whom worked closely with the juvenile courts in various cities, were based on such theories. These writers advocated a clinical approach (using the medical model)—one that stressed the need for a scientific laboratory to study delinquents. One such laboratory was the juvenile court.

The child savers claimed that they had ushered in new innovations in penology, especially with the establishment of industrial schools (often called industrial and training schools). Actually, the methods used were variations of earlier methods used in houses of refuge and other institutions. Most of the new institutions of the twentieth century were placed in rural areas—a product of the popular antiurban bias among so many child savers. It was assumed that the temptations of city life would be offset by placement in such a setting. The juvenile court was to be the primary placing agency, thus serving a function similar to that of the Children's Aid Society when it placed children out west.

The emphasis within these institutions remained relatively unchanged from previous methods. Restraint, control, the teaching of good work habits (e.g., cleaning floors, waiting on tables, milking cows, cooking, etc.), respect for authority, and a quasi-military model continued to be the hallmark of these institutions.

An example of the kinds of institutions opened during this period was the Shelby County Industrial and Training School, located near Memphis, Tennessee. Opened in 1904 in a farming community, it emphasized farm labor and the development of habits of industry through various forms of work and education. A report in 1912 to the board of directors stated in glowing terms how successful this institution had become.

> The boys in the several departments of work and in the school room have shown commendable interest in work and study. . . . In the several departments of work, habits of industry have been cultivated which must prove a helpful training for future usefulness. The half-day work and half-day school, which has been in practice in these institutions for years, is now appealing to our public school authorities as a necessary advance in youthful development. . . .
>
> Our work in all departments is necessary, practical and productive. On the farm and in the garden the actual use of the implement in the hand of the boy, under intelligent supervision, must produce results—and does—which means an abundance of fresh vegetables in their season for our tables and feed for our dairy cows and other stock. . . . The laundry force and the boys who do the endless scrubbing, sweeping and dusting are all being taught the necessity of work.[94]

Thus, even the most menial work was made respectable, so that these youths would fit into their appropriate labor force position after release. This institution was closed in 1935 amid a great deal of controversy, with two grand jury reports criticizing its methods and lack of results (in terms of a high recidivism rate and overcrowding).[95]

All institutions for juveniles emphasized menial labor that helped produce profits for both the state and private industry. For instance, the Illinois State Reform School (opened in 1871 at Pontiac) signed contracts with a Chicago shoe company, a brush company, and a chair company; the institution referred to its the production of commercial products as an educational program.[96] Frederick Wines said the training in institutions should correspond to the mode of life of working people and should "be characterized by the greatest simplicity in diet, dress and surroundings, and *above all by labor.*"[97]

In many of these institutions (such as the one in Memphis) a lot of emphasis was placed on agricultural training, despite the fact that the United States was fast moving toward an industrial society. The reformatory regime aimed to teach middle-class values but lower-class skills. Bookishness was expressed as something undesirable, while menial labor was described as an educational experience. Reformers aimed to "get the idea out of the heads of city boys that farm life is menial and low."[98]

The San Francisco Industrial School

The movement to establish special institutions for juveniles spread westward. The first institution for juvenile offenders in California was the San Francisco Industrial School. It was established in 1858. The Gold Rush (1848–1855) brought about 300,000 people to California, the largest mass migration in US history; it introduced a period of general lawlessness.[99] The Industrial School was described "as an enlightened response to the surging numbers of 'idle and vicious' youths wandering the streets of San Francisco."[100] The aim of the institution was "the detention, management, reformation, education, and maintenance of such children as shall be committed or surrendered thereto."[101]

The city's leaders noted the growing number of vagrant and destitute children and the necessity of insuring that they did not create problems for themselves or for society. The growth of the juvenile population paralleled the growth of the adult population. Civic leaders "feared that many of these children would inevitably threaten the social order by forming a permanent pauper class."[102] For guidance, they "looked to the well-established houses of refuge that existed in most of the large East Coast cities as their guide for establishing the San Francisco Industrial School."[103] As in other major cities in the country, the leaders in San Francisco belonged to the merchant class. Their goals were "the promotion of a favorable business climate, restricting government spending, and maintaining law and order."[104]

One of the leaders was Colonel J.B. Crockett, who had been involved in the reform school movement in Missouri. He urged that San Francisco follow the examples of other cities to in establishing an institution to address the urgent needs of the children of migrants, who arrived in the state sick and destitute. The social conditions result in children being neglected and roaming the streets where they "fall into bad company and quickly become thieves and vagabonds."[105] Like others promoting the industrial school, he argued that children needed to be prevented from succumbing to evil associations. The industrial school would wean the children from destructive practices.

The industrial school, like houses of refuge and similar institutions for youth, was plagued by overcrowding, corruption and violence throughout its history. In San Francisco,"the Industrial School's tumultuous and controversial 33 year history foreshadowed the realities and inherent failings of institutional care that characterized the state's youth corrections system and confounded state reform efforts ever since."[106]

DELINQUENCY, PUBLIC SCHOOLS, AND INDUSTRY

Most of the reformers tended to accept the version of *Social Darwinism* known as *Reform Darwinism*—the view that man was not completely helpless and that man's progress enabled him, through positive science, to step in and improve his lot. With the help of such writers as Charles Cooley and Charles Henderson, reformers accepted the nature versus nurture view, with a heavy emphasis on the nurture side.[107] Beliefs that children needed to be saved from an environment of dysfunctional homes and corrupting influences dominated the thinking throughout the nineteenth and early twentieth centuries. There is little evidence that the prevailing views have changed very much.

The beliefs that intervention should be stressed and that potential criminals and delinquents could and should be identified and treated at the earliest age possible continued to be dominant themes. The juvenile court was intended to be one of the chief means through which intervention would be made; the court also enlisted the help of other programs and institutions. Public schools, recreation programs, public playgrounds, boys' clubs, YMCAs, and other organizations all helped in dealing with the problem of delinquency, especially in their role of identifying and containing those labeled pre-delinquents.[108]

The desire to use public schools for social control had been stated early in their development. Brace declared in 1880:

> We need, in the interests of public order, of liberty, of property, for the sake of our own safety and the endurance of free institutions here, a strict and careful law, which shall compel every minor to learn to read and write, under severe penalties in case of disobedience.[109]

It can certainly be argued that the school system ultimately meant upward mobility for some. For the majority, however, it meant remaining in their original class position.

Compulsory schooling, the new factory system, and various forms of punishment in penal institutions were connected. The emphasis on discipline in industrial capitalism influenced both schooling and punishment.

> The more general concern of industrialists was that schools produce an individual who was cooperative, knew how to work well with others, and was physically and mentally equipped to do his job efficiently. A cooperative and unselfish individual not only worked well with his fellows in the organization *but was more easily managed.*[110]

Representatives of the business world began a concerted campaign to support new forms of education that would train the future workers of the United States.[111] They also offered their own educational programs. For example, The Plymouth Cordage Company established nurseries because: "The company believed that by removing the children from the house for part of the day the mother could give her undivided attention to housework."[112] The rationale for the innovation was that the husband would function better at work coming from a clean home with hot meals. Throughout this time period, the emphasis was on preparing the next generation of male workers and reinforcing traditional female roles within the home.

> These industrial programs for the management of workers became models for the type of activities adopted by the public school. . . . In some cases actual programs, like home economics, were transferred from factory education activities to the public schools to produce workers with the correct social attitudes and skills.[113]

William H. Tolman, cofounder of the American Institute of Social Service, commented in 1900 on the importance of the kindergarten program.

> The lessons of order and neatness, the discipline of regulated play . . . are acquisitions, making the child of greater value to himself, and, if he can follow up the good start which has been made for him, tending to make him of greater wage earning capacity.[114]

Such innovations in public schooling as kindergarten, extracurricular activities, home room, and organized playgrounds combined to teach children the benefits of cooperative work, discipline, punctuality, respect for authority, accountability for one's work, and submission to the needs of the group. Education socialized the student for a life of cooperation; it also trained pupils in the specialized skills required by corporations. "To a great extent children became a form of natural resource that was to be molded by the schools and fed into the industrial machine."[115]

Rather than eliminating inequality and increasing upward social mobility, the school system effectively maintained class differences. A report by the National

Education Association in 1910 stated: "The differences among children as to aptitudes, interests, economic resources, and prospective careers furnish the basis for a rational as opposed to merely a formal distinction between elementary, secondary, and high education."[116] Ellwood Cubberly, an educational reformer, wrote in 1909:

> Our city schools will soon be forced to give up the exceedingly democratic idea that all are equal, and our society devoid of classes . . . and to begin specialization of educational effort along many lines in an attempt to adapt the school to the needs of these many classes.[117]

As noted earlier, reforms in public schooling were closely related to the problem of juvenile delinquency.[118] Henry Goddard, one of the leaders in the development of the Alfred Binet Intelligence Test implemented in 1916, believed that intelligence testing was the key to reducing delinquency and claimed that the public schools could be used as clearing houses to pick out potential delinquents, especially the category he called the low intelligent, "defective delinquent."[119] Teachers, guidance counselors, truant officers, school social workers, and school psychologists became part of this vast network of social control within the school system.

Twentieth-Century Developments in Juvenile Justice

During the period roughly between 1920 and the 1960s there were relatively few structural changes within the juvenile justice system. In Illinois, beginning around 1909, the juvenile court began experimenting with the intensive psychological study and treatment of youthful deviance. The Juvenile Protective League, under the leadership of such notables as Julia Lathrop (head of the U.S. Children's Bureau), Jane Addams (reformer and founder of Hull House[120]), Julian Mack (judge of the Boston juvenile court), and William Healy (psychologist), established a child guidance clinic. The clinic embodied the medical model of delinquency. Under the direction of Healy, child guidance clinics focused their attention and energies on the individual delinquent, one who was generally viewed as maladjusted to his or her social environment. By 1931 there were over 200 such clinics around the country.[121]

During the 1920s and 1930s the profession of social work grew to prominence.[122] This field began to dominate the treatment of individual delinquents and interpreted delinquency as stemming from conflicts within the family. Even today, social work methodology has a strong influence within the juvenile justice system.

The Chicago Area Project, theoretically based on the works of the Chicago School of Sociology and those of Clifford Shaw, focused on community organization to prevent delinquency. From this perspective, delinquency stemmed from the social disorganization of slum communities. Hence, the solution would be found in "fostering local community organizations to attack problems related to delinquency," such as poverty, inadequate housing, and unemployment.[123] Much of the effort focused on reducing gang delinquency, which was prevalent in Chicago and other large cities.[124] But such programs did little to alter the social reality of economic deprivation and other structural sources of delinquency.

> Chicago at that time was caught in the most serious economic depression in the nation's history. Tens of thousands of people were unemployed, especially immigrants and blacks. During this period, a growing radicalization among impoverished groups resulted in urban riots. The primary response by those in positions of power was an expansion and centralization of charity and welfare systems. In addition, there was considerable experimentation with new methods of delivering relief services to the needy [e.g., Hull House]. No doubt, Chicago's wealthy looked favorably upon programs like the Area Project, which promised to alleviate some of the problems of the poor without requiring a redistribution of wealth and power.[125]

The decade of the 1960s brought two significant changes. One was interventions by the United States Supreme Court in cases including *In re Gault* (1967),[126] *Kent v. United States* (1966),[127] and *In re Winship* (1970).[128] Sadly, most of the promise of reform inherent in these rulings was never realized. Chapter 11 includes a discussion of these and other cases.

The second development came on the heels of the efforts of Jerome Miller, who managed to close most of the reform schools opened in the nineteenth century in the state of Massachusetts.[129] Despite the success of the closure of these types of institutions and the development of workable alternatives throughout the country, get-tough policies beginning in the 1980s threatened the progress made. Many jurisdictions continued to rely on placement in institutions. Children were warehoused in large correctional facilities, under conditions reminiscent of reform schools 100 years earlier[130] Increasing numbers of institutions were populated with urban African Americans.[131] Young women were subject to a double standard; minor offenses too often resulted in some form of incarceration.[132] Many institutional systems became huge bureaucracies with a vested interest in keeping a certain percentage of youth incarcerated. Punitive trends in the late 1990s included zero tolerance policies and the war on drugs, which are discussed in chapters 11 and 12.

INTO THE TWENTIETH-FIRST CENTURY

As the new century dawned, it became obvious to most observers that getting tough was not working. Scandals surrounding juvenile training schools and local detention centers drew attention to the abusive practices of these institutions and how counterproductive they had become. The situation became so bad within the

California Youth Authority that they were forced to close many institutions and even changed their name to one that represented a more innovative approach (see chapter 12).

New models for dealing with juvenile crime began to emerge, highlighted by alternative programs in the community and a nationwide attempt to reduce minority overrepresentation inside juvenile institutions. Among the most popular models was one that emerged in the state of Missouri as they began to close down their large institutions and institute community-based programming and one in San Francisco, the Detention Diversion Advocacy Project. Several large foundations, such as the Annie E. Casey Foundation, began to fund alternative programs. The results so far have been promising, as recidivism rates have declined significantly and youth crime continues to decrease. These and other model programs will be discussed in more detail in the last chapter of this book.

SUMMARY

The history of the juvenile justice system in the United States demonstrates that a class, race, and gender bias has pervaded the institution since its inception. The standard definitions of delinquency reflect such biases. The roots of this pattern can be traced to colonial embellishments of the *parens patriae* doctrine. The first and most significant legal challenge to this doctrine, *Ex Parte Crouse*, involved the incarceration of a girl on the grounds that she was incorrigible.

Changes in the labor market and several other structural changes in society during the nineteenth century brought new conceptions of and responses to youthful deviance. The House of Refuge movement during the first half of the nineteenth century was one result of those changes. The primary function of these institutions (and those that followed) was to control and reform children of the poor. The general aim of reform was to inculcate habits of industry and respect for authority, which would help maintain the existing class structure.

The last half of the nineteenth century brought additional changes in the social structure and more reforms of the juvenile justice system. With thousands flocking to large cities in the Northeast and Midwest, unemployment and vagrancy became widespread. The juvenile system as we know it today began to take shape. One of the most notable changes was the establishment of the juvenile court system and industrial and training schools. The basic structure of modern juvenile justice was created between 1900 and 1910. The *parens patriae* doctrine and the medical model of deviance provided the philosophical justification for state intervention into the lives of youth. Child guidance clinics and the Chicago Area Project were two significant forms of youth control that followed the establishment of the juvenile court. The most recent reforms have focused on disproportionate minority contact and a resurgence in efforts to find alternatives to confining juveniles in institutions.

Notes

1   For more detail on the history of juvenile justice see the following: Anthony M. Platt, *The Child Savers: The Invention of Delinquency*, 40th anniversary edition (New Brunswick, NJ: Rutgers University Press, 2009); Robert M. Mennel, *Thorns and Thistles: Juvenile Delinquents in the U.S., 1820–1940* (Hanover, NH: University Press of New England, 1973); Thomas J. Bernard and Megan C. Kurlychek, *The Cycle of Juvenile Justice*, 2nd ed. (New York: Oxford University Press, 2010).

2   Neil Postman, *The Disappearance of Childhood* (New York: Vintage, 1994), xi.

3   Ibid., 53.

4   Philippe Ariès, *Centuries of Childhood* (New York: Knopf, 1962).

5   Postman, *The Disappearance of Childhood*, 15–16.

6   Shulamith Firestone, *The Dialectic of Sex: The Case for Feminist Revolution* (New York: Bantam Books, 1970) 78.

7   Barbara Tuchman. *A Distant Mirror* (New York: Alfred A. Knopf, 1978) 53.

8   For background on the invention of the printing press see the following web site: http://inventors.about.com/od/gstartinventors/a/Gutenberg.htm

9   Postman, *The Disappearance of Childhood*, 36.

10   Ibid., 41–42.

11   Ibid., 42.

12   Elizabeth Eisenstein, *The Printing Press as an Agent of Change* (Cambridge, UK: Cambridge University Press, 1979) 133–34.

13   Postman, *The Disappearance of Childhood*, 46.

14   Joel Spring, *Education and the Rise of the Corporate State* (Boston: Little, Brown, 1972), 37–38.

15   Joseph Hawes, *Children in Urban Society: Juvenile Delinquency in Nineteenth-Century America* (New York: Oxford University Press, 1971), 18. See also David J. Rothman, *The Discovery of the Asylum: Social Order and the Disorder in the New Republic*, Rev. ed. (New Brunswick, NJ: Transaction Publishers, 2002); John R. Sutton, *Stubborn Children: Controlling Delinquency in the United States, 1640–1981* (Berkeley: University of California Press, 1988).

16   Robert H. Bremner, (ed.), *Children and Youth in America: A Documentary History, Vol. I, 1600–1865* (Cambridge, MA: Harvard University Press, 1970); Bernard and Kurlychek, *The Cycle of Juvenile Justice*, 55; Doug Rendleman, "Parens Patriae: From Chancery to Juvenile Court," In F. Faust and P. Brantingham (eds.), *Juvenile Justice Philosophy*, 2nd ed. (St. Paul, MN: West, 1979).

17   Sutton, *Stubborn Children*, 11.

18   Platt, *The Child Savers*; Postman, *The Disappearance of Childhood*.

19   Sutton, *Stubborn Children*.

20   Rendleman, "Parens Patriae," 63.

21   Lee E. Teitelbaum and Leslie J. Harris, "Some Historical Perspectives on Governmental Regulation of Children and Parents," In L. E. Teitelbaum and A. R. Gough (eds.), *Beyond Control: Status Offenders in the Juvenile Court* (Cambridge, MA: Ballinger, 1977).

22   R. Emerson Dobash and Russell Dobash, *Violence against Wives: A Case against the Patriarchy* (New York: Free Press, 1979), chapter 1.

23   Bernard and Kurlychek, *The Cycle of Juvenile Justice*, 44.

24   Rothman, *The Discovery of the Asylum*, 70.

25   One of the persistent problems in our response to crime and delinquency is that when trying to make predictions based on risk factors (as is done with various health problems,

there are too many false positives where the prediction that someone will become a delinquent turns out to be false. Most kids, even those at high risk, will never become adult criminals.

26 Robert S. Pickett, *House of Refuge Origins of Juvenile Reform in New York State 1815–1857* (Syracuse: Syracuse University Press, 1969), 48; David Lewis, *From Newgate to Dannemora: The Rise of the Penitentiary in New York, 1796–1848* (Ithaca, NY: Cornell University Press, 2009; originally published in 1965), 47.

27 This group was formerly called the Society for the Prevention of *Pauperism* (another word for poverty). For a discussion of this group and a detailed description of its upper-class backgrounds see Pickett, *House of Refuge*, 21–49. A list of the managers and officers is available at http://books.google.com/books?id=-NUXAAAAYAAJ&pg=PA3&output=text. The members were among the most prominent families in New York Society.

28 Hawes, *Children in Urban Society*, 28.

29 "An Act to Incorporate the Society for the Reformation of Juvenile Delinquents in the City of New York," Chap. 126, Laws of 1824, passed on March 29, 1824.

30 Society for the Reformation of Juvenile Delinquents (SRJD), *Documents Relative to the House of Refuge* (New York: Mahlon Day, 1832), 304, https://books.google.com/books?output=text&id=YrkqAAAAMAAJ&q=bind#v=snippet&q=bind&f=false

31 Ibid., 21.

32 The title of Howard's book was: *State of the Prisons in England and Wales with Preliminary Observations and an Account of Some Foreign Prisons and Hospitals.*

33 Thorsten Sellin: "The House of Correction for Boys in the Hospice of Saint Michael in Rome," *Journal of the American Institute of Criminal Law and Criminology*, 1930, 20(4): 533–553, http://www.jstor.org/pss/1134675.

34 Ibid.

35 Thomas Eddy, a wealthy businessman and Quaker, was influential in designing the New York House of Refuge. He had helped design and build the first penitentiary in New York (Newgate) and had been influenced by Howard and Bentham. For further background on Eddy see Pickett, *House of Refuge* and Lewis, *From Newgate to Dannemora.* For more on Bentham and the panopticon design see Randall G. Shelden and Pavel V. Vasiliev, *Controlling the Dangerous Classes: A History of Criminal Justice in America*, 3rd ed. (Long Grove, IL: Waveland Press, 2018), chapter 4.

36 For a discussion of the connection between religion and punitiveness see Randall G. Shelden, *Our Punitive Society: Race, Class, Gender and Punishment in America* (Long Grove, IL: Waveland Press, 2010), 9–12.

37 The upper class apparently did not approve of the lower classes attending theatres, which were growing in popularity. In their 1838 annual report, the managers of the House of Refuge claimed that theatres played a major role in the depravity of 59 out of 130 children committed to the refuge. It was noted that one boy sold his father's Bible in order to get money for tickets (Pickett, *House of Refuge*, 18). The city eventually levied a tax on theatres to help finance the refuge. Religious fanaticism was prevalent. Frances Trollope, a European traveler who observed the fulmination over theatres, came to the conclusion that "religious enthusiasm and narrow provincialism combined to freeze out cultural activities" (19–20). Religious instruction took on a primary role in the daily routine of the refuge.

38 Ibid., 21–49. The charges that brought juveniles into the early juvenile courts included immorality. This was especially true for girls, as discussed later in the chapter.

39 Ibid., 15.

40 Grace Abbott, *The Child and the State* (Chicago: University of Chicago Press, 1938), 362.

41 Pickett, House of Refuge, 15.

[42] Mennel, *Thorns and Thistles*, 6.

[43] Ibid., xxvi.

[44] Platt, *The Child Savers*, 53.

[45] Bremner, *Children and Youth in America*, 613.

[46] Hawes, *Children in Urban Society*, 44, emphasis added.

[47] Platt, *The Child Savers*, 107. Platt was writing about the later nineteenth century, but his comments applied to the next century as well. "If, as the child savers believed, criminals are conditioned by biological heritage and brutish living conditions, then *prophylactic* [preventive] measures must be taken early in life." Platt quoted prison reformer Enoch Wines, who reinforced the belief that criminals of the next generation must be prevented from pursuit of criminal careers: "They are born to it, brought up for it. They must be saved." (45).

[48] Hawes, *Children in Urban Society*, 45–46.

[49] Society for the Prevention of Pauperism, *Report on the Penitentiary System in the United States*, 1822, 95, http://books.google.com/books?id=yNHf851WemcC&pg=PP8&ots=EK7H0ewdjn&dq=Report+on+the+Penitentiary+System+in+the+United+States&output=text

[50] Mennel, *Thorns and Thistles*, 103.

[51] Alexander Pisciotta, "Saving the Children: The Promise and Practice of *Parens Patriae*, 1838– 98." *Crime and Delinquency*, 1982, 28: 410–25.

[52] Ibid., 72–73.

[53] SRJD, *Documents*, 127–128. Multiple shops created many different items in 1828. For example, the shoe shop completed 1,214 pair of pumps; the chair shop completed 9,834 cane seats and 330 backs for large arm chairs; the brass nail shop completed 14,976 brass nails, 228 dozen bits, and 2,196 pair of stirrups; the tailor shop created 350 canvas pantaloons and 175 jackets.

[54] Bremner, *Children and Youth in America*, 672.

[55] Ibid., 689–91; Hawes, *Children in Urban Society*, 47–48

[56] Rothman, *The Discovery of the Asylum*, 210.

[57] Hawes, *Children in Urban Society*, 44.

[58] The wording used here is taken *verbatim* from the law, passed in Pennsylvania in 1826, which authorized the House of Refuge "at their discretion, to receive into their care and guardianship, infants, *males under the age of twenty-one years, and females under the age of eighteen years*, committed to their custody" (emphasis added). Note the distinction of age based on gender. This exact same statute was reproduced in numerous state laws throughout the nineteenth century. See, for example, Randall G. Shelden, "Rescued from Evil: Origins of the Juvenile Justice System in Memphis, Tennessee, 1900–1917," Ph.D. dissertation, Carbondale: Southern Illinois University, 1976; Randall G. Shelden and Lynn T. Osborne, "'For Their Own Good': Class Interests and the Child Saving Movement in Memphis, Tennessee, 1900–1917," *Criminology*, 1989, 27: 801–21.

[59] Shelden and Vasiliev, *Controlling the Dangerous Classes*, 195.

[60] Pickett, *House of Refuge*, 76–77. Pickett also notes that on some occasions where the parents challenged the Refuge officials legally, officials backed off to avoid further legal problems. In hindsight, we might wonder what would have happened if several dozen or more parents filed a class action lawsuit. In all likelihood, most parents were too poor and/or too unaware of their rights to challenge the officials.

[61] *Ex Parte Crouse*, 4 Wharton (Pa.) 9 (1938); for the significance for girls see Randall G. Shelden, "Confronting the Ghost of Mary Ann Crouse: Gender Bias in the Juvenile Justice System." *Juvenile and Family Court Journal*, 1998, 49: 11–26.

[62] *Ex Parte Crouse.*

[63] See Mennel, *Thorns and Thistles*; Hawes, *Children in Urban Society*; Bremner, *Children and Youth in America*; Pisciotta, "Saving the Children."

[64] Pisciotta, "Saving the Children."

[65] Quoted in Pickett, *House of Refuge*, 159.

[66] Bernard and Kurlychek, *The Cycle of Juvenile Justice*, 60–61.

[67] For further discussion of this issue see Meda Chesney-Lind and Randall G. Shelden, *Girls, Delinquency, and Juvenile Justice*, 4th ed. (Malden, NJ: Wiley-Blackwell, 2014).

[68] *Commonwealth v. Fisher*, 213 Pa. 48 (1905).

[69] During the decade of the 1830s, just under 600,000 immigrants arrived, followed by about 1.7 million during the 1840s, and another 2.6 million in the 1850s. Most came from northern and western Europe (especially Ireland and Germany). In Ireland, the potato famine in 1845 caused the death of thousands; an estimated 1.5 million Irish immigrated to the United States between 1845 and 1860 to escape the misery. New York City alone received between 62 and 70 percent of all immigrants between1846 and 1855 (http://www.latinamericanstudies.org/immigration-statistics.htm). For a general discussion of the immigration to the Midwest, see http://www.wisconsinhistory.org/turningpoints/tp-018 / The Midwest experienced massive population growth between 1820 and 1840: Ohio grew by 140%; Indiana went up by 308%; Illinois grew by 765% (http://www.connerprairie .org/Learn-And-Do/Indiana-History/America-1800-1860/Western-Immigration.aspx).

[70] Charles L. Brace, *The Dangerous Classes of New York* (New York: Wynkoop and Hallenbeck, 1872).

[71] For background see: "An Act Concerning the Attendance of Children at School," http://www.mhla.org/information/massdocuments/mglhistory.htm

[72] Bremner, *Children and Youth in America*, 456, 739, 820.

[73] Barbara Brenzel, "Lancaster Industrial School for Girls: A Social Portrait of a Nineteenth Century Reform School for Girls," *Feminist Studies* 1975(3): 40–53.

[74] Bremner, *Children and Youth in America*, 705.

[75] Platt, *The Child Savers*, 61–66. One supporter of this plan stated that such cottages would be "furnished with all the necessities and comforts of a well ordered home, presided over by a Christian gentleman and lady," 63.

[76] Robert Mennel, "Attitudes and Policies toward Juvenile Delinquency in the United States: A Historiographical Review," In M. Tonry and N. Morris (eds.). *Crime and Justice: An Annual Review of Research*, 1983, 4:191–224.

[77] The Children's Aid Society website, http://www.childrensaidsociety.org/about/history

[78] Marilyn I. Holt, *The Orphan Trains* (Lincoln: University of Nebraska Press, 1992).

[79] Hawes, *Children in Urban Society*, 101.

[80] In a study of the origins of the juvenile justice system in Memphis, Shelden found several instances where commitments to the county training school were challenged in court, some successfully. See Shelden, "Rescued from Evil," and Randall G. Shelden, "A History of the Shelby County Industrial and Training School," *Tennessee Historical Quarterly*, 1992, 51: 96–106.

[81] Bremner, *Children and Youth in America*, 693–94.

[82] Rendleman, "Parens Patriae," 104, 106.

[83] Rothman, *The Discovery of the Asylum*, 204.

[84] Bernard and Kurlychek, *The Cycle of Juvenile Justice*, 76–77.

[85] Platt, *The Child Savers*, 138.

[86] Anne M. Knupfer, *Reform and Resistance: Gender, Delinquency, and America's First Juvenile Court* (New York: Routledge, 2001), 199.

87 R. T. Shannon (ed.), *Code of Tennessee* (Nashville: Marshall and Bruce, 1896), 1087–88.

88 Platt, *The Child Savers*, chapter 6.

89 James Finckenauer, *Juvenile Delinquency and Corrections* (New York: Academic Press, 1984), 116

90 Steven Schlossman, *Love and the American Delinquent: The Theory and Practice of "Progressive" Juvenile Justice, 1825–1920,* (Chicago: University of Chicago Press, 1977), 92.

91 John Augustus, a Boston shoemaker, is credited with originating probation. During the 1840s, he volunteered to take on the responsibility of supervising offenders in the community as a substitute to sending them to prison or jail. Since then, his idea has become highly bureaucratized with the average probation officer supervising between 50 and 100 offenders. The spirit of volunteerism and the offering of a helping hand in the name of true benevolence toward another human being has turned into a job as a career bureaucrat. Many who engage in this line of work are overwhelmed by the responsibilities and often care little about the persons they supervise. In fact, the supervision is often little more than surveillance, which usually consists of a few phone calls. Some probation officers follow the motto found on the wall of a California probation office: "Trail 'em, Surveil 'em, Nail 'em, and Jail 'em."

92 Schlossman, *Love and the American Delinquent*, 99.

93 Ibid., emphasis added.

94 *Memphis Commercial Appeal*, July 16, 1912.

95 Shelden, "A History of the Shelby County Industrial and Training School."

96 Platt, *The Child Savers*, 105.

97 Ibid., 50, emphasis added.

98 Ibid., 59–60.

99 History Net (2016). "California Gold Rush." Retrieved from: http://www.historynet.com/california-gold-rush

100 Dan Macallair, *After the Doors Were Locked: A History of Youth Corrections in California and the Origins of Twenty-First-Century Reform* (Lanham, MD: Roman and Littlefield, 2015), 3.

101 Ibid.

102 Ibid., 10.

103 Ibid., 3.

104 Ibid., 10.

105 Ibid.

106 Ibid., 3.

107 Charles Cooley, "Nature v. Nurture in the Making of Social Careers," in F. Faust and P. Brantingham (eds.), *Juvenile Justice Philosophy*, 2nd ed. (St. Paul, MN: West, 1974); Charles Henderson, "Relation of Philanthropy to Social Order and Progress," in F. Faust and P. Brantingham (eds.), *Juvenile Justice Philosophy*, 2nd ed. (St. Paul, MN: West, 1974).

108 Shelden, "Rescued from Evil" and Shelden and Osborne, "For Their Own Good."

109 Brace, *The Dangerous Classes of New York*.

110 Spring, *Education and the Rise of the Corporate State*, 43, emphasis added.

111 Samuel Bowles, "Unequal Education and the Reproduction of the Social Division of Labor," in M. Carnoy (ed.), *Schooling in a Corporate Society* (New York: David McKay, 1975).

112 Spring, *Education and the Rise of the Corporate State*, 36.

113 *Education and the Rise of the Corporate State*, 22.

114 Quoted in Spring, *Education and the Rise of the Corporate State*, 36–37.

115 Ibid., xii.

[116] David Cohen and Marvin Lazeron, "Education and the Corporate Order," in R. C. Edwards, M. Reich, and T. E. Weisskopf (eds.), *The Capitalist System* (Englewood Cliffs, NJ: Prentice Hall, 1972), 186.

[117] Quoted in Ibid., 187.

[118] For a fuller discussion of this topic from the perspective of an active reformer of the period see Jane Addams, *The Spirit of Youth and the City Streets* (Champaign: University of Illinois Press, 2001). Originally published in 1909.

[119] Mennel, *Thorns and Thistles*, 96–99.

[120] See Jane Addams, *Twenty Years at Hull-House Streets* (Champaign: University of Illinois Press, 1990). Originally published in 1910.

[121] Barry Krisberg and James Austin, *Reinventing Juvenile Justice* (Thousand Oaks CA: Sage, 1993), 32–35.

[122] Roy Lubove, *The Professional Altruist: The Emergence of Social Work as a Career, 1880–1930* (Cambridge, MA: Harvard University Press, 1965).

[123] Krisberg and Austin, *Reinventing Juvenile Justice*, 35–42.

[124] Alexander Liazos, "Class Oppression: The Functions of Juvenile Justice," *Insurgent Sociologist*, 1974, 12; Frederic Thrasher, *The Gang* (Chicago: University of Chicago Press, 1927).

[125] Krisberg and Austin, *Reinventing Juvenile Justice*, 33.

[126] The case of *In Re Gault* involved a 15-year-old Arizona boy named Gerald Gault who was adjudicated delinquent in juvenile court and committed to the Arizona Industrial School for the "period of his majority" (21 years old) because he and some friends made an obscene phone call to a neighbor. The U.S. Supreme Court ruled that Gault had been denied certain fundamental rights (similar to the ruling by the Illinois court in the O'Connell case), such as the right to counsel. Writing for the majority, Justice Abe Fortus stated that "Under our Constitution, the condition of being a boy does not justify a kangaroo court." For the full text of this case (and many others, including the O'Connell case) see Faust and Brantingham, *Juvenile Justice Philosophy*; see also Platt, *The Child Savers*, 161–63.

[127] *Kent v. United States* (383 U.S. 541, 1966).

[128] *In re Winship* (397 U.S. 358, 1970).

[129] Jerome G. Miller, *Last One Over the Wall: The Massachusetts Experiment in Closing Reform Schools*, 2nd ed. (Columbus: Ohio State University Press, 1998).

[130] Krisberg and Austin, *Reinventing Juvenile Justice*, 49.

[131] Carl Pope and William Feyerherm, "Minority Status and Juvenile Justice Processing: An Assessment of the Research Literature" (Parts I and II), *Criminal Justice Abstracts*, 1990; Miller, *Search and Destroy*.

[132] Chesney-Lind and Shelden, *Girls, Delinquency and Juvenile Justice*.

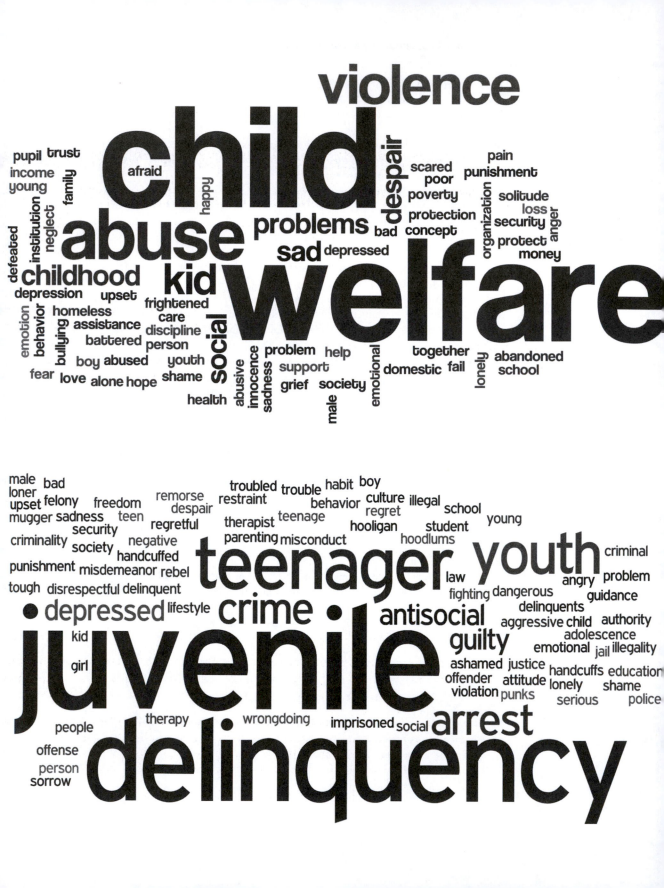

Chapter 2

The Extent of Delinquency

The actual amount of crime committed in the United States is not known and is probably unknowable. There are 4,500 federal criminal laws described in 27,000 pages of the US federal code.[1] Thousands of acts are prohibited by law; undoubtedly many violations are undetected by authorities. Many illegal acts are committed out of public view (such as possession and/or sale of illegal drugs), and victimless crimes generally do not involve anyone reporting the incident. Even in criminal cases involving victims, the crime is not always reported (see discussion later in the chapter). Criminologists and sociologists describe undiscovered or unreported criminal acts as the *dark figure of crime.* Determining the true extent of crime would mean that each individual would have to be monitored 24 hours a day, which would be impossible (and incredibly invasive and undesirable). Therefore, the sources for statistics about crimes are those known by local police or other authorities (from actual observation or reported by citizens), admissions from perpetrators, or victimization surveys.

MEASURING DELINQUENCY

The same factors affect the measurement of the amount of delinquent behavior in the United States. Consider, for example, the measurement of youth gang activities. A government report claimed that the number of counties reporting gang problems had increased by more than 1,000% between 1970 and1998.[2] The figures were alarming if accepted uncritically. There are, however, important questions to ask about the statistics. First, the definition of *gang* varies across jurisdictional lines. Given varying definitions, how were the statistics collected? Did the researchers have a list of gangs to consider, and how was it compiled? (Gangs do not keep records that can be searched.) The numbers were generated largely from law enforcement agencies—the same agencies that improve their chances of receiving additional funding by making a case that their communities have gang problems. The fact is that many of the youth labeled as gang members were probably not gang members at all. Indeed, some of the acts were committed by people legally classified as adults. We are not suggesting that people should disregard government reports, but it is essential to employ critical analysis before reaching any conclusions.[3]

Before discussing the extent of delinquency in the United States, we will take a close look at where we obtain the information on this subject and how crime and delinquency are measured. The most frequently consulted sources of data are: (1) *Crime in the United States* and *National Incident-Based Reporting System* (NIBRS) both published annually by the Federal Bureau of Investigation; (2) *Juvenile Court Statistics*, which provides data from the various juvenile courts in the country (3) various self-reports (questionnaires and/or interviews) in which young people list the delinquent activities in which they have engaged recently; and (4) the *National Crime Victimization* survey (NCVS). The first category is discussed below; the others are addressed later in the chapter.

FBI Uniform Crime Reporting

The International Association of Chiefs of Police proposed the Uniform Crime Reporting (UCR) program in 1929 to gather national crime statistics. One year later, the Federal Bureau of Investigation (FBI) was given the task of collecting and publishing the statistics. The annual report, *Crime in the United States*, consists of data sent to the FBI by 18,000 city, county, university/college, state, tribal, and federal law enforcement agencies; it covers about 93% of the population.

Crime in the United States consists of two major sections: (1) offenses known to law enforcement (crimes that are reported or otherwise come to the attention of local police departments) and (2) persons arrested. The first section reports the *number* of incidents known to law enforcement and the *crime rate* per 100,000 people in the general population. The crime rate is established by dividing the number of crimes by the population and multiplying by 100,000. The second section reports the number of arrests and includes tables on age and race and ethnicity.[4] Until 2013, Hispanics were included with whites on the report. Since that time, the report includes the total number of arrests by race (white, black, Native American, Asian, and Native Hawaiian) plus a total number of arrests by ethnicity (Hispanic/Latino and not Hispanic/Latino). The totals reported differ because not all agencies provide ethnicity data. In 2017, the total number of arrests of people under the age of 18 *by race* was 625,099; the total number of juvenile arrests *by ethnicity* was 466,450.[5] Thus, for example, one cannot determine the percentage of arrests of Hispanics (113,244) compared to the percentage of arrests of blacks—only the percentage of Hispanics versus non-Hispanics.

Part I Crimes (formerly index crimes)

Part I crimes are considered the most likely to be reported and the most likely to occur with sufficient frequency across jurisdictions. They include: (1) murder, (2) forcible rape, (3) robbery, (4) aggravated assault, (5) burglary, (6) larceny-theft, (7) motor vehicle theft, and (8) arson. The media generally cover the FBI's annual release (usually mid-September) of the numbers for the previous year, reporting whether the numbers or rate of serious crime decreased or increased.

Crime in the United States also includes a section called crimes cleared by an arrest. Relatively few crimes known to the police are ever cleared by an arrest. The percentage varies according to the type of crime committed. For instance, in 2017, 45.6% of the violent crimes known to the police were cleared by an arrest (61.6% of murders; 34.5% of rapes; 29.7% of robberies; and 53. 3% of aggravated assaults). Property crimes have always been the least likely to be cleared by an arrest. In 2017, 17.6% of property crimes were cleared by arrest (13.5% of burglaries, 19.2% of larcenies. 13.7% of motor vehicle thefts. and 21.7% of arsons).[6] Of the property crimes involving juveniles, 9.4% were cleared (9.3% of burglaries; 9.2% of larceny thefts; 11.6% of motor vehicle thefts; and 20.4% of arsons).[7]

Part II Offenses

The persons arrested section of *Crime in the United States* includes the eight part I offenses plus 20 other *categories* of crimes. *Other assaults* is a very broad category covering a variety of altercations and/or threats (ranging from a barroom brawl to a couple of teenagers fighting after school).[8] The category *all other offenses* includes such crimes as public nuisance, failure to appear on a warrant, bigamy, and—strangely enough—kidnapping, which can carry a penalty harsher than murder or rape if there is a ransom demand.

Critique of the UCR Reporting

Shortly after the death of actor Philip Seymour Hoffman of a drug overdose in February 2014, then Attorney General, Eric Holder, warned that the abuse of heroin and prescription drugs was an urgent and increasing public health crisis. He relied on data showing an increase of heroin overdoses by 45% between 2006 and 2010.[9] One of the most common criticisms of FBI and other national data is that they are always out of date. As Rick Rosenfeld, a criminologist at the University of Missouri-St. Louis, stated: "Using 2010 data to tell us about a heroin problem in 2014 is ludicrous. I don't think we know if we're in the midst of a heroin epidemic. I do know there are localities where the numbers are up. But to use numbers from four years ago as evidence of an urgent national problem today is pointless and silly. It just shows you how primitive the crime information infrastructure remains in this country."[10]

Similarly, most data from the Bureau of Justice Statistics are dated the moment they are released. Melissa Sickmund, director of the National Center for Juvenile Justice in Pittsburgh, said "I often joke to reporters that when we look at the national data it's like driving while looking in your rearview mirror, always looking at past years' data."[11] For example, *Juvenile Court Statistics 2016* was published in August 2018.

Perhaps the most important problem with UCR data is that its accuracy depends primarily on how well participating agencies adhere to the reporting procedures.

Criminologists and many police agencies acknowledge that *uniform* crime reporting is rarely the case.[12] A 157-page handbook from the FBI defines types of crimes and provides guidelines for agencies to follow when submitting their data. The choices made in categorizing certain crimes—especially assaults—have a major impact on the statistics generated.

Law enforcement agencies (like other bureaucracies) need to protect themselves—to prove that they are doing their job. They are not above manipulating crime statistics in order to obtain more local, state, or federal funding or to improve their public image. Crime statistics are easy to manipulate. For instance, some crimes are never counted officially. Some police administrators may knowingly falsify crime reports by undervaluing the cost of stolen goods. Conversely, they may report an ordinary pickpocketing incident as a robbery. The number of gangs, gang members, and gang-related crime can be inflated to receive federal funding to create or increase the size of a gang unit or to divert the public's attention away from internal problems within the police department.[13]

Henry Brownstein found that in the mid-1990s the media, politicians, and criminal justice officials in New York exaggerated a relatively modest fluctuation of reported crime to further private and political ambitions.[14] His analysis demonstrates how easily local data can be miscounted. The most easily manipulated category of crime—drug offenses—creates serious doubts about official statistics. Brownstein noted that in New York City in 1980 there were a reported 14,339 drug sales, while in 1981 there were only 4,317, a decrease of 70%. Two informal, unwritten policy changes affected how drug sales were counted. The first change was that phone calls from citizens reporting drug sales were no longer counted. The second change was that instead of counting an arrest of one drug dealer as one crime, the police began counting each drug sales *scene* as one crime, *no matter how many people were arrested.*

Decades later, examples of problems with data continue. A retired New York City police captain surveyed 400 retired NYPD police commanders who said that they were under enormous pressure to "underreport or misclassify serious crimes, which were then excluded from the city's crime reports to the state and FBI."[15] One New York commissioner accused another of deflating the number of shootings by directing officers not to count people injured by broken glass caused by gunfire.[16] Reporting often relies on the subjective assessment of law enforcement personnel. Many police departments massage their crime numbers, including Philadelphia, New Orleans, Chicago, and Milwaukee. In Milwaukee more than 500 violent crimes in 2009 were classified as minor assaults and were not included in the city's violent crime rate.[17] Crime reporting and data collection are *human enterprises and hence subject to ordinary human error*; critical analysis is essential when using data to make decisions about policies.

Another problem with UCR data is that most crimes are never reported to the police at all.[18] In 2016, about 42% of violent crimes and 36% of property crime were reported. Underreporting is particularly pervasive for rape.[19] Citizens may be reluctant to report crimes because they believe that nothing can be done, that the police do not want to be bothered, that the incident was essentially a private matter, or that reporting the crime will bring retaliation. In the case of rape, the victims fear (often justifiably) that the criminal justice system will not take their victimization seriously and will further victimize them, primarily by blaming them for their own victimization. This has been well documented in studies spanning more than 30 years.[20] Recent studies continue to note that rape is the most underreported crime.[21]

Arrest figures are also problematic. If someone is arrested and charged with more than one crime, only the most serious of these crimes is counted in the final tabulation of arrest data. Further, in some cases each *act* is counted as a separate offense, while in others multiple acts are counted as a single offense. If several people are robbed in an incident at a restaurant, it would be counted as one robbery. However, if the same offender physically attacked four people, the attacks would be listed as four assaults. For the crime of murder, the data list the number of people arrested—*not the number of victims murdered.* A mass murderer counts as one person arrested for homicide—the number of murders committed by that person is not known.

There is also an issue with the statistics not including resolution. How many of the arrestees were released? If indicted, was the person convicted? Many arrestees are *overcharged* by the police because they anticipate that the district attorney will bargain down the charges. Someone arrested for burglary could be convicted of trespassing. The UCR does not cover the outcomes of the millions of arrests the police make each year.

Interpreting crime *rates* presents another problem. First, the rates are based on the *total* population, which is far different from the population *at risk* for a particular crime—that is, the population of potential victims. For instance, rates of forcible rape are not based on the number of women in the population (the major at risk group). Since the female population is about 50% of the total population, the actual rate of reported rapes should be about double the UCR figures. Similarly, motor vehicle theft should be based on the number of motor vehicles, since not every person owns a motor vehicle (at a minimum, the rate should be based only on the population 16 and over). Second, changes in crime rates may be more a reflection of changes in the population or various demographic characteristics (e.g., increases or decreases in the proportion of youth), rather than the number of crimes committed. Quite often the actual number of specific crimes may increase, while the rate will decrease during a given period (and vice versa).

Finally, several types of crimes are excluded from UCR data. *Crime in the United States* focuses almost exclusively on street crimes involving a direct, one-on-one harm. Corporate crimes, crimes of the state, and child abuse and neglect are not included. The common definitions of crime and the popular images of crime are shaped and determined by the dominant classes in society and the state itself.[22] There are built-in class and racial biases in the very definition of crime.[23]

National Incident-Based Reporting

In response to many of these criticisms, the FBI developed the National Incident-Based Reporting Program (NIBRS) in 1991; the first published compilation of statistics was in 2011. Incident-based reporting captures more detailed information for each single crime occurrence. NIBRS subdivides offenses into 3 categories: crimes against persons, crimes against property, and crimes against society. It covers 52 offenses; in 2016, identity theft and hacking were added to the fraud category, and animal cruelty was added as one of the crimes against society. The data collected include characteristics of victims and perpetrators (including relationship), when and where a crime took place, property involved, injury sustained, the presence of alcohol or drugs, whether the incident was attempted or completed, and the circumstances of the incident. NIBRS data is not yet nationally representative; 37.1% of law enforcement agencies that participated in the UCR program in 2016 submitted their data via NIBRS. One fundamental flaw is that NIBRS (like UCR) depends on voluntary reporting from police agencies.[24] Another issue is that a huge database has its own potential problems, Too much information on citizens is a problem waiting to happen. There is always the danger of information being misused. Minorities are especially at risk; for example, data collected on gangs often disproportionately targets minorities.[25]

How Much Delinquency Is There?

FBI figures provide data on the number of arrests of people under the age of 18. Juveniles commit a wide variety of offenses, ranging from the most serious (such as murder and assault) to the most trivial (such as curfew violation and loitering). As will be noted shortly, self-report studies indicate that practically every youth at some point in their teenage years does something that could theoretically result in an arrest. Most are never arrested, and only a very small percentage end up in the juvenile justice system. What about those arrested? What are they arrested for?

Arrest Figures

Table 2-1 shows the total number of arrests of people under the age of 18. Juveniles accounted for 7.7% of all arrests in 2017. The table also gives the percentage of all juvenile arrests for each offense. The majority of juvenile arrests are for part II offenses, with all other offenses constituting the largest chunk of these arrests (see table 2-2). Other assaults are mostly minor personal crimes, resulting in few injuries. The number of arrests for other assaults depends on the willingness to resort to a formal arrest for minor forms of fighting on and off school grounds and for domestic disturbances. The zero tolerance mentality of recent years contributes to arrests. In Las Vegas, where the authors live, school police make thousands of arrests

Table 2-1   Total Arrests, Ages under 18, 2017

	Number	Percent of Juvenile Arrests
Total Arrests	634,535	100.0
Murder	717	0.1
Rape	3,030	0.5
Robbery	15,282	2.4
Aggravated assault	22,155	3.5
Burglary	24,223	3.8
Larceny-theft	93,738	14.8
Motor vehicle theft	12,798	2.0
Arson	1,766	0.3
Violent crime totals	41,184	6.5
Property crime totals	132,525	20.9
Other assaults	96,523	15.2
Forgery & counterfeiting	957	0.2
Fraud	3,714	0.6
Embezzlement	499	0.1
Stolen property	8,243	1.3
Vandalism	28,842	4.5
Weapons	14,384	2.3
Prostitution	218	*
Sex offenses	6,644	1.0
Drugs	74,088	11.7
Gambling	213	*
Offenses against the family and children	2,895	0.5
Driving under the influence	4,692	0.7
Liquor laws	26,107	4.1
Drunkenness	3,395	0.5
Disorderly conduct	49,041	7.7
Vagrancy	583	0.1
Curfew & loitering	23,699	3.7
All other offenses**	116,023	18.3

* Less than .1%

**Other offenses category includes trespassing, public nuisance, failure to appear on warrants, contempt, violation of probation, and certain status offenses.

Source: FBI, Crime in the United States, 2017, table 38.

Table 2-2 Rank Order of Juvenile Arrests, 2009 and 2017 (percent distribution)

2009	2017
1. All Other Offenses (18.0%)	1. All other offenses (18.1%)
2. Larceny-theft (15.0%)	2. Other assaults (15.0%)
3. Other assaults (12.0%)	3. Larceny-theft (15.7%)
4. Disorderly conduct (10.0%)	4. Drugs (11.5%)
5. Drugs (9.0%)	5. Disorderly conduct (7.7%)
Sub-total: 64% of all juvenile arrests	68% of all juvenile arrests

Source: FBI, Uniform Crime Reports 2017, table 38.

each year, and most of the crimes are ordinary fighting among students. A generation ago, teachers and other school employees would break up such fights, and an
arrest was a rare occurrence. When juveniles commit part I offenses, the majority
of arrests are for property offenses (some serious, but mostly minor). Larceny-theft,
which includes shoplifting , accounts for most arrests. Figure 2-1 shows the trends
in arrest rates from 1994 to 2016. From the peak of 8,476 arrests per 100,000 persons ages 10 to 17 in 1996, rates declined almost 76% by 2016.

National statistics that report a juvenile violent crime rate without listing the
rates for specific offenses are misleading. Most referrals to juvenile court are for
simple assault. Very often, however, news reports will give a single rate for all person
offenses or will use the label *violent crime* without pointing out that the bulk of the

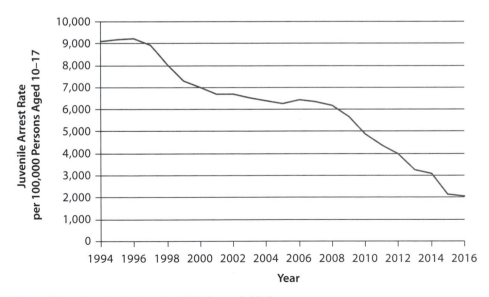

Figure 2.1 Arrest rate trends, 1994 through 2016.

offenses are simple assaults. The authors have seen articles in newspapers on numerous occasions with headlines that violent crime is up among juvenile court referrals.

Most (76%) of the public forms opinions about crime based on media reports; that is particularly true with juvenile crime because a very small percentage is committed by youth.[26] In addition, most of the public has no direct personal experience with crime by minority youth; thus, the public images are based on media presentations. In a review of research studies that investigated the race of perpetrators, Lori Dorfman and Vincent Schiraldi found that 75% of the studies concluded that people of color were disproportionately associated with violent crime as suspects in news stories, and 86% found consistent underreporting of people of color as victims of crime. More recent studies have found that the exaggerations have continued.[27]

Juvenile Court Statistics

The most common source for national figures has been the Office of Juvenile Justice and Delinquency Prevention (OJJDP), which publishes surveys of juvenile court case processing based on the voluntary submission of data from both state and local agencies. The data are grouped into the following major categories: person, property, drugs, and public order.

In 2016 juvenile courts across the nation processed 850,000 cases—33% were property offenses, 29% were person offenses, 25% were public order offenses, and 13% were drug law violations.[28] Relatively few (6.5%) were serious violent offenses (homicide, rape, robbery and aggravated assault. From 2005 through 2016, delinquency cases declined 49%. Property cases decreased 54%, public order 51%, person 44%, and drugs 42%. Most juvenile crime is relatively minor; larceny-theft (chiefly shoplifting) accounts for 45% of property offenses, and simple assault accounts for 65% of person offenses. This is quite different from the media image of juvenile predators running wild; the superpredator image was a myth.[29]

We have only an incomplete picture of status offenses. Published national data are cases actually petitioned to court—not all status offense referrals. In 2016 an estimated 94,700 status offense cases were petitioned, a decrease of 43% since 2005. The most common status offense was truancy (57% of the total) with liquor-law violations ranking second (12%), followed by ungovernability (9%) and runaway (8%).[30] OJJDP provides an online tool to access case counts of petitioned and non-petitioned status offense cases by state. In 2016, 20 states reported 71,557 non-petitioned status offense cases; the other 30 states did not provide that information.[31]

Self-Report Studies

One of the most popular methods of determining the extent of crime is the self-report survey. Since the 1940s there have been a number of such studies. Some researchers rely on anonymous questionnaires. Other studies check the accuracy of the answers to the questionnaires with follow-up interviews. Some studies use interviews plus validation by looking at police records.[32]

As long ago as the mid-1930s researchers noted the large amount of delinquent behavior that never came to the attention of the police and juvenile court officials. About one-third of delinquent behaviors known to social service agencies in New York City at that time never became juvenile court cases.[33] A study of boys in a counseling program found that many had committed delinquent acts but were never arrested, while many others were handled informally by the police. A mid-1940s study of college students discovered that they committed a variety of delinquent offenses while in high school. Self-report studies continued to be published in the 1950s and 1960s. One study compared the delinquent behaviors of a group of high school students with those of institutionalized delinquents and found that the behaviors were quite similar.[34]

Martin Gold and Jay Williams conducted a comprehensive study of 13- to 16-year-old boys and girls in 1967, the first national survey of youth.[35] For another study, the researchers drew data from interviews and records of that national sample of 847 youths and conducted in-depth interviews that lasted an average of about 105 minutes.[36] Each interview covered a wide variety of both delinquent and nondelinquent activities; 88% of the interviewees had committed at least one delinquent act during the previous three years. While most were rather trivial acts, some were serious felonies. Moreover, higher status white male youth committed more serious delinquencies than lower status youth. Less than 3% of the offenses were detected by the police, and only 9% of those interviewed had any contact with the police in the 3 years prior to the survey. The researchers concluded that official measures of delinquency do not accurately reflect delinquent behavior.

Most misleading has been the interpretation that whatever differentiates official delinquents from "non-delinquents" is a clue to the causes of delinquent behavior. In fact, the differentials result from the various behaviors of actors in the social system that include juveniles, police officers, judges, and less directly, others in the community and society. The delinquent behavior of the juvenile is but one element in the behavior of the whole social system that generates official delinquency.[37]

Several different agencies and organizations have investigated various forms of youth behavior over the past couple of decades. The Office of Applied Studies in the Substance Abuse and Mental Health Services Administration (SAMHSA) conducts an annual survey of the population age 12 and older to collect information on health issues, primarily the prevalence, patterns, and consequences of substance abuse. The National Survey on Drug Use and Health also asks youths if they have engaged in delinquent behaviors in the year prior to the survey. Some of the key findings are found in table 2-3. Note the low prevalence of most of these behaviors and that the most common was engaging in a fight. Notice too that there were few differences among the races for drug sales. One of the most comprehensive surveys is conducted by the Centers for Disease Control and Prevention. The Youth Risk Behavior Surveillance survey is published every two years. Some of the results from

Table 2-3   Participation in a Physical Delinquent Behavior in the Past Year among Persons
Aged 12 to 17, 2017

	Got into a Serious Fight at School or Work	Took Part in a Group-against-Group Fight	Attacked Someone with Intent to Seriously Hurt
Total	16.40%	11.3%	4.6%
Male	19.7	12.3	5.6
Female	12.9	10.4	3.7
White	14.1	10.2	3.4
Black	25	15	8.7
Hispanic	17.2	11.7	5.1

	Carried a Handgun	Sold Illegal Drugs	Tried to/ Stole Anything of More than $50 Value
Total	4.60%	2.10%	3.05%
Male	6.8	2.8	3.5
Female	2.4	1.4	2.6
White	5.7	2.3	2.6
Black	3	1.8	4.3
Hispanic	3.6	2.1	3.2

Center for Behavioral Health Statistics and Quality. *Results from the 2017 National Survey on Drug Use and Health: Detailed Tables*, Rockville, MD: Substance Abuse and Mental Health Services Administration, September 7, 2018, tables 3.14B, 3.15B.

2017 are summarized in table 2-4. Again, note the similarities for most behaviors across races.

In general, these studies have demonstrated that just about every juvenile has committed some act that could be designated as criminal or delinquent, but few people have been caught. Most juveniles have not committed serious forms of criminal or delinquent behavior, and they have not committed these acts on a regular basis. Crime and delinquency are distributed throughout the social class structure, and blacks and whites have about the same average of deviance. Class and racial differences are most apparent when considering persistent forms of lawbreaking.

Self-report studies can be criticized on several grounds. First, there are problems with the research methods used. The social settings where the research is conducted differ (e.g., some in high school classrooms, some at institutions, some in the home, etc.). Also, there are problems inherent in asking people questions about their past behavior. This is especially the case when asking about behaviors that violate the law. There is the problem of the loss of memory (e.g., we often tend to forget an experience that was unpleasant), some people exaggerate (e.g., youths may want to seem tough), the wording of questions and even the meaning of different acts may be interpreted differently by different people, and there is always the problem of bias on the part of the interviewer. Another problem is how to measure

Table 2-4 Proportion of High School Students Engaging in Delinquent Behavior, by Race and Gender, 2017

	Male			Female		
	White	**Black**	**Hispanic**	**White**	**Black**	**Hispanic**
Behavior						
Carried weapon to school	5.9	5.4	4.5	1.7	1.7	2.5
Threatened/injured by weapon on school property	6.5	10.0	8.3	3.6	5.5	3.8
Got in a physical fight	28.7	37.2	29.9	13.5	29.1	21.1
Physical fight on school property	10.1	16.9	11.6	3.1	13.7	7.0
Ever drank alcohol	60.5	44.8	62.3	62.8	57.3	67.1
Current alcohol use	31.6	16.9	26.8	33.2	24.3	35.9
Ever used pot	31.7	40.5	42.1	32.1	44.9	42.7
Current use pot	18.1	25.4	23.1	17.2	25.0	23.8
Ever used cocaine	5.5	4.2	8.1	3.4	1.2	4.6
Ever used heroin	1.8	2.9	2.7	0.4	1.3	1.0
Ever used meth	2.9	3.5	4.0	1.0	1.5	1.7
Ever used prescription pain medicine illegally	12.9	11.9	14.0	14.0	12.5	16.1
Offered, sold or given illegal drug on school property	19.6	19.6	25.8	15.9	18.2	25.0
Ever had sexual intercourse	38.5	52.7	44.1	38.7	39.4	37.9
Sexual intercourse before age 13	2.3	12.8	6.0	1.8	2.5	1.9

Source: Centers for Disease Control and Prevention, *Youth Risk Behavior Surveillance—United States, 2017*. Atlanta: Author, June 15, 2018, 67(8). Tables 18, 22, 24, 26, 94, 98, 106, 110, 114, 118, 120, 127, 131, 133, 135.

social class. Some surveys use income levels of individuals (or their parents), some use median income of census tracts, and some use occupation.

Many of these surveys have been validated through one or more methods. The most common methods include: comparing incarcerated youth with youth groups in the community; asking friends about a subject's delinquent acts; longitudinal testing where the same questions are asked at different points in time; and comparing self-reports with official arrest or juvenile court records. These methods have shown that most of the youths responding to self-report questionnaires have been telling the truth.[38]

JUVENILES AS VICTIMS

The victimization of juveniles takes two forms. First, there is the traditional victimization from a standard crime—an assault, a theft, etc. Second, there is the victimization by a member of one's own family, commonly referred to as *abuse and neglect*. While both of these areas will be discussed in this section, the latter will receive the most attention because it is more common and the most devastating to the victims. All states have laws that require certain professionals and institutions to refer suspected maltreatment to a child protective services (CPS) agency. Each state sets its own definitions of child abuse and neglect based on standards set by federal law.[39] Government publications often use the umbrella term maltreatment to refer to six major types of child abuse and neglect. The categories are outlined below.

Types of Child Abuse and Neglect

The Child Abuse Prevention and Treatment Act (CAPTA) as amended by the Reauthorization Act of 2010 defined child abuse and neglect, at a minimum, as: "Any recent act or failure to act on the part of a parent or caretaker which results in death, serious physical or emotional harm, sexual abuse or exploitation, or an act or failure to act, which presents an imminent risk of serious harm."[40] In 2016, 86% of victims suffered from a single type of maltreatment, which they could experience multiple times. Other children experience polyvictimization; the most common combination was neglect and physical abuse (5.2%).[41] Most states recognize the first four types of abuse listed below.

Neglect

Neglect is the failure of a parent, guardian, or other caregiver to provide for a child's basic needs. Neglect includes deprivation of adequate food, clothing, shelter, medical care, education, or supervision.[42]

Physical Abuse

Physical abuse is any nonaccidental physical injury to the child and can include striking, kicking, burning, biting, shaking, choking, or stabbing the child, or any action that results in a physical impairment.[43]

Sexual Abuse

CAPTA defines sexual abuse as "the employment, use, persuasion, inducement, enticement, or coercion of any child to engage in, or assist any other person to engage in, any sexually explicit conduct or simulation of such conduct for the purpose of producing a visual depiction of such conduct; or the rape, and in cases of caretaker or inter-familial relationships, statutory rape, molestation, prostitution, or other form of sexual exploitation of children, or incest with children."[44]

Psychological or Emotional Maltreatment

A pattern of behavior that impairs a child's emotional development or sense of self-worth is emotional abuse. This may include constant criticism, threats, and withholding love or guidance.[45]

Parental Substance Abuse

Circumstances considered parental substance abuse include: prenatal exposure due to the mother's use of harmful substances such as drugs; manufacturing a controlled substance in the presence of a child or on the premises occupied by a child; allowing a child to be present where the chemicals or equipment for the manufacture of controlled substances are used or stored; selling, distributing, or giving drugs or alcohol to a child; use of a controlled substance by a caregiver that impairs the caregiver's ability to adequately care for the child.[46]

Abandonment

Abandonment of the child occurs when the parent's identity or whereabouts are unknown; the child has been left by the parent in circumstances in which the child suffers serious harm; or the parent has failed to maintain contact with the child or to provide reasonable support for a specified period of time.[47]

In fiscal year 2016 there were an estimated 4.1 million referrals to CPS agencies, involving about 7.4 million children (more than triple the 2 million in 1986).[48] About 17% of these cases were substantiated. An estimated 1,750 children died of abuse and neglect (a decrease of 11% from 2008). Seventy percent of the children who died were younger than 3 years of age. The rate of African American child fatalities was 2.2 times greater than the rate for white children and almost 3 times greater than the rate for Hispanic children. Of the maltreated children, 40.3% were maltreated by their mother acting alone; 21.7% were victimized by their father acting alone; 20.5% were victimized by both parents. The most common type of maltreatment was neglect (74.8%), while about 18.2% were physically abused, 8.5% were sexually abused, 5.6% were psychologically maltreated. There is a correlation between maltreatment and lower socioeconomic status; maltreatment is also more likely within single-parent families—making poverty a contributing factor to maltreatment.[49]

The connection between child abuse and neglect and future behavioral problems has been clearly established. There are at least six long-term effects: *Emotional trauma* results in low self-esteem, guilt, anxiety, depression, and such physical problems as sleep disturbances, significant weight gain or loss, numerous illnesses, poor social relationships, and overall difficulties functioning in society;[50] *Running away* is another effect. The important word is *away*—not running *to* something but running *away* from what is often an unbearable situation (many who are placed in foster homes or some other alternative living arrangements continue to run, since they often experience further abuse and neglect). *Disruptive and truant behavior in school* is an understandable corollary—problems at home spill over into the schools. Problems experienced at school run the gamut from language deficiencies to learning problems to conflict with peers and teachers and the school itself (e.g., fights, vandalism, arson), not to mention poor academic performance and dropping out. *Drug and alcohol abuse* are often efforts to block the pain; this is especially common among sexual abuse victims. *Sexual behavior* involves promiscuity, prostitution, and early pregnancy; the connection between girls' sexual abuse and later prostitution has been extensively documented. *Violence and abuse* is a frequent pattern for those who have been abused themselves; they often abuse others, sometimes with severe violence, as in the case where children kill their parents. One important gender difference is that whereas boy victims generally take out their anger on others in the form of violence, girl victims tend to engage in self-destructive behavior. The adage that sparing the rod spoils the child is one of the greatest myths ever, as study after study show the clear connection between corporal punishment and children's deviance.[51] Finally, studies have shown that those who have experienced abuse are far more likely to end up somewhere in the juvenile justice system.[52]

Juvenile Victims of Violent Crime

It is sad to report that children of all ages—including those under the age of five—experienced some kind of violence in 2010. Almost half (46%) of those under 18 experienced some kind of assault. Black children were more than twice as likely to be victims of serious violence and 30% more likely to be victims of simple assault.[53] Perhaps the most dramatic statistic about juvenile victims of crime is that homicide was the fourth leading cause of death for children ages 1 to 11; it was the third leading cause of death for juveniles ages 12 to 17. Murder is most common among the oldest and youngest juveniles. Of the 1,450 juveniles murdered in 2010, 42% were under age 6 and 45% were ages 15 to 17. Black youth accounted for about 16% of the juvenile population between 1980 and 2010 but were the victims of 47% of the juvenile homicides during those 31 years. In 2014, the death by homicide rate for black male teens was 46 per 100,000 compared to 2 per 100,000 for whites and 11 per 100,000 for Hispanics.[54] The Centers for Disease Control and Prevention examined fatal and nonfatal firearm injuries among children aged 0 to 17. They found that 693 children are murdered by firearms each year; 22% are younger than 12 and 78% are ages 13 to 17. More than half (56%) of the victims are African American; 20% are white and 21% Hispanic.[55]

Research has also documented the close connection between being a victim and offending. A large study of delinquent careers in Denver (see below) found that the victimization of males predicted greater levels of violence and the victimization of girls predicted a greater level of delinquency in general (but not violence in particular).[56] Multiple studies have continued to document the connection between early experience of violence and subsequent serious delinquency.[57]

Victimization Surveys

The National Crime Victimization Survey (NCVS) began in 1973; it is a major source of crime statistics for analyzing victimization risk, consequences of victimization, and responses to crime.[58] NCVS provides an alternative to the collection of statistical data from official responses to crime. Most statistics on crime are produced from administrative records maintained by agencies such as the police or the courts.[59] The interdependence of protective services and statistical systems can introduce biases (or the perception of bias) into crime statistics. Another difference is that UCR aggregates crime rates at the jurisdictional level. There is little information about victims and the social context of crimes.

Twice a year, U.S. Census Bureau personnel interview members of a nationally representative sample of about 42,000 households—approximately 75,000 people age 12 or older. Households remain in the sample for three years. The interviewers ask a series of questions regarding household members' experiences as victims of crime, whether or not they reported a crime if they were victimized, and if they did not report it, why not. They are also asked to describe their offenders (in cases of personal crimes) and how they reacted (did they resist, etc.).[60]

The NCVS has had incremental minor changes as well as two major, multiyear redesigns to improve the accuracy and completeness of the data provided by victims.[61] The changes have been based on the need to improve the questions asked, to update survey methods, and to broaden the scope of crimes measured. When completed, the second redesign will cover stalking, identity theft, and fraud as well as improving the measurement of sexual and domestic violence and assessing perceptions of the police. The survey focuses on the crimes of rape, physical assault, robbery, burglary, larceny, and motor vehicle theft. The results of the survey have consistently shown significant differences from the annual FBI report.

NCVS illuminates the dark figure of crime. Victims may not report crimes to the police because they are afraid of reprisal or of getting an offender in trouble, or because they believe the police will not or cannot help, or because they think the crime is a personal issue or too trivial to report. In 2016, fewer than half (42%) of the violent victimizations reported to NCVS were also reported to the police.[62] Aggravated assault (58%) and robbery (54%) were more likely to be reported than simple assault (38%). Rape or sexual assault (23%) was even less likely to be reported. For property crime, motor vehicle thefts were the most likely to be reported to police (80%); half of household burglaries were reported and 30% of theft.

There were 5.7 million violent victimizations in 2016, a rate of 21 per 1,000 people age 12 or older. The most common violent crime reported to NCVS was simple assault—3.8 million victimizations at a rate of 14 per 1,000.[63] The rates for simple assault dwarf all of the other offenses included in the survey . The survey provides minimal age, offense, and race cross tabulations. For ages 12-17 the rate of serious violent crime (which does not include simple assault) per 1,000 was 8.6.[64] The rate for violent crime was 30.9. For all people age 12 or older, the victimization rate for serious violent crime for blacks and Hispanics was 8.2 compared to 6.3 for whites, while the rate for violent crime was 24 per 1,000 for blacks compared to 20 per 1,000 for whites and Hispanics.

NCVS data point to potential future problems. As already noted, the victim of today is often the offender of tomorrow. Many youths who joined gangs had been victimized and believed that gang affiliation would protect them from future victimization.[65]

A major problem with NCVS is that many crimes are *underreported,* as is the case with UCR. Crime is obviously a sensitive topic for many people, and they may understandably keep some information away from both the police and researchers. If they live in an area where there is a lot of crime, they might not remember the particulars of each and every theft, for example. When it comes to crimes committed by family members, there is a tendency to withhold information. If the victim is young enough, he or she might not even recognize that the behavior is criminal. Similarly, women who are victims of abuse by their husbands often rationalize or minimize abusive behavior; in some cases the abuse may be so frequent it is regarded as normal. Women who are raped are often reluctant to report such incidents, even to researchers.

People who move frequently may never have the opportunity to be part of the national sample. If you are homeless or a runaway, you are at increased risk for victimization but very unlikely to be included in the annual survey. An estimated 2.5 million children are homeless—an historic high of one in every 30 children.[66] The homeless are especially susceptible to victimization.[67]

Conducting household surveys is expensive, and response rates are declining.[68] Many households do not have land lines, and sampling techniques for cell phones have not been sufficiently developed. Technology allows respondents to screen incoming calls making it more difficult to reach potential participants. Many of the crimes measured in victimization surveys are increasingly rare. To obtain reliable estimates, in such cases, one needs larger samples—at a time when response rates are declining.

Finally, a common criticism is that many questions on the NCVS are about relatively minor offenses. The same can be said about UCR data, since the majority of crimes reported to the police are relatively minor offenses. However, NCVS specifically excludes homicide, arson, commercial crimes, and crimes against children under the age of 12. Survey respondents are never asked if toxic chemicals were dumped in the creek behind their house, if they were cheated out of a month's rent by the local bank or rental agent, if their children were made sick by companies selling lead-based crayons, or if they lost their union retirement benefits when the local savings and loan closed down after the president left for the Cayman Islands with $100 million. Nor are they asked about racial or sexual harassment in their schools, at work, or even on the street.[69] Moreover, children are never asked if their parents or some other adult sexually or physically abused them. This is especially important to know, since abuse and neglect have been found by many researchers to be an important link to delinquency, as already noted.

Although the subject will be discussed in more detail in chapter 10, some mention should be made of school violence. Despite media attention to the rare instances of school shootings, the school grounds continue to be the safest places for kids to be. The percentages of public schools recording incidents of crime and reporting incidents to the police were lower in the 2015–2016 school year than in every prior survey year (the survey began in 1993). Ten percent of public schools reported serious violent crime to the police. The rate per 1,000 students was 0.4.[70]

DELINQUENT CAREERS

The past several decades have witnessed considerable interest in delinquent careers and an increasing concern over the chronic delinquent. One of the most famous studies was authored by Marvin Wolfgang and his colleagues at the University of Pennsylvania.[71] Their study and a subsequent update traced the delinquent behavior of a group of adolescents over time.[72] Other researchers have completed similar longitudinal studies to explore the extensiveness of involvement in delinquent behavior. Most studies have measured delinquency by using contact with police or courts.[73]

The method of using a *cohort* (which can be all those born in a particular year, all who graduated in the same year, all those first arrested in the same year, etc.) has been used in longitudinal studies. This type of analysis is especially helpful in examining the extent, prevalence, and incidence of delinquency, since these rates may vary among specific individuals. This is important from both a practical and theoretical perspective. For instance, it is important to be able to distinguish between youths who come into contact with the juvenile court only once and those who have repeated contacts with the court. We also need to distinguish between those who cease their delinquent activities prior to their 18th birthday and those who persist into their adult years. A longitudinal approach tells us the onset, duration, and termination of delinquent careers.[74]

The data for these studies have come from a variety of sources. The study by Wolfgang and his associates used arrest records of youths in two different birth cohorts of Philadelphia; Lyle Shannon used police arrest records for three different birth cohorts in Racine, Wisconsin.[75] The Cambridge Study in Delinquency used self-report data, arrest and convictions, plus interview data.[76] Others have used self-report data, juvenile court data, and records of commitments to institutions.[77]

One of the most often quoted of these kinds of studies included in-depth surveys in three cities: Pittsburgh, Rochester, and Denver.[78] These longitudinal studies have examined a number of questions, including: (1) What factors are most strongly related to the onset, duration, and termination of delinquent careers? (2) What factors best predict who persists in their delinquent careers into their adult years? (3) Are there early warning signs for the onset of a delinquent career? (4) Do delinquents specialize in certain offense types? (5) Do delinquents progress from minor to more serious offenses during their careers?

Longitudinal research has revealed several factors that predict the length of one's career. The age at which an individual first has contact with the juvenile justice system is one of the most powerful predictors of the extent of his or her delinquent career. In general, research has found that the earlier one's contact, the greater the extent of one's career. Strongly related to this factor is exhibiting antisocial behavior at an early age (what researchers call early onset). Several studies have documented that such behavior in school, at home, and in the youth's own neighborhood are strong predictors of extensive delinquent behavior. More specifically, aggressiveness and theft at a very early age are particularly strong predictors. The research is clear that the later one begins getting into trouble, the less likely he or she will continue such behavior into their adult years.[79]

Gender, race, and social class are also related to delinquent careers. Both of the Philadelphia cohort studies, in addition to several others, suggest that African American youths not only have more extensive careers but also begin their careers at a younger age.[80] However, one study showed no connection to race.[81] While social class (or socioeconomic status) is not correlated with self-reported delinquency, it is related to *official* delinquency (partly because class is related to the seriousness of offenses committed and because class is related to police response). This fact has been noted by several researchers.[82] Gender differences appear to be the most pronounced among all the variables examined.[83]

From 1991 to 2000, arrests of girls increased more than arrests of boys for most offenses. By 2004, girls accounted for 30% of all juvenile arrests. There were questions about whether the trend indicated an increase in girls' delinquency or changes in the responses of society to girls' behavior. OJJDP convened the Girls Study Group to examine the paths taken by girls who engage in delinquent behavior. Researchers from two long-term longitudinal studies of delinquency (the Denver Youth Survey and the Fast Track Project) collaborated with academics to analyze and integrate findings on developmental patterns of girls' offending.[84] The girls in both studies were classified as high-risk, and the ages were 7 to 17 years. Most girls were involved in some form of delinquency, but the frequency of engaging in either minor or serious offenses was relatively small. The most common behavior involved status offenses, public disorder offenses, or minor crimes. Most girls began offending with less serious offenses, and there was no identifiable pattern of a specific age for committing a first offense or any particular offense to initiate offending, even for girls who were continually involved in delinquent behavior over several years. Similarly, girls stopped offending at different ages. More than half the girls were involved in status and/or minor offenses; those who did commit serious offenses generally returned to status and minor offending after 1 or 2 years. There was no dominant delinquency pathway for the girls. Researchers have noted that female status offenders rarely returned to court; when they do return, it is almost always for another status offense.[85]

The important point is that the vast majority of problem behaviors are intermittent or transitory. The OJJDP report on the surveys in Denver, Rochester, and Pittsburgh notes that most juveniles who exhibit problem behaviors do so only during a single year, and this pattern holds true for all problem behaviors.[86] The next most common pattern lasts for only two years. The report did find, however, a large proportion (20–30%) could be classified as serious delinquents. However, these surveys also found that more than half of the male serious delinquents in Denver and Pittsburgh and more than half of the female serious delinquents in Denver display no other problems; in Rochester, the figure is roughly 40% for both genders.

> A large proportion of persistent serious delinquents are not involved in persistent drug use, nor do they have persistent school or mental health problems. Although a significant number of offenders have other problems and are in need of help, persistent offenders as a group cannot be characterized as having other problems.[87]

As noted in multiple studies, even those involved in serious delinquency generally engage in the behavior for a limited amount of time.

SUMMARY

This chapter focused on the extent of delinquency in the United States. While it is impossible to determine the true extent of delinquency, many sources provide estimates, including the FBI's annual UCR and NIBRS data, statistics from juvenile courts, self-report studies, and victimization surveys. Each source of data has limitations. FBI statistics rely on voluntary submissions. In addition, subjective interpretations of guidelines affect the classifications submitted.

Victimization surveys were designed to estimate crimes that are not reported to local police departments. Although these self-report studies focus primarily on minor behavior, they do reveal that a great deal of criminal behavior never gets reported, the dark figure of crime. Surveys may not be representative of everyone in the population. The homeless, for example, are not included.

There has been a substantial decline in the number of arrests of juveniles since the late 1990s. Juveniles are consistently charged primarily with minor offenses. There has been no wave of violence, contrary to sensational media accounts. Indeed, juveniles are far more frequently on the receiving end of violence. Not only do victims suffer the trauma of physical injury but research has also shown a close connection between being a victim and offending

Although not included in the official crime statistics, children suffer from a number of forms of maltreatment, whether neglect, physical abuse, sexual abuse, and/or emotional abuse. As with criminal victimization, maltreatment is a predictor of future delinquency.

Researchers have used longitudinal studies to determine the onset, duration, and termination of delinquent careers. Studies have looked at various cohorts and have found several early warning signs. The age of first contact with the juvenile justice system is a strong predictor, as is antisocial behavior at an early age. Gender, race, and social class also affect delinquent careers. Most juvenile problem behaviors do not persist.

Notes

[1] Randall G. Shelden, William B. Brown, Karen S. Miller, and Randal B. Fritzler, *Crime and Criminal Justice in American Society*, 2nd ed. (Long Grove, IL: Waveland Press, 2016).

[2] Walter B. Miller, *The Growth of Youth Gang Problems in the United States: 1970–98*, Washington, DC: OJJDP, April 2001.

[3] For a more complete critique of the measurement of gang activities see Randall G. Shelden, Sharon K. Tracy, and William B. Brown, *Youth Gangs in American Society*, 4th ed. (Belmont, CA: Cengage, 2013).

[4] There are five categories for race: white; black; American Indian or Alaskan Native; Asian, or Pacific Islander; In 2013, UCR added an ethnicity category of Hispanic/Latino. Prior to 2016, UCR included tables on sex. In 2016 some of that information is available only by downloading supplemental tables.

[5] Federal Bureau of Investigation, "Crime in the United States, 2017," Washington, DC: Author, 2018, table 43b. The total arrests by race more nearly match the total given for arrests under the age of 18 (634.535) in table 38.

[6] Ibid., table 25.

[7] Ibid., table 28.

[8] Legal codes distinguish between assault and battery as specific crimes. A simple example will help. If someone should come up and threaten you with bodily harm, that threat is technically an assault. For example, the statement, "The next time you cross me, I'll bash your face in!" is an assault. If a person carries through on the threat, it is "assault and battery." If there were no threat but simply a case of someone attacking you without a weapon, the charge would be battery (but for statistical purposes it would be counted as an assault). Also, if someone threatens you and points a gun or other weapon at you, a charge of assault with a deadly weapon can be made. If the threat is carried out, it can result in a charge of felonious assault.

[9] David J. Krajicek, "Can We Trust Crime Numbers?" *The Crime Report*, March 31, 2014.

[10] Quoted in Ibid.

[11] Quoted in Ibid.

[12] Victor E. Kappeler and Gary W. Potter, *The Mythology of Crime and Criminal Justice*, 5th ed. (Long Grove, IL: Waveland Press, 2018).

[13] This assertion is based on personal observations of the author, confidential conversations with members of police departments in two different cities and internal memos obtained. Documentation about using gangs to divert attention away from internal problems is found in Richard C. McCorkle and Terance D. Miethe, *Panic: The Social Construction of the Street Gang Problem* (Upper Saddle River, NJ: Prentice-Hall, 2001).

[14] Henry H. Brownstein, *The Rise and Fall of a Violent Crime Wave: Crack Cocaine and the Social Construction of a Crime Problem* (Guilderland, NY: Harrow and Heston, 1996), 22.

[15] Ryan Jacobs, "Just Like in *The Wire*, Real FBI Crime Stats Are 'Juked,'" *Mother Jones*, June 19, 2012.

[16] Carl Bialik, "How to Make Sense of Conflicting, Confusing and Misleading Crime Statistics," FiveThirtyEight, January 8, 2016.

[17] Ben Poston, "Hundreds of Assault Cases Misreported by Milwaukee Police Department," *Milwaukee Journal Sentinel*, May 22, 2012.

[18] John Gramlich, "5 Facts about Crime in the US," Washington, DC: Pew Research Center, January 30, 2018.

[19] Bialik, "How to Make Sense of Conflicting, Confusing and Misleading Crime Statistics."

[20] Julie Allison and Lawrence Wrightsman, *Rape: The Misunderstood Crime* (Newbury Park, CA: Sage, 1993); Lee Madigan and Nancy Gamble, *The Second Rape: Society's Continual Betrayal of the Victim* (New York: Lexington Books, 1989).

[21] National Research Council, *Estimating the Incidence of Rape and Sexual Assault*, Washington, DC: Author, 2014; Sharon Smith et al., *National Intimate Partner and Sexual Violence Survey: 2015 Data Brief*. Atlanta, GA: Centers for Disease Control and Prevention, July 14, 2017, https://www.cdc.gov/violenceprevention/nisvs/2015NISVSdatabrief.html

[22] Jeffrey H. Reiman and Paul Leighton, *The Rich Get Richer and the Poor Get Prison*, 11th ed. (New York: Routledge, 2017).

[23] For a further discussion of this issue see Randall G. Shelden and Pavel V. Vasiliev, *Controlling the Dangerous Classes: A History of Criminal Justice in America*, 3rd ed. (Long Grove, IL: Waveland Press, 2018).

[24] Shelden et al., *Crime and Criminal Justice in American Society*.

[25] Shelden et al., *Youth Gangs in American Society*.

[26] Lori Dorfman and Vincent Schiraldi, "Off Balance: Youth, Race & Crime in the News," Washington, DC: Youth Law Center, April 2001.

[27] Justice Policy Institute, "The Youth Gang Violence Problem Is Exaggerated," *Violent Children*, edited by Roman Espejo, Greenhaven Press, 2010. At Issue. *Opposing Viewpoints In Context*, http://ic.galegroup.com/ic/ovic/ViewpointsDetailsPage/ViewpointsDetailsWindow?displayGroupName=Viewpoints&prodId=OVIC&action=2&catId=&documentId=GALE%7CEJ3010032227&userGroupName=txshracd2560&jsid=6a0eb05a3a670f5a10c33d86e864afe1

[28] Sarah Hockenberry and Charles Puzzanchera, "Juvenile Court Statistics 2016." Pittsburgh, PA: National Center for Juvenile Justice, August 2018.

[29] For a good summary of the superpredator myth, see: Equal Justice Initiative, "The Superpredator Myth, 20 Years Later," Montgomery, AL: Author, April 7, 2014. As noted in the introduction, images and stereotypes from the myth are alive today. For example, see law professor Steven Drizin's article "Trayvon and the Myth of the 'Juvenile Superpredator,'" *Huffpost Crime* (November 17, 2013).

[30] Hockenberry and Puzzanchera, "Juvenile Court Statistics 2016."

[31] Sarah Hockenberry, J. Smith, and W. Kang, "Easy Access to State and County Juvenile Court Case Counts," 2016," https://www.ojjdp.gov/ojstatbb/ezaco/

[32] Walter S. DeKeseredy and Martin D. Schwartz, *Contemporary Criminology* (Belmont, CA: Wadsworth, 1996), 135.

[33] Sophia Robison, *Can Delinquency Be Measured?* (New York: Columbia University Press, 1936).

[34] James F. Short, Jr. and F. Ivan Nye, "Extent of Unrecorded Juvenile Delinquency: Tentative Conclusions," *Journal of Criminal Law, Criminology and Police Science*, 1958, 49: 296–302; Fred J. Murphy, Mary M. Shirley, and Helen L. Witmer, "The Incidence of Hidden Delinquency," *American Journal of Orthopsychiatry*, 1946, 16: 686–96; Austin Porterfield, *Youth in Trouble* (Fort Worth, TX: Leo Potishman Foundation, 1946).

[35] Martin Gold and Jay R. Williams, "National Survey of Youth, 1967." Ann Arbor, MI: Interuniversity Consortium for Political and Social Research, March 30, 2006, ICPSR 3509.

[36] Jay R. Williams and Martin Gold, "From Delinquent Behavior to Official Delinquency," *Social Problems*, 1972, 20(2): 209–229.

[37] Ibid., 227.

[38] David P. Farrington, Rolf Loeber, Magda Stouthamer-Loeber, Welmoet Van Kammen, and Laura Schmidt, "Self-Reported Delinquency and a Combined Delinquency

Seriousness Scale Based on Boys, Mothers, and Teachers: Concurrent and Predictive Validity for African-Americans and Caucasians," *Criminology*, 1996, 34: 501–25; James P. Lynch, "The Evolving Role of self-Report Surveys of Criminal Victimization in a System of Statistics on Crime and the Administration of Justice," *Statistical Journal of the IAOS*, 2014, 30(3): 165–169.

39   Children's Bureau, *Child Maltreatment 2016* (Washington, DC: Administration on Children, Youth and Families, 2018), viii. Federal legislation addressing child abuse and neglect was passed in 1974. *The Child Abuse Prevention and Treatment Act* (CAPTA) authorized the National Center on Child Abuse and Neglect (NCCAN) to collect data annually on cases reported to child protective services. The act has been amended several times, most recently in July 2016 by the Comprehensive Addiction and Recovery Act.

40   Ibid.

41   Ibid., 20.

42   Ibid.

43   Child Welfare Information Gateway, "What Is Child Abuse and Neglect," Washington, DC: Children's Bureau, July 2013, 3.

44   Ibid., 4.

45   Ibid.

46   Ibid.

47   Ibid.

48   Children's Bureau, *Child Maltreatment 2016*, ix–x; table 3-16; table 3-8.

49   See David Zielinski, "Long-term Socioeconomic Impact of Child Abuse and Neglect: Implications for Policy," West Lafayette, IN: Family Impact Institute, 2005; Lawrence M. Berger and Jeanne Brooks-Gunn, "Socioeconomic Status, Parenting Knowledge and Behaviors, and Perceived Maltreatment of Young Low-Birth-Weight Children," *Social Science Review*, 2005, 79(2): 237–267; Child Welfare Information Gateway, "Long-Term Consequences of Child Abuse and Neglect," Washington, DC: Children's Bureau, July 2013.

50   Shelden has personally seen firsthand hundreds of incarcerated youth (in detention centers and training schools) who are very small for their age, often shorter than normal, and who have numerous serious physical ailments, including dental problems (many never saw a dentist until they were detained) and eating disorders (for many, incarceration is their first experience with three meals a day). No wonder they are angry, confused, depressed, anxious, and so often express these problems outwardly either against themselves (e.g., suicide attempts) or others (e.g., fighting, theft). A visit to a local detention center or training school quickly brings the problem into focus.

51   Murray Straus, *Beating the Devil Out of Them: Corporal Punishment in American Families* (New York: Lexington Books, 1994); Joan Durrant and Ron Ensom, "Physical Punishment of Children: Lessons from 20 Years of Research," *Canadian Medical Association Journal*, 2012, 184: 1373–1377; Matthew K. Mulvaney and Carolyn J. Mebert,. "Parental Corporal Punishment Predicts Behavior Problems in Early Childhood." *Journal of Family Psychology*, 2007, 21: 389–97; Eric P. Slade and Lawrence S. Wissow, "Spanking in Early Childhood and Later Behaviour Problems: A Prospective Study of Infants and Young Toddlers," *Pediatrics*, 2004, 113(5): 1321–30; Catherine A. Taylor, Jennifer A. Manganello, Shawna J. Lee, and Janet C. Rice, "Mothers' Spanking of 3-year-old Children and Subsequent Risk of Children's Aggressive Behavior." *Pediatrics*, 2010, 125: 1087–1065.

52   Joseph P. Ryan, Denise Herz, Pedro M. Hernandeza, and Jane Marie Marshall. "Maltreatment and Delinquency: Investigating Child Welfare Bias in Juvenile Justice Processing," *Children and Youth Services Review*, 2007, 29(8): 1035–1050. See also: Jennifer E.

Lansford, Shari Miller-Johnson, Lisa J. Berlin, Kenneth A. Dodge, John E. Bates, and Gregory S. Pettit, "Early Physical Abuse and Later Violent Delinquency: A Prospective Longitudinal Study," *Child Maltreatment*, 2007, 12(3): 233–245.

[53]   Melissa Sickmund and Charles Puzzanchera, *Juvenile Offenders and Victims: 2014 National Report* (Pittsburgh: National Center for Juvenile Justice, December 2014).

[54]   Child Trends Databank, "Teen Homicide, Suicide and Firearms Deaths," Bethesda, MD: Child Trends, December 2015.

[55]   Katherine A. Fowler, Linda L. Dahlberg, Tadesse Haileyesus, Carmen Gutierrez, and Sarah Bacon, "Childhood Firearm Injuries in the United States," *Pediatrics*, 2017, 140(1).

[56]   David Huizinga, Rolf Loeber, Terence P. Thornberry, and Lynn Cothern, "Co-occurrence of Delinquency and Other Problem Behaviors," Washington, DC: OJJDP, November 2000.

[57]   Lansford et al., "Early Physical Abuse and Later Violent Delinquency; World Health Organization"; Carlos Cuevas, David Finkelhor, Heather A. Turner, and Richard K. Ormrod, "Juvenile Delinquency and Victimization: A Theoretical Typology," *Journal of Interpersonal Violence*, 2007, 22(12): 1581–1602.

[58]   Lynn Lanton, Michael Planty, and James P. Lynch, "Second Major Redesign of the National Crime Victimization Survey (NCVS), *Criminology & Public Policy*, 16(4): 1049–1074.

[59]   Lynch, "The Evolving Role of Self-report Surveys of Criminal Victimization."

[60]   For a complete overview see http://www.bjs.gov/index.cfm?ty=dcdetail&iid=245

[61]   Langton, Planty, and Lynch.

[62]   Rachel E. Morgan and Grace Kena, "Criminal Victimization, 2016," Washington, DC: Bureau of Justice Statistics, December 2017, p. 7.

[63]   Ibid., table 2.

[64]   Ibid., table 8.

[65]   Shelden et al., *Youth Gangs in American Society*.

[66]   Ellen L. Bassuk, Carmela J. DeCandia, Corey Anne Beach, Fred Berman, "America's Youngest Outcasts: A Report Card on Child Homelessness," Waltham, MA: The National Center on Family Homelessness, 2014.

[67]   Michael Stoops, "Vulnerable to Hate: A Survey of Hate Crimes and Violence Committed against Homeless People in 2013," Washington, DC: National Coalition for the Homeless, June 2014.

[68]   Lynch, "The Evolving Role of Self-report Surveys of Criminal Victimization."

[69]   DeKeseredy and Schwartz, *Contemporary Criminology*, 132–33.

[70]   Lauren Musu, Anlan Zhang, Ke Wang, Jizhi Zhang, and Barbara Oudekerk, *Indicators of School Crime and Safety: 2018* (Washington, DC: National Center for Education Statistics, 2019), table 6.3.

[71]   Marvin E. Wolfgang, Robert M. Figlio, and Thorsten Sellin, *Delinquency in the Birth Cohort.* (Chicago: University of Chicago Press, 1972).

[72]   Paul E. Tracy, Marvin E. Wolfgang, and Robert M. Figlio, "Delinquency in Two Birth Cohorts," Washington, DC: U. S. Department of Justice, 1985.

[73]   David P. Farrington, "Offending from 10 to 25 Years of Age." in K. Van Dusen and S. A. Mednick (eds.), *Prospective Studies of Crime and Delinquency* (Boston: Kluwer-Nijhoff, 1983); David P. Farrington, "Early Precursors of Frequent Offending," in James Q. Wilson and Glenn C. Loury (eds.), *From Children to Citizens, Vol. 3: Families, Schools, and Delinquency Prevention.* (New York: Springer-Verlag, 1987); Peter J. Carrington, "Co-offending and Offending and the Development of the Delinquent Career," *Criminology*, 2009, 47: 1295–1329.

[74] David Farrington, Lloyd Ohlin, and James Q. Wilson, *Understanding and Controlling Crime: Toward a New Research Strategy* (New York: Springer-Verlag, 1986), 40–44.

[75] Lyle W. Shannon, *Assessing the Relationship of Adult Criminal Careers to Juvenile Careers* (Washington, DC: US Department of Justice), 1982.

[76] Donald West, *Delinquency: Its Roots, Careers and Prospects* (Cambridge, MA: Harvard University Press, 1982); Donald West and David P. Farrington, *The Delinquent Way of Life* (London: Heinemann, 1977); Donald West and David P. Farrington, *Who Becomes Delinquent* (London: Heinemann, 1973).

[77] The research is too vast to cite here; see the following for a good representation: Rolf Loeber, "The Stability of Antisocial and Delinquent Child Behavior: A Review." *Child Development*, 1987, 53: 1431–46; Rolf Loeber, and Thomas Dishion, "Early Predictors of Male Delinquency: A Review," *Psychological Bulletin*, 1983, 94: 68–99.

[78] Huizinga et al. "Co-occurrence of Delinquency and Other Problem Behaviors."

[79] Although somewhat dated, a very good literature review is provided by Joy G. Dryfoos, *Adolescents at Risk: Prevalence and Prevention* (New York: Oxford University Press, 1990); see also Alex R. Piquero, David P. Farrington, Daniel S. Nagin, and Terrie E. Moffitt, "Trajectories of Offending and Their Relation to Life Failure in Late Middle Age: Findings from the Cambridge Study in Delinquent Development," *Journal of Research in Crime and Delinquency*, 2010, 47(2): 151–173; Maria M. Ttofia, David P. Farrington, and Friedrich Lösel, "School Bullying as a Predictor of Violence Later in Life: A Systematic Review and Meta-analysis of Prospective Longitudinal Studies," *Aggression and Violent Behavior*, 2012, 17(5): 405–418.

[80] Huizinga et al. "Co-occurrence of Delinquency and Other Problem Behaviors."

[81] Alex R. Piquero, Carol A. Schubert, and Robert Brame (2014). "Comparing Official and Self-report Records of Offending across Gender and Race/Ethnicity in a Longitudinal Study of Serious Youthful Offenders," *Journal of Research in Crime and Delinquency*, 2012, 51(4): 526–556.

[82] For a discussion of class as a key variable, see Reiman and Leighton, *The Rich Get Richer and the Poor Get Prison*.

[83] For a comprehensive review of girls and delinquency see Meda Chesney-Lind and Randall G. Shelden, *Girls, Delinquency, and Juvenile Justice,* 4th ed. (Malden, MA: Wiley-Blackwell, 2014).

[84] David Huizinga, Shari Miller, and the Conduct Problems Prevention Research Group, Developmental Sequences of Girls' Delinquent Behavior," Washington, DC: OJJDP, December 2013.

[85] A complete review is found in Chesney-Lind and Shelden, *Girls, Delinquency and Juvenile Justice*.

[86] Huizinga et al., "Co-occurrence of Delinquency."

[87] Ibid., 5–6.

Chapter 3

The Nature of Delinquency

As we saw in chapter 1, the term *delinquency* evolved from early nineteenth-century state codes based, at least in part, on the *parens patriae* doctrine. *Juvenile delinquent* referred to both the failure to do something that is required and to someone who is not yet fixed in his or her ways and is thus subject to change and redemption.

The Illinois Juvenile Court Act of 1899 created the first juvenile court and delineated three major areas for its jurisdiction: (1) juvenile acts that violated laws applicable to adults (e.g., burglary, larceny, assault, etc.); (2) juvenile violations of local ordinances; and (3) behaviors that would eventually be called status offenses (e.g., running away from home, truancy, underage drinking, curfew violations, etc.). In time, juvenile and family courts would oversee three broad areas: (1) *delinquency*, which refers to violations of laws applicable to any age group; (2) *status offenses*, which are offenses because of the age of the offender; and (3) *abuse and neglect* (or dependency and neglect), which are cases in which the juvenile is the victim. Violations of various court orders (e.g., contempt of court, conditions of probation or parole) also fall under the umbrella of delinquency. This is important because it can override certain restrictions. For example, status offenders cannot be placed in detention, subjected to incarceration in correctional institutions, or placed in adult facilities. However, if a youth violates a court order, even if the original behavior was a status offense, he or she could be subject to detention. We will revisit this issue later in this chapter.

While juvenile codes have changed a great deal since the founding of the modern juvenile court, there are still numerous vaguely worded statutes governing the behavior of juveniles. Words such as *idle, immoral*, or *dissolute* appear in statutes that prohibit loitering or sleeping in alleys and begging—in other words, being poor. An important component of modern juvenile codes is the term *juvenile* itself. State law determines the oldest age at which a juvenile court has original jurisdiction over an individual for violating the law.

As discussed in the introduction, 46 states and the District of Columbia use 18 as the upper age limit for juvenile court jurisdiction; 4 states use 16 as the upper limit. This means that a person who reaches the age of 18 (or 16 in 4 states) is legally an adult. Vincent Schiraldi and Bruce Western are among those who believe the age should be raised to 21.[1] Neurobiology and developmental psychology have shown that the brain doesn't develop fully until the mid-20s. Until fully mature, young people are more susceptible to peer pressure and are more volatile in emotionally charged settings. In addition, adolescence extends to a later age today than in previous generations. Young people finish college, leave home, find jobs, and get married much later than their parents did. States prohibit people younger than 21 from smoking cigarettes, consuming alcohol, and possessing firearms but treat them as adults 3 years earlier in the legal system.

This chapter provides a broad overview of some of the major types of delinquency behavior and the patterns that such behavior takes. Some of the most distinctive features of delinquency are the range of behaviors covered, the degree to which such behaviors reflect various social and personal problems, the actual extent of such behavior, and the significance of such behaviors.[2]

Varieties of Delinquent Behavior

We can segment delinquency and delinquents into eight categories. Within each category, there is a continuum of behavior.

From Mentally Disturbed to Well Adjusted

At one extreme are acts committed by young people that are behavioral responses to a perceived threatening environment by persons ill equipped to cope with that environment (ranging from children who demonstrate minor forms of mental disturbances to fully developed psychopathology).[3] At the other extreme are youths who appear to be well adjusted to their environment and who may be acting in accordance with the prevailing system of norms (whether a middle-class youth who gets high at a party or a gang member who commits a crime as part of an initiation ritual). Failure to act in any other manner could be considered deviant by peers and could result in rejection by the group. The majority of juveniles who violate some law or status offense are rather well-adjusted young people who will invariably age out of the behavior and become fully functioning adults. As we saw in chapter 2, self-report studies show that almost all juveniles commit some crime or delinquent behavior before they reach adulthood.

From Striving for Acceptance to Chronic Delinquent

Some juveniles act out to gain personal recognition and/or acceptance. Gaining attention can involve wearing clothes perceived as outlandish, doing something wild with one's hair color or style, or getting multiple body piercings or tattoos. Quite often young people are just testing the boundaries of what they can do, or perhaps they got carried away at a party or group gathering and committed a crime (perhaps on a dare). Or they merely made a mistake, like we all do from time to time.

These examples constitute the typical form of delinquency engaged in by millions of adolescents the world over.

At the other extreme, there is a small minority who engage in very businesslike criminal behavior—repeatedly breaking into cars, homes, businesses, or schools in order to steal things; dealing in drugs; systematically shoplifting at malls. As discussed in chapter 2, a very small minority of juveniles (known as chronic offenders) is responsible for a disproportionate amount of the crime committed by this age group.

From Means of Survival to Hedonistic Behavior

Some youths engage in a variety of delinquent activities—especially theft and drug dealing—as a means of surviving in a very deprived environment. The typical delinquent, however, engages in behavior that more often than not reflects consumerist behavior in a capitalist society, where wants are artificially created and obtaining material things (e.g., clothes, cosmetics, cars, etc.) is linked to status. Young people often engage in minor forms of theft where the objects stolen are not necessary for survival but for demonstrating that they belong or to attract the opposite sex. As we will see later in the chapter, most theft by juveniles is of this kind. Part of this kind of criminal activity is merely a natural by-product of the relentless pursuit of the American Dream, a cultural ethos that places intense pressures on most people to want and desire what may be impossible to obtain legally.[4]

From Individual to Highly Organized Behavior

Most delinquent activities involve two or more youths. The lone delinquent offender is the exception rather than the rule.[5] He or she lies at one extreme of the continuum and acts alone for a variety of reasons. Most delinquent behavior is highly disorganized and occurs on the spur of the moment, with little or no planning involved. More often than not, a group of youths wander about with little sense of direction, perhaps merely hanging out where teenagers normally gather—on a street corner, in a park or playground, at the movies, at a mall, at video arcades, or just "cruising" around, with "no particular place to go."[6] Numerous studies have confirmed that little planning takes place during most delinquent activities.[7] At the other end of the continuum are the few who engage in highly organized behavior, sometimes for profit and sometimes just for the thrills created by engaging in the behavior.[8]

From Restricted Acts to Generic Deviation

Some juveniles tend to specialize in one form of delinquency or another. Some may engage in status offenses only or shoplift, while others steal cars, deal drugs, commit burglaries, or participate in other forms of crime. More often than not, those who engage in persistent delinquent activities engage in more than one type. Some will commit a variety of property crimes involving little or no violence; others may engage in violent types of crimes only, such as assaults (including rapes) or robberies. An examination of the rap sheets of juvenile offenders usually finds a variety of mostly property crimes, some status offenses, and some referrals to court for abuse and neglect.

From Prankish Behavior to Intended Harm

The vast majority of delinquent activities do not involve a victim who suffers a direct harm. If harm does occur, it is not serious and/or intentional. Most acts are of the public order variety (disturbing the peace, loitering, curfew violations, truancy, running away from home, drug and/or alcohol use, etc.). *Joyriding* (where youths take someone's car, usually a neighbor's, for a short ride) is an example of an offense where usually no one is physically harmed or no property damage occurs (unless there is an accident). Pranks have been a normal part of adolescence for hundreds of years and are usually viewed as an acceptable method of letting off steam. The zero-tolerance mentality (see chapter 10) closed off many outlets for youthful expression.

At the other extreme are activities where harm, often very serious harm, is the express purpose. Examples include gang retaliations, such as drive-by shootings. People may be killed or injured—sometimes bystanders rather than the intended victim.[9]

From the Isolated Act to Criminal Career

Delinquents range from those youth who are involved in a single act of deviance (or one act where they are caught) to those who engage in repeated (habitual) criminal behavior. The typical delinquent engages in just a few acts in his or her lifetime. Most longitudinal studies have found that the majority of youths who are arrested and referred to the juvenile court usually have no subsequent official contact or have perhaps one or two additional arrests or referrals to court (see section on delinquent careers in chapter 2). Most juvenile offenders never become adult offenders.

From Status Offenses to Criminal Law Violations

The two main categories of behavior that may result in a referral to juvenile court are committing an offense that is unlawful for all age groups (delinquent offenses) and committing an offense that applies to juveniles only (status offenses). While most chronic youths have engaged in both types of behaviors at one time or another, most of those referred to juvenile court specialize in one form or the other.

These eight dimensions are but a few of the factors that must be considered when explaining juvenile delinquency. The interrelationships and overlapping of the categories make this subject even more complex. We presented these variations to illustrate that delinquents, like humans in general, are not one-dimensional. There is no *typical* delinquent. In fact, as we review some of the more common varieties of delinquent behavior, we will discover that no one single act is the same as another (e.g., no two cases of shoplifting are identical, no two assaults are identical). To more fully understand a behavior, one must know the surrounding context of an act.

Even the most serious crime—such as a drive-by shooting or a kidnapping—is the result of a complex set of factors. We have heard numerous stories over the years about assaults—labeled violent crime and tabulated and categorized as if every one of them were alike. A young girl who has been habitually running away from home (often for a very good reason, such as sexual abuse) attempts to run one more time, but her mother gets in her way and the girl bumps into her on the way out the door. According to the law, the mother can file an assault charge against the daughter, which immediately transforms what is really a status offense into a delinquent offense, which carries a more serious punishment. The remainder of this chapter reviews the main categories of delinquent offenses: property crimes, violent crimes, public order offenses, and status offenses.

PROPERTY CRIMES

Shoplifting

About 27 million people shoplift each year; only 25% of shoplifters are juveniles.[10] Shoplifting is a spur of the moment behavior. Slightly more than 25% of shoplifters planned the activity before entering a store; only 3% of shoplifters are professionals. Most shoplifters do not commit other crimes. As we saw in chapter 2, larceny-theft was the second largest category of all juvenile arrests. In 2017, 13.1% of all male juvenile arrests were for larceny theft.[11] There were 58,792 arrests of males under the age of 18; the 17,709 arrests of males under the age of 15 represented 14.1% of all arrests of that age group. For females, 19% of all arrests were for larceny theft. There were 34,946 arrests of females under the age of 18; the 8,687 arrests of females under the age of 15 represented 14% of all the arrests of that age group.[12] Shoplifting accounts for 20.9% of all larceny-theft arrests.

For teenagers, going shopping (including hanging out at the shopping mall) is a very common activity. It is normal and healthy for adolescents to want to be with their peers. By the time a child has reached puberty, the peer group has already begun to take over in terms of influencing behavior. Same-sex cliques are extremely popular among youth, and the bulk of delinquency occurs within these groups. Indeed, peer influences have long been recognized as a factor in delinquency causation.[13]

Vandalism

As noted in table 2-1, there were about 28,842 arrests for vandalism, constituting about 4.5% of all arrests for juveniles in 2017.[14] Contrary to the frequent assumption that vandalism is a youthful activity, 69% of arrests for vandalism were adults. Juvenile vandalism declined 33.4% from 2012 to 2016, while the decline for adults was only 6.3%. Vandalism is primarily a male offense (in 2017 males accounted for 77.5% of all arrests for this offense).[15] Vandalism is defined as follows:

> To willfully or maliciously destroy, injure, disfigure, or deface any public or private property, real or personal, without the consent of the owner or person having custody or control by cutting, tearing, breaking, marking, painting, drawing, covering with filth, or any other such means as may be specified by local law.[16]

Vandalism is associated with more affluent societies. The term was first used to describe the behaviors of a group called the Vandals, an East German tribe that attacked Rome in the fifth century. They engaged in what was described as the senseless destruction of objects that had aesthetic appeal or were completed with great effort.[17] The concept was also used to describe the destruction of Paris during the French Revolution (*Vandalisme*).

There are three categories of vandalism: wanton, predatory, and vindictive.[18] *Wanton vandalism* is defined as nonutilitarian or just plain ornery. It is usually sporadic and done on the spur of the moment, often on a dare. *Predatory vandalism* is economically oriented; it includes breaking into parking meters, public telephones, and vending machines to collect change. *Vindictive vandalism* is, as the name implies, a hate crime directed at a specific individual or group, often of a different race, religious orientation, or social class. The majority of those who commit vandalism are not serious offenders and do not view themselves as criminals. More often than not, they view their actions as mere pranks. Most of the time, such acts are a form of entertainment or rebellion and are viewed as exciting.

Graffiti

As every parent knows, adolescents strive to create their own unique world—separate and distinct from the adult world. Modes of dress and communication styles draw the boundaries between themselves and adults. The original definition of graffiti was scratched or written public marking, and it was considered the first example of art. In New York City in the late 1960s and early 1970s, kids began writing their street names on subway cars—"the one thing that crossed every boundary of class, borough, race, and neighborhood."[19]

> When graffiti writing grew from simple signatures and stick figures to brilliantly colored calligraphic and typographical murals, the vast majority of artists [were] between the ages of twelve and eighteen, a pattern that continued well into the 1980s. Graffiti can claim something that no other art movement can: it was entirely created and developed by kids. . . . Not only was graffiti writing an invention of kids, but they also created and developed it in the face of adults' laws, arrests, beatings, and organized removal efforts. No other art movement in human history has so thoroughly confounded the deeply held concepts of public and private property; no other art movement has so thoroughly made itself a public policy issue. Long before it developed into an art, graffiti was—and remains—a crime.

Youth gangs often employ graffiti as a unique form of communication.[20] Graffiti is the primary form of communication used by gangs today, although historically a wide variety of groups have used graffiti. Not all graffiti is the product of gangs. As several studies have shown, many artists began with graffiti. The goal of such artwork is to establish an individual artist's reputation and to display one's own style of art. In contrast, the purpose of gang graffiti is usually (but not always) to expand the reputation of the gang, rather than that of an individual. Gangs use graffiti to identify their existence (to tell others who they are), to mark a specific area as their turf (for example, by writing on a wall, a building, or other structure), to challenge rival gangs, and to commemorate members who have died in battles. Graffiti can be used as a community memo.

Gang graffiti may be viewed as a form of artistic expression because it follows established styles and makes use of sophisticated principles of graphic design. One of the most common styles is the use of large block lettering. This is especially common when writing the name or initials of the gang. Graffiti is a way of gaining attention and recognition from the public. A Chicano gang member in Los Angeles remarked: "I always wonder what people think of when they ride by and see the name 'Puppet' (his nickname) there. Do they think of me?"[21]

Joyriding

There are generally four motivations for motor-vehicle theft: (1) joyriding, (2) transportation, (3) commission of other crimes, and (4) commercial theft.[22] Joyriding can be defined as taking or operating a vehicle without the owner's consent.[23] The intent is to *temporarily* deprive the owner of the vehicle. The other type of auto theft involves the intent to *permanently* deprive the owner of his or her automobile. The car can be stolen as a means of transportation, used during the commission of a crime, or stripped and the parts sold on the black market. Carjacking involves stealing a car by forcefully removing the driver, sometimes using a weapon.

While most auto thieves have extensive records, those who engage in joyriding do not. It is typically a teenage crime, very spur-of-the-moment behavior, usually done in groups where either the keys are in the car or the car belongs to a neighbor (often a parent or relative of one of the youths involved).[24] Joyriding brings momentary excitement to the daily routine. The behavior is mostly expressive and spontaneous. The automobile is extremely important in U.S. culture. Having one means freedom and independence, especially for juveniles not yet able to leave home, vote, and engage in a number of other activities. Obtaining a drivers license represents a very important rite of passage. On a hot day in Chicago, a 16-year-old decided to take a car for a joy ride; he said he liked driving around and going fast. "Who wouldn't want to be seen in a car? Who wouldn't want to be seen not walking?"[25]

Gang members sometimes recruit a juvenile to carry out a carjacking if they want to steal a car to use in a drive-by shooting.[26] The penalties for a juvenile are far less severe if caught. For example, since Illinois raised the age for juvenile jurisdiction, a carjacking charge no longer triggers automatic transfer to adult court for those younger than 18. An adult faces 4 to 15 years in prison if unarmed and 6 to 30 years if the crime was carried out with a weapon. Juveniles convicted of carjacking may be placed on probation or sentenced to a few months detention in a juvenile facility. Some law enforcement officials believe the change in the law is responsible for an increase in the number of carjackings. Juvenile advocates believe it is too soon to blame the law. From 2014 through early 2018, 100 juveniles were arrested in 75 carjackings. Stephanie Kollmann, policy director at the Children and Family Justice Center at Northwestern University asks whether those who fear being a carjacking victim would truly feel safer if young people were sentenced to lengthy prison terms. "Do we want to keep investing in responses that give us a false sense of security and help us exercise our punishment instinct? Or do we want to invest in responses that hold people accountable but focus on rehabilitation over punishment?" Nationally, arrests for motor vehicle theft constitute a small proportion of arrests among juveniles (12,798 of the 634,535 juvenile arrests in 2017—2% of all juvenile arrests; it is primarily an adult activity (more than 5.5 times the number of arrests as for juveniles).[27]

VIOLENT CRIMES

Although violent crime is declining, the United States, in comparison to similar capitalist democracies (such as Australia, Canada, France, Germany, Japan, and Great Britain), is a society where an unusual number of people die violently.[28] We fear violence, yet are fascinated by it. We spend hours viewing it on television and on the movie screen. It brings in billions of dollars in advertising revenue for the nightly news.

As discussed in the introduction, the debate, fear, and distortion about the projected violence to be committed by juvenile superpredators changed the landscape of juvenile justice for years. In a book filled with hyperbole and gross misuse of statistics, William Bennett, John DiIulio, and John Walters presented dire warnings.[29]

> A new generation of street criminals is upon us—the youngest, biggest, and baddest generation any society has ever known. . . . They live by the meanest code of the meanest streets, a code that reinforces rather than restrains their violent, hair-trigger mentality. In prison or out, the things that superpredators get by their criminal behavior—sex, drugs, money—are their own immediate rewards. *Nothing else matters to them.*

The actual figures on homicide (the crime most often linked to youthful superpredators) tell another story. The arrest rate for juveniles on homicide charges was 5.8 per 100,000 persons ages 10–17 in 1980. It peaked at 12.8 in 1993 and declined steadily and substantially to 2.6 in 2016.[30] The number of juveniles arrested for murder in 2008 was 716; there was a 26% decline to 530 homicide arrests in 2017.[31] In comparison, adult arrests declined from 7,262 to 6,696—a 7.8% decline. The percent decline of all juvenile arrests for violent crimes during that decade was 47.2% compared to an 8.5% decline for adults. As noted in the previous chapter, juveniles are far more likely to be the victims of violent crimes than to be perpetrators.

Gang Violence: A Special Case

A great deal of the violence committed by juveniles occurs within the context of youth gangs. Certain features of gangs may facilitate violence.

> Street socialization generally produces a street subculture of violence, and . . . areas with a high concentration of crime undergird a pattern of violence. The potential for street mayhem and violence in such places is a product of opportunity. A youth who spends more time with criminal offenders is more likely to participate in offending activities. In short, motivated offenders, suitable targets, and an absence of capable guardians converge in certain times and places to increase the possibility of a crime.[32]

Some point to exaggerated masculine behavior, or machismo, to explain gang violence. Joan Moore advises that the term refers as much to control as it does to aggressiveness.[33] It is especially related to unrestrained conduct on the part of a member.

> In the most marginalized and impoverished communities, for some individuals, a series of personal traumatic experiences and influences have generated a sense of rage and aggression such that lashing out violently becomes a generally predictable and expected type of behavior. In this context of social determinants and psychological propensities, street gangs have become a street-created medium and vehicle to encourage and vent this aggression.[34]

The National Gang Center (NGC) conducted an annual survey of law enforcement agencies from 1996 to 2012 to measure the presence, characteristics, and behaviors of local gangs. Of the agencies responding to the National Youth Gang Survey, 30% reported gang activity in 2012.[35] Gang activity was concentrated primarily in urban areas; 85% of larger cities, 50% of suburban counties, and 15% of rural counties reported gang activity. Intergang conflict and drug-related factors affected local levels of gang violence.[36] From 2007 to 2012, gang homicides averaged 2,000 annually (about 13% of all homicides).[37] The vast majority of gang-related homicides occurred in larger cities—67% in cities with populations of more than 100,000 and 17% in suburban counties in 2012. Chicago and Los Angeles accounted for 25% of the gang-related homicides. More than 75% of the smaller cities and rural counties reported no homicides; 5% or less of all gang homicides occurred in these areas.

The Code of the Street

Elijah Anderson explored a culture that differed substantially from middle-class expectations.[38] He noted that in poor environments the negative influences are everywhere.

> Of all the problems besetting the poor inner-city black community, none is more pressing than that of interpersonal violence and aggression. This phenomenon wreaks havoc daily on the lives of community residents and increasingly spills over into downtown and residential middle-class areas. . . . Although there are often forces in the community that can counteract the negative influences—by far the most powerful is strong, loving, "decent" (as the inner-city residents put it) family that is committed to middle-class values—the despair is pervasive enough to have spawned an oppositional culture, that of "the street," whose norms are often consciously opposed to those of mainstream society. These two orientations—decent and street—organize the community socially, and the way they coexist and interact has important consequences for its residents, particularly for children growing up in the inner city.[39]

The existence of an oppositional culture means that even youths from functional homes must be able to handle themselves in a street-oriented environment.

> The street culture has evolved a "code of the street," which amounts to a set of informal rules governing interpersonal public behavior, including violence. The rules prescribe both a proper comportment and a proper way to respond if challenged. They regulate the use of violence and so supply a rationale allowing those who are inclined to aggression to precipitate violent encounters in an approved way.[40]

The heart of the code is respect, which is defined as being treated with proper deference. In a troublesome environment, that becomes difficult to define. For example, maintaining eye contact for too long can be a sign of disrespect and could indicate imminent physical danger. Many young people feel totally alienated from mainstream society and its institutions. The code is a subcultural adaptation to the lack of faith in the justice system (especially the police). Many residents have taken on the responsibility of protecting themselves. The code of the street takes over where the police and judicial system have failed.

Children who are ignored by their parents learn to fend for themselves at a very early age. They become children of the street, and, as a popular saying goes, they "come up hard."[41] Many become employed by drug dealers and learn to fight at an early age. In the most extreme cases, a street-oriented mother may leave her children alone for several days. This is most common among women with drug and/or alcohol problems. These children learn "the first lesson of the streets: you cannot take survival itself, let alone respect, for granted; you have to fight for your place in the world."[42]

The essence of the code centers on the presentation of self. The major requirement is to prove to others that one is willing and able to use violence to defend oneself. One communicates this message through facial expressions and a certain way of walking and talking (including the words one selects). Physical appearance is also important—jewelry, certain kinds of clothing (jackets, sneakers, and so on), and the way one is groomed. In order to be respected, one must have the right look. There are always going to be challenges to one's respect. If one is assaulted or otherwise challenged, one must avenge oneself.

There is a widespread feeling that within this environment there is a limited amount of respect and that everyone must compete for affirmation. If a challenge is issued and the person does not respond, the lack of response encourages further violations. One must be constantly on guard against not only direct violations but even the appearance of potential violation. This is especially true among teenagers, whose self-esteem is already vulnerable. There are many young males who so desperately want respect that they are willing to die in order to maintain it.[43]

One major assumption is that everyone should know the code of the streets. Thus, even the victim of a mugging who does not act according to the code may cause the mugger to feel no remorse for his violence—the victim "should have known better."[44] Because even youths from decent families are familiar with the code, they too may have to resort to violence to defend their honor or respect.

One of the core beliefs associated with this concept of manhood is that one of the best ways of gaining respect (therefore proving one is a real man) is to exhibit nerve. The concept of nerve refers to the ability to take someone else's possessions, mess with someone's woman, get in someone's face, or fire a weapon. The show of nerve, however, is a very forceful method of showing disrespect—it can very easily offend others and result in retaliation.[45]

The issue of respect is very important to understand in terms of the extent to which a young person has the potential for violence. Most individuals in mainstream society are able to retreat and not seek revenge against an attack; they have gained enough self-esteem from other sources (e.g., education, jobs, and family) to withstand the insult. Other sources of self-esteem are absent for inner-city youths; thus, they have to seek revenge (even going so far as to enlist the aid of relatives or fellow gang members). Within the inner city there are few nonviolent means to maintain respect and to prove that one is in control.

Sex Offenses

Media reports about sex offenders have been replete with misinformation and have contributed to national hysteria about the issue. While the impetus for the legislation was extremely serious crimes, the reality is that sex offenses and sex offenders have been defined so broadly that even the most innocuous acts have been criminalized. During the past two decades far-reaching legislation has widened the net of social control over a vast array of sexual behaviors that previously were virtually

ignored. This is despite the fact that only 1% of all juvenile arrests are for sex offenses, and recidivism rates for sex offenders is among the lowest of all offenders.[46]
Consider the following cases.

- A 14-year old Minnesota girl sexted an explicit photo of herself to a boy at
  her school. He copied the photo and distributed it to other students without her permission. The prosecutor charged her with felony distribution of
  child pornography, which requires spending 10 years on the sex offender
  registry.[47]
- Zachery Anderson, a 19-year-old Elkhart, Indiana boy, went online in
  December 2015. He contacted a Michigan girl, who said she was 17. They
  met and had sex. The girl was 14, and police arrested Zachery. (The girl
  and her mother pleaded for the case to be dropped.) His conviction of 4th
  degree criminal sexual conduct (a plea bargain) resulted in a sentence of 90
  days in jail, 2 years probation, and 25 years on the sex offender registry. One
  night of consensual teen sex resulted in his being prohibited from living
  at home (his parent's home was near a dock where children could gather);
  being within 500 feet of a park, pre-school or municipal pool; using the
  internet or a smart phone; being out of his home from 9 p.m. to 7 a.m.; purchasing anything valued over $200 without pre-approval from his probation
  officer; being in contact with anyone younger than 18—and required him
  to notify the officer of any dating relationship. A resentencing hearing removed him from the sex offender registry, but an additional 6 months were
  added to his probation because he went online to look for a filter for his fish
  tank and information on building a skateboard ramp. The probation officer
  later told the court that Zachery had met all the requirements and merited
  release. The judge refused, saying she never allows early release to anyone in
  Zachery's situation.[48]
- In Oregon, a girl who spent the majority of her time in the Oregon Youth
  Authority (OYA) for petty theft, running away, and other minor crimes, declared herself to be a lesbian while at a juvenile institution. A staff member
  saw her putting her arm around another girl. Based on this action, she was
  sent to the sex offender unit and must register as a sex offender.[49]
- In Michigan an 11 year-old boy was adjudicated for a sex offense for touch-
  ing, without penetrating, his sister's genitals. Found guilty of one count of
  criminal sexual conduct he was placed on Michigan's sex offender registry
  and prevented by residency restriction laws from living near other children.
  Because he could not live in the house with his sister, he was placed in a
  juvenile home. He moved to Florida at the age of 18 and tried to follow that
  state's sex offender laws. Once he had to move because his house was too
  close to a school. After a period of homelessness, he failed to register a new
  address and was convicted of the felony of failure to register. Now 26, his life
  continues to be defined by an offense he committed at age 11.[50]

These few examples are a tiny sampling of the overreach of sex offender laws. In most states, intercourse with anyone under the ages of 14, 15, or 16 is considered sexual assault, regardless of consent. However, 36.2% of youth in the tenth grade and 47.3% of youth in the eleventh grade reported having had sexual intercourse.[51] Most youth behavior categorized as sex crimes is not predatory. "Many of the behaviors reported are status offenses, including things such as parking and necking, which would not be a crime if committed by an adult."[52]

Sensational media stories about children as victims of adult predators prompted public support for legislation. Public concern then extended to children as sex offenders. National anxiety about sex crimes prompted legislators to take action.[53] Since 1994, there have been ten major pieces of federal legislation concerning sex offenses.[54] The first significant piece of legislation was the Jacob Wetterling Act in 1994 that required states to create a database of people convicted of violent sex crimes or crimes against children (Jacob was kidnapped at the age of 11).[55] In 1996, Megan's Law required states to make their registries accessible to the public (Megan Kanka was 7 when raped and murdered by a neighbor who had 2 prior convictions for sexual assault). The Adam Walsh Child Protection and Safety Act, title I of the Sex Offender Registration and Notification Act (SORNA), was enacted in July 2006; it was signed on the 25th anniversary of six-year-old Adam Walsh's abduction and murder.

The Act created a national sex offender registry. Prior to the act, all fifty states already had sex offender registration lists, but they varied regarding the registration of juveniles. SORNA required the registration of juveniles at least 14 years old adjudicated delinquent for engaging in a sexual act by force, threat of serious violence, or rendering unconscious; it also reduced justice assistance funding to jurisdictions that failed to substantially implement SORNA requirements.[56] The Adam Walsh Act eviscerates a central tenet of the juvenile justice system. For more than a century, the records of youthful offenses have generally been sealed and unavailable to the public. The rationale for this protection has been that children are less responsible for their actions and more amenable to rehabilitation.[57] Some states, including New York and Georgia defied the requirements at the risk of losing funds.[58] By April 2018, only 18 states had substantially implemented SORNA.[59]

Proponents of registration argue that children must be protected from predators, regardless of the age of the perpetrator. Juvenile justice advocates want rehabilitation instead of registration. Another concern is that juveniles are subject to the same registration requirements as adults without the benefit of a jury trial or similar protections.[60] "Public notification of juvenile sex offenders hinders rehabilitation efforts in many ways. By requiring notification to an offender's school, this public outing could lead to peer harassment causing social isolation, emotional and physical harm."[61] The national hysteria over sex offenders is highly exaggerated when it comes to juveniles.[62] "People want to eradicate horrible crimes like child abduction and child sexual abuse. In their zeal to eliminate heinous crimes, other juveniles are trapped by the unintended consequences of keeping children safe."[63]

PUBLIC ORDER OFFENSES

Behaviors that fall under this category are victimless crimes (crimes without a complaining victim) or crimes that offend some vague sense of public order. Among the most common charges in this category are drug abuse violations, prostitution, pornography, illegal gambling, liquor-law violations (these are sometimes classified as status offenses, discussed in the next section), public drunkenness, disorderly conduct, and vagrancy. Some public order offenses are subsumed within the category known as *all other offenses*, discussed below. *Juvenile Court Statistics* includes the following offenses under the heading of public order: weapons offenses, nonviolent sex offenses, being in a public place while intoxicated, disorderly conduct, obstruction of justice, other offenses against public order such as bribery, gambling, hitchhiking, and false fire alarms.[64] Drugs are treated as a separate category.

Rarely discussed in the literature on delinquency cases is the catchall offense generally called *obstruction of justice*. In the UCR, these charges are usually included in the all other offenses category. They represent a sizeable proportion of cases processed through the juvenile court. As noted in table 2-1, there were 116,023 arrests in this category in 2017—the most of any UCR category. What exactly is obstruction of justice?

> intentionally obstructing court or law enforcement efforts in the administration of justice, acting in a way calculated to lessen the authority or dignity of the court, failing to obey the lawful order of a court, escaping from confinement, and violating probation or parole. This term includes contempt, perjury, bribery of witnesses, failure to report a crime, and nonviolent resistance of arrest.[65]

The description clearly covers a wide variety of behaviors. Personal observations and conversations with court personnel and juveniles over many decades suggest that this charge often stems from occasions when a youth: angers a judge or court officer (e.g., his or her parole officer); fails to display an acceptable attitude (which also can add the charge of resisting arrest); or gets caught violating one or more of the myriad rules of probation and parole. In 2016 juvenile courts handled 109,200 obstruction of justice cases (a 45% decline from 2007); 80,400 (74%) of these cases were petitioned to court and 47,400 (59%) were adjudicated delinquent.[66]

While public order offenses cover diverse behaviors, there are several commonalities.[67] First, many are victimless crimes where both participants are technically violating the law. Second, many involve the generic public as victim, as in disturbing the peace of the surrounding community. Third, many involve a simple exchange of goods or services that are in demand. Fourth, there is no consensus on the seriousness of these offenses. Fifth, some of the offenses resemble behaviors engaged in by adult citizens. This is especially the case with drunkenness and illegal drug use.[68] While the public may condemn such behavior for others and for juveniles, they may also secretly indulge in similar behavior.

Tens of thousands of juveniles are picked up by the police and at least momentarily detained for offenses that could be considered hanging out or partying. In 2017, more than 176,000 juveniles were arrested for such offenses as drunkenness, disorderly conduct, curfew violation/loitering, liquor-law and drug violations, prostitution, and other sex offenses (except rape).[69] These high numbers should come as no surprise given that the police historically have been charged with maintaining order within a community. In 2016, there were 214,700 public order case referrals to juvenile court plus another 107,400 drug case referrals for a total of 322,100 (see table 11-1).

STATUS OFFENSES

As we noted in chapter 1, the earliest juvenile codes strongly emphasized offenses applicable to those under a certain age. The behavior is a violation only because of the juvenile's age status; thus, these offenses are commonly known as *status offenses*. Chapter 2 discussed the fact that published national data on status offenses cover only the cases petitioned to court—not all status offense referrals. In 2016 an estimated 94,700 status offense cases were petitioned, a decline of 43% from 2005. Law enforcement referred 21% of the petitioned status offense disposed by juvenile courts.[70] Compared with 2005, law enforcement referred larger proportions of runaway (46% versus 36%) and ungovernability (30% versus 26%) cases. Schools referred 93% of petitioned truancy cases, and relatives referred 50% of ungovernability cases.

There are four major types of status offenses: (1) running away, (2) truancy, (3) curfew violations, (4) liquor-law violations. The catchall categories of *incorrigible* and *unmanageable* cover other status offense behaviors. Every state's juvenile code contains several of these kinds of offenses. Many status offenses are related to academic difficulties, abuse and neglect in the home, substance abuse, or physical and mental health problems. Girls and youth of color are disproportionately confined for status offense behavior.[71] Arizona defines status offenses as: "habitual truancy, being a runaway, failing to obey a court order, refusing to obey a parent or guardian, behaving in a manner which injures the morals or health of the juvenile or others." Michigan defines it this way: "desertion of the home without sufficient cause, disobedience to the commands of parents or guardians, and truancy." Some states include vague descriptions such as "beyond the control of parents" or "child in need of supervision."[72]

In many states guardians can file a status offense petition when a youth is unruly, ungovernable, or incorrigible. Such behaviors range from refusing to obey parental curfews to repeated arguments with family members to a child physically abusing a parent—cases in which the parent or guardian perceives the situation to be unmanageable and is looking for help.[73] Virginia distinguishes between a "child in need of services" and a "child in need of supervision." The former "refers to a child whose behavior, conduct or condition presents or results in a serious threat to the well-being and physical safety of the child." The latter "refers to a child who either while subject to compulsory school attendance, is habitually and without justification absent from school, or without reasonable cause and without the consent of his parent or lawful custodian, remains away from home."[74]

Title II of the Juvenile Justice and Delinquency Prevention Act (passed in 1974) prohibited the placement of status offenders in locked detention in states receiving federal funds. Between 1974 and 1980, status referrals decreased by 21%, and the detention of juveniles for status offenses was cut in half.[75] The Act was modified in 1980 to allow judges discretion if status offenders violated a valid court order (VCO).[76]

> The VCO exception allows courts to hold juvenile status offenders in a secure juvenile facility without violating the DSO [deinstitutionalizing status offenders] requirement, either under the traditional contempt authority of the court or if the state delinquency code allows judges to adjudicate a status offender as delinquent after he violates a VCO. This approach is commonly known as "bootstrapping," as it takes what had been nondelinquent behavior, protected under the DSO requirement of the JJDPA, and converts it into a category of behavior that loses that protection. For example, a runaway ordered by the court to stay in her home could be placed in secure detention if she runs again. Because many states did not increase services to address the underlying problems facing status offenders, repeat offending was common.[77]

Status offender detentions increased dramatically after the VCO modification, and the number of incarcerated status offenders quickly doubled.

In large part, the separation of status offenders from other delinquent youths has emerged in response to concerns about the rights of youths charged with status offenses. Status offense laws have been objected to on constitutional grounds. One of the most common grounds is that the statutes are too vague. For example, what is the precise meaning of *habitual disobedience* or *lawful parental demands*? Another concern is that status offense laws violate the Eighth Amendment in that punishment ensues from status rather than behavior. A major source of the bias in contemporary juvenile courts is undoubtedly parental use (some might say abuse) of the status offense category. As noted above, relatives referred half of petitioned ungovernability offenses in 2016.[78]

Chapter 5 identifies status offenses as a distinguishing characteristic of female delinquency. Females accounted for a substantially larger proportion of petitioned status offenses (43%) compared to delinquency cases handled by the juvenile courts (28%). Of status cases petitioned to court, females accounted for 56% of runaway cases. The number of petitioned truancy cases outnumbered all other status offense cases for both males and females. Males accounted for the majority of curfew (72%), liquor law violation (60%) ungovernability (57%), and truancy (54%) cases.[79]

Adolescents are less likely than adults to think about the future consequences of their actions; they are generally more focused on the present and immediate gratification. They have an imbalanced perception of risk and lack impulse control. In addition, most adolescents respond to peer influence and may gain higher social status for engaging in antisocial behavior. A truant, disruptive, or runaway youth focuses on the immediate benefits rather than long-term effects.[80]

Runaways

Experts estimate that approximately 1.6 million juveniles run away from or are thrown out of their homes each year; most return within a week.[81] Youths who leave home without permission are runaways; youths who are forced out of their homes or refused permission to return are throwaways. Runaway youth often leave their homes because of intense family conflict or abuse (physical, sexual or psychological). Most of these children are between the ages of 15 and 17.[82] OJJDP conducts periodic national incidence studies through a survey of parents and other primary caretakers to determine the number of children reported missing each year.[83] The rates of runaway or throwaway episodes in 2013 did not differ statistically from the rates in 1999. The rate in 2013 was 5.3 children per 1,000 for the estimated 413,000 runaways/throwaways (compared to a rate of 5.6 and 395,500 in 1999).

The number of petitioned runaway cases processed by juvenile courts was 18,700 in 2005 and 8,000 in 2016—a decrease of 57%.[84] Runaways accounted for 8% of the petitioned cases. As noted above, females accounted for 56% of petitioned runaway cases—the only status offense category in which females represented a larger proportion of the case load than males (11% versus 7%). From 2005 to 2015, runaway cases were more likely to be detained than any other status offense; about 33% were adjudicated and 24% involved out-of-home placement.

Most youths who run away remain within 10–50 miles from home (usually staying with friends nearby). Runaways often feel unwanted, abused, neglected, and rejected by their parents. Many believe their parents have unrealistic expectations of them, are overly strict, and use excessive punishment. Many runaways have experienced poor relationships outside of the home, often ostracized by both teachers and peers. They have also experienced failure at school, and many have had to repeat grades. In-school problems and habitual truancy are also common. Not surprisingly, most have very negative feelings toward school in general. Youth who run away from caregivers even once are more likely to experience victimization, delinquency, school problems, and substance abuse problems than those who do not run away.[85]

Runaway statutes often include phrases such as voluntary absence and without consent, which are vague, subjective, and open to interpretation.

> There is often a very active parental role in a child's running away. In many cases where a child is alleged to have stayed away from home overnight or longer—i.e.,

to have run away—the youth has a very different take on the events that caused her to leave, insisting that she was actually "put out of the house" by the parent. Many cases involve an argument between the parent and youth that eventually escalates to the point that the parent insists the youth leave the house. Rather than back down or lose face by apologizing, the youth leaves angrily. Most kids don't wander the streets. Usually the parent knows exactly where the youth went—to a relative, neighbor, or friend's home. . . .

Occasionally, kids run away from stable, healthy homes to wander the streets in search of drugs or to pursue a romantic relationship that their parents forbid. In many instances, however, children's actions are justified. The desire for a safe, loving home is innate. Under normal circumstances, obstinacy alone will not motivate a child to leave her home and fend for herself. If she does, she may be running away *from* something with good cause.[86]

The runaway statutes in some states are more defined. For example, Florida's statute requires proof that the youth has *persistently* run away. Other states insert a good cause requirement.[87] In Arkansas, running away consists of leaving home *without sufficient cause, permission, or justification.* Connecticut uses the phrase *without just cause*, and Virginia uses *without reasonable cause.* Terms such as *sufficient, just*, and *reasonable* are also very general, but they do direct the juvenile court to determine the reason for running away. Certainly, abuse or neglect by another household member would qualify as good cause. Some judges also might find good cause where a parent has kicked the child out of the home, or in cases of persistent, but nonviolent, parent-child conflict.

Some studies find that girls and boys are about equally as likely to run away, but girls are more likely to enter the justice system.[88] Girls are more likely to experience sexual assault during childhood and run away at younger ages. This places them on a trajectory of affiliation with deviant peers, increasing rates of victimization, substance use, and sexually deviant subsistence strategies.

Physically leaving a difficult situation is a common coping mechanism for many youths. Repeated runaway behavior frustrates judges, service providers, and parents—who often hope that a one-time intervention will end the behavior. Research shows that the most successful responses tackle the underlying issues that prompted the runaway behavior.[89] Some guardians are misdirected to the status offender system. They want their children located and returned but are unaware of the other components of the status offender process. When probation or child welfare brings the petition, they may believe that court involvement is required, although voluntary services or reuniting the family might also be an option. If the case is petitioned, several issues should be explored. For example, did the parent breach a legal obligation to the child? Was the child's behavior threatening, or was it only a poor response after being placed in a difficult situation by the person who is supposed to provide care and guidance?[90]

Overzealous Protection

When sociology professor Emily Horowitz began researching the panic surrounding crimes against children, she was surprised to learn

> that any given year saw exceedingly few kidnappings and murders of children by strangers. I started to think differently, and critically, about cultural attitudes and fears about child safety. . . . Statistically, these sorts of events were very rare, with data showing that the vast majority of victims of stranger murder abductions were teenage girls, not preteen children, and yet not only have such rare events determined macro-level criminal justice policies, they drive irrational fear at the micro level, too, governing adult-child interactions (e.g., no-touch daycare policies) and parenting behaviors (e.g. not letting children take the subway or walk to school alone).[91]

We reviewed how laws designed to protect children from victimization can have the opposite effect—children being prosecuted for sexting, essentially victimizing themselves. Overzealous parenting can also do real harm.[92] "The exaggerated reporting of crimes against children and a culture that encourages parents to supervise every moment of their children's lives carries its own dangers."[93]

Psychologists and educators believe the decline in independence and autonomy of children compared to a few generations ago has contributed to a surge of anxiety disorders in juveniles. Today, fewer children walk to school, ride their bicycles, or run errands for their parents. Indeed, some parents have been charged with neglect for allowing their children to walk or play unsupervised. Some states have laws specifying the minimum age when children can be home alone. Illinois states that children younger than 14 can't be left alone for an *unreasonable* amount of time—a vague description open to subjective interpretations. There has been some backlash to the pressure for parental oversight. In 2018, Utah enacted a free-range parenting law that does not classify letting a child play in a park alone or walking to a neighborhood store alone as neglect.

Overprotection can reinforce the idea of the world as a dangerous place. The absence of autonomy and independence hinders the development of self-confidence. Children innately want more independence as they get older. Denying them the opportunity to enjoy some freedom can make them angry, and they may act out as a result. Children need to develop skills and acquire a sense of mastery to become self-sufficient adults. Lenore Skenazy created an organization, Let Grow, to help communities cooperate in giving children independence.[94] The superintendent of an elementary school district on Long Island implemented a Let Grow project after noticing that students were averse to risk taking. After one year of homework once a week that consisted only of doing something new alone or with a friend (i.e. walking the dog, exploring the woods), he found that the children were more self-confident and better behaved in the classroom. One milestone for autonomy that some parents find difficult is that the independence to make one's own decisions includes the right to make a wrong decision.

Summary

Delinquent behavior encompasses a wide variety of prohibited behaviors, ranging from the petty to the most serious, from offenses applicable to youths under a certain age (status offenses) to behaviors that apply to adults as well. Many of the behaviors are motivated by the desire to obtain various kinds of property, with shoplifting from retail stores being the most common—not a surprising motivation given how much emphasis our culture places on material goods. There are also a variety of personal crimes involving some physical contact with the victim, ranging in seriousness from minor altercations to serious assaults with weapons, which can result in serious injury and in a few cases death.

Youngsters spend a lot of time together in public. Therefore, public order offenses are common, often known by such names as disturbing the peace, loitering, and curfew violation. Another category of offenses have no complaining victim, such as drug use and possession of liquor. Finally, there are millions of youngsters who suffer some form of abuse, sometimes running away to escape or exhibiting similar abusive behavior and being labeled as incorrigible. Runaway behavior often leads to the commission of various criminal behaviors as a means of survival.

Notes

[1] Vincent Schiraldi and Bruce Western, "Commentary: Time to Raise the Juvenile Age," *The Washington Post*, October 5, 2015.

[2] Shelden is indebted to his former professor, Charles H. Newton (now deceased). These are part of his lecture notes from his course on juvenile delinquency taught at Memphis State University during the late 1960s and early 1970s. They contain much information that remains relevant today; not much has changed in terms of the various dimensions of delinquent behavior over the past 50 years.

[3] As we will see in chapter 12, growing numbers of youth with serious mental issues are being detained all across the country waiting for placement in a mental health agency.

[4] Steven F. Messner and Richard Rosenfeld, *Crime and the American Dream* (5th ed.) (Belmont, CA: Wadsworth, 2012), 76.

[5] Albert Reiss, Jr. "Co-Offending and Criminal Careers," *Crime and Justice*, 1988, 10: 117–170.

[6] Many songs over the years have been based on the theme of kids just "hangin' out," including "I Get Around," "Fun, Fun, Fun," and "No Particular Place to Go."

[7] See for instance: Holly V. Miller, "Correlates of Delinquency and Victimization in a Sample of Hispanic Youth," *International Criminal Justice Review*, 2012, 22: 153–170; Margit Averdijk and Wim Bernasco, "Testing the Situational Explanation of Victimization among Adolescents," *Journal of Research in Crime and Delinquency*, 2015, 52: 151–180; Joana Carvalho and Pedro Nobre, "Dynamic Factors of Sexual Aggression: The Role

of Affect and Impulsiveness," *Criminal Justice and Behavior*, 2013, 40: 376–387. Research has found that kids with attention-deficit/hyperactivity disorder (ADHD) are very likely to commit petty crimes on the spur of the moment, compared to kids without ADHD. Jason Fletcher and Barbara Wolfe, "Long-term Consequences of Childhood ADHD on Criminal Activities," *Journal of Mental Health Policy and Economics*, 2009, 12: 119–138.

8 Callie H. Burt and Ronald L. Simons, "Self-Control, Thrill Seeking, and Crime: Motivation Matters," *Criminal Justice and Behavior*, 2013, 40: 1326–1348; John F. Rauthmann, "The Dark Triad and Interpersonal Perception: Similarities and Differences in the Social Consequences of Narcissism, Machiavellianism, and Psychopathy," *Social Psychological and Personality Science*, 2012, 3: 487–496.

9 Randall G. Shelden, Sharon K. Tracy, and William B. Brown, *Youth Gangs in American Society*, 4th ed. (Belmont, CA: Cengage, 2013).

10 National Association for Shoplifting Prevention. Retrieved from http://www.shoplifting-prevention.org/what-we-do/learning-resource-center/statistics/

11 FBI. *Crime in the United States, 2017* (Washington, DC: Author, 2018), table 39.

12 Ibid., table 40.

13 Robert Agnew and Timothy Brezina, "Relational Problems with Peers, Gender and Delinquency," *Youth and Society*, 1997, 29: 84–111; Dustin Albert, Jason Chein, and Laurence Steinberg, "Peer Influences on Adolescent Risk Behavior," *Current Directions in Psychological Science*, 2013, 22(2): 114–120.

14 FBI. *Crime in the United States, 2017*, table 38.

15 Ibid., table 42.

16 Federal Bureau of Investigation, *Summary Reporting System (SRS)*. (Washington, DC: Author, June 20, 2013), 162.

17 A. H. Merrills, "The Origins of 'Vandalism,'" *International Journal of the Classical Tradition*, 16(2): 155–175.

18 Marshall B. Clinard, Richard Quinney, and John Wildeman, *Criminal Behavior Systems: A Typology*, 3rd ed. (New York: Routledge, 2015), 65.

19 Roger Gastman and Caleb Neelon, *The History of American Graffiti* (New York: Harper Design, 2010), 20.

20 The following section is adapted from Shelden et al., *Youth Gangs in American Society*, chapter 3.

21 James D. Vigil, *Barrio Gangs: Street Life and Identity in Southern California* (Austin: University of Texas Press, 1988), 115.

22 Terance D. Miethe, Richard C. McCorkle, and Shelley J. Listwan, *Crime Profiles: The Anatomy of Dangerous Persons, Places, and Situations*, 3rd ed. (New York: Oxford University Press, 2006).

23 Ave Mince-Didier, "What Is the Difference between Joyriding and Stealing a Car?" Nolo.com, http://www.criminaldefenselawyer.com/resources/criminal-defense/criminal-offense/what-difference-between-joyriding-stealing-a-ca

24 Miethe et al., *Crime Profiles*.

25 Jeremy Gorner, "Youth Arrests Rise with Carjacking Spike," *Chicago Tribune*, June 13, 2018, 8.

26 Ibid.

27 FBI, *Crime in the United States, 2017*, table 38.

28 Kieran Healy, "America Is a Violent Country," *The Washington Post*, October 3, 2017.

29 It is highly recommend that you read the book by Bennett, DiIulio, and Walters. It is an eye-opening example of not only the alarmist rhetoric noted here but also the misuse of crime statistics, especially the tendency to look only at *numbers* (e.g., going from

1 homicide to 3 homicides represents a 300% increase) rather than *rates*, plus the tendency to use "maximum starting and stopping points" to back up an exaggerated claim. It is also interesting to note that both Bennett and Walters held the office of Director of the Office of National Drug Control Policy. Criminologist John DiIulio was briefly Director of the White House Office of Faith-based and Community Initiatives. Bennett, W., J. DiIulio, and J. P. Walters, *Body Count: Moral Poverty and How to Win America's War against Crime and Drugs* (New York: Simon and Schuster, 1996).

30 OJJDP Statistical Briefing Book, Juvenile Arrest Rate Trends, Online. December 6, 2017, http://www.ojjdp.gov/ojstatbb/crime/JAR_Display.asp?ID=qa05200

31 FBI, *Crime in the United States, 2017*,table 32.

32 Vigil, *Gang Redux*, 61.

33 Joan Moore, *Going Down to the Barrio: Homeboys and Homegirls in Change* (Philadelphia: Temple University Press, 1991), 57–58.

34 Vigil, *Gang Redux*, 24.

35 The survey was based on a nationally representative sample of more than 2,500 law enforcement agencies serving larger cities, suburban counties, smaller cities, and rural counties. The annual response rate was 85%. Arlen Egley, Jr., James C. Howell, and Meena Harris, *Highlights of the 2012 National Youth Gang Survey* (Washington, DC: OJJDP, December, 2014).

36 National Gang Center, National Youth Gang Survey Analysis, Factors Influencing Gang-Related Violence, Tallahassee, FL: National Gang Center, https://www.nationalgangcenter .gov/Survey-Analysis/Gang-Related-Offenses#related

37 Ibid., Number of Gang-related Homicides, http://www.nationalgangcenter.gov/Survey-Analysis/Measuring-the-Extent-of-Gang-Problems#homicidesnumber

38 Elijah Anderson, *The Code of the Street: Decency, Violence, and the Moral Life of the Inner City* (New York: W. W. Norton, 1999).

39 Ibid., 32–33.

40 Ibid., 33.

41 Ibid., 49. This has also been noted by Vigil, *Barrio Gangs.*

42 Ibid., 49.

43 The authors connected a local example with similar behavior at the national level. A gang member at a local alternative school attacked someone else merely because he heard a rumor that the other person was out to get him for some reason. The code he lived by dictated that he attack this person before he was attacked in order not to be embarrassed or "dissed."

44 Anderson, "The Code of the Streets," 92.

45 Ibid.

46 Nancy G. Calleja, "Deconstructing a Puzzling Relationship: Sex Offender Legislation, the Crimes that Inspired It, and Sustained Moral Panic," *Justice Policy Journal*, 2016 13(1) 1–17; Alissa R. Ackerman and Marshall Burns, "Bad Data: How Government Agencies Distort Statistics on Sex-Crime Recidivism." *Justice Policy Journal*, 2016, 13(1): 1–23.

47 Teresa Nelson, "Minnesota Prosecutor Charges Sexting Teenage Girl with Child Pornography," ACLU of Minnesota, January 5, 2018.

48 Lenore Skenazy, "Update on Zach Anderson: Judge Shows No Mercy at All," National Association for Rational Sexual Offense Laws, December 14, 2017.

49 Debra Lee Cochrane, "Attitudes toward Megan's Law and Juvenile Sex Offenders." *UNLV Theses/Dissertations/Professional Papers/Capstones*, 2010. Shelden and William Brown of Western Oregon University interviewed the girl when she was confined in the special unit for female sex offenders.

50 Nicole Pittman, *Raised on the Registry the Irreparable Harm of Placing Children on Sex Offender Registries in the US* (New York: Human Rights Watch, 2013).

51 Centers for Disease Control and Prevention, *Youth Risk Behavior Surveillance—United States, 2017*. Atlanta: Author, June 15, 2018, 67(8), table 133.

52 Ibid., 5.

53 Quoted in Maggie Jones, "How Can You Distinguish a Budding Pedophile from a Kid With Real Boundary Problems?", *New York Times Magazine*, July 22, 2007.

54 Calleja, "Deconstructing a Puzzling Relationship."

55 Sarah Stillman, "The List," *The New Yorker*, March 14, 2016.

56 Supplemental guidelines for SORNA were issued in 2011 that allowed jurisdictions discretion in whether to post information about juveniles. A third set of guidelines were released in August 2016 regarding what constituted substantial implementation of SORNA. See https://www.smart.gov/juvenile_offenders.htm; Department of Justice, "Supplemental Guidelines for Juvenile Registration under the Sex Offender Registration and Notification Act, *Federal Register*, August 1, 016, vol. 81, no. 147.

57 Jones, "How Can You Distinguish a Budding Pedophile?"

58 Stillman, "The List."

59 Office of Sex Offender Sentencing, Monitoring, Apprehending, Registering, and Tracking, "State and Territory Implementation Progress Check," Smart.gov, April 5, 2018.

60 Jones, "How Can You Distinguish a Budding Pedophile?"

61 Cochrane, "Attitudes Toward Megan's Law and Juvenile Sex Offenders," 11.

62 More information can be obtained from the National Center for Sexual Behavior of Youth at http://www.ncsby.org/

63 Victor E. Kappeler and Gary W. Potter, *The Mythology of Crime and Criminal Justice*, 5th ed. (Long Grove, IL: Waveland Press, 2018), 88.

64 Sarah Hockenberry and Charles Puzzanchera, "Juvenile Court Statistics 2016," Pittsburgh: National Center for Juvenile Justice, August 2018.

65 Ibid., 98.

66 Ibid., 9, 36, 42.

67 Miethe et al., *Crime Profiles*, chapter 8.

68 Clinard et al., *Criminal Behavior Systems*, 101.

69 FBI, *Crime in the United States, 2017*, table 38.

70 Hockenberry and Puzzanchera, "Juvenile Court Statistics 2016."

71 Shay Bilchik and Erika Pinheiro, "What the JJDPA Means for Lawyers Representing Juvenile Status Offenders," In Sally Inada and Claire Chiamulera (eds.), *Representing Juvenile Status Offenders* (Chicago: American Bar Association, 2010), 1–14.

72 These definitions are found on the OJJDP website: http://www.ojjdp.gov/ojstatbb/structure_process/qa04122.asp?qaDate=2013

73 Claire Shubik, "What Social Science Tells Us about Youth Who Commit Status Offenses: Practical Advice for Attorneys," In Sally Inada and Claire Chiamulera (eds.), *Representing Juvenile Status Offenders* (Chicago: American Bar Association, 2010), 23–24.

74 Department of Social Services, City of Virginia Beach (2017). Retrieved from: http://www.vbgov.com/government/departments/courts/court-services-unit/Pages/child-in-need.aspx

75 Bilchik and Pinheiro, 5–6.

76 Nancy Gannon Hornberger, "Improving Outcomes for Status Offenders in the JJDPA Reauthorization," *Juvenile and Family Justice Today*, 2010, 15.

77 Ibid., 6–7.

78 Hockenberry and Puzzanchera, "Juvenile Court Statistics 2016," 76.

[79] Ibid., 69.

[80] Shubik, 19–20, 22.

[81] Michelle N. Jeanis, "Chronic Runaway Youth: A Gender-based Analysis," Tampa: University of South Florida, July 2017.

[82] Shubik, 29.

[83] NISMART-1 was conducted in 1988; NISMART-2 in 1999; NISMART-3 in 2011. Andrea J. Sedlak, David Finkelhor, and J. Michael Brick, "National Estimates of Missing Children: Updated Findings from a Survey of Parents and Other Primary Caretakers," Washington, DC: OJJDP, June 2017.

[84] Hockenberry and Puzzanchera, "Juvenile Court Statistics 2016."

[85] Jeanis, "Chronic Runaway Youth."

[86] Tobie J. Smith, "Preadjudication Strategies for Defending Juveniles in Status Offense Proceedings," In Sally Inada and Claire Chiamulera (eds.) *Representing Juvenile Status Offenders* (Chicago: American Bar Association, 2010), 59–76, 69, 70.

[87] Ibid.

[88] Jeanis, "Chronic Runaway Youth."

[89] Shubik, 31.

[90] Smith, 69.

[91] Emily Horowitz, *Protecting Our Kids?: How Sex Offender Laws Are Failing Us* (Santa Barbara, CA: ABC-CLIO, 2015), xv, xvi, xvii.

[92] Andrea Petersen, "The Overprotected American Child: Children Left to Themselves," *The Wall Street Journal*, June 2, 2018.

[93] Kappeler and Potter, *The Mythology of Crime and Criminal Justice*, 81.

[94] Petersen, "The Overprotected American Child."

PART II

Specific Delinquency Contexts

Chapter 4

Youth Gangs

Youths have formed groups (usually with their own age cohorts) from the beginning of time. Some of these groups have committed various kinds of harmful activities, including crimes. Some of these groups have been called gangs; many have been labeled with other negative terms, including: hoodlums, punks, rowdies, or troublemakers.

A BRIEF HISTORY

Youth groups known as gangs are not recent inventions of U.S. society. Gangs were a prominent feature of early Roman society.[1] They have existed since at least the fourteenth and fifteenth centuries in Europe Descriptions of life in England in the 1700s included references to gangs committing various forms of theft and robbery, along with extortion and rape.[2] Citizens in London were

> terrorized by a series of organized gangs calling themselves the Mims, Hectors, Bugles, Dead Boys . . . who found amusement in breaking windows, demolishing taverns, assaulting the watch . . . The gangs also fought pitched battles among themselves dressed with colored ribbons to distinguish the different factions.[3]

In France during the Middle Ages, there were groups of youths who fought with rival groups from other areas and schools, and who committed a variety of crimes. Youth gangs or groups reportedly existed in Germany during the seventeenth and eighteenth centuries.[4]

The emergence and growth of youth or street gangs in the United States differed by region. The Northeast was first, followed by the Midwest, the West, and the South.[5] The largest cities (New York City, Chicago, and Los Angeles) were notable for the rapid development of gangs and for serving as springboards for the diffusion of gang cultures within the regions. Street gangs developed on the East Coast around 1783 in rapidly growing cities. Large-scale immigration and urban overcrowding created the conditions from which the gangs emerged. The following criteria identified the urban adolescent street gang: (1) recurring gatherings (2) at locations outside homes (3) with affiliation based on self-defined criteria for inclusion (4) with subgroup delineations based on age, authority, roles, or prestige and (5) varied activities of which hanging-out, mating, recreation, and illegal activity were centrally important.

The first street gangs on the East Coast consisted primarily of white youth fighting over local turf. The second phase began in 1820 as immigration from northern and western regions of Europe increased. The third wave arrived in the 1930s and 1940s as Latino and black populations arrived in large numbers. The first gang in New York, the Forty Thieves, formed around 1826 in the Five Points district. Other gangs soon formed in the Bowery. Battles between Bowery Boys and Five Points gangs and the gangs they spawned (claiming more than 1,000 members each) were epic.[6] A third cluster of gangs, composed primarily of adolescents, operated along the docks and shipyards, stealing cargo. Gangs in Boston, primarily Irish youth with some Italians, were reported in the 1840s. White gangs in Philadelphia emerged between 1840 and 1870. By the 1990s, urban renewal, slum clearances, and ethnic migration created conflict between gangs of black, Puerto Rican, and Euro-American youth to maintain their turf and honor.

Chicago was the industrial hub after the Civil War. Immigration from southern and eastern Europe to find jobs created the circumstances for the emergence of gangs.[7] Black gangs formed in the 1920s to combat aggressive all-white gangs. The large number of black migrants were forced to settle on the south side of Chicago; most lived in abject poverty. The Chicago Housing Authority constructed 20,000 low-income family apartments, primarily in high-rise buildings. Gangs grew stronger in the buildings, sometimes taking control. Public housing was a common denominator of gang growth in New York City, Chicago, and Los Angeles. Concentrated poverty in high-rise public buildings provided a clearly identified and secure home base for gangs. The policy was most widely implemented in Chicago, stimulating more gang growth than in either of the other two cities. Gang wars erupted over drug-trafficking turf. Black, Puerto Rican, and Mexican American gangs proliferated in the late 1950s. The influence of Chicago gangs extended throughout the Great Lakes Basin. Chicago gangs are larger, have more sophisticated organizations, and are heavily involved in large-scale drug dealing more than gangs in other cities.

The emergence of gangs in the West is covered in detail in the section on gang classifications below. Contrary to the Northeast and Midwest, there was no history of white ethnic gangs. Gangs in the South emerged much later than other regions.[8] Despite nascent gangs in San Antonio and El Paso in the 1920s, those cities may have been too isolated geographically to extend gang influence through the Southern youth culture. From the 1970s through 1995, the South region led the nation in the number of new gang cities. Miami reported gang activity in the mid 1980s. Houston had only a borderline gang problem in 1980. The first gangs there were barrio gangs resembling those in Los Angeles. Gang problems surfaced in New Orleans in 1996. Gangs incubated in public housing projects in Atlanta at about the same time.

There were common denominators (including the need to belong) in the emergence of gangs in all regions.

> Immigrant families felt marginalized between their society of origin and the dominant American culture to which they had migrated. Once children and adolescents experienced this discomfort, gangs emerged as a group that provided relief on an ongoing basis. Having been left out of mainstream society because of language, education, cultural, and economic barriers, this situation left them with few options or resources to develop socially. Naturally, they drew comfort from places where they were not marginalized, often in the streets and in gangs. In this way, gangs helped immigrant youth adapt to tribulations from social disorganization.[9]

Racially locked out of the dominant Anglo culture and economically locked out of the middle class, youth sought to satisfy social needs with those who had similar problems. Gangs offered relief from double marginalization by providing a sense of identity and bonding.

Beginning in the 1980s, the escalation of media presentations about youth gangs—particularly those gangs located in inner cities—has raised the public's level of fear about youth gangs.

> Newspapers, television, and films were suddenly awash with images of gun-toting, drug-dealing, hat-to-the-back gangstas. With the hue-and-cry came a massive mobilization of resources. Federal, state, and local funds were allocated to create anti-gang units in law enforcement and prosecution agencies.[10]

The rapid deployment of technology and databases augmented the proliferation of gang experts (typically police officers or former gang members). The alarm was sounded that gangs were everywhere. "In public schools across the country, gang awareness and resistance techniques were incorporated into the curriculum, gang-related clothing was banned from campuses, and teachers instructed on how to identify gang members and spot concealed weapons."[11] More often than not, the media totally ignore the surrounding social context of issues. Focusing on gang members communicates the idea that these offenders exist in a social vacuum. The media "breeze past the complexities that cast doubt on the very system that has produced the criminal activity in the first place."[12]

Gangs have become somewhat permanent institutions of large urban areas with a heavy concentration of adolescents and young adults living in poverty and racial minorities. Youth gangs exist, in some form, in all 50 states.[13] As Émile Durkheim once proposed, there is a certain inevitability of crime.[14] So too there will probably always be some groups in society that will be labeled *gangs*. Gang members come from an array of economic and ethnic backgrounds (for example, African American, Asian, Latino, and a multiplicity of European ethnic groups). Each of these ethnic groups, at various junctures in history, has been viewed as representing a threat to the existing order.

Gangs emerged in the United States in a rainbow of colors, beginning with the White ones, reflecting both outside immigration and internal racial/ethnic and territorial conflicts. Understanding the history of evolving gangs in America also engenders a stark realization that gang joining is typically a logical choice for powerless and marginalized youths who have been relegated to the fringes of society.[15]

Substantive attributes of youth gangs have not changed significantly since the early part of the twentieth century.[16] However, gangs have taken advantage of technological advancements (social media) and the abundance of automatic weapons. They have expanded their business-venture options (drug dealing) and have increased violence to protect their interests (drive-by shootings). These changes in gang activities parallel economic, social, and technological transformations that shape social change in the greater society (for example, declining employment opportunities, widespread acceptance of violence promoted by the mass media, social fascination with draconian modes of punishment, and the development and sanitized/impersonal use of high-tech war machinery). Gangs are also an adaptation to "racial and ethnic oppression, as well as poverty and slums, and are reactions of despair to persisting inequality."[17]

Fifty years ago, membership in gangs was a transitory experience of recent immigrant groups. Most members eventually matured out of the gangs and settled down to jobs and families. In the 1990s research indicated that gang membership had become more permanent.[18] During a follow-up study of the original 47 gang founders in Milwaukee, John Hagedorn found that over 80% of them were still involved in the gang despite having reached their mid-20s, an age when previously most members would have matured out of the gang.[19] In contrast, a detailed study in Rochester, New York found that membership in a gang was a brief experience for most youths. Half of the males were in a gang 1 year or less, while two-thirds of the females were in a gang for 1 year or less.[20] Gang membership now is usually a temporary status—one to two years in duration, although longer for some. Disengagement from gangs is not rare; about 400,000 youths leave gangs each year in the United States.[21]

WHAT IS A GANG?

What exactly constitutes a gang or gang membership? If four youths are standing on a street corner or are simply walking down the street, are they a gang? If these same youths hang out together frequently and occasionally engage in some form of deviant activity, are they gang members? Suppose this same group invents a name for itself and purchases special shirts or jackets and invents slogans or hand-signs—does this mean it is a gang? If a young person is seen giving special hand signals or heard uttering gang phrases because he thinks it is cool or hip to do so (whether he fully understands the implications or not), should he be considered a gang member?

Or, if a youth lives in a neighborhood that has an established gang (but no one in the gang considers him a member) and is passing the time on a street corner with a gang member he has known for several years, will the police officer who decides to question the group fill out a field investigation card on him? Should he be counted as a gang member? How does race enter into the picture of defining gangs?

We suspect that the average white citizen (and many police officers) would respond to a group of three or four white youths differently than they would to a group of three or four African American teenagers hanging out together (for example, at a shopping mall). Forty percent of young white Americans identify as gang members, but police undercount them at 10% to 14%. Criminal law professor Babe Howell says police see groups of young whites as individuals, with each person responsible for his or her conduct, but they see people of color in street gangs as criminally liable for the conduct of their peers.[22] These few examples illustrate the difficulty in defining gangs and gang members.

The term *gang* can have many different definitions. Gil Geis suggested that the etymology of the term from Middle English provided a useful guide: "a going, a walking, or a journey."[23] One dictionary defined a gang as "(1) a group of persons working together (2) a group of persons working to unlawful or antisocial ends; esp: a band of antisocial adolescents."[24] Synonyms for the term include: band, clan, clique, club, coterie, crew, guild, league, squad, team, tribe.[25]

Not surprisingly, there has been little consensus among social scientists and law-enforcement personnel as to the definition. One writer defined gangs as "groups whose members meet together with some regularity, over time, on the basis of group-defined criteria of membership and group-defined organization."[26] Researchers have often used a police definition of the term. Many researchers have apparently confused the term *group* with the term *gang* and have proceeded to expand the definition in such a way as to include every group of youths who commit offenses together. One of the most accepted definitions comes from Malcolm Klein, who has studied gangs for more than thirty years:

> [A gang is] any denotable . . . group [of adolescents or young adults] who (a) are generally perceived as a distinct aggregation by others in their neighborhood, (b) recognize themselves as a denotable group (almost invariably with a group name), and (c) have been involved in a sufficient number of [illegal] incidents to call forth a consistent negative response from neighborhood residents and/or enforcement agencies.[27]

The National Gang Center finds a general consensus on the following elements in defining a gang:[28]

- The group has three or more members, generally aged 12–24.
- Members share an identity, typically linked to a name, and often other symbols.
- Members view themselves as a gang, and they are recognized by others as a gang.

- The group has some permanence and a degree of organization.
- The group is involved in an elevated level of criminal activity.

"In general, law enforcement agencies report that group criminality is of greatest importance and the presence of leadership is of least importance in defining a gang."[29] Omitted from this definition were such groups as motorcycle gangs, hate/ideology groups, prison gangs, and exclusively adult gangs.

Other researchers distinguish between the terms *gang, street gang, traditional youth gang*, and *posse/crew*. A *gang* is

> a group or collectivity of persons with a common identity who interact in cliques or sometimes as a whole group on a fairly regular basis and whose activities the community may view in varying degrees as legitimate, illegitimate, criminal, or some combination thereof. What distinguishes the gang from other groups is its communal or fraternal, different, or special interstitial character.[30]

In contrast, *street gang* is "a group or collectivity of persons engaged in significant illegitimate or criminal activities, mainly threatening and violent."[31] The emphasis is placed on the location of the gang and their gang-related activities. The *traditional youth gang*

> refers to a youth or adolescent gang and often to the youth sector of a street gang. Such a group is concerned primarily with issues of status, prestige, and turf protection. The youth gang may have a name and a location, be relatively well organized, and persist over time. [They] often have leadership structure (implicit or explicit), codes of conduct, colors, special dress, signs, symbols, and the like. [They] may vary across time in characteristics of age, gender, community, race/ethnicity, or generation, as well as in scope and nature of delinquent or criminal activities.[32]

Still another variation is the *posse* or *crew*, which, while often used in conjunction with the terms *street* or *youth gang*, is more commonly "characterized by a commitment to criminal activity for economic gain, particularly drug trafficking."[33]

Researchers have also distinguished between *delinquent groups* and *criminal organizations*. The former are far less organized and criminal and do not have distinctive dress, colors, signs, and so on. The latter refers more to a relatively well-organized and sophisticated group of either youths or adults (often a combination of both) organized mainly around the illegal pursuit of economic gain. Finally, there are gang *cliques* or *sets* that are often smaller versions (or subgroups) of larger gangs, usually based on age.[34]

Ronald Huff distinguishes between youth gangs and organized crime. He defines a *youth gang* as a

> collectivity consisting primarily of adolescents and young adults who (a) interact frequently with one another; (b) are frequently and deliberately involved in illegal activities; (c) share a common collective identity that is usually, but not always,

expressed through a gang name; and (d) typically express that identity by adopting certain symbols and/or claiming control over certain "turf" (persons, places, things, and/or economic markets).[35]

In comparison, an *organized crime group* is a

collectivity consisting primarily of adults who (a) interact frequently with one another; (b) are frequently and deliberately involved in illegal activities directed toward economic gain, primarily through the provision of illegal goods and services; and (c) generally have better defined leadership and organizational structure than does the youth gang.[36]

There are several key differences between these two groups. First, they differ significantly in terms of age, with youth gangs being much younger than organized crime groups. Second, whereas the organized crime group exists almost exclusively for the purpose of economic criminal activity, youth gangs engage in a variety of both legal and illegal activities, with their illegal activities usually committed by individuals or small groups of individuals, rather than by the entire group.

Several researchers argue that gangs should not be defined as purely criminal or delinquent organizations. Huff regards group experience as a normative component in youth subculture. "In analyzing youth gangs, it is important to acknowledge that it is normal and healthy for adolescents to want to be with their peers. In fact, adolescents who are loners often tend to be maladjusted."[37] James Howell and Elizabeth Griffiths describe the gradations of behavior in embryonic gangs.

> Starter gangs often emerge somewhat spontaneously among authority-rejecting children and adolescents who have been alienated from families and schools. Finding themselves spending a great deal of time on the street, youths may form gangs with other socially marginalized adolescents and look to each other for protection and street socialization. Although most youths who join are on average in a gang for less than a year, some of these gangs increase their criminal activity, especially when conflict with other street groups solidifies them, becoming a formidable force in the streets. Girls often are active participants in youth gangs, and they commit very similar crimes to those of boys.[38]

Hagedorn believes that gangs are not merely criminal enterprises or bureaucratic entities with formal organizational structures. Rather, as other researchers have noted, gangs are age-graded groups or cliques "with considerable variation within each age group of friends."[39] More recently Hagedorn has argued that gangs "are not stable, clearly defined entities. Today's youth gang might become a drug posse tomorrow or, in some places, even transform into an ethnic militia or a vigilante group the next day."[40]

Most gang members spend the bulk of their time simply hanging out or engaging in other nondelinquent activities. Many researchers have spent a considerable amount of time (perhaps months) "waiting for something to happen."[41] Malcolm Klein described gang member life as very dull, with the occasional exception of a fight or an exciting rumor.

> For the most part, gang members do very little—sleep, get up late, hang around, brag a lot, eat again, drink, hang around some more. It's a boring life; the only thing that is equally boring is being a researcher watching gang members.[42]

An equally difficult task is trying to determine what constitutes a *gang-related offense*. If a gang member kills another gang member in retaliation for the killing of a fellow gang member, few would argue over whether this would be gang related. However, what if a gang member is killed as a result of a love triangle? What if a gang member kills someone while committing a robbery on his own? How does one characterize the murder of a gang member by someone who is not in a gang? Decisions about these kinds of incidents must be made, and police officials have procedures for such reporting. However, as Malcolm Klein and Cheryl Maxson observe, such procedures are conducted "not always according to reliable criteria, not always with adequate information regarding the motive or circumstances of the crime, not always with extensive gang-membership information on file, and *most clearly*—not by the same criteria from city to city."[43]

Klein and Maxson reviewed reporting procedures in five cities and found that each city had somewhat different methods for defining gang-related incidents. For example, in two cities, only violent incidents were counted. In one city the policy was to include only gang-on-gang crimes, but the authors found that robberies where the offenders (but not the victims) were gang members constituted gang-related crimes. In another city any offense committed by a gang member was counted as gang related.[44]

Other than homicides and graffiti, most law enforcement agencies do not record whether criminal offenses are gang-related. From 1996 through 2012, the National Gang Center conducted an annual survey of law enforcement agencies to assess the extent of gang problems.[45] One-third or less of the responding agencies reported that they regularly recorded aggravated assault, firearms use, drug sales, robbery, burglary, motor vehicle theft or larceny/theft as gang-related. They were slightly more likely to record person offenses than property offenses as gang-related. "The relative lack of definitive and comprehensive gang-crime statistics for violent and nonviolent offenses alike signifies that much remains unknown about gang crime trends."[46]

How Many Gangs and Gang Members Are There?

Gangs exist in all cities with populations of 100,000 or more, as well as in federal and state prison systems and most juvenile correctional systems. Gangs are found within almost every major urban high school in the United States.[47] Exactly how many gangs and how many gang members there are in the country is not known with any degree of certainty. In fact, there are as many estimates as there are estimators![48] In the 1920s Frederic Thrasher estimated that there were 1,313 gangs in Chicago alone.[49] Walter Miller's nationwide survey in the 1970s estimated anywhere from 700 to almost 3,000 gangs in the largest cities in the country.[50]

Most estimates are from law enforcement sources. Until 1997, the estimated numbers showed yearly increases—and the amount of money going to police departments increased as well, in addition to the number of gang units and police officers assigned to those units. As noted earlier, in virtually every survey in recent years the definition of gang and gang member has been left entirely up to the reporting law enforcement agencies. This enables local criminal justice agencies to vary their estimates depending on their goals. Some provide conservative estimates to project an image of their city as safe or to promote tourism, while others exaggerate the numbers to obtain more funding. Field researchers emphasize that local politics shape gang intelligence and record keeping on gangs in law enforcement agencies. Gang problems can be exaggerated or denied in law enforcement reporting depending on local political considerations.

Other researchers have noted that official data on gangs more often reflect "the organization of social control agencies than empirical realities about gang membership or gangs," and police data "provide rather subjective assessments of gang behavior."[51] The Justice Policy Institute observes:

> It is difficult to find a law enforcement account of gang activity that does not give the impression that the problem is getting worse by the day. . . . The most comprehensive survey of law enforcement data on gang activity shows no significant changes in estimated gang membership or the prevalence of gang activity—both of which are down significantly since the late 1990s. Further, law enforcement depictions of the gang population are sharply at odds with youth survey data when it comes to the geography of gang activity as well as the race and gender of gang members.[52]

From 2005 to 2012 (the final National Youth Gang survey), only one third of the jurisdictions participating in the survey reported having a gang problem.[53] The estimated number of gangs fluctuated over the 16-year study period (1996–2012). In 1996, there were an estimated 30,800 gangs in the country.[54] The estimated number declined each year to a low of 20,100 in 2003. Estimates then increased yearly to 30,700 in 2012. The age of gang members during the survey years ranged from 50% under 18 in 1996 to 33.2% in 2001. The average percentage of juveniles was 39%.[55] The average percentage of girls was 6.9%.

Criminologists David Pyrooz and Gary Sweeten estimate that there are over one million juvenile gang members in the United States.[56] The overall prevalence of gang membership was 2%; involvement was highest at age 14 (5%) before falling to 1% in the late teens. While gang members were disproportionately male, black,

Latino, from single-parent households, and in families living below the poverty line, youth in gangs came from all types of backgrounds. A recurring stereotype is that once someone joins a gang, they cannot leave. Turnover rates are about 36%. Gang membership is highly transient; rarely did youth remain in gangs longer than two years. The numbers of gang members are higher than law enforcement estimates because the latter focus more on criminally-involved youth and ignore younger and peripherally gang-involved youth.

Schools sometimes serve as a gathering place for gangs. In 1995, 37% of students reported that gangs were present at their school.[57] By 2001, the percentage declined to 20%, and in 2017, the percentage was 9%.[58] A higher percentage of students from urban areas (11%) reported a gang presence than did students from suburban (8%) and rural (7%) areas. Demographically, 17% of black students reported a gang presence at school compared to 12% of Hispanic students, 5% of white students, and 2% of Asian students. During the 2015–16 school year, the percentage of all public schools reporting disciplinary problems from gang activities was 1.2%.[59] The largest percentage (4.2%) was reported by high schools with an enrollment over 1,000. A survey of gang-involved youth found that gangs did not impact their school lives despite some victimizations and incivilities.[60]

GANGS AND CRIME

There is some evidence that gang members commit a disproportionate amount of crime, especially violent crime. It is quite probable that this aspect of the problem is exaggerated, since violence captures the public imagination and makes the headlines. Also, the violence is heavily concentrated within certain neighborhoods in large cities. If we consider an entire city or county, we find that gang members do not contribute significantly to the overall crime problem.[61] Most of the offenses committed by gang members continue to be property crimes (often committed by gang members independently, rather than as part of an organized gang activity).

The stereotype of the gang member and the gang revolves around criminal activity—a characterization perpetuated by both the media and the police.[62] The media embrace gang stories because they are easy to report and generate viewer interest.[63] Gang activity marked by graffiti, colors, hand signs, and rivalries is memorable and newsworthy. Law enforcement and the media discuss all gang activity as criminal activity. They also connect the entire gang with any crime committed by an individual gang member. As a result, public perception of gangs is distorted. It is important to keep this in mind throughout our discussion of the various crimes committed by gang members.

In the late 1980s and early 1990s, media reports stoked fears that gangs were violent organizations posing a unique threat to society.[64] Public concern over gang activity has skyrocketed since 2000, despite youth crime rates steadily decreasing to historic lows. Policymakers characterize gangs as one of the most pressing law enforcement concerns. To allay public fear of violent crime, policymakers have prioritized suppressing gangs. Suppression tactics include targeting gang members with severe criminal punishments, forming gang units in police departments, aggressively policing high-crime neighborhoods, and creating gang databases to facilitate oversight.

In California, gang enhancements became law in the late 1980s. The State Legislature passed the Street Terrorism Enforcement and Protection Act (STEP Act), which adds anywhere from two years to life to the prison sentence, depending on the severity of the underlying conviction. Thirty-one states enacted similar laws.[65] In 1997, California created a statewide database, CalGang. By 2012, it included the names of more than 200,000 individuals, including some as young as 10; 66% percent were Latino. California uses the following criteria for identifying gang members: (1) self-reported affiliation, (2) association with known gang members, (3) tattoos indicating gang affiliation, (4) wearing clothing or other symbols associated with a specific gang, (5) using hand signs of a gang or being photographed with known gang members, (6) appearance of suspect's name on a gang document, hit list, or graffiti, (7) accusation of gang membership by a reliable source, (8) arrested with identified gang members, (9) correspondence to or from known gang members about gang activity, (10) creating gang graffiti.[66]

In many counties across the United States, law-enforcement officers keep databases of individuals they have identified as gang members. Databases generally consist of the names of suspected gang members, photographs, addresses, school attended, affiliations, and tattoos or other identifying marks.[67] The Chicago Crime Commission released a 400-page book on street gangs in 2018 that includes more than 1,000 mug shots of mostly young African American and Latino men.[68] The book was compiled primarily from information provided by the Chicago police. The city's gang database includes 128,000 names of people police have arrested or stopped on the street. They have not necessarily been convicted or charged with a crime, and 95% are African Americans and Hispanics. Community organizations and activists filed a class-action lawsuit against Chicago in June 2018 alleging that the database is inaccurate, outdated, and racially skewed.[69] Officers have unlimited discretion to add individuals to the database; current practices include adding people based on distinctive tattoos and information from informants.

Researchers have found that white gang membership tends to be underestimated and undercounted, while the opposite is true for black and Latino youth. People are categorized as gang members based on the color of clothes they wear or posing in a picture giving hand signs. In some communities, it might be difficult to avoid contact with a gang member, but any association can be used as criteria for an enhancement charge. "Every young person who lives on a block where there is gang activity is not a gang member. That doesn't stop law enforcement officials from labeling them as such. . . . Once someone is labeled a gang member, whether it is true or not, there is little recourse for undoing the damage."[70] Critics of gang enhancements ask the pertinent question: Are people to be held responsible for their actions or for whom they are perceived to be?

Prosecutors increasingly use gang enhancements, sometimes to make weak cases seem stronger.[71] Gang allegations introduce inflammatory information rather than concrete evidence related to the criminal charge. At the bail hearing, prosecutors often submit documentation from law enforcement that the defendant is a gang member.[72] Gang membership triggers perceptions of violence, which factors into a judge's decision about the risk the defendant poses to society if released pretrial. Considerations of dangerousness generally result in higher bail or detention. Being detained has a significant negative impact on the defendant in the eventual disposition of the case. The threat of the gang enhancement influences defendants to accept a plea bargain.

John Hagedorn provided details of gang enhancement that resulted in the ultimate penalty. Robert Butts, Jr. was 18 when he and his companion killed a man during a robbery. Prosecutors took extreme measures to label the crime gang-related.[73] The sheriff testified that the bullet type was "F shot," and the "F" stood for "Folks" (see discussion below about Folks as one coalition of gangs). Another witness testified that Folks was an acronym for followers of Satan. In closing arguments, the prosecutor told the jury that their county was in the midst of a violent crime wave by vicious gangs, which was pure invention. "The jury didn't sentence a human being, Robert Butts, to death. They sentenced a caricature of a gang member, a dehumanized monster of the jury's darkest nightmares . . . an offender so unalterably evil there is literally no choice to the jury but to sentence him to death." Georgia executed Robert Butts, Jr. on May 4, 2018.

Gang enhancements are not the only tool used to suppress gangs. Since the late 1980s, authorities in the city of Los Angeles obtained gang injunctions. A prosecutor would file a civil public nuisance injunction against a particular gang for conduct harmful to the community; it would be granted by default.[74] Police would then serve people alleged to be members of the gang with copies of the injunction, which turned common behavior in areas deemed to be gang territory into crimes—possessing a cell phone, drinking alcohol on one's front porch or in a restaurant, associating with people alleged to be gang members (including family members and friends), or wearing certain types of clothing in specific neighborhoods. The geographical area over which the provisions of the injunction are enforced is the "safety zone." Sizes of the zones ranged from four square blocks to one square mile to almost seven square miles.[75] Because the injunctions are civil orders, alleged gang members are not entitled to a public defender if they want to appeal the order.[76]

Critics alleged the injunctions were overly broad, subjecting thousands of people to restrictions for knowing or being related to a gang member.[77] Many included in the orders had never been convicted of a crime. In addition, the injunctions disproportionately targeted Latinos and Latin Americans. Since 2000, Los Angeles enforced injunctions against 79 gang sets, affecting about 8,900 people. After a citywide audit in 2017, the city released 7,300 people from injunctions. On March 15, 2018, the federal district court ordered release of the remaining people placed on injunctions granted before January 19, 2018; the injunctions violated due process rights.

It should be emphasized that for most gangs the bulk of their time is *not* spent committing crimes. Recall Klein's comments above about how most gang members spend their time.[78] The Milwaukee gangs Hagedorn studied spent most of their time partying and hanging out.[79] When gang members hang out, it is usually by a park, by a taco stand, and they are "smoking, drinking, roughhousing, playing a pickup ball game, messing with a few girls, or sauntering up a street in a possessive, get-outta-our-way fashion."[80] The minimal amount of violence actually engaged in by gangs has been corroborated by other studies. Property crimes remain the major type of offense committed by gangs.[81] One study found the consumption of alcohol was the most common activity of gang members.[82] A more recent study reinforces the observation that gangs spend the bulk of their time *not* committing crimes.[83] Many researchers say the reality is that most gang members are more likely to talk than to take action.[84]

The criminal activities of gangs vary according to the type of gang, with some committing little crime and others heavily involved in criminal activity. Overall, the typical crimes committed by gangs have consistently covered a variety of offenses (for example, burglaries, petty theft, vandalism, fighting, and truancy). The major victims of gang violence are other gang members. Innocent bystanders are rarely the victims, despite claims from law enforcement and other officials to the contrary.[85] If an innocent bystander is killed by a gang member, the media report the tragedy in a highly sensational manner.[86] Sometimes a report does not mention that violence against a victim was gang related but the audience, conditioned by previous shocking reports, assumes it was.

The commission of crime is rarely an activity in which the entire gang participates; rather, it is usually committed by a small group of gang members. Moreover, "the crimes themselves are not committed on behalf of the gang, nor are proceeds shared. The individuals (or groups, which may include non-gang members as well as homeboys) who commit such crimes do so for their own reasons and by their own rules—and that includes drug dealing."[87] This fact is extremely important. It contradicts the theory underlying most gang-enhancement statutes, which increase the punishment if the crime is gang related.[88]

There are many ways to think about gangs, but media narratives and law enforcement approaches have conditioned the public to view gang activity as a dangerous subclass of crime.[89] In summary, the following are common myths about gangs and crime: (1) gang members are hardened criminals, (2) gang members spend most of their time planning or committing crimes, (3) gang members are responsible for most violent crime, and (4) gang leaders organize and direct the criminal activity of their members. While these myths may apply to a select few gangs and their members, the stereotypes fail to account for the majority of gang affiliations. Replacing the myths with the following gives a more accurate description of the relationship between gangs and crime: (1) the extent of criminal involvement of individual gang members varies widely, (2) gang members spend most of their time in noncriminal pursuits—even those members who do sometimes engage in criminal activity, (3) gang members commit only a small proportion of all crime, including violent crime, (4) when gang members commit crime, it is often to serve personal rather than gang interests.

GANG AND GANG MEMBER TYPOLOGIES

Gangs and gang members can be differentiated by multiple criteria including: age, race or ethnicity, gender, setting, type of activity, purpose of the gang activity, degree of criminality, level of organization, and group function.[90] Remember that much of the terminology used to discuss gangs is the invention of outside observers, and the terms applied can be influenced by the backgrounds of those observing.

Klein found that a number of police gang experts he surveyed knew little about the structural nature of the gangs in their cities. "Because they were concentrating on crime patterns and investigative issues, they found little relevance in the forms that their gangs took."[91] When he asked the police respondents about terminology applied to gang groups and members he heard such an array that he was concerned that the patterns reported might not be reliable. He cautioned: "The dismaying array of terms makes it clear that consensus is not a feature of the current American police knowledge of gangs."[92] He found the terminology far more varied than the activities to which it was being applied. "Officials are applying self satisfying terms to arbitrary distinctions."[93]

Most gangs are rather loosely structured groups who "come together for periods of weeks, months, or as long as a year, but then disintegrate."[94] On the youth/street gang continuum, starter gangs designate short-lived, embryonic gangs.[95] Schools are generally the settings for these gangs, which develop from a variety of interest groups. Members range in age from 10 to 13 and are usually formed by rejected, alienated, and rebellious children. They are unsuccessful at school, aggressive toward others, punished more frequently, and reject everything that represents order. Feelings of powerlessness and exclusion in school provide a basis for identification with others who share the same feelings.

One of the more stable types is the traditional area gang, often described as a vertical organization because of its age-graded structure of cliques within the group. Characterized by a common territory, these gangs are typically all male (often with female auxiliary groups) ethnic minorities (usually African American and Hispanic, but often Asian).

Another variation is the horizontally organized groups in which divisions cut across different neighborhoods and include youths in different age brackets. Many have spread across cities, states, and even countries. Often they are referred to as supergangs and nations. Examples of these horizontal alliances include the Crips and Bloods (who started in Los Angeles) and the People and Folk (starting in Illinois).

It should be emphasized that these large groupings often consist of gangs with very little in common with one another, other than their affiliation. To a gang member, the particular *set* or neighborhood of origin is of prime importance. "See, 'Crip' doesn't mean nothin' to a membership. Like 'I'm a Crip, you're a Crip—so what? What set are you from? What neighborhood are you from? What street do you live on? I may live on Sixty-ninth, he may live on Seventieth.'"[96]

Small groups clustered by age or friendship are the basic building blocks of gangs. Gangs are loosely organized into small age/friendship cohorts or cliques. Age groupings vary by location and time frame. In the early 1960s in New York City, age divisions included Tots (11 to 13 years of age), Juniors (13 to 15 years of age), Tims (15 to 17 years of age), and Seniors (17 and older). By the 1970s the most common groupings in New York included the Baby Spades (9 to 12 years), the Young Spades (12 to 15 years old), and the Black Spades (16 to 30 years of age). In Philadelphia the age groupings were identified as: Bottom-Level Midgets (12 to 14 years), Middle-Level Young Boys (14 to 17), and Upper-Level Old Heads (18 to 23 years old). Members of gangs are often further categorized by levels of participation. Hard-core, confirmed members spend more time with the gang than fringe, associates, marginals, and wannabes. The latter group is normally composed of the very young (usually 12 or younger).[97] In Los Angeles, barrios sometimes have at least two or three cohorts defined by age and status: 12- to 16-year-olds who are just getting into the gang; 14- to 18-year-olds who are somewhat proven gang members; and 18- to 20-year olds who are seasoned. Diego Vigil notes: "This age grading, with its informal and formal processes of socialization and encultura-tion, ensures that the barrio gang always has a new clique to take over the duties of defending the turf."[98]

Leadership in gangs can best be described as shifting, permeable, and elastic—thus inherently resistant to outside intervention. "It presents not a cohesive force but, rather, a sponge-like resilience."[99] Gang leadership is usually divided among a number of members depending on the type of activity. "Gang leadership is func-tional, not positional. It exists more, and less, because of its context."[100] If the gang is involved in protecting its turf, the leader will be someone who is cool under pres-sure and has the skills required for protection. If the gang needs a spokesperson, the leader will be someone with good verbal skills. If the gang is involved in an athletic contest, the leader will be someone who can manage the team and is respected by other members.

Leadership is also a function of time and the availability of members. As time passes, members may not be available because of work, marriage, or incarceration. The stereotype of the gang leader is someone who is tough, with a long criminal history, and a strong influence over the members. In actuality, the typical leader does not maintain influence over a long period of time for the reasons described above. Gangs with centralized authority are probably a small minority, but they fit a convenient stereotype.

One possible reason that gangs with centralized authority are seen as more prevalent is that they appear to be more amenable to methods of gang control frequently advocated by the police and the courts. If one attributes crime by gang members primarily to the presence and influence of a single strong leader (key-personality model), all one has to do is to locate and remove that leader to curb or eliminate crime.[101]

The reality is that if one gang leader is removed, there will be someone else to fill the needed function.

One of the most important distinguishing features of gangs has been territory or *turf*. However, there have been changes. Autonomous gangs occupy smaller territories than was once the pattern. Examples include single blocks, a school, public housing, etc. These gangs have shorter histories, fewer ties to neighborhoods, and are less cohesive than the more traditional gangs. Geographically connected gangs are branches of another gang located in a neighboring territory or sharing an affiliation but residing in totally separate geographical areas.[102] The declining importance of turf for some gangs could be a function of growing sophistication and the increasing use of the automobile.

Turf or neighborhood remains of critical importance to the more traditional gangs. In many areas, especially in Los Angeles, the term *gang* is often synonymous with *barrio* or *neighborhood*.[103] The notion of turf centers around two important ideas—identification and control—with control being the most important. There are three primary types of turf rights. The first is basic ownership rights; the gang attempts to control practically everything that occurs in a particular area. The second is occupancy rights; different gangs share an area or tolerate one another's use. The third is enterprise monopoly; one gang controls certain activities within a specified area.[104] Contested areas between gangs can consist of actual territory involving homes and family or "symbolic space or 'turf' that must be defended from pecuniary intruders."[105] Disputes over market space are somewhat recent developments. It should be noted that turf is less important to gangs now, with the exception of Hispanic gangs, who still define themselves as protectors of their own neighborhoods.[106]

When categorizing gangs, there are two prevalent methods: types of *gangs* and types of gang *members*. More than a dozen types of gangs have been identified, and about an equal number of categories of gang *members*. This coincides with a point made previously; namely, there are a variety of adolescent groups existing at any one time. In fact, the adolescent subculture is famous for the infinite variety of groupings.[107]

Researchers in all fields of study organize a vast array of research findings using *ideal types*, a useful concept in that there are no pure types of anything.[108] What normally happens is that the researcher suggests that a phenomenon *tends to fit into one or another type*. The following typologies should be considered ideal types. For instance, there may not be a pure hard-core gang member, but a particular individual may come close despite having certain characteristics that resemble those of peripheral members. Similarly, a specific gang could be characterized as predatory despite having some characteristics of a territorial gang. The predatory tendencies would be prominent while the territorial characteristics would be less defining. The most commonly used criteria to classify types of gangs are behavioral characteristics, especially deviant and/or criminal behavior, although certain non-deviant or traditional group behaviors are also factors.

Types of Gangs

Research in six different cities by three different researchers identified the following major types of gangs.[109]

- *Hedonistic/social* gangs. With only moderate drug use and offending, these gangs like having a good time, use drugs to get high, and have little involvement in crime, especially violent crime.
- *Party* gangs. These groups have relatively high use and sales of drugs but only one major form of delinquency (vandalism).
- *Instrumental* gangs. The main criminal activity of these gangs is committing property crimes. Most members use drugs and alcohol but seldom engage in the selling of drugs.
- *Predatory* gangs. These gangs are heavily involved in serious crimes (for example, robberies and muggings) and in the abuse of addictive drugs. Some may engage in the selling of drugs, although not in any organized fashion, and some have lower involvement in drug use and drug sales than the party gang.
- *Scavenger* gangs. These loosely organized groups of youths are urban survivors, preying on the weak in the inner cities, engaging in petty crimes (but sometimes violent) often just for fun. The members have no greater bond than their impulsiveness and the need to belong. They have no goals and are low achievers, often illiterate, with poor school performance.
- *Serious delinquent* gangs. Although heavily involved in both serious and minor crimes, these gangs have much lower involvement in drug use and drug sales than the party gang.
- *Territorial* gangs. Gangs associated with a specific area or turf; they are often involved in conflicts with other gangs over their territories.
- *Organized/corporate* gangs. Resembling major corporations, with separate divisions handling sales, marketing, discipline, and so on, these gangs are heavily involved in all kinds of crime including sales of drugs. Discipline is strict, and promotion is based on merit; drug use is also heavy.
- *Drug* gangs. These gangs are smaller than other gangs and focused on the drug business. They are much more cohesive with strong, centralized leadership.

Some people use the all-inclusive term, *street gang*, to describe most of the above gangs (except for drug gangs).[110]

More recently Klein and Maxson provided the following typology of gangs.[111]

- *Traditional.* Large size (100+ members); long duration (more than 20 years); subgroups (e.g., O.G.s, seniors, juniors, midgets, etc.); territorial; wide age range (20–30 years); criminally versatile.
- *Nontraditional.* Medium-large size (more than 50 members); short duration (less than 10 years); subgroups; territorial; no pattern for age range; criminally versatile.
- *Compressed.* Small size (up to 50 members); short duration (less than 10 years); no subgroups; no territorial pattern; narrow age range (less than 10 years); criminally versatile.
- *Collective.* Medium-large size (more than 50 members); medium duration (10–15 years); no subgroups; no territorial pattern; medium-wide age range (more than 10 years); criminally versatile.
- *Specialty.* Small size (less than 50 members); short duration (less than 10 years); no subgroups; territorial; narrow age range (less than 10 years); not criminally versatile.

Types of Gang Members

The most common method of distinguishing types of gang *members* is based on the *degree of attachment to and involvement in the gang*. Think of a continuum running from very little attachment to complete involvement. The following gang *member* types have been identified by researchers.[112]

- *Regulars/hard core.* These members are strongly attached to the gang, participate regularly, and have few interests outside of the gang. They lacked a consistent male adult in their lives, became street oriented earlier, experimented with drugs at an earlier age, became gang members sooner, and participated in destructive patterns over a longer period of time. Smaller in numbers, these are the most influential and active members of the gang. They interact frequently and relate easily to one another, thriving on the gang's activity. Individuals in the inner clique are the key recruiters and make key decisions. They have few friends outside the gang and recognize no authority beyond the gang.
- *Peripheral* members. Also known as *associates*, these individuals have a strong attachment to the gang but participate less often than the regulars because they have other interests outside the gang. The *associates* are sometimes called *fringe* members. They may claim gang affiliation and wear gang colors, but they infrequently participate.
- *Temporary* members. Marginally committed, these members join the gang at a later age than the regulars and peripherals; they remain in the gang only a

short period of time. The less intense commitment lasts only during a particular development phase.

- *Situational* members. These members are very marginally attached and join the gang only for certain activities (avoiding the more violent activities whenever possible).
- *At risk.* These *pre-gang* youths are not really gang members. They do not yet belong to a gang but have shown some interest. They live in neighborhoods where gangs exist. They often fantasize about being members and also might have friends or relatives whom they admire who belong to the gang. Often they begin experimenting with certain gang attire and/ or language. This may begin as early as the second grade.
- *Wannabe.* Gangs themselves use this term to describe recruits, who are usually in their preteen years and know and admire gang members. They are perhaps one notch above the at risk youths in terms of commitment and involvement. They have already begun to emulate gang members in terms of dress, gang values, and so on. They may be called *Pee Wees* or *Baby Homies.*
- *Veteranos/O.G.s.* This group usually consists of men in their 20s or 30s (possibly older) who still participate in gang activities (sometimes referred to as *gang banging*). There are two major subtypes within this category. *Veteranos* are somewhat retired statesmen who still command respect. *O.G.s* are *original gangsters.* They earned respect through a combination of longevity and achievement. Often they are expected to teach younger members the ways of the gang and/or to straighten out younger members causing trouble within the gang. They are sometimes the founding member(s) of the gang.
- *Auxiliary.* These members hold limited responsibility within a gang; this is a very common role for female members. These individuals do not participate in all gang activities. A related type is the *adjunct* member, who is a permanent part-time member by choice, often because of holding down a regular job.

GANG CLASSIFICATIONS

Gangs are most commonly characterized by ethnicity or race. After discussing an example of a supergang, we will look at the most frequent ethnic groupings. Some gangs have united into supergangs to achieve uniform objectives (especially self-protection). Others are gang nations or gang sets. Examples of the latter include the Bloods and Crips that began in the Los Angeles area.

People and Folks

In the 1960s a youth group in Chicago known as the Black P-Stone Rangers evolved into a criminal organization, largely through the efforts of Jeff Fort.[113] He eventually organized a group of about 50 gangs into the Black P-Stone Nation.

The leaders (21 in all) described themselves as a "socially conscious, self-help or-ganization that would help uplift themselves and their community." They obtained $1.4 million in federal anti-poverty money. Eventually Fort was indicted by a fed-eral grand jury, convicted, and sent to prison.

Shortly thereafter, two other Chicago gangs (Black Disciples and Gangster Dis-ciples) combined to form the Black Gangster Disciple Nation. Throughout the dec-ade of the 1970s Black P-Stone Nation and Black Gangster Disciple Nations fought over control of the illegal drug market in Chicago. Many from each nation ended up in prison, including Larry Hoover (leader of the Gangster Disciples) who is serving a life sentence at a supermax prison in Colorado. At the end of that decade, two major alliances emerged—People Nation and Folk Nation.[114] Gangs that were originally part of the Black P-Stone Nation aligned with the People Nation; those that were part of the Black Gangster Disciple Nation aligned with the Folk Nation.

Although alliances are weaker with the growth of factions, most Chicago gangs still identify as either Folk or People.[115] The Chicago Crime Commission iden-tified 59 active Chicago gangs; once cohesive, disciplined gangs have splintered into 2,400 factions. Police estimate 100,000 gang members are in the city; more than half that number belong to the Gangster Disciples, Latin Kings, and Black P. Stones. Thousands of members are not active. The book includes gang-turf maps and describes how social media has altered gang culture in recent years, sometimes making gang conflicts deadlier. Police in Cicero say 70% of gang conflict is due to taunts on social media. No longer are gangs well-disciplined and controlled by older leaders. Smaller factions run by younger members are more violent.

Chicano Gangs

Chicano gangs have a long history. Non-territorial, age-graded friendship associations—palomilla—originated in Mexico and were brought to the United States in the early 1900s on a route through El Paso and Albuquerque to Los An-geles.[116] In 1924, 20 to 25 gangs of 300 to 400 boys were reported in El Paso; 80% were younger than fifteen. The first reported Mexican-American gang members in El Paso were called *Pachucos*—"a Mexican-Spanish term for a young Mexican living in El Paso, especially one of low social status who belongs to a more tightly knit group, a street gang."[117] Gangs in Los Angeles were outgrowths of this foundation.

The earliest cliques in Los Angeles, such as El Hoyo Maravilla, were similar to the palomilla.[118] Age-graded associations provided adolescents with channels for social growth. In contrast to later gangs, palomillas were not identified with a par-ticular territory, did not have a group name, and were sometimes short-lived. An important heritage from the palomilla is the age-graded clique. "Most barrio gangs are made up of age cohorts, or klikas, separated in age by two to three years."[119] After World War II, the cliques began to change. Although there had been con-frontations at school and parties that involved fighting, those events were usually personal and did not always involve associates. As the number of barrios grew and larger groups of unsupervised youth were in the streets, conflicts among groups escalated. In response, gangs became more structured, and territorial affiliations were formalized.

Physical and cultural marginalization served as incubators for Mexican street gangs. Mexican immigrants settled in barrios—geographically isolated areas that others had rejected for habitation.[120] Prejudices in the Anglo-American community contributed to urban social pressures and discrimination in schools, which made acculturation difficult. As a result, people in the barrio developed a subculture. Cholo (derived from the Spanish *solo* meaning alone) youth were the poorest of the marginalized immigrants. Gangs were the outgrowth of culturally and socially alienated youths.

> Through the decades the gang subculture has established itself as an alternative coping strategy with socialization and enculturation processes of its own. Only a small percentage of the barrio youth population is attracted to it, and of that number an even smaller portion become thoroughly immersed in it, usually members of the underclass or the most marginal ones. The external reasons for the variance in involvement and participation are multiple—type and degree of family stress, amount of street socialization, peer and model influences, barrio traditions and sense of territoriality, and so on.[121]

Two of the oldest gangs in East Los Angeles are White Fence and El Hoyo Maravilla. White Fence traces its beginnings to the 1930s when it was a sports group associated with a local church. The younger brothers and cousins of the original group started the gang in 1944 after most of the founders were drafted into World War II. By that time, there were already several established gangs in the area.[122] The first clique of El Hoyo Maravilla was actively involved in sports and often competed with White Fence neighborhood kids. Like the original White Fence group, World War II left many younger kids to carry on the tradition.

By the late 1940s the gangs became permanent fixtures, essentially agents of socialization in the form of peer groups. An age-graded structure developed as the older members matured and broke with the gang, and younger kids formed their own cliques.

> It is a process that begins with where people live and raise their families; what type of work and status they've attained; how place and status, in turn, shape the patterns of parenting, schooling, and policing; and finally, the personal and group identities that emerge in this marginalized context. A broad linking and sequencing of these features show the additive and cumulative nature of the emergence of gangs and the generation of gang members.[123]

Various cultural changes and conflicts have made some Chicano youth especially vulnerable to becoming gang members. Victims of *multiple marginality* are the youths most likely to become gang members.[124]

> [They] are often the most unsupervised and reside in crowded housing conditions where private space is limited. These youngsters are driven into the public space

of the streets where peers and teenaged males, with whom they must contend, dominate. . . . Thus, because of the *situations* (e.g. exposure only to run-down and spatially separate enclaves; lack of or limited access to and identity with dominant institutions; social and cultural conflicts between first- and second-generation family members; and so on) and *conditions* (e.g. inferior, crowded housing; low or inadequate income; and so on) many urban youths are compelled to seek the dynamics of the street.[125]

Joan Moore studied three major Chicano gangs in the Los Angeles area. "The age-graded gang is one among many barrio structures in which boys play a role; it may be the only structure in which they play a reasonably autonomous role." She also notes that the Chicano subculture is more than just machismo, as there is a sense of belongingness, a feeling of family—referring to themselves as homies or homeboys.[126] Family and community ties are most apparent among Chicano gangs. The individual gang member is expected to assist other gang members in times of need and to uphold the neighborhood gang name.

Gangs developed a cohort—clique—tradition.[127] Since their inception, the three long-standing barrios—El Hoyo Maravilla, White Fence, and Cuatro Flats— each generated a succession of separate age-graded cliques. Each have two or three cohorts defined by age and status, usually 12- to 14-year olds in middle school beginning their affiliation, 14- to 18-year-olds in high school who are somewhat proven members, and 18- to 20-year olds who are seasoned members. In some barrios there are also veteranos in their mid- to late 20s. The informal and formal processes of socialization in these age-graded cliques ensures that there is always someone to assume the duties of defending the turf.

The estimates of Chicano gangs in Los Angeles County exceed 500, constituting about half of all gangs in this area.[128] Hispanic youth often join gangs to improve their self-esteem (including their sense of masculinity) and to satisfy their sense of honor. The young men make connections in groups with others who understand and share the Chicano honor code and cultural history. They seek ways to defend and uphold the Chicano way of life rejected by mainstream standards.[129] "Isolationism and stigmatization were major contributing factors to gang regeneration and growth. The intense bonding to barrios and gangs is unique to Los Angeles and other Southwestern cities because of their long-standing youth subculture underpinnings."[130]

Asian Gangs

Nationally less than 10% of American gangs are classified as Asian.[131] Asians who enter gang life generally pursue the same kind of activities that were pursued historically in their countries of origin. As a result, Cambodian, Chinese, Filipino, Korean, Japanese, Taiwanese, and Vietnamese gang members engage in different behaviors. Police find that Asian gangs are difficult to penetrate, because they are extremely secretive. Most members are clean-cut, polite, and act with respect toward law enforcement.

> In many East Asian cultures, rituals and protocols guiding social interactions are well defined and reinforced through a variety of highly developed feelings of obligation, many of which are hierarchical in nature. This facilitates some control over the behavior of younger Asian gang members by elders in the gang.[132]

Adaptation to a new country, failures in acculturation, and breakdowns in family connections contribute to the formation of Asian gangs. Parents working long hours may not provide the necessary emotional support. Conflicts arise in the family over language barriers; parents cannot help with homework to alleviate stress at school. Generational conflicts (for example, over talk of returning to the home country) surface. Youth spend time in two different worlds but are only partially socialized into each; they are not accepted as wholly Asian or wholly American. Gang culture alleviates the strains and frustrations of double marginalization. The Asian gang experience is a product of the need to belong.[133]

Asian gangs are highly entrepreneurial in nature. They generally victimize people from their own culture, because the victims usually fail to report the crimes to the police.[134] The gangs do not generally claim turf.[135] Some Asian street gangs are connected to adult criminal organizations, assisting in extortion activities and protecting illegal gambling enterprises.[136]

Vietnamese Gangs

After the Vietnam War, a large number of Vietnamese sought refuge in the United States; often they were young, unskilled, and unable to speak English. Many were the sons and daughters born to American soldiers who had brief relationships with Vietnamese women while serving during the Viet Nam War.[137] Southern California towns like Garden Grove, San Gabriel, and Westminster have Vietnamese gangs, which are also found in Atlanta, Houston, New Orleans, St. Petersburg, Washington, D.C., Boston, New York, Denver, St. Louis, Chicago, and Vancouver, British Columbia.[138]

Schools placed recent arrivals in grades according to age rather than accounting for the lack of proficiency in English and failed to provide effective guidance and tutoring. Unable to understand what was being taught in class, many gave up.

> Many children who were high achievers in Vietnam have failed here, and failure in school drives too many of these youngsters into gangs. Embarrassed, humiliated, lacking self-esteem and self-confidence, students on the edge of failure begin cutting classes. Then they become truant and drop out.[139]

Uncomfortable at home and unsuccessful at school, juveniles joined gangs to feel a sense of belonging. They resent what they perceive as society's indifference to them.

Vietnamese gangs have become a permanent part of Southern California life. The first generation of Vietnamese gang youth from the early and mid-1980s have died, are imprisoned, or are no longer involved. Second-generation Vietnamese youth gangs are more street-socialized than their predecessors.[140] Vietnamese and Asian American gangs differ from black and Chicano/Mexican gangs that are demarcated by streets and blocks. They have "very different residential and settlement patterns than other racialized populations. Vietnamese American youth gangs are not spatially bound."[141]

The ages of Vietnamese gang members range from mid- to late-teens to the early 20s. They have been described as youths who are frustrated by their lack of success in both school and the community and their inability to acquire material goods. Many were harassed by Chicano gang members when they were growing up and formed gangs as a method of protection.[142] Unlike African American or Hispanic gangs, Vietnamese gangs do not adopt particular modes of dress and often do not have a gang name. They tend to be very secretive and loyal, making it difficult to conduct research. Fighting is infrequent. Members avoid drug dealing, wearing tattoos, and using hand signs so that they do not draw attention to their activities. They are organized very loosely, and membership changes constantly. Unlike Chinese gangs, they have few ties to adult groups.[143]

Money is the focal point of gang behavior. As with most other Asian gangs, Vietnamese groups are extremely entrepreneurial. Their crimes include mostly auto theft, burglary, robbery, and extortion, and they travel rather extensively. They are very pragmatic; they victimize other Vietnamese citizens, taking advantage of their inability to understand and/or utilize the American legal system. Many Vietnamese Americans keep large amounts of cash and gold at home rather than in banks.[144] Youth gangs survey a residence. Then, in small groups (usually four or five persons) they enter the home armed with handguns. Victims are beaten and coerced into revealing the location of their valuables.[145]

Chinese Gangs

The immigration or refugee experience of Asian Americans affects the emergence of various ethnic gangs.[146] The Chinese experience differed from that of the Vietnamese. Chinese Americans are the oldest and largest Asian ethnic group in the United States, with immigration dating from the late 1840s. Like western Europeans, the Chinese immigrated for economic reasons versus the refugee experience of the Vietnamese who fled to escape political persecution. Chinese, Japanese, and Filipinos were highly educated immigrants.

Chinese gangs have strong roots in China, Taiwan, and Hong Kong, tracing back to the Tongs and Triads. These gangs are the most likely to have connections to organized crime groups. They can now be found in San Francisco, Los Angeles, Boston, Toronto, Vancouver (British Columbia), and New York City.[147] In the 1960s and 1970s most Chinese gang members were from Hong Kong. The second generation of Chinese youths were either born in this country or brought here at an early age. As with other second-generation adolescents, many formed gangs, often simply to protect themselves from other students in local schools. Most of the youths who are recruited are those who are vulnerable, are not doing well in school, or have dropped out. Their English is usually very poor, and they have few job skills. Many who dropped out of school began hanging out on street corners where they were recruited by adult Tong groups (hiring them to run errands for gamblers and to provide protection for gambling places). Unlike other groups, Chinese gangs had an existing organized crime network to emulate or within which to operate.[148]

Chinese gangs are different from African American and Hispanic gangs in that (1) they are not based on youth fads or illicit drug use and are closely related to their community's social and economic life; (2) they do not operate in deteriorated, poor neighborhoods; and (3) they are embedded in the legendary Triad subculture and so are able to claim legitimacy in the Chinese community.[149] Chinese gangs are composed predominantly of males, whose ages range from 13 to 37, with an average age of 22. Each gang has between 20 and 50 hard-core members. Gangs tend to have a hierarchical structure nearly parallel to organized crime groups. Most gangs have two or more cliques constantly at battle with each other, so that the intergang conflicts are more threatening. Gang members are most often killed by other members of the same group rather than attacks from external sources, such as rival gangs.[150]

African American Gangs

There were three phases in the formation of black gangs in Los Angeles. In the 1920s and early 1930s, black gangs were strictly juvenile gangs. In the 1940s, black gangs formed because of school-based conflicts. Beginning in the 1960s, black gangs emerged from segregated housing conflicts.[151] Black youths in the 1940s experienced residential segregation, police brutality, and racially motivated violence.[152] The civil rights conflicts in the 1960s in which national and local leaders were assassinated were a breeding ground for gang formation in the early 1970s. Economic restructuring, deindustrialization, population shifts and poverty are factors in recent gang phenomena and contributed to gang proliferation, but they played lesser roles in early gang formation processes. Racial intimidation by whites, residential and school segregation, and marginalization were the significant factors.

Several Los Angeles area high schools during the late 1940s and early 1950s experienced racial conflicts. African American gangs emerged as a *defensive* response to discrimination. Gangs at that time differed from current gangs. They usually did not consider neighborhoods where they lived as their turf. They did not commonly fight other gangs; they had no colors; they did not paint graffiti.

Young African Americans were seen in an even more negative light by the media and by the rest of society after the Watts riots of 1965. At the same time, African American youths began to see themselves differently. Many banded together to fight police brutality and other injustices.[153] They were aware of the benefits Chicano gangs derived from the bonding of cohorts in the barrio. "The cocky, dangerous style of the Latino gangs had a strong appeal for African American youths. It responded perfectly to the need for repackaging defeat as defiance, redefining exclusion as exclusivity."[154]

The emergence of groups that eventually called themselves Crips transformed the gang landscape. There is some debate as to the exact origin of the name. One version is that the Crips were founded by a group of youths from Fremont High School. One of them was referred to as a crip (short for cripple) because he walked with the aid of a stick. Still another version alleges that because walking sticks were a symbol for the original gang, the police and the media began to apply the name, and the gang eventually adopted it.[155] One version of the origin of the Crips gang was that the first set formed in reaction to the destruction of housing and neighborhood ties when the Century Freeway was built. Another version is that the Crips emerged in the wake of the demise of the Black Panther Party.[156] Many believe that the decline of the Panthers led directly to a resurgence of gangs, including the Bloods and Crips, in the early 1970s.[157]

The Crips borrowed one of the cholo traditions of wearing bandannas and emphasized the color blue. Other Crip sets soon began wearing other blue clothing to set themselves apart. One group of African American youths who lived on Piru street in Compton began to get together for protection from attacks by Crip sets. They called themselves the Compton Pirus and are believed to be the first gang to apply the term *blood brothers* to their association.[158] They chose the color red as the gang's color and called themselves Blood. Soon Blood sets wore red bandannas, shoes, and jackets to set themselves apart from the Crips.

Within just a few years Blood and Crip sets spread throughout the Los Angeles area. These gangs began to borrow other traditions of Hispanic gangs—flying colors, defending their turf, using graffiti, hanging with homeboys, and jumping in new members. Crips currently outnumber Bloods by about three to one in Los Angeles. The Crips and Bloods have so influenced African American street gangs in Los Angeles that the only distinction between the thousands of gang members is the blue and the red colors. Crips do not use words starting with the letter "B," and Bloods do not use words starting with the letter "C." Crips often refer to themselves as cuzz, while bloods often call each other Piru. They often include rival gang abbreviations along with the slant sign and the letter "K," which means killers. Thus the letters C/K may mean Crip killers and the letters B/K will stand for Blood killers. Typically African American gang members will ask the question, "What set you from?" This is asking for the individual's gang affiliation.[159]

In recent years African American gang members have struggled for economic survival; as a result, they have engaged in a great deal of drug trafficking.[160] One of the most famous African American gangs is the Black Gangster Disciples of Chicago. Enforcement officials and the media too often place street gangs in the same category as drug cartels. "Street gangs are for the most part incapable of behaving like organized crime groups, although there are a few large street gangs that occasionally bridge this gap, most notably Chicago's Black Gangster Disciples, Vice Lords, Latin Kings, and Black P Stone Nation."[161]

White Gangs

Official statistics listed the average percentage of white gang members from 1996 to 2011 as 10.5%.[162] The percentage was higher in smaller cities (14.6%) and rural counties (14.9%). As mentioned earlier, official statistics underestimate the number of white gang members. Gang researchers estimate that 40% of gang members are white.[163] White gangs are covered less by the media and are less likely to be punished by the criminal justice system.[164] The Mississippi Association of Gang Investigators report that 53% of verified gang members in the state are white, yet all of the 97 people prosecuted under the state's gang law from 2010 to 2017 were black.

Children raised in poverty, sometimes by parents addicted to drugs, can be attracted to a world that promises brotherhood, loyalty, and respect. The Simon City Royals is one of the largest white gangs in the United States. It began on the north side of Chicago in 1952 when two greaser gangs (the Ashland Royals and Simon City) guarded their turf as Puerto Ricans moved in. Early greasers were immigrants who worked at blue-collar jobs and were labeled by whites because their work involved greasing machines. The Royals joined the Folk Nation alliance, which included the Black Gangster Disciples. Simon City eventually had Hispanic and women members.[165] In Los Angeles, white gangs emerged partly in response to "the growing encroachment of African American families in South Los Angeles."[166]

Skinheads

The skinhead movement is a militant racist organization that employs a distinct clothing style, symbols and signs (swastikas, SS lightning bolts, and 88, the numerical code for "Heil Hitler") as identifiers.[167] Gang scholars have excluded youths who are active in white supremacy groups from street gang studies for 30 years.[168] More recently, some gang scholars have suggested that street gangs and white supremacy groups are more analogous to gangs than originally thought. Like street gangs, white separatist movements are not singular monoliths. They are loosely-structured, youth-oriented factions that regularly feud. While skinheads straddle the line between gang and extremist group, other groups such as the American Nazi Party and Ku Klux Klan have little in common with gangs.[169]

Youths have belonged to white power organizations since the early 1980s. However, not all members are avowed racists. The racist skinheads advocate white supremacy, and the nonracist skinheads have a multiracial membership. They are rivals and often engage in violent confrontations. These groups are scattered and have erratic membership, although in some areas they claim territory and are classified as a street gang. One example of a nonracist skinhead gang is the SHARPs (Skinheads Against Racial Prejudice) or SARs (Skinheads Against Racism).[170] A variation is the kind of group known as a separatist group. These are youths who consider themselves survivalists, concerned only with their personal welfare if confronted with disaster.[171] These groups do not care much about what is going on around them and try to avoid overt racial violence.

The skinhead movement in Southern California began in the late 1970s. Music was an important component. Punk rock provided a subcultural foundation for the development of skinheads. Other groups contributing to the formation of skinheads were surfers, skaters, bikers, stoners, and peckerwoods. All of these groups were white youth subcultures. Punks can be viewed as a rejection of left-wing political movements—a result of the anxiety of a rapidly changing world that ignored the white working class. Although they held a variety of views on social issues, one of the most important was the perception that white youth were victimized by several outside social forces (e.g., minority street gangs, affirmative action programs, etc.).[172] The shaved heads of many of these individuals made a strong statement, an "in your face" protest. Much of the punk subculture evolved into a more aggressive attitude, often expressed through random violence. Punk rock music reflected this aggressiveness, with very loud and hard tones. Skinhead music is as important to these youths as rap is to African American youths. This music is radical and often reflects the racial and political attitudes of the skinheads.

Eventually, skinheads began to construct a racist ideology that included, in part, neo-Nazism. Some of the early skinhead gang members became involved with Nazism when they were punks and long before they shaved their heads and became skinheads. Furthermore, some of the surfers, such as those living in La Jolla (an upscale town just north of San Diego) were a version of Nazi punks. The skinheads in Los Angeles were reacting to some very specific trends that they perceived as threatening to them and their class and especially their race. Increased immigration was one of the most important of these changes occurring in Southern California.[173]

The classic skinhead look is a shaved head, black Doc Martens boots, jeans with suspenders, and racist tattoos.[174] Before the 1980s, racist skinheads were regarded as another example of rebellious youth subculture. Not very organized at first, many groups dissolved quickly. Eventually they became very aggressive groups with shared interests and identification with specific turfs. Skinheads engage in violent acts against those they perceive as different or a threat to the white majority—homosexuals, racial and ethnic groups, and religious minorities.

> Hate rock from racist skinhead bands has bled into the flow of rebellious teen music. And skinheads have taken their "boot parties" from the street to the Internet, targeting young people for recruitment into their supposed movement.[175]

Stoners

Youths known as *stoners* are distinguishable from traditional street gangs by their secretiveness and the difficulty in identifying them. Often referred to as cults, they engage in many ritualistic activities. They are white suburban youths from a higher socioeconomic background than most other gangs. Stoner gangs constitute only about 5% of all gangs in California and an even smaller percentage of all white youths in the correctional system.[176]

Researchers found that the majority (62%) of stoners surveyed in the California Youth Authority came from homes described as having either adequate or more than adequate incomes. Most (72%) scored above average on standard intelligence tests, and almost all had some work history prior to their incarceration. Despite their high intelligence, none had graduated from high school, while two-thirds had been placed in special education classes. More than 40% had dropped out of high school. Most were described as either low achievers or nonachievers. Most had been heavily involved in the abuse of both alcohol and drugs, with the majority (69%) beginning their drug use before the age of 13. Their most common offense was burglary (70%).[177]

Stoner gangs are heavily involved in the use of drugs and have an especially high rate of toxic vapor use. They are almost always into heavy metal music. Stoners use graffiti to mark territory—usually to claim music groups or types of music rather than geography. They generally do not have any organized leadership, are antiestablishment, and often dabble in Satanism, participating in animal sacrifice and ritual crimes (e.g., grave or church desecrations). Stoners typically dress in red or black clothing, with athletic jersey tops depicting heavy metal music stars, metal-spiked wrist cuffs, collars and belts, earrings, long hair, and tattoos. They often wear Satanic relics or sacrilegious effigies.[178]

Taggers

The final variation of white subcultures is *taggers*. Chapter 3 outlined the origins of graffiti and its use by youth gangs. Tagging is graffiti, but it is not done to mark turf or to communicate gang threats or challenges. Rather it is a way for mostly white middle-class youths to call attention to themselves.[179] Taggers do not have common features of gangs; they typically engage only in tagging.[180]

Areas targeted varies by the age of the tagger. Younger taggers (10 to 15) usually mark school grounds. Older youths will go after bigger targets, such as freeway overpasses or bridges, public transportation (especially buses), streetlight poles, and so on. "Less geographically bound to protecting a particular neighborhood turf than are ethnic and inner-city gangs, the taggers spread their marks far and wide on their nightly runs."[181] Taggers consider all public buildings as the turf where they display their art versus ethnic gangs that limit their graffiti to the gang's neighborhood boundaries. Taggers are driven to gain fame—to establish identity and recognition for themselves among their peers. Placing their tag names in highly visible areas or dangerous places increases recognition. The longer a tag is visible, the more fame—which is why municipalities remove the marks as quickly as possible at considerable taxpayer expense. Los Angeles spends about $7 million annually and has 80 one-person abatement crews.[182] A mayoral candidate counted 27,754 graffiti tags in one day in one of fifteen council districts.

Tagger pseudonyms, or nicknames, usually have four to six letters or numbers, usually three. They usually adopt a name comprised of two or three words, e.g., Clever Writing Kings (CWK) or Oxnard Piecers Unite, written as 678K to correspond to the letters OPU on the telephone; the K is for "krew." A tagger can have two nicknames and may belong to several tagging crews at once. There may be several tag names and/or crew names put up by the taggers in the same incident. One explanation given for the rise of these tagger groups is that middle-class, suburban white youths have been influenced by the ethnic gangs of the inner cities and their gangsta rap and have tried to emulate them. Members often drift in and out of groups; they often change their names (monikers) when they get tired of the old ones. "Play groups, break-dancing groups, taggers, and school peer groups experiment with gang life. The diffusion of street gang culture in modern-day movies, music, and clothing merchandizing has served to intertwine gang culture with the general youth subculture."[183]

SUMMARY

Gangs are not something new to the social arena. They existed in fourteenth- and fifteenth-century Europe and colonial America. In this chapter we have pointed out that public perception (and fear), crucial to policy development, is shaped largely by the mass media. It is clear that the media have done little to differentiate fact from fiction in the portrayal of youth gangs; they have contributed to the stereotypical images of how we think about gangs and gang members.

The only agreement about what constitutes a gang, its members, and its activities is disagreement. Often, this discord is linked to location (e.g., type of neighborhood), age (e.g., adolescent versus young adult), and purpose (e.g., play group, organized crime, drugs). We have found that one of the major problems associated with the study of gangs is the identification of gang-related crime. Each jurisdiction seems to create its own criteria to determine whether or not a crime is gang related.

This chapter also addressed the issue of *how many*. How many gangs are currently active in the United States? How many individuals are in these groups? There are a significant number of projections and estimates related to these questions. Frequently, the argument is raised that because gangs come and go, it is difficult to determine accurately the number of gangs and gang members. It is our contention, however, that the most critical factor in determining how many gangs or gang members are active is to first determine what exactly a gang or gang member is.

We reviewed attempts to categorize gangs and gang members. It is impossible to provide a profile of a gang member that covers all socioeconomic factors and motivations for affiliation. It is equally difficult to precisely identify a pure type of gang. Any attempt to identify a typical gang falls short. While many gangs are identified by ethnic composition, others cross gender, racial, and ethnic boundaries. Organizational structures are difficult to categorize. The fairly traditional idea of a vertically organized street gang contrasts dramatically with loosely organized starter or scavenger gangs. Social scientists have created several typologies to describe the many varied groupings, but there are no universally applicable labels.

Notes

1. Mike Davis, "Foreword" to John M. Hagedorn, *A World of Gangs: Armed Young Men and Gangsta Culture.* (Minneapolis: University of Minnesota Press, 2008), xi–xii.
2. Douglas Hay, Peter. Linebaugh, John Rule, E. P. Thompson, and Cal Winslow (eds.), *Albion's Fatal Tree: Crime and Society in Eighteenth-Century England.* (New York: Pantheon, 1975); Geoffrey Pearson, *Hooligan: A History of Reportable Fears.* (New York: Schoeken Books, 1983).
3. Pearson, *Hooligan*, 188.
4. Herbert C. Covey, Scott Menard, and Robert Franzese, *Juvenile Gangs.* (Springfield, IL: Charles S. Thomas, 1992). 90–91.
5. James C. Howell and Elizabeth Griffiths, *Gangs in America's Communities*, 3rd ed. (Thousand Oaks, CA: Sage Publications, 2019).
6. The 2002 movie, "Gangs of New York" depicted the violence of these gangs.
7. Howell and Griffiths, *Gangs in America's Communities.*
8. Ibid.
9. Ibid., Kindle Edition.
10. Richard McCorkle and Terance Miethe, *Panic: The Social Construction of the Street Gang Problem.* (Upper Saddle River, NJ: Prentice-Hall, 2001), 3.
11. Ibid.
12. Debra Seagal, "Tales from the Cutting-Room Floor: The Reality of 'Reality-Based' Television." *Harper's Magazine.* November, 1993, 50–57.
13. Randall G. Shelden, Sharon K. Tracy, and William B. Brown, *Youth Gangs in American Society*, 4th ed. (Belmont, CA: Cengage, 2013).
14. Émile Durkheim, *The Rules of Sociological Method and Selected Texts on Sociology and Its Method.* (New York: The Free Press, 1982), 98. (Originally published in 1895.)
15. Howell and Griffiths, *Gangs in America's Communities*, Kindle Edition.
16. Clifford R. Shaw and Henry D. McKay, *Juvenile Delinquency in Urban Areas.* (Chicago: University of Chicago Press, 1942); Frederic Thrasher, *The Gang: A Study of 1,313 Gangs in Chicago.* (Chicago: University of Chicago Press, 1927, 1936, 1963).
17. Hagedorn, *A World of Gangs*, xxiv.
18. For an extensive review see Shelden et al., *Youth Gangs.*
19. John M. Hagedorn, *People and Folks: Gangs, Crime and the Underclass in a Rustbelt City*, 2nd ed. (Chicago: Lakeview Press, 1998).
20. Terence P. Thornberry, David Huizinga, and Rolf Loeber, "The Causes and Correlates Studies: Findings and Policy Implications," *Juvenile Justice*, 2004, 9: 3–19.
21. James A. Densley and David C. Pyrooz, "A Signaling Perspective on Disengagement from Gangs," *Justice Quarterly*, 2017.
22. Donna Ladd, "Dangerous, Growing, Yet Unnoticed: the Rise of America's White Gangs," *The Guardian*, April 5, 2018.
23. Quoted in Malcolm W. Klein, *The American Street Gang: Its Nature, Prevalence, and Control.* (New York: Oxford University Press, 1995), 22.
24. *Merriam-Webster's Collegiate Dictionary*, 11th ed. (Springfield, MA: Merriam-Webster, Incorporated, 2014).

25 *Merriam-Webster's Collegiate Thesaurus*, 2nd ed. (Springfield, MA: Merriam-Webster, Incorporated, 2010).

26 James F. Short, "Gangs, Neighborhoods, and Youth Crime." *Criminal Justice Research Bulletin*, 1990, 5: 3.

27 Malcolm W. Klein, *Street Gangs and Street Workers*. (Englewood Cliffs, NJ: Prentice-Hall, 1971), 111.

28 National Gang Center. "What Is a Gang?" http://www.nationalgangcenter.gov/About/FAQ#q1

29 http://www.nationalgangcenter.gov/Survey-Analysis/Defining-Gangs

30 Irving A. Spergel and G. David Curry, "Strategies and Perceived Agency Effectiveness in Dealing with the Youth Gang Problem." In C. Ronald Huff (ed.), *Gangs in America*. (Newbury Park, CA: Sage Publications, 1990), 388.

31 Ibid.

32 Ibid., 389.

33 Ibid.

34 Ibid.

35 C. Ronald Huff, "Gangs in the United States," in A. P. Goldstein. and C. R. Huff (eds.), *The Gang Intervention Handbook* (Champaign, IL: Research Press, 1993), 4.

36 Ibid.

37 Ibid., 5.

38 Howell and Griffiths, *Gangs in America's Communities*, Kindle Edition.

39 Hagedorn, *People and Folks*, 86.

40 Hagedorn, *A World of Gangs*, xxv.

41 Patrick G. Jackson, "Theories and Findings about Youth Gangs," *Criminal Justice Abstracts*, 1989 (June): 314. A close friend and colleague, Bud Brown, who spent a considerable amount of time hanging out with a Detroit gang, noted the same thing.

42 Klein, *The American Street Gang*, 11.

43 Malcolm W. Klein and Cheryl L. Maxson, "Street Gang Violence," in Marvin E. Wolfgang and Neil A. Weiner (eds.), *Violent Crime, Violent Criminals* (Newbury Park, CA: Sage, 1989), 206.

44 Ibid., 208.

45 National Gang Center, "National Youth Gang Survey Analysis," http://www.nationalgangcenter.gov/Survey-Analysis

46 National Gang Center, "Gang-Related Offenses," http://www.nationalgangcenter.gov/Survey-Analysis/Gang-Related-Offenses

47 Shelden et al., *Youth Gangs*, chapter 1.

48 This concern over how many gangs and gang members there are is typical of the positivistic orientation in the social sciences—and in the larger society in general. Numbers assume enormous importance. What is lost in the quest for numbers are people (both the victims and the victimizers) and their circumstances. Also lost are the various social conditions that create gangs. Imagine doctors spending their time counting the number of cases of cancer and AIDS rather than trying to locate and eliminate the causes.

49 Thrasher, *The Gang*.

[50] Walter B. Miller, *Violence by Youth Gangs and Youth Groups as a Crime Problem in Major American Cities* (Washington, DC: U.S. Department of Justice, 1975); see also Walter B. Miller, *Crime by Youth Gangs and Groups in the United States* (Washington, DC: U.S. Department of Justice, 1982).

[51] G. David Curry, "Self-Reported Gang Involvement and Officially Recorded Delinquency." *Criminology*, 2000, 3: 1254–55.

[52] Judith Greene and Kevin Pranis, "Gang Wars: The Failure of Enforcement Tactics and the Need for Effective Public Safety Strategies," *Justice Policy Institute*, 2007, 33.

[53] National Gang Center, "Prevalence of Gang Problems in Study Population," https://www.nationalgangcenter.gov/Survey-Analysis/Prevalence-of-Gang-Problems

[54] National Gang Center, "Measuring the Extent of Gang Problems," https://www.nationalgangcenter.gov/Survey-Analysis/Measuring-the-Extent-of-Gang-Problems

[55] National Gang Center, "Demographics," https://www.nationalgangcenter.gov/Survey-Analysis/Demographics

[56] David C. Pyrooz and Gary Sweeten, "Gang Membership between Ages 5 and 17 Years in the United States. *Journal of Adolescent Health*, April 2015, 56(4): 414–419.

[57] James C. Howell and James P. Lynch, *Youth Gangs in Schools* (Washington, DC: Office of Juvenile Justice and Delinquency Prevention, 2000).

[58] Lauren Musu, Anlan Zhang, Ke Wang, Jizhi Zhang, and Barbara Oudekerk, *Indicators of School Crime and Safety: 2018* (Washington, DC: National Center for Education Statistics, 2019).

[59] Melissa Diliberti, Michael Jackson, and Jana Kemp, *Crime, Violence, Discipline, and Safety in U.S. Public Schools: Findings from the School Survey on Crime and Safety: 2015–16* (Washington, DC: National Center for Education Statistics, 2017).

[60] Dena C. Carson and Finn-Aage Esbensen, Gangs in School: Exploring the Experiences of Gang-Involved Youth. November 7, 2017, https://doi.org/10.1177/1541204017739678

[61] Terence P. Thornberry, Marvin D. Krohn, Alan J. Lizotte, Carolyn A. Smith, and Kimberly Tobin, *Gangs and Delinquency in Developmental Perspective.* (Cambridge, UK: Cambridge University Press, 2003).

[62] The website of a defense attorney in Orange County, California (http://www.william-weinberg.com/lawyer-attorney-1472296.html) gives specific instructions to other attorneys on how to provide a defense against an offender when the prosecutor alleges gang involvement. "It should be noted that many agencies receive funding for investigation and arrest for suspect gang members. This creates a conflict of interest that should be exposed to the public. There are many instances where a person commits a criminal offense and should be punished, but the prosecutor decides to allege gang charges in addition to the substantive offense (e.g., drug sales, assault with a firearm) because he or she knows that when a jury hears about a gang, jurors will fold their hands in their laps and wait to convict."

[63] Michael Cannell, "Assumed Dangerous until Proven Innocent: The Constitutional Defect in Alleging Gang Affiliation at Bail Hearings," *DePaul Law Review*, Summer 2014, 63(4): 1027–1062.

[64] Ibid.

[65] Daniel Alarcón, "Guilt by Association," *The New York Times Magazine*, May 30, 2015, 47.

[66] Cannell, "Assumed Dangerous until Proven Innocent."

[67] Ibid.

[68] Dahleen Glanton, : "'Gang Book' Long on Blame, Short on Solutions," *Chicago Tribune*, June 14, 2018: 3.

[69] Annie Sweeney, "Suit Says CPD Gang Database Discriminatory, Error-ridden," *Chicago Tribune*, June 20, 2018, 4.

[70] Ibid.

[71] Alarcón, "Guilt by Association."

[72] Cannell, "Assumed Dangerous until Proven Innocent."

[73] John Hagedorn, "Stereotypes Killed Robert Butts," GangResearch.net, May 6, 2018, http://gangsandthemedia.blogspot.com/2018/05/stereotypes-killed-robert-butts.html

[74] Melanie Ochoa, "LAPD Gang Injunctions Gave Cops a License to Harass and Control Black and Latino Residents," ACLU, March 23, 2018.

[75] Wesley F. Harward, "A New Understanding of Gang Injunctions," *Notre Dame Law Review*, 2015, 90(3): 1345–1370.

[76] Ana Muniz, "Maintaining Racial Boundaries: Criminalization, Neighborhood Context, and the Origins of Gang Injunctions," *Social Problems*, May 2014, 61(2): 216–236.

[77] James Queally, "Los Angeles Barred from Enforcing Nearly All Gang Injunctions, Federal Judge Rules, *Los Angeles Times*, March 15, 2018.

[78] The stereotypes have often become so ludicrous that there are many times when adolescents are mistaken for gang members simply because they "look like one." Much gang attire, plus slang, tattoos, and so on, have been borrowed by millions of teenagers all over the country, perhaps trying to mimic the rebellious image of gangs. The authors of *Youth Gangs in American Society* have had students in their classes who were once gang members. Lead author Shelden has taught many students originally from Southern California who were members of various gangs. Likewise, Tracy has had former gang members from Atlanta, while Brown teaches ex-gang members from Portland, Oregon. In all likelihood, the reader is sitting in a class with a few ex-gang members. These observations reinforce one of the key findings from gang research: Many gang members leave the gang eventually and lead normal lives, including going to college and majoring in criminal justice.

[79] A similar finding was reported by C. Ronald Huff, "Youth Gangs and Public Policy," *Crime and Delinquency*, 1989, 35: 524–37.

[80] Hagedorn, *People and Folks*, 22.

[81] Ruth Horowitz, "The End of the Youth Gang." *Criminology*, 1983, 21: 585–600; Ruth Horowitz, "Community Tolerance of Gang Violence." *Social Problems*, 1987, 34: 437–50; Miller, *The Growth of Youth Gang Problems*.

[82] Jeffrey Fagan, "Gangs, Drugs and Neighborhood Change." In Rebecca D. Peterson (ed.), *Understanding Contemporary Gangs in America*. (Upper Saddle River, NJ: Prentice Hall, 2004).

[83] Robert J. Durán, *Gang Life in Two Cities: An Insider's Journey*. New York: Columbia University Press, 2013).

[84] Cannell, "Assumed Dangerous until Proven Innocent."

85 Klein, *The American Street Gang*, 22. Data collected by Klein and Maxson found that only 2% to 5% of gang homicides involved innocent, non-gang victims (Klein and Maxson, "Street Gang Violence," 231).

86 Emily I. Troshynski and Laura Finley. "Gang Violence, Against Bystanders," in Laura L. Finley (ed.), *Encyclopedia of Juvenile Violence*. (Westport, CT: Greenwood Press, 2007), 90.

87 Ira Reiner, *Gangs, Crime and Violence in Los Angeles: Findings and Proposals from the District Attorney's Office* (Arlington, VA: National Youth Gang Information Center, 1992), 58–59.

88 This is reinforced by Duran's research in *Gang Life in Two Cities.*

89 Cannell, "Assumed Dangerous until Proven Innocent."

90 Irving. A. Spergel, *The Youth Gang Problem: A Community Approach*. (New York: Oxford University Press, 1995), 60.

91 Klein, *The American Street Gang*, 101.

92 Ibid., 102.

93 Ibid., 103.

94 Klein and Maxson, "Street Gang Violence," 209–10.

95 Howell and Griffiths, *Gangs in America's Communities.*

96 Leon Bing, *Do or Die*. (New York: Harper/Perennial, 1992), 244.

97 Spergel, *The Youth Gang Problem*, 55–56.

98 James Diego Vigil, *Gang Redux: A Balanced Anti-Gang Strategy*. (Long Grove, IL: Waveland Press, 2010), 62.

99 Klein and Maxson, "Street Gang Violence," 211.

100 Klein, *The American Street Gang*, 64.

101 Ibid., 64.

102 Ibid., 102.

103 Joan W. Moore. *Homeboys: Gangs, Drugs, and Prisons in the Barrios of Los Angeles*. (Philadelphia: Temple University Press, 1978) and Joan W. Moore, *Going Down to the Barrio: Homeboys and Homegirls in Change*. (Philadelphia: Temple University Press, 1991).

104 Spergel, *The Youth Gang Problem*, 71–72.

105 Vigil, *Gang Redux*, 61.

106 Ibid. and James Diego Vigil, *The Projects: Gang and Non-Gang Families in East Los Angeles*. (Austin: University of Texas Press [Kindle edition], 2007).

107 For an overview of the gang subculture in particular, see Shelden et al., *Youth Gangs.*

108 Max Weber (1864–1920) developed the concept of the ideal type. He was a prolific writer on subjects ranging from law to economy to religion.

109 Huff, "Youth Gangs and Public Policy"; Jeffrey Fagan, "The Social Organization of Drug Use and Drug Dealing Among Urban Gangs." *Criminology*, 1989, 27: 633–67; Carl S. Taylor, *Dangerous Society*. (East Lansing: Michigan State University Press, 1990).

110 Klein, *American Street Gang*, 132.

111 Malcolm W. Klein and Cheryl L. Maxson, *Street Gang Patterns and Policies* (New York: Oxford University Press, 2006), 176.

112 James Diego Vigil, *Barrio Gangs: Street Life and Identity in Southern California* (Austin: University of Texas Press, 1988); James Diego Vigil, "Cholos and Gangs: Culture Change

and Street Youths in Los Angeles," in C. R. Huff (ed.), *Gangs in America* (Newbury Park, CA: Sage, 1990), 116–28; James Diego Vigil and J. M. Long, "Emic and Etic Perspectives on Gang Culture: The Chicano Case," in C. R. Huff (ed.), *Gangs in America* (Newbury Park, CA: Sage, 1990), 55–70; and Reiner, *Gangs, Crime and Violence in Los Angeles*.

[113] Florida Department of Corrections, "Street Gangs—Chicago Based or Influenced," http://www.dc.state.fl.us/pub/gangs/chicago.html

[114] Florida Department of Corrections, "People Nation and Folk Nation 'Sets,'" http://www.dc.state.fl.us/pub/gangs/sets.html

[115] Associated Press, "Chicago Crime Commission's Latest Street Gang Book Lists More Than 2,400 factions," *Chicago Tribune*, June 12, 2018.

[116] James C. Howell and John P. Moore, "History of Street Gangs in the United States," National Gang Center Bulletin, May 2010, no. 4.

[117] James C. Howell, *The History of Street Gangs in the United States: Their Origins and Transformations* (Lanham, MD: Lexington Books, 2015), 29.

[118] Vigil, *Barrio Gangs*.

[119] Ibid., 92.

[120] Howell, *The History of Street Gangs in the United States*.

[121] Vigil, *Barrio Gangs*, 124.

[122] Joan W. Moore, "Gangs, Drugs, and Violence" in Scott Cummings and Daniel J. Monti (eds.), *Gangs: The Origins and Impact of Contemporary Youth Gangs in the United States.* (Albany: SUNY Press, 1993), 25–44.

[123] Vigil, *Gang Redux*, 3.

[124] Vigil, *Barrio Gangs*.

[125] Vigil, *Gang Redux*, 6.

[126] Moore, *Homeboys*, 52–53.

[127] Vigil, *Gang Redux*.

[128] "Hispanic Gangs in Los Angeles County," http://www.streetgangs.com/hispanic#sthash.UZB4HiL1.dpbs

[129] Ramiro Martinez, Jr., Meghan E. Hollis, and Jacob I. Stowell (eds.), *The Handbook of Race and Crime* (Malden, MA: Wiley, 2018).

[130] Howell, *The History of Street Gangs in the United States*, 31.

[131] Shelden et al., *Youth Gangs in American Society*, chapter 2.

[132] Anthony A. Braga, "Police Gang Units and Effective Gang Violence Reduction," in Scott H. Decker and David C. Pyrooz (eds.), *The Handbook of Gangs* (Malden, MA: Wiley, 2015), 309–327, 324.

[133] Sou Lee, "Asian Gangs in the United States: A Meta-Synthesis. Theses," 2016, paper 1875. Carbondale: Southern Illinois University.

[134] Reiner, *Gangs, Crime and Violence in Los Angeles*, 46; Kay Pih, Mario De La Rosa, Douglas Rugh, and Kuoray Mao, "Different Strokes for Different Gangs? An Analysis of Capital among Latino and Asian Gang Members," *Sociological Perspectives*, 2008, 51(3): 473–494.

[135] G. David Curry, Scott H. Decker, and David C. Pyrooz, *Confronting Gangs: Crime and Community* (New York: Oxford University Press, 2014).

[136] Braga, "Police Gang Units and Effective Gang Violence Reduction."

[137] Yarborough, *Surviving Twice*; Van Do, "Between Two Cultures."

138 Klein, *The American Street Gang*, 109–110; Kien Nguyen, *The Unwanted: A Memoir of Childhood* (Boston: Back Bay Books, 2002); Patrick Du Phuoc Long with Laura Ricaud, *The Dream Shattered: Vietnamese Gangs in America* (Boston: Northeastern University Press, 1997); Trin Yarborough, *Surviving Twice: Amerasian Children of the Vietnam War* (Herndon, VA: Potomac Books, 2005); Peter Van Do, "Between Two Cultures: Struggles of Vietnamese Adolescents," *The Review of Vietnamese Studies*, 2002, 2(1): 1–19.

139 Long and Ricaud, *The Dream Shattered, 95*.

140 Kevin D. Lam, "Racism, Schooling, and the Streets: A Critical Analysis of Vietnamese American Youth Gang Formation in Southern California," *Journal of Southeast Asian American Education and Advancement*, 2012, 7(1): 1–16.

141 Ibid., 3.

142 Ibid.; See also Kevin D. Lam, *Youth Gangs, Racism, and Schooling: Vietnamese American Youth in a Postcolonial Context* (New York: Palgrave Macmillan, 2015).

143 Studies confirming this information date back to the late 1980s and 1990s. See for example the following: James Diego Vigil and Steve C. Yun, "Southern California Gangs: Comparative Ethnicity and Social Control," in C. Ronald Huff, *Gangs in America II* (Thousand Oaks, CA: Sage Publications, 1996); Spergel, *The Youth Gang Problem.*

144 C. N. Le, "Asian American Gangs." Asian-Nation: The Landscape of Asian America, June 12, 2018, http://www.asian-nation.org/gangs.shtml#sthash.sj5SEl4U.dpbs

145 Vigil and Yun, "Southern California Gangs."

146 Lee, "Asian Gangs in the United States."

147 Hua-Lun Huang, "From the Asian Boyz to the Zhu Lian Bang (the Bamboo Union Gang): A Typological Analysis of Asian Gangs." *Asian Criminology*, 2007, 2(2): 127–143.

148 Hannah Kim, "The Origin of Asian and Chinese Gangs in Chicago's Chinatown," http://www.gangresearch.net/ChicagoGangs/tongs/kimpri.html

149 Triad societies formed 300 years ago to fight the corruption of the Qing dynasty. "Triad" refer to the unity of 3 elements: heaven, earth, and humanity. Triad values include loyalty, secrecy, brotherhood, and righteousness. After 1911, some Triad societies became involved in criminal activities. See Lee, "Asian Gangs in the United States."

150 Peter Huston, *Tongs, Gangs, and Triads: Chinese Crime Groups in North America.* (Lincoln, NE: Authors Choice Press, 2001), chapter 6; Chin, *Chinatown Gangs.*

151 Howell, *The History of Street Gangs in the United States*, 31.

152 Alejandro A. Alonso, "Racialized Identities and the Formation of Black Gangs in Los Angeles," in Cheryl L. Maxson, Arlen Egley, Jr., Jody Miller, and Malcolm W. Klein (eds.), *The Modern Gang Reader*, 4th ed., 230–243. (New York: Oxford University Press, 2014).

153 Alonso, "Racialized Identities." See also Mike Davis, *City of Quartz: Excavating the Future in Los Angeles* (New York: Vintage Books, 1992), 297.

154 Reiner, *Gangs, Crime and Violence in Los Angeles*, 5.

155 Davis, *City of Quartz*, 299; Reiner, *Gangs, Crime and Violence in Los Angeles*, 6.

156 The FBI and other police organizations engaged in a systematic elimination of the Black Panther Party in the 1960s largely through COINTELPRO, a counterintelligence program established by the FBI to "disrupt, harass, and discredit groups that the FBI decided were in some way 'un-American.'" This included the American Civil Liberties Union and

just about every African American political organization in the country whose views were in any way militant. William J. Chambliss, "State Organized Crime," in William Chambliss and Marjorie Zatz (eds.), *Making Law: The State, the Law and Structural Contradictions* (Bloomington: Indiana University Press, 1993), 290–314, 308; Noam Chomsky, "Domestic Terrorism: Notes on the State System of Oppression," *New Political Science*, 1999, 21(3): 303–324.

[157] Davis, *City of Quartz*, 298; Alonso ("Racialized Identities") also makes this argument.

[158] Ibid.

[159] Shelden et al., *Youth Gangs*, chapter 2.

[160] Louis Kontos, David C. Brotherton, and Luis Barrios (eds.), *Gangs and Society: Alternative Perspectives.* (New York: Columbia University Press, 2003); Alex Alonzo, "New Anti-gang Strategy Is Introduced by Chief Bratton," *Streetgangs.com Magazine*, January 15, 2003; Brenda C. Coughlin and Sudhir A. Venkatesh, "The Urban Street Gang After 1970," *Annual Review of Sociology*, 2003, 29:41–64.

[161] Malcolm Klein and Cheryl L. Maxson, "Gang Structures," in Cheryl L. Maxson, Arlen Egley, Jr., Jody Miller, and Malcolm W. Klein (eds.), *The Modern Gang Reader*, 4th ed. (New York: Oxford University Press, 2014), 137–153.

[162] National Gang Center, "Race/Ethnicity of Gang Members, 1996–2011, https://www .nationalgangcenter.gov/survey-analysis/demographics. The low estimate may reflect both the definitions of gangs and a racial bias or stereotype of what gangs are. If criteria used to define gang were expanded to include taggers and biker groups, the numbers of white gangs and white gang members would increase.

[163] Cannell, "Assumed Dangerous until Proven Innocent."

[164] Ladd, "Dangerous, Growing, Yet Unnoticed."

[165] Ibid.

[166] Scott H. Decker, Frank van Gemert and David C. Pyrooz, "Gangs, Migration, and Crime: The Changing Landscape in Europe and the USA," *International Migration and Integration*, 2009, 10: 393–408, 400.

[167] Pete Simi and Robert Futrell, *American Swastika*: *Inside the White Power Movement's Hidden Spaces of Hate*, 2nd ed. (Lanham, MD: Rowman & Littlefield, 2015).

[168] Matthew Valasik and Shannon Reid, "Alt-right Gangs and White Power Youth Groups," Oxford Bibliographies in Criminology, May 2018.

[169] Howell and Griffiths, *Gangs in America's Communities.*

[170] Wayne Wooden and Randy Blazak, *Renegade Kids, Suburban Outlaws*, 2nd ed. (Belmont, CA: Wadsworth, 2001).

[171] Ibid., 136.

[172] Pete Simi, "Rage in the City of Angels: The Historical Development of the Skinhead Subculture in Los Angeles." Unpublished doctoral dissertation, Department of Sociology, University of Nevada–Las Vegas, 2003.

[173] Ibid.

[174] Southern Poverty Law Center, "Racist Skinhead," http://www.splcenter.org/fighting-hate/extremist-files/ideology/racist-skinhead

[175] Ibid.

176 Wooden and Blazak, *Renegade Kids, Suburban Outlaws*.

177 Ibid.

178 Simi, "Rage in the City of Angels."

179 Wooden and Blazak, *Renegade Kids, Suburban Outlaws*.

180 Ibid.

181 Ibid., 120.

182 Aaron Mendelson, "LA Scrubs Away 30 million Square Feet of Graffiti Each Year," 89.3KPCC, September 10, 2015.

183 James C. Howell, "Gang Prevention: An Overview of Research and Programs," Washington, DC: Office of Juvenile Justice and Delinquency Prevention, December 2010.

Chapter 5

Female Delinquency

While the numbers of girls and boys arrested have declined for two decades, the percentage of girls arrested has increased. In 1985, 20% of the youths arrested were girls; in 2017 the percentage was 29%.[1] These arrests were primarily for offenses that pose little threat to public safety (i.e. larceny-theft, liquor law violations, disorderly conduct). Most of the behaviors for which girls are criminalized are nonviolent, minor offenses. Girls are more likely to be detained for status offenses, technical violations, and misdemeanors. "Research indicates that decisions to detain girls have more to do with problems in their homes, while decisions to detain boys are guided by concerns about public safety."[2]

Similarly the share of girls placed on probation for all offense categories increased from 62% in 2005 to 64% in 2016, despite a 48% decline in the number of delinquency cases for both boys and girls in that time frame.[3] Researchers attribute increases in the portion of girls involved in the juvenile justice system to more vigorous enforcement of non-serious offenses and to paternalism on the part of system players who believe that girls engaging in certain behaviors need more supervision for their own protection.[4]

Who is the typical female delinquent? What behavior brings her in contact with the juvenile justice system? How do her violations differ from those committed by boys? How are they similar? What causes her to get into trouble? What happens to her if she is arrested? These are complex questions that few members of the general public could answer quickly. When the public talks about delinquency or youth crime, they generally mean male behavior. Furthermore, certain racial and ethnic subgroups of girls (Black, American Indian/Alaska Native, Latina) are left out of the conversation altogether. Very little is known/discussed about the role of girls' gender identity and delinquency.

Girls in the juvenile justice system have many characteristics in common: experiencing poverty, an unstable family life, neglect, histories of sexual, physical, or emotional abuse, academic disconnection, self-harm, substance abuse, and mental health challenges.[5] Their experiences of trauma, separation, and family loss differ from the experiences of many boys. Nationally, 73% of girls in the juvenile justice system have experienced physical or sexual abuse. Justice-involved girls are four times more likely than boys to have experienced childhood sexual abuse. The rates of major depression are more than twice those of justice-involved boys. Experiences of trauma and marginalization are directly correlated to girls' delinquency.

There are six common pathways for the entry of girls into the juvenile justice system:

1. the abuse to prison pipeline—offenses directly related to being victims of abuse lead to justice-system involvement
2. disproportionate criminalization of girls for status offenses
3. crossover of child welfare and juvenile justice systems—girls are overrepresented among youth dually-involved in the two systems
4. domestic violence and mandatory arrest policies increase the number of girls arrested for conflicts within their homes, even if the behavior is a defense against abuse or in response to family chaos
5. school to prison pipeline—girls, especially black girls, are increasingly referred to the juvenile justice system through discriminatory application of school discipline policies that criminalize normal adolescent behavior
6. poverty and housing instability can cause girls to engage in behaviors such as larceny or curfew violations that put them at risk for justice involvement.

The impact of gendered and racial attitudes on decisions to arrest, detain, adjudicate, and place girls in the juvenile justice system are especially acute for girls of color.[6] These girls are more likely to be treated harshly in the criminal justice system. One study found that 68% of girls in adult court were black (compared to 59% of boys); 88% were girls of color (compared to 83% of boys). The disproportional representation is the result of implicit biases beginning with high levels of surveillance in low-income communities of color and continuing through key decision-making points. Black girls are only 14% of the general population, yet they are 33% of detained and committed girls.

Approximately 27% of girls in the justice system are and lesbian, gay, bisexual, transgender, and gender non-conforming youth (LGBTQ). They are stereotyped as hyper-masculine, aggressive, and delinquent. They are at significantly greater risk of being expelled from school, a key component in delinquent behavior and a contributing factor in the school-to-prison pipeline. LGBTQ youth are only 7 to 9% of all youth but 40% of girls in juvenile justice facilities.[7]

Although there are many similarities between male and female delinquent behaviors, there are also significant differences. First, girls' pathways into and through the juvenile justice system are unique. Second, the social contexts associated with girls' behavior and involvement in the juvenile justice system are also diverse, compared to boys. Third, and perhaps most important, girls tend to be arrested for offenses that are less serious and less violent than those committed by boys. In 2017, girls' made up approximately 37% of arrests for larceny-theft, 41% of arrests for liquor law violations, 36% of arrests for disorderly conduct, and 30% of arrests for curfew/loitering violations (see table 5-3).[8] Boys accounted for 81% of arrests for violent crime.

Girls are often arrested for offenses that are not actual crimes—running away from home, violating curfew, being incorrigible, or ungovernable (i.e. acting out beyond parental control). This is not a recent development. In the early years of the juvenile justice system, most of the girls in juvenile court were charged with status offenses—a trend that continues today. In 2015, 37% of girls detained before trial and 34% of girls sentenced to juvenile confinement were punished for either status offenses or a violation of probation. In contrast, 23% of detained males and 19% of confined males received the punishment for violations or status offenses.[9]

Girls are most frequently arrested for running away, substance abuse, and truancy—which are also the most common symptoms of abuse.[10] Research confirms that girls' problem behavior generally relates to a traumatizing home life. Girls self-report that victimization is a key factor in their offending significantly more frequently than do boys. The relationship between girls' problems, their attempts to escape victimization by running away, and the traditional reaction of the juvenile justice system are all unique aspects of girls' interaction with the system.[11]

THE EXTENT OF FEMALE DELINQUENCY

Like all criminal and delinquent behavior, female delinquency encompasses a very wide range of activities. Girls can be labeled as delinquent for the commission of crimes (e.g., burglary, larceny, assault) or for status offenses, which play a major and controversial role in female delinquency. This section looks at data from a variety of sources to determine not only how much female delinquency exists but also its manifestations. We compare the portraits of girls' offending drawn by official agencies (the police and the juvenile courts) with those based on self-reports. We also look at gender differences in delinquency and trends in girls' delinquency over time.

Recent Trends: National Arrest Data

Crime in the United States includes information on persons under the age of 18 arrested for a variety of offenses. In 2017, there were 634,535 juvenile arrests. There are considerable gender differences in the picture of delinquency derived from statistics maintained by law enforcement officers (see table 5-1). More than twice as many males were arrested. Boys are far more likely than girls to be arrested for violent crimes and for the most serious property crimes.

Girls (41%) approach the percentages for boys (59%) in the commission of some status offenses, such as liquor-law violations. Boys outnumber girls by a considerable margin for burglary, robbery, vandalism, drug abuse violations, and weapon charges. The male/female percentages of arrests are closest for larceny theft and other assaults. Males account for 63% of all juvenile arrests in both

Table 5-1 Ten-Year Arrest Trends of Persons under 18 by Sex (2008 and 2017)

Offense charged	Male Under 18			Female Under 18		
	2008	2017	Percent Change	2008	2017	Percent Change
TOTAL	1,138,281	450,360	−60.4%	484,802	184,175	−62.0%
Murder and nonnegligent manslaughter	909	660	−27.4%	65	57	−12.3%
Rape[1]	2,465	2,918		40	112	
Robbery	24,966	13,692	−45.2%	2,556	1,590	−37.8%
Aggravated assault	32,855	16,286	−50.4%	10,114	5,869	−42.0%
Burglary	56,616	21,389	−62.2%	7,802	2,834	−63.7%
Larceny-theft	140,554	58,792	−58.2%	110,929	34,946	−68.5%
Motor vehicle theft	16,107	10,443	−35.2%	2,961	2,355	−20.5%
Arson	4,406	1,510	−65.7%	615	256	−58.4%
Violent crime[2]	61,195	33,556	−45.2%	12,775	7,628	−40.3%
Property crime[2]	217,683	92,134	−57.7%	122,307	40,391	−67.0%
Other assaults	116,883	60,430	−48.3%	60,636	36,093	−40.5%
Forgery and counterfeiting	1,340	748	−44.2%	663	209	−68.5%
Fraud	3,726	2,496	−33.0%	1,965	1,218	−38.0%
Embezzlement	569	284	−50.1%	424	215	−49.3%
Stolen property; buying, receiving, possessing	13,064	6,928	−47.0%	2,996	1,315	−56.1%
Vandalism	71,434	23,673	−66.9%	11,007	5,169	−53.0%
Weapons; carrying, possessing, etc.	27,830	12,878	−53.7%	2,974	1,506	−49.4%
Prostitution and commercialized vice	280	84	−70.0%	878	134	−84.7%
Sex offenses (except rape and prostitution)	9,950	5,877	−40.9%	1,079	767	−28.9%
Drug abuse violations	116,660	56,440	−51.6%	21,298	17,648	−17.1%
Gambling	1,269	174	−86.3%	26	39	50.0%
Offenses against the family and children	2,795	1,829	−34.6%	1,583	1,066	−32.7%
Driving under the influence	9,063	3,538	−61.0%	2,938	1,154	−60.7%
Liquor laws	62,837	15,375	−75.5%	38,007	10,732	−71.8%
Drunkenness	9,099	2,369	−74.0%	2,835	1,026	−63.8%
Disorderly conduct	97,402	31,203	−68.0%	47,530	17,838	−62.5%
Vagrancy	2,209	452	−79.5%	889	131	−85.3%
All other offenses (except traffic)	204,249	83,213	−59.3%	72,304	32,810	−54.6%
Curfew and loitering law violations	71,675	16,628	−76.8%	32,493	7,071	−78.2%

[1]The 2008 rape figures are based on the legacy definition, and the 2017 rape figures are aggregate totals based on both the legacy and revised Uniform Crime Reporting definitions. For this reason, a percent change is not provided.

[2]Violent crimes are offenses of murder and nonnegligent manslaughter, rape, robbery, and aggravated assault. Property crimes are offenses of burglary, larceny-theft, motor vehicle theft, and arson.

Source: Federal Bureau of Investigation, *Crime in the United States, 2017* and *Crime in the United States, 2008*, tables 39 and 40.

categories, while females account for 37%. Table 5-1 shows that the bulk of offenses for which both males and females are arrested are relatively minor; many do not have a clearly defined victim. Of all the arrests of girls in 2017, only 4% of were for violent crime.

The UCR arrest figures understate the extent of status offense arrests. Since 2010, the only separate statistics compiled are for curfew violations (through 2009 there were also statistics for runaways). Other status offenses (such as incorrigibility, unmanageability, and truancy), which are important components of both male and female delinquency, are placed in the "all other offenses" category—17.8% of all girls' arrests in 2017 and 18.5% of all boys' arrests. This category ranked highest for boys in both 2008 and 2017 (see table 5-2). Table 5-1 shows the 10-year trend in the offenses for which males and females were arrested.

What are the trends in female delinquency? Are there more female delinquents today? Are they more likely than their counterparts of a previous time period to commit offenses previously connected with boys? The number of girls arrested increased during the 1960s and early 1970s. Some believed that the women's movement had transformed the roles of women in society—in the criminal world as well as in the conventional world. As women gained more equality, their level of criminal activity would increase.[12] While aspects of that theory have not survived

Table 5-2 Rank Order of Arrests for Juveniles, 2008 and 2017 (percent distribution within each sex cohort)

	Male				Female		
	2008		**2017**		**2008**		**2017**
1. All other offenses[1]	17.9%	All other offenses	18.5%	Larceny	22.9%	Other assaults	19.6%
2. Larceny-theft	12.3%	Other assaults	13.4%	All other	14.9%	Larceny	19.0%
3. Other assaults	10.3%	Larceny theft	13.1%	Other assaults	12.5%	All other offenses	17.8%
4. Drug violations	10.2%	Drug violations	12.5%	Disorderly	9.8%	Disorderly	9.7%
5. Disorderly	8.6%	Disorderly	6.9%	Liquor Laws	7.8%	Drug violations	9.6%
Serious violent[2]	5.4%		7.5%		2.6%		4.1%
Property crime	19.1%		20.5%		23.7%		25.2%
Status offenses[3]	6.3%		3.7%		6.7%		3.8%

[1]Includes variety of offenses depending on state and local ordinances; the most common include public nuisance, trespassing, failure to appear on warrants, contempt of court, and, for juveniles especially, violation of various court orders (e.g., probation, parole) and certain status offenses. This category does not include traffic offenses.

[2]Arrests for murder, robbery, rape, and aggravated assault.

[3]Arrests for curfew and loitering.

Source: Federal Bureau of Investigation *Crime in the United States, 2017*; *Crime in the United States, 2008*, tables 39 and 40.

current research,[13] the emphasis on the intersection of race, class and gender and how gender shapes involvement in drugs, sex-related, and white-collar crimes—as well as the differential and sexist treatment of women in the criminal justice system—have all had a significant impact.[14]

Increases in the number of arrests of girls do not indicate that girls are becoming more like boys.[15] Rather, minor violence committed by girls that had previously been ignored was criminalized. If juvenile girls had become more violent, the proportion of female arrests for each violent crime category should have increased. This did not happen. Instead, scholars suggest that (1) context specific factors influenced the rate and/or nature of delinquent behaviors experienced by boys and girls, and/or (2) differential responses by law enforcement existed for how boys and girls were treated.

> Juveniles' arrests for violence may reflect real differences in rates of offending by gender or they may reflect differences in how police and courts respond to boys and girls. Police arrest proportionally fewer girls than boys, and their arrest patterns have diverged over the past decades. . . . Recently, arrests of females for violent offenses have either increased more or decreased less than those of their male counterparts.[16]

The juvenile male arrest rate for aggravated assault in 2016 was 121.4 per 100,000 persons ages 10–17 compared to 215.2 in 1980—a decrease of 56%.[17] For girls, the rate increased more than 10% from 40.3 in 1980 to 44.5 in 2016. The simple assault rate for arrests of boys was 427.2 in 1980 versus 471.7 in 2016.[18] The rate for girls went from 118.8 to 289.2. The increase for boys was slightly more than 10%, while the rate for girls was almost 2.5 times higher.

> Girls' increased arrest rates for simple assaults and boys' decreased arrest rates for aggravated assaults constitute the most conspicuous gendered changes in youth violence. Despite these gendered changes, one must ask whether girls' arrests reflect real changes in their underlying behavior or police reclassification of assault with a gendered dimension. Unlike murder and robbery, which have relatively well defined elements and clearer indicators, police exercise considerable discretion when they characterize behavior as an assault, whether they classify it as simple or aggravated assault, and the meanings of these offenses have changed over time. Because elements of assault are not objective constants, their subjective definition may change from one observer to another. Proactive policing of disorder and minor crimes, a lower threshold to arrest or charge those offenses or more aggressive policing in private settings may create the appearance of a juvenile crime wave where none exists. Police exercise considerable discretion to classify low-level offenses, and policy changes rather than actual behavior may account for girls' increased arrests for minor assaults.[19]

The decline in the number of arrests for females and males was almost identical in the decade from 2008 to 2017. The arrests of girls declined from 484,802 to

184,175; the arrests of boys declined from 1,138,281 to 450,360 (see table 5-1). The arrest rates have been decreasing for **both** males and females since 1997 (see figure 5-1).

There are several possible explanations for the increased percentage of girls' share of arrests for other assaults from 34.2% in 2008 to 37.4% in 2017 (see table 5-3). First, some of the increase could be attributed to greater attention given to the problem of domestic violence, which has resulted in more arrests for both males and females.[20] Second, it is possible that many of the recent arrests on assault charges are due to greater attention to normal adolescent fighting and/or girls fighting with their parents or legal guardians.[21] Previously this type of aggression was ignored or dealt with informally.

As discussed in chapter 2, the decade of the 1990s was marked by a contradiction between media representations of juvenile delinquency (for **both** boys and girls), the law-and-order rhetoric of most politicians, and the reality of arrest statistics and self-reports of experiences with delinquency. Despite media images of

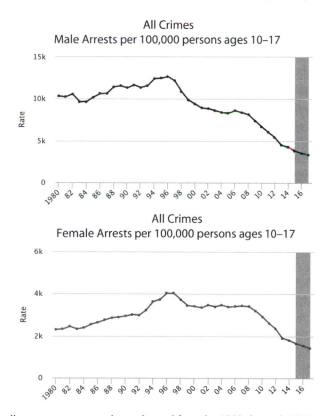

Figure 5-1   Juvenile arrest rate trends, male and female, 1980 through 2017.
(Source: OJJDP Statistical Briefing Book, Online, December 6, 2017. http://www.ojjdp.gov/ojstatbb/crime/JAR_Display. asp?ID=qa05230)

Table 5-3 Girls' Share of All Juvenile Arrests, 2008 and 2017

Offense charged	2008	2017
TOTAL	**29.9%**	**29.0%**
Murder and nonnegligent manslaughter	6.7%	7.9%
Forcible rape	1.6%	3.7%
Robbery	9.3%	10.4%
Aggravated assault	23.5%	26.5%
Burglary	12.1%	11.7%
Larceny-theft	44.1%	37.3%
Motor vehicle theft	15.5%	18.4%
Arson	12.2%	14.5%
Violent crime[2]	17.3%	18.5%
Property crime[2]	36.0%	30.5%
Other assaults	34.2%	37.4%
Forgery and counterfeiting	33.1%	21.8%
Fraud	34.5%	32.8%
Embezzlement	42.7%	43.1%
Stolen property; buying, receiving, possessing	18.7%	16.0%
Vandalism	13.4%	17.9%
Weapons; carrying, possessing, etc.	9.7%	10.5%
Prostitution and commercialized vice	75.8%	61.5%
Sex offenses (except forcible rape and prostitution)	9.8%	11.5%
Drug abuse violations	15.4%	23.8%
Gambling	2.0%	18.3%
Offenses against the family and children	36.2%	36.8%
Driving under the influence	24.5%	24.6%
Liquor laws	37.7%	41.1%
Drunkenness	23.8%	30.2%
Disorderly conduct	32.8%	36.4%
Vagrancy	28.7%	22.5%
All other offenses (except traffic)	26.1%	28.3%
Curfew and loitering law violations	31.2%	29.8%

[1] Because of rounding, the percentages may not add to 100.0.

[2] Violent crimes are offenses of murder and nonnegligent manslaughter, forcible rape, robbery, and aggravated assault. Property crimes are offenses of burglary, larceny-theft, motor vehicle theft, and arson.

Source: Federal Bureau of Investigation. Crime in the United States, 2017; Crime in the United States, 2008. tables 38, 39, 40.

wild, uncontrollable youths preying on citizens everywhere, in actuality there was a significant *decrease* in youth crime for both sexes in that decade—a trend that continues today. With significant declines in almost all categories of offenses, there is little data to support the belief that girls are becoming more violent. As discussed previously, small increases in some of the arrest categories may reflect changes in official crime control policies targeting certain kinds of youthful behaviors (e.g., ungovernability, drug use, schoolyard fights, and domestic disturbances.)

Arrest statistics are based on juvenile police contacts that result in an arrest; however, the police do not arrest everyone who has committed an offense. Further, police officers contact many more youths than they arrest.[22] As a result, arrest statistics are as much a measure of police behavior as they are of criminal behavior. For a more complete picture of the extent of female delinquency, we turn to self-report surveys. In such surveys, individuals respond anonymously to questionnaires or participate anonymously in interviews about their delinquent activities, especially about acts (offending behavior as well as victimization) that never come to the attention of the police.

Self-Report Surveys

Researchers have long used self-report surveys to attempt to gain information about the extent of juvenile delinquency. Typically, the surveys reveal that female delinquency is more common than arrest statistics indicate and that there are more similarities than official statistics suggest between male and female juvenile delinquency. They also show males are more involved in delinquency, especially the most serious types of offenses (i.e. violent crime). Compared to FBI data, self-report data suggest that boys and girls commit similar status offenses at similar rates. The discrepancy between the two sources of data points to possible gender biases operating within the juvenile justice system.

Self-report survey data were first collected in the 1940s to determine the distribution and patterns of delinquency and crime that were not available from official arrest data.[23] In a comprehensive review of self-report studies published between 1955 and 1977, Darrell Steffensmeier and Renée Steffensmeier noted that male–female differences were greater for crimes of violence and serious property crimes.[24] Males and females reported similar rates for such offenses as truancy, driving without a license, running away from home, and minor forms of theft. Another study compared girls' arrests for running away and incorrigibility with girls' self-reports of these two activities. It found a 10% overrepresentation of girls arrested for running away and a 31% overrepresentation in arrests for incorrigibility.[25] Rachelle Canter analyzed data from the National Youth Survey over time and found much similarity between female and male delinquency.[26] There was no behavior in which girls were significantly more involved than boys—even in offenses traditionally ascribed to girls (such as prostitution and running away from home).

The unexpected similarity in girls' and boys' violence against parents and/or legal guardians highlights another problem with some of the offense categories used in arrest statistics. Categories can obscure significant differences in specific behaviors and in responses to those behaviors. For example, when simple assault against parents is considered, the gender gap in assaults decreases. The settings in which delinquent behavior occurs and the relationships between victim and assailant often differ for males and females.

The 2017 National Survey on Drug Use and Health reported similar findings for male and female involvement in a number of activities. As shown in table 2-3, the male percentage of youths who self-reported trying to steal anything worth more than $50 in the past year was 3.5%, versus 2.6% of females. Serious fights at school or work had larger differences, with 19.7% of males reporting such activity and 12.9% of females. The percentages for participation in a group-against-group fight in the past year were more similar: 12.3% of males and 10.4% of females. Attacks with intent to seriously hurt others were reported by 5.6% of male respondents and 3.7% of females. A higher percentage of females (22.3% versus 15.4% of males) reported arguing with at least one parent 10 times or more in the past year.[27]

THE NATURE OF FEMALE DELINQUENCY

The remainder of this chapter will look at some of the major forms of delinquent behavior committed by girls: shoplifting, status offenses, running away (and the corresponding problem of prostitution), and violent offenses. A detailed look at the many dimensions of these offenses reveals the context-specific reality of juvenile delinquency. In so doing, they also tell us much about the lives of the girls who become enmeshed in the juvenile justice system.

Shoplifting: The Prototypical Girls' Crime?

As discussed previously, 41% of girls arrested are charged with larceny-theft; the section on shoplifting in chapter 3 mentioned that the behavior accounts for almost 21% of the arrests for larceny theft. In such a consumer culture, this is not a surprising statistic. Studies consistently document the frequency of shoplifting.[28]

Most studies on shoplifting were published four to six decades ago.[29] One study compared girls' self-reports of delinquency in Florida with official arrest statistics. The police tended to arrest fewer girls than boys for major felonies, but they arrested more girls than boys for petty property crimes. The researchers suggested that this might have been a product of police bias because shoplifting was seen as a stereotypical female crime.[30] Another study found that private security personnel charged with identifying and apprehending shoplifters used race, gender, and perceived age to profile potential offenders.[31] Because stereotypes link women with shopping and the acquisition of clothes, jewelry, and makeup, there is an assumption that shoplifting is a female offense. "A closer examination suggests that shoplifting may be gender neutral or male-gender-related."[32]

Only a small fraction of shoplifters are caught. As a result, official data are extremely limited as a source for understanding the nature of the offense. Researchers have used self-report data to study shoplifting. All the surveys indicate that shoplifting is one of the most prevalent forms of criminal activity.[33] The National Association of Shoplifting Prevention estimates that one in 11 people shoplift and that men are as likely to shoplift as women.[34] Shoplifting occurs across all sociodemographic segments of the population, but it is more common among those with higher education and income. About two-thirds of shoplifting cases occur before age 15; thus, shoplifting has a limited time course. Several recent self-report studies have also shown little or no difference in shoplifting between girls and boys and a few show boys with slightly higher rates. A survey of adolescents in Montana found that males were more likely than females to engage in shoplifting.[35] A study of college students also found that males were more likely than females to shoplift.[36]

Explanations of male and female shoplifting have generally been simplistic and gender biased.[37] One explanation for shoplifting among girls is that it is an outlet for sexual frustration; another is that it is the result of being led astray. Many studies focused on the abnormalities of those who shoplift, such as kleptomania, depression, or low self-esteem. Shoplifting by males is usually seen as rational and based on economic considerations. One consideration that rarely appears in shoplifting research is that young people, especially girls, may be inordinately sensitive to the consumer culture: they steal things they feel they need or cannot afford. The temptation to steal may be more pronounced for girls who feel that popularity is linked to physical appearance and participation in fashions and fads.

The college student study found that those who engaged in shoplifting had personality characteristics and belief systems that placed greater emphasis on individualist values (e.g., hedonism) and less emphasis on such collectivist values as benevolence and conformity that were shared by those who did not shoplift.[38] Shoplifting behavior is most likely to be influenced by peers who also shoplift, especially those who have not yet been caught. The most influential factor in the decision to shoplift was money (mentioned by 41% of the shoplifting subjects), while 21% reported that they shoplifted for the thrill, and another 18% did so because of peer pressure.

It is also important to note that shoplifting often occurs within the context of serious life problems among some girls. For instance, a study of 38 drug-addicted women found a direct link between early life trauma and later criminal activities, including shoplifting and prostitution. Most of the women in this study were African American and grew up in the inner cities of Philadelphia and Camden, New Jersey. Their early lives were marked by constant abuse, both physical and sexual (many victimized by alcoholic parents), and they began to engage in drug use at an early age. Eventually, they were drawn into the world of crime, as shoplifters and sex workers. Most started drinking and using drugs at around the age of 12 or 13 and some even younger than that.[39] These studies document the connections between early abuse and later criminal behavior.

In general, shoplifting by girls must be placed within the context of girls' lives in a youth- and consumer-oriented culture. As noted in chapter 3, to fully understand a behavior, one must know the circumstances surrounding an act. All cases of shoplifting are not identical; motivations and frequency vary. Some girls are strongly influenced by peers or by thrill seeing; others perceive the behavior as the only means of meeting a perceived need.

Status Offenses

As emphasized earlier, one of the distinguishing characteristics of female delinquency is the role played by status offenses. "The line between status offenses and delinquency is as imprecise and malleable as the definition of assaults. Ambiguous differences between incorrigible or unruly behavior—status offenses—and disorderly conduct or simple assault readily lend themselves to relabeling girls' behavior."[40]

As discussed in chapter 3, the early juvenile justice system developed the concept of status offenses specifically to distinguish between delinquent and criminal behavior. Despite the intent, status offenses have subjected many youths to court action. The Juvenile Justice and Delinquency Prevention Act (JJDPA) prohibited placing status offenders in locked detention. Proponents of the act argued that community agencies rather than police departments and juvenile courts were more appropriate entities to deal with youths who were not guilty of criminal behavior.[41]

For many years, statistics showing large numbers of girls arrested and referred to court for status offenses were taken as evidence of the different types of male and female delinquency. As we have seen, self-report studies of male and female delinquency do not reflect such differences. A persuasive explanation for the differences between official and unofficial rates of female delinquency is that the juvenile justice system's historic commitment to the idea of the state as parent has encouraged abuse of the status offense category. Because parents are likely to set different standards of obedience for their male and female children, and because there are few legal guidelines concerning what constitutes a reasonable parental request, parents are able to refer their children to court for a variety of activities. Research dating back many decades has affirmed this.[42] "The decision to arrest and detain girls in these cases is often based in part on the perception that girls violated conventional norms of feminine behavior."[43]

Gender-specific socialization patterns have not changed very much over the years, and this is especially true for parents' relationships with daughters. A study conducted in the 1970s found that even parents who opposed sexism in general, felt "uncomfortable tampering with existing traditions."[44] Parents find multiple reasons to enforce a sexual double standard that treats girls differently. Concerned about sexual harassment, rape, and HIV/AIDS, parents and other adults mix protection with punishment and "often tighten control of girls when they become adolescents, and sexuality becomes a terrain of struggle between the generations."[45] Girls use sexuality as a proxy for independence.

Girls may use cosmetics, discussions of boyfriends, dressing sexually, and other forms of exaggerated "teen" femininity to challenge adult, and class and race-based authority in schools. . . . But the pleasurable and powerful dimensions of heterosexual femininity contain a series of traps and double binds. The double standard persists, and girls who are overtly sexual run the risk of being labeled "sluts."[46]

Peggy Orenstein also observed the durability of the sexual double standard—sex "ruins girls; it enhances boys."[47] Multiple research studies have found evidence of gender differences and traditional sex role expectations where girls are chastised for expressing sexuality while boys are commended.[48] While parents and authorities may have been concerned about preventing pregnancy and protecting the sexual reputations of girls (while essentially sanctioning the same behavior by boys), "the outcome has often been unfettered parenting, policing, and court decisions criminalizing girls for noncriminal behaviors, and even punishing them for being victims of sexual abuse."[49]

Increased reliance on formal social control practices and a decreased tolerance by law enforcement for female delinquency have led to more arrests of girls for simple assaults. Most of those incidents involve family conflicts.

Parents' differing expectations for their sons' and daughters' behavior may affect how the justice system responds to girls when they act out at home. Girls who deviate from traditional gender norms may be at greater risk of arrest for domestic violence than their brothers. . . . Girls fight with family members or siblings more frequently than do boys, while males more often fight with acquaintances or strangers. Girls are three times as likely to assault a family member as are boys. . . . Many girls charged with assault were involved in a nonserious altercation with a parent who oftentimes was the initial aggressor.[50]

If girls behave aggressively, their behavior may be judged as atypical for their sex role and in need of more control than boys who behave similarly.

Childhood sexual abuse often leads girls into behaviors such as running away from home, difficulties in school, and truancy.[51] Girls experience sexual abuse at much higher rates than boys, and at an earlier age than boys do. Their abuse is more likely to be perpetrated by family members (usually the father or the stepfather); consequently, it has a longer duration than abuse of boys. All of these factors are associated with more severe trauma, causing dramatic short- and long-term effects in victims, including fear, anxiety, depression, anger and hostility, and inappropriate sexual behavior. The behaviors of victims are directly related to their traumas. Their homes are not safe environments, and detention rarely proves better.

All studies find higher rates of victimization for girls than boys, although the specific findings of rates of sexual abuse may vary.[52] A literature review in 2011 found that the most consistent finding among 19 studies of the prevalence of trauma by gender was that girls suffered a dramatically higher rate of sexual abuse. One study found that girls in correctional institutions were more often diagnosed with major types of depression than were boys.[53] A study of youth in a Hawaii Youth Correctional Facility found that in comparison to their male counterparts, the female juvenile offender is more likely to: "be arrested for status offenses, especially runaway; to have tried ice; to have histories of trauma, suicidal ideation, and suicide attempts; to suffer from depression/PTSD; and to engage in self-injurious behaviors."[54]

A report on girls in the New York youth prison system found that incarcerated girls had frequently experienced emotional, physical, and/or sexual abuse at home—and that the history of abuse could be the most significant underlying cause of delinquent behavior.[55] In Maryland, 24% of the girls in the juvenile justice system have a history of physical abuse versus 11% of boys; 30% have a history of sexual abuse versus 5% of boys; and 62% have a substantial need for mental health treatment versus 41% of boys.[56]

Sexual abuse is a primary predictor of girls' entry into the juvenile justice system; 93% of girls in the juvenile justice system in Oregon and 81% of the girls in California have been sexually or physically abused.[57] Nationally, the rate of sexual abuse of girls (31%) in the juvenile justice system is 4 times higher than the rate for boys (7%).

> Girls are at much greater risk than boys of having their parents turn them into the police or juvenile courts. Parents are often less tolerant of their daughters' than their sons' identical behaviors, whether they are status offenses (e.g. running away, breaking curfews, drinking alcohol, and being sexually active) or more traditional offenses (e.g., larceny and assaults).[58]

Particularly troubling is that parents are also more likely to physically and sexually abuse their daughters.

In summary, girls may well have legitimate reasons to differ with their parents and/or legal guardians—reasons that may bring them into court as status offenders. The juvenile justice system, because of its history and structure, has tended to ignore children's rights in favor of judicial support for family authority and power over offspring. Girls who may in fact be victims find themselves arrested and referred to court for noncriminal offenses.

Runaways

Over the past twenty years, 60% of runaway cases involved girls.[59] As mentioned in chapter 3, it is the only petitioned offense other than prostitution where the majority of offenders are girls. As discussed above, running away is often a response to sexual abuse, which often initiates cyclical harm. Girls with a history of sexual abuse who run away are more likely to be sexually exploited or to engage in other behavior that increases the likelihood of becoming involved in the criminal justice system. Runaway cases are the most likely to result in an adjudication of detention and out-of-home-placement. Repeat runaways are incarcerated more frequently and for longer periods than girls accused of other offenses and boys accused of status offenses.[60]

There are two reasons why girls, compared to boys, are more likely to run away from home: (1) higher rates of sexual abuse by family members and (2) stricter regulation of girls by parents, creating family conflict.[61] Most male status offenders are reported by school or law enforcement officials; the majority of girl status offenders are reported by parents. The juvenile justice system ignores the reasons why girls disobey their parents or run away from home. Rather, it focuses on defiance of parental and court authority, which transforms the girls from victims to offenders. For example, when a girl has a physical altercation with a family member, the system may charge her with assault rather than incorrigibility. Assault is a delinquency offense that can be punished with confinement. Incorrigibility is a status offense; confinement would violate the JJDPA.

The punitive system does not address underlying issues, such as sexual or physical abuse, substance abuse, and family discord. Rather, it stigmatizes and re-traumatizes the victims, exacerbating the problem.[62] This is particularly true of runaways—repeated detention does not stop girls from running away. Girls who run away generally pose a very low risk to others. They themselves, however, are very vulnerable.

As already noted, most runaways have fled homes where abuse was an everyday event; their lives on the streets are almost always even more abusive. Sex trafficking includes the commercial sexual exploitation of children (CSEC). Children who are homeless, runaways, LGBTQ, African American, Latino, or youth interacting with the child welfare system are more vulnerable to CSEC.[63] The internet has facilitated selling children for sex. Human trafficking is the second largest illegal business in the world.[64] Traffickers prey on the vulnerable. Large cities like Dallas, Houston, and Los Angeles are home to many runaway and throwaway youth. Texas has about 6,000 runaways annually. An estimated 33% of children who run away are lured into sex trafficking within 48 hours of leaving home. The following factors elevate vulnerability: past sexual/physical/emotional abuse, learning disabilities, depression/mental health issues, homelessness, drug/alcohol addiction, lack of education, low self-esteem, and looking for attention. The average age of entry is 12 to 14.[65]

> Child sex trafficking is child sexual abuse. And it is abuse that is often layered over pre-existing trauma: children who have been sexually abused are especially vulnerable to traffickers. Yet many jurisdictions still view victims of child sex trafficking as perpetrators. These girls are arrested on charges of prostitution even though they are too young to legally consent to sex.[66]

Uneducated, unloved, and often abused, many runaways/thrownaways turn to prostitution to survive.[67] Traffickers target vulnerable children, luring them by offering food, clothes, a place to sleep, and attention.[68] After engendering a false sense of trust, the trafficker forces the child into prostitution and uses physical, emotional, and psychological abuse to maintain control. The Internet provides a convenient marketing channel for advertising, scheduling, and purchasing sexual encounters with minors. The exact number of child victims of sex trafficking in the United States is not known because of the hidden nature of the problem and varying methodologies used in studies.[69]

New technologies facilitate the online sexual exploitation of children, including the live-streaming of sexual abuse. Mobile devices are used to target, recruit, and coerce children to engage in sexual activity. Sextortion is a form of online sexual exploitation where exploiters obtain incriminating photos or information and then threaten exposure if the child does not perform sex acts via web cameras. After recruiting a potential child victim and psychologically manipulating them, the exploiter connects via the Internet with paying clients.[70]

Prostitution

The juvenile justice system uses status offenses to regulate sexual behavior and obedience.[71] New York and a few other states have decriminalized prostitution for some minors because they are too young to legally consent to sex. However, they continue to arrest and detain girls as status offenders. Prostitution is closely connected to running away, with about 60% of prostituted children nationwide having a runaway history. In New York, 61% of runaway girls engaged in survival sex. Runaway girls with a history of abuse are particularly vulnerable to pimps, who survey bus stations and homeless shelters to identify prospects. Girls who lack stable housing are at increased risk for commercial sexual exploitation; 67% of homeless girls were offered money in exchange for sex, and 20% were trafficked for sex.[72]

How is it that thousands of teenage girls end up as prostitutes? There are several interrelated reasons. The first was discussed in the previous section: it is a form of survival. The most common form of teenage prostitution today may be for *survival sex*—sex in return for basic needs (i.e. food and shelter). Whatever term one applies, teenage prostitution is widespread, often beginning before the girl reaches 15. Most girls are from dysfunctional families characterized by alcoholism or drug abuse, physical and sexual abuse, and neglect. Many can be classified as chronic homeless (three or more months on their own). They often live in abandoned buildings with no bathrooms or utilities.

Several additional factors may lead to prostitution. Girls may be coerced, tricked, seduced, or even blackmailed by a pimp. Further, a lack of shelters may leave few alternatives to prostitution. Family conditioning could have caused very low self-esteem, resulting in the belief that prostitution is deserved. Some girls may move from a few isolated sexual encounters for money to a situation in which they feel they have no access to more acceptable roles such as housewife or student. In other words, being a prostitute becomes a girl's major role. The most vulnerable are female children 13 and younger who have been abused, suffer from family instability and dislocation, live in poverty, have run away, or are homeless.[73]

Las Vegas is a hub for sex trafficking because of conventions and the gaming industry.[74] Recruitment of girls can begin through friends at school, at a party, in a club, or through the Internet. The pimp-prostitute relationship may begin as a romance. After a relationship begins, the pimp may allege the need for money and ask the girl to help by selling sex. Mary Swanson met Kobe Hogue when she was a junior in high school. Her mother saw that Mary, who suffered from low self-esteem, was happy. At first Andrea Swanson trusted Hogue. Hogue paid for provocative outfits for Mary and for having her hair and nails done; he also designed a tattoo for her. Mary's parents assumed the changes were signs of rebellion, but they also noticed occasional bruises. Even after Hogue served time in prison for stealing vehicles, they allowed him to continue dating their daughter. Mary then became verbally abusive; she was rarely home and any question became an argument. Shortly before her graduation from high school, she was arrested for prostitution. Hogue was her pimp and arranged for her to work in Strip hotels and along Boulder Highway. She gave all her earnings to Hogue. He was arrested and sentenced to Three Lakes Valley Conservation Camp after pleading guilty. Mary and Andrea have worked on repairing their relationship, but Mary intends to be with Hogue after his release from custody, although she says she will not work as a prostitute.

Jasmine lived with her mother, father, and grandfather in Oakland.[75] Her mother left the family when she was 2; her father left when she was 4, and her grandmother died shortly after. She and her brother entered California's foster care system for a year. When their father resurfaced in Las Vegas, they moved to live with him. They were removed to foster care when he started using drugs and alcohol. Her brother was eventually adopted. When Jasmine was about 11, her father regained custody. Her uncle raped her when she was 13, and her father and uncle forced her into the sex trade with several other girls kept in cages in the basement of a suburban Las Vegas house. Nationally, 86% of child sex trafficking victims were under the care of social services when they ran away. Foster youth have unique vulnerabilities that make them targets for traffickers, including transiency, history of abuse and neglect and need for familial bonds. They have a history of bouncing between foster care and family—an unstable environment separated from siblings and the feeling of being thrown away. Girls who are trapped in abusive situations usually don't leave; they depend on the abuser for survival. Jasmine was fortunate. A customer realized she was too young and dropped her off at Child Haven when she was 14. She spent the next four years in the Clark County foster care system. She cycled through foster homes and got in fights with other children. After landing at St. Jude's Ranch for Children, she enrolled in a new school and attended programs and therapy to help her understand her history. Her caseworker found her brother and a half-sister, and the ranch arranged visits with her siblings. After attending nine schools, she graduated from high school in 2017. When she was 18 she moved to Sacramento and began studying psychology so she can counsel teens with substance abuse problems.

Prostitution among girls, then, is not so much a choice as a survival mechanism for those who have few other options once forced onto the streets. For many young people who cannot stay at home, there is little help from the social service and criminal justice systems. Safe harbor laws are one means of ending the detention of minors for prostitution.[76] They provide immunity from arrest and prosecution when the charged offense is related to exploitation and victimization.

Girls and Violence

Previous chapters have discussed the effects of sensational media stories—whether the inaccurate predictions of superpredators, the inflated accounts of school violence, the overestimates of sex offenders, or the impact of reports on public opinion regarding the amount of crime. Another point of media emphasis since the 1990s has been *mean* girls. The stories emphasize violent behavior by girls. While isolated incidents of violence by girls do occur, the media does not report the infrequency of such incidents. Instead, it suggests a new breed of violent female offenders who are as wicked and evil as their male counterparts.

Labeling girls as violent or more violent than at some point in the past is a process of social construction. Feminist criminologists have criticized traditional schools of criminology for assuming that male delinquency, even in its most violent forms, was somehow an understandable response. Girls who shared the same social and cultural influences as delinquent boys but who were not violent were labeled abnormal or over-controlled.[77] Law-abiding behavior on the part of boys is taken as a sign of character, but when girls avoid crime and violence, it is an expression of weakness. "The other side of this equation is that *if* girls engage in even minor forms of violence, they are somehow more vicious than their male counterparts."[78] The media often react to increases in male violence with the attitude of "so what else is new?" However, when reporting an increase in girls' violence, the conclusion is that something fundamental is wrong or there is a new breed of violent girls roaming the streets and threatening the social order.

Such is clearly not the case. Criminologists Meda Chesney-Lind and Katherine Irwin explored the disconnect between the reality of the lives of girls and the media constructions of those girls.[79] While a gap between media claims and reality is not new, this gap was particularly problematic and punitive—and the misinformation was widely believed by people with substantial power over girls.

> The masculinization of female defiance also brings the role of race and class forward. In a society that has long sought to keep all women in line with negative images, breaking gender norms has very real consequences for all girls who are seen as challenging their assigned place.[80]

The mean girl media narrative continues a historic trend of identifying and denouncing girls who break feminine norms and, thus, appear to threaten the moral fiber of society. In the fifties, promiscuous girls were identified; in the seventies, it was the revolutionary; in the eighties, there were girl gangsters, at the turn of the century it was the mean girl, and the new millennia has the violent girl. Media attention to girls' violence was based on exaggerated reports and anecdotal evidence. "The institutions that have historically socialized and controlled girls *informally* (families, schools, peer groups) are changing the way they monitor and control girls—with bad consequences for girls."[81]

Virtually all news stories on girls and violence follow the same inaccurate pattern. Typically, an egregious example of female violence is described, followed by a quick review of the FBI's latest arrest statistics showing what appear to be large increases in the number of girls arrested for violent offenses, accompanied by quotations from "experts"—usually police officers, teachers, or various social service workers, and occasionally criminologists. Much of the "evidence" cited is anecdotal, and the focus is almost always on a few, isolated and exceptional cases (otherwise it would not be "news") followed by gross generalizations.

Jerry Kurelic offers the acronym W.I.S.E. to explain the framing of sensational events by the media and political pundits: *withhold* information that is contrary to their opinion; *identify* that which is consistent with their opinion; *sensationalize* that which illustrates their perspective; *expand* information as if it represents the whole. So in the case of girls and violence, journalists will seek out (identify) a few cases that fit their preconceived notions that girls are getting more violent; withhold any information that contradicts this position; sensationalize it with inflammatory headlines in bold, large type; and finally, make it seem as if this behavior is typical all over the country.[82]

Before looking at whether girls are becoming as violent as boys, we want to reemphasize that words like *violence* and *assault* are value laden and cover a wide variety of behaviors, most of which are relatively harmless. As suggested in chapter 3, official statistics about juvenile arrests and dispositions should be scrutinized to find more specific details about offenses beyond the broad categories of *person crimes*, *other assaults*, and *simple assaults*. Assaults with deadly weapons leading to serious injuries (aggravated assaults) as well as minor fistfights on high school campuses or fights between children and their parents (simple assaults) are all person crimes. Only aggravated assaults are categorized as violent crime, but the distinction is sometimes overlooked.

Self-report data of youthful involvement in violent offenses shows a decline. The Youth Risk Behavior Survey asks students in grades nine through twelve in public and private schools questions about a number of topics, including violence; the results are published every two years. In 1991, 34.4% of girls and 50.2% of boys surveyed said that they had been in a physical fight one or more times in the 12 months before the survey; in 2001, the percentages were 23.9% for girls and 43.1% for boys; in 2009, 22.9% for girls and 39.3% for boys[83] and in 2017, 17.2% for girls and 30% for boys.[84] When asked about carrying a weapon on at least 1 day in the month prior to the survey, 10.9% of girls in 1991 and 40.6% of boys had done so; in 2001, the percentages were 6.2% for girls and 29.3% for boys; in 2009,

7.1% for girls and 27.1% for boys. In 2017, the percentage was 7.4% for girls and 24.2% for boys.

Earlier research also revealed significant decreases in girls' involvement in felony assaults, minor assaults, and hard drugs, and no change in a wide range of other delinquent behaviors—including felony theft, minor theft, and index delinquency.[85] Self-report data showing increased involvement of girls in assaultive behavior needs to be viewed with a very clear idea of what behavior is included in each category. As discussed above, the percentage of arrests of girls increased for other assaults over the last decade. The increase may be due to changes in public policies concerning domestic violence and school fighting.

Chesney-Lind and Irwin note that the increasing number of arrests for girls on relatively minor offenses like simple assaults stems from what they term *hyper policing*, rather than a change in actual behavior.[86]

> Girls' increased arrests came, we argue, not because they were becoming more like boys, but instead because girls would bear the brunt of an intensified system of social control . . . girls who were "acting out" in the home, in their peer groups, or in the school are now being punished formally, and often labeled as violent criminals in the process.[87]

The idea that girls have "gone wild" in recent years is a complete fraud. Mike Males and Chesney-Lind provide a more accurate picture.

> We have examined every major index of crime on which the authorities rely. None show a recent increase in girls' violence; in fact, every reliable measure shows that violence by girls has been plummeting for years. Major offenses like murder and robbery by girls are at their lowest levels in four decades. Fights, weapons possession, assaults and violent injuries by and toward girls have been plunging for at least a decade. . . . This mythical wave of girls' violence and meanness is, in the end, contradicted by reams of evidence from almost every available and reliable source. Yet news media and myriad experts, seemingly eager to sensationalize every "crisis" among young people, have aroused unwarranted worry in the public and policy arenas. The unfortunate result is more punitive treatment of girls, including arrests and incarceration for lesser offenses like minor assaults that were treated informally in the past, as well as alarmist calls for restrictions on their Internet use.[88]

Relabeling Status Offenses

Policy makers have been alarmed over the increase in arrests of girls for simple and aggravated assault. As discussed earlier, the increases may be the result of the public's desire to control violence, changes in parental attitudes, or changes in law enforcement policies regarding domestic violence, which disproportionately affects girls. One study found that policy changes for domestic violence ended up lowering the risk of arrest for men and actually increased the risks for women and girls.[89]

Most assault charges involve nonserious, trivial, combative situations with parents, who decide to call the police. A girl might throw food at her mother during an argument, or she might shove her mother who slapped her.[90] Some critics have called the trend toward criminalizing behaviors previously ignored or treated informally as "upcriming."[91]

> Female arrest gains for violence are largely a by-product of net-widening enforcement policies, like broader definitions of youth violence and greater surveillance of girls that have escalated the arrest proneness of adolescent girls today relative to girls in prior decades and relative to boys.[92]

What previously would have been classified as disagreements are now taken as evidence of increased violence. Barry Feld analyzed data on changes in arrests and confinement for boys and girls who were charged with simple and aggravated assault and found that the charges were mostly a relabeling of status offenses.[93] The social construction of girls' violence may reflect policy changes in the juvenile justice system itself, especially the deinstitutionalization of status offenders mandated by the 1974 Juvenile Justice and Delinquency Prevention Act. The mandate encouraged relabeling female status offenders as delinquents to retain access to confinement facilities.[94] Girls who would have originally been charged with the status offenses of incorrigibility or ungovernability were instead charged with simple assault, a delinquency offense.

Changes in New York's domestic violence policies resulted in an increase in arrests of girls, mostly charged with simple assault.[95] An analysis of the National Incident Based Reporting System data found that both male and female juveniles were more likely to be arrested in states with mandatory or pro-arrest policies than in states with discretionary arrest policies.[96] Beyond the effects of domestic arrest laws, girls were increasingly more likely to be arrested for assaults against parents.

Girls' case files in various states highlight the trend of relabeling domestic violence incidents as more serious offenses. In Maryland's juvenile justice system, young women are disproportionately locked up for misdemeanors.[97] They are more likely to appear before a judge for probation offenses such as running away, breaking curfew, and defying their parents. An African American Baltimore teen and her mother fought for months; sometimes the fights were physical. One night she came home late, shoved her mother, and the mother called the police. At age 14, she was charged with second-degree assault. As a delinquent, coming home late or leaving the house without permission were offenses that resulted in her being confined in a maximum-security lockup about six times a year for the next two years. If she had been a boy, the outcome would probably have been different. Once in the system, girls are detained longer. Although girls are less likely to be committed for felonies or violent offenses, they spend 25% more time in the state's most secure facilities. Much of the increase in girls' arrests for violent crimes is an artifact of policy changes, rather than actual behavior. There is not, nor has there ever been, a new wave of violent girls.

Aggression and Gender

Is there any truth to the claim that girls are just as aggressive as boys? Are girls becoming more violent? Research literature largely refutes both these claims. Women commit less crime than men, and their crimes are typically less serious, violent, and profitable.[98] However, the existence of a male co-offender increases women's criminal involvement. In general, research on the effects of gender on crime employs either gender-neutral approaches (psychopathy and risk assessment tools) or gender-specific approaches (victimization, family support/dysfunction, housing safety, and mental health factors).[99] Research is often affected by small sample sizes.[100]

Early research concluded that boys exhibit significantly higher levels of aggression than girls.

> The perception that males are more aggressive, however, might be more of a factor of how aggression is defined, which historically tended to reflect more overt manifestations. Increasingly, in both the empirical and popular literature, the concept of "relational aggression" has been discussed and associated with girls.[101]

Relational aggression involves a number of passive, indirect behaviors (i.e. ostracizing, ignoring, spreading rumors). Adding covert, non-physical behaviors to overt, physical forms expands the range of behaviors considered aggressive. Relational aggression research essentially posits that girls are manipulative, mean, and backstabbing—a set of attributes long associated with girls but now equating these behaviors to boys' violence. The gender stereotype carried the implication that there were significant gender differences in relational aggression, although research on the question has been mixed, with some studies finding that boys are more relationally aggressive than girls.

One method of looking at underlying motivations for violence distinguishes between instrumental versus reactive violence. Instrumental aggression (also known as proactive or premeditated aggression) is used to achieve a specific goal. Reactive aggression (also known as impulsive aggression) occurs when defending oneself from a threat. Personality disorders were the most predictive of instrumental violence in both males and females. Juveniles who engaged in instrumental aggression had a history of poor school performance, parental substance abuse or violence, conduct disorders, fighting, and delinquency. Reactively violent females experienced trauma at an early age and had low verbal skills versus reactive males who were impulsive and exhibited ADHD. Males and females engage in reactive and proactive relational aggression differently. Girls who use relational aggression as a strategy to gain control and status (i.e., befriending someone to gain their trust in order to exploit them or spreading rumors to elevate one's social status even if the target never inflicted personal harm) feel restrained by their parents and gravitate toward relationships that support their behavior.[102]

Violent crimes are not exclusively the acts of boys and men, but men greatly outnumber women in those types of offenses. Mass shootings are almost always committed by young men. There are occasional violent acts by girls, such as the beating of a 15-year-old girl by 6 other girls between the ages of 15 and 18 at a Brooklyn McDonald's. The leader of the attackers was 16 and had been arrested six times in the previous six months, once for stabbing her teenage brother in the arm and once for beating her grandmother.[103] Sources said she suffered from mood and conduct disorders; prior to sentencing, she was sent for psychiatric treatment at a facility for adolescents but was remanded to Rikers because of unruly behavior. She was sentenced to 4 years in prison. Despite such sensational cases that garner significant media coverage, female violence remains relatively rare.

The research is clear that aggression among girls usually occurs within the context of the home or *intrafemale* (girl-on-girl) scenarios. Traditionally, this kind of violence was rarely reported to authorities. Female motivations are driven by relational concerns.[104] Most cases of girls arrested for simple assault involved a female-on-female fight in retaliation for spreading rumors or for involvement with another's boyfriend or a mother and daughter fight over breaking curfew. Female violence is less likely to be directed at strangers. Girls most frequently commit minor thefts, low-level drug dealing, prostitution, and simple assaults against family members or acquaintances.

A longitudinal study found that boys in elementary school who exhibited behaviors such as arguing, disobedience, and fighting (*externalizing factors*) were more likely to commit crimes as adults; girls whose behavior was similar were not.[105] Rather, the girls who were socially withdrawn or exhibited signs of anxiety or depression (*internalizing factors*) were more likely to commit crimes as adults, while boys who showed the same characteristics were not.

A combination of factors helps explain why some female victims of abuse become involved in the criminal justice system while most do not.[106] Abused girls who have repeatedly internalized their feelings during childhood may reach a threshold as teenagers; their repressed emotions can surface violently and be directed towards others. If they perceived their parents as overly restrictive, they may manipulate peer relationships to gain a sense of power and control. Girls who are abused as children are at increased risk of forming relationships where they experience the same abuse. Some abused girls may choose abusive partners who introduce them to a criminal lifestyle. As teens, girls are more likely to use more extreme and premeditated forms of relational aggression than boys to gain status and control and to deal with painful emotions.

A teen girl may use social media to post something derogatory about an ex boyfriend's new girlfriend. While the behavior is not admirable, most juveniles who engage in it eventually mature into well-adjusted adults. Many adolescent girls gossip, spread rumors, manipulatively attempt to ruin relationships, and intentionally exclude others. One study examined the effects of individual, peer, and parent-related variables on low aggressors, reactive aggressors, and combined proactive/reactive aggressors.[107] Those in the latter group were young, exhibited greater callous-unemotional traits, had fewer male peers, and a greater perception of parental control than either of the other two groups. The low aggressive group had less delinquency than the other groups.

In a study of relational-aggression among girls, focus group interviews revealed that girls' aggression revolved around competition with other girls to fit in and be accepted. Several interviewees described cases of bullying, but only one said there was actual violence. The authors found that "meanness did not drive girls into horrible risk-taking behaviors, nor did it propel them into the depths of depression."[108] In addition, meanness, pettiness, and nastiness is not unique among girls—it is also common among boys. Why, therefore, so much attention toward this behavior only on girls?

> It is because the rules of the game seriously disadvantage girls. If they conform to feminine ideals such as being kind to everyone and attractive, they are negatively labeled as shallow creatures who are overly concerned with popularity and appearances. And if they reject or challenge these impossible feminine goals, they are "fat cows," "bitches," or "mean girls." Even covert social skills, like the ability to recognize and deploy indirect aggression, is demonized in girls while in the adult male world, it is seen as an extremely clever political strategy. In a world where people are regularly nasty to one another, it is girls who become the focus of our attention and the subject of books, television shows, and newspaper articles. For girls, it shows clearly and poignantly that the game is rigged against them.[109]

Indeed, aggression and meanness is a huge part of the business world, a world dominated by men. Whenever women behave like men (which they have to do to survive in a world dominated by men), they are subjected to negative labels (bitch, etc.). All of these examples speak further to the gendered nature of aggression specifically and of delinquency more broadly.

Criminologist Walter DeKeseredy notes that the "ideology of familial patriarchy . . . supports the abuse of women who violate the ideals of male power and control over women." This ideology is acted out by those males and females who insist on women being obedient, respectful, loyal, dependent, sexually accessible and sexually faithful to males.[110] Girls who accept these beliefs and police other girls' behaviors preserve the status quo—including, ironically, their own continued oppression. People in oppressed situations or those who suffer various forms of prejudice and discrimination typically take it out on similarly situated others rather than on the perpetrators of their oppression.[111]

Chesney-Lind notes that from 1995 through 2007 when cultural images of girls' violence proliferated, the arrest rates of girls for murder, robbery, rape, and felony assault fell sharply.[112] Felony assault rates rose through 1995 before declining. Only misdemeanor assault arrests increased—for both sexes and for all age groups.

What could explain this pattern of girls' arrests for murder, robbery and other serious crime *declining* sharply, while the only offense to increase is assault? If girls are becoming more violent, wouldn't we expect all types of violent crime by girls to increase? And if girls' assaults are rising dramatically, wouldn't we expect homicide to increase as well simply as a result of more attacks causing more deaths? It's odd that 90% of the supposed increase in girls' violence has been for simple assault, *the least serious offense.* . . . This pattern is best explained by new law enforcement initiatives authorized by stronger laws beginning in the 1980s to make arrests for street, school, workplace, and (especially) domestic violence in cases that once brought warnings or informal discipline.[113]

Girls and Robbery

The crime of robbery has traditionally been included in the broad category of violent crime. While typically a masculine crime, the percentage of arrests of girls increased slightly in the last decade. The small increase does not substantiate the sensational reports of violent girls. Of all juvenile arrests for robbery, girls comprised 10% (see table 5-3). Girls' arrest rates for robbery are down 23% from 1975.[114]

In order to investigate whether girls now participate more frequently in the traditionally male offense, we must first examine the concept of robbery. There are many more nuances than the stereotypes of this crime suggest. In some cases, the offenses resemble criminal mischief. Because of the increased risk of a felony charge and the relatively low yield involved in robbery, its appeal decreases with age as peer support declines and societal bonds strengthen.[115] Popular youth culture stresses the importance of status (i.e. name-brand athletic shoes, gold jewelry, and expensive electronics), which can play a major role in juvenile robbery. Youths are less likely to victimize the elderly and most likely to victimize their peers. The thrill and excitement associated with street robbery is another possible motivation. Most juvenile robberies are not sophisticated and planned offenses; rather they are impulsive and spontaneous events.

The majority of juvenile robberies involved male offenders.[116] About 34% of the victims of juvenile robbers were acquaintances, and 26% of the victims were female. Multiple offenders were more likely in juvenile robbery—31% were victimized by two or more juveniles and 30% were victimized by juveniles acting with adults. Guns were more frequently involved in instances with multiple offenders. Women are more likely to participate in robbery, burglary, and drug sales when co-offending with men and are more likely to use guns than women who work alone.[117] For most crimes, women more frequently co-offend in mixed-gender groups than in all-female groups. Women are several times more likely to be involved in gender atypical offenses when they have at least one male co-offender compared to working alone or in a same-sex group.

In a qualitative review of the role of gender in robbery, Jody Miller analyzed interviews with youthful robbers in St. Louis. She concluded that the acquisition of money and status-conferring goods, such as jewelry, are the primary motivations for committing the offense for both males and females.[118] Males are most likely to use weapons when committing a robbery. Males use physical violence and weapons to display masculinity. Female robberies tend not to include weapons because females typically prey on other females, and female victims are less likely to fight back.

In an analysis of robbery arrests in Honolulu between 1991 and 1997, the percentage of girls increased from 5% to 17%. However, the researchers found that there was no major change in the overall pattern of robberies committed; rather, they found that less serious incidents had been labeled robberies. The age of offenders had declined, as did the value of the items taken (from a median of $10 to a median of $1.25. Frequently, the robberies were committed by older youth bullying younger youth for small amounts of cash.[119] These types of robberies accounted for almost all of the increases in formal arrest statistics. A key to the increases were changes in school policies, which involved calling the police versus handling the problem at the school. The police labeled the offenses robberies, whereas before they would have been labeled as thefts. As with virtually all offenses, crimes must be analyzed within a social context. Details of the incidents may well indicate a relabeling of behavior rather than an increase in violence.

Summary

Girls commit a variety of offenses but are less likely than boys to engage in serious, violent delinquency. Some research (especially self-report studies) suggests that there are more similarities than previously imagined in male and female delinquency. In essence, most delinquency is quite minor, and the differences between boys' and girls' misbehavior are not pronounced. Female delinquency has changed little in the past three decades. Girls are still arrested and referred to court primarily for minor property offenses and for status offenses. There is little or no evidence of any major change in girls' delinquent behavior.

Most girls in the juvenile justice system have experienced poverty, an unstable family life, problems at school, and sexual, physical, or emotional abuse. Their experiences of trauma, separation, and family loss differ from the experiences of many boys. The offenses they commit are often directly related to their victimization. The abuse to prison pipeline, the school to prison pipeline, and the disproportionate criminalization of girls for status offenses are common pathways to the juvenile justice system for girls. Changes in policies and law enforcement practices have contributed to the risk for justice involvement for girls.

Status offenses have always been closely identified with female delinquency. Running away from home and being unmanageable or incorrigible have long been seen as typical female offenses. The prevalence of status offenses in girls' delinquency stems, in part, from the parental desire to control the behavior of girls. Self-report studies show that boys and girls are about equally as likely to commit status offenses, but referrals to juvenile court show a gender bias. The bias is even more troubling when one considers that persistent status offense behavior in girls, notably running away, is linked to abuse, especially sexual abuse, within the home. Running away very often leads girls to commit a variety of crimes in order to survive. Girls who join the ranks of street youth often end up in the world of prostitution or trafficking, where their abuse continues at the hands of pimps and customers alike.

Larceny-theft and shoplifting have consistently been the most common property offenses committed by girls. From the few available studies, it appears that girls and boys are about equally as likely to shoplift, but girls are more likely to be detected by store personnel, arrested by the police, and referred to juvenile court. Items stolen by girls are of lesser value than those stolen by boys, and girls are more apt to be amateurs. Most of the items girls steal are for personal use and may be linked to their desire to conform to a standard of female beauty and appearance that is otherwise inaccessible, particularly to poorer girls.

Overall, there has not been sufficient research on girls' delinquency. The investigation of girls' lives, identities, and circumstances has begun only within the past few decades. To understand delinquency in girls, we need to overcome stereotypical thinking and implicit biases about girls whose behavior or appearance differs from social expectations. Objective inquiry into the impact of gendered and racial attitudes on decisions to arrest, detain, adjudicate, and place girls in the juvenile justice system will provide a more nuanced perspective on the delinquency of girls.

Notes

1 Charles Puzzanchera and Samantha Ehrmann, "Spotlight on Girls in the Juvenile Justice System," Washington, DC: Statistical Briefing Book, January 2018.

2 Yasmin Vafa, Eduardo Ferrer, Maheen Kaleem, Chrice Hopkins, and Emily Feldhake, "Beyond the Walls: A Look at Girls in DC's Juvenile Justice System," Washington, DC: Rights4Girls and the Georgetown Juvenile Justice Initiative, March 2018, 2.

3 Sarah Hockenberry and Charles Puzzanchera, "Juvenile Court Statistics 2016," Pittsburgh, PA: National Center for Juvenile Justice, August 2018.

4 Vafa et al., "Beyond the Walls."

5 Ibid.

6 Ibid.

7 Ibid.

8 FBI, *Crime in the United States, 2017* (Washington, DC: Author, 2018), tables 38, 40.

9 Puzzanchera & Ehrmann, "Spotlight on Girls in the Juvenile Justice System."

10 Malika Saar, Rebecca Epstein, Lindsay Rosenthal, Yasmin Vafa, "The Sexual Abuse to Prison Pipeline: The Girls' Story," Washington, DC: Center for Poverty and Inequality, October 2015.

11 For a more complete analysis, see Meda Chesney-Lind and Randall G. Shelden, *Girls, Delinquency, and Juvenile Justice,* 4th ed. (Malden, MA: Wiley-Blackwell, 2014), chapters 2 and 3. In order to understand why girls become involved in activities that are likely to land them in the juvenile justice system, it is essential to consider gender in all its dimensions.

Girls undergo a childhood and adolescence that is heavily colored by their gender (a case can be made that the lives of boys are also affected by gender roles). Girls and boys do not have the same choices. This is not to say that girls do not share some problems with boys (notably the burdens of class and race), but even the way in which these similarities affect the daily lives of young people is heavily mediated by gender.

12   Freda Adler, *Sisters in Crime* (New York: McGraw-Hill, 1975). Adler's book has a significant legacy for its role in inspiring scholars to bring gender into criminology.

13   See Chesney-Lind and Shelden, *Girls, Delinquency, and Juvenile Justice*, chapter 2.

14   Francis T. Cullen, Pamela Wilcox, Jennifer L. Lux, and Cheryl Lero Johnson, *Sisters in Crime Revisited* (New York: Oxford University Press, 2015).

15   Joanne Belknap, *The Invisible Woman: Gender, Crime, and Justice*, 4th ed. (Stamford, CT: Cengage Learning, 2015).

16   Barry Feld, *The Evolution of the Juvenile Court: Race, Politics, and the Criminalizing of Juvenile Justice* (New York: New York University Press, 2017), 160.

17   OJJDP Statistical Briefing Book Online, December 6, 2017, http://www.ojjdp.gov/ojstatbb/crime/JAR_Display.asp?ID=qa05235

18   Ibid., http://www.ojjdp.gov/ojstatbb/crime/JAR_Display.asp?ID=qa05241

19   Feld, *The Evolution of the Juvenile Court*, 163–164.

20   Kevin Strom, Tara Warner, Lisa Tichavsky, and Margaret Zahn, "Policing Juveniles: Domestic Violence Arrest Policies, Gender, and Police Response to Child-Parent Violence," *Crime & Delinquency*, 2014, 60(3): 427–450.

21   Although there are no hard data on this, several sources inside the juvenile justice system have told the authors about the following trend. Because juvenile courts have been restrained in recent years from responding vigorously to cases of runaways, some police and probation officers are suggesting that parents do the following: when a girl threatens to run away, the parent should stand in her way; if she runs into the parent or pushes the parent out of the way, then the parent can call the court and have the girl arrested on "simple assault" or "battery" or some other "personal" crime that would fit into the FBI category "other assaults." Although it is uncertain how often this happens or how this could shape arrest figures that are reported to the FBI, it illustrates that FBI categories are just that: *categories* encompassing a wide variety of behaviors and different social contexts. As discussed in chapter 2, official arrest statistics like those discussed in this chapter should be interpreted cautiously.

22   Chesney-Lind and Shelden, *Girls, Delinquency, and Juvenile Justice*, chapter 7.

23   Scott Menard, Lisa C. Bowman-Bowen, Yi-Fen Lu, "Self-Reported Crime and Delinquency," in Beth M. Huebner and Timothy S. Bynum, *The Handbook of Measurement Issues in Criminology and Criminal Justice* (Malden, MA: John Wiley & Sons, 2016, 473–495).

24   Darrell Steffensmeier and Renee Steffensmeier, "Trends in Female Delinquency: An Examination of Arrest, Juvenile Court, Self Report, and Field Data," *Criminology*, 1980, 18: 62–85.

25   Katherine Teilmann and Pierre Landry, "Gender Bias in Juvenile Justice," *Journal of Research in Crime and Delinquency*, 1981, 18: 47–80.

26   Rachel J. Canter, "Sex Differences in Self-Report Delinquency." *Criminology*, 1982, 20: 373–93.

27   Center for Behavioral Health Statistics and Quality. *Results from the 2017 National Survey on Drug Use and Health: Detailed Tables*. Rockville, MD: Substance Abuse and Mental Health Services Administration, September 7, 2018, table 3.16B.

[28] An interesting history of shoplifting is presented by Kerry Segrave, *Shoplifting: A Social History* (New York: McFarland & Company, 2001). Until the 1920s, shoplifting was mostly a male activity. Then it shifted to a mostly female activity, in part because of the significant increase in women shoppers.

[29] Belknap, *The Invisible Woman*.

[30] Ruth Horowitz and Anne Pottieger, "Gender Bias in Juvenile Justice Handling of Seriously Crime-Involved Youths," *Journal of Research in Crime and Delinquency*, 1991, 28(1): 75–100.

[31] Dean Dabney, Laura Dugan, Volkan Topalli, and Richard Hollinger, "The Impact of Implicit Stereotyping on Offender Profiling: Unexpected Results from an Observational Study of Shoplifting," *Criminal Justice and Behavior*, 2006, 33(5): 646–674.

[32] Belknap, *The Invisible Woman*, 133.

[33] Dean Dabney, Richard Hollinger, and Laura Dugan, "Who Actually Steals? A Study of Covertly Observed Shoplifters," *Justice Quarterly*, 2004, 21(4): 693–728.

[34] Carlos Blanco et al., "Prevalence and Correlates of Shoplifting in the United States: Results from the National Epidemiologic Survey on Alcohol and Related Conditions," *American Journal of Psychiatry*, 2008, 165(7): 905–913.

[35] Kirk Astroth and George Haynes, "More Than Cows & Cooking: Newest Research Shows the Impact of 4-H," *Journal of Extension*, 2002, 40.

[36] Joanne Sweeney, "The Impact of Individualism and Collectivism on Shoplifting Attitudes and Behaviors," *The UCI Undergraduate Research Journal*, 2007, 61–68.

[37] Chesney-Lind and Shelden, *Girls, Delinquency, and Juvenile Justice*.

[38] Sweeney, "The Impact of Individualism and Collectivism." Sweeney explains: "Individualism is a multifaceted outlook on life that emphasizes, among other things, independence and self-reliance. In contrast, collectivism focuses on duty and obedience" (62).

[39] Gail Caputo, "Early Life Trauma among Women Shoplifters and Sex Workers," *Journal of Child and Adolescent Trauma*, 2009, 2: 15–27.

[40] Feld, *The Evolution of the Juvenile Court*, 164–165.

[41] Chesney-Lind and Shelden, *Girls, Delinquency, and Juvenile Justice*, chapter 3.

[42] Andrews and Cohn found that in New York parental concerns varied from serious problems (like running away from home) to "sleeping all day" and "refusing to do household chores." Despite the petty nature of some complaints, court personnel routinely failed to make independent determinations about youthful behaviors and typically responded to parental wishes. R. Hale Andrews and Andrew H. Cohn. "Ungovernability: The Unjustifiable Jurisdiction," *Yale Law Journal*, 1974, 83(7): 1383–1409, 1404.

[43] Saar et al., "The Sexual Abuse to Prison Pipeline," 7.

[44] Phyllis A. Katz, "The Development of Female Identity," in Claire B. Kopp (ed.), *Becoming Female: Perspectives on Development* (New York: Plenum, 1979, 3–28.

[45] Barrie Thorne, *Gender Play: Girls and Boys in School*. (New Brunswick, NJ: Rutgers University Press, 1993), 156. Observations of students in our classes, plus conversations with colleagues, reinforce these research findings, showing that such behaviors extend into the university setting.

[46] Ibid.

[47] Peggy Orenstein, *Schoolgirls* (New York: Anchor Books, 2000), 57.

[48] See, for example: Michael Cassano, Carisa Perry-Parrish, and Janice Zeman, "Influence of Gender on Parental Socialization of Children's Sadness Regulation," *Social Development*, 2007, 16(2): 210–231; Campbell Leaper and Carly Kay Friedman, "The Socialization of Gender," in Joan Grusec and Paul Hastings (eds.), *Handbook of Socialization: Theory and*

Research (New York: Guilford Publications, 2007), 561–587; Tara Chaplin, Pamela Cole. and Carolyn Zahn-Waxler, "Parental Socialization of Emotion Expression: Gender Differences and Relations to Child Adjustment," *Emotion*, 2005, 5(1): 80–88.

49 Belknap, *The Invisible Woman*, 178.

50 Feld, *The Evolution of the Juvenile Court*, 166.

51 The literature is nicely summarized in Clifford K. Dorne, *An Introduction to Child Maltreatment in the United States: History, Public Policy and Research*, 3rd ed. (Monsey, NY: Criminal Justice Press, 2002).

52 Saar et al., "The Sexual Abuse to Prison Pipeline."

53 Seena Fazel, Helen Doll, and Niklas Langstrom, "Mental Disorders among Adolescents in Juvenile Detention and Correctional Facilities: A Systematic Review and Metaregression Analysis of 25 Surveys," *Journal of the American Academy of Child & Adolescent Psychiatry*, 2008, 47: 1010–1019.

54 Lisa Pasko, "The Female Juvenile Offender in Hawaii: Understanding Gender Differences in Arrests, Adjudications, and Social Characteristics of Juvenile Offenders," Washington, DC: OJJDP, May 2006, 2.

55 Human Rights Watch, "Custody and Control: Conditions of Confinement in New York's Juvenile Prisons for Girls," New York: Human Rights Watch, 2006.

56 Erica L. Green, "Lost Girls: Young Women Face Harsher Punishment in Maryland's Juvenile Justice System," *The Baltimore Sun*, December 16, 2016.

57 Saar et al., "The Sexual Abuse to Prison Pipeline."

58 Belknap, *The Invisible Woman*, 176.

59 Saar et al., "The Sexual Abuse to Prison Pipeline."

60 Cynthia Godsoe, "Contempt, Status, and the Criminalization of Non-conforming Girls," *Cardoza Law Review*, 2014, 35: 1091–1116.

61 Ibid.

62 Ibid.

63 THORN, "Child Sex Trafficking Is a Cycle of Abuse," Author, n.d., https://www.wearethorn.org/child-trafficking-statistics/

64 Louise Greeley-Copley, "FAUSA Focus on Human Trafficking in the USA," FAUSA.org, March 5, 2015.

65 STARCourt, "Commercially Sexually Exploited Children," January 2014, http://www.courts.ca.gov/documents/LosAngeles-STARCourt-TrainingPresentations_ikc.pdf

66 Saar et al., "The Sexual Abuse to Prison Pipeline," 19.

67 Matt Evans, "Missing Teen's Slaying in KCK Shines Spotlight on 'Throwaway Children,'" KMBC News, August 19, 2015.

68 Child Exploitation and Obscenity Section, "Child Sex Trafficking," Washington, DC: US Department of Justice, July 25, 2017.

69 Kristin Finklea, Adreienne Fernandes-Alcantara, and Alison Siskin, "Sex Trafficking of Children in the United States: Overview and Issues for Congress, Washington, DC: Congressional Research Service, January 28, 2015.

70 Office to Monitor and Combat Tracking in Persons, "Online Sexual Exploitation of Children: An Alarming Trend," Washington, DC: US Department of State, June 2017.

71 Godsoe, "Contempt, Status, and the Criminalization of Non-conforming Girls."

72 Vafa et al., "Beyond the Walls."

73 Camalot Todd, "Combating Underage Sex Trafficking in Las Vegas," *Las Vegas Sun*, February 22, 2018.

74 Jackie Valley, "Sex Trafficking of Children: Las Vegas' Deep, Dark Secret," *Las Vegas Sun*, November 1, 2012.

[75] Todd, "Combating Underage Sex Trafficking in Las Vegas."

[76] Saar et al., "The Sexual Abuse to Prison Pipeline."

[77] Chesney-Lind and Shelden, *Girls, Delinquency, and Juvenile Justice.*

[78] Ibid., 16.

[79] Meda Chesney-Lind and Katherine Irwin, *Beyond Bad Girls: Gender, Violence and Hype* (New York: Routledge, 2008).

[80] Ibid., 3.

[81] Ibid., 4.

[82] Jerry Kurelic, *Our Indispensable Delusions: Why Humans Can't Handle the Truth*, 2005. Unpublished manuscript, on file with Shelden.

[83] Centers for Disease Control and Prevention, *Youth Risk Behavior Surveillance—United States, 2009.* Surveillance Summaries, June 4, 2010, MMWR; 59 (No. SS-5);Centers for Disease Control and Prevention, *Youth Risk Behavior Surveillance—United States, 2001.* Surveillance Summaries, 2002, MMWR; 51 (No. SS-4); Kann et al., "Results from the National School-Based 1991 *Youth Risk Behavior Survey* and Progress Toward Achieving Related Health Objectives for the Nation," *Public Health Rep*, 1993, 108(Suppl. 1): 47–67.

[84] Centers for Disease Control and Prevention, *Youth Risk Behavior Surveillance—United States, 2017.* Atlanta: Author, June 15, 2018, 67(8), tables 16 and 24.

[85] David Huizinga. *Over-Time Changes in Delinquency and Drug Use: The 1970s to the 1990s.* Boulder: University of Colorado, Research Brief, 1997.

[86] Chesney-Lind and Irwin, *Beyond Bad Girls*, 27–28.

[87] Ibid., 31.

[88] Mike Males and Meda Chesney-Lind, "The Myth of Mean Girls," *The New York Times*, April 1, 2010, A23.

[89] Peter Hovmand, David Ford, Ingrid Flom, and Stavroula Kyriakakis, "Victims Arrested for Domestic Violence: Unintended Consequences of Arrest Policies," 2009, Wiley Online Library, 25(3): 161–181.They also report that women constitute about 20% of arrests for domestic violence. See also: Mary Finn and Pamela Bettis, "Punitive Action or Gentle Persuasion: Exploring Police Officers' Justifications for Using Dual Arrest in Domestic Violence Cases," *Violence Against Women*, 2006, 12: 268–287.

[90] Recent statistics have identified the rising use of detention for girls and the disproportionate representation of girls of color in detention. These issues are discussed at length in Chesney-Lind and Shelden, *Girls, Delinquency, and Juvenile Justice*, chapter 7.

[91] Meda Chesney-Lind and Katherine Irwin, "Still the 'Best Place to Conquer Girls': Girls and the Juvenile Justice System," in Randall Shelden and Dan Macallair (eds.), *Juvenile Justice in America: Problems and Prospects.* (Long Grove, IL: Waveland Press, 2008, 115–136).

[92] Darrell Steffensmeier quoted in Feld, *The Evolution of the Juvenile Court,* 165.

[93] Barry Feld, "Violent Girls or Relabeled Status Offenders? An Alternative Interpretation of the Data," *Crime and Delinquency*, 2009, 55(2): 241–265.

[94] Feld, *The Evolution of the Juvenile Court.*

[95] Victoria Frye, Mary Haviland, and Valli Rajah, "Dual Arrest and Other Unintended Consequences of Mandatory Arrest in New York City: A Brief Report," *Journal of Family Violence*, 2007, 22(6): 397–405.

[96] Strom et al., "Policing Juveniles."

[97] Green, "Lost Girls."

[98] Sarah Becker and Jill McCorkel, "The Gender of Criminal Opportunity: The Impact of Male Co-offenders on Women's Crime," *Feminist Criminology*, 2011, 692):79–110.

[99] Patricia Van Voorhis, Emily Wright, Emily Salisbury, and Ashley Bauman, "Existing Risk/Needs Assessment: The Current Status of a Gender-Responsive Supplement," *Criminal Justice and Behavior*, 2010, 37(3): 261–288.

[100] April Louise Beckman, *Female Offending and the Question of Gender Specificity*. (Birmingham, England: University of Birmingham Thesis, 2014.)

[101] Meda Chesney-Lind, *Fighting for Girls: New Perspectives on Gender and Violence*. (Albany: State University of New York, 2010), 110.

[102] Joni Johnston, "Violent Female Offenders: A Girl's Path to a Life of Crime," *Psychology Today*, Jan 29, 2018.

[103] Nicole Spector, "Why Boys Are More Likely To Be Violent—and What We Can Do To Stop It," NBC News, February 28, 2018.

[104] Jennifer Schwartz and Darrell Steffensmeier, "The Nature of Female Offending: Patterns and Explanation," in Ruth Zaplin (ed.), *Female Offenders: Critical Perspectives and Effective Interventions* (Sudbury, MA: Jones and Bartlett, 2008, 43–75).

[105] Hyunzee Jung et al., "Gendered Pathways from Child Abuse to Adult Crime through Internalizing and Externalizing Behaviors in Childhood and Adolescence," *Journal of Interpersonal Violence*, 2017, 32(18): 2724–2750.

[106] Johnston, "Violent Female Offenders."

[107] Luna Munoz Centifanti, Kostas Fanti, Nicholas Thomson, Vasiliki Demetriou, and Xenia Anastassiou-Hadjicharalambous, "Types of Relational Aggression in Girls are Differentiated by Callous-Unemotional Traits, Peers, and Parental Overcontrol," *Behavioral Sciences*, 2015, 5(4): 518–536.

[108] Chesney-Lind and Irwin, *Beyond Bad Girls*, 50.

[109] Ibid., 55–56.

[110] Walter DeKeseredy, *Women, Crime and the Canadian Criminal Justice System*. (Cincinnati: Anderson, 2000), 46.

[111] Gordon Allport, *The Nature of Prejudice* (New York: Bantam Books, 1954).

[112] Chesney-Lind, *Fighting for Girls*.

[113] Ibid., 26–27.

[114] Ibid.

[115] Chesney-Lind and Shelden, *Girls, Delinquency, and Juvenile Justice*.

[116] Carl McCurley and Howard Snyder, "Victims of Violent Juvenile Crime," Washington, DC: OJJDP, July 2004.

[117] Sarah Becker and Jill McCorkel, "The Gender of Criminal Opportunity: The Impact of Male Co-offenders on Women's Crime," *Feminist Criminology*, 2011, 6(2) 79–110.

[118] Jodi Miller, "Up It Up: Gender and the Accomplishment of Street Robbery." *Criminology*, 1998, 36: 37–65.

[119] Chesney-Lind and Irwin, *Beyond Bad Girls*, 149.

PART III
Explaining Delinquency

Chapter 6

Individualistic Theories of Delinquency

Theory is an important part of any academic discipline. Two broad schools of thought have dominated the thinking about crime and criminal justice during the past 200 years: the *classical* and the *positivist*. Whereas the classical perspective has been the dominant theoretical backbone of criminological research, the positivist paradigm has also dominated most theories attempting to explain criminal behavior. Both theoretical perspectives have also provided some of the major assumptions behind the juvenile justice system. Within the positivist tradition, there have been two major categories of theories that, for simplistic purposes, can be described as either *individualistic* (discussed in this chapter) or *sociological approaches* (chapter 7) that focus on the environment. When explaining crime and criminal behavior, one can emphasize two individualistic approaches—the offender's body (biological) or mind (psychological).

THE CLASSICAL SCHOOL

The work of Englishmen Thomas Hobbes (1588–1678) and Jeremy Bentham (1748–1832) and an Italian publicist named Cesare Beccaria (1738–1794 heavily influenced the classical school of thought. It was a time of great social change, the most notable being the ending of the old feudal order and the emergence of the capitalist order. Age of Reason (seventeenth century) and Enlightenment (eighteenth century) thinkers such as John Locke, Montesquieu, Jean-Jacques Rousseau, Claude Helvetius, and Denis Diderot also provided the foundation for the core ideas of the classical school.[1] It is safe to say that just about everyone associated with this school of thought "affirmed their belief in the principles of reason, in the precision of the scientific method, and in the authority of nature."[2]

From the perspective of the classical school, an unwritten *social contract* emerged during the Renaissance (1300–1600), a period during which a vast social movement swept away old customs and institutions and promoted intellectual development. The social contract was an agreement defining the right and duties of individuals for the good of society. As described by philosophers such as Hobbes and Rousseau, the social contract involves a *responsible* and *rational* person apply-ing *reason*. The ability to reason places humans above animals. This perspective also stressed that humans have *free will*. Theoretically, there is no limit to what they can accomplish. So, the principle of rationality suggests that human beings have free will and that their actions are the result of choice.

Furthermore, humans are essentially *hedonistic*. By their very *nature*, humans will choose actions that *maximize pleasure and minimize pain*. More importantly, social contract thinkers claim that the main instrument of the control of human behavior is *fear*, especially fear of *pain*. Fear of punishment and the pains it causes influence humans to make the right choice. This focus on the rewards and pun-ishments associated with choice is a hallmark associated with the classical school of thought where punishment is viewed as the logical means to control behav-ior. Criminals have control over their individual behavior; they choose to commit crimes, and they can be deterred by the threat of punishment. Therefore, society has a right to punish the individual and to transfer this right to the state to insure it will be carried out. Finally, some code of criminal law, or better, some system of punishment is deemed necessary to respond to crime.[3]

Thomas Hobbes, in writing *Leviathan* (1651), describes men as neither good nor bad but creatures of their own volition; individuals who desire certain things and will fight when their desires are in conflict. In the Hobbesian classical tradi-tion, people pursue their self-interests (i.e. personal safety, material gain, reputa-tion) and make enemies without caring if they harm others in the process. Hobbes also suggested that humans are rational enough to realize the self-interested nature of man, including those interests that would lead to crime. To avoid living with conflict, crime, and war, Hobbes theorized that people would enter into a social contract with the government to insure their protection.

Social contract theorists based their theories on some unproven assumptions about human nature, yet their views were taken as given by the new democratic governments in the seventeenth and eighteenth centuries. The concept of a social contract became a convenient ideology for justifying a strong central government to protect the interests of individuals (only the ruling class), private property, and prof-its. The social contract theory justified the buildup of police forces and other formal methods of handling conflicts and disputes. The formal criminal justice system in-cluded a definition of crime as harm to the state and to the people—terms often used interchangeably—individuals would be punished for violating the social contract.

Rousseau wrote that the ultimate source of inequality was man taking a plot of ground and claiming it as his own. This is exactly what happened during the *Enclosure Movements* in England during the sixteenth century when powerful landlords built fences around common ground (land formerly used by all) and claimed it as their own. This resulted in thousands of vagrants (homeless people) flocking to European cities in search of work and eventually being labeled the "dangerous classes."

The Elizabethan Poor Laws passed during the sixteenth century declared two kinds of poor: (1) the *worthy*: those who could be reformed and be useful to society; and (2) the *unworthy*: those who were unreformable, useless, and requiring a sentence to the poorhouse/workhouse (early forms of jails and prisons). The prevailing view that crime was a *voluntary* violation of the social contract became an essential idea in much of the subsequent thinking about crime, especially classical views. Such a view largely ignored the gross inequalities existing at the time. These inequalities included illiteracy, leading to the question of whether the people in the new social orders unanimously agreed on the social contract, since so few could actually read or write.

Cesare Beccaria published *On Crimes and Punishment* in 1764.[4] Beccaria and other liberal thinkers believed that the major governing principle for any legislation should be that it provide the greatest happiness for the greatest numbers. This philosophical doctrine is known as *utilitarianism*—the idea that human behavior is rational, purposeful, and not motivated by outside supernatural forces. Additionally, utilitarianism promotes the idea that punishment is based on its *usefulness* or *utility* or *practicality*. Beccaria concluded his book with this advice.

> In order for punishment not to be, in every instance, an act of violence of one or of many against a private citizen, it must be essentially public, prompt, necessary, the least possible in the given circumstances, proportionate to the crimes, dictated by the laws.[5]

In other words, punishment should not be excessive; *it should fit the crime*. Beccaria also argued that the punishment should closely follow the commission of a crime, making it more just and useful. The major thrust of the classical school, however, is that the purpose of the criminal justice system should be to *prevent* crime through *deterrence* (see below). A potential criminal, according to this line of thinking, will decide not to commit a crime because the punishment will be too costly.

In writing *An Introduction to the Principles of Morals and Legislation* (1780), Jeremy Bentham also suggested that criminal behavior (like all human behavior) is a rational choice, born of man's free will. He argued that, "nature has placed mankind under the governance of two sovereign masters, *pain* and *pleasure*."[6] Bentham's view of the state, then, was to promote happiness of the greatest number, by punishing and rewarding. In order to prevent crime we must make the punishment (i.e., pain) associated with that act *worse* than the pleasure one would receive because they committed the act.

In summary, the classical school assumes that (1) all people by nature are hedonistic and self-serving; they are likely to commit crime to get what they want; (2) in order to live in harmony and avoid strife against each other (as Thomas Hobbes stressed), the people agree to a social contract and give up certain freedoms in order to be protected by a strong central state; (3) punishment is necessary to deter crime, and the state has the prerogative (which has been granted to it by the people) to administer it; (4) punishment should fit the crime and not be used to rehabilitate the offender; (5) punishment, in excess of deterrence, is unjustified; the use of law should be limited, and due process rights should be observed; (6) each individual is responsible for his or her actions; mitigating circumstances are not a consideration.[7] The ideas of Hobbes, Beccaria, and Bentham influenced one of the most popular perspectives on crime and crime control: deterrence.

Deterrence Theory

To deter someone means to discourage, to inhibit, or to prevent from acting.[8] Synonyms include hinder, divert, impede or stop. In large part the theory of deterrence is based on *fear*—fear of consequences/punishment. For example, a young person might be warned by his or her parents "if you stay out past midnight, you'll be grounded" or "if you do that again, we'll take the car away!"

The theory of deterrence as developed via the works of Hobbes, Beccaria, and Bentham relies on three individual components: severity, certainty, and celerity. First, *severity* promotes the idea that the more severe a punishment, the more likely that a rationally calculating individual will refrain from committing the criminal act. To prevent crime, law must emphasize penalties to encourage citizens to obey. Punishment that is too severe is unjust, while punishment that is not severe enough will not deter criminals from committing crimes. Second, *certainty* of punishment means that the state has to make sure that punishment takes place whenever a criminal act is committed. Moreover, the punishment must have *celerity*—the elapsed time between the illegal act and the punishment should be minimal; celerity refers to the swift application of a sanction.[9]

Applying the deterrence idea to the prevention of crime, we have two variations. *General deterrence* sends a message to the general public about what will happen if they break a law. "Clearly announced laws backed up with aggressive enforcement, prosecution, and punishment send a message to the community that crime will not be tolerated. Potential offenders—who learn from the experiences of others—will mostly choose not to offend.[10] The assumption is that the general public will be discouraged from law-breaking behavior by the example of how the state punishes offenders.[11] *Special (or specific) deterrence* is based on experiential learning. The punishment received by an individual offender will deter him or her from future offenses. The offender will think twice before committing another crime. The assumption is that the state must apply enough pain via punishment for a specific individual to offset the potential pleasure that could be derived from future criminal acts.

The conservative belief system that dominates the United States is rooted in the classical school and all of its modern variations. The war on drugs and crime policies such as three-strikes legislation and mandatory sentencing are based on the belief that punishment deters crime and severe punishment deters more crime. We need to look deep into the culture to understand the high degree of punitiveness that characterizes US society.[12] At the heart of this philosophy is a simplistic view of the world—a world divided into rigid categories of good and evil. To become a good and moral person, a child must learn to obey the rules and to respect authority. Proper behavior is taught through the use or threat of punishment. Within such a system, "the exercise of authority is itself moral; that is, it is moral to reward obedience and punish disobedience."[13]

Punishment, according to this philosophy, is the only way to become a self-disciplined and moral person. More importantly, rewarding someone who has not earned it is immoral. This is why conservatives reject welfare, affirmative action, lenient punishments, and the like; they view such actions as rewarding deviance, laziness, etc.[14] According to the conservative view, self-control equates with morality. One must be morally strong to stand up to evil, and one becomes morally strong through a system of rewards and punishments that teaches self-discipline. If one is too self-indulgent, he or she is immoral. Teenage sex, drug use, and other perceived deviant behaviors stem from a lack of self-control. A person, including a child or juvenile, with proper self-discipline should be able to "just say no," and those who do not must be and deserve to be punished.[15]

Does deterrence work? Does putting fear into potential offenders keep them from committing crime? With some exceptions, the answer to this question is no.[16] "The empirical evidence leads to the conclusion that there is a marginal deterrent effect for legal sanctions, but this conclusion must be swallowed with a hefty dose of caution and skepticism."[17] Research on the general deterrent effects of the death penalty have been conducted for at least 60 years, and the results show little if any effect on murder. Collectively, empirical results of death penalty studies have concluded that the death penalty does not deter homicide.[18]

The death penalty, as a potential general deterrent, does not relate to juveniles since the Supreme Court in March 2005 ruled the penalty unconstitutional for anyone who committed a capital crime when under the age of 18.[19] Programs for juveniles, based on theories of deterrence, include boot camps for teenage offenders, "scared straight" programs that frighten kids away from becoming a criminal, and other "get-tough" policies based on both actual and threatened punishments. As for the deterrent effect of punishment in general on juveniles, most research has shown that there is little, if any, impact.

A study of the incarceration rates of juveniles in California during a 30-year period (1970-2000) found that as incarceration rates went down so did the crime rate for juveniles.[20] As will be shown in chapter 12, the number of youths incarcerated has declined since 2001—as has the overall youth crime rate. Another study followed 1,300 serious juvenile offenders for 7 years after their conviction; there was no meaningful reduction in offending or arrests in response to more severe punishment (correctional placement, longer lengths of placement).

> Although the idea that increasing the severity of punishment should serve as a strongly motivating deterrent from crime is intuitive and popular, the majority of deterrence research indicates that the certainty of the punishment, rather than its severity is the primary mechanism through which deterrence works.[21]

The major problem with applying deterrence theories to juveniles is the fact that most of their crimes are done without much planning; therefore, juveniles do not weigh the potential costs versus potential gains of their actions—nor are they generally considered rational. More often than not, their behavior is the result of spur-of-the-moment decisions. Therefore, the threat—both at the individual and general level—of punishment has little impact.[22] Because psychosocial development (impulse control, emotion regulation, future orientation, delayed gratification, resistance to peer influence) lags behind logical reasoning capabilities, it weakens the reasoning abilities of adolescents and results in higher vulnerability for engaging in risk-taking behaviors.[23]

The extent to which offenders apply decision-making processes and the amenability to deterrence varies widely.[24] Some offenders abruptly desist from crimes; others desist over time or shift to less serious crimes. Differences in maturity, cognitive impairment, and prior experiences affect risk-taking behavior. Internalizing the rules of society plus the perceived legitimacy of authority to deal fairly with violators influence decisions to offend. Encouraging a sense of belonging and self-worth has an impact on juveniles and their propensity to commit crimes. The strongest factors in preventing youths from committing crimes include: increasing employment, reducing poverty, increasing family income, and increasing family supervision.[25] These factors are not addressed in the traditional classical school of thought.

During the last half of the twentieth century, several variations to the classical approach appeared. One theory that became popular in the 1970s and 1980s took the position that crime was a product of rational choices and decisions that people made in their daily lives. Various terminologies have been used almost interchangeably, such as *criminal opportunity theory*, *routine activity theory*, and *situational choice model*.[26]

Rational Choice Theory

The classical approach to crime assumed that all humans behave rationally all the time—that they consistently, carefully calculate the pros and cons of their behaviors. Modern versions of the classical approach—including *rational choice theory*—recognize that choices are often not based on pure reason and rationality; rather, they are determined by a host of factors. There are constraints on our choices because of lack of information, differing moral values, the social context of the situation, and other situational factors. In short, not everyone acts logically and rationally all the time, which may be especially true for young offenders. Modern rational choice theory continues to assume that people freely choose to commit crime. Acting out of self interest, their goal is to maximize their pleasure and minimize their pain.

Another modern variation, known as *routine activities theory*, suggests that criminals plan very carefully by selecting specific targets based on vulnerability (e.g., elderly citizens, unguarded premises, lack of police presence) and commit their crimes accordingly. The theory suggests there will always be motivated offenders and an insufficient number of capable guardians.[27] Active criminals weigh the odds of getting caught when they select their targets. The theory implies that increasing guardianship and decreasing the suitability of targets will deter offenders.[28] One of the flaws in this thinking is the assumption that people should stay home to avoid becoming a victim when, in fact, certain groups (especially women and children) are more vulnerable at home.[29]

Studies of gangs have noted that there are many logical reasons why a youth may want to join a gang.[30] Rational choice theory could be used to explain the motivation to join. On the other hand, the threat of punishment (e.g., so-called enhancement statutes that increase the penalty for the commission of a crime if a person is a gang member) could predict against joining a gang. Malcolm Klein used a crackdown on gangs by the Los Angeles Police Department (Operation Hammer) to illustrate the problem of deterrence. This operation resulted in mass arrests of almost 1,500 individuals; about 90% were released with no charges filed. Klein presents two scenarios of the return of the gang member to his neighborhood following his release.

> Does he say to them [his homies], "Oh, gracious, I've been arrested and subjected to deterrence; I'm going to give up my gang affiliation." Or does he say, "Shit man, they're just jivin' us—can't hold us on any charges, and gotta let us go." Without hesitation, the gangbanger will turn the experience to his and the gang's advantage. Far from being deterred from membership or crime, his ties to the groups will be strengthened when the members group together to make light of the whole affair and heap ridicule on the police.[31]

In other words, human behavior is far more complex than the simplistic notion that we all use free will to make choices. Decisions hinge on the availability of alternative choices. A good analogy is that of a menu at a restaurant. Some restaurants have several items to choose from, while others have a limited selection. Likewise, some youths may have a variety of choices (stemming mostly from their environment), while others may have extremely limited selections. A youth growing up in a community with gangs may have the choice of joining or getting attacked. Other youths in other communities may have other options, such as moving with their parents to a new community.[32] A *situational choice model* asserts that criminal behavior is a function of choices and decisions that are made within a surrounding context of various opportunities and constraints.[33]

Each of the variations of the classical school eventually is reduced to the key notion of *free will*, an idea that has been debated for several centuries among philosophers and scientists. It is beyond the scope of this chapter to deal with this issue in any detail, but we will briefly raise several issues. We often ask our students why they are attending our university, rather than Harvard or Stanford. The students usually reply that they wanted to attend our university. When we ask why they did not choose to attend Harvard or Stanford, the students talk about their family backgrounds, the income level of their parents, the communities where they grew up, their grades in high school, etc. We could continue to explore each of these variables. For example, does family income affect high school grades? The bottom line is that almost everything has multiple causes. We can categorize the causes as genetic or environmental—nature v. nurture. To reduce the complexities of human behavior, delinquent or otherwise, to some simple formula of rational choice ignores the continuum of variables that influence every decision.

Our entire legal system is based on deterrence. We have laws, police, and courts that mete out punishments for wrongdoing. All of these systems operate on the assumption that people freely choose to commit crime, and it is up to the legal system to deter such choices by demonstrating that the pain of being caught outweighs any potential pleasure gained by committing a crime. Actions by the legal system—including the probability of apprehension by law enforcement and sentencing offenders to long periods of incarceration—are the foundation of the legal order. This system does not address the possibility that there are multiple causes beyond an individual's control for some crimes.

The Crime Control and Due Process Models

The classical school of thought has generally led to two contrasting models of the criminal justice system, which are roughly the equivalent of two differing political ideologies, namely, conservatism and liberalism. These models have been termed the crime control and due process models.[34]

From the conservative ideology comes the *crime control model*. Essentially, the crime control model is based on the assumption that the fundamental goal of the criminal justice system is the repression of crime through aggressive law enforcement, strict enforcement of the law, and harsh punishments including the death penalty. From this point of view, it is better to emphasize protecting citizens from crime than protecting the civil liberties of citizens. In other words, supporters of this model would prefer that no criminals be set free on technicalities, even at the expense of depriving innocent persons of their constitutional rights. The primary concern is public safety rather than individual rights. The appropriate response to crime is repression through arrest and conviction. Discussion of causes are ignored, dismissed, or reduced to clichés: "if you can't do the time, don't do the crime."[35]

From the liberal ideology comes the *due process model*. While the crime control model may resemble an assembly line, the due process model resembles an obstacle course. The due process model stresses the importance of individual rights and supports the general belief that it is better to let a few criminals go unpunished than to falsely imprison an innocent person. This model is based on the assumption that the criminal justice process is plagued by human error. Discretion by criminal justice personnel—especially the police—should be limited; the accused should receive equitable treatment at each stage of the proceedings and should have adequate legal counsel to safeguard individual rights.

The classical school and its modern derivatives are subject to several major criticisms. As we have noted already, the assumptions that people always act rationally and that all people are hedonists and self-serving can be challenged.

Over 100 years of social science research has demonstrated that this is clearly not the case; humans are much more complex than such a simplistic view.[36]

The classical school of thought assumes that people are equal in the ability to reason and that they are equally likely to commit a crime. In point of fact, people in society (especially when the classical school emerged) are hardly equal by any method of measurement. You can't have equal justice in an unequal society. The French philosopher Anatole France wrote that being a citizen for the poor means "supporting and maintaining the rich in their power and their idleness. At this task they must labor in the face of the majestic equality of the laws, which forbid rich and poor alike to sleep under the bridges, to beg in the streets, and to steal their bread."[37]

This point leads us directly into the third objection, namely that the classical school does little to address the causes of crime. Classical writers particularly avoided any discussion of the relationship between inequality and crime and instead focused on problems associated with the control of crime.[38] Probing the multiple *causes* of crime would lead to an emphasis on *prevention*. The prevention of crime is reduced to finding ways to deter people through the threats of the legal system, usually in the form of more cops on the street and harsher punishments. What is really the topic is the *control* of crime, rather than true prevention. The classical approach is, in essence, administrative criminology—justice consists of specified punishment for a specific behavior regardless of the circumstances.

The problems associated with the classical approach were evident as soon as legislatures attempted to put them in place. The French Code of 1791, for instance, tried to fix an exact amount of penalty for every crime. Social determinants of human behavior were ignored, with courts proceeding as though "punishment and incarceration could be easily measured on some kind of universal calculus."[39] Eventually, lawyers and jurists primarily in Europe revised the classical approach to account for practical problems in the administration of justice (sometimes called the neoclassical school). Reformers attacked the French Code as unjust because of its rigidity and recognized the necessity of looking at factors other than the crime itself. The offender's past record, the degree of incompetence, insanity, and the impact of age on criminal responsibility were considered.[40] There was some recognition that all offenders did not possess the same degree of free will; because of this, imprisonment was not a suitable punishment for every offender.

It is important to note, however, that the basic thrust of the classical school's vision of human beings and the proper response to crime was, for all practical purposes, left unchanged. What began as a general theory of human behavior became a perspective on government crime control policy.[41] The administration of justice continued to be guided, as it still is today, with one overriding principle: that criminal behavior can be shaped, molded, and changed through the *fear of punishment;* all that is needed to prevent people from committing crime is to make the punishment (the *pain* that is associated with it) exceed the *pleasure* (profit from the crime). Almost as soon as Beccaria's proposals were being debated, a rival school of criminology challenged these assumptions.

The Positivist School

In the nineteenth century, a new trend emerged that used observation and measurement to study social phenomena. The *scientific method* represented a sharp break from the past. Rather than relying on religious beliefs, people used objective processes to seek answers to fundamental questions about human beings and the universe around them.[42] After careful study and experiments, Charles Darwin explained the process of natural selection in his book *On the Origin of Species* (published in 1859, which became the foundation for evolutionary biology. The first scientific studies of crime and criminal behavior began at about the same time.

Positivism is a *method of inquiry* that attempts to answer questions through the scientific method. The researcher tests hypotheses with the goal of arriving at facts and laws (e.g., the law of falling bodies, the law of relativity).[43] Therefore, the basic premise of positivism includes measurement (quantification), objectivity (neutrality), and causality (determinism).

The positivist mode of inquiry gained respectability in the social sciences largely through the work of Auguste Comte (1798–1857). "While Comte recognized that positive methods to study society cannot be completely identical to mathematical and physical science methods, he maintained that positive knowledge can be gained by using observation, experiment, comparison, and historical method."[44] Using the scientific approach, human beings are able to discover regularities among social phenomena resulting in the establishment of predictability and control.[45]

Four elements emerged in applying Comte's approach to criminology: a focus on the criminal actor (instead of the criminal act); a deterministic model to assess the actor (usually biological or psychological); the use of scientific method to establish the model; and an emphasis on the rehabilitation of "sick" criminals (instead of the punishment of "rational" actors). Overall, the positivist school of criminology argues that humans do not have free will—their behavior is determined by various biological, psychological, and sociological factors. Thus, responsibility for one's actions is diminished.

The solution to the problem of crime, from this perspective, is to eliminate the various factors thought to be primarily responsible for the occurrence of crime. Such a task might include (but is not limited to) the reduction of poverty; greater emphasis on education, psychiatric, and or psychological testing and treatment; monitoring nutrition and adjusting or supplementing one's diet. The goal of the criminal justice system is to reduce crime by *making the punishment fit the offender* rather than fit the crime, as the classical school proposed. *Rehabilitation* of the offender is accomplished through the wide use of discretion among criminal justice officials and some form of *indeterminate* sentence.

The scientific study of crime began with Adolphe Quetelet (a Belgian astronomer and mathematician) and Andre-Michel Guerry (a French lawyer and statistician) in Europe during the 1830s and 1840s. The first annual national crime statistics were published in France in 1827; Guerry was appointed director of criminal statistics for the French Ministry of Justice. He used maps to indicate crime rates and to display social factors. He found higher rates of property crimes in wealthier regions and concluded that the primary contributing factor was opportunity—there was more to steal.[46] He also found that the areas with the highest levels of education had the highest rates of violent crime.

Quetelet used probability theory to search for the causes of crime and to predict future trends in criminal activity. His quest was to identify law-like regularities in society by applying traditional scientific methods to official crime data for France. He concluded that, "criminal behavior was as much a product of society as of volition."[47] Quetelet found that the frequency of criminal acts decreased as reading and writing proficiency increased. For example, looking at the years 1828 and 1829, he was able to identify over 2,000 crimes against the person committed by people who could not read or write. During the same period, he noted that only 80 similar offenses had been committed by people who had received superior academic instruction. He found that the educated were much less likely to commit property crimes than their uneducated counterparts. He identified 206 property offenses committed by the well educated compared to 6,617 like offenses committed by illiterate offenders during the same time period.

> The knowledgeable class implies more affluence and, consequently, less need to resort to the different varieties of theft which make up a great part of crimes against property; while affluence and knowledge do not succeed as easily in restraining the fire of the passions and sentiments of hate and vengeance.[48]

He also looked at the criminal justice process in France for crimes committed between 1826 and 1829. He found consistencies in the number of defendants who failed to appear in the courts and certain courts that were more likely to impose particular sanctions for particular offenses.

> So, as I have had occasion to repeat several times before, one passes from one year to the other with the sad perspective of seeing the same crimes reproduced in the same order and bring with them the same penalties in the same proportions.[49]

Later, he turned his attention to the propensities for crime and found striking correlations between crime and independent variables such as age, sex, climate, and socioeconomic status of offenders. Young males between the ages of 21 and 25 were found to have the highest propensity for crime, while women had the lowest. When Quetelet compared female and male offenders he discovered that males committed nearly four times as many property offenses as women, and they were involved in over six times the number of violent offenses. He also noted that violent offenses were more likely to occur in the summer months, and property offenses were more commonly committed during the winter. The poor and the unemployed were found to have a higher propensity for crime than members of the working and upper classes. He also discovered that economic changes were related to crime rates, surmising that society itself, through its economic and social attributes, was responsible for crime.

Although recognizing that all people had the capacity to commit crime (an idea that would later be adopted by neo-Freudians), Quetelet argued that the average person rarely transferred that option into action. He eventually turned away from the social influences of criminal behavior and focused on the correlation between crime and morality, suggesting that certain people were more prone to criminal behavior than others (e.g., vagabonds and gypsies).

In 1876 an Italian doctor named Cesare Lombroso published *Criminal Man*.[50] He emphasized the *biological* basis of criminal behavior and argued that criminals had distinctive physical *stigmata* that distinguished them from noncriminals. Some of Lombroso's examples of physical stigmata were: a large jaw, high cheekbones, eye defects, deformed or oddly shaped ears, protruding foreheads, and excessive body hair. This early form of positivism saw criminals as "throwbacks," defective and/ or inferior. Classical deterrents to crime (i.e. sure and certain punishment) did not apply to these "natural-born" criminals.

Lombroso's work (now largely considered sexist) was, at the time, a breakthrough for positivist criminology, which has since branched out in several directions. There are now three major versions of positivist criminology: biological (which began with Lombroso), psychological, and sociological. Biological positivism locates the causes of crime within the individual's physical makeup; psychological positivism suggests the causes are in faulty personality development; sociological positivism stresses social factors within one's environment or surrounding culture and social structure.[51]

The positivist approach suffers from several problems. First, it assumes that pure objectivity is possible—that research is value free without any biases. Max Weber, perhaps fully understanding the potential for intellectual and/or academic arrogance, strongly cautioned researchers to recognize the subjectivity in research.[52] "There is no absolutely 'objective' scientific analysis of culture . . . independent of special and 'one-sided' viewpoints according to which—expressly or tacitly, consciously or un-consciously—they are selected, analyzed and organized for expository purposes."[53] Second, there is an assumption that the scientific method is the *only way* of arriving at the truth. Third, positivism takes for granted the existing social and economic order; that is, it generally accepts the status quo and the official definition of reality. Part of the reality that is accepted includes the standard definitions of crime—the state's def-initions. Because of this, positivists have focused their research almost exclusively on those who violate the criminal law rather than on the law itself. Their efforts focus on controlling and/or changing the lawbreaker rather than the law or the social order.

The positivist method does not assist us in seeking alternatives to the pres-ent social and economic order and the current method of responding to crime.[54] Finally, as David Shichor notes, there is the concern that, "biological theorizing and research can lead to profiling, racial discrimination, selective law enforcement, discriminatory preventive policies, and sentencing based on 'dangerousness.'"[55] Granting individuals the power to identify what types of people commit crimes or to prescribe punishment or treatment can endanger the rights of others.

What is most interesting about both the classical and the positivist's perspectives is that they are primarily concerned with the *control* of crime, rather than the amelioration of the social conditions that create crime, although the positivist approach gives at least some lip service to the causes of crime. Even the positivists, however, have been concerned primarily with the offender and how he or she can be controlled and/or changed, rather than changing the existing social and economic conditions.

BIOLOGICAL THEORIES

The central thesis of this perspective is that criminals are biologically different from noncriminals—and that criminals are *inferior* to noncriminals because of those biological characteristics. As mentioned in the previous section, Cesare Lombroso is the most famous representative of this perspective. Lombroso (1836–1909) and his followers, such as Enrico Ferri (1856–1928) and Rafaele Garofalo (1852–1934), have been referred to as the Italian School. Following this school of thought, criminal anthropologists believed that criminals had certain *atavistic* physical features—that they were biological throwbacks to a more primitive time with inferior and criminal genetic characteristics.

Lombroso's theory included five propositions. The first was that criminals are, at birth, a distinct type of human being. The second was that the criminal type can be recognized by certain stigmata (described above). Lombroso arrived at these and other conclusions as a result of his work performing autopsies on the bodies of hundreds of Italian prisoners who had died in confinement. He never explored whether the physical conditions of these prisoners could have been the *result of their confinement* rather than the *cause* of their criminal behavior—an entirely plausible explanation given the horrible conditions in Italian prisons and jails of the time. Third, exhibiting five or more of these stigmata identifies a person as a criminal. Lombroso also believed that women offenders were more inferior than male criminals.[56] Fourth, these stigmata do not so much cause criminal behavior as they are indicators of someone who is *predisposed* to becoming a criminal. Fifth, because of their genetic inheritance, these individuals will become criminals unless they grow up under extremely favorable conditions.[57]

Although the concept of being able to identify a criminal because of certain physical features has been thoroughly rejected within academic circles, certain variations still exist today.[58] It is interesting to note that people in US society (with the media playing a major contributing role) continue to subscribe to stereotypes of the appearance of criminals.[59] Unfortunately many of these stereotypes center on race (mostly African American and Hispanic) and class (mostly lower or underclass). A large number of studies over the last three decades have attempted to predict criminal behavior; the conclusions have not been uniform.[60]

A variation of Lombroso's views is the general theory of *body types* (sometimes referred to as *physiognomy*), which gained popularity during the first half of the twentieth century.[61] According to this view, humans can be divided into three basic *somatotypes*. These body types correspond to certain *temperaments*. The first type is the *endomorph*, characterized by excessive body weight and having an extroverted personality (the stereotype of the "jolly fat man"). The second type is the *mesomorph*, who is athletically built and muscular. These individuals are described as being active and behaving aggressively. They are believed to be the most likely to be involved in serious criminal activity and to join gangs. The third type is the *ectomorph*, who is thin and delicate with an introverted personality (characterized as loners unlikely to engage in crime).

A closely related view is known as *phrenology*, which was popular for a time in the nineteenth century. According to this view, character and behavior is determined, in part, by the shape of the head. There is an assumption (false) that a person's mental faculties are located in brain "organs" on the surface of the skull that can be detected by visible inspection. The individual most responsible for the popularity of phrenology was Joseph Gall, who wrote the first book on the subject.[62] He believed that, similar to muscles, protrusions on the cranium grew with use and that skilled phrenologists could use touch to interpret psychological qualities revealed by the bumps. According to phronology, "visible curves, indentations, and bumps on the skull were external manifestations of internal mental abilities, talents, and personal traits."[63] Although it has been discredited as a viable explanation of crime, it still remains popular, as witnessed by the existence of a website devoted to the theory.[64]

The belief in the connection between physiological features of the body and human behavior persists.

> A small band of economists has been studying how height, weight and beauty affect the likelihood of committing—or being convicted of—a crime. Looking at records from the 19th, 20th and 21st centuries, they have found evidence that shorter men are 20 to 30 percent more likely to end up in prison than their taller counterparts, and that obesity and physical attractiveness are linked to crime.[65]

Biological determinism (a genetic predisposition to crime) has been discredited. However, economists found that the absence of genetic predispositions does not mean that human biology and physiology have zero effect on criminal activity.[66] Heritable physical attributes, which include attractiveness or obesity, translate into different labor market opportunities. Crime can be viewed, at least partially, as an alternative labor market. Individuals whose physical attributes disadvantage them in the labor force may find crime an attractive alternative.

This area of study is sometimes called anthropometric economics. One study found that students ranked as unattractive (on a 5-point scale) had lower grade point averages and more problems with teachers.[67] They were also more likely to commit crimes (such as burglary or selling drugs) than average or attractive students. Shorter students were less likely to participate in clubs, often resulting in lower self-esteem and underdeveloped social skills that could be useful later in life.

Some biological positivists focus on the functioning of the central nervous system, which is involved in conscious thought and voluntary motor activities.[68] Abnormal brain wave patterns, measured through electroencephalographs (EEGs), have been associated with various abnormal behavioral patterns in individuals. Researchers have also studied neurological impairments, minimal brain dysfunction (MBD), hormonal influences, diet (especially sugar intake), and attention deficit hyperactivity disorder (ADHD). Many studies of biological variables to assess criminality have been conducted without reaching uniform conclusions.

Criminality as an Inherited Trait

Another popular variation of the biological approach claims that criminal behavior is genetically transmitted from one generation to another. Throughout the twentieth century, various researchers reported evidence in support of this view, primarily in the studies of twins. While correlations have been found when studying identical twins raised in different geographical locations, the samples have been much too small to be able to generalize.[69] Criminality in the family is correlated with becoming an offender. For example, having a father with a criminal record is highly correlated with a juvenile's chance of being a delinquent. This, however, could easily be the result of socialization. The juvenile could be modeling his or her behavior on that of the father or the lack of parenting skills could affect socialization—rather than any kind of genetic predisposition.

An additional view holds that certain individuals have an extra Y chromosome, and this genetic abnormality makes them "supermales" who exhibit more aggressive behavior than males who have one X and one Y chromosome.[70] However, this extra Y chromosome is only found in about one male out of every 1,000.[71] Despite the hoopla surrounding this research (including the fact that these individuals are overrepresented in the criminal justice system), the vast majority of male offenders (including most violent offenders) do not have the extra Y chromosome.

Biocriminology has generated a great deal of controversy over the past 150 years. While molecular and behavioral genetics have demonstrated that there may be a genetic basis for many behaviors, other factors play significant roles in shaping human conduct.[72] Biological factors should be viewed as one of multiple factors influencing behavior. They certainly do not influence whether or not certain behaviors will be *defined by society as criminal.* Perhaps more importantly, we should stress the idea that these kinds of theories, based as they are on alleged biological inferiority, have consistently been used to describe people of certain races and ethnic groups (e.g., European immigrants, African Americans). This can be seen more clearly in recent efforts to link genetics with abnormal behavior, especially with regard to poor and/or minority children. Critics of research to find a biological predisposition to crime point to the long, tragic history of using poorly understood genetic science to justify social policies affecting classes of people deemed dangerous or inferior.[73]

A relatively recent variation of biological theories is that of *sociobiology*.[74] This line of thinking attempts to link both genetic and environmental factors with criminality. One line of research tries to link neuropsychological factors with delinquency; another focuses on the relationship between temperament and delinquency.

Terrie Moffitt offered a *developmental theory* identifying two trajectories in the life patterns of delinquent youth.[75] Some children become *life-course persistent offenders* starting with antisocial behavior as early as 3 years of age because of the interaction between neuropsychological deficits and disadvantaged environments.[76] Those on the second trajectory are *adolescence-limited offenders* whose delinquent behavior stems from peer pressure and desists around the age of 18. Prenatal and perinatal (such as low birth weight) complications disrupt the central nervous system leading to temperament difficulties, cognitive deficiencies, and poor verbal test scores. Children in inner cities are more vulnerable to lack of prenatal care, premature births, infant malnutrition, and possible exposure to toxic agents.[77]

Neuropsychological differences disrupt normal development and increase vulnerability to the criminogenic aspects of family adversity/distressed environments.[78] The interaction of biological and physiological characteristics with environmental conditions predicts those most at risk for early onset and persistent offending. The double hazard of neuropsychological deficits and social disadvantage increase the likelihood for deviant behavioral outcomes. Young boys who had both low neuropsychological test scores and adverse home environments had a mean aggression score four times higher than boys with only one of the factors. Although the interaction of neurological deficits and disadvantaged environments is similar for boys and girls, life-course-persistent offenders are rarely female.[79] Gender differences affect exposure to risk factors for life-course persistent antisocial behavior. For females, the causes of delinquency were more social, especially relating to social relationships.[80]

Some research as early as 1993 indicated that carriers of a low-activity variant of the MAOA gene (which regulates dopamine, norepinephrine, and serotonin in the brain) were at risk for impulsive aggression.[81] Moffit researched the role of the MAOA gene in males who had been severely mistreated in childhood and found they were more likely to engage in antisocial behavior than males with the other common form of the gene who had also been mistreated.[82] Moffitt urges a nuanced understanding of the interplay between genes and the environment where, "in the absence of a person's lifestyle and social relationships, the gene was not a powerful force."[83] In another study, researchers found several genetic variations linked to delinquency and to social factors. Genetic variants are conditional and interact with family processes, school processes, and friendship networks.[84]

As with most biological explanations, the percentage of delinquents who exhibit various neuropsychological problems is extremely small. Most of those who engage in delinquent behavior are relatively normal and well-adjusted youth. Moreover, such explanations do not fit well with various social factors to be discussed in the next chapter.[85] More importantly, attempts to link various biological defects with criminality have some very serious negative side effects, with important social and political ramifications often linked to class, race, and gendered assumptions of normality. Troy Duster, a New York University sociologist cautions: "Even in its earliest stages, gene screening has produced a series of new concerns about the nature of state monitoring and information control and the relative vulnerability of differing groups because of the uneven social and political power of those being screened."[86] He cautions that screening at the genetic level misses the complex interactions between genes and environment; the screening presumes a precision that does not exist. Pierre Bordieu concurs: "Today the new genetics brings a 'halo of legitimacy' to racist and reactionary stereotypes. Purely genetic arguments are invoked with increasing frequency to account for behaviors which, like intelligence and the propensity to violence, are the results of complex combinations of factors."[87]

Duke University law professor Nita Farahany is a leading scholar on the ethical, legal, and social implications of biosciences.

> The frequency and application of this evidence [behavioral genetics and neuroscience] in the criminal justice system is increasing, although its use continues to be haphazard, ad hoc, and often ill conceived. Defense attorneys have introduced biological and neurological predisposition evidence to exculpate defendants, to bolster preexisting legal defenses, and to mitigate a defendant's culpability and punishment. Prosecutors have seized up the double-edged potential of this evidence, using it to denigrate the defendant's character and to demonstrate a defendant's likely future dangerousness. And as the science continues to develop, its potential use in criminal investigations, interrogations, and predictions of dangerousness has been widely speculated.[88]

Gene Warfare[89]

A social movement known as *eugenics* developed during the late nineteenth and early twentieth centuries in the context of widespread fear and nativism.[90] In Britain in the late nineteenth century, Francis Galton based his concept of eugenics on what he saw as the logical extension of Darwin's survival of the fittest philosophy applied to humans.[91] Galton attributed invariant character to genes and believed they were stronger than any traits developed through nurture. History professor Edward Larson notes that eugenics built on public acceptance of a competitive struggle for existence as the driving force for social and economic progress. "It only took a slight twist of reasoning to transpose accepting the natural selection of the fit into encouraging the intentional elimination of the unfit.[92]

Social Darwinism looked at human society in terms of natural selection and believed science could engineer progress by attacking problems believed to be hereditary, including moral decadence, crime, venereal disease, tuberculosis, and alcoholism. Eugenicists believed science could solve social problems, and they looked at individuals in terms of their economic worth. If an individual possessed traits that, through propagation, would weaken society, the scientific remedy was sterilization.[93]

Eugenics was, quite literally, an effort to breed better human beings—by encouraging the reproduction of people with "good" genes and discouraging those with "bad" genes. Eugenicists effectively lobbied for social legislation to keep racial and ethnic groups separate, to restrict immigration from southern and eastern Europe, and to sterilize people considered "genetically unfit." Elements of the American eugenics movement were models for the Nazis, whose radical adaptation of eugenics culminated in the Holocaust.[94]

The movement's research was funded in part by some of the wealthiest men in the United States at the time—including Andrew Carnegie, John Rockefeller, and Henry Ford. These and other industrial leaders were feeling threatened by a growing labor movement. Eugenics fit in well with the prevailing ideology that white Protestant Europeans were naturally superior, and just about every other racial stock was inferior. The rich and powerful deserved to rule over the less fit. The unfit—generally, the poor and nonwhite races—could not compete. Just as nature weeds out the unfit, society should do the same. This view justified the vast discrepancies in the distribution of wealth in society—the rich deserve to be rich because of their superiority.

Investigative journalist Edwin Black explored the history of eugenics. He and his team collected documentation

> that clearly chronicled a century of eugenic crusading by America's finest universities, most reputable scientists, most trusted professional and charitable organizations, and most revered corporate foundations. They had collaborated with the Department of Agriculture and numerous state agencies in an attempt to breed a new race of Nordic humans, applying the same principles used to breed cattle and corn. The names define power and prestige in America: the Carnegie Institution, the Rockefeller Foundation, the Harriman railroad fortune, Harvard University, Princeton University, Yale University, Stanford University, the American Medical Association, Margaret Sanger, Oliver Wendell Holmes, Robert Yerkes, Woodrow Wilson, the American Museum of Natural History, the American Genetic Association and a sweeping array of government agencies from the obscure Virginia Bureau of Vital Statistics to the U.S. State Department.[95]

In 1924, Virginia passed a sterilization law based on a template drafted by the Eugenics Education Society with funding from the Carnegie Institute.[96] In 1927, the Supreme Court upheld the constitutionality of Virginia's law in *Buck v. Bell*, enabling the sterilization of a young women falsely labeled feebleminded. The court that decided the case included William Howard Taft (chief justice), Louis Brandeis, and Oliver Wendell Holmes, Jr., who wrote the decision. Adam Cohen, in his book about the case wrote that Holmes "included in it one of the most brutal aphorisms in American jurisprudence."[97]

> Holmes, the Harvard-educated scion of several of Boston's most distinguished families, was scornful of the poorly educated Carrie and her working-class mother. Based on scant information about the two Buck women—and about Carrie's daughter, who was a small child at the time—he famously declared: "Three

generations of imbeciles are enough." Holmes's opinion for an 8–1 majority did not merely uphold Virginia's sterilization law: it delivered a clarion call to Americans to identify those among them who should not be allowed to reproduce—and to sterilize them in large numbers. The nation must sterilize those who "sap the strength of the State," Homes insisted, to "prevent our being swamped with incompetence." In words that could have been torn from the pages of a eugenics tract, he declared: "It is better for all the world, if instead of waiting to execute degenerate offspring for crime, or to let them starve for their imbecility, society can prevent those who are manifestly unfit from continuing their kind."[98]

On the seventy-fifth anniversary of the decision, the governor of Virginia apologized for his states' forcible sterilization of about 8,000 people between 1927 and 1979, more than any state except California.

The *Winston-Salem Journal* published a series of articles exploring the eugenics program in North Carolina under which 7,600 people between 1929 and 1974 were sterilized.[99] One article describes how the Southern Poverty Law Center, a civil rights organization that watches hate groups such as the Ku Klux Klan, began tracking university professors who suggested that a modern version of eugenics should be used to eliminate weak parts of the population.[100]

A study by André Sofair and Lauris Kaldjian of Yale University found that physicians participated in state-authorized sterilization programs to prevent people believed to possess undesirable characteristics from having children.[101] The alliance between the medical profession and the eugenics movement in the United States was not short-lived. The first state eugenics law was passed in Indiana in 1907. Forced sterilization was legal in 18 states, and most left the decision to a third party. The study found that more than 40,000 people classified as insane or feebleminded in 30 states had been sterilized by 1944; by 1963, another 22,000 had been sterilized.

Eugenics was eventually discredited, but the search for scientific solutions to social problems continues to target minorities and the poor. For example, *The Bell Curve* argued that social stratification and economic inequality depend on one criterion: cognitive ability as measured by IQ tests. Using this measure, blacks and other minority races were deemed genetically inferior.[102]

In 1989, the Department of Health and Human Services and the Public Health Service issued a report calling for strategies of intervention in minority homicide and violence. Ironically the report cited factors like poverty, unemployment, homelessness, the availability of guns, and the glorification of violence within U.S. culture as causes of violence. Yet, its recommendation for prevention focused on identifying *individuals* and *modifying their behavior*—mostly, as it turned out, with medication. The report flatly stated that: "Targeting individuals with a predisposition to, but no history of, violence would be considered primary as in programs to screen for violent behavior."[103] This would require screening of high-risk individuals for early intervention. Such screening would target hospital emergency rooms, health centers, jails, and schools where "acting out" behavior could be identified.

The program would conduct research "on the biomedical, molecular, and genetic underpinnings of interpersonal violence, suicidal behavior, and related mental and behavioral disorders."[104]

Soon thereafter, the Department of Justice sponsored the Program on Human Development and Criminal Behavior. The co-directors of this project were Felton Earls (Professor of Child Psychiatry at Harvard Medical School) and Albert Reiss (Professor of Sociology at Yale's Institute for Social and Police Studies). As was the case with eugenics, academics led the search for the genetic source of criminal behavior. The program was designed to identify children who could be potential offenders. Specifically, the research would target nine age groups: infancy, 3, 6, 9, 12, 15, 18, 21, and 24. The key question to be answered would be: "What biological, biomedical, and psychological characteristics, some of them present from the beginning of life, put children at risk for delinquency and criminal behavior?"[105]

A program called the Violence Initiative Project received funding from the National Institute of Mental Health. Led by psychiatrists and funded by some of the largest pharmaceutical companies (Lilly, Pfizer, Upjohn, Hoffman-La Roche, Abbott Laboratories and many more), the program sought genetic explanations for violent crime. The National Institutes of Health provided a $100,000 grant for a conference on genetic factors in crime. The promotional brochure stated: "Genetic and neurobiological research holds out the prospect of identifying individuals who may be predisposed to certain kinds of criminal conduct . . . and of treating some predispositions with drugs and unintrusive therapies.[106]

In her funding proposal to establish a behavioral disorders center at the Department of Child Psychiatry at Columbia University. Gail Wasserman said: "It is proper to focus on blacks and other minorities as they are overrepresented in the courts and not well studied."[107] Wasserman and her colleague Daniel Pine conducted a study at the New York State Psychiatric Institute with 34 healthy, minority boys, ages 6 to 10, each of whom had an older sibling who had been ruled delinquent by family court. These children, who had no criminal record, were deemed high risk (often a code word for poor urban minorities) for future violence. They were given a dose of a dangerous drug called fenfluramine to examine the effects of environmental stressors on serotonin levels. Some scientists correlated low serotonin levels with aggressive behavior. Administering fenfluramine was an attempt to counter presumed genetic predispositions to violence by increasing serotonin levels to prevent future violent acts. Of course, the only "predisposition" was a family member who had been declared delinquent, and none of the children had committed any violent acts. In addition, their serotonin levels were normal.

Dr. Peter Breggin and Ginger Ross Breggin campaigned against the Violence Initiative Project to identify inner-city children with alleged defects that would make them violent as adults.

Children's disorders and disruptive or violent behavior in particular remain growth markets. Powerful vested interests, including giant pharmaceutical firms, stand to profit mightily from proposed applications of biological research. Biomedical researchers and their labs and institutes will not readily fold or refrain and retool for wholly different kinds of research.[108]

The research cited by such biological theories is very selective and ignores the vast research that disproves any linkage between biology (including genetics) and crime, especially violent crime. Numerous studies have shown that those who commit the most heinous acts of violence have suffered, from an early age, incredible humiliation and brutality from their caretakers (often witnessing one violent act after another). Inevitably they begin to engage in similar acts against others; the victim becomes the victimizer.

Biological and genetic approaches to human behavior, including criminality, have a long history. Popular magazines (including *Life, Atlantic Monthly, New Republic, U.S. News and World Report, Time*, and *Newsweek*) ran cover stories in the late 1980s and throughout the 1990s

> emphasizing the contribution of genes to our social behavior. Coat-tailing on major advances in genetic biotechnology, these articles portray genetics as the new "magic bullet" of biomedical science that will solve many of our recurrent social problems. The implication is that these problems are largely a result of the defective biology of individuals or even racial or ethnic groups.[109]

Some see a connection between the modern use of the genome to solve certain problems and the old eugenics programs. With the completion of the human genome map, some worry that blaming criminal behavior on genes will once again surface. Eugenics was one of many attempts to explain criminality and other human problems as individual defects rather than the result of social conditions.

Over the last decade, sociogenomics—the identification of social factors that affect the activity of the genome—has gained prominence. It integrates evolutionary biology, behavioral biology, neuroscience, and genomics; social researchers work with biologists and geneticists as genomics collaborators. Researchers have published studies linking genetics and educational attainment, gang membership, and life satisfaction. "The essential and innate drives that concern social genomics researchers most are the drive for cooperation, for conflict, or the drive to take risks to avoid them.[110]

Sociologist Catherine Bliss recognizes the possible promise of this interdisciplinary science but also points to the dark history of the search for genetic similarities that cause groups of people to behave similarly. Unlike the debates that raged over research linking IQ to race, there has not been a major backlash against sociogenomics. Bliss argues that the public needs to be skeptical of any study that reduces human nature to a sequence of genes. She argues that funding drives sociogenomic science to reproduce genetic determinism. "While researchers do not intend to lift the focus off of the environment, they are forced to recast social phenomena as 'evolutionary phenotypes' so they can make scientific claims."[111]

> New genomic characterizations of behavior may therefore create powerful genetically deterministic stereotypes for already stereotyped youth. This can lead to problems with identity construction and social participation throughout childhood and adolescence, setting off a negative chain reaction in self-image, family relationships, and life planning, and eventually leading to worse life outcomes and possibly even shorter life spans. No one has examined these specific ramifications for disadvantaged youth. . . . None have explored how tests and other forms of genomic knowledge affect youth in the institutional contexts that are programmed to serve them, like schools and juvenile justice centers.[112]

The Adolescent Brain

The Supreme Court ruled in *Roper v. Simmons* in 2005 that the Eighth and Fourteenth Amendments forbid the execution of offenders who commit their crimes when younger than 18. Justice Anthony Kennedy wrote the opinion and stated: "When a juvenile offender commits a heinous crime, the State can exact forfeiture of some of the most basic liberties, but the State cannot extinguish his life and his potential to attain a mature understanding of his own humanity."[113] We will discuss this case in detail in chapter 11. Here we present some background information about the differences between adolescent and adult reasoning that was used by lawyers who opposed the imposition of the death penalty on juveniles. Following similar reasoning that juveniles are less culpable than adults because they are not yet as capable of controlling their behavior, the Supreme Court in *Graham v. Florida* in 2010 ruled that a sentence of life without parole is cruel and unusual punishment for juveniles who commit a crime other than homicide.[114]

The existence of a juvenile court indicates recognition that kids differ from adults. The term *juvenile* means "young, immature, redeemable, subject to change." Temple University psychologist Laurence Steinberg notes that the classic stereotype of adolescence is that it is a time characterized by confusion—but that adults are even more bewildered by adolescence. "Our current approach to raising adolescents reflects a mix of misunderstanding, uncertainty, and contradiction, where we frequently treat them as more mature than they really are, but just as frequently treat them as less so.[115] The same society that tries teenagers who commit serious crimes in adult court does not allow them to see R-rated movies.

Longitudinal neuroimaging studies show that the adolescent brain continues to mature halfway through the third decade of life. The frontal lobes that include neural circuitry for planning and impulse control are among the last areas of the brain to mature.[116] The prefrontal cortex is responsible for prioritizing thoughts, thinking in the abstract, and anticipating consequences. Although teens are capable of thinking logically, the process is more easily derailed by emotions and other distractions than is the case for most adults.

Steinberg notes that the brain's facility for cognitive processes reaches levels equivalent to an adult by mid-adolescence but that the areas of the brain that are active in self-regulation mature much later.[117] That is, adolescents mature intellectually before they mature socially or emotionally. Abilities for impulse control, thinking of future consequences, and resisting peer pressure slowly mature through the twenties. The circumstances surrounding decision making can differ significantly. Adolescents are capable of competent decisions under certain circumstances, but they may be less capable in other situations. Emotions and peer pressure increase impulse behavior and sensation seeking.

By tracing brain development throughout the teenage years, researchers at Harvard Medical School, the National Institute of Mental Health, and UCLA have found physiological changes that may help explain such typical adolescent behaviors as emotional outbursts and reckless behavior (violating rules and taking enormous risks). During most of the teenage years, there is a release of hormones (starting around puberty) that cause areas of the brain (such as the amygdala, which governs emotional responses) to expand, prompting some very irrational and impulsive behavior.[118]

Ronald Dahl at the University of Pittsburgh School of Medicine notes that passions in adolescence can derail the brain's ability to make decisions and control behavior. "The system is precarious, tipping on one side toward strong emotions and drives and on the other side not yet supported well enough by self-control."[119] He urges parents, coaches, teachers and other responsible adults and social systems to support adolescents so that they can take some risks, experiment, and develop some self-control without spiraling into terrible outcomes.

Despite the lack of brain development, every youth does not go out and kill someone. What factors are present in the cases that do result in murder? The background characteristics of people on death row who committed their crimes when under the age of 18 are revealing. Chris Mallett found that about 75% experienced various kinds of family dysfunction, 60% were victims of abuse and/or neglect, 43% had a diagnosed psychiatric disorder, 38% were addicted to drugs, and 38% lived in poverty.[120] Mallett also noted that 30% had experienced six or more distinct areas of childhood trauma with an overall average of four such experiences per offender. Few children and adolescents experience even one of these traumas, yet less than half of the juries who convicted the juveniles heard these mitigating circumstances. In another study, well over half of the 14 death row inmates had either a major neuropsychological disorder or a psychotic disorder, and all but two had IQ scores under 90. Just three had average reading abilities, while three learned to read while on death row.[121]

Although we have acquired a much greater understanding of brain development in general, there are still many unanswered questions. There is no universally accepted normal model of brain functioning. "Each individual is not an exact map, and the difficulties in determining what the range of variations are is really dangerous. The data is incredibly easy to be over-interpreted."[122]

A lot of research in the medical field on the development of the adolescent brain has consistently found a close connection between environmental factors and brain development, especially poverty. For example, researchers at the Washington University School of Medicine in St Louis conducted a longitudinal study of preschool children who participated in neuroimaging at school. They concluded: "The finding that exposure to poverty in early childhood materially impacts brain development at school age further underscores the importance of attention to the well-established deleterious effects of poverty on child development."[123] The researchers also note that: "Children exposed to poverty have poorer cognitive outcomes and school performance, and they are at higher risk for antisocial behaviors and mental disorders."[124] Other researchers have arrived at the same conclusion.[125]

The relationship between poverty, children's development and academic performance is well documented.[126] More specifically, what educators perceive as readiness for school before entry to kindergarten is very critical for future success, and living in poverty hinders such readiness.[127] "School readiness has been shown to be predictive of virtually every educational benchmark (e.g., achievement test scores, grade retention, special education placement, dropout, etc.)."[128] Lack of readiness predicts increased likelihood of truancy, dropping out and delinquency. Children in poor families have both lower cognitive and academic performance and overall behavior problems than children not living in poverty.[129] Nurturing caregiving can protect children from exposure to stressful life events; this important factor may positively influence brain development.[130] Such nurturing cannot be accomplished within a congregate care correctional setting.

Some critics contend that adolescent brain science uses biology to oppress a less powerful group of people—that it is a prejudicial stereotype of young people cloaked in pseudoscience.[131] Others charge that it reduces adolescence to little more than a network of neurons and suggests behavior is dictated by individual biology rather than shaped by external forces. Steinberg argues that we need to be aware of stereotypes but that there has been important progress in the study of brain development in the years between puberty and the early twenties. "Pointing this out is no more biased against teenagers than it is prejudiced against babies to note that infants can't walk as well as preschoolers. Adolescence is not a deficiency, a disease, or a disability, but it is a stage of life when people are less mature than they will be when they are adults."[132]

PSYCHOLOGICAL THEORIES

Psychological theories of criminal behavior focus on the link between such factors as intelligence, personality, various abnormalities of the brain, and crime. As biological views stressed that criminals were biologically inferior, psychological views stress that criminals are psychologically or mentally inferior.

Feeblemindedness and Crime

Early in the twentieth century, psychologist Henry Goddard began to study intelligence and argued that there was a correlation between low intelligence and crime. He administered an IQ test to inmates at the New Jersey Training School for the Feebleminded and found that none of the inmates scored higher than a mental age of 13. Goddard established feeblemindedness as a mental age of 12 or an IQ of 75.[133] Over the years, the link between feeblemindedness and crime has been discredited, primarily because of poor measurement tools and the recognition that the motivation for such tests could be the desire to control (or even eliminate) certain segments of the population. It is easier to justify controlling people if science validates inferior traits. The Nazi genocides, the practice of slavery, and the eugenics movement all claimed to be based on scientific theories and research.[134]

The IQ-crime connection surfaced again in the late 1960s with claims by William Shockley that genetics accounted for lower African American IQ scores and Arthur Jensen finding that all races were equal for associative learning (retention of information) but whites scored higher in conceptual learning (problem solving).[135] Robert Gordon argued that IQ was a better predictor of delinquency than socioeconomic status. As mentioned earlier, Richard Herrnstein and Charles Murray argued in *The Bell Curve* that there is a consistent link between low intelligence and criminality. Recently, the IQ-crime debate has centered on the biogenic origins of intelligence.

The debate continues about exactly what IQ tests measure and the effects of the environment and culture.[136] Some believe the questions on IQ tests do not measure the capacity for learning reliably or that they are culturally biased. Some studies have found that IQ increases an average of 3 points per year of education, which calls into question the impact of heredity.

Psychoanalytic Theories

While Sigmund Freud did not specifically study criminal behavior, a good deal of what he had to say about the human personality and the *id*, *ego*, and *superego* has been used to explain criminality. This view maintains that crime is a symptom of deep-seated mental problems, which in turn stem from defects in one's personality. Causes of criminal behavior include: (1) difficulties or problems during one of the psychosexual stages of development (e.g., anal, phallic, Oedipal); (2) an inability to sublimate (or redirect) sexual and aggressive drives; (3) an inability to successfully resolve the *Oedipal* (in men) or *Electra* (in women) complex, and; (4) an unconscious desire for punishment.[137]

Often researchers claim that specific crimes are associated with certain stages of development. For example, problems during the so-called *phallic* stage (in which a child begins to understand the pleasure associated with his or her sexual organs) can be related to such crimes as sexual assault, rape, or prostitution. Problems during the *oral* stage may result in crimes associated with alcoholism or drug addiction.

Other works related to criminal behavior that can be traced back to Freud's theories include studies of antisocial personalities, sociopaths, and psychopaths—people characterized as having no sense of guilt and no sense of right and wrong.

Personality Trait Theories

Various standardized tests have been devised to study personality traits. The Minnesota Multiphasic Personality Inventory (MMPI) is one of the most frequently used tests to identify personality structure and psychopathology.[138] It consists of 567 true and false questions. Different scales have been used to assess responses to the questions. The psychopathic deviate scale (scale 4) measures conflict, struggle, anger, and respect for society's rules. Psychopathic personalities display an array of maladaptive attributes and behaviors including callousness, lack of remorse, sensation seeking, impulsivity, and lack of responsibility.[139] "Psychopathic individuals are more likely to engage in criminal behavior at a young age and are responsible for a large proportion of violent crime and violent recidivism."[140]

There is an assumption that we can easily distinguish between criminals and noncriminals. As self-report studies have shown, most high school and college students have done something that could have landed them in jail. Yet they are viewed in these kinds of research projects as the nonoffender control group. Research using personality inventories of delinquents versus nondelinquents has not produced strong findings that personality variables are major causes of criminal and delinquent behavior.[141]

Psychologist Robert Hare is an internationally renowned expert on psychopathology. He developed and revised the psychopathy checklist (PCL-R is the current version) that measures 4 factors (interpersonal, affective, lifestyle, and antisocial) that make unique contributions to the prediction of violence, treatment outcome, and institutional behavior.[142] From large and diverse samples of offenders, he identified 4 profiles of factor scores: psychopath, callous-conning offender, sociopath, and general offender. Hare discusses the possibility that psychopathy is an evolutionary adaptive life-strategy rather than a disorder; the cognitive, affective and behavioral processes of psychopaths differ from those of others but do not necessarily reflect deficits. Researchers are sometimes too quick to interpret brain functions in psychopathy as abnormal. Hare cautions that the PCL-R can be abused and misused; he states clearly that he and his colleagues do not consider criminality to be essential to the psychopathology construct. However antisociality is a fundamental component. Hare's research on psychopathology has been applied to the behavior of large corporations. This is highly unusual, for these kinds of traits are normally alleged to be associated with those occupying the lower socioeconomic sectors of society.[143]

Mental Illness and Crime

Occasionally someone commits an outrageous crime that attracts widespread media attention. On February 14, 2018, former student Nikolas Cruz, 19, killed 17 people at Marjory Stoneman Douglas High School in Parkland, Florida.[144]

On October 1, 2017 from his room in the Mandalay Bay Resort and Casino, Stephen Paddock, 64, killed 58 people and injured 500 attending a concert. On November 5, 2017, Devin Patrick Kelley killed 25 and wounded 20 in a church in Sutherland Springs, Texas. On June 12, 2016 Omar Saddiqui Mateen, 29, killed 49 people and injured 50 others inside a gay nightclub. The images from these and other high-profile incidents sear into the national conscience and leave the impression of frequency, but compared to the thousands of serious crimes committed each year, they are aberrations. Yet, many in the media, and some experts, immediately attribute the criminal behavior to mental illness, as if the term had a precise and agreed upon meaning.

Juvenile murderers—a very small minority—have often been described as anxious, depressed, and overly hostile. Many have been labeled as schizophrenic and with other personality disorders.[145] Actually, there is serious question as to whether or not there is a direct link between mental disorders and criminality. The fact is that most people with mental illness are far more likely to withdraw from other people or to harm themselves rather than engage in aggressive behaviors with and against others.

In fact, the recidivism rate of prisoners who had been hospitalized with mental disorders is actually lower than the rate for others. If they do commit more crime, they do so for the same reasons as other offenders—long histories of crime, unemployment, lack of education, drug and alcohol abuse, etc.[146] This is not to say that juveniles do not suffer from some serious mental health problems, for indeed they do. As we will see in chapter 12, many are held in detention centers awaiting placement in mental health centers, even though few have committed serious crimes.

Summary

The theories reviewed in this chapter focus on individual characteristics of offenders, specifically as these theories relate to the human body and the mind. Many questions about biological and psychological theories remain unanswered. One problem is that cross-cultural research has failed to arrive at similar findings. Why is the risk of being a crime victim higher in the United States than in most other countries? Is there a US crime gene or US personality trait?

One problem with these types of theories is what criminologist Elliott Currie has called the "fallacy of autonomy"—the idea that people act totally on their own, without the influence of others, and are totally unaffected by their surrounding culture and social institutions.[147] If some inferior gene or a certain personality trait causes crime, then do the upper-class, white males who commit corporate and white-collar crimes have that gene? Why is it that the crime rates have remained the highest in certain parts of large urban areas, regardless of the kinds of people who live there, over about a 100-year period? Why are crime rates higher in urban than in rural areas? And, why do males have a crime rate about four times higher than the rate of females? For these and other questions, we turn to sociological theories of crime discussed in the next chapter.

Notes

[1] For a simple and easy-to-read overview of the Enlightenment, see Lloyd Spencer and Andrzej Krauze, *Introducing the Enlightenment: A Graphic Guide* (London: Icon Books, 2010). The series of graphic guides written by experts and illustrated by leading graphic artists provide overviews of topics ranging from Freud to Postmodernism and includes books on Marx, Jung, Kant, Sartre, and many others.

[2] Piers Bierne, *Inventing Criminology: Essays on the Rise of "Homo Criminalis"* (Albany: SUNY Press, 1993), 20. This book is an excellent source for the early development of criminology. See also: Ian Taylor, Paul Walton, and Jock Young, *The New Criminology: For a Social Theory of Deviance* (London: Routledge & Kegan Paul, 1973).

[3] Taylor et al., *The New Criminology*, chapter 1.

[4] This classic book is available in many bookstores and libraries. One edition was published by Bobbs-Merrill: Cesare Beccaria, *On Crimes and Punishment* (New York: Bobbs-Merrill, 1963).

[5] Ibid., 99.

[6] Jeremy Bentham, *The Principles of Morals and Legislation* (Amherst, NY: Prometheus Books, 1988), 1.

[7] Taylor et al., *The New Criminology*, 2.

[8] *Merriam-Webster's Collegiate Dictionary*, 11th ed. (Springfield, MA: Merriam-Webster, Incorporated, 2014).

[9] L. Thomas Winfree, Jr., and Howard Abadinsky, *Essentials of Criminological Theory*, 4th ed. (Long Grove, IL: Waveland Press, 2017).

[10] Thomas A. Loughran, Robert Brame, Jeffrey Fagan, Alex R. Piquero, Edward P. Mulvey, and Carol A. Schubert, "Studying Deterrence Among High-risk adolescents." Washington, DC: OJJDP, August 2015.

[11] Mark Stafford and Mark Warr, "A Reconceptualization of General and Specific Deterrence," *Journal of Research in Crime and Delinquency*, 1993, 30(2): 123–135.

[12] Randall G. Shelden, *Our Punitive Society: Race, Class, Gender and Punishment in America* (Long Grove, IL: Waveland Press, 2010). The "get tough" approach will be discussed in more detail in chapter 14.

[13] George Lakoff, *Moral Politics: What Conservatives Know that Liberals Don't* (Chicago: University of Chicago Press, 1996), 67.

[14] Ibid., 68.

[15] Ibid., 74–75.

[16] Daniel S. Nagin and Greg Pogarsky, "Integrating Celerity, Impulsivity and Extralegal Sanctions Theories into a Model of General Deterrence: Theory and Evidence," *Criminology*, 2001, 39: 865–892; Loughran et al., "Studying Deterrence Among High-risk Adolescents."

[17] Raymond Paternoster, "How Much Do We Really Know about Criminal Deterrence?", *Journal of Criminal Law and Criminology*, 2010, 100(3): 765–824, 765.

[18] One of the oldest studies was Robert Dann, "The Deterrent Effect of Capital Punishment," *Friends Social Service Series*, 1935, 29; Thorsten Sellin (ed.), *Capital Punishment* (New York: Harper & Row, 1967); a study in Texas, the state that leads the nation in executions, found that the death penalty had no impact on murder rates: Jon Sorenson, Robert Wrinkle, Victoria Brewer, and James Marquart, "Capital Punishment and Deterrence: Examining the Effect of Executions on Murder in Texas," *Crime and Delinquency*, 1999, 45(4): 481–493; Michael L. Radelet and Traci L. Lacock, "Recent Developments: Do Executions Lower Homicide Rates? The Views of Leading Criminologists," *The Journal of Criminal Law & Criminology*, 2009, 99(2): 489–508; Daniel S. Nagin and

John V. Pepper (eds.), *Deterrence and the Death Penalty* (Washington, DC: The National Academies Press, 2012). For more studies see Death Penalty Information Center, https://deathpenaltyinfo.org/discussion-recent-deterrence-studies

[19] *Roper, Superintendent, Potosi Correctional Center v. Simmons* 543 US 551 (2005).

[20] Mike Males, Daniel Macallair and Megan Corcoran, "Testing Incapacitation Theory; Youth Crime and Incarceration in California," in Randall Shelden and Daniel Macallair (eds.), *Juvenile Justice in America: Problems and Prospects* (Long Grove, IL: Waveland Press, 2008, 63–81).

[21] Loughran et al., "Studying Deterrence Among High-risk Adolescents," 4.

[22] Laurence Steinberg, Elizabeth Cauffman, Jennifer Woolard, Sandra Graham, and Marie Banich, "Are Adolescents Less Mature Than Adults?", *American Psychologist*, 2009, 64(7): 583–594.

[23] Loughran et al., "Studying Deterrence Among High-risk Adolescents," 4.

[24] Ibid.

[25] H. Naci Mocan and Daniel I. Rees, "Economic Conditions, Deterrence and Juvenile Crime: Evidence from Micro Data," *American Law and Economics Review*, 2005, 7(2): 319–349.

[26] Philip J. Cook, "The Demand and Supply of Criminal Opportunities," *Crime and Justice*, 1986, 7: 1–27; Lawrence E. Cohen and Marcus Felson, "Social Change and Crime Rate Trends: A Routine Activity Approach," *American Sociological Review*, 1979, 44(4): 588–608; Werner J. Einstadter and Stuart Henry, *Criminological Theory: An Analysis of Its Underlying Assumptions*, 2nd ed. (Lanham, MD: Rowman & Littlefield, 2006); Derek B. Cornish and Ronald V. Clarke (eds.), *The Reasoning Criminal: Rational Choice Perspectives on Offending* (New York: Routledge, 2017 (originally published 1986 by Springer-Verlag; published 2014 by Transaction Publishers).

[27] Winfree and Abadinsky, *Essentials of Criminological Theory.*

[28] Bruce A. Jacobs, "Deterrence and Deterrability," *Criminology*, 2010, 48(2): 417–441.

[29] Michael G. Maxfield, "Household Composition, Routine Activities, and Victimization: A Comparative Analysis," *Journal of Quantitative Criminology*, 1987, 3(4): 301–20. Steven F. Messner and Kenneth Tardiff, "The Social Ecology of Urban Homicide: An Application of the Routine Activities Approach," *Criminology*, 1985, 23(2): 241–267.

[30] Randall G. Shelden, Sharon K. Tracy, and William B. Brown, *Youth Gangs in American Society*, 4th ed. (Belmont, CA: Cengage, 2013).

[31] Malcolm W. Klein, *The American Street Gang: Its Nature, Prevalence, and Control* (New York: Oxford University Press, 1995), 163.

[32] Robert Agnew, "Determinism, Indeterminism, and Crime: An Empirical Exploration," *Criminology* 33(1): 83–109.

[33] Ronald V. Clarke and Derek B. Cornish (eds.), *Crime Control in Britain: A Review of Policy and Research* (Albany: SUNY Press, 1983).

[34] Herbert L. Packer, *The Limits of the Criminal Sanction* (Palo Alto, CA: Stanford University Press, 1968).

[35] Shelden recalls mention of a theory of crime articulated by a police officer in a criminology class, which he termed the asshole theory of crime because assholes cause crime. Period. End of discussion. No need to seek why some people are assholes and others are not!

[36] For a good discussion of human nature and the fact that humans are not inherently hedonistic see Raymond J. Michalowski, *Order, Law and Crime* (New York: Macmillan, 1985), chapter 3. See also Taylor et al., *The New Criminology*, for a critique of the classical school of thought. For an excellent discussion of deterrence (which is a central feature of the classical school) see Franklin E. Zimring and Gordon J. Hawkins, *Deterrence: The Legal Threat in Crime Control* (Chicago: University of Chicago Press, 1973).

37 Quoted in Randall G. Shelden and Pavel V. Vasiliev, *Controlling the Dangerous Classes: A History of Criminal Justice in America* (Long Grove, IL: Waveland Press, 2018), 54.

38 Taylor et al., *The New Criminology*, 5.

39 Taylor et al., *The New Criminology*, 7.

40 Ibid., 8.

41 David Shichor, "The French-Italian Controversy: A Neglected Historical Topic in Criminological Literacy," *Journal of Criminal Justice Education*, 2010, vol. 21, #3.

42 The scientific method consists, generally, of four main stages: (1) identify a problem by observing something occurring in the universe (e.g., certain groups of people seem to commit more crime than others); (2) derive from this a hypothesis that suggests a possible answer (e.g., those from single-family homes commit more crime than those from two-family homes); (3) test this hypothesis through an experiment or some other kind of observations (e.g., collect data on court cases); and (4) draw conclusions from your research. A possible fifth step is to modify your original hypothesis and derive a competing hypothesis. From this procedure you eventually derive a theory to explain what you discovered. One of the great advantages of this method is that it is *unprejudiced* in that the conclusions are independent of religious persuasion, ideology, or the state of consciousness of the investigator and/or the subject of the investigation. In direct contrast, faith refers to a belief in something that does not rest on any logical proof or material evidence. Faith does not determine whether a scientific theory is adopted or discarded. Knowledge based on faith was the dominant paradigm until the discovery of the scientific method. For an excellent book on the subject see, Thomas S. Kuhn, *The Structure of Scientific Revolutions*, 4th ed. (Chicago: University of Chicago Press, 2012).

43 The word *empirical* is defined in the Random House Dictionary as "derived from or guided by experience or experiment"; a related term is empiricism, which means "the doctrine that all knowledge is derived from sense experience." A *hypothesis* is a key ingredient of the *scientific method*, and it can be defined as a proposition about the expected or anticipated relationship between two or more variables, usually expressed as the dependent and independent variable. When using the scientific method you use a hypothesis in order to find out what causes something. It is sort of like testing a hunch you have about the cause of something, such as trying to determine why your car is not starting. In this case, the "car not starting" is the dependent variable in that it is dependent on some other variable—the independent variable. You might hypothesize that your car not starting is caused by being out of gas.

44 Shichor, "The French-Italian Controversy," 214.

45 Tom Bottomore, Lawrence Harris, V. G. Kiernan, and Ralph Miliband (eds.), 2nd ed., *A Dictionary of Marxist Thought* (Cambridge, MA: Harvard University Press, 1991).

46 Thomas J. Bernard, Jeffrey B. Snipes, and Alexander L. Gerould, *Vold's Theoretical Criminology*, 7th ed. (New York: Oxford University Press, 2015).

47 Quoted in Shichor, "The French-Italian Controversy," 215.

48 Adolphe Quetelet, *Research on the Propensity for Crime at Different Ages* (Cincinnati: Anderson, 1984 [originally published in 1831]), 69.

49 Ibid.

50 Cesare Lombroso, *Criminal Man* (Montclair, NJ: Patterson-Smith, 1911 [originally published in 1876]).

51 Francis T. Cullen and Karen E. Gilbert, *Reaffirming Rehabilitation*, 2nd ed. (Cincinnati: Anderson, 2013), 33.

52 Max Weber (1864–1920) was one of the pioneers in the early years of sociology. He is most famous for his book *The Protestant Ethic and the Spirit of Capitalism*, originally

published in 1904, translated by Talcott Parsons, and published by Scribner's in 1958. A good summary of his works is found in Max Weber, *From Max Weber: Essays in Sociology* (trans. H. H. Gerth and C. W. Mills) (New York: Oxford University Press, 1946).

[53] Max Weber, "'Objectivity' in Social Science and Social Policy," in Edward A. Shils and Henry A. Finch (eds.), *Max Weber on the Methodology of the Social Sciences* (Glencoe, IL: The Free Press, 1949) 72.

[54] Richard Quinney and John Wildeman, *The Problem of Crime: A Peace and Social Justice Perspective*, 3rd ed. (Mountain View, CA: Mayfield, 1991) 32–33.

[55] Shichor, "The French-Italian Controversy," 224.

[56] Cesare Lombroso and William Ferrero, *The Female Offender* (New York: D. Appleton, 1895).

[57] Robert M. Bohm and Brenda L. Vogel, *A Primer on Crime and Delinquency Theory*, 3rd ed. (Belmont, CA: Wadsworth, 2011) 35.

[58] Bernard et al., *Vold's Theoretical Criminology.*

[59] The television program *Cops* on Fox is a good representation of many stereotypes. For instance, nearly everyone they arrest is a black man who is shirtless; he is invariably shown spread-eagled on the ground or against the hood of a police car.

[60] These studies are too numerous to mention here. A good overall review is found in Terrie E. Moffitt, "The Neuropsychology of Juvenile Delinquency: A Critical Review," *Crime and Justice*, 1990, 12: 99–169; David Rowe, *Biology and Crime* (Los Angeles: Roxbury Press, 2001).

[61] Sheldon Glueck and Eleanor Glueck, *Physique and Delinquency* (New York: Harper and Row, 1956); Earnest A. Hooton, *The American Criminal: An Anthropological Study* (Cambridge, MA: Harvard University Press, 1939); William H. Sheldon, *Varieties of Delinquent Youth* (New York: Harper, 1949). Each of these authors was on the faculty of Harvard University at one time, lending credibility to the views expressed.

[62] Gall lived between 1758 and 1828. His most important book was called *On the Functions of the Brain and of Each of Its Parts*, which was published after his death in 1835 (Boston: Marsh, Capen & Lyon). For more about Gall and Phrenology see the following website: http://www.whonamedit.com/doctor.cfm/1018.html

[63] Martin S. Lindauer, *The Expressiveness of Perceptual Experience: Physiognomy Reconsidered* (Philadelphia: John Benjamins Publishing Company, 2013), 25.

[64] Phrenology, http://www.phrenology.org/

[65] Patricia Cohen, "For Crime, Is Anatomy Destiny?", *New York Times*, May 11, 2010, C1.

[66] Howard Bodenhorn, Carolyn Moehling, and Gregory N. Price, "Short Criminals: Stature and Crime in Early America," National Bureau of Economic Research, April 2010, working paper 15945.

[67] Naci Mocan and Erdal Tekin, "Ugly Criminals," National Bureau of Economic Research, January 2006, working paper 12019.

[68] See, for example, Adrian Raine, *The Anatomy of Violence: The Biological Roots of Crime* (New York: First Vintage Books, 2014).

[69] English scientist Cyril Burt was discredited for using fabricated data in his studies of twins to prove that certain races are born with low intelligence, leading to the propensity to commit crime. Despite research debunking such theories, supporters continue to search for a crime gene, arguing that the environment is only indirectly responsible by triggering behaviors to which one is genetically predisposed.

[70] Winfree and Abadinsky, *Essentials of Criminological Theory.*

[71] Eric Bank, "Extra Y Chromosome in Men," *Sciencing*, April 25, 2017.

[72] Winfree and Abadinsky, *Essentials of Criminological Theory.*

73 Trine Tsouderos, "Genes, Crime and Ties that Bind," *Chicago Tribune*, February 26, 2010, 4.

74 The most popular statement of this view is Edward O. Wilson, *Sociobiology* (Cambridge, MA: Harvard University Press, 1975).

75 Terrie E. Moffitt, "Adolescent-Limited and Life-Course-Persistent Antisocial Behavior: A Developmental Taxonomy," *Psychological Review*, 1993, 100(4): 674–701.

76 Stephen G. Tibbetts, *Criminological Theory: The Essentials*, 3rd ed. (Thousand Oaks: Sage Publications, 2019).

77 Stephen G. Tibetts and Alex R. Piquero, "The Influence of Gender, Low Birth Weight, and Disadvantaged Environment in Predicting Early Onset Offending: A Test of Moffitt's Interactional Hypothesis," *Criminology*, 1999, 37(4): 843–878.

78 Terrie E. Moffitt, Donald R. Lynam, and Phil A. Silva, "Neuropsychological Tests Predicting Persistent Male Delinquency," *Criminology*, 1994, 32(2): 277–300.

79 Chris L. Gibson, Alex R. Piquero, and Stephen Tibbetts, "The Contribution of Family Adversity to Criminal Behavior," *International Journal of Offender Therapy and Comparative Criminology*, 2001, 45(5): 574–592.

80 Terri E. Moffitt, Avshalom Caspi, Michael Rutter, and Phil A. Silva, *Sex Differences in Antisocial Behaviour: Conduct Disorder, Delinquency, and Violence in the Dunedin Longitudinal Study* (Cambridge, England: Cambridge University Press, 1993).

81 Rose McDermott, Dustin Tingley, Jonathan Cowden, Giovanni Frazzetto, and Dominic Johnson, "Monoamine Oxidase-A Gene (MAOA) Predicts Behavioral Aggression Following Provocation," *Proceedings of the National Academy of Sciences*, 106(7): 2118–2123.

82 Avshalom Caspi, Joseph McClay, Terrie E. Moffitt, et al., "Role of Genotype in the Cycle of Violence in Maltreated Children," *Science*, 2002, 297(2): 851–854.

83 Tsouderos, "Genes, Crime and Ties that Bind," 4.

84 Guang Guo, Michael E. Roettger, and Tianji Cai, "The Integration of Genetic Propensities into Social Control Models of Delinquency and Violence among Male Youths," *American Sociological Review*, 2008, 73(4): 543–568.

85 These approaches have received their share of criticisms over the years. See especially James W. Messerschmidt, *Masculinities and Crime: Critique and Reconceptualization of Theory* (New York: Rowan and Littlefield, 1993).

86 Troy Duster, *Backdoor to Eugenics*, 2nd ed. (New York: Routledge, 2003), 39.

87 Pierre Bourdieu, "Foreword," in Ibid., vii.

88 Nita Farahany (ed.), *The Impact of Behavioral Sciences on Criminal Law* (New York: Oxford University Press, 2009), xi.

89 This section is taken from Randall G. Shelden, "Gene Warfare," *Social Justice*, 2000, 27: 162–67.

90 Nicole Hahn Rafter (ed.), *White Trash: The Eugenic Family Studies, 1899–1919* (Boston: Northeastern University Press, 1988).

91 Edward J. Larson, "A Race to Nowhere," *The American Interest*, 2017, 13(1), https://www.the-american-interest.com/2017/06/30/a-race-to-nowhere/

92 Ibid.

93 André N. Sofair and Lauris C. Kaldjian, "Eugenic Sterilization and a Qualified Nazi Analogy: The United States and Germany, 1930–1945," *Annals of Internal Medicine*, 2000, 132(4): 312–319.

94 Cold Spring Harbor Laboratory, "Image Archive on the American Eugenics Movement," http://www.eugenicsarchive.org/eugenics/list3.pl; see also James Q. Whitman, *Hitler's American Model: The United States and the Making of Nazi Race Law* (Princeton, NJ: Princeton University Press, 2017).

95　Edwin Black, *War against the Weak: Eugenics and America's Campaign to Create a Master Race*, expanded ed. (Washington, DC: Dialog Press, 2012).

96　Larson, "A Race to Nowhere."

97　Adam Cohen, *Imbeciles: The Supreme Court, American Eugenics, and the Sterilization of Carrie Buck* (New York: Penguin Press, 2016), 2.

98　Ibid.

99　*Winston-Salem Journal*, "Against Their Will: North Carolina's Sterilization Program," https://www.journalnow.com/specialreports/againsttheirwill/; the series of articles were published in book form. Kevin Begos, Danielle Deaver, John Railey, and Scott Sexton, *Against Their Will: North Carolina's Sterilization Program and the Campaign for Reparations* (Apalachicola, FL: Gray Oak Books, 2012, 2011, 2004, 2002, 2002).

100　Danielle Deaver, "Stirring Up Academia," *Winston-Salem Journal*, December 9, 2002.

101　Sofair and Kaldjian, "Eugenic Sterilization and a Qualified Nazi Analogy."

102　Space does not permit a complete examination of this controversy. It began in 1969 with the publication of Arthur Jensen's "How Much Can We Boost IQ and Scholastic Achievement?", *Harvard Educational Review*, 1969, 39: 1–123). Richard Hernstein then wrote an article simply called "I.Q.," *The Atlantic*, September 1971, 43–64. James Q. Wilson and Hernstein wrote *Crime and Human Nature: The Definitive Study of the Causes of Crime* in 1985 (New York: Simon and Schuster). This book resurrected some of the oldest biological theories from the nineteenth century and dressed them up in twentieth-century jargon. Note the subtitle, revealing a bit of elitism. The most controversial publication was by Hernstein and Charles Murray (1994). *The Bell Curve: Intelligence and Class Structure in American Life* (New York: The Free Press). Critiques include: Stephen Jay Gould, "Curveball," *The New Yorker*, November 28, 1994, 139–49; E. Herman, "The New Onslaught," *Z Magazine*, December, 1994, 24–26, Robert M. Hanser, H. F. Taylor, and Troy Duster, "Symposium: the Bell Curve," *Contemporary Sociology*, 1995, 24(2): 149–161. Rafter, *White Trash*, is an excellent source for information about the eugenics movement.

103　Cited in Peter R. Bregin and Ginger R. Bregin, *The War Against Children of Color: Psychiatry Targets Inner City Youth* (Monroe, ME: Common Courage Press, 1998), 15.

104　Ibid., 16.

105　Ibid., 38.

106　Cited in Mitchel Cohen, "Beware the Violence Initiative Project," *Z Magazine*, April 2000, https://zcomm.org/zmagazine/beware-the-violence-initiative-project-by-mitchel-cohen/

107　Ibid. Fenfluramine was the main ingredient in the diet drug "fen phen." Shortly after this experiment was completed in late 1997, the drug was withdrawn from the market because it could cause potentially fatal heart valve impairments in many patients and brain cell death in others.

108　Bregin and Bregin, *The War Against Children of Color*, 40. The violence targeted is that committed by the poor and racial minorities. No one suggested testing the children of members of Congress or the children of Fortune 500 CEOs, despite the fact that some of those individuals have been responsible for a great deal of death and destruction around the world (as any cursory review of white collar and corporate crime research will reveal). But no one has put that type of violence under the microscope to determine genetic influences. Rather, the poor and racial minorities pose the same threat to those in power that European immigrants posed in the late nineteenth and early twentieth centuries.

109　Garland Allen, "Is a New Eugenics Afoot?", *Science*, 2001, 294: 59–61, 59.

110　Catherine Bliss, *Social by Nature: The Promise and Peril of Sociogenomics* (Palo Alto, CA: Stanford University Press, 2018), 63.

111　Ibid., 61.

112 Ibid., 7.

113 *Roper v. Simmons.*

114 N. Koppel, "Judges Forced to Revisit Juveniles' Life Sentences," *The Wall Street Journal*, A3.

115 Laurence Steinberg, *Age of Opportunity: Lessons from the New Science of Adolescence* (Boston: Mariner Books, 2015), 1.

116 Sara Johnson, Robert Blum, and Jay Giedd, "Adolescent Maturity and the Brain: The Promise and Pitfalls of Neuroscience Research in Adolescent Health Policy," *Journal of Adolescent Health*, 2009, 45(3): 216–221.

117 Laurence Steinberg, "Should the Science of Adolescent Brain Development Inform Public Policy?", *Issues in Science and Technology*, 2012, XXVII(3).

118 Lee Bowman, "New Research Shows Stark Differences in Teen Brains," *Scripps Howard News Service*, May 11, 2004, http://www.deathpenaltyinfo.org/new-research-shows-stark-differences-teen-brains

119 Cited in Kotulak, R. (2006, April 24). "Teens Driven to Distraction," *Chicago Tribune*, pp. 1, 21.

120 Christopher A. Mallett, "Socio-Historical Analysis of Juvenile Offenders on Death Row," *Criminal Law Bulletin*, 2003, 39(4): 455–468.

121 D. O. Lewis, J. H. Pincus, B. Bard, E. Richardson, L. S. Prichep, M. Feldman, and C. Yeager, "Neuropsychiatric, Psychoeducational, and Family Characteristics of 14 Juveniles Condemned to Death in the United States," *American Journal of Psychiatry*, 1988, 145(5): 584–589.

122 Sonia Miller, New York attorney cited in Bowman, "New Research."

123 Joan Luby, et al., "The Effects of Poverty on Childhood Brain Development: The Mediating Effect of Caregiving and Stressful Life Events," *Journal of the American Medical Association Pediatrics*, 2013, 167(12): 1135–1142, 1135.

124 Ibid., 1136.

125 Hirokazu Yoshikawa, J. Lawrence Aber and William R. Beardslee, "The Effects of Poverty on the Mental, Emotional, and Behavioral Health of Children and Youth: Implications for Prevention," *American Psychologist*, 2012, 67(4): 272–284.

126 Maureen M. Black, Christine Reiner Hess, and Julie Berenson-Howard, "Toddlers from Low-Income Families Have Below Normal Mental, Motor, and Behavior Scores on the Revised Bayley Scales," *Journal of Applied Developmental Psychology*, 2000, 21(6): 655–666; Doris R. Entwisle, Karl L. Alexander, and Linda Steffel Olson, "First Grade and Educational Attainment by Age 22: A New Story," *American Journal of Sociology*, 2005, 110: 1458–1502.

127 Edward Zigler, Walter S. Gilliam, and Stephanie M. Jones, *A Vision for Universal Preschool Education* (New York: Cambridge University Press, 2006).

128 Ibid., 21.

129 National Institute of Child Health and Human Development Early Child Care Research Network, "Duration and Developmental Timing of Poverty and Children's Cognitive and Social Development from Birth through Third Grade," *Child Development*, 2005, 76: 795–810.

130 Luby et al., "The Effects of Poverty on Childhood Brain Development," 1141.

131 Steinberg, *Age of Opportunity.*

132 Ibid., 5.

133 Winfree and Abadinsky, *Essentials of Criminological Theory.*

134 Peter Kraska, "The Sophistication of Hans Jurgen Eysenck: An Analysis and Critique of Contemporary Biological Criminology," *Criminal Justice Research Bulletin*, 1989, (4)5: 1–7.

[135] Winfree and Abadinsky, *Essentials of Criminological Theory.*

[136] Ibid.

[137] Bohm and Vogel, *A Primer on Crime and Delinquency Theory*, 55

[138] Michael W. Adamowicz, "Psychological Testing: Minnesota Multiphasic Personality Inventory," MentalHelp.net, August 31, 2016.

[139] Brandee E. Marion, Martin Sellborn, Randall T. Salekin, Joseph A. Toomey, L. Thomas Kucharski, and Scott Duncan, "An Examination of the Association between Psychopathy and Dissimulation Using the MMPI-2-RF Validity Scales," *Law and Human Behavior*, 2013, 37(4): 219–230.

[140] Ibid., 219.

[141] Ronald Akers, Christine Sellers, and Wesley G. Jennings, *Criminological Theories*, 7th ed. (New York: Oxford University Press, 2016).

[142] Robert D. Hare, "Psychopathy, the PCL-R, and Criminal Justice: Some New Findings and Current Issues," *Canadian Psychology*, 2016, 57(1): 21–34.

[143] The adaptation to the behavior of corporations is found in Joel Bakan, *The Corporation: The Pathological Pursuit of Profit and Power* (New York: Free Press, 2004).

[144] CNN Library, "Deadliest Mass Shootings in Modern US History," May 23, 2018.

[145] James M. Sorrells, "Kids Who Kill," *Crime and Delinquency*, 1977, 23(3): 312–320; Ellen Hochstedler Steury, "Criminal Defendants with Psychiatric Impairment: Prevalence, Probabilities and Rates," *Journal of Criminal Law and Criminology*, 1992, 84(2): 352–376.

[146] Robin S. Engel and Eric Silver, "Policing Mentally Disordered Suspects: A Reexamination of the Criminalization Hypothesis," *Criminology*, 2001, 39(2): 225–252; James A. Bonta, Moira Law, and R. Karl Hanson, "The Prediction of Criminal and Violent Recidivism among Mentally Disordered Offenders: A Meta-Analysis," *Psychological Bulletin*, 1998, 123(2): 123–142.

[147] Elliott Currie, *Confronting Crime: An American Challenge* (New York: Pantheon, 1985), 185.

Chapter 7

Sociological Theories of Delinquency

Chapter 6 looked at theories that sought to find measurable characteristics of offenders that set them apart from those who do not commit delinquent behavior. The focus was on biological and psychological processes that affect behavior. The biological theories looked at genetics to determine if people are born with delinquent tendencies. The psychological theories looked at mental problems that affect behavior and learning. Learning, however, is affected by more than just personality traits and mental ability. In addition to biological and psychological theories of delinquency, there are many major social theories about the causes of delinquency.

In order to evaluate theories about delinquency, we also need to look at the various sociological factors that contribute to delinquent behavior. These include social relations, community and cultural conditions, economic circumstances, and gender and racial disparity, as well as experiences with poverty and violence. All of these social factors play a role in the way juveniles' experience their lives—including the expectations they have about these experiences. Sociologists focus on the influence of society, culture, and groups on how we behave. The probable influences of social conditions are the point of focus rather than potential causal factors of individual traits.

This chapter presents a general overview of seven sociological perspectives: (1) social disorganization/social ecology, (2) strain/anomie, (3) cultural deviance, (4) control/social bond, (5) social learning, (6) labeling, and (7) critical/Marxist. Box 7-1 provides a summary of each of these perspectives.

SOCIAL DISORGANIZATION/SOCIAL ECOLOGY THEORY

Social disorganization theory has been one of the most popular and enduring sociological theories of crime and delinquency. One variation, the *social ecology* perspective, focuses on the spatial or geographical distribution of crime and delinquency.[1] Modern versions of this perspective began with the work of sociologists at the University of Chicago during the first three decades of the twentieth century. The original idea behind the spatial distribution of crime can be traced to two scientists introduced in chapter 6: Adolphe Quetelet and Michel Guerry. Their work

Box 7-1 Sociological Theories of Delinquency

Theory	Major Points/Key Factors
1. Social disorganization	Crime stems from certain community or neighborhood characteristics, such as poverty, dilapidated housing, high density, high mobility, and high rates of unemployment. *Concentric zone theory* is a variation that argues that crime increases toward the inner-city area.
2. Strain/anomie	Cultural norms of success emphasize such goals as money, status, and power, but the means to obtain success are not equally distributed. As a result of blocked opportunities, many among the disadvantaged resort to illegal means, which are more readily available.
3. Cultural deviance	Certain subcultures, including a gang subculture, exist within poor communities, which contain values, attitudes, beliefs, and norms that are often counter to the prevailing middle-class culture. An important feature of this subculture is the absence of fathers, thus resulting in female-headed households, which tend to be poorer. Youths are exposed to this subculture early in life and become *embedded* in it.
4. Control/social bond	Delinquency persists when a youth's bonds or ties to society are weak or broken, especially bonds with family, school, and other institutions. When this occurs, a youth is likely to seek bonds with other groups, including gangs, to meet his/her needs.
5. Learning	Delinquency is *learned* through association with others, especially gang members, over a period of time. This involves a *process* that includes the acquisition of attitudes and values, the instigation of a criminal act based on certain stimuli, and the maintenance or perpetuation of such behavior over time.
6. Labeling	Definitions of delinquency and crime stem from differences in power and status in the larger society. Those without power are the most likely to have their behaviors labeled as delinquent. Delinquency may be generated—and perpetuated—through negative labeling by significant others and by the judicial system. One may associate with others similarly labeled, such as gangs.
7. Critical/Marxist	Gangs are inevitable products of social (and racial) inequality brought about by capitalism; power is unequally distributed, and those without power often resort to criminal means to survive.

collecting and analyzing crime data and matching them with various socioeconomic variables (such as poverty, infant mortality, unemployment, etc.) became known as the Cartographic School of Criminology. It involved plotting the location of criminals and various social indicators on a city map with colored dots. Police departments do the same today when, for example, they plot the sites of certain crimes, such as the locations of a series of muggings, auto thefts, etc.[2]

This idea of mapmaking and the more general notion that crime is *spatially* distributed within a geographical area became the hallmarks of the *Chicago School* of sociology. Researchers noticed that crime and delinquency rates varied by areas of the city (just as Guerry and Quetelet had done almost a century earlier). They found the highest rates of crime and delinquency in areas that exhibited high rates of many other social problems, such as single-parent families, unemployment, multiple-family dwellings, welfare cases, and low levels of education.

One of the key ideas of the social ecology of crime is that high rates of crime and other problems persist within the same neighborhoods over long periods of time *regardless of who lives there*. As several gang researchers have noted, some gangs have existed for as long as 50 or more years in certain neighborhoods, often spanning three generations. East Los Angeles is a prime example of this phenomenon.[3] Thus there must be something about the *places* themselves, perhaps something about the *neighborhoods*, rather than the people living there that produces and perpetuates high crime rates.[4]

The social ecology perspective borrows concepts from the field of plant biology, studying human life using ideas derived from studies of the interdependence of plant and animal life. From this perspective, people are seen as being in a relationship to one another and to their physical environment. Further, just as plant and animal species tend to *colonize* their environment, humans colonize their geographical space.[5] The Chicago sociologists "argued that the urban topography of industry, railroads, crowded tenements, and vice districts influenced a person's alienation, detachment, and amorality."[6] In contrast, the suburbs away from the city's core had boulevards, spacious parks, and manicured lawns that reflected community stability and organization.

Robert Park and Ernest Burgess of the Chicago School developed the *concentric zone* model of city life to explain such patterns.[7] They identified five specific zones emanating outward from the central part of the city: (1) central business district—the Loop; (2) zone in transition; (3) zone of workingmen's homes; (4) residential zone; and (5) commuter zone.

According to this theory, growth is generated (from mostly political and economic forces) outward from the central business district. Expansion occurs in concentric waves, or circles. The expansion and movement affects neighborhood development and patterns of social problems. Studies of the rates of crime and delinquency, especially by sociologists Henry Shaw and David McKay, demonstrated that over an extended period of time, the highest rates were found within the first three zones *no matter who lived there*. These high rates were strongly correlated with social problems such as mental illness, unemployment, poverty, infant mortality, and many others.[8]

For these early social ecologists, a breakdown of institutional and community-based social controls occurred within these first three zones, thus leading to higher crime rates. This breakdown was said to be the result of three general factors: industrialization, urbanization, and immigration. People living within these areas often lack a sense of community because the local institutions (e.g., schools, families, and churches) are not strong enough to provide nurturing and guidance for the area's children. It is important to note the political and economic forces at work here. The concentration of human and social problems within these zones is not the inevitable, natural result of some abstract laws of nature. Rather, they are the result of the actions of some of the most powerful groups in a city (urban planners, politicians, wealthy business leaders, etc.).

A subculture of criminal values and traditions develops in such environments and replaces conventional values and traditions. These criminal values and traditions persist over time regardless of who lives in the area. (See also the section on cultural deviance theory.) Frederic Thrasher wrote one of the classic works about gangs from a social disorganization perspective. *The Gang*, published in 1927, is equally relevant today. For Thrasher, gangs originate from

> the spontaneous effort of boys to create a society for themselves where none adequate to their needs exists. What boys get out of such association that they do not get otherwise under the conditions that adult society imposes is the thrill and zest of participation in common interests, more especially in corporate action, in hunting, capture, conflict, flight, and escape. Conflict with other gangs and the world about them furnishes the occasion for many of their exciting group activities.[9]

Thrasher's view of the origin of gangs was consistent with the social disorganization perspective. Thrasher noted that gangs are *interstitial*—situated within but not necessarily characteristic of the space occupied. In nature, there are cracks and crevices, where matter of a different nature collects. Similarly, there are fissures in social organization. Gangs are an interstitial element in the social framework of society; they are created in the cracks and boundaries of society and fill gaps when families and schools are weak in socialization. Gangland occupies an interstitial region in the geography of the city. Gangs collect in regions "characterized by deteriorating neighborhoods, shifting populations, and the mobility and disorganization of the slum."[10] Gangs are most frequently found in areas bordering the central business district.

Thrasher found evidence of at least 1,313 gangs in Chicago, with an estimated 25,000 members. No two of these gangs were alike; they reflected the great diversity characteristic of the city of Chicago in the 1920s (Chicago and its gangs today continue to reflect this diversification). Much like today, gang delinquency in Thrasher's day ranged from the petty (such as truancy and disturbing the peace) to the serious (property crime and violent crime).

Thrasher summarized his theory of why gangs exist:

> The failure of the normally directing and controlling customs and institutions to function efficiently in the boy's experience is indicated by the disintegration of family life, inefficiency of schools, formalism and externality of religion, corruption and indifference in local politics, low wages and monotony in occupational activities; unemployment; and lack of opportunity for wholesome recreation. All these factors enter into the picture of the moral and economic frontier, and,

coupled with deterioration in the housing, sanitation, and other conditions of life in the slum, give the impression of general disorganization and decay.[11]

The gang offers a substitute for what society fails to give, and it provides relief from suppression. It fills a gap and affords an escape.

Thrasher viewed gang membership as offering youths the opportunity to acquire a personality and name—conferring status and prescribing a role. The gang "not only defines for him his position in society . . . but it becomes the basis for his conception of himself."[12] The gang becomes the youth's reference group from which he obtains his main values, beliefs, and goals. In a sense, the gang becomes his family. Moreover, groups of youths progress from what Thrasher called *spontaneous play groups* to gang status when adults began to disapprove of them. When this occurs, particularly if coupled with legal intervention, the youths bond together, become closer, and develop a *we* feeling.[13] Thrasher clearly believed that gangs provided certain basic needs for growing boys, such as a sense of belonging and self-esteem.

Several subsequent studies have focused on the community or neighborhood as the primary unit of analysis. Such a focus begins with the assumption that crime and the extent of gang activities vary according to certain neighborhood or community characteristics. In *Racketville, Slumtown and Haulberg*, Irving Spergel wrote that the three neighborhoods he studied in 1964 varied according to a number of criteria and had different kinds of traditions, including delinquent and criminal norms. For example, Racketville, a mostly Italian neighborhood, had a long tradition of organized racketeering. Gangs were mostly involved in the rackets because criminal opportunities for such activities existed in their neighborhood.[14] In contrast, Slumtown was primarily a Puerto Rican neighborhood with a history of conflict and aggression. The gangs in this area were mostly involved in various conflict situations with rival gangs (usually over turf). Haulberg was a mixed ethnic neighborhood (Irish, German, Italian, and others) with a tradition of mostly property crimes; thus, a theft subculture flourished. Research that compares neighborhoods highlights that community characteristics (and not the people who live there) contribute to delinquency.

The ethnographic fieldwork of Mercer Sullivan provides a variation on this theme. He studied three neighborhoods in Brooklyn (which he called Projectville, La Barriada, and Hamilton Park).[15] Socioeconomic indicators varied in the three communities, and the neighborhoods also had significantly different patterns of crime. La Barriada was a mixed Latino and white area; Projectville was a largely African-American neighborhood; Hamilton Park was predominantly white. The two neighborhoods with the highest crime rates (Projectville and La Barriada) also had (1) the highest poverty level, with more than half the families receiving public assistance; (2) the highest percentage of single-parent families; (3) the highest rate of non-home owners or renter-occupied housing; (4) the highest rate of school dropouts; and (5) the lowest labor-force participation rates and, correspondingly, highest levels of unemployment.

Sullivan explained the concentration of high-risk, low return theft in the two impoverished, minority neighborhoods:

> The primary causes for their greater willingness to engage in desperate, highly exposed crimes for uncertain and meager monetary returns were the greater poverty of their households, the specific and severe lack of employment opportunities during these same mid-teen years, and the weakened local social control environment, itself a product of general poverty and joblessness among neighborhood residents.[16]

A key to understanding these differences, argues Sullivan, is that of personal networks rather than human capital.

> Personal networks derived from existing patterns of articulation between the local neighborhoods and particular sectors of the labor market. These effects of labor market segmentation were important for youth jobs both in the middle teens and during the ensuing period of work establishment. The Hamilton Park youths found a relatively plentiful supply of temporary, part-time, almost always off-the-books work through relatives, friends, and local employers during the middle teens, most of it in the local vicinity.[17]

When these youths reached their late teens, they were able to make use of these same contacts to get more secure and better-paying jobs. The minority youths from Projectville and La Barriada never developed such networks. Thus, social factors such as participation in social networks were found to be important (see discussion below on social embeddedness).

For most of the juveniles Sullivan studied, one important precursor to a criminal career was involvement in some gang or clique of youths. Delinquent behavior typically began with fighting with age peers whether individually or in group confrontations. Street fighting preceded involvement in economic crime and was motivated by status and territory. Beginning in their early teens, these youths would spend a great amount of time within what they considered their own territory or turf. The cliques and gangs these youths belonged to "were quasi-familial groupings that served to protect their members from outsiders."[18]

Rodney Stark also suggested that criminal behavior persists within specific neighborhoods over time *because of certain characteristics of the neighborhoods*, rather than the people who inhabit them.[19] He argued that there are five key characteristics of perpetually high-crime neighborhoods: (1) high density, (2) high rates of poverty. (3) mixed-use (poor dense neighborhoods mixed together with light industry and retail shops), (4) a high rate of transience among residents, (5) dilapidation. His theory also incorporates the impact of these five characteristics on people's responses to the social conditions surrounding them. He identified (1) moral cynicism, (2) increased opportunities for crime, (3) an increase in the *motivation* to commit crime and, (4) diminished social control, especially among residents via informal methods of control. The neighborhood characteristics and people's responses to them drive away the least deviant people—further reducing social control and attracting crime-prone people into the neighborhood.

This theory is useful in thinking about increased delinquency rates associated with certain neighborhoods. For example, in high-density neighborhoods, homes and apartments are crowded. As a result, more people congregate outside, and there is less supervision of children. Less supervision of children almost inevitably leads to poor school achievement, resulting in an increase in deviant behavior by such children. Moreover, with overcrowding comes greater family conflict, further weakening attachments (see discussion of control theory).[20]

More recent studies have continued to confirm the connection between neighborhoods (especially lower socioeconomic areas) and delinquency, continuing the work that began with Quetelet and Guerry and later the Chicago School.[21] The Justice Mapping Center, for example, plots the residential addresses of inmates in various prison systems.[22] The maps illustrate single census blocks where taxpayers spend more than $1 million annually on incarceration of residents of that neighborhood. The visual representation illustrates the magnitude of the problem. Tools like mapping help designers of reentry programs understand how incarceration, reentry, and recidivism affect communities—facilitating better use of resources.

STRAIN/ANOMIE THEORY

Strain theory originated with Robert Merton, who borrowed the term *anomie* from the French sociologist Émile Durkheim[23] and applied it to the problem of crime in the United States.[24] The concept of *anomie* refers to the absence of norms due to inconsistencies between societal conditions and opportunities for growth, fulfillment, and productivity within a society. It also involves the *weakening of the normative order* of society—that is, norms (mores, rules, laws, and so on) lose their impact on people. The existence of anomie within a culture can also produce a high level of flexibility in the pursuit of goals, including the endorsement of deviation from accepted norms concerning the methods of achieving success within any given culture.

Durkheim, writing during the late nineteenth century, suggested that when individuals are not fully integrated into society they are left to their own devices. With the weakening of social bonds, social regulations also break down, and the controlling influence that a society has is thus ineffective. Under capitalism, there is a more or less chronic state of deregulation and industrialization that removes traditional social controls on aspirations. This breakdown of moral regulation results in an increase of deviance and social unrest. The capitalist culture produces in humans a constant dissatisfaction, a never-ending longing for something more. This longing for more means that there is never enough—whether this be money, material things, or power. There is a morality under capitalism that dictates an attitude of anything goes—especially when it comes to making money.

Again, according to Durkheim, the desires and self-interests of individuals within a society are checked by institutional forces outside of the individual (i.e. family, schools, religious institutions, etc.). What Durkheim was hinting at (but never stated as forcefully as Karl Marx) was that a very strong social structure is needed to offset or place limits on the "anything goes" perspective. In other words, strong institutions, such as the family, religion, and education, are needed to place some limits on us. The ideas, values, beliefs, norms, rules, and moral boundaries an individual receives from these social institutions and external factors are known as the *collective conscience* of a society. Inadequate regulation of members of society by institutions results in higher crime rates compounded by the domination of the economic institution over all others.

Writing in the 1940s, Robert Merton theorized how anomie is experienced within the United States. The basic thesis of Merton's strain theory (sometimes referred to as means-ends theory) is that there is often a disjunction between a society's goals and the legitimate means for achieving those goals. In the United States, the dominant goal is economic success. "The goal of economic success is placed within the realm of culture, while the system of legitimate opportunities is classified as part of the society's social structure."[25] Culture, in this sense, consists of the main values and goal orientations of society. Social structure consists of the basic *social institutions* of society, especially the economy, but also such institutions as the family, education, and politics, which distribute access to the legitimate means for obtaining goals.

The "lack of fit" between the culture's norms about what constitutes success in life (*goals*) and the culture's norms about the appropriate ways (*means*) to achieve those goals creates *strain* within individuals. Individuals experiencing strain (i.e. stress of working toward culturally appropriate goals yet never fully attaining them) respond with various forms of deviance. People who find themselves at a disadvantage relative to legitimate economic activities are motivated to engage in illegitimate activities (perhaps because of unavailability of jobs, lack of job skills, education, and other factors).

Moreover, success goals have become *institutionalized*—they are deeply embedded in the psyches of everyone via a very powerful system of corporate propaganda.[26] At the same time, the legitimate means are not as well defined nor as strongly ingrained. In other words, there is a lot of discretion and a lot of tolerance for deviance from the means (i.e. striving for cultural notions of success) but not the goals (actually attaining success). One result of such an inconsistent system is high levels of crime.

Another important point made by strain theory is that our culture contributes to crime because the opportunities to achieve success goals are not equally distributed. The strong class structure creates incredible inequality within our society, which means that some are extremely disadvantaged compared to others.[27] Many minority and subgroup populations within the U.S. experience access to success as very limited and/or difficult to obtain. Another way of saying the same thing is that the *culture promises what the social structure cannot deliver*. How then do individuals respond to this disjuncture between the goals and means? The strains of this contradiction cause people to seek alternatives.

Merton refers to the possible alternatives as *modes of adaptation*. His typology of adaptations includes the following:

1. *conformity*—accepting both the legitimate means and the success goals;
2. *ritualism*—accepting the means but rejecting the goals (one goes to work every day but has given up on the goal of success);
3. *innovation*—accepting the goals of success but rejecting the legitimate means to obtain them (one who breaks the rules and/or laws in order to achieve success);
4. *retreatism*—rejecting both the goals *and* the means and more or less dropping out of society to become part of a subculture (such as the drug subculture);
5. *rebellion*—rejecting both the goals and the means, substituting *new* definitions of success and the means to obtain them.

The *innovation* adaptation directly relates to criminal activity. Socially acceptable incentives for success are provided by the prevailing values of society, yet the opportunities for working toward success are limited by the class structure. The combination of a strong cultural emphasis on success/goals with an inadequate social structure in place to achieve them produces a desire to deviate. Thus anomie/strain theory would suggest that an individual participating in gang-related activities (illegal and deviant) to achieve success (i.e. economic and/or social) would be an example of being *innovative* in the pursuit of success.

According to Steven Messner and Richard Rosenfeld, such strain explains high rates of crime not only among the disadvantaged but also among the more privileged. All individuals are under strains to make more money, often by any means necessary. This theory helps explain corporate crime in this country.[28] Messner and Rosenfeld's revision of strain theory added an important component—the relationship of social institutions with the *American Dream*.

Crime and the American Dream

Messner and Rosenfeld extended Merton's strain theory to include an analysis of *institutional anomie*. They believed it was necessary to understand how the American Dream sustains an institutional structure in which one institution—the economy—dominates all others (i.e. family, religion, education). This imbalance results in other institutions failing to insulate individuals from illegal/deviant pressures to succeed. First, it is important to understand their definition of the American Dream: "a broad cultural ethos that entails a commitment to the goal of material success, to be pursued by everyone in society, under conditions of open, individual competition."[29]

The American Dream contains four deeply embedded core values summarized in box 7-2. The dark side of the American Dream stems from a contradiction in U.S. capitalism: the same forces that promote progress and ambition also produce a lot of crime, since there is such an incredible pressure to succeed and to do so at any cost. The emphasis on competition and achievement produces selfishness that drives people apart, weakening a collective sense of community. The fact that monetary rewards are such a high priority results in noneconomic tasks receiving little cultural support (e.g. homemakers and child-care workers receiving little to no pay for a day's work).

The existence of such a high degree of inequality produces feelings of unworthiness. Those who fail are looked down on, and their failure is too often seen as an *individual* failure rather than a failure affected by societal, institutional, and cultural factors. Even education is only seen as a means to an end—the end being a high-paying job or any secure job. For example, advertisements for local universities often encourage people to "go back so you can get ahead." Rather than encouraging people to obtain a degree for the sake of expanding their knowledge base and other noneconomic benefits, the cultural goal is to get a degree to get a job. Furthermore, common societal understandings about higher education support the idea that if an individual does have a degree and cannot acquire a job, then there is something wrong with that individual—rather than analyzing whether something is wrong with the economic and/or societal system.

One of the keys to understanding the link between the American Dream and crime is knowing the meaning and importance of the term *social institution*. Social institutions can be defined as a persistent set of organized *methods* of meeting basic

---

Box 7-2   Core Values of American Culture

1. *Achievement.* One's *personal worth* is typically evaluated in terms of monetary success and/ or fame. This stems from a culture that emphasizes "doing" and "having" rather than "being." Failure to achieve is equated with the failure to make a contribution to society. This value is highly conducive to the attitude "it's not how you play the game; it's whether you win or lose." A similar attitude is "winning isn't everything; it's the *only* thing."
2. *Individualism.* People are encouraged to "make it" on their own. This value discourages a value that could (and has been proven to) successfully reduce crime, namely cooperation and collective action. A corollary to this value is "I don't need any help." (Note how this is reinforced in many movies and television series, where one man conquers evil or solves a crime, etc.) Intense individual competition to succeed pressures people to disregard normative restraints on behavior when they interfere with the realization of personal goals.
3. *Universalism.* The value claims everyone has the same opportunity to succeed, as long as you "work hard." Part of the value derives from the Protestant work ethic.
4. *Fetishism of Money.* Money is so important in our culture that it often overrides almost everything else. It is often worshiped like a God. Money is the *currency* for measuring just about everything. Moreover, there is no end point; the striving is incessant. In the *consumerist culture* everyone is socialized from the day they are born to be a *consumer.* (Witness the emergence of corporate-sponsored programs within elementary schools, including the omnipresent McDonald's.)

Source: Steven F. Messner and Richard Rosenfeld, *Crime and the American Dream,* 5th ed. (Belmont, CA: Wadsworth).

human needs. There are relatively stable groups and organizations (complete with various norms and values, statuses, and roles) that help humans (1) adapt to the environment, (2) mobilize resources to achieve collective goals, and (3) be socialized to accept society's fundamental normative patterns.[30] The most important of these institutions include (1) the economy, (2) the family, (3) schools, and (4) politics. Other important institutions include health care, media, religion, and the law (many would place law within the much larger political institution).

It is important to understand that, when these institutions fail to meet the needs of members of the society (or a sizable proportion of the population) alternative institutions will begin to develop and different forms or *methods* of meeting these needs will transpire. For example, if the prevailing economic system is failing, more and more people will engage in alternative means of earning a living; if organized religion is not meeting such needs as answers to fundamental life questions, then people will seek out unorthodox religious forms (e.g., cults like the Branch Davidians or Heaven's Gate) to find answers; if the legal institution is not perceived as providing justice, then people may take the law into their own hands; and if the mainstream media provides too much disinformation and does not allow dissenting views, then alternative media sources will emerge.

Again, gangs are one example of alternative institutions. Note in figure 7-1 that straight lines connect all of the major institutions. Because every institution

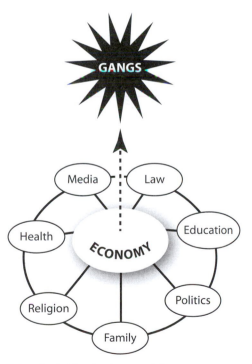

Figure 7-1   Social Institutions and Gangs.
Source: Randall G. Shelden, Sharon K. Tracy, and William B. Brown, *Youth Gangs in American Society,* 4th ed. (Belmont, CA: Cengage, 2013).

is connected in some way with all the others, problems in one cause problems in another. As suggested in chapter 4, gangs function as sort of *quasi-institutions* in many ways. For example, many gang members feel that their "homies" are like a family. Gangs provide methods and incentives to seek alternative ways of earning money. They also provide an alternative media (graffiti) and an alternative religion (RIP graffiti on walls). They even have their own informal legal system. In short, gangs provide many of the needs that are supposed to be provided by mainstream institutions.

As Messner and Rosenfeld suggest, what is unique about US society is that the economic institution almost completely dominates all other institutions. John Dewey expressed a similar view when he stated that, "politics is the shadow that big business casts over society."[31] American capitalism, unlike capitalism in other countries, emerged with virtually no interference from previously existing institutions. Unlike other societies, there were no other existing institutions that could tame or offset the economic imperatives.[32] European and Japanese cultures, in contrast, place almost equal importance on the family, religion, education, and other institutional concerns. Under US capitalism, other institutions are subordinate to the economy (which is why it appears in the middle in figure 7-1). The goal is to make a *profit*, and everything else becomes secondary. Over time this has become a market society in contrast to a market economy. In the former, the pursuit of private gain dominates all other pursuits (e.g., education, the arts, or family support).[33]

The emphasis on economics can have devastating consequences. Princeton sociologist Matthew Desmond argues that eviction is one of the most pressing problems in the United States. "For decades, we've focused mainly on jobs, public assistance, parenting, and mass incarceration. No one can deny the importance of these issues, but something fundamental is missing. We have failed to fully appreciate how deeply housing is implicated in the creation of poverty."[34] The majority of the poor spend over half their income on housing—one in four spends 70%.

Desmond surveyed more than 1,000 households in Milwaukee's low-income private housing sector from 2009–2011; the data were compiled as the Milwaukee Area Renters Study (MARS). The 250 survey questions covered landlord interactions, residential history, employment, material hardship, and social networks.[35] After beginning his research, Desmond recognized that eviction was rarely studied; there were no national data on the topic. The techniques Desmond developed for his groundbreaking study were integrated into the Census Bureau's 2017 American Housing Survey.[36] Desmond's research also involved ethnography. He lived in a trailer park in a poor, predominantly white neighborhood near the airport in Milwaukee for four months and in a rooming house in a poor, predominantly black neighborhood on Milwaukee's north side for nine months. The research is a resource for studying the causes and consequences of eviction, urban poverty, inner-city neighborhoods, the low-income housing market, and social networks.

Desmond launched the open-source Eviction Lab at Princeton University, which built the first nationwide database.[37] The database was compiled from

83 million court records back to 2000. In 2016, there were 900,000 eviction judgments—1 in 50 (2%) renters.[38] Cities with the highest rate of eviction judgments were North Charleston, SC (16.5%), Richmond, VA (11.4%), Hampton, VA (10.5%), and Newport News, VA (10.2%). One of the problems for renters in Virginia is that it has fewer tenant rights than other states. Richmond's mayor says the state favors property owners, as it has since plantation days. The database tracks only legal (formal) convictions. As Desmond discovered in Milwaukee, many tenants are convicted informally—the door to the apartment is removed or the landlord offers money to motivate the tenants to leave.

Desmond's books and articles encourage readers to reexamine how they think about poverty and race.[39] He stresses that poverty is not innate—it is influenced by social structures and relationships. Many who are evicted end up in shelters or homeless. A record of eviction limits future housing to lodgings in disrepair in unsafe neighborhoods. Children's performance in school and emotional well-being are affected by transient living. Adults may suffer job loss and depression. Women generally fare worse than men in similar neighborhoods because they earn less and are more likely to be caring for children. Eviction compounds racial discrimination and the effects of poverty. This is one recent illustration of the links between institutions and the strain experienced by some members in society.

Differential Opportunity Structures

Richard Cloward and Lloyd Ohlin developed a variation of strain theory in 1960.[40] These authors argued (1) that blocked opportunity aspirations cause poor self-concepts and feelings of frustration and (2) that these frustrations lead to delinquency. A key concept here is *differential opportunity structure*—the uneven distribution of legal and illegal means of achieving economic success, particularly the inequalities because of class, race, and gender. Cloward and Ohlin argued that while legitimate opportunities are blocked for significant numbers of lower-class youths, the same cannot be said for illegitimate opportunities (e.g., selling drugs and other crimes).

> The disparity between what lower class youth are led to want and what is actually available to them is the source of a major problem of adjustment. Adolescents who form delinquent subcultures, we suggest, have internalized an emphasis upon conventional goals. Faced with limitations on legitimate avenues of access to these goals, and unable to revise their aspirations downward, they experience intense frustrations; the exploration of nonconformist alternatives may be the result.[41]

Among the specific assumptions of this theory is that blocked opportunities (or aspirations) create feelings of frustration and low self-esteem, often leading to delinquency. Cloward and Ohlin postulate that three different types of gangs emerge and that these types correspond to characteristics of the neighborhoods rather than to the individuals who live there. *Criminal gangs* are organized mainly around the commission of property crimes and exist in areas where there are already relatively organized forms of adult criminal activity, which serve as models for the youths who live there. *Conflict gangs* engage mostly in violent behavior, such as gang fights over turf; they exist in neighborhoods where living conditions are unstable and transient, resulting in the lack of any adult role models, whether conventional or criminal. *Retreatist gangs* engage mostly in illegal drug use and exist in neighborhoods dominated by a great deal of illegal drug activity. Cloward and Ohlin describe retreatist gang youth as double failures—juveniles who have neither criminal opportunities to succeed nor access to the status/prestige gained through participation in conflict groups. Differential opportunity theory focuses on the availability of either legitimate or illegitimate opportunities. It also addresses how illegitimate opportunity structures regulate access to different forms of deviance and crime, particularly for individuals in different segments of society.

Social Embeddedness

John Hagan[42] borrows the term *social embeddedness* from economist Mark Granovetter[43] to describe a developmental view of involvement in delinquency, a very interesting variation of strain theory. Instead of unemployment *preceding* involvement in criminal behavior (a common view in criminology), *the reverse is actually the case* for young offenders. For these youths, involvement in crime begins well before they can legally be involved in the labor market. Granovetter asserts that becoming a regularly employed person involves much more than an individual's skills and education; it involves being connected to a social network of contacts that accrue over time. One needs to be socialized into the labor market at a very early age. This means, among other things, that a youth begins to earn money doing odd jobs such as mowing lawns, babysitting, washing windows, shoveling snow, delivering papers, and so on long before turning 16. These activities start the process of social embeddedness. Youths who live in declining neighborhoods, who do poorly in school, and who do not have a large support network rarely aquire the contacts to be socialized into the labor market.[44]

Hagan argues that the process of becoming embedded in a network of crime and deviance develops in a parallel sequence to the process of becoming embedded in the world of work because of the networks available. In most of the high-crime, inner-city neighborhoods, the odd jobs of middle-class youths noted above do not exist in large numbers (e.g., there are no lawns to be mowed in high-rise buildings). Rather, parental involvement in crime can integrate youths into networks of criminal opportunities. Likewise, association with delinquent peers or contacts with drug dealers can also integrate youths into criminal networks. Moreover, delinquent acts tend to cause youths to become further isolated from legitimate networks of employment. A snowballing effect takes place whereby each delinquent act and/or contact with the world of crime further distances a youth from the legitimate world of work. Thus the perspective of social embeddedness identifies the process of separation from conventional employment networks that has a time sequence with a "lagged accumulation of effect that should build over time."[45]

Ethnographic research on delinquency supports this view. Elijah Anderson notes: "For many young men the drug economy is an employment agency. . . . Young men who 'grew up' in the gang, but now are without clear opportunities, easily become involved; they fit themselves into its structure, manning its drug houses and selling drugs on street corners."[46] Felix Padilla noted that gang youths he studied "began turning to the gang in search of employment opportunities, believing that available conventional work would not sufficiently provide the kinds of material goods they wished to secure."[47] He also noted that youths were between the ages of 13 and 15 when they first became gang members. Increasing involvement in the gang further embedded them, making entry into the legitimate world of work a serious problem for them later in life. The process of estrangement from the legitimate world of work and embeddedness in the world of criminal opportunities are amply documented by research in Chicago, Los Angeles, Milwaukee, New York, Boston, and many other urban areas.[48] Research in all of these areas found evidence of the socialization of inner-city youths (especially minority youths) into the world of criminal opportunities and their subsequent isolation from the social networks of legitimate work.

CULTURAL DEVIANCE THEORIES

Cultural deviance theory proposes that delinquency results from a desire to conform to cultural values that may conflict with those of conventional society. In part, this perspective is a direct offshoot of social disorganization theory, which suggests that criminal values and traditions emerge within communities most affected by social disorganization.

Cohen's Subcultural Theory

Albert Cohen's research on delinquent boys found that Merton's strain theory, which emphasized the frustration resulting from the inability to achieve financial gain, was inadequate to explain the noneconomic deviance of gang members. His subcultural theory of delinquent gangs argued that delinquency was best understood as a collective reaction to the frustration of not being able to achieve status in a society dominated by middle-class norms.

There are two key concepts in Cohen's theory: (1) *reaction formation*, openly rejecting aspirations that one cannot achieve and (2) *middle-class measuring rod*, evaluations of behavior based on norms and values associated with the middle class, such as punctuality, neatness, cleanliness, nonviolent behavior, drive and ambition, achievement and success (especially at school), deferred gratification, and so on.[49] Cohen's view incorporates the following assumptions: (1) a high proportion of lower-class youths (especially males) do poorly in school; (2) poor school performance relates to delinquency, (3) poor school performance stems from a conflict between dominant middle-class values of the school system and values of lower-class youths; and (4) most lower-class male delinquency is committed in a gang context, partly as a means of meeting some basic human needs, such as self-esteem and belonging.

Cohen found that even when lower working-class youths successfully completed their education, they were still at a disadvantage when compared to (and competing against) middle-class youths applying for the same work/job opportunities. Potential employers, when faced with a number of equally qualified applicants, would defer to middle-class criteria (i.e. religious upbringing, style of speech, attire, etc.) that discriminates against those with lower socioeconomic status. Failure to secure a job made youths more likely to withdraw from legitimate norms and to turn to delinquency. Cohen argues that when lower working-class youths realize that they have little chance of successfully gaining a higher status in society, the result is *status frustration*. This leads to delinquents often developing a culture that is at odds with the norms and values of the middle class; they rebel against those norms by turning them upside down.

Over more than six decades, many studies have examined the four components of Cohen's subcultural perspective. "On balance, the totality of Cohen's theory has not been empirically verified."[50] However, Cohen's thesis highlighted the effects of social stratification and class differences on school performance and identified the link between failure in school and delinquency. He also pointed to the distinction between youthful law breaking and adult criminality—one of his contributions to understanding delinquency.

Lower-Class Focal Concerns

As with Cohen's work, the perspective proposed by anthropologist Walter B. Miller remains relevant today even though his study was also done in the 1950s. Within certain communities in the Boston area, Miller discovered what he called the *focal concerns* of a distinctive lower-class culture (see box 7-3). Miller argues specifically that (1) there are clear-cut focal concerns (norms and values) within the lower-class culture and (2) that *female-dominated households* are an important feature within the lower class and are a major reason for the emergence of street-corner male adolescent groups in these neighborhoods.[51]

Two key concepts here are (1) *focal concerns* and (2) *one-sex peer units*. First, *focal concerns* include trouble, toughness, smartness, excitement, fate, and autonomy. For example, Miller suggests that individuals within the lower-class subculture value *toughness* as an important trait—yet this trait sometimes leads to violence (delinquency). They also value *smartness*—activities associated with trying to outsmart or con others. Yet this trait sometimes results in individuals stealing from others (delinquency). Valuing *excitement*—thrills from, for example, drinking or gambling—is another trait that can lead to delinquency. Embracing a mixture of these focal concerns that are at odds with mainstream middle-class society leads to a subculture that accepts deviance as normal.

Second, the concept of *one-sex peer units* serves as an alternative source of companionship and male role model development outside the home. The one-sex peer group is important to Miller's theory in the sense that gangs provide male members opportunities to prove their masculinity in the absence of an adequate male role

Box 7-3   Miller's "Focal Concerns" of Lower-Class Culture

1. *Trouble* is a defining feature of lower-class life. Unlike the middle class, where judgment is usually based on one's achievements (e.g., education, career advancement), the lower-class concern is whether one will pursue the law-abiding route or its reverse. Further, membership in a gang is often contingent on demonstrating a commitment to law-violating behavior, acts that carry much prestige.

2. *Toughness* is associated with stereotypical masculine traits and behaviors, featuring an emphasis on physical prowess, strength, fearless daring, and a general macho attitude and behavior (or machismo). It also includes a lack of sentimentality, a disdain for art and literature, and a view of women as sex objects. Concern about toughness may derive from being reared in a female-headed household and lack of male role models. The need to demonstrate toughness precludes behaviors that could be interpreted as feminine, such as caring for one's children or acting responsibly to avoid fathering children out of wedlock.

3. *Smartness* revolves around the ability to *con* or outwit others—to engage in hustling activities. Skills in this area are continually being tested and honed; the most skillful have great prestige. Many leaders of gangs are more valued for smartness than toughness, but the ideal leader possesses both qualities.

4. *Excitement* refers to a constant search for thrills to offset an otherwise boring existence. Alcohol, sex, and gambling play large roles. The night on the town is a favorite pastime and involves alcohol, sex, and music. Fights are frequent, so "going to town" is an expression of actively seeking risk and danger, hence excitement. Most of the time between episodes of excitement is spent doing nothing or hanging around—common for gang members.

5. *Fate* involves luck and fortune. According to Miller, most members of the lower class believe that they have little or no control over their lives—that their destiny is predetermined. Much of what happens is determined by luck. If one is lucky, life will be rewarding. If one is unlucky, then nothing one does will change one's fate—so why bother working toward goals?

6. *Autonomy* involves a contradiction. On the one hand, there is overt resentment of external authority and controls ("No one is going to tell me what to do!"). On the other hand, there are covert behaviors that show a desire for such control. External authority and controls provide a somewhat nurturing aspect. If one is imprisoned and subjected to rigid rules and regulations, one may overtly complain while locked up. However, behavior after release sometimes seems designed to ensure reimprisonment and a return to a controlled existence. Rebellion over rules is a test of the firmness of the rules and an attempt to seek reassurance that nurturing will occur. Youngsters often misbehave in school because they do not get such reassurance.

model within their family of origin. The principal unit in lower-class society is an age-graded, one-sex peer group constituting the major psychic focus and reference group for young people. The adolescent street-corner group is one variant of the lower-class structure, and the gang is a subtype distinguished by law-violating activities. For boys reared in female-headed households, the street-corner group provides the first real opportunity to learn essential aspects of the male role—by learning from other boys in the group with similar sex-role identification problems. The group also acts as a selection process in recruiting and retaining members.

Echoing Thrasher's earlier work, Miller states that two central concerns of the adolescent street-corner group are belonging and status. One achieves belonging by adhering to the group's standards and values and continues to achieve belonging by demonstrating such characteristics as toughness, smartness, and autonomy. When there is conflict with middle-class norms, the norms of the group are far more compelling, because failure to conform means expulsion from the group. Status is achieved by demonstrating the qualities valued by lower-class culture. Status in the adolescent group requires *adultness*, that is, the material possessions and rights of adults (e.g., a car, the right to smoke and drink, etc.) but *not the responsibilities of adults*. The desire to act like an adult and avoid "kid stuff" results in gambling, drinking, and other deviant behaviors and compels the adolescent more than the adult to be smart, tough, and so on. He will seek out ways to demonstrate these qualities, even if they are illegal.

There is also a pecking order among different groups, defined by one's "rep" (reputation). Each group believes its safety depends on maintaining a solid rep for toughness compared with other groups. One's rep refers to both law-abiding and law-violating behavior. Which behavior will dominate depends on a complex set of factors, such as which community reference groups (criminals or police) are admired or respected or the individual needs of the gang members. Above all, having status is crucial and is far more important than the means selected to achieve it. Pride becomes a fiercely guarded commodity in some areas, and showing weakness invites trouble. "Youths are particularly concerned about their reputation and status among peers, seeking justice, and the risks to their personal safety. From the youths' perspectives, there are not only safety risks associated with being violent and with others using violence against them, but there are also status risks associated with backing down from a provocation."[52]

Violence is a learned behavior that can be unlearned. Gary Slutkin of Chicago's Cure Violence program sees violence as a contagious or infectious disease. Experts believe many factors put children at risk of falling into a pattern of violent thinking and behavior: "growing up in poverty, living in violent circumstances, failing to read at grade level by third grade, not graduating from high school, and not being surrounded by caring, protective adults."[53] Cure Violence works to interrupt transmissions of violence, often using violence interrupters who were once violent themselves. "The modern practice of behavior change requires the use of credible messengers, as well as ensuring that the new behaviors are acceptable and feel right socially, including being able to overcome social, physical, and other barriers (for example, the pressure that other groups are doing it."[54] Greg Boyle, a Jesuit priest, has worked with gang members in Los Angeles for 30 years He founded Homeboy Industries, now the largest gang intervention, rehab, and reentry program in the country.[55] "It's not about thinking or behavior. It's about infusing a sense of hope so the kid starts to care. No one scares them straight—you care them straight."[56]

Several recent studies have found that lower class offenders are often singled out for excessive punishments (especially minority males) by a court system that fails to take into account the importance and real consequences of these subcultures. Essentially, a mostly white, middle–class, bureaucratic subculture passes judgment on a very different lower- and/or working-class subculture. The focal concerns perspective applied to the court explains disparities in sentencing decisions. The focal concerns of courtroom workgroup members are: blameworthiness (culpability and insuring punishment fits the crime or harm caused), protection of the community (through incapacitation and assessments of dangerousness and potential recidivism), and practical constraints and consequences (concerns about organizational costs incurred by the criminal justice system).[57] "The focal concerns may be influenced by the offender's position in the social structure in ways that contribute to disparate treatment of some status categories relative to others.[58] Punishment reflects inequalities of class, status, and power in society and the organizational interests and concerns of justice officials. "Because judges rarely have enough information to accurately determine an offender's culpability or dangerousness, they develop a perceptual shorthand based on stereotypes and attributions that are themselves linked to offender characteristics such as race, sex, and age.[59] Combinations of status characteristics have larger effects on decisions than the presence of an isolated characteristic.

Control/Social Bond Theory

The essence of *control theory* (sometimes called *social bond theory*) is that the weakening, breakdown, or absence of effective social control accounts for delinquency. A unique feature of this perspective is that it asks "Why *don't* they do it?" rather than "Why do they do it?" In other words, this theory wrestles with what it is that keeps or prevents people from committing crime and offers justifications for why individuals obey rules and laws. In this sense, control theory is really a focus on those individuals who do not commit a crime—in effect, a theory of prevention.

The basic assumption of control theory is that proper social behavior requires proper socialization; if bonds to conventional society are weak or broken, individuals are free to deviate.[60] Thus, proper socialization leads to conformity, while improper socialization leads to nonconformity. Delinquency is one consequence of improper socialization. Carl Bell, director of the Institute for Juvenile Research at the University of Illinois at Chicago, says adults provide a protective shield in controlling youthful behavior. "To a great extent, children are all gasoline and no brakes. It's incumbent on parents, families, schools and society to provide them with those brakes—with expectations, rules, monitoring, and social-emotional skills."[61]

The essence of control theory is that delinquent behavior occurs because it is not prevented in the first place. Family, friends, and neighbors serve as informal control mechanisms, while schools, police and the courts serve as formal mechanisms—if informal controls are weak, there is greater reliance on formal controls.[62] There are several variations of control theory.

Containment theory looks at the restraining forces that prevent criminal behavior.[63] This social-psychological explanation is based on the assumption that delinquency results from poor self-concepts; a positive view of oneself insulates against pressures toward delinquency.[64] There are four types of pressures and containments: outer pressures, outer containments, inner containments, and inner pressures. Outer containment comes from the family and support groups, the structure of roles and expectations in society, and the sense of acceptance relative to a group or society; inner containment comes from one's self-concept, including personal strengths such as self-control, the ability to internalize societal norms, goal orientation, and frustration tolerance.

Drift theory looks at why delinquent youths violate society's norms—despite generally supporting them. The theory is a situational explanation of delinquency that transitions from deterministic depictions of delinquency to a focus on factors that influence the description of behavior as delinquent rather than the causes of the behavior.[65] Behavior is not fixed; inclinations change according to situational circumstances. The same general social conditions produce both delinquent and nondelinquent behavior. Youths commit delinquent acts because they rationalize deviance before it occurs— that is, they neutralize) the normal moral beliefs they have learned while growing up (see discussion in section on social learning theory). For example, they deny that there is a victim by saying things like "He had it coming," or they deny that there was any real harm by saying something like, "No one was really hurt," or "They won't miss it."[66]

Travis Hirschi noted that strain theorists assume that conformity is universal and that deviance needs to be explained. Hirschi's *social bond theory* looked at the inverse: deviance is assumed; conformity must be explained.[67] Hirschi theorized that "strong wants are conducive not to crime but to conformity because they tie us to the future and because crime is an inefficient means of realizing one's goals."[68] Hirschi said deviant behavior occurs when the bond of the individual to society is weak. He defined society as a "potentially large array of persons, groups, institutions, and even future states of the individual—e.g. parents, teachers, families, schools, peers, gangs, churches, education, marriage, children."[69] The strength of each element of the bond is a function of characteristics of the individual and the element.

The four major elements of this bond (see box 7-4) are: *attachment* (bonds to significant others), *commitment* (investment to conventional behavior), *involvement*

Box 7-4 Hirschi's Four Elements of the Social Bond

1. *Attachment* refers to ties of affection and respect between kids and parents, teachers, and friends. Attachment to parents is most important as the source from whom children learn and internalize the norms and values of society.
2. *Commitment* refers to the extent to which kids adhere to conventional behavior, such as getting an education, postponing participation in adult activities (e.g., working full-time, living on your own, getting married), and dedication to long-term goals. If children develop a stake in conformity, then engaging in delinquent behavior would endanger their future.
3. *Involvement* is similar to the conventional belief that "idle hands are the devil's workshop." In other words, large amounts of unstructured time may decrease the ties to the social bond; those busy doing conventional things (e.g., chores, homework, sports, camping, working, or dating) do not have time for delinquency.
4. *Belief* refers to an acceptance of the law, especially the morality of the law (e.g., belief that stealing is just plain wrong).

Source: Travis Hirschi, *Causes of Delinquency* (Berkeley: University of California Press, 1969), pp. 16–34.

(participation in conventional activities), and *belief* (acceptance of the conventional moral and social-value system). When individuals experience strong bonds to each of these elements, the chances of them ever becoming delinquent are low. Conversely, those who fail to form or maintain these four elements of bonds to society are much more likely to become delinquent.

This theory is very popular (although many do not consider it a control theory). Most people accept the four social bonds as appropriate role behaviors for young people. Juvenile justice workers try to *reattach* delinquents to family, school, and other primary social institutions; to get them to *commit* themselves to the demands of childhood; to *involve* themselves in conventional activities; and to help them acquire a *belief* system and respect for the law. This theory becomes an important starting point for the social development model and the risk-focused approach to delinquency prevention.

John Johnstone suggests that purely ecological explanations of gangs are limited; they do not explain why gangs influence only some boys in the neighborhood but not others. He notes that the opportunity to join a gang

> is established by the external social environment, but the decision to do so is governed by social and institutional attachments and by definitions of self. . . . The transition from unaffiliated to gang-affiliated delinquency occurs at the point that a boy comes to believe that he has nothing further to gain by not joining a gang.[70]

An extensive study of various ethnic gangs by Diego Vigil and Steve Yun led them to conclude that the common theme for all these gangs is that the weakening of the bonds identified by Hirschi frees them from social control and encourages deviant behavior. Interviews with 150 incarcerated gang members from four ethnic groups (Vietnamese, Chicano, African American, and Hispanic) confirmed the social control thesis.[71]

Informal social control networks within communities contribute to social bonding. Todd Clear notes that three levels of informal social control lessen the extent of crime: (1) what people do *privately* within their intimate relationships; (2) what people do *collectively* in their relationships with others in the community; and (3) people's attitudes toward criminal behavior.[72] The most common forms of social control originate in the privacy of child rearing. Collective methods of social control extend the lessons through a variety of associations and groups: churches, businesses, social clubs, volunteer groups, youth groups, neighborhood associations, and many more. Participation in these groups occupies a lot of free time for young people and increases bonds. This is one reason why after-school and summer activities are so important. Research verifies that students with low commitments to education are more likely to become delinquent.[73] Studies have found that youths who participated in structured activities were less likely to engage in delinquent behavior.[74] This relates to the involvement part of the social bond. Collective social controls fall between the most formal controls (e.g., police) and family controls.

Michael Gottfredson and Travis Hirschi outlined *self-control theory* as part of their general theory of crime.[75] Self-control is the ability to reject immediate pleasures in favor of longer-term interests. Individuals who lack self-control will be attracted to short-term pleasures that require minimal effort; they have little concern for the long-term consequences of their behavior—a precursor to crime and delinquency.[76] Parents are instrumental in teaching children self-control. Poor parental management results in little restraint on self-centeredness, the need for immediate gratification, and the impulse to take risks. Socialization differences early in childhood result in individual variations in self-control abilities that remain relatively stable throughout life (*stability effect*). Individuals fall on a continuum from those with a strong focus on longer-term goals (high self-control) to those who focus on short-term pleasures (low self-control).

The theory inspired numerous empirical studies testing the link between low self-control and crime.[77] While low self-control is an important predictor of crime, it does not reduce the importance of other factors such as differential associations.[78] Some studies have supported the stability effect, while others found that levels of self-control do change over time, including among adolescents. Other studies found that low self-control was one of several factors explaining delinquency, including delinquent peers, social bonds, poverty, and general strains. "Overall, low self-control seems a plausible explanation of general expressions of crime and delinquency, but neither complete or overwhelming."[79]

Some have noted that parental criminality contributes to low self-esteem and, in turn, high levels of delinquency.[80] Parental involvement in various kinds of criminal behavior has consistently been correlated with juvenile delinquency. This has been especially underscored through longitudinal studies of delinquency.[81]

SOCIAL LEARNING THEORY

According to this theory, people become delinquent or criminal through the same kind of process as learning to become anything else. One learns behavior through one's association with other human beings—just as one learns values, beliefs, and attitudes. (An example was noted in the section on focal concerns in the case of learning violence.) Edwin Sutherland developed the theory of *differential association*, one of the earliest variations of social learning theory that applies to delinquency.[82] According to this theory, one becomes a delinquent not only through contact with others who are delinquent but also through contact with various values, beliefs, and attitudes supportive of criminal/delinquent behavior. One of the central points of this theory is the proposition that one becomes a delinquent/criminal "because of an excess of definitions favorable to violation of law over definitions unfavorable to violation of law."[83] Delinquency is transient; exposure to delinquent norms is inconsistent (not entirely favorable or unfavorable) and accompanied by simultaneous exposure to nondelinquent norms.

Albert Bandura's observational learning/modeling theory was based on his research into aggression.[84] His experiments involved children watching an adult attack Bobo, a plastic clown doll. When children were subsequently placed in a room with toys they could not touch, they were visibly agitated. When moved to a room with a Bobo doll, 90% imitated the adult aggressive behavior; eight months later, 40% reproduced the same behavior. Individuals who observe aggressive behavior and are reinforced for acting aggressively learn to be aggressive. Bandura indentified four steps in the process of observational learning: (1) attention, (2) retention, (3) reproduction, (4) motivation.

The learned behavior is reinforced through the modeling influences of one's family, the immediate subculture (especially the peer subculture), and symbolic modeling (e.g., via television or other mass media). A child who witnesses violence within the home is apt to engage in violence later in life. This is especially true if violence within the home is rewarded or no sanctions are applied. Once a person has acquired the behavior, learning theory suggests five key factors that can instigate the performance of the behavior.

1. *Aversive* events—situations marked by frustration, deprivation, verbal insults, and actual assaults. For those who are especially violent, threats to one's reputation and status, especially those occurring in public, are very important instigators of violent acts.
2. *Modeling influences*—observing delinquent or criminal behavior by someone who serves as a role model can be an immediate instigator.
3. *Incentive inducements*—anticipated rewards. One can be motivated to commit a crime by some perceived reward, usually monetary.
4. *Instructional control*—following orders from someone in authority. A gang member, for example, may obey a direct order from a leader of the gang.
5. *Environmental control*—factors in one's immediate environment, which include crowded conditions (including traffic), extreme heat, pollution, and noise.

Each of these factors can cause someone to "lose it" and act out, sometimes in a violent manner.[85] In order for delinquent or criminal behavior to persist, there needs to be consistent reinforcement or *maintenance*. Social learning theory suggests four specific kinds of reinforcement:

1. *Direct reinforcement* refers to extrinsic rewards that correspond to an act (e.g., money, or recognition).
2. *Vicarious reinforcement* includes seeing others get rewards and/or escape punishment for delinquent or criminal acts (e.g., a youth sees someone carrying a lot of money obtained by selling drugs).
3. *Self-reinforcement* happens if a person derives his or her self-worth or sense of pride from criminal acts.
4. *Neutralization of self-punishment* is the process whereby one justifies or rationalizes delinquent acts.

One long-standing sociological theory is commonly referred to as *techniques of neutralization*.[86] Gresham Sykes and David Matza suggest that delinquents often come up with rationalizations or excuses that absolve them of guilt. Thus, for example, a youth may say that no one was harmed or that the victim deserved it ("He had it coming to him"), or a youth may condemn those who condemn him or her (e.g., by saying that adults do these kinds of things, too), appeal to higher loyalties (e.g., "I'm doing it for the 'hood'"), or merely put the blame on various external factors. Two significant outcomes of neutralization techniques is that the victim is dehumanized and there is a gradual desensitization to the use of violence or other means of force to get one's way.

Most of the perspectives summarized previously do not question the nature of the existing social order. Possible exceptions are social disorganization and strain theories which, to some extent, provide at least an indirect critique of the existing order. Most of the theories focus on how offenders and at-risk youths can be made to accommodate to the existing social order. Beginning with the labeling perspective, theorists questioned the nature of the status quo, specifically the social order of advanced capitalism in the late twentieth century. The final two perspectives discussed in this chapter call for changing the nature of the existing social order so that fewer people will be drawn into criminal behavior.

THE LABELING PERSPECTIVE

The labeling perspective (also known as the *societal reaction* perspective) does not directly address the causes of criminal/deviant behavior but rather focuses on three interrelated processes: (1) how and why certain behaviors are defined as criminal or deviant, (2) the response to crime or deviance on the part of authorities (e.g., the official processing of cases from arrest through sentencing), and (3) the effects of such definitions and official reactions on the person or persons so labeled.[87] Howard Becker summarizes the key to this perspective: "Social groups create deviance by making the rules whose infraction constitutes deviance, and by applying those rules to particular people and labeling them as outsiders."[88]

One key aspect of the labeling perspective is that the criminal justice system itself (including the legislation that creates laws and hence defines crime and criminals) helps to perpetuate crime and deviance. For example, several studies during the late 1960s and 1970s focused on the general issue of how agents of the criminal justice system (especially the police) helped to perpetuate certain kinds of criminal behavior (for example, how gangs and gang-related behavior may be perpetuated by the criminal justice system's attempts to control the problem).[89]

One of the most significant perspectives on crime and criminal behavior to emerge from the labeling tradition was Richard Quinney's theory of the *social reality of crime*. In a landmark textbook on crime and criminal justice, Quinney organized his theory around six interrelated propositions.[90]

1. Crime is a definition of human conduct that is created by authorized agents in a politically organized society.
2. Criminal definitions describe behaviors that conflict with the interests of the segments of society that have the power to shape public policy.
3. Criminal definitions are applied by the segments of society that have the power to shape the enforcement and administration of criminal law.
4. Behavior patterns are structured in segmentally organized society in relation to criminal definitions, and within this context persons engage in actions that have relative probabilities of being defined as criminal.
5. Conceptions of crime are constructed and diffused in the segments of society by various means of communication.
6. The social reality of crime is constructed by the formulation and application of criminal definitions, the development of behavior patterns related to criminal definitions, and the construction of criminal conceptions.

Key to Quinney's theory are four interrelated concepts: (1) process, (2) conflict, (3) power, and (4) action. By *process*, Quinney means that all social phenomena have duration and undergo change. The *conflict* view of society and the law is that conflicts in any society are the normal consequences of social life; conflict between persons, social units, or cultural elements are inevitable. Further, society "is held together by force and constraint and is characterized by ubiquitous conflicts that result in continuous change."[91] *Power* is an elementary force in our society. Power "is the ability of persons and groups to determine the conduct of other persons and groups. It is utilized not for its own sake, but is the vehicle for the enforcement of scarce values in society, whether the values are material, moral, or otherwise."[92] Power is important if we are to understand public policy including crime-control policies shaped by groups with special interests. In a class society, some groups have more power than others and therefore are able to have their interests represented in policy decisions, often at the expense of less powerful groups. Thus, for example, white upper-class males have more power, and their interests are more likely to be represented than those of working- or lower-class minorities and women. Finally, by *social action*, Quinney refers to purposive and voluntary behavior. By conceiving of an individual as "able to reason and choose courses of action, we may see him [/her] as changing and becoming, rather than merely being."[93] Humans are shaped by their physical, social, and cultural experiences, but they also have the capacity to change and achieve maximum potential and fulfillment.

It is important to note the distinctions between primary and secondary deviance. *Primary deviance* involves rule breaking by people who see themselves—and are seen by others—as essentially conformist.[94] Although the behavior departs from social norms, reactions are generally not stigmatizing, and there are no long-term consequences. This type of rule breaking is common behavior that has only marginal implications for one's status and psychological structure as long as one maintains an acceptable self-image and an image acceptable to others/society. If the behavior is persistent, reactions are stronger and more punitive. *Secondary deviance* results from stigmatization created by societal reaction to the deviance. Identity and behavior become organized around the deviant label imputed by others. Deviance becomes secondary "when a person begins to employ his deviant behavior or a role based upon it as a means of defense, attack, or adjustment to the overt and covert problems created by the consequent societal reaction to him."[95]

This perspective eventually led some scholars to question not only the criminal justice system but also the very social structure and institutions of society as a whole. In particular, some research in the labeling tradition directed attention to such factors as class, race, and gender in the formulation of criminal definitions and the major causes of crime itself.

CRITICAL/MARXIST PERSPECTIVES

Quinney and John Wildeman place the development of a critical/Marxist line of inquiry in the historical and social context of the late 1960s and early 1970s.

> It is not by chance that the 1970s saw the birth of critical thought in the ranks of American criminologists. Not only did critical criminology challenge old ideas, but it went on to introduce new and liberating ideas and interpretations of America and of what America could become. If social justice is not for all in a democratic society—and it was clear that it was not—then there must be something radically wrong with the way our basic institutions are structured.[96]

The critical perspective focuses on

> those social structures and forces that produce both the greed of the inside trader as well as the brutality of the rapist or the murderer. And it places those structures in their proper context: the material conditions of class struggle under a capitalist mode of production.[97]

The material conditions include the class and racial inequalities produced by the contradictions of capitalism (which produce economic changes that negatively affect the lives of so many people, especially the working class and the poor).

Quinney linked crime—and the reaction to crime—to the modern capitalist political and economic system. He theorized that the capitalist system produces a number of problems because of attempts by the capitalist class to maintain the basic institutions of the capitalist order. In attempting to maintain the existing order, the powerful commit various crimes, which Quinney classified as crimes of control, crimes of economic domination, and crimes of government. At the same time, oppressed people engage in various kinds of crimes related to accommodation and resistance, including predatory crimes, personal crimes, and crimes of resistance.[98]

Much of what is known as criminal and delinquent behavior can therefore be understood as an attempt by oppressed people to accommodate and resist the problems created by capitalist institutions. Many gang members, for example, adapt to their disadvantaged positions by engaging in predatory and personal criminal behavior. Much of their behavior, moreover, is in many ways identical to normal capitalist entrepreneurial activity.[99]

According to Mark Lanier and Stuart Henry, there are six central ideas common to critical/ Marxist theories of crime and criminal justice.[100]

1. *Capitalism shapes social institutions, social identities, and social action.* The mode of production in any given society determines many other areas of social life, including divisions based on race, class, and gender plus the manner in which people behave and act toward one another.

2. *Capitalism creates class conflict and contradictions.* Since a relatively small group (a ruling class consisting of perhaps 1–2% of the population) owns and/or controls the means of production, class divisions have resulted, as has the inevitable class conflict over control of resources. The contradiction is that workers need to consume the products of the capitalist system, but in order to do so they need to have sufficient income to spur the growth of the economy. However, too much growth may cut into profits. One result is the creation of a *surplus population*—a more or less steady supply of able workers who are permanently unemployed or underemployed (also called the underclass).

3. *Crime is a response to capitalism and its contradictions.* This notion stems in part from the second theme in that the surplus population may commit crimes to survive. These can be described as crimes of *accommodation*.[101] Crimes among the more affluent can also result (see next point) in addition to crimes of *resistance* (e.g., sabotage and political violence).

4. *Capitalist law facilitates and conceals crimes of domination and repression.* The law and legal order can often be repressive toward certain groups and engage in the violation of human rights, which are referred to as *crimes of control and repression*. Crimes of *domination* also occur with great frequency as corporations and their representatives violate numerous laws (fraud, price-fixing, pollution, etc.) that cause widespread social harms but are virtually ignored by the criminal justice system.

5. *Crime is functional to capitalism.* There is a viable and fast-growing *crime control industry* that stimulates the economy by creating jobs and profits for corporations (e.g., building prisons; providing various products and services to police departments, courthouses, and detention centers).[102]

6. *Capitalism shapes society's response to crime by shaping law.* Those in power (especially legislators) define what a crime is and what constitutes a threat to the social order. Perhaps more importantly, they determine *who* constitutes such a threat—the answer is usually members of the underclass.

Various problems that threaten the dominant mode of production become criminalized (e.g., illicit drug use by minorities rather than the use of drugs produced by corporations, such as cigarettes, prescription drugs, and alcohol).

Many scholars have sought an explanation of crime and delinquency by examining changes in the economic structure of society and how such changes have contributed to the emergence of an underclass, similar to what Marx called the surplus population.[103] This perspective can be viewed as an extension of some of the basic assumptions and key concepts of social disorganization/ecology, strain, and cultural deviance theories. People ask serious questions about the nature of capitalism and whether or not an alternative system can emerge. Therefore, it seems that a critical/Marxist view of crime and justice is more relevant than ever before.[104]

SUMMARY

With few exceptions (e.g., social learning theory) the theories in this chapter stress the importance of the external socioeconomic environment in explaining delinquency. Beginning with social disorganization/ecology (especially the early work of Thrasher), these theories link delinquency to such environmental factors as poverty, social inequality, lack of community integration, and lack of meaningful employment and educational opportunities, along with the larger economic picture of a changing labor market and the corresponding emergence of a more or less permanent underclass mired in segregated communities.

A second theme is that adolescents who grow up in such environments face daily struggles for self-esteem, a sense of belonging, protection from outside threats, and some type of family structure. Primary social institutions such as the family, the school, the church, and the community are not meeting the basic human needs for significant numbers of youngsters. The sociological theories in the chapter discuss what happens when these institutions fail to support youngsters.

A third theme is that becoming a delinquent is a social process that involves learning various roles and social expectations within any given community. It involves the reinforcement of expectations through various rationalizations or techniques of neutralization in addition to the perpetuation of various lifestyles, attitudes, and behaviors modeled by significant others. Beginning at a very early age, a youth becomes embedded in his or her surrounding environment and the cultural norms of that environment.

A fourth theme is that delinquency is shaped to a large degree by societal reaction to behavior and to the individuals who engage in such behavior. The consequences of being labeled deviant make it difficult to leave the world of delinquency. Society's response perpetuates the very problem it is trying to solve.

A fifth and final theme is that one cannot possibly explain the phenomenon of delinquency without considering the economic context of capitalism. Much delinquency is consistent with basic capitalist values, such as the law of supply and demand, the need to make money (profit), and the desire to accumulate consumer goods.

Notes

[1] Mark M. Lanier, Stuart Henry, and Desiré Anastasia, *Essential Criminology*, 4th ed. (New York: Routledge, 2015), chapter 8.

[2] For a more detailed discussion of the work of Guerry and Quetelet as well as the Chicago School, see Ibid., 181–189; see also Richard Quinney and John Wildeman, *The Problem of Crime: A Peace and Social Justice Perspective*, 3d ed. (Mountain View, CA: Mayfield, 1991), 48–50.

[3] For documentation of this phenomenon, see Joan Moore, *Going Down to the Barrio: Homeboys and Homegirls in Change.* (Philadelphia: Temple University Press, 1991); and Joan Moore, *Homeboys: Gangs, Drugs, and Prisons in the Barrio of Los Angeles.* (Philadelphia: Temple University Press, 1978).

[4] Rodney Stark, "Deviant Places: A Theory of the Ecology of Crime," *Criminology*, 1987, 25(4): 893–909.

[5] Lanier and Henry, *Essential Criminology*, 180.

[6] Anne Meis Knupfer, *Reform and Resistance: Gender, Delinquency, and America's First Juvenile Court* (New York: Routledge, 2001), 25.

[7] Ernest W. Burgess, "The Growth of the City," in Robert E. Park, Ernest W. Burgess, and Roderick D. McKenzie (eds.), *The City* (Chicago: University of Chicago Press, 1925).

[8] Clifford R. Shaw and Henry D. McKay, *Juvenile Delinquency in Urban Areas.* (Chicago: University of Chicago Press, 1972; originally published in 1942).

[9] Frederic Milton Thrasher, *The Gang: A Study of 1,313 Gangs in Chicago* (Chicago: University of Chicago Press, 1927), 32–33.

[10] Ibid., 20–21.

[11] Ibid., 33.

[12] Ibid., 228–31.

[13] James Diego Vigil, *Barrio Gangs* (Austin: University of Texas Press, 1988) 89–90. Vigil concludes that the gang provides many of the functions of a family. "The gang has become a 'spontaneous' street social unit that fills a void left by families under stress. Parents and other family members are preoccupied with their own problems, and thus the street group has arisen as a source of familial compensation" (90). Vigil notes that about half of those he interviewed mentioned how important the group was to them, that the gang was something they needed, and that it gave them something in return. Close friends become like family to the gang member, especially when support, love, and nurturance are missing from one's biological family.

[14] Irving A. Spergel, *Racketville, Slumtown and Haulberg* (Chicago: University of Chicago Press, 1964).

[15] Mercer L. Sullivan, *Getting Paid: Youth Crime and Work in the Inner City* (Ithaca, NY: Cornell University Press, 1989).

[16] Ibid., 203.

[17] Ibid., 103.

[18] Ibid., 110.

[19] Stark, "Deviant Places."

[20] Ibid., 896–97.

21 Among others see Robert J. Sampson, "Neighborhood and Crime: The Structural Determinants of Personal Victimization," *Journal of Research in Crime and Delinquency*, 1985, 22: 7–40; Robert J. Sampson, Stephen W. Raudenbush, and Felton Earls. "Neighborhoods and Violent Crime: A Multilevel Study of Collective Efficacy," *Science*, 1997, 277: 918–924; John H. Laub and Robert J. Sampson, *Shared Beginnings, Divergent Lives: Delinquent Boys to Age 70* (Cambridge, MA: Harvard University Press, 2006); Robert J. Sampson and John H. Laub, *Crime in the Making: Pathways and Turning Points through Life* (Cambridge, MA: Harvard University Press, 1995).

22 Randall G. Shelden, William B. Brown, Karen S. Miller, and Randal B. Fritzler, *Crime and Criminal Justice in American Society*, 2nd ed. (Long Grove, IL: Waveland Press, 2016).

23 The classic statement about anomie was made in Émile Durkheim's *Suicide*. (New York: Free Press, 1951).

24 Robert K. Merton, *Social Theory and Social Structure* (New York: Free Press, 1968, enlarged ed.).

25 Donald J. Shoemaker, *Theories of Delinquency: An Examination of Explanations of Deviant Behavior*, 7th ed. (New York: Oxford University Press, 2018), 121.

26 For an excellent discussion of the role of corporate propaganda see Edward S. Herman and Noam Chomsky, *Manufacturing Consent: The Political Economy of the Mass Media* (New York: Pantheon, 1988); Elizabeth A. Fones-Wolf, *Selling Free Enterprise: The Business Assault on Labor and Liberalism, 1945–60* (Indianapolis: University of Indiana Press, 1994); Alex Carey, *Taking the Risk Out of Democracy: Corporate Propaganda versus Freedom and Liberty* (Chicago: University of Illinois Press, 1995).

27 For a quick and easy-to-read look at inequality see Jonathan Teller-Elsberg, Nancy Folbre, James Heintz, and the Center for Popular Economics, *Field Guide to the US Economy: A Compact and Irreverent Guide to Economic Life in America* (New York: The New Press, 2006).

28 Steven F. Messner and Richard Rosenfeld, *Crime and the American Dream*, 5th ed (Belmont, CA: Wadsworth, 2013).

29 Ibid., 6.

30 Ibid., 72.

31 Quoted in Noam Chomsky, *Class Warfare* (Monroe, ME: Common Courage Press, 1996), 29.

32 A good illustration of this dominance is shown in Charles Derber, *Corporation Nation: How Corporations are Taking Over Our Lives and What we Can Do About It* (New York: St. Martin's Press, 1998).

33 Messner and Rosenfeld note that the United States lags far behind other countries (whose economic institutions are not nearly as dominant) in paid family leave, 80.

34 Matthew Desmond, *Evicted: Poverty and Profit in the American City* (New York: Broadway Books, 2017), 5. Desmond became the second sociologist to win a Pulitzer Prize when *Evicted* was selected for the award in 2017; the book was also chosen for the National Book Critics Circle Award, the Andrew Carnegie Medal, the Order of the Coif Biennial Book Award, and the Silver Gaval Award from the ABA.

35 Elizabeth Gudrais, "Disrupted Lives," *Harvard Magazine*. January–February 2014.

36 Andrew Flowers, "How We Undercounted Evictions by Asking the Wrong Questions," FiveThirtyEight, September 15, 2016.

37 Visit https://evictionlab.org to create custom maps, charts, and reports.

38 Emily Badger and Quoctrung Bui, "In 83 million Eviction Records, a Sweeping and Intimate New Look at Housing in America," *The New York Times*, April 7, 2018.

39 Ibid.

40 Richard A. Cloward, and Lloyd E. Ohlin, *Delinquency and Opportunity: A Theory of Delinquent Gangs* (New York: Free Press, 1960).

41 Ibid., 86.

42 John Hagan, "The Social Embeddedness of Crime and Unemployment," *Criminology*, 1993, 31(4): 465–91.

43 Mark Granovetter, "Economic Action and Social Structure: The Problem of Embeddedness," *American Journal of Sociology*, 1985, 91: 481–510.

44 Although not mentioned by Hagan, one also needs social or cultural capital to become embedded in the labor market. Steady employment is quite difficult for those who lack the necessary social or cultural capital. See Jay MacLeod, *Ain't No Makin' It: Leveled Aspirations in a Low-income Neighborhood*, 3rd ed. (Boulder, CO: Westview, 2009).

45 Hagan, "The Social Embeddedness of Crime and Unemployment," 469.

46 Elijah Anderson, *Streetwise: Race, Class and Change in an Urban Community* (Chicago: University of Chicago Press, 1990), 244.

47 Felix Padilla, *The Gang as an American Enterprise* (New Brunswick, NJ: Rutgers University Press, 1992), 101–2.

48 Anderson, *Streetwise*; John M. Hagedorn, *People and Folks: Gangs, Crime and the Underclass in a Rustbelt City*, 2nd ed. (Chicago: Lakeview Press, 1998); Moore, *Going Down to the Barrio*; Padilla, *The Gang as an American Enterprise*.

49 Albert Kircidel Cohen, *Delinquent Boys: The Culture of the Gang* (New York: Free Press, 1955).

50 Shoemaker, *Theories of Delinquency*, 150.

51 Walter B. Miller, "Lower Class Culture as a Generating Milieu of Gang Delinquency," *Journal of Social Issues*, 1958, 14(3): 5–19.

52 Deanna Wilkinson, "An Emergent Situational and Transactional Theory," in Barry C. Feld and Donna M. Bishop, *The Oxford Handbook of Juvenile Crime and Juvenile Justice* (New York: Oxford University Press, 2012, pp. 336–352), 345.

53 Deborah Shelton, "Changing Violent Youths," *Chicago Tribune*, February 22, 2010, 4.

54 Gary Slutkin, "Violence Is a Contagious Disease," in Forum on Global Violence Prevention, *Contagion of Violence* (Washington, DC: National Academies Press, 2013), 109.

55 Gregory Boyle, *Barking to the Choir: The Power of Radical Kinship* (New York: Simon & Schuster, 2017).

56 Quoted in Shelton, "Changing Violent Youths," 4.

57 Darrell Steffensmeier, Noah Painter-Davis, and Jeffery Ulmer, "The Intersectionality of Race, Ethnicity, Gender, and Age on Criminal Punishment," *Sociological Perspectives*, 2016, 60(4): 810–833. Other studies addressing the same issue include: Rebecca D. Ericson and Deborah A. Eckberg, "Racial Disparity in Juvenile Diversion: The Impact of Focal Concerns and Organizational Coupling," *Race and Justice*, 2016, 6(1): 35–56; Jeffery T. Ulmer and Julia Laskorunsky, "The Role of Juvenile Adjudications in the Disproportional Incarceration of African American and Hispanic Defendants," *Journal of Crime and Justice*, 2016, 39(1): 9–27; Darrell Steffensmeier, Jeffery Ulmer, and John Kramer, "The Interaction of Race, Gender, and Age in Criminal Sentencing: The Punishment Cost of Being Young, Black, and Male," *Criminology*, 1998, 36(4): 763–797.

58 Steffensmeier et al., "Intersectionality," 814.

59 Richard D. Hartley, Sean Maddan, and Cassia Spohn, "Concerning Conceptualization and Operationalization: Sentencing Data and the Focal Concerns Perspective," *Southwest Journal of Criminal Justice*, 2007, 4: 58–78, 59.

60 Travis Hirschi, *Causes of Delinquency* (New York: Routledge, 2017, Transaction Edition; original copyright 1969 by University of California Press).

61 Shelton, "Changing Violent Youths," 4; see also Carl C. Bell and Dominica F. McBride, "Affect Regulation and Prevention of Risky Behaviors," *JAMA*, 2010, 304(5): 565–566.

62 Winfree and Abadinsky, *Essentials of Criminological Theory.*

63 Walter C. Reckless, "A New Theory of Delinquency and Crime," *Federal Probation*, 1961, 25: 42–46.

64 Shoemaker, *Theories of Delinquency.*

65 Ibid.

66 Gresham Sykes and David Matza, "Techniques of Neutralization," *American Journal of Sociology*, 1957, 22(6): 664–770.

67 Hirschi, *Causes of Delinquency*, 10.

68 Ibid., xvi.

69 Ibid., xvii.

70 Johnstone, "Recruitment to a Youth Gang," *Youth & Society*, 1983, 14(3): 281–300, 297.

71 James Diego Vigil and Steve C. Yun, "Southern California Gangs: Comparative Ethnicity and Social Control," in C. Ronald Huff (ed.), *Gangs in America*, 2nd ed. (Thousand Oaks, CA: Sage, 1996), 139–156.

72 Todd R. Clear, "The Problem with 'Addition by Subtraction': The Prison-Crime Relationship in Low-Income Communities," in Marc Mauer and Meda Chesney-Lind (eds.), *Invisible Punishment: The Collateral Consequences of Mass Imprisonment* (New York: New Press, 2002), 181–193.

73 Angela Duckworth and Martin Seligman, The Science and Practice of Self-Control," *Perspectives on Psychological Science*, 2017, 12(5): 715–718; Lisa M. McCartan and Elaine Gunnison,. "Examining the Origins and Influence of Low Self-Control," *Journal of Crime and Justice*, 2007, 30(1): 35–62.

74 Meredith B. Weinstein, Kenethio Fuller, Timothy Mulrooney, and Glenn Koch, "The Benefits of Recreational Programming on Juvenile Crime Reduction: A Review of Literature and Data," National Recreation and Parks Association, September 2, 2014, http://www.nccu.edu/formsdocs/proxy.cfm?file_id=2907; Development Services Group, "Afterschool Programs: Literature Review," OJJDP, 2010.

75 Michael Gottfredson and Travis Hirschi, *A General Theory of Crime* (Stanford, CA: Stanford University Press, 1990).

76 Winfree and Abadinsky, *Essentials eeof Criminological Theory.*

77 Alexander T. Vazsonyi, Jakub Mikuška and Erin L. Kelley, "It's Time: A Meta-analysis on the Self-Control-Deviance Link," *Journal of Criminal Justice*, 2017, 48: 48–63; Travis C. Pratt and Francis T. Cullen, "The Empirical Status of Gottfredson and Hirschi's General Theory of Crime: A Meta-analysis," *Criminology*, 2000, 38(3), 931–964; Brie Diamond, "Assessing the Determinants and Stability of Self-Control into Adulthood," *Criminal Justice and Behavior*, 2016, 43(7): 951–968; Alex R. Piquero, Wesley G. Jennings, Brie Diamond, David P. Farrington, Richard E. Tremblay, Brandon C. Welsh, and Jennifer Reingle Gonzalez, "A Meta-analysis Update on the Effects of Early Family/Parent Training Programs on Antisocial Behavior and Delinquency," *Journal of Experimental Criminology*, 2016, 12(2): 249–264.

78 Shoemaker, *Theories of Delinquency.*

79 Ibid., 251.

80 Peggy C. Giordano, *Legacies of Crime: A Follow-up of the Children of Highly Delinquent Girls and Boys* (New York: Cambridge University Press, 2010); George E. Higgins, "Parental Criminality and Low Self-control: An Examination of Delinquency," *Criminal Justice Studies*, 2009, 22: 141–152.

81 David P. Farrington, Rolf Loeber, Magda Stouthamer-Loeber, Welmoet Van Kammen, and Laura Schmidt, "Self-Reported Delinquency and a Combined Delinquency Seriousness Scale Based on Boys, Mothers, and Teachers: Concurrent and Predictive Validity for African-Americans and Caucasians," *Criminology*, 1996, 34: 501–25.

82 Edwin H. Sutherland and Donald R. Cressey. *Criminology*, 8th ed. (Philadelphia: Lippincott, 1970).

83 Shoemaker, *Theories of Delinquency*, 185. This was one of Sutherland's seven original propositions; two additional propositions were added later.

84 Winfree and Abadinsky, *Essentials of Criminological Theory*.

85 The movie *Falling Down* starring Michael Douglas illustrates how one can "lose it" because of some of these instigators.

86 Sykes and Matza, "Techniques of Neutralization."

87 Edwin Schur, E. (1971). *Labeling Deviant Behavior*. New York: Harper & Row.

88 Howard S. Becker, *Outsiders: Studies in the Sociology of Deviance* (New York: Free Press, 1963). 8–9.

89 Examples can be cited endlessly. Two are: William J. Chambliss and Robert B. Seidman, *Law, Order, and Power* (Reading, MA: Addison-Wesley, 1971) and Carl Werthman and Irving Piliavin, "Gang Members and the Police," in David Bordua (ed.), *The Police: Six Sociological Essays* (New York: John Wiley, 1967), 56–98.

90 Richard Quinney, *The Social Reality of Crime* (Boston: Little, Brown, 1970), 15–25.

91 Ibid., 10.

92 Ibid., 11.

93 Ibid., 13.

94 Michael J. Rosenberg, "Lemert, Edwin M.: Primary and Secondary Deviance," in Francis T. Cullen & Pamela Wilcox (eds.), *Encyclopedia of Criminological Theory* (Thousand Oaks: Sage Publications, 2010), 550–552.

95 Edwin Lemert, *Social Pathology: A Systematic Approach to the Theory of Sociopathic Behavior* (New York: McGraw-Hill, 1951), 76.

96 Quinney and Wildeman, *The Problem of Crime*, 72.

97 Ibid., 77.

98 Richard Quinney, *Class, State, and Crime: On the Theory and Practice of Criminal Justice* (New York: David McKay, 1977), 33–62.

99 Randall G. Shelden, Sharon K. Tracy, and William B. Brown, *Youth Gangs in American Society*, 4th ed. (Belmont, CA: Cengage, 2013), chapter 4.

100 Lanier and Henry, *Essential Criminology*, 256–58.

101 Quinney, *Class, State, and Crime*.

102 Randall G. Shelden and Pavel V. Vasiliev, *Controlling the Dangerous Classes: A History of Criminal Justice in America*, 3rd ed.(Long Grove, IL: Waveland Press, 2018); Randall G. Shelden and William B. Brown, "The Crime Control Industry and the Management of the Surplus Population," *Critical Criminology*, 2001, 9: 39–62.

103 Marx used the term *lumpenproletariat* to refer to the bottom layer of society—the social junk, rabble, etc—seen as the criminal class. He used *surplus population* to refer to working-class men and women who, because of various fluctuations in the market (caused chiefly by contradictions within the capitalist system), were excluded—either temporarily or permanently—from the labor market.

104 For a detailed exposition of alternatives to capitalism, see Richard D. Wolff, *Capitalism's Crisis Deepens: Essays on the Global Economic Meltdown* (Chicago: Haymarket Books, 2016).

Chapter 8

Delinquency in Context

In the previous chapter we reviewed strain and critical/Marxist theories that pointed to the role of the economic institution in generating crime and delinquency. In this chapter, we will briefly introduce concepts that define US capitalism followed by a discussion of the changing economic structure of capitalism and how this relates to crime and delinquency.

John Maynard Keynes listed unemployment and excessive inequality as two of the principle faults of capitalism.[1] Wages are a major source of incomes; the inability to obtain a job relegates individuals to poverty. "The burden of joblessness is borne unequally, always concentrated among groups that already face other disadvantages: racial and ethnic minorities, immigrants, younger and older individuals, women, people with disabilities, and those with lower educational attainment."[2] The availability of jobs reduces poverty, although it does not address the issue of inequality between the top 10% and the remaining wage earners.

In July 2018, the overall unemployment rate was 3.9% (down from 9.5% in July 2009).[3] The black unemployment rate was 6.6% (down from 14.8% in 2009); the Hispanic unemployment rate was 4.5% (down from 12.5% in 2009), and the white rate 3.5%.[4] Since the Bureau of Labor Statistics began collecting data by race in 1972, the black unemployment rate has never been less than 66% higher than the rate for whites; the lowest white/Hispanic ratio was in 2006 when the unemployment rate for Hispanics was 22% higher than for whites.[5]

In some cities the unemployment differential is far worse; national numbers can be misleading. For example, the black unemployment to white unemployment ratio in Washington, DC is the highest in the country—8.5 to 1.[6] Neighborhoods within cities have even more variation. Kansas City has been revitalized since the 2008 recession; its unemployment rate in July 2018 was 3.5%. However, in the 91% black Blue Hills neighborhood, the unemployment rate is 17%; in the 86% black Ivanhoe neighborhood, the unemployment rate was 26%.[7]

> A tight labor market alone can't undo a legacy of unequal school funding, residential segregation or the disproportionate rate of incarceration for black Americans.

Nor can it reverse the gradual shift of well-paying jobs from inner cities to mostly white suburbs. Studies have found that discrimination in hiring and pay persists even in good economic times, making parity an elusive goal.[8]

Unemployment for youths is even worse, especially for blacks. In 2018, the rate for white teens (16–19) was 11.7%; for black teens, 23.1%, and for Hispanic teens 13.7%.[9] In Chicago in 2016 almost one-third of African American men between the ages of 20 and 24 were neither working nor in school (down from 39.5% in 2014).[10] Out of school and out of work percentages increased for Hispanics from 18.2% in 2014 to 21,2% in 2016. Reports on several other large urban areas cite similar statistics.[11]

There are six alternative measures that address labor underutilization. U-3 has been the official concept of unemployment since 1940—all jobless individuals who have actively sought work in the past four weeks. U-4 is total unemployed plus discouraged workers—people who are not in the labor force and had looked for a job in the previous year. They are not counted as unemployed because they had not searched for work in the previous four weeks, believing no jobs were available for them. The rate in July 2018 was 4.2% versus 3.9% for U-3. U-6 is defined as "total unemployed, plus all persons marginally attached to the labor force, plus total employed part time for economic reasons, as a percent of the civilian labor force plus all persons marginally attached to the labor force, seasonally adjusted." The rate in July 2018 stood at 7.5%.[12] A higher percentage of women (60%) were underemployed than were men (40%).[13]

In the United States in 2017, 12.8 million children (17.6% of all children) lived in poverty.[14] Children represented 23% of the total population and 32.6% of the people in poverty. For related children (12.8 million) living in married-couple families, 8.4% were in poverty compared to 42.1% of related children living in families with a female householder and 19.9% in male-householder families. Eighteen percent of whites under the age of 18 lived in poverty compared with 20.8% of blacks and 26.6% of Hispanics.

In 2017, 5.8% of children lived with an unemployed parent, a noteworthy improvement since 2010 when the figure was 11%.[15] For white families, the percentage was 5.2 compared with 9.5% for black families and 7.7% of Hispanic families.[16] Extreme poverty is defined as families with incomes less than 50% of the federal poverty level. In 2016, 9% of children lived in extreme poverty.[17] In the world's largest food-producing nation, 41 million people struggle with hunger. Households that are food insecure have uncertain access to enough food to live a healthy life.[18] One in six children face hunger; they are challenged daily with getting enough healthy food to obtain the energy they need to learn and grow. Children facing hunger experience developmental impairments in areas like language and motor skills. They are likely to struggle in school, and they have more social and behavioral problems.

The Child and Youth Well-Being Index (CWI) project at Duke University tracks the quality of life of children in the United States from birth to age 18. The index is composed of 28 key indicators of well-being: family economics, safe/risky behavior, social relationships, emotional/spiritual well-being, community engagement, educational attainment, and health. The annual results are compared to the 1975 base-year value of 100.[19] In 2013, the index was 102.9. Overall it's not a pretty picture, especially when you consider the fact that the United States is the richest country in the world. The CWI increased less than 3%. How do we explain these problems? To seek some answers it is necessary to examine the larger context of our economic system and the systemic inequality in the United States.

THE CAPITALIST ECONOMIC SYSTEM

Capitalism is a controversial concept—frequently not defined and difficult to delineate because of the areas it encompasses.[20] It is an economic (some would say social) system characterized by the deployment of capital, competition, exchange, orientation to market prices, and the search for profit. Karl Marx rarely used the term; instead he referred to the capitalist mode of production.[21]

The mode of production consists of two essential parts: (1) the *means of production* (the raw materials, tools, instruments, machines, buildings, etc., plus the current state of science and technology, and the skills, abilities, and knowledge of the people themselves) and (2) the *relations of production*.[22] These relations are essentially *class* relations, the most common of which are between the *owners/ managers* and the *workers* (salary and wage earners). The more popular term is that of *social class*, which may be defined as "a group of individuals or families who occupy a similar position in the economic system of production, distribution, and consumption of goods and services in industrial societies."[23]

The most common indicator of social class position is one's occupation. Indeed, it can be said that the work people engage in limits their financial status (income and wealth), their social status or prestige, the stability of their employment, the chances for upward social mobility, and their general health and longevity. It plays a key role in the way they think of themselves, places them within the larger systems of power and authority, and has significant implications for the future of their children. There is probably no other social variable that has a more significant bearing on one's lifestyle, including the probability of becoming defined as a criminal or delinquent.[24]

Several key questions immediately arise when analyzing capitalism, such as who owns the means of production and who decides how the *surplus* is to be distributed. The term *surplus* refers to the "difference between the volume of production needed to maintain the workforce and the volume of production the workforce produces"—meaning, very generally, the margin over and above what is required to meet basic needs.[25] Under most forms of capitalism today, the relations of production are marked by an almost total separation of the workers (i.e., producers) from the means of production. One class (a small group, around 1–2% of the total population) owns most of the means of production—the factories, land, buildings, wealth, income, and other assets. This *capitalist class* or *ruling class* has an enormous amount of power in society. Wealth frequently is not an end in itself; rather, it is a "*means for gathering more wealth,*" which in turn serves "to augment the power of a dominant class."[26]

The *drive for profit* can become an obsession. Robert Heilbroner aptly defines this unique feature of capitalism as "the restless and insatiable drive to accumulate capital."[27] The possession of capital "confers on its owners the ability to direct and mobilize the activities of society."[28] Control over capital gives people more than prestige and distinction; access to capital is power. Moreover, wealth itself becomes *a social category inseparable from power*. "Wherever there is great property, there is great inequality. For one rich man, there must be at least five hundred poor, and the affluence of the rich supposes the indigence of the many."[29]

The accumulation of capital, and hence great wealth and inequality, would not be possible without the assistance of the state. Profits are secured with the assistance of the government, both state and local, in the form of tax abatements, cash subsidies, loans, and other forms of what is essentially taxpayer assistance.[30] Big business could not exist (and has never existed) without strong support from the government—and hence taxpayers.

> Business subsidies that allow politicians to channel economic resources toward their preferred ends distort investment and trade. Moreover, turning government into an engine of illicit profit encourages what economists call rent-seeking. Well-organized special interests usually triumph over the broader public and national interest.[31]

Rent, for economists, is "the excess payment made to any factor of production (land, labor, or capital) due to scarcity."[32] Government policies that grant advantages to special interests create artificial scarcity—allowing narrow interests to enjoy political windfalls. "In both the economic and political realms, the prevalence of rent-seeking is a measure of institutionalized corruption."[33]

States and localities offer subsidies through grants, free property, and tax preferences. Estimates of these annual costs run between $50 and $80 billion.[34] Tariffs and quotas are another form of corporate welfare (about $40 billion annually). Many corporations have benefited from their abilities to get their taxes reduced or eliminated. Between 2008 and 2015, the corporate tax rate was 35%, but about half of Fortune 500 companies that were consistently profitable over those years paid 21.2%. Eighteen of them, including General Electric and Priceline.com, paid no federal income taxes in those 8 years.[35]

Since 2008 a total of $110 billion in subsidies has been awarded to just 965 companies in the Fortune 500. These companies include Boeing ($13 billion), Alcoa ($5.6 billion) and Intel ($3.9 billion), among others.[36] Corporate welfare and crony capitalism undermine public trust in both the free market and the government.[37] It wastes taxpayer resources on well-connected interest groups. Each dollar spent to benefit the well connected is no longer available to US families; with chronic deficits, corporate welfare dollars are taken from the next generation. "Targeted incentives entail an opportunity cost. Incentives direct taxpayer dollars to particular firms and industries which might have been used to provide public goods or to lower tax rates for all."[38]

Capitalism, while bringing about a virtual cornucopia of goods and a standard of living that is the envy of the world, also has negative effects—namely, it produces a tremendous amount of inequality. Within a capitalist system, especially as it exists in the United States, *such inequality is inevitable and a natural by-product of the system itself.*

Class Distinctions

Karl Marx used the terms *reserve army* or *surplus population* to refer to a more or less chronically unemployed or underemployed segment of the population. The industrial revolution created the reserve workers who became redundant as mechanization increased. They were superfluous in terms of producing profits. A closely related concept is what Marx and Engels called the *lumpenproletariat.* In the various English translations of *The Communist Manifesto* since the original publication in 1848, *dangerous class* has been used instead of *lumpenproletariat.* In its original usage, Marx and Engels referred to this segment of society as "the social scum, that passively rotting mass thrown off by the lowest layers of old society."[39] Included in the lumpenproletariat were "thieves and criminals of all kinds, living on the crumbs of society, people without a definite trade, vagabonds, people without a hearth or home."[40] Marx believed this segment of society was inevitable under capitalism because it was not integrated into the labor system (see discussion of the underclass later in the chapter).

There is a dual character to the dangerous classes or surplus population. The surplus population has at times been viewed by those in power as a threat (social dynamite—as was the case with almost the entire working class in the early years of the labor movement during the last half of the nineteenth century) or as a possible resource (a form of cheap labor or a group to exploit in order to keep wage levels down).[41] Moreover, the exact nature of this class has changed over the years, ranging from the working class in general in the nineteenth and early part of the twentieth centuries, to very specific categories in more recent years, such as racial minorities, the underclass, and gangs.

Capitalism produces several *contradictions.* One such contradiction occurs between capital and labor (owners and workers). The owners want more profit, while workers want higher wages and/or more benefits. This has been a continuous conflict throughout the history of capitalism; many believe *class conflict* is inevitable in capitalist societies. The battles have usually been won by the owners, although workers also achieved some very significant gains over the years. The chief executive officers of large corporations have made the most gains. In 1980, the average CEO earned 42 times more than the average worker; in 1990, it was 107 times higher; in 2000 it was 525 times higher . The ratio declined to 361 in 2017.[42] For individual companies the gap is even greater. For example, the CEO of Mattel toys made 4,987 times the amount paid to median employees.

Barbara Ehrenreich titled her best-selling book *Nickel and Dimed: On (Not) Getting by in America.*[43] Ehrenreich spent the better part of a year working at six different low-paying jobs and trying to make ends meet with the minimal wages earned. The stories she tells of the lives of herself and coworkers (primarily women) reveal the underside of the American Dream and the failure of our market economy. The $6 or $8 an hour these workers earned put them all under the official poverty level. Most had to augment their meager wages with either a second job or depend on other workers in the household. Even with additional help, they all struggled.

A decade later, Ehrenreich wrote an afterword for a special anniversary edition. She reported that the most shocking thing she discovered from her research when revisiting some of the workers was the extent to which poverty had been criminalized. In most cities there are ordinances that prohibit the behavior of the poor—making it a crime to loiter, have in your possession a shopping cart, or sleep on park benches. In some places it is against the law for a citizen to share food with a homeless person in public places.

> In what has become a familiar pattern, the government defunds services that might help the poor while ramping up law enforcement. Shut down public housing, then make it a crime to be homeless. Generate no public-sector jobs, then penalize people for falling into debt. The experience of the poor, and especially poor people of color, comes to resemble that of a rat in a cage scrambling to avoid erratically administered electric shocks. . . . The safety net, or what remains of it, has been transformed into a dragnet.[44]

If Ehrenreich's picture is gloomy, think for a moment that these are the *working* poor (defined as people who spend 27 weeks in a year working or looking for work whose incomes fall below the poverty level). In 2016, there were 7.6 million individuals classified as working poor—4.9% of all individuals in the labor force for at least 27 weeks.[45] The working-poor rate for women was 5.8% compared to 4.2% for men. The working-poor rate for blacks was 8.7% compared to 8.5% for Hispanics, 4.3% for whites, and 3.5% for Asians. The *nonworking* poor are among what William Julius Wilson has called the *truly disadvantaged* (see a discussion of his work later in this chapter).

Changes in the U.S. Economy

We are presently in the midst of an important era in history, the last stage of the Industrial Revolution.[46] Several forces are producing this change: (1) technology, (2) the globalization of the economy, (3) the movement of capital, and (4) the overall shift of the economy away from manufacturing to information and services. Some have termed this stage *deindustrialization*.[47] Between 2006 and 2016, jobs in the production of goods sector (mining, construction and manufacturing) declined from 15.1% to 12.6% (manufacturing went from 9.5% to 7.9%). In contrast, the service providing sector increased from 77% in to 80.3%.[48]

Cities like Rochester, Baltimore, Camden, Detroit, Memphis, and Richmond typify the deindustrialization process.[49] The state of Indiana has cities at opposite extremes. Indianapolis has thriving high-tech industries. Gary is plagued by high unemployment, business closures and poverty.[50] The movement of capital overseas, the relocation of plants to countries with lower wages, and mergers with other corporations have all had the effect of eliminating the jobs of many workers. All of this has resulted in a drastic change in educational requirements for employment in industries paying the most money (job growth has generally been in areas requiring the most education).[51] The most-common occupations in the United States are retail salesperson, cashier, food and beverage server, and office clerk.[52] Almost 10% of the labor force (15.4 million people) are employed in these low-paying jobs.

Young African Americans have found jobs in industries that generally pay the least. College access has increased for blacks, but they are overrepresented in majors that lead to low-paying jobs.[53] Areas with occupations that are growing and pay well include: STEM (science, technology, engineering, math), health, and business. African Americans account for 8% of engineering majors, 7% of math majors, 7% of finance and marketing majors, and 5% of computer engineering majors. While blacks account for 10% of health majors, many are in the lowest-earning portion of the field—21% in administrative services compared to 6% in pharmacy. A bachelor's degree in a STEM-related major produces earnings as much as 50% higher than a bachelor's degree in art, psychology, and social work. Unemployment rates are consistently the highest for those who drop out of high school (see chapter 10).[54] In July 2018, the unemployment rate for individuals with a bachelor's degree or higher was 2.2% versus 3.2% for individuals with some college, 4% for high school graduates, and 5.1% for those with less than a high school diploma.

Unequal America: Income, Wealth and Poverty

The purpose of Occupy Wall Street (OWS) when it began in September 2011 was to fight the influence of banks, multinational corporations, and the richest 1% over the democratic process. "We are the 99%" was the movement's call for economic justice. It targeted the influence of money in politics, corporate greed, and income inequality.[55] Until OWS, the extent of inequality was a debated topic only on out of the mainstream websites.[56]

The *Gini Index* is a statistical measure of inequality. The index has been criticized for being overly sensitive to changes in the middle but not picking up changes at the extremes, where much inequality research is focused.[57] A value of 0 means perfect equality—everyone earns the same amount; a value of 100 means perfect inequality—one person earns all. For five decades, the Gini index of the United States has increased steadily: from .397 in 1967 to .482 in 2017.[58] One example of increasing inequality are bonuses. In 2016, Wall Street bonuses to 177,000 employees totaled $24 billion; the annual earnings of all 1,075,000 full-time minimum wage workers totaled $15 billion.[59]

During the past four decades, the weekly wages of the top 10% of the population have been increasing (see figure 8-1), while the wages of the rest of the population

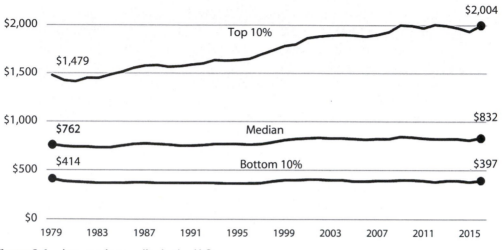

U.S. Real Weekly Wages, 1979–2016

Figure 8-1 Income Inequality in the U.S.

Source: Bureau of Labor Statistics. Real-World Economics Review Blog. https://rwer.wordpress.com/2018/03/05/
u-s-real-weekly-wages-1979-2016/

stagnated. Figure 8-2 shows the distribution of income in 2016 and the distribution of wealth. Wealth is more concentrated than income. The top 1% of income distribution received almost 25% of all income in 2016, while the top 1% of wealth distribution held almost 40% of all wealth.[60] *Wealth gaps between upper-income families and lower- and middle-income families are at the highest levels recorded.*[61]

The 2008 recession triggered a prolonged decline in the wealth of many US families. The losses of upper-income families were smaller, and their recovery was stronger. The median wealth of upper-income families in 2016 was at the highest level since the Federal Reserve started collecting data in 1983.[62] Other households had not recovered. The median wealth of all households was $97,300 compared to $139,700 before the beginning of the recession. Lower-income white families experienced greater losses in wealth during the recession than lower-income black and Hispanic families. The black/white gap decreased from 9.8 in 2007 to 4.6 in 2016, and the Hispanic/white gap decreased from 5.1 to 2.9. Among middle-class families, whites fared better. The gap increased from 3 to 4 for white to black households and from 2.2 to 3.4 for white to Hispanic households.

The racial wealth divide is affected by a stark racial disparity in homeownership and home equity. In June 2017, 71.8% of white Americans owned their homes versus 42.3% of African Americans and 45.5% of Latinos.[63] The median wealth of 18 million black households in 2017 was $4,300 compared to the median wealth of 13 million Latino households at $6,200 and 82 million white households at $151,800.[64] The top 5% of the population holds 65% of the nation's net worth.[65] In 2016, a record 30% of households had no wealth.

Distribution of before-tax income, 2016

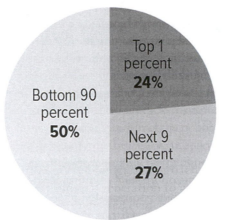

Distribution of wealth, 2016

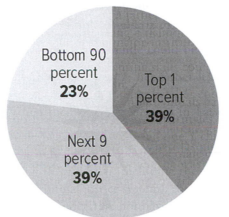

Figure 8-2　Comparison of Income and Wealth Distribution, 2016.

Source: Chad Stone, Danilo Trisi, Arloc Sherman, and Roderick Taylor, "A Guide to Statistics on Historical Trends in Income Inequality." Center on Budget and Policy Priorities, May 15, 2018, p. 15. https://www.cbpp.org/wealth-is-even-more-concentrated-than-income-0

The impact on families has not been good. According to the latest census report, the percentage of people below the official poverty rate in 2017 was 12.3%—39.7 million people living in poverty (see figure 8-3).[66] Female-headed households are the most likely to be living in poverty—sometimes described as the *feminization of poverty*. In 2016, 28.8% of female-headed families lived under the poverty level compared to 10.7% of all families. For black female-headed households; 34.2% lived under the poverty level, in comparison to 21.9% in families with a white female householder and 34.7% of families with a Hispanic householder.

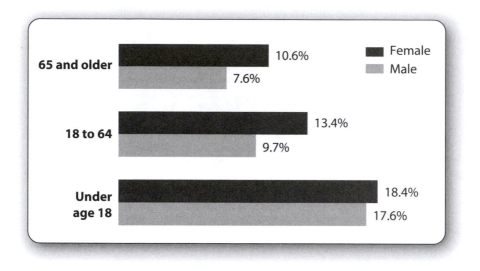

Figure 8-3   Percentage of Poverty Rates by Age and Sex, 2016.

Source: U.S. Census Bureau, Current Population Survey, 2017 Annual Social and Economic Supplement. https://www.census.gov/content/dam/Census/library/publications/2018/demo/p60-263.pdf

Over the last quarter of a century, many safeguards that people once counted on to shield them from financial harm have been weakened or completely lost. These include formal protections such as guaranteed corporate pensions and state and federal unemployment benefits. And they include informal ones, like the loyalty that employers once showed their workers by offering secure jobs with relatively little prospect of long-term layoffs. The informal social contract with corporate America that provided workers benefits in exchange for their production is no longer there. Part of the American Dream is the financial stability that comes with a college education, which is too often beyond the reach of poor families today.

THE DEVELOPMENT OF THE UNDERCLASS

The term *underclass* has been the subject of considerable debate. Herbert Gans refers to the term as an example of new wine in old bottles. It has replaced characterizations such as dangerous classes, the undeserving poor, the rabble, and so on. While it is synonymous with persistent and extreme poverty, it is also a "behavioral term invented by journalists and social scientists to describe poor people who are accused, rightly or wrongly, of failing to behave in the 'mainstream' ways of the numerically or culturally dominant American middle class."[67] The term essentially stigmatizes those who fall within the general category of the underclass—the homeless, those who live in public housing, addicts, and young poor women with babies. The term is often used interchangeably with racial minorities. However, it is misleading to conclude that the underclass is synonymous with African Americans and other minorities. In sheer numbers, whites comprise the majority of the underclass and the poor in general.[68]

Even families earning above the federal poverty level struggle to afford housing, food, health care, and transportation. United Way launched a project called ALICE—Asset Limited, Income Constrained, Employed—a grassroots movement that attempts to redefine financial hardship.[69] Working at low-paying jobs, the men and women in 34.7 million families have little or no savings and are one emergency away from poverty. They are often not included in economic indicators and policy discussions.

Economic security programs have lifted individuals above the poverty line, which has positive long-term effects on children.[70] Yet many families continue to face serious hardship. States cut educational funding, health care, and human services as a result of the 2008 recession. Since 2010, the amount of per-pupil funding in schools in New York City has been cut four times despite increased operating costs.[71] Public investment in schools declined dramatically in the last decade in some states; 29 provided less funding per student than in 2008, and local funding in 19 states also fell.[72] Poor children are more likely to complete high school and have lower poverty rates in adulthood if they attend better-funded schools.

The social and economic positions of African Americans—especially young African-American males, whom one author in the 1980s called an "endangered species"—have deteriorated.[73] By the turn of the century, many young black men had become superfluous—part of the surplus population. William Julius Wilson studied the black underclass and identified a significant difference between inner-city ghettos toward the end of the twentieth century and those of an earlier era. Until the 1960s, inner-city areas were inhabited by *multiple classes* of African Americans (lower-class, working-class, and middle-class professionals), providing much stability and reinforcing dominant cultural norms and values (e.g., hard work, stability, importance of family, obeying the law). Youths growing up in these areas had a variety of stable role models.

> Even if the truly disadvantaged segments of an inner-city area experience a significant increase in long-term spells of joblessness, the basic institutions in that area (churches, schools, stores, recreational facilities, etc.) would remain viable if much of the base of their support comes from the more economically stable and secure families. Moreover, the very presence of these families during such periods provides mainstream role models that help keep alive the perception that education is meaningful, that steady employment is a viable alternative to welfare, and that family stability is the norm, not the exception.[74]

Unfortunately, this social buffer has almost disappeared with the relocation of many families to better neighborhoods. African Americans who are poor are far more likely than previously to live in areas where just about everyone else is poor. The individuals who make up the underclass are mostly the children of previous generations of the poor—whose own children will also remain poor. Many of them have more or less permanently dropped out of the lower class and lack the skills and education to succeed in conventional society. One result is the growth of alternatives to the mainstream labor force, including crime. "The social transformation of the inner city has resulted in a disproportionate concentration of the most disadvantaged segments of the urban African-American population, creating a social milieu significantly different from the environment that existed in these communities several decades ago."[75]

The relatively new social subgroup of the disadvantaged who interact and live only with similarly situated people can be distinguished from the traditional lower class by its lack of mobility. In the twenty-first century, mobility remains a problem. Rural America is coping with socioeconomic problems once found only in inner cities.[76] Despite the decline of manufacturing, struggling residents don't leave for both economic and cultural reasons. In 2017, the overall mobility of the US population reached its lowest level since the 1940s; it fell by almost half from its most recent peak in 1985. Rural mobility has fallen faster than the mobility rate in metropolitan areas. The lack of mobility keeps rural residents from moving to find better jobs, and it means fewer workers are available for employers in areas where jobs are plentiful. The cost of housing is one of the reasons for declining mobility. State licensing requirements are also a barrier; a range of workers from barbers to bartenders to cosmetologists to florists to scrap-metal recyclers must be relicensed if they relocate to a new state. There is also a growing cultural divide; small-town residents may be distrustful of urban attitudes toward immigrants, same-sex marriage, and secularism.

Douglas Massey and Nancy Denton linked the origins and perpetuation of the African-American urban underclass to specific patterns of *segregation*.[77] Until about 1900 most African Americans lived in areas that were largely white. Massey and Denton document the changes since that time using five dimensions of segregation. *Unevenness* looks at overrepresentation and underrepresentation of African Americans in an urban area. *Isolation* refers to African Americans rarely sharing the same neighborhood with whites. *Clustering* occurs when African-American neighborhoods are grouped together so that they either form one continuous enclave (occupying a large area of land) or are scattered about the city. *Concentrated* describes a focus in one small area or sparsely settled throughout a city. *Centralization* measures location within the central core of a city versus spread out along the periphery.

> A high score on any single dimension is serious because it removes blacks from full participation in urban society and limits their access to its benefits. . . . Blacks . . . are more segregated than other groups on any single dimension of segregation, but they are also more segregated on all dimensions simultaneously; and in an important subset of U.S. metropolitan areas, they are very highly segregated on at least four of the five dimensions at once, a pattern we call hypersegregation.[78]

The patterns Massey and Denton described continue today. Areas that are heavily populated by black residents generally form a few very large blocs within metropolitan areas, such as the southern half of Atlanta, central Detroit, South Central Los Angeles, and the eastern half of Washington, DC.[79] Largely Hispanic concentrations are usually smaller clusters scattered across metropolitan areas. Los Angeles is an exception; there is a large bloc in the center/northeast that is heavily populated by Hispanics. Not all centrally located neighborhoods are low-income or non-white, and many low-income or non-white neighborhoods are located at some distance from city centers.[80] In some cities, centrally located neighborhoods have been gentrified in the past 20 years. Generally, black residents are more likely than Hispanics and Asians to be concentrated near central cities. Spatial concentration of non-white neighborhoods is more prevalent than concentration of low-income neighborhoods.

Housing policy authority Richard Rothstein meticulously traced the practices that created segregation. He presents evidence that segregation is not the result of individual choices but of

> public policy that explicitly segregated every metropolitan area in the United States. The policy was so systematic and forceful that its effects endure to the present time. Without our government's purposeful imposition of racial segregation, the other causes—private prejudice, white flight, real estate steering, bank redlining, income differences, and self-segregation—still would have existed but with far less opportunity for expression. Segregation by intentional government action is not de facto. Rather, it is what courts call de jure: segregation by law and public policy.[81]

Explicit racial zoning began in the 1920s during the migration of African Americans from the south to the north.[82] The Federal Housing Administration (FHA) was established in 1934. Its *Underwriting Manual* said that incompatible racial groups should not be permitted to live in the same communities. It sanctioned *redlining*, a practice through which developers and housing brokers would steer black home buyers and renters into the least desirable zones. FHA maps showed those districts in red, hence the term. Whites were directed to areas with access to better schools, infrastructures, and roads. The manual also recommended highways as a good way to separate African Americans from white neighborhoods.

After World War II, suburbs flourished, spurred by FHA subsidies to builders on the condition that no homes would be sold to African Americans, based on the unproven assertion of protecting property values for the homes they were insuring. The Fair Housing Act of 1968 provided modest enforcement against discrimination, but it could not reverse years of segregated residential patterns. "We have created a caste system in this country, with African Americans kept exploited and geographically separate by racially explicit government policies. Although most of these policies are now off the books, they have never been remedied and their effects endure."[83]

POVERTY AND FAMILY STRUCTURE

The American Dream incorporates the ideal that children will have a higher standard of living than their parents. Harvard economists Raj Chetty and Nathaniel Hendren have analyzed data on 20 million children and their parents across generations.[84] Among their findings is that the prospect of children earning more than their parents has fallen from 90% to 50% over the last fifty years. The Equality of Opportunity Project looks at what has caused this erosion and possible solutions. Black children have much lower rates of upward social mobility—and higher rates of downward social mobility—than white children. Black/white income disparities persist across generations. Although Hispanic and black Americans often have comparable incomes, the former group has seen income increase steadily across generations.

The number of people living below the federal poverty line grew rapidly during the 2000s. In addition, there were shifts in the geography of poverty, which spread beyond urban and rural locations. It rose rapidly in smaller metropolitan areas. It also became more concentrated in distressed and disadvantaged areas. The majority of poor people (55%) now live in high poverty or extremely poor areas—and 72.7% of poor people live in metropolitan areas. Almost 14 million people, including 6.3 million poor people, lived in neighborhoods with poverty rates of 40% or more in 2014, which was more than twice the number in 2000—13.5% of poor people faced the double burden of being poor in a very poor place.[85]

> The intersection between poverty and place matters. Poor neighborhoods come with an array of challenges that negatively affect both the people who live in those neighborhoods—whether they themselves are poor or not—as well as the larger regions in which those neighborhoods are located. Residents of poor neighborhoods face higher crime rates and exhibit poorer physical and mental health outcomes. They tend to go to poor-performing neighborhood schools with higher dropout rates. Their job-seeking networks tend to be weaker and they face higher levels of financial insecurity. . . . The concept of concentrated poverty reflects the fact that while pockets of deep neighborhood poverty can affect the well-being of all residents, they are especially troubling for poor families who already face burdens associated with their low incomes, and who may have fewer housing and neighborhood choices available to them. These challenges disproportionately fall to people of color, and, while they have long been particularly pronounced in inner cities, as poverty has spread beyond the urban core, so too has concentrated disadvantage.

Although whites made up 44% of the nation's poor in 2014, they were 18% of poor residents living in extremely poor neighborhoods.[86] Poor blacks were 5 times as likely to live in such neighborhoods, and poor Hispanics were 3 times as likely. Almost a third of the largest metropolitan areas had more than 30% of poor black residents living in concentrated poverty. Syracuse had the highest percentage

(59%). In 17 metropolitan areas, more than 30% of poor Latino residents lived in concentrated poverty, with rates reaching well above 40% in Buffalo, Fresno, Rochester, and Syracuse. High levels of neighborhood distress were a much more prominent feature in the lives of poor blacks and Hispanics than in the lives or whites.

Where families live profoundly affects access to opportunity.[87] It determines daily interactions—from casual associations to classmates to professional networks. Neighborhoods are the entry points to schools, transportation, jobs, health care, parks, and other amenities. An analysis of the data from the last three censuses found that less segregated regions of the 100 most populous metropolitan areas had higher average incomes and educational attainment and lower homicide rates.[88] In areas where low-income people live, access to quality education, jobs, housing, and public services is severely limited. People need to travel farther to find better paying jobs, if they can afford the transportation. People who live in affluent neighborhoods benefit from good schools, low crime rates, and access to better jobs. Educational attainment and job prospects improve with access to safer neighborhoods and better schools. Steady, high-paying jobs provide income, and cash flows back into communities through taxes, consumer spending, and home ownership.

Neighborhoods shape children's opportunities for economic mobility.[89] Each year a child spends in an area where permanent residents have higher incomes increases his or her income. Factors that affect economic mobility are: residential segregation, income inequality, proportion of single mothers in the neighborhood, social capital, and school quality.[90] Children who live in counties with less concentrated poverty, less income inequality, better schools, a larger share of two-parent families, and lower crime rates have better outcomes. Areas with a larger share of black residents have much lower rates of upward mobility; residential segregation by race amplifies racial inequality across generations.

The outcomes for boys vary more than the outcomes for girls. Poverty and exposure to disadvantaged neighborhoods during childhood are particularly harmful for boys. Boys respond to greater levels of income inequality by dropping out of school more frequently.[91] Boys who grow up in concentrated poverty in highly segregated neighborhoods have much lower employment rates than girls from the same areas.[92]

> Growing up in poverty may induce low-ability boys to switch from formal employment to crime or other illicit activities, perhaps because of lower perceived returns to work. . . . The secular decline in male labor force participation rates in the U.S. has been attributed to factors such as the aging of the population, changes in industrial structure, and globalization. Our findings suggest that part of the explanation may instead lie in the growth of residential segregation, income inequality, and the fraction of children raised in single-parent households—all factors associated with lower employment rates for boys relative to girls.[93]

Comparing families with comparable incomes, black men will eventually earn substantially less than white men, while black women will earn slightly more than white women.[94] Of black men born into the lowest-income families, 21% will be incarcerated, a far higher percentage than for any other low-income family groups. Black children are more likely to grow up in single parent households with less wealth, and their parents have lower levels of education. Two factors are associated with better outcomes and smaller black/white gaps for black men in low-poverty neighborhoods: less racial bias and higher rates of black fathers present in the neighborhood. Unfortunately, less than 5% of black children live in such neighborhoods versus 63% of white children.

Rutgers professor of public policy Paul Jargowsky refers to an architecture of segregation.[95] His analysis of census data found that the number of people living in areas where 40% or more of the residents are below the poverty level doubled since 2000. Impoverished families suffer both the disadvantages of living in poverty and in areas ravaged by the social problems that flow from it.

> Concentration of poverty is the product of larger structural forces, political decisions, and institutional arrangements that are too often taken for granted. Our governance and development practices ensure that significant segments of our population live in neighborhoods where there is no work, where there are underperforming schools, and where there is little access to opportunity.[96]

Effects of Economic Changes on Delinquency

It would be misleading to conclude that the emergence of the underclass is the leading cause of crime. Some areas of the country have experienced some of the economic changes described in this chapter but have not shown a significant rise in crime. Joan Moore describes the U.S. labor market as *structurally segmented*. The *primary labor market* consists of jobs with good pay, security, and opportunities for advancement, which are relatively scarce. Barrio and ghetto residents do not have ready access to these kinds of jobs. Instead, the majority are most likely to be found within the *secondary labor market*, which consists of unstable jobs with low wages (often part-time jobs) and with little or no career advancement opportunities.[97]

One consequence of this system is the existence of *supplemental economic structures*, specifically a welfare economy and an illegal economy. These economic structures supplement the more marginal or peripheral sectors of the secondary labor market. Individuals may move back and forth between the secondary market and this peripheral market. In many instances the welfare and illegal economy subsidizes the marginal industries of the secondary labor market. These are fall-back sources of income since minimum wages are not enough to support a family.

> This is a world of limited opportunities, with legitimate jobs offering little prospect for lifetime satisfaction. In this respect, the segmented labor market becomes an essential concept for understanding the structure and context of the Chicano gang, the use and marketing of illegal drugs and stolen merchandise, and the prison involvements of the residents of the Los Angeles barrios.[98]

The geographic distribution of jobs tends to eliminate many minorities, making them part of the surplus population.[99] Most live within areas where industry has left; long commutes are required to try to find a job and to go to work if hired. High-tech jobs have replaced manufacturing jobs, leaving many minorities jobless. The good jobs of an earlier generation have been replaced by low-wage jobs with little security and no fringe benefits (the secondary labor market).

Urban decline contributes to social disorganization, weakening communities and lessening social control. The poor, the unemployed, and the unemployable are left behind while others leave the area for jobs, better schools, and better housing. Higher crime rates may be a byproduct of the changing socioeconomic factors, since illegal activities are some of the only options that remain for the uneducated and underemployed.

Cultural critic Henry Giroux advocates for pedagogy to be central to politics to create a culture that provides the foundation for developing critical citizens and substantive democracy. He believes the ultimate test of morality resides in what a society does for its children. By that standard, US society has failed as public schools and colleges are defunded, job-creating programs for young people dismantled, and social protections eliminated, particularly for youths marginalized by class and color.[100]

> At stake here is not merely how American culture is redefining the meaning of youth, but how it constructs children in relation to a future devoid of the moral and political obligations of citizenship, social responsibility, and democracy. . . . The relations between youth and adults have always been marked by strained generational and ideological struggles, but the new economic and social conditions that youth face today, along with a callous indifference to their spiritual and material needs, suggest a qualitatively different attitude on the part of many adults toward American youth—one that indicates the young have become our lowest national priority. . . . Punishment and fear have replaced compassion and social responsibility as the most important modalities mediating the relationship of youth to the larger social order. . . . Many young people, especially those who are poor and underprivileged, are considered excess, if not disposable, especially to a government that denies the importance of social protections and long-term investments, and is unconcerned about the social costs of what might be called the reign of casino capitalism.[101]

A study, focusing on Chicago, found that black children suffer a great deal as a result of their exposure to concentrated disadvantage (based on six characteristics: receipt of welfare, poverty, unemployment, female-headed households, racial composition, density of children). No whites and only a few Latino families lived in the most disadvantaged quartile of Chicago's neighborhoods. Concentrated disadvantage was experienced almost solely by the black population. The effects of exposure to concentrated disadvantage included long-lasting consequences for black children's cognitive ability equivalent to missing 1 year of schooling.[102]

As noted in chapter 6, poverty is one of the leading causes of poor cognitive skills and educational outcomes, which in turn directly relate to dropping out of school and delinquency rates.

There are structural and institutional causes of the disproportionate representation of low-income children in the juvenile justice system.[103] In delinquency courtrooms, the vast majority of children live at or below the poverty level. One or both of their parents are unemployed; those who are employed earn minimum wage. The children are chronically absent from school and may have learning disorders or mental illnesses. The most common points of entry to delinquency court are the child welfare system, public schools, retail stores, and neighborhood police presence. At each stage of the process, the court gives weight to the perceived needs of the child and his or her family—often more weight than to the evidence of criminal responsibility. The standard of proof depends on the socioeconomic class of the accused, lowering the state's burden of proof for indigent juveniles and raising it for affluent youth. The practice perpetuates negative stereotypes based on class. Juvenile court involvement stigmatizes youth and increases the likelihood of continued involvement in the courts as adults.

The correlation between economic conditions within urban areas and rates of delinquency has been noted for more than 150 years. Indeed, as the classic studies by Clifford Shaw and Henry McKay and others have noted (see chapter 7), delinquency and crime cannot be separated from surrounding economic conditions. Solutions that fail to address these variables are doomed to be little more than band-aids.

THE DEATH OF CHILDHOOD IN THE INNER CITIES

Children under the age of 18 constitute 37% of the homeless population—51% of the children are under the age of six.[104] California is one of the worst states in the extent of child homelessness; only Mississippi and Alabama rank lower. The common perception of homelessness is substance abusers and the mentally ill living on skid row.[105] The economically homeless are men, women, and families who have no place to live because of a setback, whether divorce, illness, loss of a job, or eviction.

The problem is particularly acute in Los Angeles because of its high cost of housing. Of the 58,000 homeless people in Los Angeles County, 5,000 are children and 4,000 are elderly. The most vulnerable are generally those with no place to live—about 33% are mentally ill, 40% are African American, veterans, plus young people from L.A. County's overwhelmed juvenile justice system and its foster care programs. All pressing social issues play out in homelessness—inequality, racial injustice, poverty, violence, and sexism.[106] Most of California's homeless children are not homeless in the traditional sense; more than 202,000 (3% of enrolled K–12 students, which is twice the national rate) students live with their families and share living quarters with other families or live in cars or shelters. Privacy and quiet are nonexistent, and most face extreme poverty. Many are exhausted and drop out of school.[107] Students who perceive themselves to be of lower social status suffer emotional distress, which negatively affects academic performance.[108]

The failure of the American Dream to satisfy the needs and wants of people can be clearly seen in downtown Los Angeles, literally a stone's throw from many symbols of wealth. (The city of Las Vegas, where the authors live, is perhaps the most extreme expression of massive symbols of wealth juxtaposed with signs of poverty.) Giroux warns that young people facing social problems such as pervasive racism and poverty are themselves often seen as the problem. The increasing presence of police and security personnel turns public schools into containment centers for populations of disposable youth destined for incarceration. "Young people are increasingly defined through a youth crime-control complex that is predatory in nature and punishing in its consequences, leaving a generation of young people with damaged lives, impoverished spirits, and bankrupted hopes."[109] We create and sustain social conditions that give rise to predictable responses like gangs and violence—and then blame those who exhibit the behavior. To quote seventeenth-century poet John Milton (author of *Paradise Lost*) "They who have put out the people's eyes reproach them of their blindness."[110]

SUMMARY

There are many ways economic changes are related to delinquency and gang activity. Unemployment, poverty, and general despair lead young people to seek out economic opportunities in the growing illegal marketplace. The free market is largely a myth, and a surplus population is constantly being created and reproduced. Most criminal activity is consistent with basic capitalist values, such as the law of supply and demand, the need to make money (profit), and the desire to accumulate consumer goods.

The term *underclass* has become a moral condemnation of various groups not falling within mainstream society. Closely correlated with this concept is the *feminization of poverty* and the general economic decline of the inner cities. Labor market changes, particularly deindustrialization and capital flight, have propelled and perpetuated these problems. An architecture of segregation of minorities isolates them from mainstream society and the contacts that lead to a good education and decent jobs, removing opportunities for social mobility.

Notes

[1] L. Randall Wray, "The Social and Economic Importance of Full Employment," The Levy Economics Institute of Bard College, working paper no. 560, April 2009.

[2] Ibid., 6.

[3] Bureau of Labor Statistics, "Labor Force Statistics from the Current Population Survey," https://data.bls.gov/timeseries/LNS14000000

4 Kori Hale, "Black Unemployment Rate Ticks Up While Homeownership Declines," *Forbes*, July 19, 2018.

5 Philip Bump, "Black Unemployment Hits a New Low—But Still Trails White Unemployment Significantly, "*The Washington Post*, May 4, 2018.

6 Janelle Jones, "In 14 States and DC, the African American Unemployment Rate Is at Least Twice the White Unemployment Rate, Economic Policy Institute, May 17, 2018.

7 Caleb Gayle, "The Truth about Black Unemployment in America," *The Guardian*, July 7, 2018.

8 Natalie Kitroeff and Ben Casselman, "The Limitations of a Rising Tide," *The New York Times*, February 22, 2018, B1.

9 Bureau of Labor Statistics, "E-16. Unemployment Rates by Age, Sex, Race, and Hispanic or Latino Ethnicity," July 6, 2018, https://www.bls.gov/web/empsit/cpsee_e16.htm

10 Matthew D. Wilson and Teresa L. Córdova, "Industrial Restructuring and the Continuing Impact on Youth Employment in Illinois," Chicago: Great Cities Institute, University of Illinois at Chicago, May 2018.

11 NPR Staff, "The Youth Unemployment Crisis Hits African-Americans Hardest," National Public Radio, July 21, 2014; Martha Ross and Nicole Prohal Svajlenka, "Employment and Disconnection among Teens and Young Adults: The Role of Place, Race, and Education," The Brookings Institution, May 24, 2016; Jordan Bruneau and Michael Saltsman, "Young Adults: California's Forgotten Class," Employment Policies Institute, April 2017.

12 Bureau of Labor Statistics, "Alternative Measures of Labor Underutilization," August 3, 2018, table A-15, U-6, http://www.bls.gov/news.release/empsit.t15.htm; the alternative measures are published monthly in The Employment Situation news release.

13 Bureau of Labor Statistics, "Persons Not in the Labor Force and Multiple Jobholders by Sex, Not Seasonally Adjusted," August 3, 2018, table A-16

14 Kayla Fontenot, Jessica Semega, and Melissa Kollar, "Income and Poverty in the United States: 2017," United States Census Bureau, September 2018. The poverty level depends on the size of the family; for four people, the poverty threshold in 2017 was $25,283.

15 National Kids Count, "Children with at Least One Unemployed Parent," Annie E. Casey Foundation, February 2018.

16 Bureau of Labor Statistics, "Employment Characteristics of Families—2017," April 19, 2018, USDL-18-0589, table 1, https://www.bls.gov/news.release/famee.t01.htm

17 National Kids Count, "Children in Extreme Poverty," Annie E. Casey Foundation, September 2017.

18 Feeding America, "Hunger and Poverty Facts" and "Child Hunger Facts," Chicago: Author, 2018.

19 Kenneth C. Land, *Child and Youth Well-Being Index (CWI) Report*, Duke Center for Child and Family Policy, 2014.

20 Jürgen Kocka, *Capitalism: A Short History* (Princeton, NJ: Princeton University Press, 2016).

21 Other modes of production have included mercantilism, feudalism, socialism, and communism. In primitive societies, the mode of production was hunting and gathering.

22 Randall G. Shelden and Pavel V. Vasiliev, *Controlling the Dangerous Classes*, 3rd ed. (Long Grove, IL: Waveland Press).

[23] Robert A. Rothman, *Inequality and Stratification: Race, Class, and Gender,* 5th ed. (New York: Routledge, 2005; reissued 2016), 5.

[24] There is a wide body of literature documenting the relationship between social class and crime. Among other works, see Jeffrey H. Reiman and Paul Leighton, *The Rich Get Richer and the Poor Get Prison*, 11th ed. (New York: Routledge, 2017); Gregg Barak, Paul Leighton, and Allison Cotton, *Class, Race, Gender, and Crime: The Social Realities of Justice in America*, 5th ed. (New York: Roman and Littlefield, 2018); on inequality generally see Thomas M. Shapiro (ed.), *Great Divides: Readings in Social Inequality in the United States*, 3rd ed. (New York: McGraw-Hill, 2004); Kathryn Neckerman (ed.), *Social Inequality* (New York: Russell Sage Foundation, 2004).

[25] Robert L. Heilbroner, *The Nature and Logic of Capitalism* (New York: W. W. Norton, 1985), 33.

[26] Ibid., 35.

[27] Ibid., 42.

[28] Ibid., 45.

[29] Ibid., 46.

[30] Matthew D. Mitchell and Tamara Winter, "The Opportunity Cost of Corporate Welfare," Mercatus Center, May 22, 2018, https://www.investors.com/politics/commentary/subsidies-corporate-welfare-politics/

[31] Doug Bandow, "Subsidies Galore: Corporate Welfare for Politically-Connected Businesses Is Bipartisan," *Investor's Business Daily*, July 11, 2018.

[32] Brink Lindsey and Steven Teles, *The Captured Economy: How the Powerful Enrich Themselves, Slow Down Growth, and Increase Inequality* (New York: Oxford University Press, 2017), 16.

[33] Ibid., 17.

[34] Bandow, "Subsidies Galore."

[35] Aimee Picchi, "Meet the 18 Profitable Companies that Paid No Taxes over 8 Years," CBSNews.com, March 10, 2017.

[36] Philip Mattera, "Subsidizing the Corporate One Percent," Washington, DC: Good Jobs First, February 2014. Good Jobs First implemented the first national search engine for economic development subsidies and other forms of government financial assistance to business; use https://www.goodjobsfirst.org/subsidy-tracker to track state and federal subsidies and loans/bailouts to companies.

[37] Romina Boccia, "Corporate Welfare Wastes Taxpayer and Economic Resources," Testimony before the Subcommittee on Federal Spending Oversight and Emergency Management, United States Senate, June 10, 2015.

[38] Matthew Mitchell, Daniel Sutter, and Scott Eastman, "The Political Economy of Targeted Economic Development Incentives, *The Review of Regional Studies*, 2018, 48: 1–9, 3.

[39] Max Eastman, Trans. and Ed. *Capital, The Communist Manifesto and Other Writings.* (New York: The Modern Library, 1959). 332.

[40] Anthony Giddens, *Capitalism and Modern Social Theory* (New York: Cambridge University Press, 1971), 38.

41 Steven Spitzer, "Toward a Marxian Theory of Deviance," *Social Problems*, 1975, 22(5): 638–51.

42 Kenneth Quinnell, "Executive Paywatch 2018: The Gap Between CEO and Worker Compensation Continues to Grow," AFL-CIO, May 22, 2018.

43 Barbara Ehrenreich, *Nickel and Dimed: On (Not) Getting By in America.* (New York: Henry Holt, 2001).

44 Barbara Ehrenreich, *Nickel and Dimed: On (Not) Getting By in America, Tenth Anniversary Edition* (New York: Picador, 2011), 236–237.

45 Bureau of Labor Statistics, "A Profile of the Working Poor, 2016," July 2018, Report 1074.

46 D. Stanley Eitzen, Maxine Baca Zinn, and Kelly Eitzen Smith, *In Conflict and Order: Understanding Society*, 14th ed. (Boston: Pearson, 2017).

47 Barry Bluestone and Bennett Harrison, *The Deindustrialization of America* (New York: Basic Books, 1982). For updated discussions of this topic see Paul Craig Roberts, *The Failure of Laissez Faire Capitalism and Economic Dissolution of the West* (Atlanta, GA: Clarity Press. 2013).

48 Bureau of Labor Statistics, "Employment by Major Industry Sector," October 24, 2017, table 2.1.

49 For a review of jobs lost and technological displacement, see Derek Thompson, "A World Without Work," *The Atlantic*, July/August 2015.

50 "The Two Worlds of Deindustrialization," *The Economist*, March 4, 2015.

51 Susan Ockert (ed.), *Business Statistics of the United States 2016: Patterns of Economic Change*, 21st ed. (Lanham, MD: Berman Press, 2017).

52 Thompson, "A World Without Work."

53 Anthony Carnevale, Megan Fasules, Andrea Porter, and Jennifer Landis-Santos, "African Americans: College Majors and Earnings," Center on Education and the Workforce, Georgetown University, 2016.

54 Bureau of Labor Statistics, "Employment Status of The Civilian Population 25 Years and Over by Educational Attainment," August 3, 2018, table A-4.

55 Michael A. Gould-Wartofsky, *The Occupiers: The Making of the 99 Percent Movement* (New York: Oxford University Press, 2015).

56 The publication of two books by French economist Thomas Piketty pushed inequality to the forefront of public debate. See Thomas Piketty, *The Economics of Inequality*, Arthur Goldhamer, Trans. (Cambridge, MA: Harvard University Press, 2015); Thomas Piketty, *Capital in the Twenty-First Century*, Arthur Goldhamer, Trans. (Cambridge, MA: Harvard University Press, 2014).

57 Datablog, "Inequality Index: Where are the World's Most Unequal Countries? *The Guardian*, April 26, 2017.

58 Fontenot et al., "Income and Poverty in the United States: 2017."

59 Sarah Anderson, "Off the Deep End: The Wall Street Bonus Pool and Low-Wage Workers," Institute for Policy Studies, March 2017.

60 Chad Stone, Danilo Trisi, Arloc Sherman, and Roderick Taylor, "A Guide to Statistics on Historical Trends in Income Inequality." Center on Budget and Policy Priorities, May 15, 2018, 15. For additional information on inequality, see G. William Domhoff, *Who Rules America? The Triumph of the Corporate Rich*, 7th ed. (New York: McGraw-Hill, 2014) and Domhoff's website: https://whorulesamerica.ucsc.edu/power/wealth.html

61 Rakesh Kochhar and Anthony Cilluffo, "How Wealth Inequality Has Changed in the U.S. Since the Great Recession, by Race, Ethnicity and Income," PEW Research Center, November 1, 2017.

62 Ibid.

63 Stone et al, "A Guide to Statistics on Historical Trends in Income Inequality."

64 Chuck Collins and Josh Hoxie, "Billionaire Bonanza: The Forbes 400 and the Rest of Us," Institute for Policy Studies, November 2017.

65 Peter Hooper, Matthew Luzzetti, Brett Ryan, Justin Weidner, Torsten Slok, and Rajsekhar Bhattacharyya, "US Income and Wealth Inequality," Deutsche Bank, January 2018.

66 Fontenot et al., "Income and Poverty in the United States: 2017," table B-1.

67 Gans, H. (1995). *The War Against the Poor: The Underclass and Antipoverty Policy.* New York: Basic Books, 2.

68 Fontenot et al., "Income and Poverty in the United States: 2017" table 3. In 2017, approximately 27,000 whites lived in poverty compared to 9,000 blacks and 11,000 Hispanics.

69 Quentin Fottrell, "50 million American Households Can't Even Afford Basic Living Expenses," June 9, 2018, MarketWatch.com.

70 Center on Budget and Policy Priorities, "Chart Book: Economic Security and Health Insurance Programs Reduce Poverty and Provide Access to Needed Care," March 21, 2018.

71 Valerie Strauss, "This Is What Inadequate Funding at a Public School Looks and Feels Like—as told by an Entire Faculty," *The Washington Post*, February 9, 2018.

72 Michael Leachman, Kathleen Masterson, and Eric Figueroa, "A Punishing Decade for School Funding," Center on Budget and Policy Priorities, November 29, 2017.

73 Jewelle Taylor Gibbs, ed., *Young, Black, and Male in America: An Endangered Species* (Westport, CT: Auburn House, 1988).

74 William Julius Wilson, *The Truly Disadvantaged: The Inner City, the Underclass, and Public Policy*, 2nd ed. (Chicago: University of Chicago Press, 2012), 56.

75 Ibid., 58.

76 Janet Adamy and Paul Overberg, "One Nation Divisible: Struggling Americans Once Sought Greener Pastures—Now They're Stuck," *The Wall Street Journal*, Aug. 2, 2017.

77 Douglas S. Massey and Nancy A. Denton, *American Apartheid: Segregation and the Making of the Underclass* (Cambridge, MA: Harvard University Press, 1993).

78 Ibid., 74.

79 Jenny Schuetz, "Metro Areas Are Still Racially Segregated," The Brookings Institution, December 8, 2017.

80 Jenny Schuetz, Jeff Larrimore, Ellen Merry, Barbara Robles, Anna Tranfaglia, and Arturo Gonzalez, "Are Central Cities Poor and Non-white?" *Journal of Housing Economics*, 2018, 40: 83–94.

81 Richard Rothstein, *The Color of Law: A Forgotten History of How Our Government Segregated America* (New York: Liveright Publishing, 2017), viii.

82 Shelden and Vasiliev, *Controlling the Dangerous Classes.*

83 Rothstein, *The Color of Law*, xvii.

84 Raj Chetty, Nathaniel Hendren, Maggie R. Jones, and Sonya R. Porter, "Race and Economic Opportunity in the United States: An Intergenerational Perspective," Working

paper, March 2018, http://www.equality-of-opportunity.org/assets/documents/race_paper.pdf

[85] Elizabeth Kneebone and Natalie Holmes, "U.S. Concentrated Poverty in the Wake of the Great Recession," The Brookings Institution, March 31, 2016, https://www.brookings.edu/research/u-s-concentrated-poverty-in-the-wake-of-the-great-recession/

[86] Ibid.

[87] Schuetz, "Metro Areas Are Still Racially Segregated."

[88] Gregory Acs, Rolf Pendall, Mark Treskon, and Amy Khare, "The Cost of Segregation: National Trends and the Case of Chicago, 1990–2010," The Urban Institute, March 2017.

[89] Raj Chetty and Nathaniel Hendren, "The Effects of Neighborhoods on Intergenerational Mobility I: Childhood Exposure Effects," *Quarterly Journal of Economics*, 2018, 133(3): 1107–1162.

[90] Chetty and Hendren, "The Effects of Neighborhoods," 1163–1228.

[91] Melissa S. Kearney and Phillip B. Levine, "Income Inequality, Social Mobility, and the Decision to Drop Out of High School," Brookings Papers on Economic Activity, Spring 2016.

[92] Raj Chetty, Nathaniel Hendren, Frina Lin, Jeremy Majerovitz, and Benjamin Scuderi, "Childhood Environment and Gender Gaps in Adulthood," American Economic Review Papers and Proceedings, 2016, 106(5) 282–288.

[93] Ibid., 288.

[94] Chetty et al., "Race and Economic Opportunity in the United States: An Intergenerational Perspective."

[95] Paul A. Jargowsky, "Architecture of Segregation: Civil Unrest, the Concentration of Poverty, and Public Policy," Issue Brief, The Century Foundation, August 9, 2015.

[96] Ibid., 14.

[97] Joan W. Moore, *Homeboys: Gangs, Drugs, and Prisons in the Barrio of Los Angeles.* (Philadelphia: Temple University Press, 1978).

[98] Ibid., 33.

[99] Shelden and Vasiliev, *Controlling the Dangerous Classes*; Shelden et al., *Crime and Criminal Justice in American Society.*

[100] Henry A. Giroux, *Disposable Youth, Racialized Memories, and the Culture of Cruelty* (New York: Routledge, 2012).

[101] Ibid., xiv–xv.

[102] Robert J. Sampson, Patrick Sharkey, and Stephen W. Raudenbush, "Durable Effects of Concentrated Disadvantage on Verbal Ability among African-American Children." Proceedings of the National Academy of Sciences, 2008, 105: 845–852.

[103] Tamar R. Birckhead, "Delinquent by Reason of Poverty," *Washington University Journal of Law and Policy, 2012*, 38: 53–107.

[104] Ellen L. Bassuk, Carmela J. DeCandia, Corey Anne Beach, and Fred Berman, "America's Youngest Outcasts: A Report Card on Child Homelessness," The National Center on Family Homelessness at American Institutes for Research, November 2014.

[105] Editorial, "The Homeless in L.A. Are Not Who You Think They Are," *The Los Angeles Times*, February 26, 2018.

106 Editorial, "Los Angeles' Homelessness Crisis is a National Disgrace," *The Los Angeles Times*, February 25, 2018.

107 Carolyn Jones and Daniel J. Willis, "Shelters, Cars, and Crowded Rooms," EdSource, October 2, 2017.

108 Kearney and Levine, "Income Inequality, Social Mobility, and the Decision to Drop Out of High School."

109 Giroux, *Disposable Youth*, 4.

110 Retrieved from: http://www.goodreads.com/quotes/308420-they-who-have-put-out-the-people-s-eyes-reproach-them

Chapter 9

Delinquency and the Family

Families are the primary institution in which children receive care, support, identity, and a sense of belonging.[1] Changes in marriage and childbearing have reshaped the family in the United States over the last 50 years. Adults marry later in life, and many no longer marry. The percentage of children living with an unmarried parent increased from 13% in 1968 to 32% in 2017.[2] About 7% live with unmarried, cohabiting parents. Of the 24 million children younger than 18 living with one unmarried parent, 15 million live with their mother, 3 million with their father.

Contrary to popular belief, the traditional U.S. family is not always a very safe and secure institution. Consider some of the following numbers:

- 676,000   Number of children abused or neglected[3]
- 1,750   Number of children who died of abuse or neglect;[4]
- 39%   Percentage of children sexually assaulted by a family member;[5]
- 143,866   Number of children who were removed from their home because of abuse or neglect;[6]
- 12.3%   Proportion of homicides involving family members;[7]
- 8.5 million   Estimated number of intimate partner related assaults on women each year; 40% of female homicide victims are killed by an intimate partner.[8]

While there have been countless discussions about making schools (see next chapter) and streets safer, the home is usually assumed to be a safe haven. For some—especially women and children—the home can be a very dangerous place. In 2016, for example, 78% of perpetrators of child maltreatment were parents and 4% were unmarried partners of parents.[9] The institution of the family often does not match idealized images.

The array of domestic arrangements that constitute a family today is much larger than in decades past. Widespread divorce and cohabitation have made marriage only one option of many.[10] Family diversity, including same-sex marriage, can be a divisive issue. Some believe the breakdown of the traditional family indicates social decay. The family is a cultural symbol as well as a social arrangement; there are strong moral connotations connected with the family as a social institution. Mythological views of families distort the realities experienced by many.

1. *The myth of a stable and harmonious family in the past.* There has been no golden age of the family, according to historians. There have always been divorces, desertions, and abuse. The main reasons for higher divorce rates today compared to earlier generations are the lessening of strong prohibitions against divorce and longer life spans.

2. *The myth of separate worlds.* The image of the family as a place of love and intimacy where people can escape the dehumanization of the external world is an unobtainable ideal. The distinction between private and public realms assumes families are self-sufficient units free from outside pressures—a haven in a heartless world. This myth ignores the reality of family life, which can be filled with physical and emotional aggression. It also ignores the multiple connections of the family to the outside world; family life is affected by other social institutions, including schools, the workplace, and the welfare system.

3. *The myth of the monolithic family form.* From politicians, religious leaders, and television we often hear about the typical family—a two-parent family with two children living in a home in the suburbs. The reality is that this kind of family constitutes about 7% of all families in the United States.

4. *The myth of a unified family experience.* There is often an assumption that everyone in a family experiences it the same way. Men and women experience family life differently; on most measures of mental and physical health, married men fare much better than married women, while single women fare much better than single men. There are also noteworthy differences in experiences among children. Gender is a prime factor for different experiences; it determines many of the differences in rates of delinquency between girls and boys.[11]

5. *The myth of family consensus.* The myth assumes harmonious interests of all family members. It ignores power relations, competition, and varying interests. As with relations in other social institutions (i.e. school and work), negotiation, exchange, conflict, and inequality exist in family relationships.

6. *The myth of family breakdown as the cause of social problems.* This myth (the background for the rhetoric of "family values") suggests that all sorts of social problems—poverty, crime, drugs, etc.—are the result of single-parent homes or women in the workplace. This ignores the important effects of economic conditions on families.

THE FAMILY IN CONTEMPORARY SOCIETY

The history of the family in the United States has been closely connected to the development of capitalism. With the coming of the industrial age, work shifted from the home to the factory. Men went off to toil in low-wage, alienating work, while their wives took care of the home and children. While some men earned enough to support a family, others did not. For large numbers of immigrants and racial minorities, one-earner incomes were inadequate to provide the necessities of life. Many women also worked outside the home. In addition, many families combined together to form extended kinship groups. Starting in the twentieth century with the G.I. Bill (including VA loans for housing), some families received various kinds of social supports. Government funding of highways enabled millions of mostly white families to live in the suburbs and to commute to their jobs. These benefits were not as often available to minorities.[12]

Although some politicians talk about the importance of family values, rarely do policies affecting family life (such as paid time off, parental leave, and unemployment) benefit families. There is no mandated paid maternity or paternity leave in the United States, whereas European Union (EU) countries mandate a minimum of 14 weeks for new mothers.[13] Time off and compensation vary by country. In the United States, the Family and Medical Leave Act allows new parents to take 12 weeks of unpaid leave per parent. There is no statutory regulation for paid time off or sick leave in the United States. The average provided by companies is 10 paid vacation days plus 6 public holidays. In the EU, the minimum paid days off is 20 days. Unemployment benefits in the United States vary by state; they are generally 40 to 50% of prior earnings for up to 26 weeks. The least generous EU countries pay 90% of earnings for up to two years.

Families living in the poorest neighborhoods rarely enjoy even the limited benefits discussed above. Households with low incomes have a much higher incidence of *family stressors*, leading to *multiple marginality* (see chapter 4).

> The long history of racism and poverty has had lingering effects on a number of levels, such as where people live and what types of jobs are available to them, which in turn affects the extent to which their family life is structured and organized to effectively participate in society. Many people affected by racism and poverty live in deteriorating neighborhoods, crowded conditions, and their children attend schools that have crumbling infrastructures, insufficient staff, and no resources to fix these problems.[14]

The stress from the interactions of all these factors can cause maladaptive behaviors.

> When family or other normative social forces and influences do not function, as they should, street subcultures arise to fill the void. . . . Such social control breakdowns completely transform and undermine human development trajectories that affect cognitive, physical, social, and emotional needs and desires.[15]

As discussed later in the chapter, effective parental supervision can mitigate high risk factors for delinquency. The degree to which children are supervised may vary depending on the number of children in the home, the number of rooms in the home, the type of family residence (e.g., government housing project versus single-family residence), the family income, and the presence of a father. In families experiencing multiple stresses, especially those with many children, there is a loosening of control networks. One result is that children spend more unsupervised time in the streets with other similarly situated youths.

> An individual's connections, or social bonds, with significant others ordinarily begin with the family and gradually extend to others outside kinship networks starting mainly at school. However, multiple marginalization erodes social bonds and contributes to the breakdown of family life and schooling routines, resulting in a generally untethered existence for a youth, which leads to more time spent on the streets. . . . This street-based socialization becomes a key factor in developing not only different social bonds but also different aspirations for achievement, levels and intensities of participation, and belief patterns.[16]

We need to remember that external factors can affect both the structure and internal dynamics of the family as we review some of the research on the connection between family variables and juvenile delinquency. By focusing too closely on a delinquent's family, we may lose sight of the external causes of family dysfunction. For instance, the discussion of parenting styles as they relate to delinquency could result in an inclination to blame the parents (as people often do). The important question is why some parents engage in negative parenting styles and others do not. The family does not exist in a social vacuum.

THE ROLE OF THE FAMILY IN DELINQUENCY

Many criminological theories discuss parenting and families as socializing and restraining factors (see, for example, Gottfredson and Hirschi's self-control theory in chapter 7). Research articles have identified single parenting, young mothers, abusive households, and criminal fathers as factors correlated with antisocial behaviors.[17] Family influences can increase the risk of youths becoming involved in delinquency or can serve as protective factors to reduce the likelihood of delinquent behavior.

Research has looked at family factors that involve both the *structure* of the family and the *nature of relationships within the family*. Structure of the family includes such variables as the broken home (a home where one or both parents is absent because of death, desertion, or divorce), the size of the family, family income, and other variables. The quality of relationships within the family includes such factors as parental conflicts, parent–child relationships, criminality of parents, and methods of discipline and supervision.[18]

Broken Homes

Numerous studies, dating as far back as the 1920s and 1930s, have consistently shown that juvenile delinquents are far more likely than non-delinquents to come from broken homes. Sheldon and Eleanor Glueck began studying Boston delinquents in the 1930s. Their famous studies found that delinquents were about twice as likely as non-delinquents to come from broken homes (60% vs. 35%).[19]

The studies have been criticized because they focus on official delinquents—juveniles already involved in the criminal/juvenile justice system. The relationship between broken homes and delinquency may thus have been a function of juvenile justice workers and police officers deciding to process such juveniles, whereas they may have made different decisions regarding juveniles from intact homes.[20] A meta-analysis of 50 studies about the relationship between broken homes and delinquency found that delinquency in homes with only one parent present was 10%–15% higher than in homes with both parents present and that the correlation was strongest for minor offenses.[21] A recent study found only a small and temporary association between changes in family structure and adolescent delinquency.[22] Another recent study looked at three theoretical areas in the relationship of the family to youth delinquency: the role of family structure, psychological processes and interactions between children and their parents, and economic factors related to family functioning. In all three areas, attachment between parents and adolescents impacted participation in delinquency.[23]

In general, the type of household is not a significant predictor of delinquency, but maternal attachment is an important determinant of delinquent behavior across all family types.[24] The research literature indicates that the family encourages conformity of youth by monitoring behavior, applying consistent discipline, and developing parent-child attachments. Much of the research literature collapses all single-parent households into one category; it does not distinguish between families headed by a single parent because of death or never married that have differing effects on family bonds. Unlike divorced or unmarried single mothers who have unplanned pregnancies, single mothers by choice make an active decision to parent alone. Children of single mothers by choice experienced similar levels of parenting quality to a comparison group of children in two-parent families.[25] Children of these single mothers were not exposed to parental conflict or to maternal psychological problems that commonly result from divorce or an unplanned pregnancy. Adverse outcomes for children in single-parent families are primarily associated with socioeconomic disadvantage, lack of social support, parental conflict, and maternal depression.[26]

Adolescents growing up in single-parent families may suffer from several disadvantages. One of the main problems is poverty—the single greatest threat to children's well-being that negatively impacts physical health, mental health, cognitive and social capacities, and learning.[27] Changes in income following a family disruption often place single-parents in a position where they cannot afford to offer extracurricular activities and other opportunities that might give youth less time to engage in delinquency. Loss of economic resources in single-parent families may also be associated with moves to lower-income neighborhoods which may, in turn, also place youth at higher risk for delinquent behavior. Indeed, poverty is considered one of the strongest risk factors associated with juvenile delinquency.

Urie Bronfenbrenner, who has written a great deal about families, provides a succinct summary of the effects of poverty.

> The developmental risks associated with a one-parent family structure are relatively small . . . in comparison with those involved in two other types of environmental contexts. The first and most destructive of these is poverty. Because many single-parent families are also poor, parents and their children are in double jeopardy. But even when two parents are present, research in both developed and developing countries reveal that in households living under stressful economic and social conditions, processes of parent-child interaction and environmentally oriented child activity are more difficult to initiate and to sustain.[28]

Research indicates that when the mother, or some other adult committed to the child's well-being, establishes and maintains a pattern of progressive reciprocal interaction, the disruptive impact of poverty on development is significantly reduced. The presence of supportive, involved parents may mediate the negative influence of poverty to lessen a juvenile's chance of becoming delinquent. Unfortunately, the proportion of parents who are able to provide quality care despite their stressful life circumstances is not very large. Even for those who are successful, the buffering effect of parents can decline sharply by the time children reach the ages of five or six and are exposed to impoverished and disruptive settings outside the home.

Family Relationships

Surveys in a community with frequent data collection from childhood to adulthood provide the best information about family factors predicting delinquency.[29] Longitudinal studies also have the advantage of looking at reciprocal influences—parenting influencing child behaviors and child behaviors influencing parenting. *Family relationships* usually refer to parental interaction, affection, supervision, and discipline.

In a unique longitudinal study, researchers used the records of youths referred to a child guidance clinic in St. Louis in the 1920s. The juvenile court referred about half of the youths for antisocial conduct, including theft, running away, and truancy. Thirty years later, the researchers located records (juvenile court, police, prison, hospital, welfare, marriage, military, etc.) of and/or interviewed more than 500 of the people in the records or their relatives. The clinic referrals were compared to a control group of 100 children from public school records. The subjects were predominately white males from families with low socioeconomic status. The families had a high degree of disruption. Clinic subjects were more maladjusted as adults than the control subjects. Poor supervision and poor discipline were strong predictors of delinquency, in addition to antisocial or alcoholic parents.[30] Researchers found that if parents had criminal or juvenile delinquent records, their children followed the same pattern.

Joan McCord studied a sample of 250 delinquent and nondelinquent youth from the early 1940s through the 1970s.[31] She found that the best predictor for delinquency was *poor parental supervision*. Parental aggressiveness (e.g., harsh discipline) and conflict were found to be strong predictors of *violent crime* but not property crime. A passive or rejective attitude by the mother predicted property crime but not violent crime. McCord also found that boys raised in a home without affectionate mothers and where there was conflict were more likely to have a juvenile record regardless of whether the home was broken (i.e., the incidence of delinquency is lower in broken homes with affectionate mothers than in intact homes that had conflict).

In London, a longitudinal study began in 1961 and 1962 with 411 boys between the ages of 8 and 9 and continued until they reached their 20s. The *best early-life predictors* included harsh or erratic discipline; a cruel, passive, or neglecting attitude on the part of the parents; poor supervision; and conflict within the family. Delinquents came from families where parenting skills were negligible. Again, low family income was the strongest predictor for the most frequent offenders (65% vs. 18% of the non-offenders and 28% of the occasional offender).[32] The Cambridge study was conducted in another country; the results were similar to the studies conducted in the United States.

The Gluecks found that four family factors strongly predicted, at an early age, which males would most likely become a delinquent.

1. Overly strict, erratic, threatening, or lax discipline by parents;
2. Low parental supervision;
3. Parental rejection/lack of affection toward the child;
4. Weak emotional attachment to the parents or the overall *cohesiveness* of the family.[33]

A reanalysis of the original statistics, using more modern statistical procedures, found that the variables that best explained delinquency were: erratic punishment by the father, erratic punishment by the mother, mother's supervision, parental rejection of the child, and the emotional attachment to the parent.[34]

In a study that took place near Chicago, researchers conducted interviews with 2,000 parents of children around the age of 13. Parents' lack of knowledge about their children's friends and the use of physical punishment were strongly related to delinquency. However, the variable that was the most significantly related was the *attachment* between parent and child—the closer the reported relationship, the lower the delinquency.[35] Recall the importance of attachment in control/social bond theory discussed in chapter 7.

Rolf Loeber and Magda Stouthamer-Loeber identified four models of family functioning that relate to delinquency.[36]

> *The neglect model* focused on parent–child/child–parent involvement and parental supervision. Poor supervision and spending little time with children were the specific behaviors that *best* predicted delinquency.
> *The conflict model* focused on discipline practices and parent–child/child–parent rejection. *Rejection* best predicted *serious* forms of delinquency, although inconsistent and overly strict physical discipline was also a strong predictor.

The parental deviance and attitudes model focused on parental criminality and deviant attitudes and whether parents approve of, ignore, or encourage a child's deviance. *Parental criminality was one of the strongest predictors of serious delinquency.*

The disruption model focused on marital conflict (including disagreements about how to raise the kids, thus resulting in inconsistent parenting) and the absence of one or both parents. Conflict was more strongly related to delinquency than a broken home per se.

In many families several of these models may be operating simultaneously (e.g., there could be both neglect and conflict), which is a stronger predictor of delinquency. These *interaction* variables increase over time in their capacity to predict persistent delinquency—the longer these problems persist and go untreated, the greater will be the likelihood of persistent delinquency.

For example, a survey of a sample of 824 adolescents in a Midwestern city concluded that there were several different patterns of family interaction that can have varying impacts on self-reported delinquency.[37] Indirect patterns include emotional and communicative factors, and direct problems include control and supervision. The most delinquent youths were those who had the most conflict with their parents. The conflicts often concerned the youths' choice of friends.

The research is firm on one point: socializing variables, such as lack of parental supervision, parental rejection, and parent–child involvement, are the most powerful predictors of juvenile delinquency. To be more specific, *affection, supervision,* and *discipline* are the three key variables that best predict delinquency.[38] In general the parents of the most persistently delinquent youths have either (1) not cared or (2) even if they cared, did not have the time or energy to monitor the children's behavior, or (3) even if they cared and monitored, they did not see anything wrong with the deviant conduct, or (4) even if they did all of these, they may not have had the inclination or the means to apply sanctions to the behavior. Overall, weak family control over the behavior of children has been found to be the *most consistent* variable that distinguishes between delinquents and non-delinquents.

The level of familial communication is also related to delinquency; families with the poorest level of communication produce the most delinquents.[39] Youths with the least amount of parental supervision during the after-school hours (police arrest data report the highest number of delinquent acts during these hours) have the highest rates of delinquency.[40] Low parental monitoring (supervision) of children was associated with higher levels of delinquency, especially violent offenses, along with drug abuse and vulnerability to peer pressure.

A great deal of research has focused on parenting behaviors linked to children's delinquency. Most studies have not investigated whether social and economic pressures have affected the behavior of both parents and children. A meta-analysis of more than seventy studies in 1986 found that the best predictors of delinquency were lack of parental supervision, parental rejection, and parent-child involvement. Parental discipline was a weaker predictor than other family variables.[41] A meta-analysis in 2009 extended the original work.[42] The researchers supported the conclusion that parental rejection and poor supervision were among the best predictors of delinquency. There were moderate effects for psychological control and overprotection. Compared to other relatives (mother, siblings, grandparents), a father's arrest was the strongest predictor of male delinquency. The longer antisocial fathers lived with their families, the higher the risk for their children to engage in antisocial behavior.

Family Models

The circumplex model integrates three dimensions—cohesion, flexibility, and communication—that are considered relevant in family theory models. Family cohesion is the emotional bonding between family members; the model looks at four levels: disengaged, separated, connected, and enmeshed. Flexibility measures leadership, role relationships, and relationship rules; its four levels are: rigid, structured, flexible, and chaotic. Communication is critical for facilitating movement on the other two dimensions.[43] Families need both stability and change; the ability to change when appropriate distinguishes functional families from dysfunctional ones.

Researchers designate families that have the greatest amount of affection toward their children and who have the highest degree of supervision and discipline as cohesive families.[44] Families should be able to do the following: (1) cope with stress and problems in an efficient and effective way; (2) utilize coping strategies and resources from within and from outside the family; (3) have the ability to end up being more cohesive, more flexible, and more satisfied as a result of effectively overcoming stress and problems. Therefore, a strong family is based on family interaction rather than the characteristics of the individual family members.[45]

Family cohesion is necessary for learning healthy social skills. Studies have consistently shown that attachment to one's parents is especially crucial; this affects the friendships formed by adolescents, which in turn relates to levels of delinquency. Even when adolescents are with their peers, those who are strongly attached to their parents often find that the parents are psychologically present.[46] A balance between cohesion and adaptability creates more positive communication, which is characterized by empathy, supportiveness, and reflective listening among family members.[47] The lack of cohesiveness often leads to child abuse.[48]

Most of the family variables discussed impact delinquency rates for all racial groups. Within Hispanic families, there are two elements of family life that strongly relate to delinquency: family solidarity and familism (adherence to the *value and importance* of the family).[49]

In his study of inner-city Puerto Rican youths in the South Bronx, Edward Pabon found that the least delinquent youths spent more time with family members in the evenings and on weekends. Consistent with Gottfredson and Hirschi's control theory, Pabon concluded that the more time youths spend on activities in the evenings or on weekends, the less the opportunity there will be for involvement in delinquency behavior.[50]

Parenting Styles

Researchers have identified four types of *parenting styles*. The *authoritarian* is characterized by high demands on children and low responsiveness to their needs. Authoritarian parents are very rigid and controlling with an emphasis on punishment or the threat of punishment to make children behave in a certain way. The *authoritative style* is characterized by high expectations, firm enforcement of rules and standards, and open communication with children. These parents do not constantly use punishment to achieve results, and they try to listen to their children and understand what is going on in their lives. The *permissive/indulgent style* is more of a laissez faire approach; rules are either nonexistent or inconsistently enforced. Methods of discipline are more passive, and parents make few demands on their children, giving them too much freedom to do as they please.[51] The *disengaged/indifferent style* involves parents who are unresponsive to their children and only minimally demanding of them. Children from such families are virtually ignored unless they make demands, which usually receive hostile responses.[52]

Children from families with authoritative styles are the least delinquent and do the best in school.[53] This style of parenting has been found to be associated with "better psychological development, school grades, greater self-reliance, and lower levels of delinquent behavior among adolescents."[54] Youths from authoritarian and permissive families tend to have the highest rates of delinquency. Social class affects the type of parenting style. In general, the lower the social class, the greater the likelihood of authoritarian parenting styles.[55]

An interesting study was conducted in Chicago that focused on poor, black, urban families.[56] The researchers compared mothers of children who were high achievers with the mothers of low achievers. Mothers of high achievers emphasized developing their children's inner sense of self-direction, motivation, and trust in their own judgment; they emphasized cooperation, consideration, and sharing responsibilities. The mothers of the low achievers were concerned mostly with control and believed that the child should obey the authority of adults. They were overly protective about keeping their children out of trouble and shielding them from outside threats, rather than encouraging their children to strive for personal growth. Their children were hesitant to take on difficult challenges, were easily discouraged, and tended to perform badly in school—all of which led to higher rates of delinquency.)

THE SOCIAL CONTEXT OF THE FAMILY

What the majority of researchers have neglected to emphasize is that the family, including all that occurs within it, can be viewed as both an independent and dependent variable. By this we mean it is usually assumed that the family exists independently of the surrounding social, economic, and political environment. The ability of the family to function properly can certainly be a cause of delinquency, but it can also be the *result* of many factors outside of the family.

Research from an earlier era indicated that what went on within the family was more influential than what went on outside of the family. Such beliefs fit Elliott Currie's fallacy of autonomy (see chapter 6). He describes the fallacy as "the belief that what goes on inside the family can usefully be separated from the forces that affect it from the outside: the larger social context in which families are embedded for better or for worse."[57] Beginning in the early 1800s, writers and researchers continuously placed the blame for delinquency on the family. In the majority of cases, that meant the poor immigrant family or a minority family living in a depressed neighborhood. Parents in these families have always been viewed as unfit, as if the problems they had parenting were not affected by outside forces—poverty, poor housing, lack of educational and work opportunities, etc. Can anyone argue that being a parent is just as easy for a single mother with three children living in public housing with a high crime rate as it is for a working mother living with her working husband in a middle-class suburb with a low crime rate?

One group of researchers conducted a National Youth Survey of 1,725 boys and girls between the ages of 11 and 17. The study began in 1976 and followed the participants into their thirties.[58] Their study was instrumental in standardizing the characteristics necessary for reliable self-report studies: questions covering a wide range of delinquent behaviors; the inclusion of serious offenses; scales that reliably separated high-rate from low-rate offenders; follow-up questions to remove trivial acts reported that were unlikely to elicit official reactions. The researchers analyzed environmental factors and family backgrounds.[59] They found that involvement with delinquent peers was significant in the learning of delinquency. Other factors included differences in aspirations/expectations between youths and their parents, bonding to family, peers, and school as revealed in interactions, bonds to conventional norms, and attitudes toward deviance.

Most of these youths were black (73%), while 19% were white and 8% were Hispanic.[60] In 42% of the families, there was violence between the parents; 32% of the parents hit the youths, mostly with some sort of object. About 40% of the parents had been arrested, 17% for a violent crime. In 44% of the cases, a sibling also had an arrest record, with 20% being arrested for a violent crime. Clearly violence was a pattern in these families. Social environmental factors outside of the family were even stronger predictors than family factors, with delinquency among one's peers ranking first, followed by violence among peers, and property crimes by peers. Next in order came a youth's perceptions of work opportunities in the area, school integration (the extent of their bonds to the school), and whether or not they had committed a crime at school. Other factors correlated with delinquency were family physical health (the poorer the health, the higher the rate of delinquency) and family involvement in cultural activities. The researchers concluded that the role of the family as far as violent crime is concerned is not nearly as significant as what occurs outside of the family. Especially important are peer groups and the school. When violent or other antisocial acts are considered normal outside the family (e.g., among peers), families may not be able to prevent youths from being influenced. Most of the families lived in high-crime neighborhoods where local institutions were weak. The fact that the majority of the families were poor meant that they lacked access to resources that could be used as a positive force in preventing delinquency, especially violence.

Research has always documented the strong association between the behaviors of one's peer group and delinquency. As predicted by Sutherland's differential association theory (see chapter 7), strong and persistent association with delinquent peers will lead to greater delinquent involvement. However, strong family bonds and especially parental supervision can mediate this relationship.[61]

A unique study examined the relationship between delinquency and family poverty in connection with poverty rates within the surrounding community.[62] The study found that delinquency rates were highest for families living in communities with high rates of poverty and lower for families whose incomes were beneath the poverty level but living in communities with lower rate of poverty. The effect of family poverty on delinquency more than doubles when levels of community poverty are one standard deviation above the average and more than quadruples when community poverty is two standard deviations above the average. Community poverty has an amplifying effect.

Discussions about the decline of traditional family values typically translate into: mom should stay home, dad should work, and the kids should receive the proper amount of punishment for their misdeeds. Some have even argued that working mothers are a major cause of crime, which is without any foundation in fact. The evidence strongly supports the opposite: children whose mothers work are *less* delinquent, *except in cases where wages are extremely low and low-cost child care is unavailable*. Children of working mothers are "not significantly different from those of children whose mothers are not in the labor force. Moreover, even when the experiences are different, their development and educational outcome do not seem to be."[63]

GIRL OFFENDERS AND THEIR FAMILIES

Research on risk and protective factors for delinquency are often different for male and female juveniles. The mechanisms behind these differences are complex but important to understand. Jean Bottcher found that certain social practices of gender were intertwined with delinquent behavior. Her research has influenced the study of gender and delinquency by recognizing gender as an active, dynamic, everyday social practice and by suggesting that theories of delinquent behavior must include a contextually sensitive concept of gender.[64] Bottcher identified the activities that high-risk adolescent boys and girls do every day to establish masculine or feminine identities.[65] Examining the social practices of gender reveals social conditions and activities that affect involvement in delinquency. Making friends was one social practice affected by gender. Adolescent males were more likely to participate in segregated friendship groups, which overlapped with segregated delinquent group activity. The male pattern of having fun also enabled delinquent activity. Adolescent males had more access to privacy and spent more time with unsupervised peers. Adolescent female social practices included teenage child care, parental responsibilities, and limited social support for delinquency—all of which discouraged delinquent activity.

Researchers have theorized that girls experience stronger connections to family than boys do and that this connection serves as a protective factor. However, research has also found that when the protective bond is weakened (by violence, abuse, lack of parental supervision, etc.) girls engage in risk-taking behavior that may lead to delinquency.[66]

A study that looked at the influence of parents as important predictors of disruptive behavior among young girls found two specific domains of parenting that contributed to early disruptive behavior—low parental warmth and harsh discipline.[67] The findings about girls' antisocial behavior were similar to the findings of previous studies about boys. Harsh treatment by parents contributes to coercive parent-child interactions and models aggressive behavior. Children internalize standards for behavior through exposure to harsh interactions with parents, such as yelling, arguing, and slapping. Punitive discipline by parents can lead to displays of anger and defiance by children. The failure of parents to form a warm, supportive relationship with their children impedes the development of emotional understanding and empathy. Children do not learn to consider the feelings of others. One additional contribution of this study was its examination of outcomes of parenting practices across ethnic groups—there were no variations between African-American and European-American girls.

As noted in chapter 5, female delinquency consists primarily of minor offenses. Research conducted on girls also shows that minor offenses often indicate serious problems experienced by girls. For example, status offenses like running away from home and truancy are common among female delinquents. Studies of girls who are chronic runaways highlight their experiences with sexual and physical violence, suggesting that they may be leaving serious problems associated with victimization. Similarly, research on aggressive girls also suggests that these offense patterns are best understood in the context of family, peer groups, and schools. One study found that girls who had experienced severe child abuse were more than seven times as likely as nonabused girls to commit a violence offense.[68] Another study also found that girls who experienced sexual abuse had an increased likelihood of juvenile arrests for violence offenses.[69]

As can be readily seen from these studies, the family situation of delinquents is an important component of their lives and a major causative factor in their delinquency. However, as we have already noted, we cannot focus exclusively on the family as if it exists in a social vacuum. Many parents struggle daily against incredible odds to cope with the fast-changing world around them.

CHILDREN WITH PARENTS IN PRISON

One of the strongest predictors of whether or not a child will become a chronic delinquent is parental criminality, especially if a parent has spent time in jail or prison. From 5 to 8 million children have been exposed to parental incarceration.[70] By their teenage years, 1 in 4 African American and 1 in 10 Latino children will experience parental incarceration compared to 1 in 25 white children. Children of incarcerated parents are frequently younger than 10. Children living in poverty are 3 times more likely to experience the incarceration of a parent than children not living in poverty. For children of high school dropouts, 62% of African American children will experience parental incarceration before the age of 17 compared to 15% of white children. For children of parents with some college, the percentages drop to 10% and less than 2%.

Precise estimates of the number of parents in the criminal justice system are problematic. The numbers of parents in state and federal prison are more reliable, but reports often lag behind the annual surveys. Tracking the number of parents in jail is more problematic because of the constant churning of individuals arrested, confined without bail, awaiting sentencing, or serving jail sentences of varying lengths. On any given day, there are more than 6.6 million adults somewhere in the criminal justice system: prison, jail, probation, or parole; 1 in 38 adults in the U.S. are under correctional supervision.[71]

For the children of individuals taken into custody, the experience can be a very traumatic experience.[72]

> While parental absences can occur through marital separation or even death, the removal of a parent through incarceration creates unique stressors in a child's life, many of which go unnoticed to the outside world. The stigma and shame associated with parental incarceration makes identifying children of incarcerated parents difficult for schools and social service agencies. Children of incarcerated parents are also subject to significant uncertainty and instability, as many incarcerated parents repeatedly cycle in and out of prison. Moreover, while most children have a means of personal contact with a parent who is absent because of marital separation, the barriers to communication between a child and his or her incarcerated parent are tremendous and are complicated by the fact that caregivers may be reluctant to facilitate such contact.[73]

Most incarcerated parents are fathers. In state and federal prisons, about 45% of men age 24 or younger are fathers.[74] The percentage of women who are mothers is higher—55% of women in state prisons and 48% in federal prisons, but the total number of mothers is a fraction of the total number of fathers. While the number of women in prison has been growing, there were 111,360 women in prison in 2017 compared to 1,378,003 men.[75] Most of the women in jail are mothers; 79% have young children at home and another 5% are pregnant at the time of their incarceration.[76] Between 4 and 7% of women entering prison are pregnant.[77] After giving birth, most prison mothers have less than 48 hours before the child is taken away. Nine states have prison nursery programs that allow newborns to remain with their incarcerated mother for up to 18 months; mothers who give birth shortly before incarceration are ineligible.

Mothers are more likely to have been the primary caregiver.[78] Children with incarcerated mothers are more likely to live in foster care or with grandparents or family friends than are the children of incarcerated fathers, subjecting them to greater disruption and instability.[79] Young children who lose a parent to incarceration are deprived of support at a critical time for healthy development.

> Their bonds to that parent are weakened, or sometimes never formed, as distance may keep them from making regular visits. The loss of that bond is especially devastating for children with incarcerated mothers. The trauma of being separated from a parent, along with a lack of sympathy or support from others, can increase children's mental health issues, such as depression and anxiety, and hamper educational achievement. Kids of incarcerated mothers, in particular, are at greater risk of dropping out of school.[80]

It is difficult for children to visit their incarcerated parents; 62% of parents in state prisons and 84% of parents in federal prisons were incarcerated more than 100 miles from their previous residence.[81] Visiting areas are often small, cramped, and inhospitable for children. Telephone rates in prison can be prohibitively expensive. Visiting hours within jails and prisons are tightly regulated, and the strictly enforced rules can be inconvenient. The Adoption and Safe Families Act of 1997 made it difficult for many parents to maintain custody of their children. Foster care agencies can initiate termination proceedings if a child has been in foster care for 15 of the previous 22 months. Restrictions on employment, housing, education, and public aid for ex-offenders make it difficult to meet the requirements of Child Protective Services to maintain custody.

Children of incarcerated parents

> experience a broad range of emotions, including fear, anxiety, anger, sadness, loneliness, and guilt. They may exhibit low self-esteem, depression, and emotional withdrawal from friends and family. They may also begin to act out inappropriately, become disruptive in the classroom, or engage in other antisocial behaviors. Often, their academic performance deteriorates and they develop other school-related difficulties. These emotional and behavioral difficulties have been linked to a variety of factors, including the stress of parent-child separation, the child's identification with the incarcerated parent, social stigma, and attempts to deceive children about their parents' incarceration.[82]

It should be noted that it is hard to disentangle the effects of incarceration from other factors that existed long before a parent went to prison.

One major challenge confronting researchers is disentangling the effects of parental incarceration from the effects of other factors that could have existed long before incarceration, such as child maltreatment, parental use of alcohol or drugs, parental mental illness, and domestic violence.[83]

The incarceration of an abusive parent could have positive effects. Identifying the unique effects of parental incarceration on children is difficult because of links with numerous other risk factors. For example, people living in poor communities are more likely to be incarcerated.[84] The child of an incarcerated parent could have problems in school, but the loss of income or living in extreme poverty could be factors in addition to the incarceration.

Adverse childhood experiences (ACEs) are stressful or traumatic events, which include abuse, neglect, witnessing domestic violence, growing up with family members who have substance abuse disorders or mental illness, parental separation, and an incarcerated household member.[85] More than half of the children who ever had an incarcerated parent lived with someone who had a substance abuse problem; 60% experienced parental separation; 33% witnessed violence between their parents or guardian, and 25% lived with someone who was mentally ill.[86] The harm associated with parental incarceration can compound the already difficult circumstances of vulnerable children.

One study used data from the Fragile Families and Child Wellbeing Study to examine the effects of paternal incarceration on children.[87] Incarceration forcefully removes fathers from households, many of whom contributed economically and emotionally to their families. Incarceration increases economic hardship, facilitates relationship dissolution and conflict, impairs parenting, and increases parental health problems—factors linked to children's problem behaviors and cognitive skills. For some children, it is possible that paternal incarceration exerts no independent effects. Most children of incarcerated parents are from poor families and are more likely to have experienced the absence of fathers through divorce or separation. Their parents are more likely to suffer from depression, experience high levels of parenting stress, and to abuse drugs or alcohol prior to the incarceration. The negative consequences of paternal incarceration may be strongest among children from relatively advantaged circumstances—a stable home environment in families and neighborhoods that have resources. Family disruption may be more dramatic for these children, who are unprepared for hardship. Disadvantaged children have been saturated in disadvantages.

The risk of child abuse and neglect may be exacerbated during and after the incarceration of parents.

> Prior to an incarceration, a parent's criminal justice involvement may be symptomatic of family problems or issues that prevent the parent from providing appropriate care. During a parent's incarceration, children may be at risk if placed with caregivers who are unwilling or unable to provide appropriate care. When a parent is released, the stresses associated with community and family reintegration may also increase the risk of abuse or neglect.[88]

Incarceration affects children and their families—and their communities.

In areas where a sizable portion of residents are behind bars, the effect is cumulative: The sheer number of absent people depletes available workers and providers, while constraining the entire community's access to opportunity—including individuals who have never been incarcerated. The continual cycle of residents going to and returning from prison makes for places, and faces, constantly in flux. Just living in a neighborhood with a high incarceration rate increases residents' chances of suffering from depression and anxiety. Even for residents who have had no contact with the criminal justice system, heightened police vigilance can cast a shadow over their children, families and homes. And the absence of parents, most of them fathers, weakens neighborhoods and tears apart social networks, which, in turn, affects the local economy. Parents' inability to find work when they return home further destabilizes their communities and increases their likelihood of reverting to criminal activity. . . . All of these challenges—financial and housing instability, stress, emotional difficulties, broken family relationships and communities ill-equipped to bolster children amid great uncertainty—are a minefield nearly impossible for kids to traverse without incident.[89]

As vital social services are cut in virtually every state, the juvenile justice system, along with the child welfare system, become the last resort—and often the first resort—in dealing with problems. This situation will continue to grow as the incarceration rates continue to rise.

SUMMARY

The family is one of the most crucial institutions in human existence, but in U.S. society it is often troubled. High divorce rates and high rates of domestic violence provide the starkest evidence. Several myths about the U.S. family continue to survive, such as the myth of a harmonious unit and its breakup as one of the leading causes of most social problems in the country. In reality, the cause works in the opposite direction, as important social changes have had very negative impacts on the family, not the least of which is the growing inequality of wealth. Families at the bottom of the social class ladder are suffering from severe economic hardships.

Various problems associated with the family are linked to delinquency, as many years of social science research demonstrate. Both the structure of the family and the quality of relationships within the family are linked to delinquency. The authoritarian style of parenting is most frequently associated with high rates of delinquent behavior. Socializing variables, especially the degree of supervision and the extent of parental involvement, are the most powerful predictors of delinquency. The family should not be viewed as an independent variable causing delinquency; rather it is also a dependent variable affected by various outside forces. A final critical factor in delinquency is having one or more parents involved in criminal activities, especially if sentenced to prison. Millions of children, particularly black children, are growing up with one or more parents (especially fathers) serving time in a jail or prison.

Notes

1 Stephanie Kollmann, "Parents as Partners: Family Connection and Youth Incarceration," Children and Family Justice Center, February 2018, vol. 2.

2 Gretchen Livington, "About One-Third of U.S. Children Are Living with an Unmarried Parent," Pew Research Center, April 27, 2018.

3 Children's Bureau, *Child Maltreatment 2016* (Washington, DC: Administration on Children, Youth and Families, 2018), 18.

4 Ibid., 53.

5 Melissa Sickmund and Charles Puzzanchera, *Juvenile Offenders and Victims: 2014 National Report* (Pittsburgh: National Center for Juvenile Justice, December 2014), 46.

6 *Child Maltreatment, 2016*, table 6–4.

7 Federal Bureau of Investigation, *Crime in the United States, 2017*. Expanded Homicide Data, table 10.

8 Centers for Disease Control and Prevention, "Preventing Intimate Partner Violence," 2017.

9 *OJJDP Statistical Briefing Book*, June 1, 2018, https://www.ojjdp.gov/ojstatbb/victims/qa02111.asp?qaDate=2016

10 Maxine Baca Zinn, D. Stanley Eitzen, and Barbara Wells, Diversity in Families, 10th ed. (Boston: Pearson, 2015).

11 Meda Chesney-Lind and Randall G. Shelden, *Girls, Delinquency, and Juvenile Justice*, 4th ed. (Malden, MA: Wiley-Blackwell, 2014).

12 D. Stanley Eitzen, Maxine Baca Zinn, and Kelly Eitzen Smith, *In Conflict and Order: Understanding Society*, 14th ed. (Boston: Pearson, 2017).

13 Glassdoor Team, "The US Lags behind Europe in Workplace Benefits and Paid Leave," Glassdoor.com, February 17, 2016.

14 James Diego Vigil, *Gang Redux: A Balanced Anti-Gang Strategy* (Long Grove, IL: Waveland Press, 2010), 7–8.

15 Ibid., 99, 101.

16 Ibid., 10.

17 James H. Derzon, "The Correspondence of Family Features with Problem, Aggressive, Criminal, and Violent Behavior: A Meta-analysis, *Journal of Experimental Criminology*, 2010, 6(3): 263–292.

18 David P. Farrington, "Crime and the Family," *The Criminologist*, 2010, 35(2): 1–6; Lee Ellis, David Farrington, and Anthony Hoskin, *Handbook of Crime Correlates*, 2nd ed. (San Diego: Academic Press, 2019); David P. Farrington and Brandon C. Welsh, *Saving Children from a Life of Crime: Early Risk Factors and Effective Interventions* (New York: Oxford University Press, 2007).

19 Sheldon Glueck and Eleanor Glueck, *Unraveling Juvenile Delinquency* (Cambridge, MA: Harvard University Press, 1950); John H. Laub and Robert Sampson, "Unraveling Families and Delinquency: A Reanalysis of the Gluecks' Data," *Criminology*, 1988, 26(3): 355–380. See also: Rolf Loeber and Magda Stouthamer-Loeber, "Family Factors

as Correlates and Predictors of Juvenile Conduct Problems and Delinquency," *Crime and Justice*, 1986, 7: 29–149.

20 C. R. Fenwick, "Juvenile Court Intake Decision Making: The Importance of Family Affiliation," *Journal of Criminal Justice*, 1982, 10(6): 443–453.

21 L. Edward Wells and Joseph H. Rankin, "Families and Delinquency: A Meta-Analysis of the Impact of Broken Homes," *Social Problems*, 1991, 38: 87–88.

22 Cashen M. Boccio and Kevin M. Beaver, "The Influence of Family Structure on Delinquent Behavior," *Youth Violence and Juvenile Justice*, 2017, DOI: 10.1177/1541204017727836

23 Christina Sogar, "The Influence of Family Process and Structure on Delinquency in Adolescence—An Examination of Theory and Research, *Journal of Human Behavior in the Social Environment*, 2017, 27: 206–214.

24 Kristin Y. Mack, Michael J. Leiber, Richard A. Featherstone, and Maria A. Monserud, "Reassessing the Family-Delinquency Association: Do Family Type, Family Processes, and Economic Factors Make a Difference?" *Journal of Criminal Justice*, (2007), 35: 51–67.

25 Susan Golombok, Sophie Zadeh, Susan Imrie, Venessa Smith, and Tabitha Freeman, "Single Mothers by Choice—Child Relationships and Children's Psychological Adjustment," *Journal of Family Psychology*, 2016, 30(4): 409–418.

26 Susan Golombok and Fiona Tasker, "Socioemotional Development in Changing Families," in Richard M. Lerner (ed.), *Handbook of Child Psychology and Developmental Science*, 419–463 (Hoboken, NJ: John Wiley & Sons, Inc., 2015).

27 Mary Walsh and Maria D. Thodorakakis, " The Impact of Economic Inequality on Children's Development and Achievement," *Religions*, 2017, 8(4).

28 Quoted in Commission on Behavioral and Social Sciences and Education, *Losing Generations: Adolescents in High-Risk Settings* (Washington, DC: National Academy Press, 1993), 49–50.

29 Farrington, "Crime and the Family."

30 Lee N. Robins, *Deviant Children Grown Up* (Baltimore: Williams and Wilkins, 1966); Lee N. Robins, "Deviant Children Grown Up," *European Child and Adolescent Psychiatry*, 1996, 5: 44–46.

31 Joan McCord, "A Forty Year Perspective on Effects of Child Abuse and Neglect," *Child Abuse and Neglect*, 1983, 7: 265–270; Joan McCord, "Some Child-rearing Antecedents of Criminal Behavior in Adult Men," *Journal of Personality and Social Psychology*, 1979, 37: 1477–1486.

32 D. J. West and D. P. Farrington, *The Delinquent Way of Life: Third Report of the Cambridge Study in Delinquent Development* (London: Heinemann, 1977); D. J. West and D. P. Farrington, *Who Becomes Delinquent? Second Report of the Cambridge Study in Delinquent Development* (London: Heinemann, 1973).

33 Glueck and Glueck, *Unraveling Juvenile Delinquency*.

34 Laub and Sampson, "Unraveling Families and Delinquency"; Robert J. Sampson and John H. Laub, "Urban Poverty and the Family Context of Delinquency: A New Look at Structure and Process in a Classic Study," *Child Development*, 1994, 65(2): 523–540.

35 Walter R. Gove and Robert D. Crutchfield, "The Family and Juvenile Delinquency," *Sociological Quarterly*, 1982, 23(3): 301–319.

36 Loeber and Stouthamer-Loeber, "Family Factors as Correlates and Predictors of Juvenile Conduct Problems and Delinquency."

37 Stephen A. Cernkovich and Peggy Giordano, "Family Relationships and Delinquency" *Criminology*, 1987, 16: 295–321.

38 Ibid.

39 Richard D. Clark and Glenn Shields, "Family Communication and Delinquency," *Adolescence*, 1997, 32(125): 81–92.

40 Daniel J. Flannery, Laura L. Williams, and Alexander T. Vazsonyi, "Who Are They With and What Are They Doing? Delinquent Behavior, Substance Use, and Early Adolescents after School Time," *American Journal of Orthopsychiatry*, 1999, 69(2): 247–53.

41 Loeber & Stouthamer-Loeber, "Family Factors as Correlates and Predictors of Juvenile Conduct Problems and Delinquency."

42 Machteld Hoeve, Judith Semon Dubas, Veroni I. Eichelsheim, Peter H. van der Laan, Wilma Smeenk, and Jan R. M. Gerris, "The Relationship between Parenting and Delinquency: A Meta-Analysis," *Journal of Abnormal Child Psychology*, 2009, 37(6): 749–775.

43 David H. Olson, "Circumplex Model of Marital and Family systems," *Journal of Family Therapy*, 2000, 22:144–167.

44 Craig S. Cashwell and Nicholas A. Vacc, "Family Functioning and Risk Behaviors: Influences on Adolescent Delinquency," *School Counselor*, 1996, 44(2): 105–114.

45 David H. Olson, "Circumplex Model VII: Validation Studies and FACES III," *Family Process*, 1986, 25(3), 337–351.

46 Mark Warr, "Parents, Peers, and Delinquency," *Social Forces*, 1993, 72(1): 247–264; M. Eileen Matlack, M. S. McGreevy, Robert E. Rouse, Charles Flatter, and R. F. Marcus, "Family Correlates of Social Skill Deficits in Incarcerated and Nonincarcerated Adolescents," *Adolescence*, 1994, 29(113): 117–132.

47 Matlack et al., "Family Correlates of Social Skill Deficits."

48 Willard W. Mollerstrom, Michael A. Patchner, and Joel S. Milner, "Family Functioning and Child Abuse Potential," *Journal of Clinical Psychology*, 1992, 48(4): 45–54.

49 E. Pabon, "Hispanic Adolescent Delinquency and the Family: A Discussion of Sociocultural Influences," *Adolescence*, 1998, 33(132): 941–55.

50 Ibid.

51 Diana Baumrind, "The Influence of Parenting Style on Adolescent Competence and Substance Use," *Journal of Early Adolescence*, 1991, 11: 56–95.

52 Commission on Behavioral and Social Sciences and Education, *Losing Generations*, 53.

53 Joy G. Dryfoos, *Adolescents at Risk: Prevalence and Prevention* (New York: Oxford University Press, 1990), 88.

54 Commission on Behavioral and Social Sciences and Education, *Losing Generations*, 53.

55 Loeber and Stouthamer-Loeber, "Family Factors as Correlates and Predictors of Juvenile Conduct Problems and Delinquency." The following study found that a punishing

style of parenting (which the authors placed under the category of "neglectful parenting" was more predictive of serious delinquency. Machteld Hoeve, Arjan Blokland, Judith S. Dubas, Rolf Loeber, Jab Gerris, and Peter van der Laan, "Trajectories of Delinquency and Parenting Styles," *Journal of Abnormal Psychology*, 2008, 36: 223–235.

56 Daniel R. Scheinfeld, "Family Relationships and School Achievement among Boys of Lower-Income Black Families," *American Journal of Orthopsychiatry*, 1983, 53(1): 127–143.

57 Elliot Currie, *Confronting Crime* (New York: Pantheon, 1985), 185.

58 Terence P. Thornberry and Marvin D. Krohn, "The Self-Report Method for Measuring Delinquency and Crime," in David Duffee, "Criminal Justice 2000, Volume 4," July 2000, 33–83, NCJ 182411.

59 Delbert Elliott, David Huizinga, and Suanne Ageton, *Explaining Delinquency and Drug Use* (Beverly Hills, CA: Sage, 1985).

60 Ibid.

61 Christian Connell, Tamika Gilreath, Will Akin, and Robert Brex, "Social-ecological Influences on Patterns of Substance Use among Non-metropolitan High School Students, *American Journal of Community Psychology*, 2010, 45: 36–48; Thomas J. Dishion, Deborah Capaldia, Kathleen M. Spracklen, and Fuzhong Lia, "Peer Ecology of Male Adolescent Drug Use." *Development and Psychopathology*, 1995, 7:803–824; Joan Tucker, Maria Orlando Edelen, and Wenjing Huang, "Effectiveness of Parent-Child Mediation in Improving Family Functioning and Reducing Adolescent Problem Behavior: Results from a Pilot Randomized Controlled Trial, *Journal of Youth and Adolescence*, 2017, 46(3): 505–515; Jennifer Stuart, Mark Fondacaro, Scott Miller, Veda Brown, and Eve Brank, "Procedural Justice in Family Conflict Resolution and Deviant Peer Group Involvement Among Adolescents: The Mediating Influence of Peer Conflict," *Journal of Youth and Adolescence*, 2008, 37(6): 674–684; Ellen Reitz, Peter Prinzie , Maja Deković, and Kirsten Buist, "The Role of Peer Contacts in the Relationship Between Parental Knowledge and Adolescents' Externalizing Behaviors: A Latent Growth Curve Modeling Approach," *Journal of Youth and Adolescence*, 2007, 36: 623–634.

62 Carter Hay, Edward Fortson, Dusten Hollist, Irsgad Altheimer, and Lonnie Schaible, "Compounded Risk: The Implications for Delinquency of Coming from a Poor Family that Lives in a Poor Community," *Journal of Youth and Adolescence*, 2007, 36: 593–605.

63 Ibid., 191.

64 Kathryn A. Branch, "Bottcher, Jean: Social Practices of Gender," in Francis T. Cullen and Pamela Wilcox (eds.), *Encyclopedia of Criminological Theory* (Thousand Oaks, CA: Sage Publications, 2010), 100–103.

65 Jean Bottcher, "Social Practices of Gender: How Gender Relates to Delinquency in the Everyday Lives of High-risk Youths," *Criminology*, 2001, 39(4): 893–931.

66 Terrie E. Moffitt and Avshalom Caspi, "Childhood Predictors Differentiate Life-Course Persistent and Adolescence-Limited Antisocial Pathways among Males and Females," *Development and Psychopathology*, 2001, 13(02): 355–375. See also Patricia Chamberlain,

Treating Chronic Juvenile Offenders: Advances Made through the Oregon Multidimensional Treatment Foster Care Model (Washington, DC: American Psychological Association, 2003).

[67] Shari Miller, Rolf Loeber, and Alison Hipwell, "Peer Deviance, Parenting and Disruptive Behavior among Young Girls," *Journal of Abnormal Child Psychology*, 2009, 37(2): 139–152.

[68] Veronica Herrera and Laura McCloskey, "Gender Differences in the Risk for Delinquency among Youth Exposed to Family Violence," *Child Abuse & Neglect*, 2001, 25(8): 1037–1051.

[69] Jane A. Siegel and Linda M. Williams, "The Relationship between Child Sexual Abuse and Female Delinquency and Crime: A Prospective Study," *Journal of Research in Crime and Delinquency*, 2003, 40(1), 71–94.

[70] Christopher Wildeman, Anna R. Haskings, and Julie Poehlmann-Tynan (eds.), *When Parents Are Incarcerated: Interdisciplinary Research and Interventions to Support Children* (Washington, DC: American Psychological Association, 2018).

[71] Danielle Kaeble and Mary Cowhig, "Correctional Populations in the United States, 2016," Bureau of Justice Statistics, April 2018, NCJ 251211.

[72] This is made poignantly clear in Nell Bernstein, *All Alone in the World: Children of the Incarcerated* (New York: The New Press, 2005).

[73] Nancy La Vigne, Elizabeth Davies, and Diana Brazzell, "Broken Bonds: Understanding and Assessing the Needs of Children with Incarcerated Parents," Urban Institute, 2008, 1.

[74] Annie E. Casey Foundation, "A Shared Sentence: The Devastating Toll of Parental Incarceration on Kids, Families, and Communities," April 2016.

[75] Jennifer Bronson and E. Ann Carson, "Prisoners in 2017," Bureau of Justice Statistics, April 2019, NCJ 252156.

[76] Elizabeth Swavola, Kristi Riley, and Ram Subramanian, "Overlooked: Women and Jails in an Era of Reform," Vera Institute of Justice, August 2016.

[77] Emily Halter, "Parental Prisoners: The Incarcerated Mother's Constitutional Right to Parent," *The Journal of Criminal Law and Criminology*, 2018, 108(3): 539–567.

[78] David Murphey and P. Mae Cooper, "Parents behind Bars: What Happens to Their Children?", Child Trends, October 2015.

[79] Annie E. Casey Foundation, "A Shared Sentence."

[80] Ibid., 3.

[81] Halter, "Parental Prisoners."

[82] Cynthia Seymour and Creasie Finney Hairston, *Children with Parents in Prison: Child Welfare Policy, Program and Practice Issues* (New York: Routledge, 2017; original copyright Child Welfare League of America, 1998 and 2001), 4.

[83] Steve Christian, "Children of Incarcerated Parents," National Conference of State Legislatures, March 2009, 2.

[84] Murphey and Cooper, :Parents behind Bars."

[85] Center for the Application of Prevention Technologies, "Adverse Childhood Experiences, Substance Abuse and Mental Health Services Administration, July 2018.

[86] Murphey and Cooper, "Parents behind Bars."

[87] Kristin Turney, "The Unequal Consequences of Mass Incarceration for Children," *Demography*, 2017 54(1): 361–389.

[88] Seymour and Hairston, "Children with Parents in Prison," 5–6.

[89] Annie E. Casey Foundation, "A Shared Sentence," 4.

Chapter 10

Schools and Delinquency

Study after study shows a correlation between years of schooling and a number of positive social and personal indicators, ranging from where you work and how much money you will earn in your lifetime to how long you will live.[1] Many studies show that the pathway to educational success starts early in life. Children from families in higher socioeconomic circumstances enjoy numerous advantages, including an environment that promotes the intellectual skills needed to succeed in school. Students in the most advantaged school districts have test scores that are more than four grade levels above students in the most disadvantaged districts. The socioeconomic context of a school district is a significant predictor of students' academic performances.[2]

Chapter 8 mentioned the growing impact of globalization on employment. While higher education has always promised a number of benefits, it is even more critical today when most new jobs require at least some college experience. As we shall see in this chapter, both social class and race are closely related to educational achievement and to delinquency. The association between community socioeconomic status and academic performance becomes more pronounced as children progress through school. Very few African American and Hispanic students live in school districts where the average achievement is at the national average for grade level.[3]

> The repercussions from stressed families carry over onto learning and schooling. Schools . . . usually represent society's first opportunity to participate in the socialization and development of its children. Where the family might fail or falter, somehow the public school must fill the void in fulfilling its obligatory role in socializing all youths.[4]

SCHOOLING IN A CLASS SOCIETY

As noted in the previous chapter, we live in a highly stratified and unequal society. One of the most important social institutions of our society, the educational system, plays a key role in perpetuating class and racial inequalities. One of the goals of our schools is to preserve the culture by indoctrinating students in culturally prescribed ways.[5]

We can see this goal clearly by tracing the historical origins of schooling in the United States. As noted in chapter 1, the first compulsory school law was passed in Massachusetts in 1852. It created a new category of delinquent, the truant—and a new method of controlling youths. The objective of these laws was control rather than education. Mass education was set up largely to train a mostly rural workforce for manufacturing plants in the cities. Businesses experienced problems with industrial workers: attendance was irregular, turnover was high, and tolerance for the routinization and monotony of factory work was low. They looked to public schools to instill the discipline necessary for factory production.[6] The business community "encouraged schools to adopt a corporate model of organization and called for the education system to more explicitly prepare workers for the labor market through testing, vocational guidance, and vocational education."[7]

An 1887 quotation from one of the famous social reformers of the era, Jane Addams, explained the need to train children to be obedient.

> The businessman has, of course, not said to himself: "I will have the public school train office boys and clerks for me, so that I may have them cheap," but he has thought, and sometimes said, "Teach the children to write legibly, and to figure accurately and quickly; to acquire habits of punctuality and order; to be prompt to obey, and not question why; and you will fit them to make their way in the world as I have made mine!"[8]

Lest the reader think that such practices were relegated to the past, Jonathan Kozol's analysis of modern schooling informs us that they still exist. He quotes a principal who told executives at a power breakfast: "I'm in the business of developing minds to meet a market demand."[9] Similarly, what children learn is referred to as a "product" of the school. Children are often "regarded as investments, assets, or productive units—or else, failing that, as pint-sized human deficits who threaten our competitive capacities."[10] In another school, Kozol observed that children in the early grades were asked to list what kind of managers they want to be—a program created and financially backed by a businessman in Texas.

SCHOOLS AS "DAY PRISONS"

As the above discussion makes abundantly clear, schools historically and currently perform a *social control* function. Henry Giroux notes that in many cases today schools have become surveillance zones.

> The dismantling of schools as sites for creativity, critical thinking, and learning constitutes both a war on the imagination and the establishment of a set of disciplinary practices meant to criminalize the behavior of children who do not submit to overbearing control. No longer considered democratic public spheres intended to create critically informed and engaged citizens, many schools now function as intermediary sites that move between the roles of warehousing students in low-income communities and creating pathways that will lead them into

the machinery of the criminal justice system and eventually prison. Under such circumstances, public schooling is unmoored from the culture of education and bound instead with a culture of punishment and militarization.[11]

Alain Leroy Locke High School opened in the Watts neighborhood in South Central Los Angeles in 1967. It was a beacon of hope in a neighborhood blighted by the Watts riots of 1965. Forty years later, Locke was

> a poster child for everything wrong with education in Los Angeles' poor neighborhoods. Its kids study behind prison-like gates on a litter-strewn campus that serves as an inviting canvas for competing tagging crews. The school doesn't offer much in the way of extracurricular activities beyond its sports teams, but it is host to an on-site police station with two officers and a fully utilized open-air space for all the kids caught in its daily truancy sweeps. Reforms and programs have come and gone as quickly as the teachers and administrators assigned to implement them. The only constant has been low academic achievement.[12]

There were 1,000 students in the class of 2005—240 graduated; 30 were eligible to apply to a California state university. Only 2% of ninth-graders were proficient in algebra, and only 11% could read at grade level.

> For every 100 students who entered the ninth grade in 2001, three graduated with what they needed to go to college. Figuring out what happened to their classmates doesn't require a high school diploma. An unacceptably high number are dead or in prison. The fact that kids at Locke—and schools like it in poor minority neighborhoods—are being denied access to a quality education is old hat to anyone familiar with the history of urban education in America.[13]

In 2007, community leaders, school staff and the nonprofit Green Dot Public Schools requested that Green Dot be given operational control of Locke High School. The Locke Transformation Project marked the first time an outside organization was granted authority to operate an existing school in the Los Angeles Unified School District (LAUSD).[14] From 2004 to 2007, graduation rates ranged from 18–28%. In 2007, only 10% of Locke students earned a passing score on California's English tests.[15] More than 66% of students scored in the two lowest levels: *below basic* or *far below basic*.

Despite improvements after the Green Dot takeover, the graduation rate—55.9%—remains one of the lowest of any comprehensive high school in Los Angeles.[16] In 2017 more than 50% of the district's 11th graders met or exceeded the state's standards on English tests compared to 39% at Locke. One of the challenges faced by Locke is that incoming students read at the fourth-grade level. Slightly less than 25% of LAUSD students met or exceeded the math standards compared to 8% at Locke. In California, charters must be renewed every five years, and Locke's charter was renewed for the third time in 2018. Measuring success in transforming schools marked by years of failure remains controversial.[17] Locke demonstrates the difficulties of changing a legacy of disadvantage.

Zero Tolerance Policies

Zero tolerance school discipline policies were introduced in the late 1980s, fueled by a climate in which young people were increasingly viewed as dangerous.[18] Congress applied the tough-on-crime approach to schools when it passed the Gun Free Schools Act as part of the Elementary and Secondary Education Act of 1994. To qualify for federal education funds, states had to pass a law requiring all local school districts to expel for at least one year any student who brought a weapon to school. The shootings at Columbine High School in April 1999 elevated fears, and school officials became hypervigilant about potential troublemakers.

> In response to a widespread perception that school violence was increasing dramatically, the policy of zero tolerance, mandating harsher consequences for both major and minor violations, began to be widely implemented in schools and school districts. Although subsequent data demonstrated that school violence had in fact remained stable over a twenty year period, the implementation of zero tolerance policies led to substantial increases in the rates of out-of-school suspension and expulsion.[19]

Once confined to the possession of a weapon or illegal drugs, zero tolerance policies expanded to encompass a wide range of misconduct unrelated to threats to school safety.[20] Small infractions that would previously have been disciplined by detention or a visit to the principal's office resulted in suspension, expulsion, or a trip to the police station. Zero tolerance policies mandate specific consequences (usually suspension or expulsion) for misbehavior without consideration of the severity of the behavior, surrounding circumstances, or situational context.[21]

During the 2015–16 school year, 37% of public schools invoked at least one serious disciplinary action against a student. There were 305,700 serious disciplinary actions; 72% were suspensions for 5 days or more; 24% were transfers to specialized schools; and 4 percent were expulsions (removals with no services for the remainder of the school year). The largest category of suspensions was physical attacks or fights (178,000 actions).[22]

In 2015–16, every school was required to collect and report data to the U.S. Department of Education's Office for Civil Rights on days of lost instruction due to out-of-school suspensions. Data were collected from over 96,000 schools, which reported almost 11.4 million days of lost instruction. Black students lost 66 days of instruction compared to 14 days for white students. Students with disabilities lost 44 days of instruction compared to 20 days for students without disabilities.[23] In Texas, there were more than 26,183 out-of-school suspensions for children in pre-kindergarten through second grade; in June 2017, the state passed HB674 prohibiting discretionary out-of-school suspensions for students that young.[24]

One study found that 33% of students are suspended over a K-12 school career. Twelve years after the suspension, suspended youth are less likely to have graduated from high school or college and are more likely to have been arrested and to be on probation.[25] Students suspended from school lose important instructional time; they are more likely to repeat a grade, drop out of school, and become involved in the juvenile justice system.[26] Black students, boys, and students with disabilities were disproportionately disciplined through suspensions and expulsions in K-12 public schools.

School Resource Officers

The use of school resource officers (SROs) dates back to the 1950s when the city of Flint explored ways to foster relationships between local police and youth.[27] The roles of SROs ranged from counselors to coaches to tutors to mentors. There was a dramatic shift in purpose in the 1990s largely due to the COPS in Schools program. Between 1999 and 2005, the justice department's community-policing division awarded in excess of $750 million in grants to more than 3,000 law-enforcement agencies. The recruitment and training of more than 6,500 new SROs was overseen by conventional police departments. The Columbine shootings prompted an increase in school-based law enforcement. The Sandy Hook Elementary School (CT) shooting in 2012 renewed the emphasis on SROs, with federal funds for that purpose flowing to local police departments. In Montgomery County, Maryland, the number of SROs doubled in the year following the Sandy Hook shooting. Students were viewed as threats to be watched and policed by full-time SROs.[28] Today there are more than 14,000 SROs in schools.[29]

Police presence in schools criminalized adolescent misbehavior: a schoolyard fight became simple assault; playing catch with a teacher's hat became robbery. School districts used scarce resources to hire SROs and to install metal detectors and surveillance systems.[30] Students were subjected to searches of their bags, coats, and lockers. The stigma of suspicion affects student motivation, and expectations are lowered when institutions of learning feel more like cell blocks patrolled by guards.

J.D.B. was a 13-year-old special education student when a SRO escorted him from his classroom to a conference room where two school administrators and another police officer were waiting. His parents were not contacted. He was interrogated about recent neighborhood burglaries because one of the items reported stolen was a digital camera seen in his possession. He confessed to the crimes and was charged with larceny. Arguing that the boy was effectively in police custody when he incriminated himself, his public defender sought to have his confession suppressed because he was never read his Miranda rights. The state court denied the motion, ruling that he was never in police custody and therefore not entitled to a Miranda warning. He was adjudicated delinquent. The North Carolina Supreme Court agreed that he was not in custody and that the test for custody did not include consideration of the age of an individual questioned by the police. On June 16, 2011, the Supreme Court ruled in *J.D.B. v. North Carolina* that age was a consideration.[31] Justice Sotomayor said it was beyond dispute that children would often feel obligated to submit to police questioning when an adult in the same circumstances would feel free to leave. The Court did not, however, set an age at which custody would apply.

Two years earlier the Supreme Court addressed the strip search of a 13-year-old girl. Another student had reported to officials that Savana Reding gave her ibuprofen; possession of ibuprofen was a violation of school policy. School officials interrogated Reding and searched her belongings; finding nothing, they instructed the school nurse to conduct the strip search. The Court of Appeals for the Ninth Circuit held that the student's Fourth Amendment right to be free of unreasonable search and seizure was violated. The strip search was not justified, and the intrusion was not reasonably related to the circumstances. The Supreme Court agreed.[32] Justice Stevens referenced the magnitude of the violation of constitutional rights in a strip search of a 13-year-old child. Justice Thomas dissented in part, arguing that the judiciary should not interfere with decisions made by school administrators in the interest of keeping their schools safe.

Henry Giroux links a national mood of fear with legitimizing zero-tolerance policies in schools.

> The law has been refashioned less to protect young people than to treat the most minor behavior infractions in schools as criminal, resulting in an upsurge of children who are suspended, arrested, and jailed. . . . Put bluntly, American society at present exudes both a deep-rooted hostility and chilling fear about youth. The popular demonization of the young now justifies responses to youth that were unthinkable 30 years ago, including criminalization and imprisonment, the prescription of psychotropic drugs, psychiatric confinement, and zero-tolerance policies that model schools after prisons. School has become a model for a punishing society in which children who violate a rule as minor as a dress code infraction or slightly act out in class can be handcuffed, booked, and jailed.[33]

Since the institution of strict zero tolerance policies at schools around the country, students have been suspended or expelled for offenses that range from the relatively minor to the truly ridiculous.

- A 13-year-old boy eating lunch at Weaverville Elementary School in California shared his chicken burrito with a hungry friend. He was given a detention. Superintendent Tom Barnett said safety and liability issues prohibit allowing students to exchange meals.[34]
- In Vernon, New Jersey Ethan Chaplin, 13, was twirling his pencil. The child sitting behind him said he was making gun motions. The school sent Chaplin for a 5-hour physical and psychological evaluation; his urine was tested and blood was drawn. The superintendent Charles Maranzano said when children demonstrate behaviors that raise red flags schools must do their duty.[35]
- A 6-year-old boy was imitating a Mighty Morphin Power Ranger and pantomimed an imaginary bow and arrow to "shoot" at a classmate. He was

suspended for 3 days. The principal's note to the parents said he had no tolerance for real or imitated violence.[36]

- In Coldwater, Michigan, 12-year-old Kyler Davies found a pocket knife in a backpack his mother had purchased from Goodwill. He gave the knife to school authorities and told them it was not his. He was initially suspended for 180 days, reduced to 30 days.[37]
- Gabby Collins, who has a learning disability, was doing well in school. Her grades were improving. In December 2016 she was playing with friends; they were tossing an empty water bottle at each other. She tried to throw it at a boy down the hall and accidentally hit a teacher in the head. She was expelled for 180 days.

The average annual suspension rate increased steadily to a national annual average of 10%.[38] In some public-school districts (i.e., Pontiac, Michigan and Saint Louis, Missouri), the annual rate of suspensions reached 33%. The rate was 19% for the entire state of Florida. In Texas, almost 60% of students suffered a suspension. The prevalence of suspensions correlates more with policy than with student behavior. Administrators' beliefs about how to control students determined the number of suspensions rather than the actual misdemeanor count.

Administrators may attempt to improve the learning environment for others or to avoid the challenges of dealing with disruptive behavior by removing troublesome students through suspension and expulsion. "It can be time consuming and frustrating to sit down and talk to a disrespectful, disruptive child, but it can prevent problems in the future."[39] Suspending students without addressing the causes of their misbehavior eliminates the opportunity to prevent reoccurrence of the problem. In addition, researchers found that higher levels of exclusionary discipline were associated with lower levels of math and reading achievement for non-suspended students.[40]

The Consortium on School Research at the University of Chicago challenged the assumption that severe infractions should trigger automatic suspensions.[41] There were concerns that curtailing the use of suspensions would allow the misbehavior of a few students to disrupt the learning of other students. The students with the highest estimated risk of suspension felt safer in their schools when suspensions for severe infractions were reduced. Students at the lowest risk of suspension had the largest test score gains. Schools serving predominantly black students saw meaningful improvements in school climate when suspensions were reduced.

An overly punitive school environment is destabilizing. It can heighten students' distrust and anxiety, which stifles achievement for all students.

Disciplinary exclusion raises thorny questions.

These exclusionary practices frequently lead to poor outcomes, including an increased likelihood that more students will become involved in the justice system either immediately or in the future. For example, not only do excluded students miss classroom instruction and possibly fall behind academically, but exclusion also may stigmatize them, promote school avoidance, and preclude access to needed resources. Students who eventually return to school but are behind academically can become disengaged and exhibit disruptive behavior because they are frustrated or embarrassed by their inability to meet academic expectations. In fact, empirical evidence demonstrates that excluding students from school significantly decreases the likelihood that they will graduate from high school. Not graduating from high school leads to many other problems, including unemployment, poverty, and bad health.[42]

Discretionary expulsion of students for nonviolent, noncriminal misbehavior puts students at risk. Expulsion may introduce students to the justice system when they have broken no laws, and it may push them into dropping out of school. The establishment of zero tolerance policies and the use of suspension and expulsion at younger and younger ages have had damaging consequences—from failing a grade, dropping out, or becoming incarcerated. Suspension or expulsion removes students from classrooms and eliminates the potential protective benefits of education.[43] Students enrolled in school benefit from the daily structure of the school setting. Association with positive peers in school can discourage individuals from engaging in crime. Higher educational attainment increases patience and aversion to risk taking, lowering the impulse to engage in risky, criminal behavior. Punitive removal from school increases dropout rates, and dropping out of school increases opportunities to commit crime. Suspensions and expulsions force already marginalized youth onto the streets and away from prosocial connections at school, which can increase the attraction of joining a gang.[44]

Punishments like out-of-school suspensions severely disrupt a student's academic progress.[45] Central to the philosophy of zero-tolerance is the belief that the punishment will deter future misbehavior. Contrary to that belief, numerous large-scale research studies have found that school suspensions generally predict higher rates of future misbehavior.[46] The policies put students at risk for dropping out of school and/or entering the juvenile justice system. A single suspension or expulsion doubles the risk that a student will repeat a grade. Being retained a grade, especially while in middle or high school, is one of the strongest predictors of dropping out. A national longitudinal study found that youth with a prior suspension were 68% more likely to drop out of school.

> A large body of research findings has failed to find that the use of suspension and expulsion contributes to either improved student behavior or improved school safety. Schools with higher rates of suspension have lower ratings of school safety from students and have significantly poorer school climate, especially for students of color. In terms of student behavior, rather than reducing the likelihood of being suspended, a student's history of suspension appears to predict higher rates of future antisocial behavior and higher rates of future suspensions in the long term. . . . School exclusion also appears to carry with it substantial risk for both short- and long-term negative outcomes. Use of suspension and expulsion is associated with lower academic achievement at both the school and the individual level, and increased risk of negative behavior over time.[47]

Research shows that African American and Latino students are more frequently punished in school than are whites who engage in similar behavior.[48] Black juveniles represent 15% of all students, but they comprise 35% of students suspended once and 44% of those suspended more than once.[49] Of students who are expelled, 36% are black. African American students are suspended at three times the rate of white students. The discipline gap was so pronounced that in 2014 the Departments of Education and Justice issued a joint *Dear Colleague Letter* to public schools summarizing recent racial disparities in discipline and the adverse outcomes from discipline that excludes students from school, referencing the school-to-prison pipeline (see next section).[50]

In a study that explored student discipline disparities by race and family income, researchers cited a report by the Office for Civil Rights that found black children were 3.6 times more likely to receive an out-of-school suspension in preschool than white children, 3.8 times more likely to be suspended from school in grades K–12, and 2.2 times more likely to be referred to law enforcement or subjected to a school-related arrest.[51] In 2013–14, 18% of black boys and 10% of black girls were suspended from school compared to 5% of white boys and 2% of white girls. Looking at statewide data from Louisiana from 2000 to 2014, the researchers found clear patterns of discipline gaps. Black students were 46% of the student population but 64% of suspensions. Poor students were 62% of the population and 74% of the suspensions. Being black and being poor were significant predictors of being suspended, longer suspensions, and being suspended multiple times in the same year.

A study in North Carolina found that black students were less subject to suspension or expulsion when their teachers were black.[52] The results were especially pronounced for referrals for subjectively defined infractions such as willful defiance. The relationship held regardless of gender, socioeconomic status and grade level. Implicit bias may affect decisions about exclusionary discipline. Some school officials may "unconsciously perpetuate racial inequalities in the public school system by making adverse decisions based on unconscious stereotypes and attitudes toward students of color."[53] Empirical studies have consistently found that youth of color are treated more harshly than similarly situated white youth. Research has documented that many people implicitly associate African Americans with danger, aggression, and violence.

> Teachers are on the front lines of society's efforts to promote equality of opportunity. They spend a substantial amount of structured time with children over their developmental trajectories. When the unconscious biases of well-intentioned teachers influence their judgment toward particular students (e.g., by race, ethnicity, gender), it can influence their instructional practices, the expectations they convey, and their recommendations for relevant outcomes like course placement, special education, and discipline. For example, recent research indicates that non-black teachers have significantly lower expectations of black students.[54]

Qualitative studies suggest that differing experiences by race within schools (e.g., expectations, academic tracing, and school discipline affect educational attainment.

Many districts began to shift away from zero-tolerance school discipline toward less punitive strategies designed to keep students in school. One of the leaders was the LAUSD, which in 2013 banned suspensions for *willful defiance*.[55] Refusing to take off a hat, failing to wear a school uniform, and refusing to turn off a cell phone had been among the willful defiance infractions. LAUSD took the action after statistics showed that African Americans, who were 9% of the student population, accounted for 26% of the suspensions. Suspension rates for the 700,000 LAUSD students dropped more than 53% in two years, while graduation rates rose 12%.

In 2015, the New York City Department of Education ended suspensions without prior approval.[56] New York allocated $1.2 million to expanding restorative practices, including peer mediation, restorative circles, and group conferences. Denver Public Schools implemented a district-wide restorative justice program in the early 2000s; suspension rates were cut in half over seven years, and the discipline gap between African American and white students was reduced by a third. After a decade of using restorative justice, standardized test scores in Denver's schools have gone up, as have graduation rates.

Adopting comprehensive and flexible disciplinary policies keeps students in school and provides opportunities to address the underlying problems that motivate their misbehavior. Chief judge at the Clayton County Juvenile Court in Georgia, Steven Teske, helped implement the Juvenile Detention Alternatives Initiative to eliminate criminal charges for minor offenses and develop alternatives to traditional disciplinary actions.[57] Arrests at schools decreased 67%, and the graduation rate increased. The program has also worked in other cities.

The exceptional case that attracts media attention exacerbates fears. Politicians and the public seize on alarmist responses to an exaggerated threat.[58] Moral panic has been defined as "a situation in which public fears and state interventions greatly exceed the objective threat posed to society by a particular individual or group who is/ are claimed to be responsible."[59] The groups that benefit the most from such panics include law enforcement agencies, politicians, and the news media. Schools and the children who attend them suffer the consequences. "If educators and policymakers overlook the harmful and disparate educational impact of harsh discipline they will likely make counterproductive decisions on how to spend scarce education dollars."[60]

THE SCHOOL TO PRISON PIPELINE

School policies and practices that make it more likely that students will enter the juvenile justice system than attain a quality education are often referred to as the *school-to-prison pipeline*.[61] "The School to Prison Pipeline operates directly and indirectly. Schools directly send students into the pipeline through zero tolerance policies that involve the police in minor incidents and often lead to arrests, juvenile detention referrals, and even criminal charges and incarceration."[62] As emphasized in the previous section, schools indirectly push students toward the criminal justice system by excluding them from school through suspension and expulsion.

The focus on controlling young people—particularly those perceived as difficult to manage—is not new. Zero tolerance policies are the beginning of the pipeline and represent a shift away from informal methods of discipline. Instead of calling students into the principal's office, schools began to rely on arrests by school resource officers to maintain order.

> Their power to legally use physical force, arrest and handcuff students, and bring the full weight of the criminal justice system to bear on misbehaving children is often obscured until an act of violence, captured by a student's cell phone, breaks through to the public. Police in schools are first and foremost there to enforce criminal laws, and virtually every violation of a school rule can be considered a criminal act if viewed through a police-first lens. Schools offer an ideal entry point for the criminal justice system to gather intelligence, surveil young people, and exercise strong-arm policing tactics to instill fear and compliance. The capacity for school policing to turn against students instead of protecting them has always existed, and it continues to pose a first-line threat to the civil rights and civil liberties of young people.[63]

When students are referred to the juvenile court for school infractions, they may be adjudicated and placed on probation. If the pipeline is not disrupted, offenders are placed in juvenile facilities. Facility placements exacerbate social, educational, and mental health difficulties; more than half of adolescents released from placement recidivate.[64]

If young people are not allowed to mature out of indiscretions without getting entangled in the justice system, the long-term consequences of misbehavior can be extreme. An egregious corruption scandal involving the juvenile justice system in a central Pennsylvania county provides an appalling example. The nonprofit Juvenile Law Center in Philadelphia investigated complaints that a judge was sentencing children, without legal representation, to terms in a for-profit youth center. The kickback scheme was eventually labeled "kids for cash."

Many first-time offenders (including children as young as 10) were sentenced to for-profit centers by Luzerne County Judge Mark Ciavarella, Jr.[65] He enacted an administrative policy based on zero tolerance that dictated how probation officers should handle probation violations and other charging decisions. Ciavarella had a role in closing the county-run Luzerne County Juvenile Detention Center in favor of the private, for-profit Pennsylvania Child Care facility. He and another judge, Michael Conahan, tracked the number of children sent to the facility and how it was doing financially. Eleven people were arrested in connection with the corruption that took place from 2003 to 2008, including the two judges, the coowner of the for-profit centers, the builder of the centers, a superintendent of schools, and a court administrator.

In 2009, the Pennsylvania Supreme Court appointed a judge to review Ciavarella's cases.[66] Pennsylvania overturned approximately 4,000 convictions. Ciavarella was convicted in 2011 and sentenced to 28 years in prison. Michael Conahan pleaded guilty to racketeering and was sentenced to 17.5 years. Robert Powell (the coowner of the two private juvenile justice facilities) served 18 months in prison. Developer Robert Mericle pleaded guilty to failure to tell federal agents about more than $2 million in payments to the judges and was sentenced to a year in prison. On August 12, 2015, Powell agreed to pay $4.75 million to settle a class-action suit.

Ciavarella, who was elected to a 10-year term in 1996 after running on a platform of being tough on juvenile crime and re-elected in 2006, appears in the documentary, *Kids for Cash*. He asserts he never took bribes—describing the money he took as finder's fees and saying the facilities needed to be built because parents didn't know how to be parents. The schools in Luzerne called the police for incidents such as a student mocking an assistant principal on social media, a 14-year-old girl having a minor fight with another girl in the school gymnasium, and a 12-year-old arguing with the mother of another child at a bus stop. School authorities outsourced discipline to the police and courts, pushing low-performing students out of school. Many in the community endorsed zero tolerance policies; Ciavarella collected statements from parents and teachers thanking him for his tough rulings.

For years, court personnel—juvenile probation officers, the district attorney's office, and the public defender's office—witnessed juveniles shackled and sent to juvenile facilities. Court personnel never spoke up about the denial of constitutional protections to the children. Marsha Levick, deputy director of the Juvenile Law Center, asserted there was an internal conspiracy of silence in Luzerne County.

> I think there's a coziness that happens in courtrooms, particularly in small towns with the same lawyers coming before the same judge over and over again. It's a cocoon of silence; it's a go-along-to-get-along situation. No one wants to challenge the judge.[67]

Levick was hopeful that with Luzerne County having exposed the dark side of zero tolerance policies and with federal guidelines in 2014 targeting zero tolerance policies that disproportionately affected students of color and contributed to a school-to-prison pipeline, school discipline would return to the principal's office rather than the courtroom.

The majority of arrests of juveniles for school misbehavior do not involve criminal activity. Students are routinely arrested on disorderly conduct charges for talking back to teachers, launching spitballs, or expressing an opinion that the SRO was using excessive force. Such infractions should be handled at the school rather than in a police precinct.

> Why is behavior that used to be disciplined within the school system now being outsourced to the police? There are a number of factors, but the most notable is the increase in the number of police officers stationed on school campuses? . . .

> Arrests in New York City are typically at their highest levels on Wednesdays. The reason has nothing to do with the number of crimes committed. Wednesdays are when the NYPD is staffed at its highest levels.[68]

In the 2015–16 school year, 48% of schools reported the presence of a sworn law enforcement officer versus 36% a decade earlier.[69] Among secondary schools with any sworn law enforcement officer present at least once a week, 87% of schools in cities reported having an officer who carried a firearm compared with 95% in suburban and rural areas, and 97% in towns. Academic studies over two decades have found that involving police officers in school discipline has been counterproductive.

Civil rights advocates say students of color bear the brunt of zero-tolerance policies and state laws that lead to arrests for minor misbehavior such as classroom arguments. The presence of police in schools makes arrests and referrals more likely. Black students are the most likely to attend schools with SROs. Allison Brown, a former lawyer for the Department of Justice commented: "Far too often when police are consistently present in black and brown communities, they criminalize behavior they wouldn't in other places. Especially for young people, that is just devastating to their chances for success."[70] Once in the pipeline, systemic bias further disadvantages minorities. Black juveniles are six times more likely to be sentenced to jail than white youths convicted of similar offenses.

An analysis of civil rights data in 2013–14 found 70,000 arrests at about 8,000 schools.[71] Black students were arrested at school at disproportionately high levels. African American boys have the highest risk; they are three times as likely to be arrested at school as white male students. In schools in Virginia with at least one arrest, black students are 39% of the enrollment but 75% of school-based arrests. In Louisiana, black students are 40% of the enrollment but 69% of school arrests. In 28 states, the arrests of African American students was at least 10 percentage points higher than their share of the enrollment, and in 10 of those states, the gap was at least 20 percentage points. No other racial or ethnic groups faced such disparities. Referrals to law enforcement outnumber arrests—243,000 referrals compared to 70,000 arrests. Nationally, black students are 17% of the enrollment in schools that referred students to law enforcement but more than 25% of the students referred.

Maryland reported 2,759 school related arrests in the 2015–16 school year, which was 3.1 arrests for every 1,000 Maryland public school students compared to the national rate of 1.2.[72] Many of the infractions rely more on subjective interpretations of behavior (i.e. disorderly conduct) than on objectively observable criteria (i.e. possession of a controlled substance or possession of a firearm). Black students comprised 34.6% of the public school population but 66% of school-related arrests—black students were 3.67 times more likely to be arrested at school than non-black students. Students with disabilities represented 11% of the student population but 22% of school arrests. Students eligible for free or reduced meals (45% of the student population) accounted for 63% of school arrests. Male students (51% of the student population) accounted for 67% of school arrests; female students (49% of the student population) accounted for 33% of school arrests. In 2018, Maryland passed legislation requiring all schools to have a local law enforcement officer in the school. Previous research indicates that police presence in schools can result in increased rates of arrests and referrals to juvenile justice. Monitoring the arrests in Maryland schools as the law is implemented will add to the knowledge of how the presence of officers impacts arrest patterns.

The criminalization of education has a disproportionate impact on four at-risk groups of adolescents: the poor and minority offenders; students with past or current involvement with children's services (often victims of abuse or neglect); students in special education; and LGBT adolescents.[73] In a study using data from the National Longitudinal Survey of Adolescent to Adult Health, researchers analyzed whether being suspended from school was correlated with adverse outcomes as adults. Suspension increased the likelihood of experiencing criminal victimization, criminal involvement, and incarceration in adulthood.[74]

An incident in South Carolina in October 2015 illustrates concerns with resource officers in schools and discipline laws that disproportionately affect students. A 16-year-old girl in Spring Valley High School in South Carolina refused to leave the classroom as directed by her math teacher and a school administrator. Sheriff's deputy Ben Fields was called to remove her. Fields grabbed the student out of her desk and threw her across the room before handcuffing her. Niya Kenny, another student, captured the incident on her cell phone and called out for someone to stop the excessive use of force. The girl and Kenny were arrested, charged under the Disturbing Schools Law, and taken to a detention center. Two days later, the deputy was fired; the charges against the girls were dropped. The Richland County Sheriff, Leon Lott, supervises 87 deputies stationed at schools. He said the district needs to examine whether it is proper to call in a resource officer for a school discipline problem. "We don't need to arrest these students. We need to keep them in school."[75]

The law criminalized youth who were deemed disturbing or obnoxious at school.[76] Its vague terms invited subjective evaluations and allowed disparate and discriminatory enforcement. If an offense is not clearly defined, implicit bias is more likely to affect decisions about whom to arrest. In Charleston, disturbing school was the number one cause of youth entering the juvenile justice system. Students of color and students with disabilities were more likely to be subject to arrests in school. Black youth were nearly four times as likely as white youth to be charged with criminally disturbing school.

The experience humiliated Kenny, who withdrew from high school. In August 2016, she was a named plaintiff in a lawsuit that claimed the Disturbing Schools Law and the Disorderly Conduct Law criminalize behavior that is indistinguishable from typical juvenile behavior, which schools address on a daily basis without resorting to the criminal justice system.[77] The plaintiffs in *Kenny et al. v. Wilson et al.* claimed that criminal charges under the two statutes were among the leading reasons young people enter the juvenile justice system in South Carolina. Between 2010 and 2016, more than 9,500 youths younger than 17 in the state were referred to the Department of Juvenile Justice under the Disturbing Schools Law. The plaintiffs alleged that enforcement of the two state statutes drives large numbers of young people into the juvenile and criminal justice systems, criminalizes common youthful behavior, likely results in disparities on the basis of disability, and subjects students to punishment that is not proportionate to the charged misconduct.[78]

In November 2016, the Justice Department filed a statement of interest articulating the United States' position that laws charging juveniles must include clear standards. Then head of the Civil Rights Division, Vanita Gupta, said:

> The criminalization of everyday and ordinary childhood behavior under imprecise statutes can have disastrous and discriminatory consequences. Laws must provide officers with sufficient guidance to distinguish between innocent and delinquent conduct and ensure that all children receive the full protections of our Constitution. We must remain vigilant to ensure law enforcement practices do not unnecessarily remove children from the classroom and place them in a pipeline to prison.[79]

A district court judge had dismissed the case, but the appeals court reversed the decision and allowed the case to proceed. In May 2018, the governor signed an amendment repealing the crime of disturbing schools for students in the state of South Carolina. The amendment will eliminate a major source of the school-to-prison pipeline.

How Safe Are Schools?

Contrary to popular belief, schools are not dangerous. Violence that results in death at school is extremely rare; youths are far more likely to be harmed at home (see chapter 9).

> Powerful forces behind the proliferation of intense surveillance measures in schools include fears and insecurities that violence may erupt in the absence of these measures. Despite the fact that schools generally are safe and remain among the safest places for children to reside, widely publicized events of school violence often distort the public's perception of school safety and create "moral panic," putting pressure on school officials to demonstrate to parents and community members that they are taking concrete measures to prevent school violence.[80]

Statistics versus Fears

The Centers for Disease Control and Prevention has collected data on school-associated violent deaths since 1992; over the years, the average number of homicides at school annually has been 23.[81] During the panic caused by the Columbine killings in the 1998/99 school year, the likelihood of a child dying at school was one in two million.[82] In contrast, 71% of parents polled thought that a school shooting was "likely" to happen in their community. Student self-reports and opinions about their safety at school should have reassured their parents. The percentage of youths who said they were afraid of being the victim of a serious crime either inside or outside school was 24, down from 40% in 1994; 87% thought their schools were safe.

The most recent statistics reveal that schools continue to be safe, and violence is a rare event. From July 1, 2015 to June 30, 2016, there were 1,478 homicides of youth ages 5 to 18; of those 18 (1.2%) occurred at school, on the way to school, or while attending or traveling to a school-sponsored event.[83] In 2017, less than one-half of 1% of students ages 12–18 reported serious violent victimization (rape, sexual assault, robbery, and aggravated assault).

While poor urban areas have higher crime rates, the rare mass shooting is far more prevalent in smaller towns and suburbs with fewer than 50,000 people, a low crime rate, and good schools.[84] In 2017, 6.7% of students reported not attending school on at least 1 day in the previous month because of concerns for safety at school or on the way to school. The prevalence was higher among black (9%) and Hispanic (9.4%) than white (4.9%) students; the prevalence was higher for gay, lesbian and bisexual students (10%) than heterosexual students (6.1%). The prevalence of not attending school because of safety concerns ranged from 4.5% to 11.8% across states. Across 20 large urban districts, the prevalence ranged from 5.8 to 13.3%.[85] From 1993 to 2017, the prevalence of not going to school because of safety concerns increased from 4.4% to 6.7%. Efforts to make schools safer have not reassured some students. In 1999–2000, 19% of schools reported the use of security cameras compared to 81% in 2015–16; locked entrance or exit doors during the day increased from 38 to 78%; the presence of security guards or assigned police officers increased from 54 to 70%.

Policies were enacted without researching whether the expensive measures would improve school safety. "And more importantly, they did not give adequate attention to the potential negative consequences of using these strict measures, including whether these measures would put more students on a pathway from school to prison."[86] Indeed, the strategies adopted not only jeopardize the civil liberties of students, but they are counterproductive.

> There are indications that frequent police contact, even of a minor nature, has a great impact on the perceptions that black and Latino youth have of themselves, school, and law enforcement. If school socializes children to believe that they, themselves, are the target of police in their schools, students no longer see schools as places that nurture their development or teachers as adults who care about their future. For students with risk factors—that is students living in poverty, without access to healthcare or healthy food, or in places where they are unsafe—police contact at schools can accelerate future misbehavior, truancy, and dropout rates. Children disengage where they are not safe, and for many, schools have become unsafe places.[87]

Creating safe, supportive learning environments in high crime, high poverty areas is challenging. In the Chicago Public Schools, some teachers and students reported feeling unsafe; yet in many other Chicago schools—even in disadvantaged areas—teachers and students did feel safe.[88] The difference was the quality of relationships between staff, students, and parents. The vast majority of students felt safe in their classrooms but only half felt safe in the area outside their schools. Feelings of safety increase along with social resources in the community. Another determinant of safety is the number of high achieving versus low achieving students. Trusting, collaborative, and empathetic relationships with students can improve school achievement while the unconscious bias of teachers, principals and peers trigger outgroup populations to reduce their efforts and to conform to negative stereotypes.[89]

Keeping children safe is obviously important. The problem is that the implementation of punitive surveillance measures in the hopes of creating a safe environment is not sound educational and sociological policy. Intense surveillance can create student mistrust, alienation, resentment, and resistance.

> The real school safety problem is the policies that we have put in place to try to keep children safe in schools. These policies, which have us guard the gates of schools, police their interiors, and respond vigorously to any disorder, are the real problem because they are mostly ineffective, while causing harm to students, schools, families, and communities. Perhaps it shouldn't be surprising that our school safety practices are often ineffective and even harmful to children, since we have made massive changes to schools that are guided by assumptions rather than evidence.[90]

Alternative measures that do not rely on coercion, punishment, and fear can promote school safety without pushing students out of school and into the juvenile justice system.

> A growing body of research suggests that programs promoting a strong sense of community and collective responsibility enhance school safety much more effectively than police officers and other strict security measures without degrading the learning environment. . . . Rather than spending exorbitant amounts of money hiring SROs and installing other strict security measures to promote school safety, we should use our resources to provide students with more mentoring programs; counselors; mental health services; programs that build a strong sense of community, character, collective responsibility, and trust; and programs that help students develop anger-management skills and teach students how to resolve conflict.[91]

Bullying

Extreme incidents like school shootings attract the most attention regarding student safety. While overt violence in schools is rare, some students face daily incidents of intimidation and disrespect. Bullying is aggressive behavior distinguished by repeated acts against weaker victims. Psychological bullying consists of social exclusion, extortion, intimidation, or spreading malicious rumors. Bullying can be cruel and hateful, and social media can magnify the pain.

Until this century, adults viewed bullying as the inevitable result of some juveniles attempting to dominate others.[92] The general belief was that learning to deal with intimidation in childhood would prepare individuals to deal with similar behavior when they were adults. The Columbine shootings changed attitudes about bullying. The media portrayed the killers as taking revenge after being bullied by jocks. Politicians, parents, pediatricians, and child psychologists lobbied for prevention of bullying. The first anti-bullying laws appeared in 2000. Today all fifty states have anti-bullying laws; only 6 (ME, MN, NE, NH, NM, WY) do not have a criminal sanction for cyberbullying or online harassment.[93] Montana is the lone state that does not mandate that schools have a formal policy to identify bullying behavior and to outline possible disciplinary responses.

Where is the line between behavior that is cruel and behavior that is criminal? In the age of Facebook, YouTube, and ubiquitous cell phones with cameras, embarrassing photos and public humiliation spread virally. Bullying behavior today reaches far more people and is visually more potent than older behaviors like comments scrawled on bathroom walls. Home was once a potential respite from taunts and insults, but electronic postings remove that safe harbor unless teens resist visiting the sites. Social scientists find that bullying is no more prevalent today than it was fifty years ago, but the reaction to it has changed.[94] Law professor David Yamada comments that bullying is not just a social ill, it is a cottage industry with commentators, prevention experts, and legal scholars taking on an enemy that has always been there.

Multiple websites address bullying. Stopbullying.gov is a federal website managed by the U.S. Department of Health and Human Services. The National Bullying Prevention Center was founded in 2006 and treats bullying as a serious community issue. It provides resources for students, parents, educators, and others.[95] Another website, Noplace4hate.org, illustrates the widespread nature of fears about bullying. It refers to an epidemic and claims there are 4,400 suicides each year due to bullying.[96] These and many other organizations address bullying, cyberbullying, and youth suicide.[97]

Student bullying was the most commonly reported discipline problem among public schools across survey years.[98] The percentage (20%) of students between the ages of 12 and 18 who reported being bullied at school in 2017 was the lowest in a decade (32% in 2007; 28% in 2009 and 2011; 21.5% in 2013, and 21% in 2015); 17% of males were bullied versus 24% of females. The percentage of public schools that reported student bullying at least once a week was higher for middle schools (22%) than for high schools (15%) and primary schools (8%). Cyberbullying (the use of computers, cell phones, or other electronic devices to inflict willful and repeated harm) affected the school environment in 7% of public schools.

Types of bullying varied by gender; 18% of females at school were the subject of rumors versus 9% of males while 6% of males were pushed, tripped, or spit on versus 4% of females.[99] The percentages for insults were 16% for females and 10% for males. About 27% of students who reported being bullied at school reported that bullying affected how they felt about themselves, 19% reported that bullying affected their schoolwork and their relationships with friends or family, and 14% reported that bullying had a negative effect on their physical health. Most students are bullied once or twice during a school year; persistent bullying affects a relatively small number of students.[100]

Media coverage of bullying has intensified.[101] Headlines proclaim "Bullied to Death." While bullies should be accountable for their behavior, can they be liable for the chain of events that follow? Year after year, the media report tragic stories of suicide after bullying. Gabriella Green, a 12-year-old in Panama City Beach hung herself; police arrested two 12-year-old girls for cyberbullying in connection with her death.[102] Under similar circumstances almost four years earlier, Nancy Willard, director of a group that focuses on combating cyberbullying, had reviewed police files on the suicide of Rebecca Sedwick in Lakeland, Florida.[103] She found that law enforcement and the media were too quick to allege bullying caused a suicide when other factors might have been at work. The tragedy is compounded by blaming another child for the death of a classmate by suicide.

Mallory Grossman committed suicide after being bullied repeatedly by four classmates, including one who asked her when she was going to kill herself.[104] Her parents reported the bullying of their 12-year-old daughter multiple times to school administrators, who took no disciplinary actions. Instead, Mallory was removed from classes and ate alone in the guidance counselor's office to avoid harassment. One year after her death, her parents sued the school district and school employees for failing to enforce New Jersey's anti-bullying policies, among the toughest in the nation after the suicide of Tyler Clementi in 2011. The parents are also pushing for "Mallory's Law," which would hold parents accountable for their children's actions based on the severity of the incident. Stephanie Johnson died four days after being found in the bathroom of her middle school.[105] Her parents had notified the school that other students were bullying their daughter and telling her to kill herself. Attorneys in Minnesota were considering legal action.

Many studies have researched the relationship between bullying and the tendency for suicidal behaviors.[106] One analysis of 47 studies found that both bullies and victims of bullying were more likely to think about suicide than youths not involved in bullying.[107] The correlation was strongest for youths who were both perpetrators and victims.[108] Bully/victims are at high risk for anxiety and depression. Research indicates that factors beyond bullying contribute to suicidal behaviors; delinquency and depression were contributing factors.[109] Low self-esteem is another contributing factor, as are age, race and ethnicity, alcohol use, poor parent-child relationships, living in poverty, and poor social support. There was a strong association between bullying and suicidal tendencies among LGBTQ youth.[110]

Criminology professor Sameer Hinduja is co-director of the Cyberbullying Research Center at Florida Atlantic University. His research shows real-world bullying is much more common than online bullying; 12% of children surveyed say they have bullied others online.[111] Fewer than 1% of cyberbullying cases involve suicide, and many of the victims suffered from other stressors such as depression or family issues. He notes that many children are bullied but don't commit suicide.

Many experts believe the most powerful tools to prevent school discipline and violence problems are anti-bullying efforts and peer mediation.[112] An effective antibullying program involves altering the school climate so that bullying is no longer acceptable to staff or to students. Research on prevention and intervention recognizes bullying as a group process. In 80% of incidents of bullying, there are bystanders.[113] Only about 17% of peers try to defend the victim, whether because they fear rejection by their peers or because they are friends with the bully. Passive watching is interpreted as approval. Bullying can be reduced by educating students that peers are central to occurrence, maintenance, and escalation of bullying.[114] One study found that students at schools with anti-bullying programs were, ironically, more likely to be victimized.[115] A possible reason is that the programs identified signs of antisocial behavior; that knowledge may have helped perpetrators avoid detection.

Bullying can affect the climate of a school.[116] Youth who reported witnessing bullying had greater feelings of helplessness and less connectedness to school.[117] Widespread bullying creates a school environment of fear and insecurity that reduces school attendance and affects academic performance.

> Research has found that aspects of the school environment such as levels of bullying, classmate relationships, and teacher support have an impact on students' cognitive and noncognitive outcomes, including students' social-emotional skills, attitudes about self and others, social behaviors, and academic performance.[118]

Aggressive behavior among school-aged youth negatively impacts cognition, school connectedness, and school attendance. The lack of school engagement can lead to lower graduation rates, depression/other mental disorders, and delinquency.[119] Youth with disabilities, learning differences, cultural differences, or sexual/gender identity differences are the most vulnerable to being bullied.

Bullying is an age-old problem. One ironic aspect is that unfair rules, such as those described in the previous sections, can teach bullying to students.[120]

> The real school safety problem is not that we have too many out-of-control kids, overly lenient school discipline, or too few police in schools. Instead, the real problem is that school security and punishment are too punitive and rigid: we rely too much on policing, suspension, and expulsion instead of helping kids solve their problems and properly caring for them.[121]

REINFORCING CLASS AND RACE INEQUALITY

School shootings and tragic cases of bullying attract media attention. The disappearance of the promise of the American Dream for growing numbers of children is a less explored story. Belief in equality of opportunity limited only by talent and hard work has faded. There is "a robust and growing opportunity gap among American kids."[122] Social mobility relies most heavily on educational attainment. Extensive research conclusively demonstrates that the social class of children is one of the most significant predictors of educational success.[123]

> In this new age of urbanized knowledge capitalism, place and class combine to reinforce and reproduce socioeconomic advantage. Those at the top locate in communities that afford them privileged access to the best schools, the best services, and the best economic opportunities, while the rest get the leftover neighborhoods, which have inferior versions of all those things and hence offer less of a chance for moving up in life.[124]

Follow the Money

The education system once enabled children to rise above their birth circumstances. Of the children born in 1940, 90% earned more than their parents; for children born in the 1980s, only half earned more.[125] "The root of inequality in educational outcomes in the United States is the combination of growing poverty and resegregation, along with inequality in school funding and resources."[126] For many years, local school districts were primarily responsible for funding K–12 education, primarily through property taxes.[127] Since the 1970s, state governments have shared almost equally in the funding with federal funds totaling less than 10%. State governments use several methods to distribute funds across school districts (see discussion below).

In most states, the wealthiest districts spend at least two to three times what the poorest districts spend per pupil.[128] The differences affect both learning conditions for students and salaries for educators.

> The disparate treatment of minority students has been documented repeatedly in almost all areas of public education. For example, it is more common for students of color, especially low-income students of color, to be in overcrowded classrooms, attend schools in deplorable physical condition, and be taught by educators who are less experienced, less credentialed, and lower paid. They are more likely to be suspended, expelled, referred to law enforcement, or subject to a school-based arrest than similarly situated white students. They have less access to counselors, gifted and talented programs, music and art curricula, project-based science classes, extra-curricular activities, and higher-level science and mathematics courses. Further, they are more likely to learn in segregated environments that have lower levels of peer group competition and support.[129]

Students from privileged backgrounds begin their quest for success substantially ahead of students from the bottom of the social order. The initial advantage compounds—all the way to the best colleges.[130] The college admissions process favors the privileged and undermines professed commitments to diversity. Affirmative action, originally intended as a tool to promote social justice, has morphed into a tool that colleges use to sell themselves and to attract corporate support. Children of the privileged are on track for admission; lower and middle-class students of all races find the deck stacked against them. Money and connections influence college admissions, reinforcing wealth and privilege. Schools reward donors and alumni—increasing their endowments and reinforcing wealth and privilege.

Since public schools depend on tax dollars for financing, the fact that we live in a highly stratified and unequal society results in unequal financing of public schools. Whether we compare public school financing on a state-by-state or a district-by-district basis, the disparities are enormous. The wealthier states spend about three times what the poorer states spend. As a result, opportunities for children in the wealthiest communities in states such as New York and Connecticut are dramatically different from the opportunities for children in poor communities in Arizona and Mississippi. In 2015 New York had the highest expenditure per student ($14,769), and Connecticut was third ($11,341). Arizona spent the least ($4,015), and Mississippi was fifth to last ($4,796).[131] The U.S. average was $6,903.

The National Report Card by Rutgers University researchers and the Education Law Center in Newark, New Jersey was first published in 2010. "Since then, a growing body of research has convincingly demonstrated that money does, in fact, make a difference in improving educational opportunities for the nation's schoolchildren."[132]

- Regressive distribution patterns ignore the need for additional funding in high-poverty districts. Seventeen states had regressive funding; the most regressive were Nevada, Illinois and North Dakota. Students in high poverty districts received less than 75 cents for every dollar received by low poverty districts.
- Flat distribution allocates roughly the same amount of funding across districts with varying needs. Twenty states had flat distribution patterns.
- Progressive distribution allocates more funds to districts as student poverty increases. Eleven states (down from 22 in 2008) had progressive funding. Utah, Delaware and Minnesota were the most progressive states—the highest poverty districts averaged 30% more funding per student than low poverty districts.

The report evaluates states on four fairness measures: funding level (state comparisons per pupil funding), funding distribution (described above), effort (ratio of education spending to gross state product and personal income), and coverage (proportion of children in public schools and income ratio of public/nonpublic school families). Only New Jersey and Wyoming scored well on all four indicators. California, Florida, Louisiana, and Tennessee scored poorly on all four measures.

Congress mandates that The National Center for Education Statistics report annually on the condition of education in the United States.[133] The report includes figures on the percentage distribution of public school students by poverty level, determined by the percentage of a school's enrollment that is eligible for free or reduced-price lunches. High-poverty schools are defined as those where more than 75% of the students qualify for the program; low-poverty schools are defined as those where 25% or less of the students are eligible. In the 2015–16 school year, 24.4% of students attended public high-poverty schools; 19.7% attended public low-poverty schools. Higher percentages of Hispanic (45%), African American (45%), and Native American (37%) students attended high-poverty schools than did white students (8%).

The proportion of low-income students has increased rapidly, as has the proportion of minority students in the student population. Black and Hispanic students, even if their families are not poor, are much more likely than white or Asian students to be in high poverty schools.[134] More than half (51%) of the schoolchildren attending the nation's public schools come from low-income families compared to 32% in 1989.[135] In 21 states half or more of public school students were eligible for free or reduced-price lunches. Most of these states are located in the South (13) and the West (6). Mississippi leads the nation with 71% of school children living in low income families. In 19 other states, low income students were 40 to 49% of the public school enrollment.

Income inequality perpetuates economic disadvantages.[136] Communities with higher levels of income inequality have lower rates of social mobility. One explanation is that economically disadvantaged adolescents may perceive negative returns from an investment in education. To improve rates of upward mobility, youths need to believe they can achieve economic success. They are more likely to drop out of school if they live where the gap between the bottom and middle income distribution is high. Higher income inequality is associated with increased residential segregation and a decreasing presence of high-achieving role models. Youths who are out of school and out of work may be influenced by peers toward criminal behavior.

In most public schools the children of the poor start at a terrible disadvantage, especially those for whom English is a second language. The children in wealthier schools come from neighborhoods with good housing, reliable transportation, parks, and good public libraries. One or both parents are often professionals. Children from poorer districts face a very different reality: drug dealers on street corners; police and ambulance sirens almost nightly; many (if not most) of the men either unemployed or underemployed; and neighbors in jail or prison. As noted at the beginning of this section, children from such disparate backgrounds do not begin their education from equivalent starting points. Should we be surprised that so many children, acutely aware of the huge differences between their schools and those of the more affluent, simply give up very early in life?

Apartheid Schooling

In 1954 the Supreme Court ruled in *Brown v. Board of Education* that segregation of public schools on the basis of race was unconstitutional. Fourteen years later, the Kerner Commission warned that the United States faced a system of apartheid (two societies, one black, one white—separate and unequal) in its major cities. "Today, 50 years after the report was issued, that prediction characterizes most of our large urban areas, where intensifying segregation and concentrated poverty have collided with disparities in school funding to reinforce educational inequality."[137] The Civil Rights Project refers to the overlapping phenomena of socioeconomic and racial segregation as *double segregation.*[138]

Jonathan Kozol has studied educational and social inequalities in the United States for 50 years[139] He deplores widespread acceptance of the idea that schools in poverty-stricken areas must accept different academic and career goals than those of schools in middle-class neighborhoods. Tolerating separate schools and their unequal opportunities for offering alternatives to one's current socioeconomic status means society is confining poor, minority children to spend their lives in poverty. Urban studies theorist Richard Florida quantifies the cost.

> The economic penalty for growing up in conditions of racially concentrated poverty is considerable. The difference in lifetime earnings between those raised in the richest 20% of neighborhoods versus those raised in the bottom 20% is about the same as the difference between just completing high school and having a college degree [$910,000]."[140]

The population in a growing number of schools is almost exclusively students of color from low-income families.[141] In Chicago and New York City, more than 95% of African American and Latino students attend majority-poverty schools, and most are also majority-minority schools. The city of New York has 4 million white residents, but a Latina high school student might not have a white classmate until she attends college.[142] In 1988, 44% of African American students attended majority white schools; in 2018, the percentage was about 20%.[143]

Segregation declined significantly in districts under court oversight. Decades of desegregation efforts were reversed when Pinellas County, one of the most affluent communities in Florida, passed an ordinance in 2007 to create neighborhood schools. The result was a pocket of racially isolated, high-poverty schools known as failure factories.[144] One study found that graduation rates climbed 2% for every year an African American student attended an integrated school.[145] Attending a court-ordered desegregated school for 5 years resulted in a 15% increase in wages and an 11% decline in poverty rates. After oversight was terminated in various districts, segregation increased rapidly. Segregated minority schools have fewer qualified teachers, rapid turnover of faculty, and fewer resources; students have limited exposure to peers who positively influence academic learning.

Achievement gaps result from social class and racial spatial segregation.[146] "The democratic principles of this nation are impossible to reach without universal access to a diverse, high quality, and engaging education."[147]

> Students who attend integrated schools report being more comfortable with people of different races, are more likely to seek out diverse spaces later in life, have lower levels of bias, are more satisfied with schools and more confident in their academic abilities, and possess stronger leadership skills. Diversity in schools also leads to greater creativity among students, elevated problem-solving and critical thinking skills, increased motivation and deeper learning.[148]

Research over the last five decades has found that students perform better academically in racially and socioeconomically integrated schools. A critical issue is whether education policies can alter patterns of residential segregation.

> If the demographics of schools are inextricably tied to the demographics of neighborhoods, then the goal of having racially and economically integrated schools will need to be achieved through changes in housing patterns—not quick, easy, or certain work. But to the degree that the public school a student attends can be disconnected from the neighborhood in which the student lives through public policy, there is the possibility of quicker and easier solutions than those that require building demographically diverse residential neighborhoods.[149]

Columbia sociology and education professor Amy Stuart Wells argues that political leaders should listen to the growing demand for more diverse public schools. She notes that the issue deserves more attention because students of color comprise such a large portion of the student population plus the gentrification of urban neighborhoods. In addition to improved academic success, integrated schools have the additional advantage of helping youth challenge stereotypes and implicit biases toward people of different races and ethnicities. Fully realizing this goal requires teachers who are skilled in racially and culturally relevant teaching practices.

TRACKING

Tracking has been a feature of U.S. public schools for almost a century.[150] Originally, tracking was a response to increasing numbers of immigrant children. The rationale was that children with a limited understanding of English and limited preparation needed to be separated from native students. Eventually schools separated students by academic ability into different groups (fast, average, slow) for all subjects or for certain subjects. Tracking could enable teachers to target lessons to the ability levels of students so that they learn at an appropriate pace without falling behind. Today secondary schools use tracking to designate levels of difficulty for certain courses, dividing students into basic, honors, and college preparation groups. In theory, tracking should promote academic success.

In the 1980s, Jeannie Oaks revealed that many low-income and minority students were placed in lower tracks without consideration of their academic abilities. She raised the issue of *industrial schooling*, whereby lower-income students were funneled into vocational programs while upper-class students received more educational opportunities.[151] She provided abundant evidence of how tracking perpetuates inequality. By the early 1990s, tracking was no longer seen as an equity-neutral structure, and policymakers acknowledged the disadvantages suffered by students in the lower tracks.[152] A number of courts examined whether tracking was second-generation segregation.

The surface features of tracking changed, and the rigid system of separate academic, general, and vocational programs disappeared.

> However, the deep structure of tracking remains uncannily robust. Most middle and high schools still sort students into classes at different levels based on judgments of students' "ability." This sorting continues to disadvantage those in lower-track classes. Such students have less access to high-status knowledge, fewer opportunities to engage in stimulating learning activities, and classroom relationships less likely to foster engagement with teachers, peers, and learning. The sorting and differentiated opportunities promote gaps in outcomes of every sort: achievement, graduation rates, college going, and so on. Low-income students and students of color still suffer disproportionately from these negative effects, both because they are tracked disproportionately into the lowest classes in racially mixed schools and also because they are more likely to attend racially isolated schools where lower-level classes predominate. Thus, through tracking, schools continue to replicate existing inequality along lines of race and social class and contribute to the intergenerational transmission of social and economic inequality.[153]

Tracking is controversial because it differentiates students by skills and knowledge. Tracking stratifies opportunities to learn—denying the more beneficial opportunities to lower-tracked students. "This generally plays out in a discriminatory way, segregating students by race and socio-economic status."[154] A synthesis of more than 800 meta-analyses indicates that tracking has little effect on learning outcomes but many negative effects."[155] Lower-track classes often have less experienced teachers, lower expectations, more discipline problems, and less engaging lessons.[156]

The curriculum of the lower track retards academic development and lowers self-esteem.[157] Assumptions about what students are able to learn influences the ideas and concepts to which they are exposed. High-track students are taught mathematical concepts and read Shakespeare; low-track students are given computational exercises and reading kits.

> First, students are identified in a rather public way as to their intellectual capabilities and accomplishments and separated into a hierarchical system of groups

for instruction. Second, these groups are labeled quite openly and characterized in the minds of teachers and others as being of a certain type—high ability, low achieving, slow, average, and so on. Clearly these groups are not equally valued in the school. . . . Third, individual students in these groups come to be defined by others—both adults and their peers—in terms of these group types. In other words, a student in a high achieving group is seen as a high achieving *person*, bright, smart, quick, and in the eyes of many, *good*. And those in the low-achieving groups come to be called slow, below average. . . . Fourth, on the basis of these sorting decisions, the groupings of students that result, and the way educators see the students in these groups, teenagers are treated by and experience schools very differently.[158]

Lowered self-esteem and teacher expectation can result in a self-fulfilling prophecy. Low-track students participate less in extracurricular activities at school, exhibit more school and classroom misconduct, and are more often involved in delinquent behavior outside of school.[159] Alienated from school, they have higher dropout rates. Tracking continues to be linked to both class and race, as a disproportionate number of lower-class and minority students are placed into the lower tracks.

SCHOOL FAILURE AND DELINQUENCY

A first-time arrest when in high school almost doubles the odds of dropping out; if the arrest results in a court appearance, the odds almost quadruple.[160] If not convicted, a student who returns to school after being arrested faces embarrassment and being stigmatized by classmates and teachers. They may also face increased monitoring from school officials. Frequently, these conditions lower standardized test scores, which increases the likelihood that the student will drop out of school and face increased interaction with the justice system. For those students who do drop out of high school as a result of an arrest, the chances that they will serve time in prison increase exponentially.[161]

Falling Behind and Dropping Out

Falling behind in school and dropping out should be seen as a *process* rather than a *single event* in the life course of students. Test scores are weaker indicators of potential high school success than middle school grades and attendance.[162] Students with a high risk of failure in high school are chronically absent in the middle grades or are failing their classes.

There are key differences between youth who are pulled out of school by personal circumstances (i.e. pregnancy, the need to support their family financially) and those who are pushed out of school (expelled, history of academic and disciplinary problems, academically disengaged).[163] The latter are far more likely to be involved in criminal activity than the former. The former have much better success finding work, which in turn improves their chances of staying out of trouble.[164] The Educational Longitudinal Study ranked the reasons for dropping out as follows: pushed out—49%; pulled out—37%; falling out—14% (does not show significant academic progress; student becomes disillusioned with school completion).[165]

Ninth grade is often the bottleneck for many students who find that their academic skills are insufficient for high school. Up to 40% of ninth grade students in cities with the highest dropout rates repeat ninth grade—only 10–15% of those students will graduate. Academic success in ninth grade course work is more important than demographic characteristics or prior academic achievement in predicting who will graduate. Ninth grade is the crunch point for more than 33% of dropouts.[166] Exclusionary discipline contributes to an increased risk that a student will be held back rather than promoted, and grade retention contributes to the risk of dropping out of school.[167] A single ninth-grade suspension doubles the risk that a student will drop out of high school.[168]

Hirschi's social bond theory (see chapter 7) suggests that youths who are closely bonded to school, among other attachments, are less likely to be delinquent. Some researchers use the term *engagement* to refer to the extent to which students participate in academic and nonacademic school activities plus identify with and value schooling outcomes. Engagement includes both a *participation* and a *psychological* component. The participation component refers to such factors as class attendance, being prepared for class, completing homework, and being involved in extracurricular activities. The psychological engagement component includes a sense of belonging, social ties, and bonds with other students and teachers, a feeling of safety and security at school, and valuing school success. The lowest 25% of secondary students in terms of achievement are twenty times more likely to drop out of high school than students who rank in the highest 25% for achievement. Research indicates that a lack of engagement is an important predictor for dropping out, even after controlling for academic achievement and student background.[169]

Early warning systems alert educators, parents, and students when a student falls off track. System indicators should include strong predictors of high school graduation. The number of indicators varies by school districts, but researchers suggest districts begin with attendance, behavior incidents, and course performance.[170] Research has steadily shown a strong relationship between how often a student misses school and the probability of graduating in four years. Students who regularly miss class fall behind in coursework, and their grades decline. One suspension in grade 6 can predict whether a student graduates in four years. Behavior incidents indicate disengagement with school. Poor course performance also indicates disengagement. Studies have shown that decreases in behavioral and emotional engagement with schools lead to increases in delinquency and substance abuse. In short, students begin to disengage before officially leaving school.[171]

Quite often a youngster will become increasingly frustrated and self-conscious about his or her failure in school, which often leads directly to various forms of acting out, including delinquency. More often than not, the official response is to try to *control* the behavior, rather than finding out *why* a student is acting out and then providing a solution to the behavior. This eventually leads to the student getting more and more frustrated and embarrassed (which can be especially painful in front of peers), which in turn leads to getting suspended or expelled from school, and ultimately dropping out entirely.

Among the proposals to reform public schools, the most prominent are choice (school vouchers and charter schools) and testing. Education policy analyst Diane Ravitch gives both of these reforms a failing grade.[172] "If we are unable to change the root causes of low performance, nothing will change. We may continue to spend billions of dollars on testing and choice, pretending to 'reform' our schools, but poverty and racial segregation will continue to be the shame of the nation."[173]

Charter schools and vouchers generally have not provided significant gains for students. Testing has resulted in teachers "teaching to the test," with little improvement in learning. "The purpose of American education is to prepare our children for the duties of citizenship in a democracy. The federal and state policies of the recent past have aimed to turn education into a competition for higher test scores, despite the fact that testing always favors the advantaged over the disadvantaged."[174]

The No Child Left Behind Act (NCLB) linked school funding to performance on standardized tests and authorized the closure of low-performing schools and the creation of alternative schools.[175] When school funding is linked to test scores, the high stakes may motivate some school officials to increase their surveillance of students in an effort to exclude low-performing students (and their poor test scores) from their schools.[176] The No Child Left Behind era from 2002 to 2015 was marked by states focusing on testing without investing in the resources needed to raise achievement levels.[177]

"Teaching to the test" undermines student engagement and limits the curriculum.[178] When teachers are under scrutiny to produce positive test results with dwindling resources, classroom management becomes more punitive. The students most in need of academic, social, and economic help are the ones pushed out of school. In one Texas jurisdiction, standardized test scores increased—but tens of thousands of primarily African American and Latino students were no longer enrolled.[179] Public officials praised a Massachusetts school district for the most improved standardized test scores for 10th graders while ignoring the fact that it had the second-highest ninth-grade student dropout rate. In a study of Florida school district records, David Figlio found that schools gave harsher punishments to low performing students than to high performing students. The gap was significantly wider for students in grades where the high stakes testing occurred.[180]

> Ironically, some of the hallmarks of modern education reform—including demands for greater accountability, extensive testing regimes and harsh sanctions imposed on schools and teachers—actually encourage schools to funnel out those students whom they believe are likely to drag down a school's test scores. Rather than address the systemic problems that lead to poor educational performance, harsh discipline policies provide schools with a convenient method to remove certain students and thereby mask educational deficiencies.[181]

The Every Student Succeeds Act (ESSA) replaced NCLB. Then Department of Education Secretary Arne Duncan commented: "For the first time, the law will focus on low-performing schools, focus on the dropout factories. For decades, these schools were left to languish and fail."[182] ESSA requires states to identify any high school enrolling 100 or more students with a graduation rate of 67% or less for comprehensive improvement starting in the 2018–19 school year.[183] In 2016, there were 2,425 low-graduation rate high schools with an enrollment of almost 1.1 million. More than half (57%) of the schools were in cities; 27% were in suburban areas; 6% were in small towns; 5% were in rural areas. Approximately 60% of the students in low-graduation rate schools are low income compared to 46% in all high schools. Black students are overrepresented; they comprise 15.5% of students in similarly sized high schools but 28.3% in low-graduation-rate schools. In contrast, whites are 51.5% of the high school population but 31.5% of students in low performing schools. Hispanics are 23.8% of the high school population but 31.5% in low-graduation rate schools.

Duncan criticized NCLB as a top-down, very punitive, very prescriptive program.[184] ESSA contains early childhood education requirements and sets high standards to counteract the actions of 20 states that had reduced their standards. The NCLB requirement to link teacher evaluation to test scores was removed. However, ESSA still requires state-wide annual tests on math and reading in grades 3 through 8 plus once in high school and statewide testing in science once in elementary school, once in middle school, and once in high school.

The graduation rate for public high school students in 2015–16 was 84%. The rates for individual states varied from 68% in New Mexico to 94% in Nebraska. For white students, the percentages ranged from 76% in New Mexico to 94% in New Jersey (national average 88%).[185] The rates for black students ranged from 57% in Nevada to 88% in West Virginia (national average 76%). The rates for Hispanic students ranged from 65% in Minnesota to 89% in Nevada and West Virginia (national average 79%). Dropout rates do not include institutionalized individuals.[186] Young adults who have not graduated from high school are incarcerated at higher rates than those with higher levels of educational attainment. Male are more likely to drop out of school than females; 7% of males ages 16 to 24 were high school dropouts in 2016 compared to 5% of females.

Black and Hispanic students make up more than half of the nation's non-graduates. In Minnesota, Nevada, New York, Ohio, and Wisconsin, the graduation gap between Black and white students is greater than 20%. The gap between Hispanic and white students in New York and Minnesota is also greater than 20%. More than two-thirds of non-graduates are low income. Although graduation rates for low-income students increased faster than the overall rate in the majority of states, the graduation gap between low-income students and more affluent peers increased in 16 states over the last 6 years.

Consequences of Dropping Out

A high school diploma is an initial marker on the path to postsecondary education, a good job, and civic engagement.[187] For much of the twentieth century, high school graduation was the finish line between childhood and adulthood. With the growth of the knowledge economy in the twenty-first century, a high school diploma was a requirement for the next level of training and education. The high wage industrial and manufacturing jobs that had been available to high school graduates disappeared. Without some training beyond high school, securing a stable, well-paying job is unlikely. People who do not graduate from high school are more likely to be unemployed, will earn less than high school graduates, will have worse health and lower life expectancy, are more likely to require social services, and are more likely to be involved in the criminal justice system.

The national high school dropout rate has declined, but specific student groups experience a very different kind of education than their peers.[188] Many of the students who drop out have complex behavioral and academic problems. Reducing the dropout rate is essential; a good education levels the playing field for students facing challenges such as living in an unstable home or a poor neighborhood. Completing high school provides both health and economic benefits.[189]

In addition to the cost to individuals of failing to graduate, there is also a cost to society. A study of youths in California estimated that students who dropped out of high school after being suspended would cost the state about $2.7 billion in lost tax revenue from wages, increased crime, and higher welfare and health costs.[190] A Florida study estimated that students who drop out of high school earn about $200,000 less over their lifetimes than do high school graduates. A Texas study found that grade retentions due to school discipline (approximately 6,600 per year) cost the state $76 million annually in additional instruction costs plus additional economic effects of $100 million, including lost tax revenue because of delayed workforce entry.[191] School discipline is linked to a 24% increase in high school dropouts, with a significant economic effect. Student suspensions cost the nation more than $35 billion in lost tax revenue and increased social expenditures.[192] Tenth grade school suspensions result in more than 67,000 high school dropouts nationally.[193] Over his or her lifetime, each dropout accounts for $163,000 in lost tax revenue and $364,000 in social costs, such as health care and criminal justice expenses. The aggregate cost of 67,000 dropouts exceeds $35 billion.

Students of color are far more likely to be suspended than are white students. Black students comprise 13% of all 10th graders but 25% of suspended students. Reducing the discipline gap promotes equity and fairness. California has reduced suspensions almost 40% since eliminating suspensions for disruption or defiance. Some schools in Richmond County, Georgia, have reduced suspensions by more than 90% after introducing alternative discipline models.[194] Cutting suspension rates by 50% for one cohort of students would result in economic savings of $3.1 billion for California and $817 million for Florida. Cutting the suspension rate in half nationally would result in $17.8 billion in savings, including $5.5 billion in additional tax revenue, $2 billion in health savings, and $3 billion in crime savings.

Over the lifetime of every high school dropout, the US economy loses at least $262,000 because of more criminal activity, lower tax contributions, poor health, and a greater reliance on welfare and Medicaid.[195] A longitudinal study found that by the age of 27 the outcomes between high school dropouts and graduates were noteworthy. Individuals who did not finish high school were more than 3 times as likely to have been arrested since the age of 18. They were twice as likely to have used drugs in the last 6 months and twice as likely to report being in poor health. They were also twice as likely to have been fired two or more times and 4 times more likely to be receiving government assistance.[196] Increasing the national high school graduation rate by 10% would have positive effects on the national economy by boosting gross domestic product by $11.5 billion annually; increasing annual earnings by $7.2 billion, increasing annual spending by $5.3 billion, and increasing federal tax revenue by $1.1 billion.[197]

Summary

Schools are some of the most important US social institutions, providing building blocks for a better life. Before children reach the age of 18, about three-fourths of their lives are spent in the public school system. Money spent on public schooling pays enormous returns down the road. Likewise, failure at this stage of one's life results in a heavy toll for all of us.

Schooling has always been closely related to social class and often perpetuates class differences. Rather than equalizing differences through education, public schools sometimes seem only to perform the function of social control. In the modern era, "zero tolerance" has often led to policies that make schools more like prisons than places of learning. Virtually every school district in large urban areas now has police officers either inside or nearby schools.

The public school experience is closely related to delinquency and juvenile justice. A great amount of delinquent behavior is directly related to a youth's performance in school. Below-average grades, suspension, and expulsion lead to dropping out. Problems at school have a tendency to continue out of school and can lead eventually to the juvenile court.

Notes

[1] Harold R. Kerbo, *Social Stratification and Inequality*, 8th ed. (New York: McGraw-Hill, 2011). Kerbo provides a good brief summary of the literature on education and achievement.

[2] Sean F. Reardon, "School District Socioeconomic Status, Race, and Academic Achievement," Stanford Center for Education Policy Analysis, 2016.

[3] Ibid.

4 James Diego Vigil, *Gang Redux: A Balanced Anti-Gang Strategy* (Long Grove, IL: Waveland Press, 2010), 47.

5 Aaron Cooley. "Failed States in Education: Chomsky on Dissent, Propaganda, and Reclaiming Democracy in the Media Spectacle," *Educational Studies*, 2010, 46(6): 579–605.

6 Juliette Schor, *The Overworked American: The Unexpected Decline of Leisure* (New York: Basic Books, 1991).

7 Elizabeth Fones-Wolf, *Selling Free Enterprise: The Business Assault on Labor and Liberalism, 1945–1960* (Urbana: University of Illinois Press, 1992), 190.

8 Quoted in Merle Eugene Curti, *The Social Ideas of American Educators* (Totowa, NJ: Littlefield, Adams, 1959), 203.

9 Jonathan Kozol, *The Shame of the Nation: The Restoration of Apartheid Schooling in America* (New York: Three Rivers Press, 2005), 96.

10 Ibid., 94.

11 Henry A. Giroux, *American Nightmare: Facing the Challenge of Fascism* (San Francisco: City Lights Books, 2018), 47.

12 Donna Foote, "Rewriting the Locke Story," *Los Angeles Times*, May 20, 2008, http://articles.latimes.com/2008/may/20/opinion/oe-footc20

13 Ibid.

14 Joan Herman, Jordan Rickles, Mark Hansen, Larry Thomas, Alice Gualpa, and Jia Wang, "Evaluation of Green Dot's Locke Transformation Project: Findings from the 2007–200, 2008–2009, and 2009–2010 School Years," Los Angeles: University of California, National Center for Research on Evaluation, Standards, and Student Testing (CRESST), July 2011 (CRESST Report 799).

15 Kyle Stokes and Carla Javier, "LA's Notorious Locke High School Is Improving. Is It Still 'Failing'?", 89.3KPCC, February 20, 2018.

16 Ibid.

17 For good critiques of charter schools and privatization in general see two books by Diane Ravitch: *The Death and Life of the Great American School System: How Testing and Choice Are Undermining Education* (New York: Basic Books, 2010) and *Reign of Error: The Hoax of the Privatization Movement and the Danger to America's Public Schools* (New York: Vintage Books, 2014).

18 Jacob Kang-Brown, Jennifer Trone, Jennifer Fratello, and Tarika Daftary-Kapur, "A Generation Later: What We've Learned about Zero Tolerance in Schools," Vera Institute, 2013.

19 Russell J. Skiba, Suzanne E. Eckes, and Kevin Brown, "African American Disproportionality in School Discipline: The Divide between Best Evidence and Legal Remedy," *New York Law School Law Review*, 2009/10, 54: 1071–1112, 1072.

20 Randall G. Shelden and Pavel V. Vasiliev, *Controlling the Dangerous Classes: A History of Criminal Justice in America*, 3rd ed.(Long Grove, IL: Waveland Press, 2018).

21 Nina Passero, "The Impact of Zero Tolerance Policies on the Relation between Educational Attainment and Crime," New York University OPUS, 2016.

22 Lauren Musu-Gillette, Anlan Zhang, Ke Wang, Jizhi Zhang, Jana Kemp, Melissa Diliberti, and Barbara A. Oudekerk, *Indicators of School Crime and Safety: 2017* (Washington, DC: National Center for Education Statistics, 2018).

23 Daniel J. Losen and Amir Whitaker, "11 million Days Lost: Race, Discipline, and Safety at U.S. Public Schools," The Center for Civil Rights Remedies and The American Civil Liberties Union of Southern California, August 24, 2018.

24 Morgan Craven, "Suspended Childhood: An Analysis of Exclusionary Discipline of Texas' Pre-K and Elementary School Students Updated with 2015–16 Data," Texas Appleseed, March 2017

25 Janet Rosenbaum, "Educational and Criminal Justice Outcomes 12 Years after School Suspension," *Youth & Society*, January 17, 2018.

26 Government Accountability Office, "K–12 Education: Discipline Disparities for Black Students, Boys, and Students with Disabilities," March 2018, GAO-18-258.

27 Melinda Anderson, "When Schooling Meets Policing," *The Atlantic*, September 21, 2015.

28 Victor Kappeler and Gary Potter, *The Mythology of Crime and Criminal Justice*, 5th ed. (Long Grove, IL: Waveland Press, 2018).

29 Bree Zender, "In the Spotlight, School Resource Officers Gear Up for Next Year," National Public Radio, July 2, 2018.

30 Kappeler and Potter, *The Mythology of Crime and Criminal Justice*.

31 *J.D.B. v. North Carolina*, 564 US_(2011).

32 *Safford Unified School District v. Redding*, 557 U.S. __ (2009).

33 Henry A. Giroux, *Disposable Youth, Racialized Memories, and the Culture of Cruelty* (New York: Routledge, 2012), xiv, xv–xvi.

34 Lenore Skenazy, "Here Are 10 Outrageous 'Zero Tolerance' Follies of 2014," *Reason*, December 29, 2014.

35 Ibid.

36 Chris Martin, "12 'Zero Tolerance' Policy Incidents That Were Too Ridiculous For Words," *Independent Journal Review*, November 12, 2015.

37 Annie Holmquist, "5 Suspensions from 2016 that Show a Common-Sense Deficiency in Our Schools," *Intellectual Takeout*, December 27, 2016.

38 Carly Berwick, "Zeroing Out on Zero Tolerance," *The Atlantic*, March 17, 2015.

39 Aaron Kupchik, *The Real School Safety Problem: The Long-Term Consequences of Harsh School Punishment* (Oakland: University of California Press, 2016), 120.

40 Brea L. Perry and Edward W. Morris, "Suspending Progress: Collateral Consequences of Exclusionary Punishment in Public Schools*," American Sociological Review*, 2014, 79(6): 1067–1087.

41 Rebecca Hinze-Pifer and Lauren Sartain, "Rethinking Universal Suspension for Severe Student Behavior," Consortium on School Research at the University of Chicago, 2018.

42 Jason P. Nance, "Student Surveillance, Racial Inequalities, and Implicit Racial Bias," *Emory Law Journal*, 2017, 66: 765–837; 790.

43 Passero, "The Impact of Zero Tolerance Policies on the Relation between Educational Attainment and Crime."

44 Randall G. Shelden, Sharon K. Tracy, and William B. Brown, *Youth Gangs in American Society*, 4th ed. (Belmont, CA: Cengage, 2013).

45 Farnel Maxime, "Zero Tolerance Polices and the School-to-Prison Pipeline," Shared Justice, January 18, 2018.

46 Lee Kern, "Detentions, Suspension, and Expulsion Do Not Curb Violent Behavior," The Hechinger Report, January 3, 2017.

47 Russell J. Skiba and Daniel J. Losen, "From Reaction to Prevention: Turning the Page on School Discipline," *American Educator*, Winter 2015–2016; 6.

48 Shelden and Vasiliev, *Controlling the Dangerous Classes*.

49 Carly Berwick, "Zeroing Out on Zero Tolerance."

50 Nora Gordon, "Disproportionality in Student Discipline: Connecting Policy to Research," Brookings Institution, January 18, 2018.

[51] Nathan Barrett, Andrew McEachin, Jonathan Mills, and Jon Valent, "Disparities in Student Discipline by Race and Family Income," Education Research Alliance, 2017.

[52] Constance Lindsay and Cassandra Hart, Exposure to Same-Race Teachers and Student Disciplinary Outcomes for Black Students in North Carolina," *Educational Evaluation and Policy Analysis*, 2017, 39(3): 485–510.

[53] Nance, "Student Surveillance, Racial Inequalities, and Implicit Racial Bias," 771.

[54] T. Dee and Seth Gershenson, "Unconscious Bias in the Classroom: Evidence and Opportunities," Stanford Center for Public Analysis and American University School of Public Affairs, 2017, 4, 6.

[55] Michael Hiltzik, "The Truth about 'Zero Tolerance': It Doesn't Work and Always Leads to Disaster," *Los Angeles Times*, June 22, 2018.

[56] Berwick, "Zeroing Out on Zero Tolerance."

[57] Saady, "Throwing Children Away."

[58] Nance, "Student Surveillance, Racial Inequalities, and Implicit Racial Bias."

[59] Scott A. Bonn, "Moral Panic: Who Benefits From Public Fear?" *Psychology Today*, July 20, 2015, https://www.psychologytoday.com/blog/wicked-deeds/201507/moral-panic-who-benefits-public-fear

[60] Losen and Whitaker, "11 million Days Lost," 2.

[61] Christopher A. Mallett, *The School-to-Prison Pipeline: A Comprehensive Assessment* (New York: Springer Publishing, 2016).

[62] New York Civil Liberties Union, "School to Prison Pipeline," 2018, https://www.nyclu.org/issues/racial-justice/school-prison-pipeline

[63] Megan French-Marcelin and Sarah Hinger, "Bullies in Blue: The Origins and Consequences of School Policing," American Civil Liberties Union, April 2017, 2.

[64] Maxime, "Zero Tolerance Polices and the School-to-Prison Pipeline."

[65] Shelden and Vasiliev, *Controlling the Dangerous Classes.*

[66] Ibid.

[67] Daryl Khan, "A Plot with a Scandal: A Closer Look at "Kids for Cash" Documentary," Juvenile Justice Information Exchange, February 10, 2014, http://jjie.org/a-plot-with-a-scandal-a-close-look-at-the-kids-for-cash-documentary/106276/

[68] Brian Saady, "Throwing Children Away: The School-to-Prison Pipeline," *The American Conservative*, August 13, 2018, https://www.theamericanconservative.com/articles/throwing-children-away-the-school-to-prison-pipeline/

[69] Musu-Gillette et al., *Indicators of School Crime and Safety: 2017.*

[70] Evie Blad and Alex Harwin, "Black Students More Likely to Be Arrested at School," *Education Week*, January 24, 2017, https://www.edweek.org/ew/articles/2017/01/25/black-students-more-likely-to-be-arrested.html

[71] Blad and Harwin, "Black Students More Likely to Be Arrested at School."

[72] Gail L. Sunderman & Erin Janulis, "When Law Enforcement Meets School Discipline: School-Related Arrests in Maryland 2015–16." Maryland Equity Project, June 2018.

[73] Mallett, *The School-to-Prison Pipeline.*

[74] Kerrin Wolf and Aaron Kupchik, "Suspensions and Adverse Experiences in Adulthood," *Justice Quarterly*, 2017, 34(3): 407–430.

[75] Matt Pearce and S. Kohli, "Classroom Arrest Touches Off Debate," *Chicago Tribune*, October 30, 2015, 11.

[76] Sarah Hinger, "South Carolina Legislature Repeals Racist 'Disturbing School' Law for Students," ACLU, May 21, 2018.

[77] United States Court of Appeals for the Fourth Circuit, No. 17-1367.

[78] Office of Public Affairs, "Department of Justice Files Statement of Interest in South Carolina Statewide School-to-Prison Pipeline Case," Department of Justice, November 29, 2016.

[79] Ibid., https://www.justice.gov/opa/pr/department-justice-files-statement-interest-south-carolina-statewide-school-prison-pipeline

[80] Nance, "Student Surveillance, Racial Inequalities, and Implicit Racial Bias," 778–779.

[81] Office of Juvenile Justice and Delinquency Prevention, *Statistical Briefing Book*, March 27, 2018, https://www.ojjdp.gov/ojstatbb/victims/qa02204.asp?qaDate=2015

[82] Kim Brooks, Vincent Schiraldi, and Jason Ziedenberg, "School House Hype: Two Years Later," Justice Policy Institute, 2000.

[83] Lauren Musu, Anlan Zhang, Ke Wang, Jishi Zhang, and Barbara Oudekerk, Indicators of School Crime and Safety: 2018 (Washington, DC: National Center for Education Statistics, 2019), iv, 32.

[84] Lisa Marie Pane, "Small Towns Amass Mass Shootings," *Chicago Tribune*, May 24, 2018, 10.

[85] Centers for Disease Control and Prevention, "Youth Risk Behavior Surveillance—United States, 2017," June 15, 2018, Surveillance Summaries, vol. 67(8).

[86] Jason P. Nance, "Students, Police, and the School-to-Prison Pipeline," *Washington Law Review*, 2016, 93: 919–987; 927.

[87] French-Marcelin and Hinger, "Bullies in Blue," 31.

[88] Matthew P. Steinberg, Elaine Allensworth, and David W. Johnson, "Student and Teacher Safety in Chicago Public Schools," Consortium on Chicago School Research at the University of Chicago, 2011.

[89] Dee & Gershenson, "Unconscious Bias in the Classroom."

[90] Kupchik, *The Real School Safety Problem*, 4.

[91] Nance, "Students, Police, and the School-to-Prison Pipeline," 927, 978.

[92] Kappeler and Potter, *The Mythology of Crime and Criminal Justice*.

[93] Cyberbullying Research Center, "Bullying Laws Across America," https"//cyberbullying.org/bullying-laws

[94] Jessica Bennett, "Phoebe Prince: Should School Bullying Be a Crime?" *Newsweek*, October 4, 2010.

[95] http://www.pacer.org/bullying/resources/info-facts.asp.

[96] http://www.noplace4hate.org/

[97] *Psychology Today* has set up a website devoted to this issue: https://www.psychologytoday.com/basics/bullying.

[98] Musu et al., *Indicators of School Crime and Safety: 2018*, 16, 57–58, table 10.1.

[99] Ibid., 67, 71.

[100] Kappeler and Potter, *The Mythology of Crime and Criminal Justice*.

[101] Sameer Hinduja, "Bullying, Cyberbullying, and Suicide among US Youth: Updated Research Findings," August 27, 2018.

[102] Associated Press, "Two 12-year-old Girls in Florida Arrested, Accused of Bullying Girl Until She Killed Herself," Scripps Media, January 26, 2018.

[103] Kelly Wallace, "Police File Raises Questions about Bullying in Rebecca Sedwick's Suicide," CNN, April 21, 2014.

[104] CBS News, "School Accused of Doing Nothing to Stop Bullying of Girl Who Took Her Life," June 21, 2018.

[105] Mary Stringini, "Bullied to Death: Parents Demand Change after 12-year-old Kills Herself in School Bathroom," ABC Action News, June 11, 2018.

[106] Melissa Holt, "Bullying and Suicide: What's the Connection," The Conversation, August 10, 2017.

107 Melissa K. Holt, et al., "Bullying and Suicidal Idation and Behaviors: A Meta-Analysis," *Pediatrics*, 2015, 135(2): 496–509.

108 Curt Bartol and Anne Bartol, *Introduction to Forensic Psychology: Research and Application*, 4th ed. (Thousand Oaks, CA: Sage Publications, 2015).

109 Dorothy Espelage and Melissa Holt, "Suicidal Ideation and School Bullying Experiences after Controlling for Depression and Delinquency," *Journal of Adolescent Health*, 2013, 53(1): 27–31.

110 Michele Ybarra, Kimberly Mitchell, Joseph Kosciw, and Josephine Korchmaros, "Understanding Linkages between Bullying and Suicidal Ideation in a National Sample of LGB and Heterosexual Youth in the United States," *Prevention Science*, 2016, 16(3): 451–462.

111 Associated Press, "Two 12-year-old Girls in Florida Arrested."

112 Dana Goldstein, "Grim Tally Obscures Statistical Reality: Schools Are 'Safest Place' for Children," *The New York Times*, May 22, 2018, A13.

113 Bartol and Bartol, *Introduction to Forensic Psychology.*

114 Anne Howard, Steven Landau, and John Pryor, "Peer Bystanders to Bullying: Who Wants to Play with the Victim," *Journal of Abnormal Child Psychology*, 2013, 42(2).

115 Seokjin Jeong and Byun Lee, "A Multilevel Examination of Peer Victimization and Bullying Preventions in Schools," *Journal of Criminology*, 2013.

116 Dewey Cornell, Anne Gregory, Frances Huang, and Xitao Fan, "Perceived Prevalence of Teasing and Bullying Predicts High School Dropout Rates," *Journal of Educational Psychology*, 2013, 105:138–149.

117 Division of Violence Prevention, "The Relationship between Bullying and Suicide," Centers for Disease Control and Prevention, April, 2014.

118 Musu-Gillette et al., *Indicators of School Crime and Safety: 2017*, 22.

119 Lara Robinson, Rebecca Leeb, Melissa Merrick, and Lauren Forbes, "Conceptualizing and Measuring Safe, Stable, Nurturing Relationships and Environments in Educational Settings," *Journal of Child Family Studies*, 2016, 25(5): 1488–1504.

120 Kupchik, *The Real School Safety Problem.*

121 Ibid., 118.

122 Robert D. Putnam, *Our Kids: The American Dream in Crisis* (New York: Simon & Schuster, 2016).

123 Emma Garcia and Elaine Weiss, "Education Inequalities at the School Starting Gate," Economic Policy Institute, September 27, 2017.

124 Richard Florida, *The New Urban Crisis: How Our Cities Are Increasing Inequality, Deepening Segregation, and Failing the Middle Class—And What We Can Do About It* (New York: Basic Books, 2017), 9.

125 Garcia and Weiss, "Education Inequalities at the School Starting Gate."

126 Linda Darling-Hammond, "Education and the Path to One Nation, Indivisible," Learning Policy Institute, February 2018, 1.

127 Matthew M. Chingos and Kristin Blagg, "Making Sense of State School Funding Policy," Urban Institute, November 2017.

128 Linda Darling-Hammond, "Education and the Path to One Nation, Indivisible," Learning Policy Institute, February 2018.

129 Nance, "Student Surveillance, Racial Inequalities, and Implicit Racial Bias," 767–768.

130 Sarah Reckhow, *Follow the Money: How Foundation Dollars Change Public School Policies* (New York: Oxford University Press, 2013); Jean Anyon, *Radical Possibilities: Public Policy, Urban Education, and A New Social Movement*, 2nd ed. (New York: Routledge, 2014).

131 U.S. Census Bureau, "Public Education Finances 2015," June 2017, GI15-ASPEF.

132 Bruce Baker, Danielle Farrie, and David Sciarra, *Is School Funding Fair? A National Report Card*, 7th ed., Rutgers Graduate School of Education and Education Law Center, February 2018, 1.

133 Joel McFarland et al., *Condition of Education 2018* (Washington, DC: National Center for Education Statistics, 2018) NCES 2018-144.

134 Martin Carnoy and Emma Garcia, "Five Key Trends in U.S. Student Performance," Economic Policy Institute, January 12, 2017.

135 Steve Suitts, "A New Majority: Low Income Students Now a Majority in the Nation's Public Schools," Southern Education Foundation, January 2015.

136 Melissa S. Kearney and Phillip B. Levine, "Income Inequality, Social Mobility, and the Decision to Drop Out of High School," Brookings Papers on Economic Activity, Spring 2016, 333–396.

137 Darling-Hammond, "Education and the Path to One Nation," 1.

138 Halley Potter, Kimberly Quick, and Elizabeth Davies, "A New Wave of School Integration: Districts and Charters Pursuing Socioeconomic Diversity," The Century Foundation, February 9, 2016.

139 Kozol, *The Shame of the Nation*.

140 Florida, *The New Urban Crisis*, 117.

141 Darling-Hammond, "Education and the Path to One Nation."

142 Potter et al., "A New Wave of School Integration."

143 Darling-Hammond, "Education and the Path to One Nation."

144 Potter et al., "A New Wave of School Integration."

145 Darling-Hammond, "Education and the Path to One Nation."

146 Carnoy & Garcia, "Five Key Trends in U.S. Student Performance."

147 Potter et al., "A New Wave of School Integration: Districts and Charters Pursuing Socio-economic Diversity."

148 Halley Potter and Kimberly Quick, "Is Separate and Unequal as Good as It Gets?" The Century Foundation, April 19, 2017, https://tcf.org/content/commentary/separate-unequal-good-gets/

149 Grover J. Whitehurst, "New Evidence on School Choice and Racially Segregated Schools," Evidence Speaks Reports, December 14, 2017.

150 Kate Barrington, "The Pros and Cons of Tracking in Schools," Public School Review, May 3, 2018.

151 Ibid.

152 Jeannie Oakes, *Keeping Track: How Schools Structure Inequality*, 2nd ed. (New Haven, CT: Yale University Press, 2005.

153 Ibid., ix.

154 William Mathis, "Moving Beyond Tracking," Boulder, CO: National Education Policy Center, May 2013, 1.

155 John Hattie, *Visible Learning: A Synthesis of Over 800 Meta-Analyses Relating to Achievement* (New York: Routledge, 2009).

156 Carol Burris, Kevin Welner, and Jennifer Bezoza, "Universal Access to a Quality Education: Research and Recommendations for the Elimination of Curricular Stratification," Education and the Public Interest Center and Education Policy Research Unit, December 2009.

157 Oakes, *Keeping Track*.

158 Ibid., 3.

159 Ibid.

160 Nance, "Students, Police, and the School-to-Prison Pipeline."

161 French-Marcelin and Hinger, "Bullies in Blue," 30.

162 Elaine Allensworth, Julia Gwynne, Paul Moore, and Marisa de la Torre, "Middle Grade Indicators of Readiness in Chicago Public Schools," The University of Chicago Consortium on Chicago School Research, November 2014.

163 Miner Marchbanks, Jamilia Blake, Danielle Smith, Allison Seibert, Dottie Carmichael, Eric Booth, and Tony, Fabelo, "More than a Drop in the Bucket: The Social and Economic Costs of Dropouts and Grade Retentions Associated with Exclusionary Discipline," *Journal of Applied Research on Children*, 2014, 5(2), Article 17.

164 David Bjerk, "Re-examining the Impact of Dropping Out on Criminal and Labor Outcomes in Early Adulthood," *Economics of Education Review*, 2012, 31(1): 110–122.

165 Jonathan Doll, Zohreh Eslami, and Lynne Walters, "Understanding Why Students Drop Out of High School, According to Their Own Reports," SAGE Open, October–December, 2013, 1–15.

166 Alliance for Excellent Education, "High School Dropouts in America," September 2010.

167 Marchbanks et al., "More than a Drop in the Bucket."

168 Kristen Loschert, "The Suspension Effect," Alliance for Excellent Education, June 28, 2016, 16(13).

169 Alliance for Excellent Education, "High School Dropouts in America."

170 Sarah Frazelle and Aisling Natel, "A Practitioner's Guide to Implementing Early Warning Systems," National Center for Education Evaluation and Regional Assistance, January 2015.

171 Ming-Te Wang and Jennifer Fredricks, "The Reciprocal Links Between School Engagement, Youth Problem Behaviors, and School Dropout During Adolescence," *Child Development*, 2014, 85(2): 722–737; see also D. Mark Anderson, "In School and Out of Trouble? The Minimum Dropout Age and Juvenile Crime," *Review of Economics and Statistics*, 2014, 96(2): 318–331.

172 Diane Ravitch, *The Death and Life of the Great American School System: How Testing and Choice Are Undermining Education*, 3rd ed. (New York: Basic Books, 2016).

173 Ibid., xi.

174 Ibid., xx.

175 French-Marcelin and Hinger, "Bullies in Blue."

176 Nance, "Student Surveillance, Racial Inequalities, and Implicit Racial Bias."

177 Darling-Hammond, "Education and the Path to One Nation, Indivisible."

178 French-Marcelin and Hinger, "Bullies in Blue."

179 Ibid.

180 Nance, "Student Surveillance, Racial Inequalities, and Implicit Racial Bias."

181 The NAACP Legal Defense and Educational Fund quoted in ibid., 32.

182 Jazelle Hunt, "No Child Left Behind Replacement Focuses on Marginalized Groups," NBC News, December 10, 2015, https://www.nbcnews.com/news/nbcblk/no-child-left-behind-replacement-focuses-marginalized-groups-n477791

183 Jennifer DePaoli, Robert Balfanz, Matthew Atwell, and John Bridgeland, "Building a Grad Nation: Progress and Challenge in Raising High School Graduation Rates," Annual Update 2018, Civic Enterprises and Everyone Graduates Center. June 5, 2018.

184 Hunt, "No Child Left Behind Replacement Focuses on Marginalized Groups."

185 National Center for Education Statistics, "Public High School Graduation Rates," The Condition of Education, May 2018.

186 Child Trends Databank, "High School Dropout Rates," Child Trends, 2018, https://www.childtrends.org/indicators/high-school-dropout-rates

187 DePaoli et al., "Building a Grad Nation."

188 Ibid.

189 Pamela Orpinas, Katherine Raczynski, Hsien-Lin Hsieh, Lusine Nahapetyan, and Artur Home, "Longitudinal Examination of Aggression and Study Skills from Middle to High School: Implications for Dropout Prevention," *Journal of School Health*, 2018, 88(3): 246–252.

190 Government Accountability Office, "K–12 Education."

191 Marchbanks et al., "More than a Drop in the Bucket."

192 Loschert, "The Suspension Effect."

193 Russell Rumberger and Daniel Losen, "The High Cost of Harsh Discipline and Its Disparate Impact," UCLA Center for Civil Rights Remedies, June 2, 2016.

194 Rumberger and Losen, "The High Cost of Harsh Discipline."

195 Joel McFarland, Jiashan Cui, and Patrick Stark, "Trends in Dropout and Completion 2014," National Center for Education Statistics, March 2018, NCES 2018-117.

196 Jennifer Lansford, Kenneth Dodge, Gregory Pettit, and John. Bates, "A Public Health Perspective on School Dropout and Adult Outcomes: A Prospective Study of Risk and Protective Factors From Age 5 to 27 Years," *Journal of Adolescent Health*, 2016, 58(6), 652–658.

197 Jason Amos, "The Graduation Effect," Alliance for Excellent Education, January 12, 2016.

PART IV

Responses to Delinquency

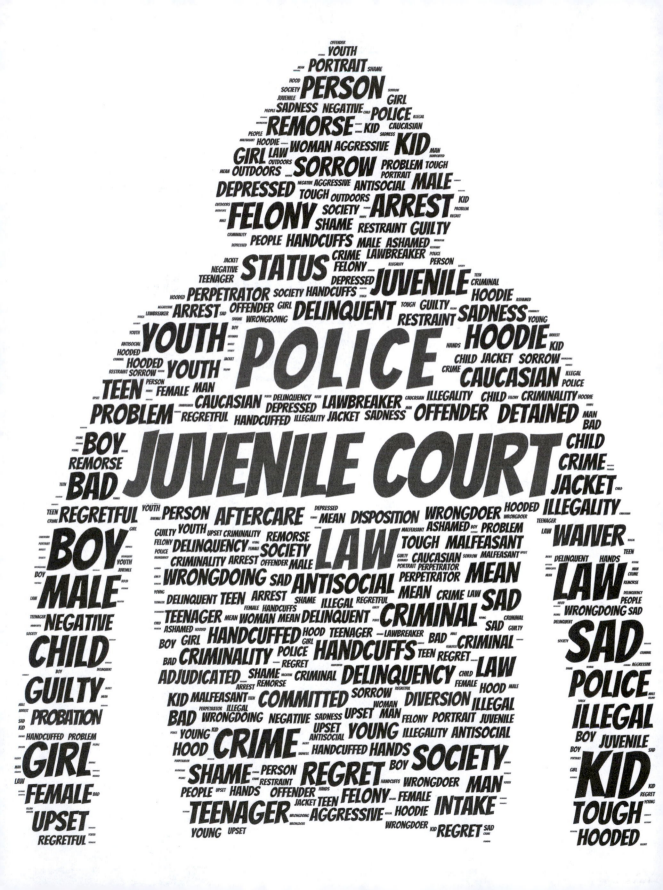

Chapter 11

Processing Offenders through the Juvenile Justice System

Some juveniles become involved with the juvenile justice system because they are accused of committing delinquent or criminal acts. Others come into contact with the system for status offenses (actions illegal only because of the age of the offender). Not all cases are formally processed through the court system. In 2016, juvenile courts handled 850,500 delinquency cases (down from the record high of 1,880,900 cases in 1997).[1] Some juveniles (less than 1% of all petitioned cases) were processed in adult courts. In 2016, criminal courts heard 3,450 cases involving juveniles (compared to the record high of 6,700 cases in 2006).

This chapter focuses on the four major components of the modern juvenile justice system: (1) juvenile laws, (2) the rights of juveniles (3) the structure of the juvenile court, and (4) the processing of youths through the court system.

Juvenile Laws

The juvenile court today has jurisdiction over youths under a certain age who (1) violate laws applicable to adults, (2) commit *status offenses*, and (3) are dependent or neglected. The upper age of juvenile court *jurisdiction* in 46 states is 17. In 4 states (Georgia, Michigan, Texas, and Wisconsin), the upper age limit is 16.[2] All states have transfer laws that allow or require juvenile offenders, regardless of age, to be prosecuted as adults for serious offenses—a process known as *certification* or *waiver* (discussed later in this chapter).

As examined in previous chapters, one of the most controversial aspects of the juvenile law involves *status offenses*. The distinguishing characteristic of juvenile law is that youths under a certain age may be arrested and processed for behavior in which adults are free to engage. Most of the controversy stems from the vagueness of the statutes; some of it stems from the *parens patriae* justification for state intervention; and much of it stems from differential and inconsistent application. For example, the ambiguity of these statutes gives those in authority a tremendous amount of discretionary power and often leads to arbitrary, subjective value judgments based on class, race, and gender biases. The double standard treatment of males and females will be discussed in more detail in the next chapter. Chapter 1 described the application of many of these offenses primarily to children of immigrant parents. After more than 150 years, juvenile laws (status offenses in particular) are still being applied more vigorously against the children of the poor, and they are just as vague as they have always been.

THE RIGHTS OF JUVENILES

During the past four decades there has been an increase in the use of attorneys in juvenile court cases and a greater emphasis on procedural rights, at least in the courts in major metropolitan areas. One reason for this change can be attributed to several important Supreme Court decisions beginning in the late 1960s that extended due process rights to juveniles. The first case was *Kent v. United States*, decided in 1966.[3] The case presented important challenges to police and juvenile court procedures in cases where juveniles commit an offense that would be a major felony if committed by an adult. In September 1961, Morris Kent (age 16 and on probation) was charged with raping a woman and stealing her wallet. He confessed to the crime, and his lawyer filed a motion requesting a hearing on jurisdiction. The juvenile court judge waived Kent to the jurisdiction of the adult court—without having talked with Kent's lawyer, without ruling on the lawyer's motion, and without a written statement of the reasons for the waiver. Kent was convicted and sentenced in adult court to a term of 30 to 90 years in prison.

The Supreme Court ruled that when a judge considers whether to transfer a case from the juvenile court to an adult court, a juvenile is entitled to a hearing and has the right to counsel. The court must provide a written statement giving the reasons for the waiver, and the defense counsel must be given access to all records and reports used in reaching the decision to waive. Justice Abe Fortas wrote the opinion and issued one of the strongest indictments of the juvenile court ever:

> There is no place in our system of law for reaching a result of such tremendous consequences without ceremony—without hearing, without effective assistance of counsel, without a statement of reasons. It is inconceivable that a court of justice dealing with adults, with respect to a similar issue, would proceed in this manner. . . . There is much evidence that some juvenile courts . . . [lack] the personnel, facilities and techniques to perform adequately as representatives of the State in a *parens patriae* capacity, at least with respect to children charged with law violation. There is evidence, in fact, that there may be grounds for concern that the child receives the worst of both worlds; that he gets neither the protection accorded to adults nor the solicitous care and regenerative treatment postulated for children.[4]

The Court reversed the conviction.

Perhaps the most significant case regarding juvenile court procedures was *In re Gault* decided in 1967.[5] The sheriff placed fifteen-year-old Gerald Gault in a detention home without notifying his parents after a neighbor complained about receiving a lewd telephone call that she believed had been made by Gault. At the time, Gault was on six months probation after having been found delinquent for being in the company of a boy who had stolen a wallet. He was not given adequate notification of the charges and was not advised that he could be represented by legal counsel—nor did his accuser appear in court. He was convicted and sentenced to the State Industrial School until the age of 21. Gault's attorneys filed a writ of habeas corpus in the Superior Court of Arizona, which was denied.

On appeal to the U.S. Supreme Court, Gault's attorneys argued that the juvenile code of Arizona was unconstitutional. The justices found in favor of Gault and held that at the adjudicatory hearing stage, juvenile court procedures must include (1) adequate written notice of charges, (2) the right to counsel, (3) privilege against self-incrimination, (4) the right to cross-examine accusers, (5) a transcript of the proceedings, and (6) the right to appellate review. Justice Fortas again wrote the decision, a very revealing account of actual juvenile court procedures.

> A boy is charged with misconduct. The boy is committed to an institution where he may be restrained of liberty for years. It is of no constitutional consequence *and of limited practical meaning* that the institution to which he is committed is called an Industrial School. The fact of the matter is that, however euphemistic the title, a "receiving home" or an "industrial school" for juveniles is an institution of confinement in which the child is incarcerated for a greater or lesser time. His world becomes "a building with whitewashed walls, regimented routine and institutional hours. Instead of mother and father and sisters and brothers and friends and classmates, his world is peopled by guards, custodians, state employees, and "delinquents" confined with him for anything from waywardness to rape and homicide.
>
> In view of this, it would be extraordinary if our Constitution did not require the procedural regularity and the exercise of care implied in the phrase "due process." Under our Constitution, the condition of being a boy does not justify a kangaroo court. . . .
>
> The essential difference between Gerald's case and a normal criminal case is that safeguards available to adults were discarded in Gerald's case. The summary procedure as well as the long commitment was possible because Gerald was 15 years of age instead of over 18. . . . For the particular offense immediately involved, the maximum punishment would have been a fine of $5 to $50, or imprisonment in jail for not more than two months. Instead, he was committed to custody for a maximum of six years. If he had been over 18 and had committed an offense to which such a sentence might apply, he would have been entitled to substantial rights under the Constitution of the United States as well as under Arizona's laws and constitution. . . . So wide a gulf between the State's treatment of the adult and of the child requires a bridge sturdier than mere verbiage, and reasons more persuasive than cliché can provide.[6]

The Court essentially found that Gault was being punished for his youth rather than being helped by the juvenile court. As in the *Kent* decision, the Court questioned *parens patriae* as the founding principle of juvenile justice. It criticized the assertion that a child had a right only to custody not to liberty, which was the basis for claiming that juvenile proceedings are civil in nature and not subject to constitutional safeguards that restrict the state when it deprives a person of liberty.[7] "Juvenile court history has again demonstrated that unbridled discretion, however benevolently motivated, is frequently a poor substitute for principle and procedure."[8]

Another significant case was *In re Winship*, decided in 1970. Justice Brennan wrote the decision, which addressed how much proof is necessary to support a finding of delinquency. Again rejecting the idea that the juvenile justice system was a civil system, the Supreme Court held that the due process clause of the Fourteenth Amendment required that delinquency charges in the juvenile system have to meet the same standard of "beyond a reasonable doubt" required in the adult system.

> In sum, the constitutional safeguard of proof beyond a reasonable doubt is as much required during the adjudicatory stage of a delinquency proceeding as are those constitutional safeguards applied in *Gault*—notice of charges, right to counsel, the rights of confrontation and examination, and the privilege against self-incrimination. . . . Where a 12-year-old child is charged with an act of stealing which renders him liable to confinement for as long as six years, then, as a matter of due process the case against him must be proved beyond a reasonable doubt.[9]

The Court noted that the New York Court of Appeals had attempted to justify a preponderance-of-evidence standard based on the grounds that juvenile proceedings are designed to save the child rather than to punish. It also noted that *Gault* rejected such justifications. "Good intentions do not themselves obviate the need for criminal due process safeguards in juvenile courts."[10]

In *McKeiver v. Pennsylvania* the Court dealt with the right of trial by jury, normally guaranteed to adults but traditionally denied to juveniles. The Court ruled in 1971 that jury trials were admissible but not mandatory within the juvenile court.

> We must recognize, as the Court has recognized before, that the fond and idealistic hopes of the juvenile court proponents and early reformers of three generations ago have not been realized. . . . Too often the juvenile court judge falls far short of that stalwart, protective, and communicating figure the system envisaged. The community's unwillingness to provide people and facilities and to be concerned, the insufficiency of time devoted, the scarcity of professional help, the inadequacy of dispositional alternatives, and our general lack of knowledge all contribute to dissatisfaction with the experiment. . . . Despite all these disappointments, all these failures, and all these shortcomings, we conclude that trial by jury in the juvenile court's adjudicative stage is not a constitutional requirement. . . . If the formalities of the criminal adjudicative process are to be superimposed upon the juvenile court system, there is little need for its separate existence. Perhaps that ultimate disillusionment will come one day, but for the moment we are disinclined to give impetus to it.[11]

The Court's decisions in *Gault* and *Winship* directed juvenile courts to insure the accuracy of the fact-finding stage. In *McKeiver*, the Court considered whether a jury is a necessary component to accurate fact finding in juvenile adjudications. It decided that juries are not more accurate than judges in the adjudication stage; moreover it expressed concerns that juries could be disruptive to the informal atmosphere of the juvenile court and could make the process more adversarial.[12] The Court reasoned that mandatory jury trials could create problems for juveniles, including publicity that would be contrary to the confidentiality usually linked with juvenile justice. Although the Supreme Court said that states do not have to provide for jury trials in the juvenile justice system, it did allow for the possibility that they could. Ten states grant juveniles the right to a jury trial if requested; in 8 states, juveniles can receive a jury trial in limited circumstances.[13] Juveniles have no right to a jury trial in 32 states. The vast majority of delinquents, similar to criminal defendants, plead guilty rather than have their cases decided by juries.[14]

Breed v. Jones was decided in 1975, nine years after *Kent*.[15] It involved essentially the same issue—waiver to the adult court. However, in this case, Jones' lawyer argued that his client had been subjected to "double jeopardy" since he was adjudicated in juvenile court (tantamount to a conviction in an adult court) and then tried again in an adult court for the same crime. The Court ruled that an adjudication in juvenile court involving a violation of a criminal statute is equivalent to a trial in criminal court. The Court also specified that jeopardy applies at the adjudication hearing when evidence is first presented. Waiver cannot occur after jeopardy attaches; juvenile courts must hold transfer hearings prior to adjudication.

In 1984, the Supreme Court issued a ruling in *Schall v. Martin* that most consider to be a setback to juvenile rights. It ruled that the courts have a right to hold youths in preventive detention if judges determine the youths pose a danger to the community. Fourteen-year-old Gregory Martin was arrested in 1977 and charged with robbery, assault, and possession of a weapon. He was detained pending adjudication because the court found there was a serious risk that he would commit another crime if released. Martin's attorney filed a habeas corpus action challenging the fairness of preventive detention. The lower appellate courts reversed the juvenile court's detention order. The Supreme Court upheld the constitutionality of the preventive detention statute, ruling that preventive detention serves a legitimate objective to protect both the juvenile and society from pretrial crime and is not intended as punishment. The Court found that there were enough procedures in place to protect juveniles from wrongful deprivation of liberty: namely, a notice, a statement of the facts and reasons for detention, and a probable cause hearing within a short time. In *Schall v. Martin*, the Court confirmed *parens patriae* in promoting the welfare of children.[16]

In his dissent, Justice Marshall (joined by Justices Brennan and Stevens) emphasized the lack of adequate criteria at a judge's disposal to determine whether or not a juvenile may, after release, commit a crime. He also noted that "Family Court judges are incapable of determining which of the juveniles who appear before them would commit offenses before their trials if left at large and which would not."[17] The district court's ruling that prompted the appeal had noted that there were no diagnostic tools that enable even highly trained criminologists to predict reliably which juveniles will engage in violent crime. Brennan also pointed to the minimal amount of data available to a judge at a youth's initial appearance, yet the judge "must make his decision whether to detain a juvenile on the basis of a set of allegations regarding the child's alleged offense, a cursory review of his background and criminal record, and the recommendation of a probation officer who, in the typical case, has seen the child only once."[18]

Even after the decision in *Gault*, the vast majority of juveniles have waived their rights to counsel in juvenile court.

> In the years following *Gault*, states moved to implement the right to counsel, but few have defined it as an absolute right by requiring that the juvenile have the advice of an attorney before the right to counsel can be waived, or by prescribing an "unwaivable" right to counsel.[19]

In some states, 50 to 90% of juveniles are unrepresented because they waive their rights to counsel.[20] Many juveniles do not understand their rights or the role of lawyers. The limited understanding of juveniles combined with their vulnerability requires greater procedural protections, such as a nonwaivable right to counsel. Judges may give minimal advice about the implications of waiving counsel, may imply that waivers are merely legal technicalities, and may find that waivers ease administrative burdens. "Juveniles' diminished competence, inability to understand proceedings, and judicial incentives and encouragement to waive counsel results in larger proportions of delinquents adjudicated without lawyers than criminal defendants."[21] Even if juveniles are represented, their lawyers often have heavy caseloads, inadequate resources, and lack of training.

Some courts have operated on the assumption that lawyers are not really needed and that they are impediments to the court's philosophy of acting in the best interest of the child. Judges in Minnesota resisted the requirements of *Gault*. Four years after the state passed a law in 1995 that required the appointment of counsel in all delinquency cases, there were still inconsistencies in the appointment of counsel.[22] In sum, the fact that juveniles have various rights approaching those of adults may be meaningless in the daily reality of juvenile court procedures.

Courts have also determined that juveniles adjudicated and committed to correctional facilities have a *right to treatment*. A case decided in 1954 ruled that juveniles could not be held in institutions that did not provide any form of rehabilitation.[23] In a 1972 case, *Inmates of the Boys' Training School v. Affleck*, a federal court ruled that since the purpose of the juvenile court is rehabilitation, youths have a right to treatment if committed to an institution.[24] This case established certain minimal standards, such as sufficient clothing to meet seasonal needs, proper bedding (sheets, pillow cases, etc.), daily showers, personal hygiene supplies, minimal writing materials, and access to books and other reading materials. It "shocks the conscience" that some jurisdictions did not follow such standards until this ruling.

The Special Litigation Section of the Department of Justice (DOJ) protects the rights of youth confined in juvenile detention and commitment facilities. The Violent Crime Control and Law Enforcement Act of 1994 gave the DOJ the authority to investigate and to seek judicial remedies to protect the rights of youth involved in the juvenile justice and detention systems. Under the law, DOJ can also determine if arrests, court procedures, and probation policies comply with the civil rights of juveniles. The Civil Rights of Institutionalized Persons Act (CRIPA) of 1997 allows the DOJ to review conditions and practices within juvenile justice institutions. Investigations have looked at medical care, mental health care, protection from staff-on-youth or youth-on-youth violence and exploitation, equal treatment for minority youth, fair court procedures, adequate educational services, programs to encourage juveniles to manage their behavior, and working with jurisdictions to explore alternatives to juvenile incarceration.[25] Despite investigations and intervention, abuses continue within juvenile institutions, a subject to be discussed in more detail in the next chapter.

Eighth Amendment Protections

Prior to 2005, about one in every 50 individuals on death row was a juvenile offender. Victor Streib found that executions for crimes committed by youths younger than 18 accounted for 1.8% of all confirmed legal executions carried out between 1642 and 2005—the 366 executions equaled about one per year.[26] From January 1, 1973 until the decision in *Roper v. Simmons* (see discussion below) on March 1, 2005, 22 juvenile offenders were executed (2.3% of the 949 executions during that time frame). One of the juveniles executed was 16 at the time of his crime; the others were all 17. Ten were white; 11 were black; 1 was Latino.[27]

In 1955, the United States ratified Article 68 of the Fourth Geneva Convention (1949), which states "the death penalty may not be pronounced on a protected person who was under 18 years of age at the time of the offense."[28] Thus, for five decades, the U.S. protected youthful offenders in other countries from the death penalty during war or armed conflict but did not offer the youth in this country the same protections during peace. The International Covenant on Civil and Political Rights was signed by the U.S. in 1977 and ratified in 1992.[29] The provisions in this covenant include that youths should be separated from incarcerated adults and receive appropriate treatment, and the death penalty must not be imposed for crimes committed by juvenile offenders. The U.S. government stated that the policy and practice of the United States are generally in compliance with and supportive of the Covenant's provisions regarding treatment of juveniles in the criminal justice system. Nevertheless, the United States reserves the right in exceptional circumstances to treat juveniles as adults.

The vast majority of juvenile offenders executed in the U.S. before 1972 were sentenced to death and executed while still teenagers. After the death penalty was reinstated in 1976, the delay between sentencing and execution increased substantially. Of the 22 juveniles discussed earlier, the youngest at the age of execution was 24 and the oldest was 38. Perhaps the fact that it was not actually a child strapped down and killed made it easier for society to allow such sentences. The fact remains, however, these individuals were executed for crimes they committed as juveniles. Many had been sentenced to death by juries that were ill informed about any mitigating factors (e.g., evidence presented in court regarding the defendant and/or circumstances surrounding the crime).

For instance, Dwayne Allen Wright was sentenced to death for murder in Virginia. Dwayne grew up in a poor family in a neighborhood characterized by illegal drug activity, gun violence, and homicides. At the age of four, Dwayne's father was incarcerated. His mother, suffering from mental illness, was unemployed for most of his life. When he was 10, his older brother was murdered, after which Dwayne developed serious mental problems. He did poorly at school, and for the next seven years spent time in hospitals and juvenile detention facilities. He was treated for major depression with psychotic episodes; his mental capacity was evaluated as borderline retarded, his verbal ability retarded, and doctors found signs of organic brain damage.[30] In their request for clemency from the governor, Dwayne's attorneys obtained affidavits from two jurors in his 1991 capital trial who stated that they would not have sentenced him to death had they known of brain damage suffered at birth, which left Dwayne prone to violent outbursts. Clemency was denied, and Dwayne was executed on October 14, 1998, for a crime he committed when he was 17.

Thompson v. Oklahoma

In 1983, when he was 15 years old, William Wayne Thompson and three accomplices (who were older than 18) murdered his sister's abusive ex-husband and dumped his body in a river. Thompson was waived to adult court and all 4 defendants were sentenced to death. The Supreme Court ruled in *Thompson v. Oklahoma* that the "cruel and unusual punishments" provision of the Eighth Amendment prohibits the execution of a person who was under 16 years of age at the time of his or her offense.[31]

> This Court has already endorsed the proposition that less culpability should attach to a crime committed by a juvenile than to a comparable crime committed by an adult, since inexperience, less education, and less intelligence make the teenager less able to evaluate the consequences of his or her conduct while at the same time he or she is much more apt to be motivated by mere emotion or peer pressure than is an adult. Given this lesser culpability, as well as the teenager's capacity for growth and society's fiduciary obligations to its children, the retributive purpose underlying the death penalty is simply inapplicable to the execution of a 15-year-old offender. Moreover, the deterrence rationale for the penalty is equally

unacceptable with respect to such offenders, since statistics demonstrate that the vast majority of persons arrested for willful homicide are over 16 at the time of the offense, since the likelihood that the teenage offender has made the kind of cold-blooded, cost-benefit analysis that attaches any weight to the possibility of execution is virtually nonexistent, and since it is fanciful to believe that a 15-year-old would be deterred by the knowledge that a small number of persons his age have been executed during the 20th century.[32]

Extending Eighth Amendment protections for juveniles was halted for a number of years. In 1989 the Court ruled in *Stanford v. Kentucky* that the Constitution did not prohibit the execution of 16- and 17-year-old offenders.[33]

Roper v. Simmons

Christopher Simmons was 17 years old when he murdered Shirley Crook in Missouri in 1993; he was sentenced to death. In 2002, the Supreme Court ruled in *Atkins v. Virginia* that the Constitution prohibits the execution of mentally retarded people. Simmons filed a new petition arguing that the Constitution prohibits the execution of people who were younger than 18 at the time of the crime. In 2003, the Missouri Supreme Court reviewed his case. The court determined that juvenile executions violated the Eighth Amendment's provision against cruel and unusual punishment under the "evolving standards of decency" test. Simmons' death sentence was vacated, and he was sentenced to life without parole.[34]

In their decision to overturn the death penalty, the Missouri Supreme Court cited *Atkins v. Virginia*. The court stated that although they often know the difference between right and wrong, mentally retarded people "have diminished capacities to understand and process mistakes and learn from experience, to engage in logical reasoning, to control impulses, and to understand the reactions of others." The court also said that, "while such deficiencies do not warrant an exemption from criminal sanctions . . . they do diminish their personal culpability."[35]

The state of Missouri appealed the case to the Supreme Court, which heard arguments in October 2004. Amicus briefs filed jointly by eight medical and mental health associations cited numerous studies in the developmental biology and behavioral literature to support the argument that the areas of the adolescent brain that relate to criminal responsibility do not develop until after the age of 18.

> Adolescents as a group, even at the age of 16 or 17, are more impulsive than adults. They underestimate risks and overvalue short-term benefits. They are more susceptible to stress, more emotionally volatile, and less capable of controlling their emotions than adults. In short, the average adolescent cannot be expected to act with the same control or foresight as a mature adult. . . . Cutting-edge brain imaging technology reveals that regions of the adolescent brain do not reach a fully mature state until after the age of 18. These regions are precisely those associated with impulse control, regulation of emotions, risk assessment, and moral reasoning. Critical developmental changes in these regions occur only after late adolescence.[36]

The 5–4 decision in *Roper v. Simmons* prohibiting the imposition of the death penalty on offenders who were under the age of 18 when they committed their crimes clearly represents a turning point in the history of juvenile justice, as did *In re Gault* and *Kent*.

> The Eighth Amendment's prohibition against "cruel and unusual punishments" must be interpreted according to its text, by considering history, tradition, and precedent, and with due regard for its purpose and function in the constitutional design. To implement this framework this Court has established the propriety and affirmed the necessity of referring to "the evolving standards of decency that mark the progress of a maturing society" to determine which punishments are so disproportionate as to be "cruel and unusual."[37]

The Court specifically reasoned that a majority of states (31) had rejected the death penalty for juveniles; execution was infrequent even in the states where it was allowed (no juveniles had been executed since 1976 in 43 states); and there was a consistent trend toward abolition of the juvenile death penalty (no juveniles were on death row in 38 states). These facts demonstrated a national consensus against the practice. Sixteen years after *Stanford v. Kentucky*, the court found that evolving standards of decency had formed a national consensus against the execution of juvenile offenders. Justice Kennedy wrote: "The age of 18 is the point where society draws the line for many purposes between childhood and adulthood. It is, we conclude, the age at which the line for death eligibility ought to rest. *Stanford* should be deemed no longer controlling on this issue."[38] The *Roper* decision affected 72 juveniles on death row in 12 states.[39]

The ruling also made reference to the fact that juveniles are vulnerable to influence and that they are inclined toward immature and irresponsible behavior. Given their diminished culpability, retribution or deterrence does not provide adequate justification for the death penalty. The Court also noted that the execution of juvenile offenders violated several international treaties, including the United Nations Convention on the Rights of the Child and the International Covenant on Civil and Political Rights. The ruling stated that the overwhelming weight of international opinion against the juvenile death penalty confirms the conclusion of the Court that the death penalty is a cruel and unusual punishment for offenders under 18.

Four justices dissented (O'Connor, Rehnquist, Scalia, and Thomas). O'Connor argued that the difference in maturity between adults and juveniles was neither universal nor significant enough to justify a rule excluding juveniles from the death penalty. Scalia argued that the Court improperly substituted its own judgment for that of the people in outlawing juvenile executions. He criticized the majority for counting non-death penalty states toward a national consensus against juvenile executions, and he stated that acknowledgement of foreign approval had no place in the legal opinion of the Supreme Court.

Life without Parole (LWOP)

On May 17, 2010, the Supreme Court ruled in *Graham v. Florida* that juveniles who commit crimes in which no one is killed may not be sentenced to LWOP. The court found that such sentences violate the Eighth Amendment prohibition against cruel and unusual punishment.

> The inadequacy of penological theory to justify life without parole sentences for juvenile nonhomicide offenders, the limited culpability of such offenders, and the severity of these sentences all lead the Court to conclude that the sentencing practice at issue is cruel and unusual. No recent data provide reason to reconsider *Roper*'s holding that because juveniles have lessened culpability they are less deserving of the most serious forms of punishment.[40]

Justice Kennedy wrote the majority opinion and explained that the State had denied Terrance Graham "any chance to later demonstrate that he is fit to rejoin society based solely on a nonhomicide crime that he committed while he was a child in the eyes of the law. This the Eighth Amendment does not permit." Bryan Stevenson, Executive Director of the Equal Justice Initiative, saw the *Roper* ruling as an opportunity. The Court had ruled that children were too immature to be sentenced to death; Stevenson reasoned that they should not be sentenced to life in prison either. He took the case of Joe Sullivan (discussed below) to the Supreme Court in 2009. The justices dismissed the case on procedural grounds the same day they heard *Graham v. Florida*. Stevenson commented on that decision.

> This is a significant victory for children. The Court recognized that it is cruel to pass a final judgment on children, who have an enormous capacity for change and rehabilitation compared to adults. I am very encouraged by the Court's ruling. It's an important win not only for kids who have been condemned to die in prison but for all children who need additional protection and recognition in the criminal justice system.[41]

Graham, age 16, and three accomplices robbed a restaurant in Jacksonville. He was sentenced to one year in jail and three years probation. The next year, he and two accomplices were involved in a home invasion. His attorney asked for a sentence of 5 years; prosecutors asked for 30; the judge sentenced him to LWOP for violating his probation. *Graham v. Florida* entitled Graham and 128 others (77 in Florida; the remainder in 10 other states) to a resentencing hearing.[42] The hearing was held February 2012 before the original judge; Graham's new sentence was 25 years. His release date is August 27, 2026, when he will be in his late 30s.

Joe Sullivan, mentally disabled and living in a home where he was physically and sexually abused, is 1 of only 2 people in the United States sentenced to LWOP for a nonhomicide offense committed at the age of 13.[43] In 1989, two older boys convinced Joe to participate in a burglary. The three boys entered an empty home, and one older boy took some money and jewelry. That afternoon, the elderly homeowner was sexually assaulted in her home but never saw her attacker. One of the older boys accused Joe of the sexual battery. Both older boys received short sentences in juvenile detention; Joe was charged and tried in adult court by a six-person jury in a one-day proceeding. During the trial, the prosecutor and witnesses repeatedly noted that Joe was African American and the victim was white. Joe was sent to an adult prison at age fourteen, where he was the victim of numerous sexual assaults. He was diagnosed with multiple sclerosis in 1996; at age 42, he is in a wheelchair.[44] After the *Graham* decision, Stevenson took Sullivan's case to the Florida trial court for resentencing. The Florida Department of Corrections reviewed his record in prison and set a release date of June 30, 2014. Three weeks before his scheduled release, he was notified that the release date had been miscalculated and should have been December 2019.

In 2012 in *Miller v. Alabama*, the Court held "a judge or jury must have the opportunity to consider mitigating circumstances before imposing the harshest possible penalty for juveniles. By requiring that all children convicted of homicide receive lifetime incarceration without possibility of parole, regardless of their age and age-related characteristics and the nature of their crimes, the mandatory sentencing schemes before us violate this principle of proportionality, and so the Eighth Amendment's ban on cruel and unusual punishment."[45]

After *Miller v. Alabama* required states and the federal government to consider the circumstances of each juvenile defendant in determining an individualized (versus mandatory) sentence, *Montgomery v. Louisiana* in 2016 applied that requirement retroactively. States can remedy the unconstitutionality of the mandatory LWOP sentences of approximately 2,100 individuals by resentencing or through parole hearings. The decision does not guarantee release of offenders, but it provides an opportunity for review.

Many of the 2,100 people serving juvenile life sentences were victims of abuse and were frequently exposed to violence.[46] A survey of individuals sentenced to life in prison as juveniles found that 79% witnessed violence in their homes regularly; 47% were physically abused growing up; 32% grew up in public housing; 40% had been enrolled in special education classes; and fewer than half were attending school at the time of the offense. Of girl defendants, 80% reported histories of physical abuse, and 77% reported histories of sexual violence. Racial disparities plague juvenile LWOP sentences. While 23.2% of juvenile arrests for murder involve an African American suspected of killing a white person, 42.4% of LWOP sentences are for African Americans convicted of this crime. In comparison, 6.4% of juvenile arrests involve a white person killing an African American, but only 3.6% receive a LWOP sentence.

Twenty-one states have banned life sentences without the possibility of parole for juveniles; in several other states, no one is serving the sentence.[47] Of the 29 states that allow juvenile LWOP, 3 states (Louisiana, Michigan, and Pennsylvania) account for about two-thirds of juvenile LWOP sentences. California now provides individuals who committed their crimes as juveniles a meaningful chance at parole after 15 to 25 years.

One researcher supports LWOP for juveniles who commit murder and notes that most of those offenders sentenced to LWOP began their offending early in life.[48] There is abundant evidence that early "age of onset" is a strong predictor of continued offending into adulthood.[49] While a cogent argument, Mike Males counters with the point that a sentence of life without parole should be decided based on circumstances, traits, and behaviors

> not whether or not the offender committed the murder before or after the stroke of midnight on his eighteenth birthday. Children do not turn into adults overnight; each individual's maturity and culpability level is different depending on the stage of his life, not the date on which he was born.[50]

In *Montgomery*, the Court said the ruling protects juveniles whose crimes reflect transient immaturity from a disproportionate sentence that violates the Eighth Amendment.[51] There are multiple reasons for reform including research that indicates adolescents lack the ability to make sound judgments and to appreciate risks and consequences. In addition, juveniles are at a substantial disadvantage in assisting in their defense. Aside from considerations of fairness and justice, the financial cost of juvenile LWOP is substantial. The incarceration of a 16-year-old sentenced to 50 years will cost society about $2.25 million.

JUVENILE COURT: THE STRUCTURE

The centerpiece of the juvenile justice system is the juvenile court. The size and functions of these courts vary from one jurisdiction to another. Some jurisdictions hear cases on special days in other courts. Other jurisdictions have facilities that range from a small courthouse with a skeleton staff to a large, bureaucratic complex with many separate divisions (often occupying different buildings over several acres of land) and employing over 100 personnel. Some juvenile courts (e.g., Honolulu, New York City, Las Vegas) are called *family courts* and handle a wide variety of family-related problems (e.g., child custody, child support, etc.).

Typically, juvenile courts are part of municipal courts, county courts, or other types of court systems, depending on an area's governmental structure. Most of the courts have the following divisions: (1) intake and detention, (2) probation, (3) records, (4) psychological services, (5) judges and personnel staff, (6) medical services (doctor and nurses), and (7) volunteer services.

Among the most important juvenile court personnel are the judges, referees, probation and parole officers, and the defense and prosecuting attorneys. Judges are usually elected officials and have a wide variety of duties, not unlike judges in the adult system. Referees (sometimes called "masters") are typically lawyers who perform some of the same functions as judges and supplement the roster of juvenile court judges.

Defense attorneys have become more common in juvenile court since *Gault* and are usually part of the public defender system. As noted above, however, many youths who appear in juvenile court are still not represented by an attorney.

The prosecutor is generally a member of the local district attorney's office assigned to the juvenile court (other district attorneys may be assigned to areas like domestic violence, gang prosecution, appeals, etc.). Like their criminal court counterparts, they are involved in every stage of the process, including such important decisions as whether or not to charge, what to charge, whether or not to detain, whether or not to certify a youth as an adult.

There are several other important personnel within a juvenile court, many of whom make some very important decisions. These include intake workers (who are generally the first personnel a youth actually sees when taken into custody and who often decide whether or not to detain), detention workers (who supervise youths who are detained), and probation and parole officers (who supervise youth placed on probation and those released from institutional care, respectively).

While the juvenile court differs in many significant ways from the adult system, there are also numerous similarities. For instance, cases proceed generally from arrest through pretrial hearings through the actual court process to disposition and finally to some form of punishment and/or treatment in a correctional institution. The juvenile court, however, has different terminology for the stages in the process. For instance, in the juvenile court a *petition* is the equivalent to an indictment, a trial is called an *adjudicatory hearing*, which is often followed by a *dispositional hearing*, roughly the equivalent of a sentencing hearing in the adult system. Parole is known as *aftercare*, while a sentence is called a *commitment*. The term *detention* is the equivalent of jailing, while *taking into custody* is the same as being arrested. Box 11-1 lists the stages of processing juveniles, along with standard definitions.

Juvenile Justice: The Process

The first stage of the juvenile justice system begins when the police apprehend a youngster for an alleged offense.

Initial Contact: The Police

Given the fact that the police make so many arrests of persons under the age of 18, it should come as no surprise that the largest percentage of referrals to the juvenile court come from the police (81%).[52] In most jurisdictions, the police have several options when contact with a juvenile is made (either because of a citizen complaint or an on-site observation of an alleged offense). First, they can, and often do, simply warn and release (for instance, telling a group of young people hanging around a street corner to "move along" or "go home"). Second, they can release after filling out an interview card ("field investigation card" or "field contact card"). Third, they can make a "station adjustment" where a youth is brought to the police station and then either (1) released to a parent or guardian or (2) released with a referral

Box 11-1   The Juvenile Court Process

Arrest

When a juvenile is arrested by the police, one of three options is usually available: they can release the youth with a simple warning, issue a misdemeanor citation (like a traffic ticket, ordering the youth to appear in court on a certain date), or physically take the youth to the juvenile court and the intake division, where he or she is booked.

Intake

This is the first step following the police decision to take the youth to court. The intake process is an initial screening of the case by staff members. Normally there are also probation officers (sometimes called "intake officers") who review the forms filled out by a staff member who collects some preliminary information (e.g., the alleged offense, various personal information about the youth, such as name, address, phone, names of the parents, etc.). During this stage, a decision is made as to whether to file a *petition* to appear in court on the charges, to drop the charges altogether (e.g., for lack of evidence), or to handle the case informally.

Diversion

In the event that the intake decision is to handle informally, probation staff, usually in cooperation with the prosecutor's office, will either release the youth without any further action or propose a diversion alternative. Diversion entails having the youth and his or her parent or guardian agree to complete certain requirements instead of going to court. This may include supervision by the probation department, plus satisfying certain requirements (e.g., curfew, restitution, community service, substance-abuse treatment, etc.). After a certain length of time, if the youth successfully completes the program, the charges are usually dropped; if not, the youth is brought back to court via a formal petition.

Detention

If the case is petitioned to court, the next major decision is whether to detain the youth or release him or her to a parent or guardian, pending a court appearance. The reasons for detaining a youth usually include: (1) safety (does the youth pose a danger to himself or to others) or (2) flight risk (does the youth pose a risk to flee or not appear in court). If the youth is detained, then a hearing must be held (called a "detention hearing") within a certain period of time (normally 24 to 72 hours), in order for a judge to hear arguments as to whether the youth should be detained any longer. Bail is not generally guaranteed.

Transfer/Waiver

In rare cases, a youth may be transferred or "waived" to the adult system. This is usually (but not always) done only in the case of extremely serious crimes or when the youth is a "chronic" offender.

Adjudication

The juvenile court equivalent of a trial in the adult system is called an *adjudication hearing*. Rather than a jury hearing the case, the final decision rests with a judge or referee. Both defense and prosecuting attorneys present their cases if the youth denies the petition (i.e., pleads not guilty). If a youth admits to the charges (which happens in the majority of all cases), the case proceeds to the next stage.

Box 11-1 *(Continued)*

Disposition

The *disposition hearing* is the equivalent of the sentencing stage in the adult system. Numerous alternatives are available at this stage, including outright dismissal, probation, placement in a community-based program (e.g., "boot camp," wilderness programs, group homes, substance abuse facility, etc.) or incarceration in a secure facility (e.g., "training school").

Aftercare

This stage occurs after a youth has served his or her sentence. It is the equivalent to "parole" in the adult system and, in fact, is often called "youth parole."

to some community agency. Fourth, they can issue a misdemeanor citation, which will require the youth and a parent or guardian to appear in juvenile court at some future date (not unlike a traffic ticket). Fifth, they can transport a youth to the juvenile court after making a formal arrest.

One of the most revealing statistics is the number of times the police use a particular option. Police today are far more likely to refer a youth to the juvenile court. In 1974, less than half (47%) of the cases where a juvenile was taken into custody by the police resulted in a referral to juvenile court; 44% of cases were handled informally within the department.[53] In 2014, 23% of the cases were handled within law enforcement agencies; 68% were referred to the juvenile court, and 9% were referred directly to criminal court.[54] These figures reflect the general trend toward increasing formality in our response to human problems.

The school-to-prison pipeline leads many juveniles to their first contact with the juvenile justice system.[55] Does this mean that the offenses committed by youths are getting more serious and thus require more formal processing? No. The offenses for which the majority of youths are charged remain minor—as they always have been. As discussed in chapter 10, the presence of school resource officers, which has increased dramatically since 1999, contributed to criminalizing adolescent misbehavior.

Police Discretion and Juveniles

Police officers make decisions largely out of public view with little public scrutiny—discretion is inherent in the job. Officers can use their discretion to detour juveniles from the juvenile justice system or to involve them with it.[56]

As described above, the police have several alternatives available when they encounter delinquent behavior. They can release with a warning, or they can release after filling out a report that does not constitute an arrest but is an official record of deviant behavior. It is important to note that this information may be used against the youth at a later date. The youth, however, does not have the opportunity to review or contest the charges in the report, a problem that has yet to be dealt with by the courts. After taking the youth to the police station, officers can decide to release him or her to a parent or guardian or release with a referral to a community agency, a mental health agency, or a social welfare agency. The last option is to decide to start the intake process.

The police are provided with few guidelines about how to determine what action to take. In most states the police are empowered to arrest juveniles without a warrant if there are reasonable grounds to believe that the child (1) has committed a delinquent act, (2) is unruly, (3) is in immediate danger from his surroundings, or (4) has run away from home. The following factors seem to be the most influential in determining the course of action the police take when confronting a juvenile who may be in violation of the law.

1. *The nature of the offense.* The more serious the offense, the more likely formal action will be taken.
2. *Citizen complainants.* If a citizen has made a complaint and remains on the scene demanding that an arrest be made, the police will comply.
3. *Gender.* Males are far more likely than females to be referred to court, since their offenses are typically more serious. There are some exceptions, such as when girls act contrary to role expectations and the complainant is a parent.[57]
4. *Race* (this is such an important issue that a separate section will be devoted to it later in this chapter). Studies have concluded that race is the most critical variable in determining how far into the system a youth is processed.[58]
5. *Social class.* In general, the lower the social class, the more likely a youth will be formally processed. Police often believe that kids from wealthier neighborhoods have parents who can handle the problem.
6. *Individual factors related to the offender.* Factors such as prior record, age, the context of the offense, the offender's family, etc. influence arrest decisions.
7. *The nature of police–youth encounters.* Much research has focused on the *demeanor* or attitude of the youth. If the youth appears cooperative and respectful, no formal action will be taken. All other things being equal, if the youth is hostile or, in police parlance, "flunks the attitude test," formal action generally follows. Race, class, and gender play a role here; lower class and minority males are far more likely than white males and females to flunk the attitude test.[59]
8. *Departmental policies.* Police departments vary with regard to policies about how to handle juveniles. Some emphasize formal handling, and others stress informal handling, with predictable results that some have much higher referral rates than others.[60]
9. *External pressures in the community.* The attitudes of the local media and the public, the social status of the complainant or victim, and the extent to which local resources are available to provide alternative service affect the decisions made.[61]

Youths who do not display deference are usually the most likely to be processed formally. This is especially the case with minor offenses and even when there is little or no evidence that a crime has been committed. Race is a factor because so many African American youths are angry at the white establishment and authority figures such as police officers. Many minority youths, especially gang members, display defiant attitudes that are interpreted as a challenge to police authority.[62] Similarly, gender dynamics associated with stereotypical understandings of how girls should behave (i.e. do what you're told and don't talk back to an authority figure) contribute to girls being arrested for incorrigibility and ungovernability.

Juvenile Attitudes toward Authorities

Adolescents have high rates of contact with the police, and most of the contacts are involuntary.

> For many youths, during pivotal developmental stages when adolescents form lasting views of the legitimacy of legal norms and legal actors, the police are the primary face of the state and the first that they are likely to encounter growing up. The growing policy preference for proactive policing over the past two decades has increased the likelihood of police encounters and changed the nature of police-youth contact.[63]

One example of proactive policing is street stops. Until the courts halted the process, police in New York City made 206,000 stops of youths between the ages of 13 and 15 from 2004 to 2012.[64] Approximately 80% of African American adolescents between the ages of 16 and 17 were stopped at least once by the police in 2006, compared to 38% of Hispanics and 10% of whites. The stops rarely resulted in arrests or seizure of evidence of a crime. Force is significantly more likely to be used against minority suspects in such encounters, which compounds the assault on dignity with physical trauma and adds the dimension of racial profiling.

The type of policing experienced by racial minorities influences their perceptions. Disproportionate police contact can foster a belief by minority youth that the police have an antipathy toward them.[65] Compared to whites, minority youth are more likely to hold negative attitudes about the police, to perceive encounters with authorities negatively, and to believe the police harass them. African American and Hispanic boys report that police violence is a possibility during each police interaction. Racial disparities in arrest rates can be the result of police policies such as stop and frisk that differentially target minorities or informal policing practices such as giving warnings to whites versus arresting minorities. Black and Latino youths, especially boys, are more likely to be the focus of policing policies, leading those youths to increased encounters with the police.

Negative attitudes have been reinforced in recent years. The death of Michael Brown in Ferguson, Missouri, in August 2014 became one of many well-publicized incidents that sparked massive protests throughout the country. Since then several news reports and websites have been monitoring police shootings. The website, Mapping Police Violence, reported that police killed 287 black people in 2017—25% of deaths at the hands of the police, although blacks comprise only 13% of the population.[66] Blacks are 3 times more likely to be killed by police than white people. The *Washington Post* also maintains a website. Fatal Force reported that 229 of the 998 people shot and killed by police in 2018 were black.[67]

Ferguson represents the "fire this time"—a modification of James Baldwin's classic book *The Fire Next Time*.[68] Bob Herbert used the modified phrase to describe the black community's reaction to what happened in Ferguson and elsewhere.

> But these tragedies all emerge from the same fetid source—the racism embedded in the very foundation of America. And it's that racism—stark, in-your-face, never-ending, frequently murderous—that has so many African Americans so angry and frustrated, so furious, so enraged. Black people all across America, not just in Ferguson, are angry about the killing of Michael Brown. And they remain angry over the killing of Trayvon Martin. And many are seething over the fatal chokehold clamped on the throat of Eric Garner by a cop on Staten Island in New York.[69]

Procedural Justice

Barry Feld advises that interactions of adolescents with the justice system affect the likelihood of cooperation and compliance with legal actors.[70] Their own experiences and their observations of the experiences of others with the legal system shape attitudes of juveniles toward authority and rules. If the system treats parties respectfully and fact-finders are neutral and fair, juveniles will more readily accept the system as legitimate and are more likely to abide by the rules. Procedural justice, however, is frequently not employed.

> Juvenile courts' procedures disregard youths' developmental limitations, deviate from accepted criminal procedural norms, use processes that few adults charged with a crime and facing confinement would accept, and undermine delinquents' feelings of fair treatment.[71]

Face-to-face encounters are a significant factor in shaping attitudes toward the police. One study identified both positive and negative elements of interactions. The first elements increase willingness to cooperate with officers versus negative outcomes with the latter treatment.

> Give citizens a reason for a stop, treat them courteously, allow them to explain their actions, and demonstrate that police procedures are fair. When a person is verbally demeaned, given no reason for being stopped, told to "shut up," detained in public for a long time, subjected to excessive force, or given a "rough ride" in a police van it is almost guaranteed that he or she will define this treatment as unjust and that these experiences will spill over and color the citizen's general opinion of the police.[72]

JUVENILE COURT PROCESSING

Table 11-1 presents the number of cases handled by juvenile courts and the percentage change from a decade earlier. The number of cases have declined substantially for almost every offense—total delinquency cases declined 48%. The majority of

Table 11-1   Referrals to Juvenile Court, 2007–2016

	Number of Cases 2016	Percent Change 2007–2016
Most serious offense		
Total delinquency	850,000	−48
Person offenses	244,900	−40
Criminal homicide	1,000	−22
Forcible rape	7,900	−20
Robbery	20,300	−37
Aggravated assault	26,200	−42
Simple assault	158,700	−39
Other violent sex offenses	7,600	−37
Other person offenses	23,200	53
Property offenses	283,600	−53
Burglary	55,300	−47
Larceny-theft	126,800	−52
Motor vehicle theft	15,700	−42
Arson	2,700	−60
Vandalism	41,900	−61
Trespassing	24,500	−56
Stolen property offenses	9,700	−52
Other property offenses	6,900	−57
Drug law violations	107,400	−41
Public order offenses	214,700	−50
Obstruction of justice	109,200	−45
Disorderly conduct	56,100	−56
Weapons offenses	18,300	−54
Liquor-law violations	5,300	−71
Nonviolent sex offenses	11,300	−3
Other public order offenses	14,500	−58

Note: Detail may not add to totals because of rounding. Percent change calculations are based on unrounded numbers.

Source: Sarah Hockenberry and Charles Puzzanchera, "Juvenile Court Statistics 2016," 7.

cases continue to be relatively minor. Public order offenses constitute 25% of all delinquency cases, with "obstruction of justice" accounting for more than half of these offenses.[73] While "person offenses" comprised 29% of all juvenile court processing, the bulk of these were "simple assaults" (65% of all person offenses; 19% of all delinquency cases). Property offenses were the largest category (33%), with larceny-theft leading the way (45% of all property offenses; 15% of all cases).[74] It should be emphasized that these are "delinquency cases" and do not include several thousand cases classified as "status," "dependency" and "abuse and neglect" (see chapter 2).

Disproportionate Minority Contact

Structural and institutional drivers that are not directly related to crime disproportionately propel young people of color into the justice system. "The racial and ethnic inequities present in our current justice system create the perception that incarceration is the most appropriate option for black and brown people with high needs, such as mental illness, but low risk for public safety."[75] An estimated 30% of children in the child welfare system subsequently become involved in the juvenile justice system.[76] These crossover youth are a high risk, vulnerable population with complex needs. Minority youth are disproportionately represented in the crossover youth population.

Disproportionate Minority Contact (DMC) results from racial biases woven into the juvenile justice system and from differences in offending patterns among ethnic groups.[77] Two theoretical perspectives frame studies of DMC.[78] The differential treatment framework (also called differential selection, bias theory, or systems factors) concentrates on justice decisions that disadvantage minority youth. The differential offending framework (also called differential involvement) looks at why some juveniles commit more crimes than others.

Differential treatment explores how the system treats minority youth more punitively at each stage of the juvenile justice decision-making process, even after accounting for legal and extralegal (age, socioeconomic status, school status) factors. Symbolic threat theory falls within this framework and focuses on social-psychological processes. Decision makers are influenced by perceptions

Table 11-2 Racial Profile of Delinquency Cases, 2005–2016

Most Serious Offense	White		Black		Hispanic	
	2005	**2016**	**2005**	**2016**	**2005**	**2016**
Total	48%	44%	33%	36%	16%	18%
Person	44%	40%	40%	40%	13%	17%
Property	53%	43%	29%	37%	15%	16%
Drugs	57%	56%	24%	18%	17%	22%
Public order	43%	41%	36%	37%	19%	20%

Source: Sarah Hockenberry and Charles Puzzanchera, "Juvenile Court Statistics 2016," 21.

that minority youth threaten public safety and middle-class standards. Attribution theory and labeling theory also contribute to this perspective.

The differential offending framework centers on individual, family, and neighborhood factors related to offending. This perspective focuses on legal factors such as prior record and severity of crime to account for differences in treatment of minority youth.[79] The legal factors are often related to risk factors more frequently experienced by minority youth: economically disadvantaged communities, low-performing public schools, delinquent peers, family risk factors such as incarcerated parents, and greater exposure to violence. Minority youth may grow up in severely compromised familial, community, and educational environments that set the stage for adverse behaviors.

DMC is a complex social problem affected by entrenched patterns of poverty, segregation, gaps in educational achievement, and residential instability.[80] Many public policies, institutional practices, and cultural representations produce and maintain racial inequities.

> Differences in arrest rates and processing of juvenile offenders are the residue of policies and practices that have disparate impact on communities of color. A litany of studies clarify the reasons DMC exists: selective enforcement, differential opportunities for treatment, institutional racism, indirect effects of socioeconomic factors, differential offending, biased risk assessment, and differential administrative practices.[81]

Congress enacted the Juvenile Justice and Delinquency Prevention Act (JJDPA) in 1974. The legislation established the Office of Juvenile Justice and Delinquency Prevention. The federal agency establishes national standards; if states receive federal funding, they are required to follow key JJDPA requirements.[82] The 1974 Act established two core requirements: (1) the separation of incarcerated juveniles and adults; (2) the deinstitutionalization of status offenders (DSO). Youths charged with status offenses could not be placed in secure detention or locked confinement. As discussed in chapter 3, the 1980 amendment to JJDPA allowed a valid court order (VCO) exception to the DSO requirement. An amendment in 1988 added requirements about disproportionate minority confinement; the 1992 amendment made DMC a core requirement and established programs to address gender bias.

States that received federal grants were required to determine whether disproportionate minority confinement existed in the state's juvenile justice system, to identify the causes, and to implement corrective strategies.[83] If the proportion of minority group youths detained in any secure detention facility exceeded the proportion of such groups in the general population, the state was required to reduce the number of minorities confined or lose a portion of its federal funds. In 2002, disproportionate minority confinement was expanded to include any disproportionate minority contact. States were required to examine representation of minority youth at *all* decision points along the juvenile justice system continuum—arrest, referral to juvenile court, diversion, secure detention, petition filed (charged), adjudication, probation, secure confinement, and transfer to criminal court (waiver)—to be eligible for federal funds.[84]

In 2003, the Relative Rate Index (RRI) was introduced as the method for states to determine the contact points in their juvenile justice systems that need more examination.[85] The previous method of assessing proportionality was not useful for measuring changes over time or for comparing disparity levels from one jurisdiction to another. This version of the RRI compared the rates of processing for minority youth to the rates of processing for white youth at each contact point in the system.

Despite the federal guidelines, disparate outcomes in juvenile court processing remain. In 2016, cases involving black youth were three times more likely (RRI of 3.0) to be referred to juvenile court for a delinquency offense than were cases involving white youth.[86] The diversion rate for cases involving black and other minority youth was less than the diversion rate for cases involving white youth: 0.6 for blacks and 0.8 for Hispanics. Probation rates were the same; the adjudicated rate for blacks was slightly lower (0.9) but slightly higher for Hispanics (1.1). Hispanic youth were 50% more likely to be detained (1.5) and to be placed (1.5) compared to an RRI of 1.4 for blacks. The waiver rate was 1.6 for blacks and 0.8 for Hispanics. See figure 11-1 for the relative rate indices between minority and white youth for delinquency offenses.

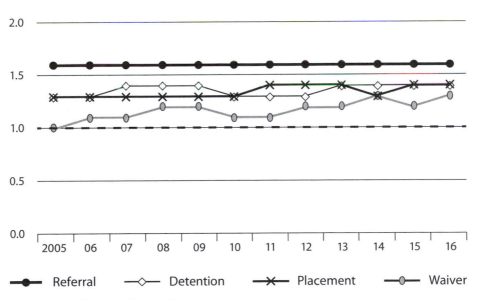

Relative Rate Indices between Minority and White Youth for Delinquency Offenses, 2005–2016

Figure 11-1   Relative Rate Indices.

Source: OJJDP Statistical Briefing Book, August 2018, https://www.ojjdp.gov/ojstatbb/special_topics/qa11602.asp?qaDate=2016

From 2003 to 2015, the rate of commitment for white juveniles fell 57% from 140 to 60 per 100,000. The rate for black juveniles fell 47% from 519 to 275 per 100,000, and the rate for Hispanics fell 61% from 230 to 89.[87] Although the commitment rates declined, the racial disparities endemic to the juvenile justice system did not. The commitment rate for minority youth was more than twice the rate for white youth. The RRI for black youth was 3.7 in 2003 but increased to 4.6 in 2015. The rate for Hispanics declined slightly from 1.6 to 1.5. Residential placement rates showed a similar pattern, increasing for blacks from 3.9 to 5 and decreasing slightly from 1.8 to 1.7 for Hispanics.

Juvenile arrest rates fell 34% from 2003 to 2013, which helps explain the decrease in juvenile commitments—fewer juveniles were placed on a path that could result in secure placement.[88] The larger decrease in commitments suggests the impact of policy initiatives. Arrests that once might have resulted in a commitment may have been diverted to probation or other lower level sanctions. Black teenagers are far more likely to be arrested across a range of offenses. Researchers have found few group differences between youth of color and white youth in the most common categories of youth arrests. Some behavioral differences exist, but African American and white youth are about equally likely to get into fights, carry weapons, steal property, use and sell illicit substances, and commit status offenses.

The differential in arrests is likely the result of police policies (e.g., targeting low-income, mostly minority neighborhoods) or the location of some offenses in more visible places. Race is related to the *visibility* of the offense, which affects the police decision to arrest. This is especially the case with regard to drug law violations. The rate per 100,000 juveniles for drug offenses in 1997 was 11 for whites and 117 for blacks; in 2006, the rate was 13 for whites and 69 for blacks; in 2015, the rate was 6 for whites and 15 for blacks.[89] While drug cases decreased more than 40% from 2005 to 2016, drug offense case rates were highest for black males in each of those years.[90] One study found a racial bias in drug sanctions where the disadvantages of minority status increased as cases moved deeper into the system.[91] Another study found that blacks were treated more harshly at intake and judicial disposition, confirming the role of selection bias in race differences in juvenile court outcomes.[92]

Racial bias is cumulative, starting long before a youth is ever contacted by the police. It is not being suggested that everyone connected with the juvenile justice system is a racist and practices discrimination, although stereotypes about youth from certain race or class backgrounds definitely exist. Cultural biases that affect police practices and the existence of various forms of racial profiling contribute to disproportionality.[93] As Kimberly Kahn and Karin Martin note: "Overall, little debate remains that officers at times can and do use race as an unwarranted factor when conducting stops or investigative actions, which is the definition of racial profiling."[94] Ascertaining evidence that individual officers are biased is difficult because "there is scant evidence about the direct role of police officers' racial attitudes on police behavior with racial minorities in the field."[95]

Part of the problem is institutional in that such negative stereotypes are deeply imbedded in our culture. Juvenile courts and police departments are largely staffed by whites. The widespread poverty and joblessness affecting minority communities result in the lack of available resources (e.g., alternatives to formal court processing) to deal with crime-related issues and the general failure of schools.

Regardless of whether race, class, gender, or demeanor is statistically more relevant, one fact remains: growing numbers of African American youths are finding themselves within the juvenile justice system. In 2016, 63% of delinquency cases involving black youth were processed formally compared to 55% of the cases involving Hispanic youth and 51% of the cases involving white youth.[96] Blacks are more likely to have their cases petitioned to go before a judge and more likely to be waived to the adult system. Once petitioned, 53% of cases involving white youth were adjudicated delinquent compared to 49% of cases involving black youth and 57% of cases involving Hispanic youth. One-third of the adjudicated cases involving Hispanic youth resulted in out-of-home placement compared to 29% of cases involving black youth and 22% of cases involving white youth.

The Influence of Gender

As discussed in chapter 1, juvenile courts historically have responded differently to girls than to boys. Sensibilities about female sexuality resulted in different approaches to regulating the behavior of girls. Chapter 5 reviewed the more recent trend of identifying girls who break feminine norms, focusing on mean girls and violence. Exaggerated reports resulted in increased arrests of girls who acted out at home or at school. Barry Feld notes: "Despite changes in practices over time—the different expectations and social construction of gender in different periods—the juvenile justice system's responses to girls have differed from those to boys."[97] Chapter 13 discusses the double standard of juvenile justice.

In 2016, 32% of all delinquency cases for girls were person offenses versus 28% for boys.[98] The percentage of girls' cases for public order offenses was 26% versus 25% for boys. Of the 614,900 male delinquency cases, 59% were petitioned; 194,600 (53%) were adjudicated. Of the 235,600 female delinquency cases, 49% were petitioned; 55,800 (49%) were adjudicated. Of the male adjudicated cases, 28% received out-of-home placement compared with 21% of girls. Probation percentages were fairly similar—62% for boys and 64% for girls. Males accounted for 57% of petitioned status offense cases. The only status offense category in which females represented a larger proportion of the caseload than males was runaway. Between 2005 and 2016, the truancy case rate was greater than the rate of any other status offense category for both girls and boys.

The Influence of Social Class

Social class is another important factor. While juvenile court and arrest statistics do not give any indication of the class backgrounds of youths, studies over the years have documented the class bias at each stage of the process. A longitudinal study of over 10,000 cases in Philadelphia determined that at every step, minorities and youths from the lowest socioeconomic backgrounds were processed further into the system than whites and those from higher-class backgrounds.[99] Some studies have suggested that social class, rather than race per se, best predicted police decisions.[100] For instance, research by Sampson found that the overall socioeconomic status of a *community* was more important than other variables, although race figured prominently.[101] In general, the lower the socioeconomic standing of the community as a whole, the greater will be the tendency for formal processing of youths.[102]

It is often difficult to find data that show social class as a variable in juvenile court cases. A good surrogate is poverty, which is often noted in case files, especially if a youth lives in government housing or is eligible for free legal representation or lives with a single parent (especially the mother, who is more often than not living in poverty). Several studies have used poverty status as a variable. For instance, one study found that youth who came from concentrated disadvantage were more likely to be confined than youth from more affluent areas.[103] Court officials perceive areas of disadvantage as high risk and dangerous for youth. Such perceptions play an important role in deciding whether youth remain in the community or are placed in confinement. Black and Hispanic youth were more likely than whites to be institutionalized.

Although dated, William Chambliss researched the relevance of social class in his study of the "Saints" and the "Roughnecks."[104] The Saints were eight white boys from upper-middle-class backgrounds, and the Roughnecks were six white boys from lower-class backgrounds. Each of the two groups engaged in a variety of mostly minor delinquencies, typical of American teenagers. The "Saints" however were viewed by teachers and the police as "good kids" engaging in pranks while the "Roughnecks" were seen as "bad kids," proving through their actions that they were headed for trouble. The differential treatment, suggests Chambliss, stemmed in part from the greater *visibility* of the Roughnecks, as they committed their acts mostly in public, while the Saints were able to drive to neighboring communities in their cars and/or in their private backyards in the suburbs. The two groups had predictable careers, with two of the Roughnecks ending up in prison and all but one of the Saints going to college and pursuing respectable careers.

By defining certain acts as delinquent, the juvenile justice system (at least in effect), helps prevent upward mobility for the majority of lower-class youths. Chambliss concluded that the juvenile justice system and other control/processing institutions (e.g., schools) help maintain the class structure by channeling youth in directions appropriate to their class background.

> The answer lies in the class structure of American society and the control of legal institutions by those at the top of the class structure. Obviously, no representative of the upper class drew up the operational chart for the police which led them to look in the ghettoes and on street-corners—which led them to see the demeanor

of lower-class youth as troublesome and that of upper-middle-class youth as tolerable. Rather, the procedures simply developed from experience—experience with irate and influential upper-middle-class parents insisting that their son's vandalism was simply a prank and his drunkenness only a momentary "sowing of wild oats"—experience with cooperative or indifferent, powerless, lower-class parents who acquiesced to the law's definition of their son's behavior.[105]

A more recent study found that interracial socioeconomic inequality in the community results in race being a factor in decisions about detention. Intergroup inequality can motivate whites to discriminate based on their perceptions that minorities threaten middle-class norms, values, and standards.[106] In another study cumulative disadvantage was used as an orienting framework for analyzing the consequences of early contact with the criminal justice system and problem behavior over the life course. Race, poverty, and lack of prosocial bonds were structural impediments to avoiding arrest. Juvenile arrest disrupts schooling and has a substantive impact on dropping out of high school. "The alarming differences in employment, wages, and family life between the never incarcerated and the incarcerated and formerly incarcerated can thus ultimately be traced to educational disadvantage."[107]

Social class helps determine many, if not most, of the life chances of people in the United States.[108] When combined with race, the restrictions can be truly devastating. Take, for instance, decisions made by the police and courts. Members of racial minorities and the lower classes tend to have their behaviors defined as felonies, while whites and more privileged youths are far more likely to be charged with misdemeanors, if charged at all. In juvenile courts all over the country, minorities and lower class youth will be processed further into the system than their more privileged and white counterparts. Even when out-of-home placements are ordered, the more privileged youth are sent to group homes or well-funded drug treatment programs paid for by insurance, while their lower class and minority counterparts are sent to public facilities.

The Intake Process and the Decision to Detain

Juveniles enter the juvenile court after having been referred to it by a law enforcement agency or a parent or guardian. Upon arrival, the juvenile faces what is known as *intake screening*, a unique feature of the juvenile court. This division is staffed by full-time employees of the court (normally probation officers), who are usually college graduates with majors such as social work, sociology, or criminal justice. Customarily, the youth and a parent or guardian is interviewed at intake. The options available to the court representative at this stage vary somewhat among jurisdictions but fall into four categories: (1) dismissal, (2) informal supervision, or "informal probation," (3) referral to another agency, and (4) formal petition to the court. Each year from 2005 to 2016, delinquency cases were more likely to be handled formally than informally.[109] In 2016, 147,600 cases (17% of all delinquency cases) were dismissed at intake (see table 11.4). An additional 223,300 cases were handled informally, with the juvenile agreeing to a voluntary sanction (e.g., restitution). Authorities filed a petition and handled 479,600 cases formally.

If it is determined that the case falls within the jurisdiction of the court, the next decision is whether the youth will be detained. The decision about whether the youth needs to be placed in detention is usually based on written court policies. The three typical reasons for detention are (1) the youth may harm others or himself or herself or be subject to injury by others if not detained; (2) the youth has no parent, guardian, or other person able to provide adequate care and supervision, is homeless, or is a runaway; and (3) it is believed that if not detained the youth will leave the jurisdiction and not appear for court proceedings. The intake staff is usually instructed to consider the nature and severity of the current offense and previous offenses (if any), the youth's age, the youth's conduct within the home and at school, ability of the parents or guardians to supervise the youth, whether the current offense is a continuation of a pattern of delinquent behavior, and the willingness of the parents or guardian to cooperate with the court.

Decisions are based on *risk assessment instruments* (see box 11-2) that were devised as a method to determine the likelihood of appearance in court and whether the youth presents a danger to self or others. However, the theory behind the instruments is seriously flawed; it assumes that there is a valid method of predicting who is most likely to commit a crime if released. Risk assessment instruments can be misused, and their predictive accuracy has been questioned. There is a polarized debate between those who promote actuarial assessments and those who advocate for blended models that combine assessment and discretion.[110] One study found that probation officers used their own set of criteria (revolving around respect for and compliance with legal institutions) that had little or nothing to do with predicting recidivism.[111] In another study it was found that about half of those that used the assessment instrument "completed tools carefully and honestly and tended to use them for decision making." But the rest filled out the forms but often made decisions that did not correspond with what the assessment showed, "and in some cases even manipulating the information included in them."[112] On the other hand, some instruments have been proven to be of value in predicting recidivism among offenders following release from incarceration.[113]

It could be argued that detention should be reserved for youths who are charged with serious crimes. This is not the case, however. In 2016, 33% of youths detained nationwide were charged with a person crime; 23% were charged with a property crime; 18% were charged with a drug offense; and 29% were charged with a public order crime.[114]

After the decision to detain has been made, the intake officer has several options. These include: (1) counsel, warn, and release, sometimes called *informal adjustment*; (2) *informal probation* (release under certain conditions, with supervision by a volunteer or a regular probation officer; after a certain period of time if no new offense is committed, the case is dismissed); (3) referral to another agency;

Box 11-2 Risk Assessment Instrument

VIRGINIA DEPARTMENT OF JUVENILE JUSTICE
DETENTION ASSESSMENT INSTRUMENT (Rev. 8/15/05)

Juvenile Name: _____ DOB: _____/_____/_____ Juvenile #: _____ ICN#

Intake Date: _____/_____/_____ Time: ____:____ ☐AM ☐PM Worker Name: _____ CSU #:

Completed as Part of Detention Decision: ☐ Completed as Follow-Up (On-Call Intake): ☐

Score

1. **Most Serious Alleged Offense** (see reverse for examples of offenses in each category)
   Category A: Felonies against persons. 15
   Category B: Felony weapons and felony narcotics distribution. 12
   Category C: Other felonies. 7
   Category D: Class 1 misdemeanors against persons. 5
   Category E: Other Class 1 misdemeanors. 3
   Category F: Violations of probation/parole. ....2 _____

2. **Additional Charges in this Referral**
   Two or more additional current felony offenses..3
   One additional current felony offense 2
   One or more additional misdemeanor **OR** violation of probation/parole offenses.........1
   One or more status offenses **OR** No additional current offenses ....0 _____

3. **Prior Adjudications of Guilt** (includes continued adjudications with "evidence sufficient to finding of guilt")
   Two or more prior adjudications of guilt for felony offenses....................................6
   One prior adjudication of guilt for a felony offense..4
   Two or more prior adjudications of guilt for misdemeanor offenses.............................3
   Two or more prior adjudications of guilt for probation/parole violations.......................2
   One prior adjudication of guilt for any misdemeanor or status offense 1
   No prior adjudications of guilt..0 _____

4. **Petitions Pending Adjudication or Disposition** (exclude deferred adjudications)
   One or more pending petitions/dispositions for a felony offense................................8
   Two or more pending petitions/dispositions for other offenses.................................5
   One pending petition/disposition for an other offense 2
   No pending petitions/dispositions..0 _____

5. **Supervision Status**
   Parole 4
   Probation based on a Felony or Class 1 misdemeanor 3
   Probation based on other offenses **OR** CHINSup **OR** Deferred disposition with conditions ..2
   Informal Supervision **OR** Intake Diversion 1
   None ....0 _____

6. **History of Failure to Appear** (within past 12 months)
   Two or more petitions/warrants/detention orders for FTA in past 12 months..................3
   One petition/warrant/detention order for FTA in past 12 months 1
   No petition/warrant/detention order for FTA in past 12 months ....0 _____

7. **History of Escape/ Runaways** (within past 12 months)
   One or more escapes from secure confinement or custody 4
   One or more instances of absconding from non-secure, court-ordered placements 3
   One or more runaways from home...1
   No escapes or runaways w/in past 12 months ....0 _____

8. **TOTAL SCORE**... _____

Indicated Decision: _____ **0 - 9 Release** _____ **10 - 14 Detention Alternative** _____ **15+ Secure Detention**

Mandatory Overrides: ☐ 1. Use of firearm in current offense
(must be detained) ☐ 2. Escapee from a secure placement
☐ 3. Local court policy (indicate applicable policy) _____

Discretionary Override: ☐ 1. Aggravating factors (override to more restrictive placement than indicated by guidelines)
☐ 2. Mitigating factors (override to less restrictive placement than indicated by guidelines)
☐ 3. Approved local graduated sanction for probation/parole violation

Actual Decision / Recommendation: _____ **Release** _____ **Alternative** _____ **Secure Detention**

(4) outright dismissal; (5) file a *consent decree* (somewhat more restrictive than informal probation); or (6) file a petition to have the youth appear in court for a formal *adjudicatory hearing*. As mentioned earlier, race figures prominently in the decision to detain. Table 11-3 presents the rate of detained juveniles by sex, race, and most serious offense. Regardless of offense, African American youths are far more likely to be detained than their white counterparts, and Hispanic youth are more likely to be detained.

After the decisions in the *Kent* and *Gault* cases, there was a movement to try to keep young offenders out of juvenile court. If they were processed, the goal was to *divert* them out of the system as quickly as possible. The research that was done in conjunction with the two court decisions (and a great deal of research immediately following them) demonstrated the need for some type of diversion. If youths are not diverted from further processing, they move to the adjudication stage of the juvenile court process.

Adjudication

Adjudication is the juvenile court counterpart to trial in adult court, but it has some significant differences. Very often the hearings are rather informal (sometimes they are merely conversations between a judge, parents, and the child), and they are closed to the public and to reporters. In recent years the procedures have become more formal, especially in large metropolitan courts—almost as formal as an adult court.

There are two types of hearings. The *adjudicatory hearing* is the fact-finding stage of the juvenile court process, which is followed by the *dispositional hearing*. These two stages are roughly the equivalent of the trial and sentencing stages of the

Table 11-3 Offense Profile of Detained Residents by Sex and Race/Ethnicity for United States, 2015 (rate per 100,000 juveniles)

Most Serious Offense	Total	Sex			Race	
		Male	Female	White	Black	Hispanic
Total	**50**	**81**	**17**	**25**	**153**	**50**
Violent Index	13	23	3	4	46	14
Other person	6	8	3	4	15	4
Property Index	8	14	2	4	28	7
Other property	2	2	1	1	4	2
Drug	2	4	1	1	5	3
Public order	6	11	2	3	22	6
Technical violation	11	17	5	6	29	13
Status offense	2	2	1	1	3	1

Source: Melissa Sickmund, T. J. Sladky, W. Kang, and Charles Puzzanchera, "Easy Access to the Census of Juveniles in Residential Placement," 2017, https://www.ojjdp.gov/ojstatbb/ezacjrp/asp/Offense_Detained.asp?state=0&topic=Offense_Detained&year=2015&percent=rate

adult system. In most urban courts, both the defense and the prosecutor present the evidence of the case. Hearsay evidence is inadmissible; the defendant has the right to cross-examine a witness; he or she is protected against self-incrimination; and a youth's guilt must be proven beyond a reasonable doubt.

In the majority of juvenile courts, the dispositional hearing is a separate hearing altogether, part of what is often referred to as a *bifurcated* system. During this hearing, the judge relies heavily on two important court documents, usually prepared by the probation department. One document is the *legal* file that contains a complete referral history, including the nature of all the offenses that brought the youth into court prior to the current offense, along with prior dispositions. The other document is probably the most important; it contains a wide range of personal information about the juvenile. This is known as the *social* file, which contains such information as family background, school records, psychological profile, and the like. Together these two documents aid the probation department in preparing what is known as the *presentence report*, roughly the equivalent of the one prepared in the adult system. Typically both a treatment plan and a sentence recommendation are prepared for the case. More often than not, the judge agrees to the recommendation.

There are several alternative dispositions available to juvenile court judges: (1) dismissal, (2) probation, (3) commitment to an institution or "out-of-home placement" (with several different security level types, ranging from group homes to training schools), and (4) waiver to an adult court.

What are the final decisions at this stage? Table 11-4 shows the outcome of the more than 850,000 juvenile court cases processed in 2016. A slight majority

Table 11-4 Juvenile Court Processing, 2016

850,500 Delinquency Cases

44% Not Petitioned; Handled Informally (370,900)

  40% Dismissed at Intake (147,600)

  16% Probation (58,800)

  44% Other Sanction (164,500)

56% Petitioned (479,600)

  1% Waived (3,500)

  52% Adjudicated Delinquent (250,400)

    27% Placed

  62% Probation

  11% Other Sanction

47% Not Adjudicated Delinquent (225,700)

  30% Probation

  14% Other Sanction

  56% Dismissed

Sarah Hockenberry and Charles Puzzanchera, "Juvenile Court Statistics 2016," 52.

of all referrals result in a petition to court (56%). Of those cases that do not result in a petition, the most common outcome is dismissal (40%) followed by other sanctions (i.e., community service, restitution, and fines) and probation. Of the petitioned cases not adjudicated delinquent, 56% are dismissed. Of those petitioned to court, 52% are adjudicated as delinquent, usually as the result of a guilty plea; 62% are granted probation; 27% are placed outside the home. Table 11-5 shows the most serious offense by gender and race of juveniles committed outside the home.

Juveniles tried as adults and committed to adult facilities face higher risks of rape, assault, and suicide. Even in juvenile facilities, children may be victimized by staff members. Of the 9,500 allegations of sexual victimization in juvenile correctional facilities in 2012, 45% involved staff-on-youth sexual victimization.[115] Many detained/committed juveniles have mental health needs; suicide rates in juvenile detention facilities are more than four times higher than for adolescents overall.

KEEPING OFFENDERS FROM GOING DEEPER INTO THE SYSTEM

It has long been recognized that the juvenile court can and often does have a negative impact on youths who are referred. Indeed, there have been a plethora of studies documenting this, starting with the President's Commission report on juvenile delinquency in 1967.[116] A meta-analysis of 29 different studies covering a period of 35 years concluded that with few exceptions "juvenile system processing

Table 11-5 Offense Profile of Committed Residents by Sex and Race/Ethnicity for United States, 2015 (rate per 100,000 juveniles)

Most Serious Offense	Total	Sex		Race		
		Male	**Female**	**White**	**Black**	**Hispanic**
Total	**100**	**168**	**29**	**60**	**275**	**89**
Violent Index	27	49	4	15	83	24
Other person	11	16	6	7	29	10
Property Index	19	34	4	10	58	16
Other property	4	6	1	2	10	3
Drug	6	9	2	5	10	6
Public order	12	22	2	8	34	11
Technical violation	15	24	6	9	40	16
Status offense	5	7	4	5	12	3

Source: Melissa Sickmund, T. J. Sladky, W. Kang, and Charles Puzzanchera, "Easy Access to the Census of Juveniles in Residential Placement," 2017, https://www.ojjdp.gov/ojstatbb/ezacjrp/asp/Offense_Committed.asp?state=0&topic=Offense_Committed&year=2015&percent=rate

appears to not have a crime control effect, and across all measures appears to increase delinquency."[117]

Diversion

Diversionary tactics have a strong theoretical background (see the discussion on labeling in chapter 7). Legal interaction by the juvenile justice system may actually perpetuate delinquency by processing the cases of children and youths whose problems might be better ignored, normalized in their original settings, or dealt with in more informal settings within the community. Courts may inadvertently stigmatize some youths for relatively petty acts.

Diversion programs are designed, in part, to deal with the problem of overcrowded juvenile courts and correctional institutions (including detention), so that greater attention can be devoted to more serious offenders. The President's Commission called for the creation of youth services bureaus to develop alternative programs for juvenile offenders in local communities. The establishment of these bureaus initiated a move toward diverting youths, especially status offenders and other nonserious delinquents, from the juvenile court. These bureaus were quickly established in virtually every community regardless of size. Unfortunately, the youth services bureau concept was far from clear and unambiguous.

> The recommendation that community services be coordinated by the bureau assumed that there was a wealth of services to be coordinated when, in fact, the lack of such agencies and services had been an impediment to successful juvenile court work.[118]

Seven theoretical perspectives influence teen courts: peer justice, procedural justice, specific deterrence, labeling, law-related education, skill building, and restorative justice. Almost 130,000 youthful offenders are referred to these programs each year; 42% are juvenile justice system-based, 36% are school-based, and 22% are community-based.[119] Few definitive studies regarding the impact of teen courts on juvenile offender outcomes exist despite the substantial growth in the number of such programs over the past 40 years.[120] Given the considerable differences across programs, it is difficult to gauge overall effectiveness.[121]

Mentoring addresses the lack of prosocial role models in the lives of youths at risk for delinquent behavior. Studies have identified improvements in self-efficacy, relationships with adults and parents, plus improved attitudes toward school as well as improved school performance and attendance.[122] The level of involvement of youths in the juvenile justice system affects the success of a mentoring program. A deficit in research to date is lack of attention to the role of risk to reoffend. Additional research is needed to identify the components of mentoring services correlated with reducing recidivism. One recent study found that to reduce further involvement in the juvenile justice system, mentoring must be packaged with other interventions.

Conflicting expectations, findings, and conclusions emerged from the widespread, disjointed, and complicated experiment with diversion. Potential benefits of diversion include: avoiding the stigma of a formal court record; receiving rehabilitative services that could reduce recidivism, and reducing court caseloads.[123] Potential harms are widening the net of social control, increased recidivism, and abuse of the discretion to place youth in diversion programs, amplifying racial and gender disparities in sanctioning. Diversion increases scrutiny of offenders.[124] A youth participating in an informal sanction faces additional justice contact. If required to admit responsibility, juveniles could be subject to adjudication in a subsequent case. If youths refuse offers of diversion, the refusal may be interpreted as a sign of defiance, prompting more severe sanctions than if diversion had not been offered.

Widening the Net or True Alternatives?

The process of diverting youth away from existing institutions and into new, theoretically more humane alternatives is not as new as we might like to think. The process began when the New York House of Refuge opened in 1824 to divert youth from adult institutions (although the word "diversion" was not used). In time, as we saw in chapter 1, it became like its adult counterparts. Over the next century, new institutions emerged to take its place. With each new institution or alternative, the number of youths being processed in a formal manner increased.

Diversion has created concern over such issues as prejudice, discrimination, civil rights violations, and net widening. The latter issue has received the most attention. Ideally, a true diversion program (and the original concept behind diversion) would remove youths from the juvenile justice system. So, for example, if 1,000 youths are usually processed through the system, a true diversion would take, say, 300 of those youths and place them in some alternative program. Essentially, net widening would occur if instead of reducing the number in the juvenile justice system to 700, diversion resulted in the same 1,000 being processed plus 300 more youths placed in diversion programs. In this example, the "net" would have been extended to envelop 1,300 youths.

> If diversion is used to expand the reach of the justice system and to impose potentially risky interventions on less serious offenders with little promise of real preventive effect, the practice should be ended and juvenile defense attorneys should fight it vigorously.[125]

PROBATION

Probation (from the Latin verb *probare*—to prove, to test) began in the mid-nineteenth century with the efforts of John Augustus.[126] In 1841 he persuaded the Boston Police Court to release an adult drunkard into his custody rather than sending him to prison (which was the most common disposition at the time). In 1843, he expanded his efforts to include children. By 1846 he was managing the cases of about 30 children ranging from 9 to 16 years old. By 1869, the Massachusetts legislature required that an agent of the state be present if court actions might result in the placement of a child in a reformatory. These agents were to search for other placement, protect the child's interests, investigate the case before trial, and supervise the plan for the child after disposition. In every respect it was a social work role before social work became a profession. In 1878 Massachusetts passed the first probation statute; other states quickly followed suit. By 1925 probation was available for juvenile offenders in every state.[127]

Social Work or Law Enforcement?

Augustus was a *volunteer*, rather than a salaried bureaucrat. What began as a true alternative to the justice process became *bureaucratized* (or what Weber called *rationalized*).[128] The humane gesture of an individual to help the unfortunate morphed over time into a huge, often impersonal, bureaucracy encompassing the conflicting roles of law enforcement and social work. It did not take long for this to happen. By the second decade of the twentieth century, probation was an established part of the juvenile court system. Many of the first probation officers were former policemen.[129]

As more and more people with social work degrees and licenses began working in probation, the social work functions evolved, but the law enforcement aspect persisted. In many states, both probation and parole officers are designated as peace officers—yet many carry both a badge and a gun.[130] The author has met many who seem to be "frustrated cop wannabes." Jerome Miller found a sign on the office wall of the chief probation officer in California that read: "Trail 'em, "Surveil 'em, Nail 'em, and Jail 'em."[131] For some, there seems to be a general attitude that social work solutions are not sufficiently punitive and that probation should be a "tough" test.

Should Probation Officers Be Armed?

The subject of probation officer safety has prompted decisions about the need to carry weapons.[132] Supporters believe firearms are necessary to manage heavy caseloads, dangerous clientele, and mandates to supervise offenders where they live. Opponents believe that firearms push officers toward enforcement rather than treatment.[133] Barry Krisberg believes carrying a weapon is inconsistent with the traditional role of probation officer. "You can't be delivering cognitive behavioral therapy with a gun strapped to your waist. The therapeutic relationship is inhibited and destroyed by someone carrying a gun openly."[134] Similarly, the head of the probation services division in Colorado stated: "There is an atmosphere created when a visibly armed staff member interacts with an offender; some feel that detracts from building the necessary relationship with the offender to allow behavioral change to occur."[135]

The question that needs to be asked is: do juvenile probation officers face more dangers than before? Have there been any significant increases in attacks in recent years? In 2016 there was one fatal injury to probation and parole officers.[136]

There is no empirical evidence that probation is a very dangerous occupation; the evidence in support of carrying weapons is anecdotal.

The Functions of Probation

Probation officers serve three important functions. The officers perform the *intake* function, providing a preliminary investigation of cases as they first come into the system. The second major function is that of *investigation*, which produces the *social history report* presented to the judge. Finally, perhaps the most important function is *supervision.* Youths are assigned to a probation officer who performs multiple duties related to supervision, such as surveillance, casework services, counseling, etc.

Many experts have suggested that workload is a better unit of measurement for juvenile probation officers than caseloads.[137] Departments need to consider the elements of the workload: risk and needs assessment; helping youth and parents set expectations and goals; helping youth meet those goals; budgeting and staffing to facilitate accomplishing those tasks. Underfunded systems make workloads unmanageable. As the number of youth in the justice system declines, probation officers will supervise fewer probationers. Youth with complex needs add more to the workload than those with straightforward needs. The number of cases in which adjudicated juveniles were placed on probation has declined steadily from a peak of 700,000 in 1997 to 155,531 in 2016.[138]

Probation departments have become huge entities within the juvenile justice system. In large urban areas it is not uncommon to employ thousands of people and to have large budgets. The budget of the Los Angeles County Probation Department is in excess of $700 million; it employs 4,400 sworn officers. Investigative reports found allegations of juvenile probation officer misconduct (including molesting or beating youths in their care) involving at least 170 department employees.[139]

Part of the bureaucratic nature of probation is the number of rules and regulations to which the probationer must adhere, such as going to school and/or work, obeying all laws, not associating with other delinquents, obeying the lawful demands of parents, contacting the probation officer periodically, etc. With varying caseloads, officers cannot provide the same services for all youths. In larger urban areas, probation officers may not be able to schedule more than a perfunctory phone call once a month.

In recent years burnout has become a significant problem as increasing numbers of probation officers have been asked to perform multiple tasks. Probation officers complete presentence investigations as well as sentencing recommendations. If a probation officer does not investigate fully, the juvenile—particularly those with rehabilitation needs—will not receive the appropriate disposition or sentence.[140] Studies on juvenile probation officers have been lacking, but researchers interviewed a sample of probation officers in the Midwest and found that about one-fourth experienced some kind of burnout.[141] The officers indicated burnout affected their relationships with clients and their families, which can result in taking out frustrations on clients, being less tolerant, and/or doing the bare minimum required for the job. Being emotionally exhausted, overwhelmed, and not connecting to others can mean that officers "may not pay attention to clients and miss important details in their lives. Officers also may spend less time interacting with juveniles and engaging in activities that could be beneficial for youth on their caseload."[142] Another study of juvenile probation officers found about one-third of the officers reported high levels of emotional exhaustion, and more than one-quarter, particularly those with high-risk clients, reported high levels of cynicism.[143]

Probation officers conduct a number of surveillance strategies over juveniles in the community, including intensive supervision, electronic monitoring, and house arrest. Intensive supervision probation is common in juvenile corrections. The effects of this supervision-oriented intervention on recidivism are mixed.[144] Evaluations of intensive supervision have consistently found that it has little impact on recidivism.[145] Increased supervision that includes more frequent contacts with probation officers makes technical violations more likely. The expense to increase the intensity of supervision could be better allocated to treatment.

House arrest is similar to "grounding." The only difference is that it is imposed by the court. It is much better than being locked up in detention or some other form of official confinement, but its effectiveness has not been demonstrated. House arrest is often used in conjunction with *electronic monitoring*, a punishment originally inspired by a *Spiderman* comic strip where someone was tracked by a transmitter attached to his wrist. An electronic bracelet is attached to the offender (usually on the ankle) that signals when the probationer travels a certain distance (usually meaning a violation of probation by leaving the home). While electronic monitoring has been a boon to various businesses that produce these products, the effectiveness for juveniles, as with house arrest, has not been demonstrated.

Electronic monitoring disproportionately affects children of color and children from low-income families, subjecting every aspect of their daily lives to surveillance and control.[146] EM has stigmatizing and marginalizing effects. Youth report feeling dehumanized—as though they were on a leash. If juveniles have mental health issues, the experiences of EM may make those conditions worse. Requiring juveniles to spend substantial time at home can aggravate family tensions. Families also face surveillance and control; EM provisions regulate who can enter the home without permission. With monitors tracking every move, the chance of a violation is high. Violations mean new penalties; not charging the device is a violation. EM is often used on juveniles who would not have been incarcerated pretrial or post-adjudication, which means that it extends the system's reach rather than diverting youth from institutions.

> Being monitored at all times and having to follow the prescribed and detailed electronic monitoring conditions is in tension with the behavioral, emotional, and intellectual development of adolescents, and is especially burdensome for those youth with mental illness or learning disabilities. This gap between the

requirements of electronic monitoring and the capacity of youth to understand and cope with its requirements calls into question its effectiveness as a tool for rehabilitation.[147]

Most programs require families to pay for the monitoring device and to set up the necessary phone lines to activate it, which may present a financial burden.[148] Jurisdictions may bill families $15 per day to reimburse the cost of monitoring.[149] Families must ensure that the child has constant access to a cellular phone and electricity; if the device is damaged or lost, replacement is several hundred dollars. The costs can push impoverished families further into debt.

Electronic monitoring is imposed as an alternative to detention or as a condition of probation; it is classified as rehabilitative. Because it does not look like traditional punishment, it falls outside discussions of due process and is not subject to judicial oversight. "As a result, electronic monitoring exists in a legal netherworld: wielded and expanded with almost no limits or review."[150]

Jerome Miller, reflecting on his own 30-plus years of working with youthful offenders, notes that one of the problems within the modern juvenile justice system is the method of diagnosing youth and recommending appropriate dispositions. He notes that the treatment options available for the diagnostician to select determine the actual diagnosis of the youth, rather than the other way around.

> The theory-diagnosis-treatment flow runs backward. The diagnostician looks first to the means available for handling the client, then labels the client, and finally justifies the label with psychiatric or sociological theory. Diagnosis virtually never determines treatment; treatment dictates diagnosis.[151]

Perhaps giving in to the "law and order" rhetoric of the past two decades, the juvenile courts have begun to rely increasingly on one of the most extreme dispositions within the juvenile justice system—certifying a youth as an adult. It is as if they have said: "We give up! We have done everything we can think of to help you." Juveniles waived to adult court are, in effect, disposable children—and they are disproportionately African American.

GIVING UP ON DELINQUENT YOUTH: TRANSFER TO ADULT COURT

One of the most talked about issues in juvenile justice in recent years is that of treating children as adults when certain crimes are committed. Moving the cases of juveniles to adult court is technically known as *waiver* or *certification*. If a juvenile court believes that an offender is too dangerous or not amenable to treatment, the court transfers (i.e., waives) its jurisdiction to the adult system by, legally speaking, making the youth an adult.[152]

Federal authorities have three options if a juvenile violates federal criminal law: (1) referral of juvenile to state authorities, (2) federal delinquency proceedings,

(3) petition the federal court to transfer the juvenile for trial as an adult. In 1938, the Federal Juvenile Delinquency Act (FJDA) separated juveniles from adults for federal crimes. The FJDA provided a procedural device for juveniles (under age 18 when the crime was committed and under 21 when the case was tried) to be adjudicated outside of adult criminal courts. State juvenile proceedings remained the preferred alternative, but the attorney general could decide to waive the case. In 1974 Congress limited the discretion of the attorney general to petitioning the federal juvenile court for transfer.[153]

Every state has some provisions for transferring offenders to adult courts. While state laws differ, most states specify a minimum age, a particular type or level of offense, a history of previous serious delinquency, or a combination of these three criteria. The crime must be serious, aggressive, and premeditated. The sophistication and maturity of juveniles are evaluated using external factors, such as emotional attitude and the juvenile's record and history. The evaluation must conclude that if the juvenile is not treated and punished as an adult, the public will not be protected from future victimizations.

States establish the ages of offenders for cases to be adjudicated in juvenile courts; in 46 states, the maximum age of juvenile court jurisdiction is 17.[154] In 4 states (Georgia, Michigan, Texas, and Wisconsin), the maximum age is 16. All states also have laws that allow juveniles younger than the upper age limits to be tried as adults. Most states have more than one mechanism for transferring cases to criminal court. There are three types of transfer laws. Concurrent jurisdiction laws allow prosecutors the discretion to file a case in juvenile or criminal court (direct file statutes). Statutory exclusion laws remove certain offenses from the jurisdiction of juvenile courts and grant criminal courts jurisdiction over those cases. Judicial waiver laws authorize or require juvenile court judges to remove certain youths from juvenile court jurisdiction and to try them as adults in criminal court.[155]

Judicial waiver includes three categories: discretionary, presumptive, and mandatory. In 2016, 46 states had discretionary waiver provisions, meaning juvenile court judges decide whether individual juveniles will be prosecuted in adult criminal court.[156] Twelve states had presumptive waiver laws, which designate specific crimes for which waiver to criminal court is presumed to be appropriate. Juveniles who meet the age, offense, or other statutory criteria will be transferred to criminal court unless they can make an adequate argument against transfer. Thirteen states had mandatory waiver provisions for specific offenses. Although the proceedings begin in juvenile court, the only role for the court is to confirm that the case meets statutory requirements for mandatory waiver. Thirty-five states had laws that specified juveniles convicted as adults must be prosecuted in criminal court for any subsequent offenses ("once an adult, always an adult").

Fourteen states have *blended sentencing laws*. Juvenile court judges can "order both a juvenile disposition and an adult criminal sentence. The adult sentence is suspended on the condition that the juvenile offender successfully completes the terms of the juvenile disposition and refrains from committing any new offenses."[157] It is like a "conditional" sentence, depending upon the behavior of the youth during the time the sentence is suspended.

In 2016, less than 1% of delinquency cases were waived—3,500 of 850,500 cases. In 1985 5,800 cases were waived; the peak number of cases waived was 12,700 in 1994.[158] The decline in cases waived after 1994 has been affected by the large increase in the number of states that passed statutory exclusion or direct file laws that automatically remove some offenders from juvenile court jurisdiction.[159] Person offenses accounted for the most cases waived (1,800) followed by property offenses (1,100), drug offenses (300), and public order offenses (300). There were 3,100 waived cases involving males and 300 involving females. There were 1,100 waived cases involving whites; 1,800 waived cases involving blacks; and 400 waived cases involving Hispanics.

Direct file legislation has come under severe criticism. The power given to prosecutors under direct file is problematic. Many prosecutors seek the most severe punishment without consideration for the circumstances in the case.[160] Twelve states (AK, AZ, CO, FL, GA, LA, MI, MT, NE, OK, VA, WY) allow direct file.[161] Florida charges more juveniles as adults than any other state—and 60% of the offenses are nonviolent felonies; 2.7% of the charges are for murder.[162] From 2006 to 2011, more than 15,600 youths were processed in the adult criminal court system for violent and nonviolent offenses; since that time yearly direct files have declined, totaling 1,592 in 2015.[163] A majority of states do not allow direct file, and some states discontinued the practice. Vermont ended direct file in 2017.

As discussed in chapter 1, California voters passed Proposition 57 on November 8, 2016 that reversed a proposition passed in 2000 that allowed prosecutors to direct file. An analysis prior to the vote had found that prosecutors made direct file decisions within 48 hours without using the statutory parameters that guide juvenile court judges when considering a waiver. There were wide disparities across California's counties. Race rather than severity of the alleged offense determined the likelihood of adult prosecution.[164] Black and Latino youth constituted less than 60% of California's population ages 14–17, but they were 90% of youth subjected to direct file prosecutions, and the gap increased substantially from 2003 to 2015. In 2003, black juveniles were 4.5 times more likely to experience direct file than whites—the disparity increased to 10.8 times more likely in 2015. Hispanic youth were 2.4 times more likely than white youth in 2003 and 3.4 times in 2015. In some counties the disparities were even larger.

There is no federal law requiring the collection of data on all transfer mechanisms that place youth in adult courts.[165] Statutory exclusion and prosecutorial direct file are more widely used than waiver. While the data on waiver are collected, there is no similar requirement for the other two mechanisms. In 2015, at least 75,900 juveniles under the age of 18 were prosecuted as adults—an estimated 66,700 because of statutory exclusion. Most are youth of color.

What is the result of waiving a youth to the adult system? There is a high risk of physical and sexual abuse of juveniles confined in adult facilities—five times higher than for youth in juvenile facilities.[166] The abuse from guards and other inmates can have devastating consequences for the juvenile victim, leading to depression, post-traumatic stress disorder, despair, persistent distrust, and withdrawal. Suicide rates are dramatically higher for juveniles in adult facilities than for those in juvenile facilities. Juveniles are also particularly vulnerable to criminal socialization. Juveniles in the adult system do not have the opportunity to acquire skills critical to their success as adults. Instead, they are confined in an environment in which adult criminals become their teachers.[167] Lack of access to critical services, education, programming, and treatment in adult facilities negatively affects the development of juveniles.

The rationale for transferring juveniles to the adult system has been public safety. Research shows the opposite results, with juveniles placed in the adult system 34 times more likely to recidivate.[168] About 80% of youth convicted as adults will be released before they turn 21; 95% will be released by the time they are 25.

Adults receive different sentences for offenses that cause the same harm because defendants differ in culpability. Such differences are even more pronounced during adolescence when decision-making abilities are undeveloped. Juveniles are impulsive, lack future orientation, and are susceptible to negative peer pressure. Brain imaging technology reveals that the teenage brain undergoes dramatic changes during adolescence. These changes affect the ability of teens to reason, to delay gratification, and to weigh the consequences of their decisions.[169]

Laurence Steinberg and Elizabeth Scott, leading scholars in law and adolescent development, have concluded that people younger than 15 should never be tried as adults.[170] They also note that trying youths in juvenile court is not the equivalent of absolving them of responsibility and that age as a mitigating factor is not the equivalent of an excuse. Youths should be punished for their crimes, but the punishment should be developmentally appropriate. Steinberg advises that juveniles are more likely to be harmed by exposure to trauma—and that they are more likely to benefit from rehabilitation. Juveniles confined in adult facilities are more likely to reoffend than counterparts released from facilities designed for adolescents.[171]

Studies routinely show that the juvenile justice system protects the public better than the criminal justice system. Jeffrey Fagan concludes that treating juveniles as adult criminals is not an effective means of crime control.[172] Exposure to harsh and toxic forms of punishment has the reverse effect of increasing criminal activity. Adolescent offenders transferred to criminal court have higher rates of re-offending than do those retained in juvenile court. "Rarely do social scientists or policy analysts report such consistency and agreement under such widely varying sampling, measurement, and analytic conditions."[173]

Another study found that transferring juveniles to adult court *does not result in a reduction of crime and may even contribute to at least a short-term increase in crime*.[174] Juveniles have reported that they attempt to fit into the inmate culture to survive. Many accept violence as a routine part of life and become more violent themselves to mask their vulnerability.

A body of evidence suggests that incarcerating juveniles in adult correctional facilities not only places the juveniles in a demonstrably more hazardous living situation but also does not fulfill commonly accepted purposes of punishment. Research indicates that incarcerating juveniles with adults, an often more experienced criminal population, may neither deter juveniles from future criminal activity nor improve public safety.[175]

SUMMARY

The processing of cases through the various stages of the juvenile justice system begins with juvenile laws, which address both criminal and misdemeanor behavior—including behavior that would not be unlawful for an adult (status offenses). More than 60 years elapsed before the Supreme Court took a serious look at the possible violation of rights for juveniles processed through the system. Despite the rulings in *Kent, Gault, Winship, McKeiver, Breed, Thompson, Roper, Graham, Miller,* and *Montgomery*, juvenile rights are still restricted.

Juvenile (or family) courts are found in most large and medium cities, with some consisting of rather elaborate and very bureaucratic organizations. Thousands of cases are processed through these courts every year, usually referred by the police, who have a great deal of discretion as to what courses of action to take. Class and race are significant predictors in how juveniles are processed. The case study of the "Saints and Roughnecks" illustrates the cultural biases.

Intake screening is the first step into the court system. At this point, a decision with important consequences is made: the decision to detain. Race again plays a key role. Minorities are far more likely to be detained, no matter the offense. This in turn affects other stages within the court process, such as adjudication and the final disposition. It was noted that at each stage of the process there are several dispositional options. The final disposition following adjudication may involve commitment to a juvenile institution. As noted, minorities receive the harshest dispositions.

The juvenile court, in spite of the promises of a century ago, has not had a very positive record of achievement. In fact, dissatisfaction with the court (accusations of being too lenient leading the way) has resulted in a movement to certify youths as adults. The results have been far from promising.

Notes

1. Melissa Sickmund, Anthony Sladky, and W. Kang, "Easy Access to Juvenile Court Statistics: 1985–2016," National Center for Juvenile Justice, 2018, https://ojjdp.gov/ojstatbb/ezajcs/

2. Anne Teigen, "Juvenile Age of Jurisdiction and Transfer to Adult Court Laws," National Conference of State Legislators, April 17, 2017, http://www.ncsl.org/research/civil-and-criminal-justice/juvenile-age-of-jurisdiction-and-transfer-to-adult-court-laws.aspx

3. *Kent v. United States* (383 US 541, 1966).

4. Ibid.

5. *In re Gault* (387 US 1, 1967).

6. Ibid.

7. Andrew Treaster, "Juveniles in Kansas Have a Constitutional Right to a Jury Trial. Now What? Making Sense of *In re L.M.*" *Kansas Law Review*, 2009, 57(5): 1275–1303.

8. *In re Gault* quoted in Juvenile Justice Bulletin, "Juvenile Justice: A Century of Change," December 1999, NCJ 178995, 4.

9. *In re Winship* (397 US 358, 1970).

10. Ibid.

11. *McKeiver v. Pennsylvania* (403 US 528, 1971). Two other cases were heard at the same time: *In re Terry* (438 Pa., 339, 265A.2d 350, 1970) and *In re Barbara Burris* (275 N.C. 517, 169 Sk. E. 2d 879, 1969k). The major decision for all three cases was issued in *McKeiver.*

12. Juvenile Justice Bulletin, "Juvenile Justice: A Century of Change."

13. National Juvenile Defender Center, "Juvenile right to Jury Trial Chart," July 17, 2014, http://njdc.info/wp-content/uploads/2017/03/Right-to-Jury-Trial-Chart-7-18-14.pdf

14. Barry C. Feld, *The Evolution of the Juvenile Court: Race, Politics, and the Criminalizing of Juvenile Justice* (New York: NYU Press, 2017).

15. *Breed v. Jones* (421 US 519, 1975).

16. Juvenile Justice Bulletin, "Juvenile Justice: A Century of Change."

17. J. Marshall Dissenting Opinion in *Schall v. Martin* (467 US 253, 1984).

18. Ibid.

19. Robert E. Shepherd, Jr., "*In re Gault* at 40: Still Seeking the Promise," *Criminal Justice*, 2007, 22(3).

20. Barry Feld, "Competence and Culpability: Delinquents in Juvenile Courts, Youths in Criminal Courts," *Minnesota Law Review*, 2017, 102: 473–576.

21. Ibid., 526.

22. Barry Feld and Shelly Schaefer, "The Right to Counsel in Juvenile Court: The Conundrum of Attorneys as an Aggravating Factor at Disposition," *Justice Quarterly*, 2010, 27(5): 714–741.

23. *White v. Reid*, 125 F. Supp. 647, D.D.C., 1954.

24. 346 F. Supp. 1354 D.R.I., 1972. An identical conclusion was rendered in *Nelson v. Heyne* concerning an Indiana training school (355 F. Supp. 451 N.D. Ind. 1973). Finally, in *Morales v. Turman* (364 F. Supp. 166 E.D. Tex. 1973) the U. S. District Court for the Eastern District of Texas made this right more specific saying a number of criteria had to be followed to insure that youths received proper treatment, such as establishing certain minimal standards.

25. Department of Justice, "Rights of Juveniles," September 14, 2017.

26. Victor L. Streib, "The Juvenile Death Penalty Today: Death Sentences and Executions for Juvenile Crimes, January 1, 1973–February 28, 2005," Issue #77, October 7, 2005, 4.

27 Ibid., table 1.

28 Amnesty International, On the Wrong Side of History: Children and the Death Penalty in the USA, October 1998, 7.

29 U.S. Reservations, Declarations, and Understandings, International Covenant on Civil and Political Rights, 138 *Congressional Record* S4781-01, April 2, 1992.

30 Amnesty International, *On the Wrong Side of History.*

31 *Thompson v. Oklahoma*, 487 US 815 (1988).

32 Ibid.

33 Stanford v. Kentucky, 492 US 361 (1989).

34 The Death Penalty Information Center provides complete coverage of this case.

35 *Atkins v. Virginia*, 536 US 304, 318, 122 S. Ct. 2242, 2250 (2002).

36 Amici curiae in support of respondent, filed with the Supreme Court in *Roper v. Simmons*, 2–3, https://www.aacap.org/App_Themes/AACAP/docs/Advocacy/amicus_curiae/Roper_v_Simmons.pdf

37 *Roper v. Simmons*, 543 US 551 (2005).

38 Ibid.

39 Josh Rovner, "Juvenile Life without Parole: An Overview," The Sentencing Project, October 2018.

40 *Graham v. Florida*, 560 US 48 (2010).

41 Equal Justice Initiative, *Graham v. Florida*, Montgomery, AL: Author, 2017. Retrieved from

42 Tessa Duvall, Jacksonville Man's Case Led to New Sentences for Juvenile Lifers—But He's Still Behind Bars, *The Florida Times-Union*, March 4, 2017.

43 Equal Justice Initiative, *Graham v. Florida.*

44 Jeffrey Toobin, "The Legacy of Lynching, On Death Row," *The New Yorker*, August 22, 2016.

45 Miller v. Alabama, 567 US_ (2012), 31.

46 Rovner, "Juvenile Life without Parole."

47 Ibid.

48 Summer L. Davidson, "The Relationship between Childhood Conduct Disorder and Antisocial Personality in Adulthood: An Argument in Favor of Mandatory Life Sentences without Parole for Juvenile Homicide Offenders." *Law & Psychology Review*, 2015, 39: 239–252.

49 Heng Choon Chan and Wing Hong Chui, "Psychological Correlates of Violent and Nonviolent Hong Kong Juvenile Probationers," *Behavioral Science and Law*, 2012, 30(2): 103–120;Anne Vries and Marieke Liem, "Recidivism of Juvenile Homicide Offenders." *Behavioral Science and Law*, 2011, 29(4): 483–498; Raymond Paternoster, "Absolute and Restrictive Deterrence in a Panel of Youth: Explaining the Onset, Persistence/Desistence, and Frequency of Delinquent Offending," *Social Problems*, 1989, 36(3): 289–309; David Farrington, "Early Precursors of Frequent Offending," in J. Q. Wilson and G. C. Loury (Eds.) *Families, Schools, and Delinquency Prevention*, 1987, 27–50; Rolf Loeber and Thomas Dishion, "Early Predictors of Male Delinquency: A Review," *Psychological Bulletin*, 1983, 94(1): 68–99.

50 Personal communication with the author, October 26, 2016.

51 Rovner, "Juvenile Life without Parole."

52 Sarah Hockenberry and Charles Puzzanchera, "Juvenile Court Statistics 2016," Pittsburgh, PA: National Center for Juvenile Justice, August 2018, 31.

53 Thomas Monahan, "Police Dispositions of Juvenile Offenders." *Phylon*, 1970, 31(2): 129–141.

54 Melissa Sickmund and Charles Puzzanchera, *Juvenile Offenders and Victims: 2014 National Report*, Pittsburgh, PA: National Center for Juvenile Justice, December 2014.

55 Libby Nelson and Dara Lind. "The School to Prison Pipeline, Explained," Washington, DC: Justice Policy Institute, February 24, 2015.

56 Ronald Claus, Sarah Vidal, and Michele Harmon, "Racial and Ethnic Disparities in the Police Handling of Juvenile Arrests, Washington, DC: National Criminal Justice Reference Service, 2017.

57 Meda Chesney-Lind and Randall G. Shelden, *Girls, Delinquency, and Juvenile Justice*, 4th ed. (Malden, MA: Wiley-Blackwell, 2014).

58 Joshua Rovner, "Racial Disparities in Youth Commitments and Arrests," Washington, DC: Sentencing Project, April, 2016.

59 Research on this issue goes back several decades. See ,for instance: Irving Piliavin and Scott Briar, "Police Encounters with Juveniles," *American Journal of Sociology*, 1964, 70 (2): 206–14; Roger Dunham and Geoffrey Alpert, "Officer and Suspect Demeanor: A Qualitative Analysis of Change." *Police Quarterly*, 2009, 12(1): 6–21; David Klinger, "Demeanor or Crime? Why 'Hostile' Citizens are More Likely to be Arrested," *Criminology*, 1994, 32(3): 475–493; Richard Lundman, "Demeanor and Arrest: Additional Evidence from Previously Unpublished Data," *Journal of Research on Crime and Delinquency*, 1996, 33: 306–323; Robert Worden and Robin Shepard, "Demeanor, Crime and Police Behavior: A Reexamination of the Police Services Study Data." *Criminology*, 1996, 34(1): 61–82; Lyn Hinds, "Youth, Police Legitimacy, and Informal Contact," Journal of Police and Criminal Psychology, 2009, 24(1), 10–21; Anne Nordberg, Marcus Crawford, Regina Praetorius, and Schnavia Hatcher, "Exploring Minority Youths' Police Encounters: A Qualitative Interpretive Meta-synthesis," *Child and Adolescent Social Work Journal*, 2016, 33(2): 137–149.

60 Feld, *The Evolution of the Juvenile Court*; Hayley Cleary and Todd Warner, "Police Training in Interviewing and Interrogation Methods: A Comparison of Techniques Used with Adults and Juvenile Suspects," *Law and Human Behavior*, 2016, 40(3): 270–284; Emily Cabanissa, James Frabutt, Mary Kendricka, and Margaret Arbuckle, "Reducing Disproportionate Minority Contact in the Juvenile Justice System: Promising Practices," *Aggression and Violent Behavior*, 2007, 12(4): 393–401.

61 Development Services Group, Inc., "Interactions between Youth and Law Enforcement," literature review, Washington, DC: Office of Juvenile Justice and Delinquency Prevention, 2018; Ronald Weitzer, Steven Tuch, and Wesley Skogan,. "Police–Community Relations in a Majority-Black City," *Journal of Research in Crime and Delinquency*, 2008, 45(4): 398–428; Gordon Bazemore and Scott Senjo, "Police Encounters with Juveniles Revisited: An Exploratory Study of Themes and Styles in Community Policing." *Policing: An International Journal of Police Strategy and Management*, 1997, 20(1): 60–82; see also Pope, C. and W. Feyerherm. (1990). "Minority Status and Juvenile Justice Processing: An Assessment of the Research Literature," (Parts I and II). *Criminal Justice Abstracts* 22 (2, 3).

62 Robert J. Durán, "Legitimated Oppression: Inner-City Mexican American Experiences with Police Gang Enforcement," *Journal of Contemporary Ethnography*, 2008, 38(2): 143–168; Arthur Lurigio, Jamie Flexon, and Richard Greenleaf, "Antecedents to Gang Membership: Attachments, Beliefs, and Street Encounters with the Police," *Journal of Gang Research*, 2008, 15: 15–33; Rod Brunson, "Police Don't Like Black People": African-American Young Men's Accumulated Police Experiences, Criminology and Public Policy, 2007, 6(1), 71–101.

63 Tom Tyler, Jeffrey Fagan, and Amanda Geller, "Street Stops and Police Legitimacy: Teachable Moments in Young Urban Men's Legal Socialization," *Journal of Empirical Legal Studies*, 2014, 11(4): 751–785.

64 Ibid.

65 Kimberly Kahn and Karin Martin, "Policing and Race: Disparate Treatment, Perceptions, and Policy Responses," *Social Issues and Policy Review*, 2016, 10(1): 82–121.

66 http://mappingpoliceviolence.org/

67 *The Washington Post*, Fatal Force 2018, https://www.washingtonpost.com/graphics/2018/national/police-shootings-2018/?noredirect=on&utm_term=.6143e7495e136

68 James Baldwin *The Fire Next Time* (New York: Vintage, 1992; originally published in 1963).

69 Bob Herbert, "The Fire This Time," HuffPost, October 20, 2014. Retrieved from: http://www.huffingtonpost.com/bob-herbert/the-fire-this-time_b_5694941.html

70 Barry Feld, *The Evolution of the Juvenile Court*.

71 Ibid., 228.

72 Ronald Weitzer, "American Policing Under Fire: Misconduct and Reform," *Social Science and Public Policy*, 2015, 52: 475–480, 476.

73 This term seems to be a catchall of several different offenses. Appendix B in "Juvenile Court Statistics 2016" defines obstruction of justice as: "intentionally obstructing court or law enforcement efforts in the administration of justice, acting in a way calculated to lessen the authority or dignity of the court, failing to obey the lawful order of a court, escaping from confinement, and violating probation or parole. This term includes contempt, perjury, bribery of witnesses, failure to report a crime, and nonviolent resistance of arrest."

74 Hockenberry and Puzzanchera, "Juvenile Court Statistics 2016."

75 W. Haywood Burns Institute, "Non-Judicial Drivers into the Juvenile Justice System for Youth of Color, San Francisco: Author, 2012, pp. 2–3.

76 Sarah Vidal, Dana Prince, Christian Connell, Colleen Caron, Joy Kaufman, and Jacob Tebes, "Maltreatment, Family Environment, and Social Risk Factors: Determinants of the Child Welfare to Juvenile Justice Transition among Maltreated Children and Adolescents," *Child Abuse Neglect*, 2017, 63: 7–18.

77 Joshua Rovner, "Disproportionate Minority Contact in the Juvenile Justice System," Washington, DC: The Sentencing Project, May 2014.

78 Development Services Group, "Disproportionate Minority Contact," Washington, DC: Office of Juvenile Justice and Delinquency Prevention, 2014.

79 Ibid.

80 National Research Council. Reforming Juvenile Justice: A Developmental Approach. (Washington, DC: The National Academies Press, 2013), 239.

81 Rovner, "Disproportionate Minority Contact in the Juvenile Justice System," 1.

82 Development Services Group, "Status Offenders," literature review, Washington, DC: Office of Juvenile Justice and Delinquency Prevention, 2015.

83 Jaya Davis and Jon Sorensen, "Disproportionate Minority Confinement of Juveniles: A National Examination of Black-White Disparity in Placements," *Crime & Delinquency*, 2010, 56(3), doi:10.1177/0011128709359653

84 Development Services Group, "Disproportionate Minority Contac."

85 Andrea Coleman, "A Disproportionate Minority Contact (DMC) Chronology: 1988 to Date," Washington, DC: Office of Juvenile Justice and Delinquency Prevention, 2010.

86 OJJDP Statistical Briefing Book. Online, https://www.ojjdp.gov/ojstatbb/special_topics/qa11601.asp?qaDate=2016, August 22, 2018.

87 OJJDP Statistical Briefing Book. Online, https://www.ojjdp.gov/ojstatbb/special_topics/ qa11803.asp?qaDate=2015, August 07, 2017.

88 Rovner, "Racial Disparities in Youth Commitments and Arrests."

89 Melissa Sickmund, W. Kang, and Charles Puzzanchera, "Easy Access to the Census of Juveniles in Residential Placement," National Center for Juvenile Justice, 2017, http:// www.ojjdp.gov/ojstatbb/ezacjrp/

90 Hockenberry and Puzzanchera, "Juvenile Court Statistics 2016."

91 Ojmarrh Mitchell and Michael Caudy, "Examining Racial Disparities in Drug Arrests," *Justice Quarterly*, 2013, 32(2): 1–26.

92 Jennifer Peck and Wesley Jennings, "A Critical Examination of 'Being Black' in the Juvenile Justice System." *Law and Human Behavior*, 2016, 40(3): 219–232.

93 William Chambliss *Power, Politics, and Crime* (New York: Routledge, 2018); David Cole *No Equal Justice: Race and Class in the American Criminal Justice System* (New York: The New Press, 1999).

94 Kahn and Martin, "Policing and Race," 84–85.

95 Ibid., 88; see also Phillip Goff and Kimberly Kahn, Racial Bias in Policing: Why We Know Less Than We Should," *Social Issues and Policy Review*, 2012, 6(1): 177–210.

96 Ibid.

97 Barry Feld, "My Life in Crime: An Intellectual History of the Juvenile Court," *Nevada Law Journal*, 2017, 17(3): 299–329, 301.

98 Hockenberry and Puzzanchera, "Juvenile Court Statistics 2016.

99 Marvin E. Wolfgang, Robert M. Figlio, and Thorsten Sellin, *Delinquency in the Birth Cohort.* (Chicago: University of Chicago Press, 1972).

100 Interested readers should start with Jeffrey H. Reiman and Paul Leighton, *The Rich Get Richer and the Poor Get Prison*, 11th ed. (New York: Routledge, 2017). Looking at case files in just about any juvenile court—from one end of the country to the next—will reveal that kids from privileged environments, with intact families and many resources available, will be far more likely to avoid a court appearance in the first place, since their cases will be settled at intake. The senior author has personally examined in detail more than 1,000 such cases in Las Vegas. Sitting in the waiting areas just outside courtrooms, he has observed that the only people dressed in clothing that would indicate a higher social class are court probation officers, judges, and lawyers.

101 Robert Sampson, "Effects of Socioeconomic Context on Official Reaction to Juvenile Delinquency." *American Sociological Review*, 1986, 51(6): 876–885.

102 Donna Bishop, "The Role of Race and Ethnicity in Juvenile Justice Processing." In Darnell Hawkins and Kimberly Kempf-Leonard (Eds.). *Our Children, Their Children: Confronting Racial and Ethnic Differences in American Juvenile Justice* (Chicago: University of Chicago Press, 2005); Stephen Brown, "The Class-Delinquency Hypothesis and Juvenile Justice System Bias," *Sociological Inquiry*, 1985, 55(2): 212–223.

103 Nancy Rodriquez, "Concentrated Disadvantage and the Incarceration of Youth: Examining How Context Affects Juvenile Justice." *Journal of Research in Crime and Delinquency*, 2013, 50(2): 189–215. See also: Michael Leiber, Jennifer Peck, and Nancy Rodriguez, "Minority Threat and Juvenile Court Outcomes," *Crime & Delinquency*, 2013, 62(1): 54–80.

104 William Chambliss, "The Saints and the Roughnecks," in *Criminal Law in Action*, ed. William Chambliss. (New York: John Wiley, 1975).

105 Ibid., 78.

106 Shaun Thomas, Stacy Moak, and Jeffery Walker, "The Contingent Effect of Race in Juvenile Court Detention Decisions: The Role of Racial and Symbolic Threat." *Race and Justice*, 2012, 3(3): 239–265.

107 David Kirk and Robert Sampson, "Juvenile Arrest and Collateral Educational Damage in the Transition to Adulthood," *Sociology of Education*, 2012, 86(1): 36–62, 54.

108 For good summaries of this literature see: Dennis Gilbert, *The American Class Structure*, 10th ed. (Thousand Oaks, CA: Sage, 2018); Macleod, J. (2008). *Ain't No Makin' It: Aspirations and Attainment in a Low-Income Neighborhood*, 3rd ed. (Denver, CO: Westview Press, 2009); Martin Marger, *Social Inequality: Patterns and Processes*, 6th ed. (New York: McGraw-Hill, 2014); Annette Lareau, *Unequal Childhoods: Class, Race, and Family Life*, 2nd ed. (Berkeley: University of California Press, 2011).

109 Hockenberry and Puzzanchera, "Juvenile Court Statistics 2016."

110 Kelly Hannah-Moffat, "Needle in a Haystack: Logical Parameters of Treatment Based on Actuarial Risk-Needs Assessment," Criminology & Public Policy, 2015, 14(1): 113–120.

111 Jeffrey Lin, Joel Miller, and Mayumi Fukushim, "Juvenile Probation Officers' Disposition Recommendations: Predictive Factors and Their Alignment with Predictors of Recidivism," *Journal of Crime and Justice*, 2008, 31(1): 1–34.

112 Joel Miller and Carrie Maloney, "Practitioner Compliance With Risk/Needs Assessment Tools: A Theoretical and Empirical Assessment," *Criminal Justice and Behavior*, 2013, 40(7): 716–736.

113 Christina Campbell, Eyitayo Onifade, Ashlee Barnes, Jodi Peterson, Valerie Anderson, William Davidson, and Derrick Gordon, "Screening Offenders: The Exploration of a Youth Level of Service/Case Management Inventory," Journal of Offender Rehabilitation, 2014, 53(1): 19–34; Kristin Bechtel, Christopher Lowenkamp, and Edward Latessa, "Assessing the Risk of Re-offending for Juvenile Offenders Using the Youth-Level of Service/Case Management Inventory," *Journal of Offender Rehabilitation*, 2008, 45: 85–108.

114 Charles Puzzanchera and Sarah Hockenberry, "Characteristics of Delinquency Cases Handled in Juvenile Court in 2016," National Center for Juvenile Justice, October 2018.

115 Allen Beck and Ramona Rantala, "Sexual Victimization Reported by Juvenile Correctional Authorities, 2007–2012," Washington, DC: Bureau of Justice Statistics, NCJ 249145, January 2016.

116 President's Commission on Law and Administration of Justice, *Task Force Report: Juvenile Delinquency and Youth Crime*. (Washington, DC: U.S. Government Printing Office, 1967).

117 Anthony Petrosino, Carolyn Turpin-Petrosino, and Sarah Guckenburg, *Formal System Processing of Juveniles: Effects on Delinquency*, Campbell Systematic Reviews, 2010, DOI: 10.4073/csf.2010.1

118 Don Gibbons and Marvin Krohn, *Delinquent Behavior*, 5th ed. (Englewood Cliffs, NJ: Prentice-Hall, 1991), 313.

119 Global Youth Justice, Statistics, 2018. Retrieved from

120 Katie Cotter and Caroline Evans, "A Systematic Review of Teen Court Evaluation Studies: A Focus on Evaluation Design Characteristics and Program Components, *Adolescent Research Review*, 2017, DOI 10.1007/s40894-017-0056-1.

121 The author has personally observed many such programs where he lives and teaches (Las Vegas) and most are positively promoted by those who operate them, but advocates can rarely offer any data. Many persist because they "make sense" or someone has a "gut feeling" that it works. This assessment is very common. Samuel Walker makes the point that many programs are based more upon "faith" than evidence. Samuel Walker, *Sense and Nonsense About Crime and Drugs*, 8th ed. (Stamford, CT: Cengage Learning, 2015).

122 Stephanie Duriez, Carrie Sullivan, Christopher Sullivan, Sarah Manchak, and Edward Latessa, "Mentoring Best Practices Research: Effectiveness of Juvenile Mentoring Programs on Recidivism, National Criminal Justice Reference Service, November 2017, document 251378.

123 Daniel Mears, Joshua Kuch, Andrea Lindsey, Sonja Siennick, George Pesta, Mark Greenwald, and Thomas Blomberg, "Juvenile Court and Contemporary Diversion: Helpful, Harmful, or Both?" Criminology & Public Policy, 2016, 15(3): 953–981.

124 Jeffrey Butts, "Critical Diversion: Juvenile Court and Diversion," *Criminology & Public Policy*, 2016, 15(3): 983–989

125 Butts, "Critical Diversion," 988.

126 Todd Clear, Michael Reisig, and George Cole, *American Corrections*, 12th ed. (Boston, MA: Cengage Learning, 2019).

127 Randall G. Shelden, William B. Brown, Karen S. Miller, and Randal B. Fritzler, *Crime and Criminal Justice in American Society*, 2nd ed. (Long Grove, IL: Waveland Press, 2016).

128 Anthony Giddens, *Capitalism and Modern Social Theory* (London: Cambridge University Press, 1971), 178–84.

129 I found this to be the case in my study of the early years of the juvenile court in Memphis. Randall Shelden, "Rescued from Evil: Origins of Juvenile Justice in Memphis, Tennessee, 1900–1917," Ph.D. dissertation, Southern Illinois University, Carbondale, 1976.

130 David Murphy and Faith Lutze, "Police-Probation Partnerships: Professional Identity and the Sharing of Coercive Power," *Journal of Criminal Justice*, 2009, 37(1): 65–76.

131 Miller, *Search and Destroy*, 131. Barry Nidorf was chief of probation for Los Angeles County from 1984 to 1997. The department was the largest in the nation with 4,000 employees supervising 16,000 juveniles and 80,000 adults. In an interview in 1984, he told a reporter: "Probation should be a form of punishment. If we can help [offenders] along the way, fine. But primarily the client has to be the community rather than the probationer." Nidorf introduced the first juvenile boot camp in the nation in 1991. Mary Rourke, "Barry J. Nidorf: Ex-Chief of L. A. County Probation Department," *Los Angeles Times*, December 17, 2004.

132 Gayle Rhineberger-Dunn and Kristin Mack, "To Carry or Not to Carry: Predictors of Support for Allowing Probation/Parole Officers to Carry Firearms," *Corrections*, 2018, 3(2): 92–104.

133 Thomas Roscoe, David Duffee, Craig Rivera, and Tony Smith, "Arming Probation Officers: Correlates of the Decision to Arm at the Departmental Level, *Criminal Justice Studies*, 2007, 20(1): 43–63.

134 Karen de Sá, "Santa Clara County Seeks to Arm Some Probation Officers," *The Mercury News*, January 29, 2010, https://www.mercurynews.com/2010/01/29/santa-clara-county-seeks-to-arm-some-probation-officers/

135 Felisa Cardona, "Colorado Probation under the Gun after Rash of Felonies," *Denver Post*, May 4, 2011, http://www.denverpost.com/2011/03/26/colorado-probation-under-the-gun-after-rash-of-felonies/

136 Bureau of Labor Statistics, 2016 Census of Fatal Occupational Injuries; Industry by Event or Exposure, 2016, https://www.bls.gov/iif/oshcfoi1.htm

137 Robert Schwartz, "A 21st Century Developmentally Appropriate Juvenile Probation Approach," Juvenile Family Court, 2018, 69(1): 41–54.

138 Sickmund et al., "Easy Access to Juvenile Court Statistics: 1985–2016"; Sarah Livesay, "Juvenile Delinquency Probation Caseload, 2009," Office of Juvenile Justice and Delinquency Prevention, October 2012.

139 Molly Hennessy-Fiske and Richard Winton, "L.A. County Probation Workers Elude Punishment for Misdeeds," *Los Angeles Times*, March 3, 2010; investigators took so long that the statute of limitations has expired and most will escape any kind of sanctions. Among other violations, the investigation found that 31 probation officers committed such acts as theft and sexual assault. Office of Independent Review, County of Los Angeles,

"Evaluation and Recommendations Concerning Internal Investigations at the Los Angeles County Probation Department," June 2, 2010.

140   Lynn Greenwood, "An Exploratory Study of Juvenile Probation Officer Job Stress and Stress-Related Outcomes," Dissertation, Texas State University, December 2016.

141   Michelle Salyers, Brittany Hood, Katherine Schwartz, Andrew Alexander, and Matthew Aalsma, "The Experience, Impact, and Management of Professional Burnout among Probation Officers in Juvenile Justice Settings," *Journal of Offender Rehabilitation* 2015, 54(3): 175–193.

142   Ibid, 17–18.

143   Laura White, Matthew Aalsma, Evan Holloway, Erin Adams, Michelle Salyers, "Job-Related Burnout among Juvenile Probation Officers, Psychological Services, 2015, 12(3), 291–302.

144   Jessica Bouchard and Jennifer Wong, "Examining the Effects of Intensive Supervision and Aftercare Programs for At-Risk Youth: A Systematic Review and Meta-Analysis, 2017, *International Journal of Offender Therapy and Comparative Criminology*, 62(6): 1509–1534.

145   Jordan Hyatt and Geoffrey Barnes, "An Experimental Evaluation of the Impact of Intensive Supervision on the Recidivism of High-Risk Probationers," *Crime and Delinquency*, 2014, 63(1): 3–38.

146   Leah Mack, "Electronic Monitoring Hurts Kids and Their Communities," Juvenile Justice Information Exchange, October 24, 2018.

147   Kate Weisburd, "Monitoring Youth: The Collision of Rights and Rehabilitation," *Iowa Law Review*, 2015, 101: 297–341, 324.

148   George Palermo, "Electronic Monitoring in the Criminal Justice System: Less Recidivism?" *International Journal of Offender Therapy and Comparative Criminology*, 2015, 59(9): 911–912.

149   Weisburd, "Monitoring Youth."

150   Ibid., 305.

151   Jerome Miller, *Last One Over the Wall: The Massachusetts Experiment in Closing Reform Schools*, 2nd ed. (Columbus: Ohio State University Press, 1998), 232.

152   Rarely discussed is the logical extension of declaring a minor an adult. If a 15-year-old youth is certified as an adult, does that mean he or she can vote, drop out of school, buy cigarettes, purchase alcohol, leave home, or do anything an adult can do? In actual fact they cannot, even if they are placed on probation by the adult court and are still under 18.

153   Charles Doyle, "Juvenile Delinquents and Federal Criminal Law: The Federal Juvenile Delinquency Act and Related Matters in Short, Congressional Research Service, November 1, 2018.

154   Anne Teigen, "Juvenile Age of Jurisdiction and Transfer to Adult Court Laws," National Conference of State Legislatures, April 17, 2017.

155   Sarah Hockenberry and Charles Puzzanchera, "Delinquency Cases Waived to Criminal Court, 2011," Office of Juvenile Justice and Delinquency Prevention, December 2014.

156   OJJDP Statistical Briefing Book, March 27, 2018.

157   Sickmund and Puzzanchera, *Juvenile Offenders and Victims: 2014 National Report*, 105.

158   Sickmund et al., "Easy Access to Juvenile Court Statistics, 1985–2016."

159   Hockenberry and Puzzanchera, "Juvenile Court Statistics 2016."

160   Brittany Harwell, "The Detriments of Direct File," Campaign for Youth Justice, February 10, 2016.

161   Campaign for Youth Justice, "Fact Sheet: Direct File," February 12, 2018.

162 Human Rights Watch, "Branded for Life: Florida's Prosecution of Children as Adults under its Direct File Statute," 2014.

163 Renata Sago, "Charging Youths as Adults Can Be A 'Cruel Wake-Up Call: Is There Another Way?" NPR, ugust 15, 2017.

164 Laura Ridolfi, Maureen Washburn, and Frankie Guzman, "The Prosecution of Youth as Adults in California: A 2015 Update," Center on Juvenile and Criminal Justice, October 2016.

165 Jeree Thomas and Mel Wilson, "The Color of Youth Transferred to the Adult Criminal Justice System," Campaign for Youth Justice, September 2018.

166 Andrea Wood, "Cruel and Unusual Punishment: Confining Juveniles with Adults after Graham and Miller," Emory Law Journal, 2012, 61(6): 1445–1491.

167 Nicole Scialabba, "Should Juveniles Be Charged as Adults in the Criminal Justice System?" Chicago, IL: American Bar Association, October 3, 2016.

168 Jessica Lahey, "The Steep Costs of Keeping Juveniles in Adult Prisons," *The Atlantic*, January 8, 2016.

169 Robert Schwartz, "Kids Should Never Be Tried as Adults," CNN, February 18, 2010.

170 Laurence Steinberg and Elizabeth Scott, *Rethinking Juvenile Justice* (Cambridge: Harvard University Press, 2008).

171 Lahey, "The Steep Costs of Keeping Juveniles in Adult Prisons."

172 Jeffrey Fagan, "Juvenile Crime and Criminal Justice: Resolving Border Disputes," *Juvenile Justice*, 2008, 18(2): 81–118.

173 Ibid., 101.

174 Donna Bishop, Charles Frazier, Lonn Lanza-Kaduce, and Lawrence Winner, "The Transfer of Juveniles to Criminal Court: Does It Make a Difference?" *Crime & Delinquency*, 1996, 42(2): 171–191.

175 Wood, "Cruel and Unusual Punishment," 1456.

Chapter 12

Prisons or "Correctional" Institutions

WHAT'S IN A NAME?

Within the formal juvenile justice system, the most severe disposition has always been commitment to some form of secure facility. As we saw in chapter 1, many terms have been used throughout the past 180 years: houses of refuge, reform schools, industrial and training schools, and juvenile correctional institutions.[1] Notice that none of these names include the word "prison." However, when one cannot leave and there are walls or fences surrounding the place you are in, you are, in fact, imprisoned. Americans have a hard time admitting what we do with young offenders, and in Orwellian fashion we hide what is going on by using "nice" terminology.[2] The plain and simple truth is that these institutions are prisons.

Justice Hugo Black's concurring opinion in the *Gault* decision said that Gault was ordered confined for six years in what was in all but name a penitentiary or jail.[3] Correctional historian David Rothman wrote in 1980 that training schools were indistinguishable from prisons. Justice Thurgood Marshall in *Schall v. Martin* wrote that pretrial detention of juveniles gives rise to injuries comparable to those associated with the imprisonment of an adult. Since the first youth facility opened, youth incarceration has followed the adult model of control, coercion, and punishment with "a little bit of programming sprinkled in. . . . Sometimes the names attempt to camouflage the nature of the facility, but whether they are called 'training schools' or 'youth centers,' nearly all of these facilities are youth prisons."[4]

> For more than a century, the predominant model for the treatment, punishment, and rehabilitation of serious youthful offenders has been static: confinement in a large, congregate-care correctional facility. . . . In most states, these institutions still house the bulk of all incarcerated youth and still consume the lion's share of taxpayer spending on juvenile justice.
>
> Unfortunately, the record of large juvenile corrections facilities is dismal. Though many youth confined in these training schools are not, in fact, serious or chronic offenders, recidivism rates are uniformly high. Violence and abuse inside the facilities are alarmingly commonplace. The costs of correctional incarceration vastly exceed those of other approaches to delinquency treatment with equal or better outcomes, and the evidence shows that incarceration in juvenile facilities has serious and lifelong negative impacts on confined youth.[5]

Commitment to an Institution

Commitment to a juvenile prison often represents the "end of the line" for some youthful offenders. Christopher Bickel argues that children committed to facilities are constructed as captives—members of a permanent, disreputable category.[6] Starting with houses of refuge, juvenile institutions have not had a very positive history, as noted in chapter 1. Conditions in many of these institutions have not improved much over the years and "treatment" can be the exception rather than the rule.

Individual states vary a great deal in where they place the juvenile, the length of stay, and the conditions of release. Various state executive-branch agencies decide on commitments to state juvenile facilities. In 18 states, an independent juvenile corrections agency makes the decision. In 11 states, a family/child welfare agency or division decides, while in 12 states general public welfare agencies decide. In 10 states, the adult corrections agency/division makes the decision.[7] In 22 states in 2016, the decision to release a youth from confinement was made by the agency where the youth was confined. In ten states, the original court made the decision. In 8 states, a paroling authority decided, and in 11 states the agency and the court decided together.[8]

Despite the euphemistic label of "residential placement," many of the facilities look and operate like prisons and jails.[9] Most (89%) are locked facilities. Of confined youth, 2 of every 3 are held in the most restrictive facilities. More than 8,500 juveniles are confined behind bars for technical violations of the requirements of their probation. Thousands of youth are held for nonviolent, low-level offenses before they have been adjudicated delinquent.[10] More than 500 confined children have not yet reached the age of 13. Less than 14% of youth under age 18 are black, but 43% of boys and 34% of girls in juvenile facilities are black.

Patrick McCarthy of the Annie E. Casey Foundation has challenged states to close all youth prisons because they undermine the development of young people, expose them to grave dangers, and fail to improve public safety. "I believe it's long past time to close these inhumane, ineffective, wasteful factories of failure. . . . We need to admit that what we're doing doesn't work, and is making the problem worse while costing billions of dollars and ruining thousands of lives."[11]

There are significant variations in how jurisdictions structure the types of confinement facilities in which juveniles are held.[12] Confinement is the most restrictive sanction versus diversionary and non-residential sanctions based in the community. Confinement is both a place (type of facility) and a process. The process involves the quality of care, the quality of staff, and their relationships with youth. Staff includes judicial and other decision makers responsible for matching the levels of restrictiveness with the needs of the individual youth.

While the harms of confinement are many, there has been progress in terms of reducing both the number of facilities and the number of juveniles confined. In 2000, there were 3,047 confinement facilities versus 1,772 in 2016—a decline of 42%.[13] The total number of juveniles held was 108,802 in 2000 compared to 45,567 in 2016—a decline of 58%. The percentage of facilities over capacity dropped from 8% in 2000 to 3% in 2016, while the percentage of juveniles confined in overcrowded facilities dropped from 20% to 4%.

Some of these institutions are public (15,095 state facilities and 17,206 local facilities in 2016); others are private (13,266).[14] More than half (54%) of juvenile facilities are publicly operated and hold 71% of justice-involved youth.[15] Residential treatment centers accounted for 57% of all private facilities, and group homes accounted for 35%.Prisons for young offenders can be further subdivided into short-term (usually ranging from a few days to a couple of months) and long-term (ranging from three or four months to one or two years) confinement.

SHORT-TERM FACILITIES

Since 2000, the Office of Juvenile Justice and Delinquency Prevention has collected information in even-numbered years about the facilities in which juvenile offenders are held. Detention centers, shelters (i.e., runaway/homeless), and reception/diagnostic centers are classified as short-term facilities. The Juvenile Residential Facility Census does not collect data on juveniles in adult prisons or jails. When a state deems a child in need of its protection, the custodial function is often filled by foster care—intended as a short-term solution but sometimes lasting far longer.

Adult Jails

The Juvenile Justice and Delinquency Prevention Act (JJDPA) in 1974 mandated that states remove juveniles who committed status offenses from adult facilities and create alternatives or be subject to a loss of federal funding. The 2018 Reauthorization requires that by 2021, the sight and sound separation from adult inmates and removal from adult jail applies to youth awaiting trial as adults. The protection previously applied only to youth held on juvenile charges.[16] As noted in chapter 3, an amendment to JJDPA in 1980 created an exception to the rule that status offenders were not to be placed in secure confinement. The amendment allowed for the detention of status offenders for violations of a valid court order (VCO). For example, probation might require a truant to stop skipping school. If the juvenile persists, he or she may be incarcerated for violating the court's order. In 2014, 26 states invoked the VCO exception to confine 7,466 youths who had committed status offenses.[17] The 2018 Reauthorization specifies that youth in violation of a valid court order may be held in detention only if the VCO is identified, the factual basis for believing the violation occurred is stated, there is no appropriate less restrictive alternative to detention, and the length of time the status offender remains in a secure detention facility does not exceed seven days and includes a plan for release from such facility.[18] The VCO cannot be extended.

Almost 1 in 10 juveniles are held in adult prisons and jails where they face greater safety risks and there are few age–appropriate services available. If families cannot afford bail, youth transferred to the adult system may be jailed in adult facilities for weeks or months without having been convicted.[19] There were 3,600 juveniles confined in adult jails in 2017—300 were held as juveniles, the other 3,200 were tried or awaiting trial as adults.[20]

Detention Centers

Detention, briefly discussed in the previous chapter, is primarily a temporary holding facility that functions like a jail. Detention centers are short-term facilities that provide temporary care in a physically restricting environment for juveniles in custody pending court disposition or juveniles adjudicated delinquent and awaiting placement or transfer to another jurisdiction.[21] Detention centers are generally public facilities—21% state operated and 71% local operated.[22]

In 2016, there were 662 detention centers (37% of all residential facilities compared to 22% in 2000) holding almost 18,000 juveniles.[23] Half of detained juveniles were in placement fewer than 21 days; 60% of youths were detained at least 15 days, 41% at least 30 days, 23% at least 60 days, 15% at least 90 days, and 6% at least 6 months.[24]

The impact of detention on juveniles has been studied extensively. Even short periods of time in detention have negative impacts on life outcomes—from economic disadvantages to mental health disturbances.[25] It has been repeatedly determined that most youths do not need to be placed in detention, that far too many have been charged with minor offenses (including status offenses), and that there are many negative consequences. Being detained

- promotes further delinquency through association with delinquent peers;
- stigmatizes and reinforces a delinquent identity;
- results in harsher treatment by decision makers throughout the process;
- accelerates further involvement in the juvenile justice system;
- diverts resources from comprehensive community-based interventions;
- reduces involvement and interaction with community-based services;
- increases rejection by local public institutions such as schools;
- promotes isolation, lethargy, and ineffectiveness;
- results in overcrowding, punitive custody, and abusive conditions.[26]

Youth in detention face abuse (violence, sexual assault, and isolation) and maltreatment.[27] Detention centers in San Diego routinely used pepper spray on youth, including minor misbehaviors such as being verbally defiant or failing to follow instructions. In Ohio, a detention center kept cells at such low temperatures that youth were frostbitten. Detention is also psychologically harmful and exacerbates preexisting traumas. About 90% of detained youth have suffered a traumatic loss, been physically assaulted, or have been threatened with a weapon. System-involved youth often struggle with other traumas such as strained family relationships, exposure to community violence, and victimization. For any juvenile, being detained away from home in an alien, impersonal environment causes psychological trauma. Detention increased the probability of dropping out of school, engaging in risky behavior, and being employed in a low-wage job.

A longitudinal study found that 12 years after detention, only 21.9% of males and 54.7% of females had achieved age-appropriate psychosocial milestones.[28] Only half of the study participants had a high school degree or equivalent compared to 88% of comparably aged juveniles. Only 20% of males and about 33% of females were working full time or were in school compared to 77% of the general population. Females were more likely to have positive outcomes for gainful activity, desistance from criminal activity, residential independence, parenting responsibility, and mental health. White males were 3 times more likely to achieve positive outcomes compared with minorities in educational attainment and 2 to 5 times more likely to have achieved gainful activity; they were less likely to abstain from substance abuse.

One of the most problematic features of detention centers is the large number of youths with mental health problems. Detention increases the rate of depression in youth; 33% of detainees report feeling that life is hopeless, and rates of suicide are between 2 to 4 times higher among youth in custody than among youth in the community.[29] Two-thirds of males and 75% of females in juvenile detention facilities meet the criteria for at least one mental health disorder.[30] Multiple studies confirm the prevalence of diagnosable mental health problems of youths in detention.[31] Overcrowding in detention facilities, lack of treatment/services, separation from support systems such as family and friends, and solitary confinement have a negative impact on youths with mental health issues.[32] Only 15% of juveniles received treatment while in detention.

Local Facilities

Status offenders and dependent, neglected, and abused children are housed in local facilities. If the state takes juveniles into its custody, it has an obligation to provide safe environments. Foster care is a temporary living situation for children who have come to the attention of child welfare agencies because their parents cannot provide adequate care.[33] Some children live in the private homes of foster parents. Others live in group settings, sometimes called congregate care. Local and state agencies manage child welfare cases, which results in substantial variety in the services provided. Length of stay varies both due to circumstances of children and families and because of choices made by agencies about care and services.

There are 437,500 children in the foster care system.[34] Black youths are twice as likely to be placed in foster care as white youths; LGBTQ youth and those with mental illnesses are also more likely to be placed in foster care. Many juveniles are institutionalized repeatedly, moving from foster homes to group homes without enough time to make lasting connections with peers or adults. Frequent moves jeopardize school progress. Youth placed in group homes are 2.5 times more likely to be involved in the justice system. One quarter of foster care alumni become involved with the criminal justice system within 2 years of leaving care, leading critics to refer to the foster care-to-prison pipeline that funnels youth from the child welfare system into the criminal justice system. By age 17, more than half of the juveniles in foster care have been arrested, convicted, or confined overnight in a correctional facility. Of youth with 5 or more foster placements, 90% will enter the justice system.

The massive bureaucracy of the nation's foster care system can result in juveniles growing up without experiencing a stable, secure family.[35] Because of turnover of foster parents and caseworkers, some children move five or six times. Disruptive moves affect behavior. As children act out, they fall deeper into the system, moving from foster homes to group homes to therapeutic centers. These juveniles age out of the system at age 18—20% will be homeless instantly; half will develop a substance dependence; only half will be gainfully employed by age 24; 70% of girls who age out of foster care become pregnant before age 21.[36] There is less than a 3% chance that children who have aged out of foster care will earn a college degree.

Oregon provides one example of longstanding questions about the ability of child welfare officials to regulate foster care providers. In 2014 the Department of Human Services closed more than half of the complaints it received during an initial screening because state law limits investigations in child welfare cases to incidents involving serious injuries or an ongoing threat.[37] As a result, neglect, denial of food or medicine, and financial fraud are not investigated. There had been reports of abuse and neglect by one Portland care provider for 15 years, yet the state continued placing children in its care. Children were forced to endure hunger, inappropriate force, lack of bedding, and mold. Allegations of rape and sexual abuse were not investigated.

The Senate Finance Committee conducted a two-year investigation of the privatization of foster care. It requested information from all 50 states, but only 33 submitted data. "The lack of oversight of the nation's child welfare system, at both the state and federal level, is unacceptable."[38] The Committee found that companies and agencies charged with keeping foster children safe often failed to provide the most basic protections.[39] One of the largest private providers of foster care services is Mentor, which has an average of 3,800 children in its foster homes in 15 states. Government assessments from 3 states show significant deficiencies by Mentor in selecting, training, and monitoring its foster parents. Children have been sexually or physically abused; 86 died over a 10-year period—a death rate among foster children 42% higher than the national average. Mentor conducted an internal investigation in only 13 cases. "The political problem for foster children is a structural one. It would be hard to think of a group with less lobbying power in Washington DC, while the group homes that warehouse children are making significant profits off each one and are loathe to see that income dry up."[40]

The lack of federal oversight plus underfunded agencies contribute to another shocking problem with foster care—missing children.[41] More than 61,000 foster children have been listed as missing since 2000. Another 53,000 are listed as runaway. In Arizona and other states, children missing for six months are dropped from the foster care rolls. Missing children are at profound risk. Most of the children bought and sold for sex are foster care children. One attorney remarked that the broken foster care system has become a supply chain to traffickers.

Boys Town: A Unique Case

Boys Town was founded by Father Edward Flanagan in 1917 in Nebraska. Several locations throughout the United States now provide care and shelter for abused, abandoned, neglected, handicapped, or otherwise troubled children. Each of the locations have child and family services, which can include group homes, in-home family services, foster care, parenting classes, and behavioral health services. More than 90% of the youth who receive services through the continuum of care at Boys Town stay with their families or are placed in family-like settings.[42] The authors have personally visited some of the facilities in the Las Vegas location, which provide a home-like environment, with no walls or bars.

Boys Town operates more than a hundred long-term, residential-care homes with family-style living in the least restrictive environment. In each home, a married couple (called Family Teachers) lives with six to eight youths. Couples are trained to teach youths how to build positive relationships with others, to reinforce appropriate behavior, to apply consequences to inappropriate behavior, and to empower youths to make responsible and meaningful decisions. The average length of stay is 12 to 18 months.[43] The residential program at Boys Town is an evidence-based, cost-effective alternative to incarceration. Rather than living in a correctional environment that can reinforce criminal behavior, juveniles are part of a family that teaches them positive behaviors and social skills.[44]

The Emergency Shelter Program provides short-term living arrangements for certain youths referred by the local juvenile court, family services, police agencies, school counselors, homeless shelters, and other local agencies. The shelter in Las Vegas has two eight-bed units, one for boys and one for girls. A certified school-teacher designs and teaches the education curriculum and several full-and part-time counselors are on staff. The overall goal of the program is to provide temporary care for youths facing some kind of crisis in their life until a long-term placement can be arranged.

Reception/Diagnostic Centers

This short-term facility screens juveniles committed by the courts and assigns them to appropriate facilities. In 2016, there were 58 diagnostic centers (3% of all facilities—about the same as in 2000); 65% screened all youth for mental health needs, while 35% screened some youth.[45] Prior to starting their sentence, offenders are evaluated by a psychologist or social worker to determine what sort of treatment will be required. These facilities are usually attached to a juvenile prison, and the stay is normally no more than a month. In 2015, 622 youths were held in diagnostic centers.[46]

LONG-TERM FACILITIES

The mental and physical health of juveniles is affected by the experience of being locked up at a critical stage in their development. Confinement affects their relationships as well as their academic and economic prospects. As noted above, the harms begin with even short-term confinement and become more pronounced with longer stays. There is a growing consensus that youth confinement should be a last resort, and a decline in the number of residential facilities and youths confined there indicates some progress.

Residential Treatment Centers

The 678 residential treatment centers in 2016 housed more than 10,000 committed juveniles.[47] In 2000, residential treatment centers were 61% of all facilities versus 38% in 2016.[48] Treatment centers provide some type of treatment program for youth (substance abuse, sex offender, mental health, etc.) in a long-term residential facility.[49] There are no federal laws that define and regulate residential treatment programs.[50] States vary in the oversight of residential treatment programs. Some have statutes that require licensing; others provide no oversight.

Ranch/Wilderness Camps

In 2016, there were 30 wilderness facilities housing fewer than 1,000 committed juveniles (886 males and 49 females).[51] In 2000, ranch/wilderness camps were 5% of all juvenile facilities versus 2% in 2016.[52] These long-term residential facilities are generally for juveniles whose behavior does not require the strict confinement of a long-term secure facility. Facilities include ranches, forestry camps, marine programs, and farms. Most camps (76%) are public facilities.[53] Programs vary widely in terms of eligibility criteria, types of activities, duration, and therapeutic goals.[54] Wilderness therapy focuses on removing juveniles from negative influences and increasing self-esteem by participating in physically challenging outdoor activities. Programs concentrate on skills such as hiking, mapping routes, making fires, and cooking. The small group environment and exposure to unfamiliar settings in which survival is facilitated by cooperation contribute to teaching interpersonal skills. Wilderness camps are grounded in experiential learning, while boot camps are based on a military model.

The Government Accountability Office (GAO) investigated boot camps and wilderness programs and found thousands of allegations of abuse, some of which involved death, at public and private residential treatment programs across the country between the years 1990 and 2007. It identified ineffective management, including the hiring of untrained staff, a lack of adequate nourishment, and reckless or negligent operating practices.

Boot Camps

Boot camps operate somewhat like their military counterparts. When juvenile crime spiked in the early 1990s, politicians decided boot camps would be a solution for juvenile offenders, despite no proven success with adults (see discussion of fad syndrome below).

> The use of these programs has always followed a pattern: Fear of growing youth crime fuels widespread skepticism about existing public policies. Seeking to quell criticism, public officials introduce military training as a quick fix. Military training as a treatment for adolescent problems is founded on the popular notion that adolescent problems result from inadequate discipline and structure.[55]

A meta-analysis found that discipline programs (mostly boot camps emphasizing a "paramilitary regimen") increased recidivism by 8%.[56] Programs with a therapeutic philosophy such as counseling and skills training were more effective than programs based on control, coercion, and discipline.

Samuel Walker refers to short-sighted, metaphorical strategies to prevent crime—ideas that attract a lot of attention and then fade away—as the fad syndrome.[57]

> Boot camps were suddenly all the rage in the 1980s and were adopted by many states. Boot camps are short-term facilities for felony offenders designed to "correct" their behavior through a rigorous military-style regimen of physical exercise along with other correctional programs. The purely military aspects caught the public eye, although the more successful programs did not emphasize that. And then, as soon as they appeared, they vanished from policy debates. The research simply did not find any evidence that they were any more effective in reducing recidivism than ordinary sentences.[58]

Interestingly, juveniles viewed the boot camp environment as more therapeutic than traditional juvenile reformatories—"which may say more about the reformatories than the boot camps. Any advantage that boot camps confer, however, appears to be offset by the potential in boot camps for psychological, emotional, and physical abuse of youngsters—particularly for children with a history of abuse and family violence."[59] In 2015, 244 juveniles were committed to boot camps.[60]

Group Homes

Group homes are long-term facilities where youth may leave the facility to attend school or go to work. The 344 group homes in 2016 (19% of all facilities versus 37% in 2000) housed approximately 4,000 youth.[61] There are many types of facilities housing a tremendously varied population of youth.[62]

Four components affect the quality of care: setting, staffing, safety, and treatment. Setting refers to attributes of the physical environment that indicate quality practice, such as cleanliness, maintenance, age-appropriate recreational opportunities, and a welcoming, home-like atmosphere.[63] Key staffing elements associated with positive outcomes are training, supervision, continuity, beneficial youth/staff ratios, and constructive attitudes and behavior toward youth. Safety includes rules and structures that safeguard the juveniles in placement from abuse by other youth or staff, discipline that is fair and not excessive, and resticted use of physical restraint and/or seclusion. Treatment is the centerpiece of a quality program, which must address the needs of youth with emotional, behavioral, and/or psychiatric problems.

Each component affects outcomes. Research on group residential treatment is limited, and the outcomes identified are inconsistent.[64] Literature that examines outcomes for group residential treatment looks at changes across time and compares group outcomes with other settings/conditions. Programs implementing the teaching family model were associated with better outcomes 8 months after discharge. Positively focused motivational systems were related to more beneficial changes during treatment. Appropriate use of humor by staff was also related to improved outcomes after release. Group homes that allowed restraint had significantly worse long-term outcomes than those that did not. Youth report that negatively focused behavior management or motivational systems result in harsh and punitive living environments, leading to fatalistic emotional consequences for youth.

Long-Term Secure Facilities

The most common placement for committed youth is in long-term, secure facilities.[65] Almost all (91%) are public facilities.[66] They are sometimes called training schools and are generally larger, older institutions. They fit the general pattern of the congregate model of institutions, dating back to the houses of refuge.

In 2016, there were 189 such facilities (11% of all facilities—the same percentage as in 2000) confining almost 12,000 juveniles.[67] The percentage of large institutions (more than 100 beds) dropped from 9% in 2000 to 5% in 2016. The percentage of juveniles confined in the large institutions dropped from 51% in 2000 to 25% in 2016. Sixty-two percent of training schools use restraints such as handcuffs, leg cuffs, waist bands, leather straps, or strait jackets; 46% of these facilities locked youth in seclusion for four hours or more.[68] Half of training schools have fences or walls with razor wire.

INSTITUTIONAL POPULATIONS

Table 12-1 presents data on the offense profile of juveniles in custody in 2015. A total of 31,487 juveniles were committed to a correctional institution—a drop of 58% from 1997 when there were 75,406 juveniles in custody.[69] The offense for which most (38%) juveniles were committed was person offenses, followed by property offenses (23%) and technical violations (15%).

Table 12-1   Detailed Offense Profile by Placement Status for United States, 2015

Most serious offense	Total	Placement Status		
		Committed	Detained	Diversion
Total	48,043	31,487	15,816	564
Delinquency	45,715	29,774	15,309	488
Person	18,119	12,015	5,831	226
Criminal homicide	767	315	446	5
Sexual assault	3,433	2,718	614	95
Robbery	4,717	3,054	1,616	40
Aggravated assault	3,910	2,479	1,390	26
Simple assault	3,910	2,608	1,233	55
Other person	1,382	841	532	5
Property	10,412	7,208	3,081	94
Burglary	4,241	2,945	1,259	35
Theft	2,346	1,686	636	17
Auto theft	1,793	1,183	576	19
Arson	325	218	106	1
Other property	1,707	1,176	504	22
Drug	2,607	1,790	774	32
Trafficking	421	280	136	4
Other drug	2,186	1,510	638	28
Public order	6,020	3,922	2,003	82
Weapons	2,360	1,344	992	21
Alcohol	118	80	37	0
Other public order	3,542	2,498	974	61
Technical violation	8,557	4,839	3,620	54
Violent Crime Index*	12,827	8,566	4,066	166
Property Crime Index**	8,705	6,032	2,577	72
Status offense	2,328	1,713	507	76
Running away	456	285	141	27
Truancy	642	484	146	10
Incorrigibility	761	568	138	30
Curfew violation	84	60	20	3
Underage drinking	260	231	26	3
Other status offense	125	85	36	3

* Includes criminal homicide violent sexual assault robbery and aggravated assault.

** Includes burglary theft auto theft and arson.

Source: Melissa Sickmund, T.J. Sladky, Wei Kang, and Charles Puzzanchera (2017), "Easy Access to the Census of Juveniles in Residential Placement."

Racial Composition of Juvenile Institutions

Table 12-2 compares the percentages of youths confined in public and private facilities and the offenses committed. For most delinquency offenses other than status offenses, 7 of every 10 juveniles are in public facilities. The percentages for drug offenses are closer (61% public, 39% private). For status offenses, the ratio is reversed with less than 3 of every 10 juveniles in public facilities. The majority of youths confined in *private* facilities are white. This is no doubt because most of the costs are paid for by family members, usually through their insurance.

The rates of incarceration of committed juveniles in the United States in 2015 were 60 per 100,000 juveniles for whites, 275 for blacks, and 89 for Hispanics.[70] Revisit table 11-5 to view the rate of committed juveniles per offense committed by race and sex. For every offense category, whites had the lowest rate, blacks had the highest, and Hispanics were in the middle. (Status offenses are the one exception; whites had a higher rate than Hispanics.) It reminds us of a popular phrase used during the 1960s: "If you're white, you're alright, if you're brown stick around, if you're black, stay back." As Bickel notes: "Not since slavery have we seen the rise of an institution that so fundamentally perpetuates and legitimates massive inequality, especially for inner city children of color."[71] The sad fact is that incarceration has become part of the life course for blacks and other minorities. Black youth are 8.6 times more likely than white peers to receive an adult prison sentence and Hispanic youth are 40% more likely.[72]

Juveniles Incarcerated in Adult Prisons

At yearend 2016, 956 juveniles age 17 or younger were in custody in federal or state prisons compared to 3,892 in 2000.[73] The number of juveniles held in adult prisons declined 82% from the peak year of 1997.[74] More than two decades of research documents the greater vulnerability to abuse and the greater incidence

Table 12-2   Juvenile Offenders in Residential Placement, in Public and Private Facilities, 2015

Most serious offense	All Facilities	Facility type	
		Public	Private
Total	**100%**	**69%**	**31%**
Delinquency	100%	71%	29%
Person	100%	73%	27%
Property	100%	70%	30%
Drug	100%	61%	39%
Public order	100%	68%	32%
Technical violation	100%	72%	28%
Status offense	100%	28%	72%

Source: Melissa Sickmund, T.J. Sladky, Wei Kang, and Charles Puzzanchera (2017), "Easy Access to the Census of Juveniles in Residential Placement."

of recidivism when juveniles are confined in adult prisons. The groundbreaking neuroscience research that young people have reduced criminal culpability because they differ from adults in maturity and impulsivity was a key element in the Supreme Court's decision to eliminate the death penalty for juveniles and restricting sentences to life imprisonment. (See discussion of *Roper, Graham, Miller,* and *Montgomery* in chapter 11.)

Since 2005, 36 states have passed 70 laws to reduce the number of youth prosecuted, tried, and incarcerated in the adult system. The justice reform trends include laws removing youth from adult jails and prisons, laws expanding juvenile court jurisdiction, laws reducing the transfer of youth from the juvenile system to the adult system, and changes to mandatory minimum sentencing laws with an emphasis on abolishing juvenile life without parole (JLWOP).[75]

Judicial decisions and state legislative reforms have reduced the number of youth serving JLWOP by 60% since 2015.[76] Almost 400 individuals previously sentenced to JLWOP have been released from prison. Approximately 1,700 youth have been resentenced, with the median sentence being 25 years. Of new cases tried since 2012 (after *Miller v. Alabama*), 72% of children sentenced to JLWOP have been black, compared to 61% before 2012. Prosecutors in Louisiana and Michigan continue to seek JLWOP at a rate that far exceeds other states. Of the approximately 70 sentences imposed since 2012, almost one-third were imposed in Louisiana. After 2016 when *Montgomery* was decided, prosecutors sought to reimpose the sentence in 30% of the cases in Louisiana and 60% of the cases in Michigan. Although Pennsylvania historically imposed the penalty frequently, fewer than 2% of resentencings have reimposed the original sentence.

Research increasingly identifies the negative effects of incarcerating youth, particularly in adult facilities.[77] Incarceration affects mental health; it fails to meet the developmental and criminogenic needs of juvenile offenders. Juveniles housed in adult penitentiaries and jails commit suicide at a far higher rate, at least two to three times that of youth in the general population.[78] Studies have found that juveniles who are prosecuted and punished as adults are more likely to re-offend and to do so more quickly, compared to juveniles who are dealt with by the juvenile justice system.[79]

Institutionalization

Erving Goffman offered excellent insight into the lives of people confined in what he termed *total institutions*.[80] Captives are subjected to various forms of status degradation; their movements are restricted; they are severed totally from the outside world—and they are reduced to a state of almost total dependency. Bickel describes a juvenile detention center he studied—which resembled an adult prison—from the standpoint of the architecture itself: "the thick steel doors, the countless locks on every door and every drawer, and the numerous gazing security cameras."[81]

John Irwin studied adult felons and found that a significant number were what he termed *state-raised youths*—offenders who more or less "grew up" in various institutions (such as juvenile detention centers, foster care, group homes, and the like). They had rarely spent any significant amounts of time in free society. Irwin described the worldview of state-raised youths as distorted, stunted, and incoherent. The prison world became their only meaningful world.[82]

Correctional environments can serve as a school for crime.[83] Recent analyses identify continuing problems.

> The harmful effects of incarceration are embedded in the physical facilities them-selves and the nature of institutionalization. Changes in leadership, training, or enriched programming ultimately are trumped by correctional physical plants, the great distance most facilities are from families and oversight mechanisms, and the bureaucratization and institutionalization such facilities engender. Large, institutional structures, surrounded by razor wire and filled with noise and harsh lighting, create a toxic environment. The staff and kids are inevitably caught in their roles of guard and prisoner, locking both into a struggle of power and resistance. Life in these places is about violence and control, submission, and defiance, leaving little room for the guidance, learning, role-modeling, and caring relationships that young people need.[84]

Scandalous conditions have plagued youth prisons since their inception, which suggests the nature of the institutions causes the problem rather than personnel misconduct. "The consistent failure of youth prisons to protect youth and improve their outcomes—along with the institutional model's stubborn resistance to trans-formation—argues for the replacement, rather than the improvement, of youth prisons."[85]

Victimization

Youths in institutions are at risk for sexual victimization. The Prison Rape Elimin-ation Act of 2003 mandated a comprehensive study of the problem. Beginning in 2008, the Bureau of Justice Statistics conducted the National Survey of Youth in Custody (NSYC), which compiles reports of victimization directly from youth. It also administers the Survey of Sexual Victimization; juvenile correctional adminis-trators from state juvenile systems and a sample of local and private facilities report allegations of sexual victimization.

NYSC-2 was conducted in 2012. An estimated 9.5% of youth in state juvenile facilities reported experiencing one or more incidents of sexual victimization by another youth (2.5%) or staff (7.7%) in the past 12 months.[86] The percentage of youths reporting sexual victimization declined from 12.6% in 2008–2009 when NYSC-1 was conducted. In 4 states (Georgia, Illinois, Ohio, and South Carolina), percentages exceeded 15%, primarily due to high rates of staff sexual misconduct. Youth who identified their sexual orientation as gay, lesbian, bisexual or other re-ported substantially higher youth-on-youth victimization (10.3%) compared to heterosexual youth (1.5%). The survey collects information only from adjudicated youth in facilities that housed them for at least 90 days. Since many youths are held for shorter periods of time, the reports probably underrepresent the problem of sexual victimization.

From 2007 to 2012, juvenile correctional administrators reported almost 9,500 allegations of sexual victimization; 55% involved youth-on-youth victimization, and 45% involved staff-on-youth victimization.[87] Females accounted for 10% of youth in state systems and 15% in local/private facilities but were 38% of victims of staff-on-youth sexual victimization in state systems and 23% in local/private facilities. While the number of youth held in state juvenile systems declined by more than half from 2005 to 2012, the rate of allegations of sexual victimization more than doubled from 19 per 1,000 to 47 per 1000. The rate in local and private facilities fluctuated but dropped from 15.4 in 2005 to 13.5 in 2012. The differences could be affected by state systems holding youth with more serious behavioral problems and risk factors associated with sexual victimization, differences in facility or staff characterisitics (i.e., size and training), and/or variations in reporting. The percentage of allegations substantiated was 18%.

Children who experience sexual abuse are often placed in foster care or residential facilities. The rates of sexual abuse in such facilities are alarmingly high compared with the rates in the general population.[88] Out-of-home placements increase the risk of revictimization through exposure to environments conducive to sexual abuse, such as association with high-risk youth and large child-to-caregiver ratios. The culture of institutional settings includes staff intimidation and adherence to a code of silence, which can contribute to victimization and can inhibit reports of sexual abuse. The risk of sexual abuse in residential settings is higher for those who have previously experienced sexual abuse.

Recidivism

A Pathways to Desistance study of serious offenders seven years after their release found no meaningful reduction in offending or arrests in response to more severe punishment such as correctional placement or longer stays.[89] Offenders placed in an institution had higher recidivism rates than those placed on probation. Individuals removed from the community to an out-of-home placement averaged twice as many new arrests. Severity of punishment has little deterrent effect.

WILL BUDGET NECESSITIES LEAD TO IMPROVEMENT?

As mentioned in chapter 1, Jerome Miller closed reformatories in Massachusetts in 1972 and returned juveniles to the community. When appointed in 1969, he observed deteriorating facilities with sanitation problems, lack of meaningful programs, and brutality. He implemented new programs and efforts to make the institutions more humane.

> Whenever I thought we'd made progress, something happened—a beating, a kid in an isolation cell, an offhand remark by a superintendent or cottage supervisor that told me what I envisioned would never be allowed. Reformers come and reformers go. State institutions carry on. Nothing in their history suggests that

they can sustain reform, no matter what money, staff, and programs are pumped into them. The same crises that have plagued them for 150 years intrude today. Though the casts may change, the players go on producing failure.[90]

Decades of inhumane tactics and patronage hires (plus intense opposition to any reform efforts) convinced Miller that the institutions could not be fixed—instead, they should be abandoned. He rejected a state system devoted to perpetuating itself by spending the equivalent of tuition at Harvard to incarcerate juveniles statistically doomed to return.[91] By 1972, he closed all the youth prisons in Massachusetts, including the Lyman School for Boys—the first state reform school in the United States, which opened in 1846.[92]

When the commissioner of the Office of Children and Family Services began closing youth prisons in New York, she also encountered fierce opposition from facility staff and local elected officials.[93] There were intense organizing efforts to fight facility closures, even when facilities were empty or confined very few juveniles. When first elected, Governor Andrew Cuomo vowed in his state-of-the-state address to end the use of an incarceration program as an employment program—saying New York does not put people in juvenile justice facilities to give people jobs. Facility staff fought Vincent Schiraldi when, as director of the Department of Youth Rehabilitation Services in Washington DC, he closed Oak Hill Youth Center, which had been under a consent decree for abusive and unconstitutional conditions for more than 20 years.

The history of youth prisons is a history of failure to protect youth and to provide programs for their developmental needs. Youth prisons are harmful, and their financial costs are enormous. Costs vary from state to state, but 34 states report expenditures of $100,000 or more for each youth confined.[94] Institutionalized youth are more likely to commit additional, more serious crimes, are less employable, are more likely to be on a path to lifelong failure, and are more likely to pass their problems on to their children. These lifelong negative effects add more financial costs after release—whether from lost future earnings and tax revenue to spending on Medicaid. The long-term societal costs generated by one year of incarcerating youth range from $8 to $21 billion.

The Missouri Model

Thirty years ago, Missouri closed their youth prisons and replaced them with smaller, treatment-oriented programs in communities. In contrast, when Wisconsin closed youth prisons in the southeastern part of the state in 2011, it retained one facility in the northern part of the state for the most serious juvenile offenders, which houses up to 600 juveniles (200 in 2017).[95] The Division of Youth Services (DYS) has jurisdiction over youth adjudicated by the 45 Missouri juvenile courts.[96] DYS stresses the importance of positive youth development through the therapeutic treatment model centered on continuous case management, decentralized residential facilities, small group peer-led services, and a restorative rehabilitation-centered environment.

Missouri has 30 facilities throughout the state. Juveniles who commit the most serious crimes are placed in facilities holding no more than 30 inmates and are placed in treatment groups of no more than 12.[97] Employees rarely impose solitary confinement or mechanical restraints. Facilities for those who have committed lesser crimes do not have fences; some are located in state parks. Living areas are similar to college dormitories. The treatment approach is applied across all programs and facilities and offers extensive individualized attention. One foundational element of the Missouri model is encouraging strong, supportive peer and adult relationships as a primary means for compliance, versus coercive techniques.[98]

There are other hopeful signs regarding juvenile prisons. More states are moving in the direction of sending youths to alternative residential programs. Prioritizing residential space for only the most chronic, violent offenses facilitates reallocating the cost savings to evidence-based strategies to reduce recidivism.[99] There are a number of initiatives to help states reform their juvenile justice systems.

Reform Initiatives

In 1993, the Annie E. Casey Foundation launched the Juvenile Detention Alternatives Initiative (JDAI) to reduce an overreliance on confinement of court-involved youth. Being placed in a locked detention center significantly increases the odds that a juvenile will be found delinquent and will be committed—seriously damaging prospects for future success. Twenty-five years later, 300 jurisdictions in 40 states participate. Detention populations decreased 42% in participating counties compared to the national average for states of 17%.[100] New Jersey became the only state-level JDAI model site in 2008; 10 years later, it became the first state in which every county participates. The daily population in juvenile detention centers in New Jersey decreased almost 70% between 2003 and 2017.[101] The reductions led to closing 8 county-operated detention facilities, and the number of detention centers dropped from 17 to 9. The reforms resulted in an annual savings of $21 million. The attorney general called the change remarkable, noting that the collaborative efforts of the juvenile justice commission, judiciary, law enforcement, public defenders, county government, advocates and other stakeholders have facilitated tens of thousands of young people remaining at home and receiving appropriate services.

The John D. and Catherine T. MacArthur Foundation launched the Models for Change initiative in 2004. The program supports a network of government and court officials, legal advocates, educators, community leaders, and families in 35 states to support reforms including community-based alternatives and aftercare.[102]

As discussed earlier, the rate at which juveniles have been arrested for violent crimes has been cut in half since the late 1990s, as has the rate at which juveniles were committed to state facilities. The Pew Public Safety Performance Project works with policy leaders in states to accelerate and lock in the positive trends.[103]

California

The California legislature passed a series of laws to reduce youth incarceration. The number of youth confined dropped to 1,700 in 2008 from almost 10,000 in 1996. The cost to incarcerate the remaining youths increased from approximately $36,000 per youth annually to $252,000. Policymakers then banned commitments of all but the most serious juvenile offenders. By 2012, California had closed 8 of its 11 large facilities. In 2018, there were 112 juvenile halls, camps, and ranches operated by county probation departments.[104] The Division of Juvenile Justice (DJJ), the state-run system, operates a fire camp and 3 large institutions at an annual cost of almost $200 million.

The capacity of county juvenile facilities would allow for a realignment of state confined youth. Moving the juveniles would generate savings, bring high-needs youth closer to home, and curb the trauma and violence endemic to DJJ. The population of confined youth has fallen 73% since 1999, yet the capacity of county juvenile justice facilities grew by 14%. California invested $300 million in the construction and renovation of county facilities, and counties receive hundreds of millions of dollars in state grant funding to develop alternatives to DJJ confinement. Despite these investments, counties continue to commit hundreds of youth to DJJ while operating local facilities at 35% of their design capacity. The 8,200 available beds could absorb 13 times the population of DJJ (638 in 2017).

In October 2018, California became the first state to forbid the transfer of children younger than 16 to adult court for any crime, including homicide.[105] Other legislation bars children younger than 12 from the jurisdiction of the juvenile court; makes individuals sentenced to LWOP as minors eligible for release during their 25th year of incarceration; and limits the amount of time youths deemed mentally incompetent can be detained in juvenile facilities—they must be given supportive mental health services or released to other placement. The governor acknowledged that protests from families of victims weighed on him when deciding whether to sign the bills, but research, data, and racial/geographic disparities convinced him to sign the legislation.

Since 2007 when it began implementing the realignment of responsibilities for youth from the state to the counties, California's approach to juveniles has undergone revolutionary reform. In a little over a decade, it went from one of the most repressive systems to one at the forefront of reform. Advocates for reform embrace the changes but warn of the necessity to remember the lessons of history.

Dan Macallair refers to California's reliance on congregate institutional care since the 1850s as *path dependency*—the practice of continuing a traditional practice even when more effective alternatives have been identified.[106] People with economic, professional, and/or political dependence on existing institutions campaign to maintain the existing system. The primary interest groups are those with a direct financial interest—the staff employed at the institutions and the companies that supply the facilities. Secondary interest groups, such as county probation departments, may resist closing the state institutions because they want to retain the ability to transfer responsibility for the most challenging youths. The community-oriented approach means counties must spend resources on juvenile justice. In smaller, less affluent jurisdictions, politicians may be reluctant to ask taxpayers for the necessary funds.

> The combination of these interest groups and the tendency of reform efforts to lose momentum and recede create a natural inclination to return to old practices. Institutional care is the option of convenience since it represents an established path and is seen as carrying fewer political risks.[107]

Some argue the necessity of retaining a state system because it is more easily monitored and has more resources to offer programs. In California, Los Angeles County rates among the worst local juvenile justice systems in the country, with institutions as brutal as any of those administered by the state.[108] However, sustaining two bad systems does not solve a problem. Innovations in other counties are models of what can be done when reform becomes necessary and local resources are utilized properly. San Francisco, a national leader in not sending youths to state institutions, relies on the local nonprofit sector to deliver community-based programs. Santa Cruz County established community partnerships and became one of the best local juvenile justice systems in the country. Counties do maintain high-security congregate facilities, but those facilities avoid "the concentration of troubled youths into three inherently violent state-run institutions where youths are forced to fight for survival."[109]

Since the nineteenth century, reforming juvenile justice has always centered on replacing old facilities with new structures—the *nicer institution syndrome*.[110] Once built, the new institutions quickly revert to conventional methods, and the same problems occur. California's history suggests the pattern of institutional abuse and the appeal for new facilities occurs in 15 to 30 year cycles. The downsizing of youth institutions in California has been remarkable, but questions remain about eliminating the remaining state-run congregate institutions.

> Arguments for preserving the state youth institutions to avoid unfavorable responses from segments of the juvenile justice system opposed to reform have the unintended effect of protecting historic bad practices and undermining the potential for long-term systemic transformation. Attempts to design reform efforts to accommodate the existing system and avoid potential risk have been successful in preserving the congregate institution since the nineteenth century. As Jerome Miller demonstrated in Massachusetts, true transformation only occurs when the last vestiges of the old system are abolished and replaced by something entirely new.[111]

Increasing evidence that punitive practices are ineffective and inhumane has added additional pressure to close state juvenile facilities.[112] In San Francisco, juvenile hall had 47 of its 150 beds filled—yet San Francisco paid the same $12 million to maintain the facility as it had spent since 2011 despite reducing the population by half.[113] San Francisco was not alone; 39 of 43 California counties had juvenile facilities that were half full but with skyrocketing costs. Of the youth confined in

San Francisco, almost 33% were charged with misdemeanors and 90% had been diagnosed with a mental health issue. Not only was a large portion of the facility unused but there were also serious questions as to why the current population was institutionalized.

The San Francisco Board of Supervisors in 2019 recommended the closing of its juvenile detention hall. As Daniel Macallair commented, it is a chance to rewrite the history of juvenile justice. This is a truly revolutionary movement.

New York

An evaluation of New York State's juvenile justice system in 2009 found that taxpayers spent more than $200,000 per youth in out-of-home placement.[114] Youth in facilities were subjected to excessive force, the use of inappropriate physical restraints, inadequate mental health care, inappropriate use of psychotropic medications, and inadequate substance abuse programming. Many youth were physically brutalized for typical adolescent behavior such as slamming a door. Almost 75% of youth in institutional placement were from New York City but were sent hundreds of miles upstate, making family visits difficult. In 2012, the legislature enacted Close to Home, shifting responsibility for placements from the state to the city. The number of juveniles sent to state facilities declined to 489. Similar to California, the per diem costs increased so that New York City paid $17 million more in 2012. Drawing on the strategies used successfully in a number of states, New York City transferred almost all city youth from upstate facilities to small, local facilities. Youth incarceration decreased 53%, and arrests declined about the same percentage.

Texas

In 2005, Texas confined almost 5,000 juveniles in state facilities.[115] After 13 boys were sexually abused in 2007, lawmakers overhauled the system with the goal of keeping youths out of remote rural facilities. They closed 7 of 12 facilities, and the number of youths in state custody decreased. By June 2018, there were 879. The Texas Juvenile Justice Department was rocked by another scandal in 2017.[116] Three female guards at the Gainesville State School were arrested on charges of sexual misconduct. Previously, another guard pleaded guilty to improper sexual activity with a juvenile in custody and was sentenced to 10 years. At least 6 other department employees have been arrested on suspicion of official oppression. Department officials blamed the problem on the inability to hire and retain qualified staff; the turnover rate was 39%—the highest of the state's five secure facilities. Juvenile justice advocates say the problems are systemic at remote, rural facilities and that Texas should adopt a model that keeps juveniles closer to home.

Virginia

In 2005, Virginia had 8 state facilities that confined more than 1,300 juveniles; by 2017, there was one with 208 occupants.[117] In 2014 Virginia invited the Annie E. Casey

Foundation to assess its juvenile justice system. The state spent a disproportionately large percentage of its juvenile justice budget to operate outdated, large facilities. It reduced the average daily population in facilities from 466 in 2015 to 216 in 2018 by reducing the length of stay, improving probation practices, and creating alternative placements.[118] Virginia reinvested the savings from the reduced number of incarcerated youth and the closure of one of its large facilities and a diagnostic center into an array of alternative residential and nonresidential options located in communities.

Pew Public Safety Performance Project

Georgia is one of seven states (the others are Hawaii, Kentucky, Kansas, South Dakota, West Virginia, and Utah) working with the Pew Public Safety Performance Project. Since 2013, it reduced mandatory minimum confinement periods, prohibited residential commitment for status offenders and some misdemeanors, and established a grant program to support counties that reduce the number of juveniles committed to state custody.[119] The number of youth in secure confinement has fallen 36%, and total commitments have decreased almost 50%. Three facilities closed, and lawmakers shifted $30 million into community-based sentencing options.

Kansas adopted reforms in 2016. In the first year, there was a 34% decrease in the juvenile out-of-home population that reduced placements in detention facilities, group homes, and secure facilities.[120] The group home population decrease of 58% was the largest decline. The state closed one of its two secure facilities. It shifted $12 million of savings from the reforms to evidence-based supervision and services in the community, helping 350 youths and families. The law requires that all savings (projected to be $72 million over five years) be reinvested in effective alternatives to incarceration.

In 2017, the governor of Utah signed comprehensive juvenile justice legislation to control costs, reduce recidivism and improve outcomes for juveniles, families, and communities. Truancy was removed from juvenile court jurisdiction. The reform is expected to cut the population of juveniles placed in state custody by 47% by 2022 and to free up more than $70 million over five years for reinvestment in evidence-based alternatives.[121] Collectively, the reform packages in the 7 states are projected to save $315 million over five years. Of the 924 votes cast in 14 legislative chambers, only 36 opposed the reforms.

REENTRY

Diverting youth from entering the system eliminates the negative experiences of confinement in youth prisons. "Research confirms that there is no intervention that is more effective when delivered in an institutional setting than when delivered in a community-based one."[122] Community programs at a cost of $75 per day achieve better outcomes than do institutional placements at $400 per day.

The Office of Juvenile Justice and Delinquency Prevention (OJJDP) urges states to create opportunities for positive youth development through which at-risk youth obtain a sense of safety and structure, a sense of belonging and membership, a sense of self-worth and social contribution, a sense of independence and control over one's life, and a sense of closeness in interpersonal relationships.[123] In contrast to prosocial, developmentally appropriate programs, interventions that place youth within a deviant group risk exacerbating antisocial behavior. The more restrictive a justice system intervention, the greater its negative impact.

Most youth prisons are located far from home, which makes it difficult to facilitate gradual transitions into community-based programming and to maintain family ties.[124] In contrast, smaller programs for juveniles who require secure placement are treatment intensive. "From the day youth walk in the door, the focus of these programs must be on helping them succeed when they return to the community. . . . High-quality, rigorous programming throughout the day is essential, not just to keep young people engaged, but also to boost their educational, social, and emotional development."[125]

Ideally, there would be a seamless transition from the institutional setting to the community setting with residential facility staff, juvenile probation or parole officers, mental/behavioral health service providers, community-based treatment providers, schools, family members, and other adults communicating about the reentry process.[126] The thereapeutic process offers the most opportunities for this type of cooperation. Juveniles confined hundreds of miles from their homes experience a more difficult transition.

Barriers to Reentry

The majority of youth released from juvenile institutions face a number of hurdles related to backgrounds of poverty, family conflicts, drug and alcohol use, and lack of education and skills. Most released juveniles are still adolescents and may suffer from delayed emotional and cognitive development. Most have not developed problem-solving or coping skills, and few have adults in their lives to help them learn the skills they need for life's challenges.[127]

By late adolescence, most youths have developed a strong sense of independence and healthy relationships with their parents, peers, and adults in general based on trust, empathy, self-disclosure, and loyalty. The vast majority of young offenders serving time are far behind their nondelinquent peers in terms of psychological development.[128] At the time of reentry, most of the released juveniles could be described as in the stage of adolescence usually exhibited at the ages of 11–14. Correctional facilities are not conducive to normal development; most inmates live in fear and distrust, blocking the acquisition of effective life skills. Institutional life dictates every move; it does not prepare youths to cope with the outside world—a world that has already rejected them and presented them with numerous problems. They are released into *the same hostile environment that spawned their delinquent behavior in the first place.*

The key to successful reentry centers on finding work, a place to live, and developing an intimate relationship. Years of research have confirmed this principle.[129] Out-of-home placement separates youth from their families. Reconnecting is an important step to successful reentry, and some programs focus on family reintegration.[130] One in four youths with a history of juvenile justice system involvement experience homelessness. Ensuring appropriate housing after release is important for successful reintegration and to reduce recidivism. The housing available is disproportionately located in low-income areas that have fewer educational and employment opportunities. Youth who return to more disadvantaged areas face an increased risk of recidivism, necessitating targeted services to help them overcome the barriers to successful reentry.

Education and employment are two strong predictors of successful reentry.[131] Juveniles who return to traditional school environments face numerous challenges and are at risk of dropping out. About 33% of youths in long-term secure custody have a learning disability compared with 8% in the general population. Youths who worked more than 20 hours per week reported significantly less aggressive antisocial behavior compared with unemployed youth.

Mental health and substance abuse disorders are prevalent among juveniles in residential facilities: 34% have substance use disorders; 20% have anxiety disorders, and 30% have disruptive behavior disorders.[132] Providing treatment is an important component of successful reentry. Targeted reentry services for mental health needs can reduce recidivism.

Types of Reentry Programs

One recent review of research found reentry interventions beneficial, particularly when targeted to higher-risk youth and involvement of the family in treatment.[133] To assist in the transition back to society following confinement, interventions aim to reduce risk factors (such as antisocial behavior and alienation) by enhancing protective factors, promoting community involvement, and reinforcing positive behavior.

Reentry interventions should assess the unique life experiences of each individual, including the effects of past trauma and the impact of stigma.[134] Interventions should also address the need for trusting relationships with adults. Some reentry programs offer a combination of different interventions such as case management combined with cognitive-behavioral programming.

In a meta-analysis of intensive supervision and aftercare programs, researchers did not find much evidence of the effectiveness of intensive forms of supervision.[135] The primary criticism of intermediate sanctions is that more intense supervision and strict conditions of compliance are not necessarily more effective in reducing recidivism for juvenile offenders compared with standard supervision, but the intensive supervision does increase the likelihood of detecting criminal/deviant behavior and leads to greater contact with the criminal justice system.

The findings suggest that intensive forms of probation are perhaps not necessary for effective supervision. However, one analysis (the effect of aftercare/reentry on alleged offenses) did demonstrate a significant reduction among treatment group participants, providing support for the deterring effect of supervision. Considering the mixed evidence (demonstrated here and in previous research), one could certainly argue that the inconsistent evidence is suggestive that, overall, these interventions do not reliably reduce recidivism and should therefore be replaced with new interventions or, at the very least, reconsidered.[136]

Case management begins with an assessment of criminogenic factors that must be addressed to decrease the risk of recidivism plus individual factors (such as cognitive ability and learning style) that could affect the effectiveness of interventions.[137] Risk-needs instruments are used to develop a plan, which can be modified as the needs and risks change. *Cognitive-behavioral treatment* focuses on problem solving and controlling impulses. Youth are encourated to develop the skills and thinking patterns necessary to succeed in the community. *Mentoring* programs pair juveniles with adults who provide encouragement and act as role models.[138] Mentors provide personal connections, guidance, skills training, exposure to positive values, a sense of self-worth, and hope for the future.

Therapeutic communities offer substance use treatment programs. They promote substance use recovery through group living, using a social learning approach to encourage changes in attitudes and actions.[139] *Reentry courts* use judicial oversight to supervise youths transitioning from residential facilities back into the community. The Court retains jurisdiction over the entirety of a youth's sentence.

Lessons from History

There have been historically low numbers of youth crime for decades. Juvenile facilities have closed, and unprecedented numbers of young people are now sentenced to community-based alternatives to incarceration. Reforms seek to provide more therapeutic and less punitive interventions in the lives of young people. Yet, reforms have happened at other times in U.S. history. The juvenile justice system was created because of a belief that children should be treated differently from adults. However, all children were not considered worth saving (see chapter 1). From the beginning, the juvenile justice system was exclusionary; it focused on confining young people deemed unworthy. Impoverished young people are at the crossroads of interlocking systems of social welfare and punishment because of their troubled family lives, risk taking, and poverty.[140] They struggle to cope with the dual philosophies of care and control in the juvenile justice system, and they face material and structural obstacles after release from custody.

David Rothman cautions that custody always wins when custody meets care.[141] He believes the character of institutions argues for their elimination, but the institutional model resists downsizing because ordinary citizens find them convenient for removing troublesome individuals from society and because those who benefit from them (i.e., employees, building contractors, suppliers) oppose change.

Good intentions motivate reforms, but the unintended consequences of those intentions have devastating effects on the youth trapped in the vice of care and control.[142] Intensive interventions and services push young people to change their behavior, yet enforced participation can also pull them away from other opportunities. Sometimes investments in treatment methods cannot overcome the realities of institutional life.[143] Monitoring devices allow juveniles to remain at home in the community but are stigmatizing and impose constant control on all aspects of the lives of children and their families (see chapter 11). Classification tools are used to identify specific needs, but the instruments can be biased, misapplied, and inaccurate.

The enduring question is whether policy makers will continue to embrace innovation, to assess new approaches, to monitor results, and to reduce marginalization. Accountability is emphasized for children who misbehave, but juvenile justice agencies too frequently look the other way at their own failures.

Summary

This chapter reviewed what are euphemistically called "correctional institutions"—in reality they are public or private *prisons*. Some confinement facilities are short-term (usually ranging from a few days to a couple of months); others are long-term (ranging from three or four months to one or two years). Detention centers, adult jails, and shelter care facilities are examples of short-term institutions. Over the years there have been many reports of substandard care. A high proportion of youths confined in these institutions suffer serious mental disorders, and the staff often are not professionally trained.

Minority youths are the most likely to be housed in youth prisons. Within many of these institutions, physical abuse is a daily occurrence; treatment is nonexistent; and recidivism rates are high. Budget constraints have pushed states to divert increasing numbers of troubled juveniles away from juvenile prisons. The fiscal restraints may result in better programs and better results. If the diversion to local facilities continues and is accompanied by treatment and skills programs, there will be fewer barriers to successful reentry.

Notes

[1] We will refrain from using the term "corrections" wherever possible in this chapter.

[2] War rhetoric is similar—killing innocent civilians is called "collateral damage."

[3] Patrick McCarthy, Vincent Schiraldi, and Miriam Shark, "The Future of Youth Justice: A Community-Based Alternative to the Youth Prison Model," National Institute of Justice, October 2016, NCJ 250142.

[4] Ibid., 1.

[5] Richard Mendel, "The Missouri Model: Reinventing the Practice of Rehabilitating Youthful Offenders," The Annie E. Casey Foundation, 2010, 4.

[6] Christopher Bickel, "From Child to Captive: Constructing Captivity in a Juvenile Institution," *Western Criminology Review*, 2010, 11(1): 37–49.

7 Juvenile Justice Geography, Policy, Practice & Statistics, "Corrections Agency," 2015, http://www.jjgps.org/juvenile-justice-services#release-decision

8 Juvenile Justice Geography, Policy, Practice & Statistics, "Release Decision," 2016, http://www.jjgps.org/juvenile-justice-services#release-decision

9 Peter Wagner and Wendy Sawyer, "Mass Incarceration: The Whole Pie 2018," Prison Policy Initiative, March 14, 2018.

10 Wendy Sawyer, "Youth Confinement: The Whole Pie," Prison Policy Initiative, February 27, 2018.

11 Annie E. Casey Foundation, "CEO Calls for States to Close 'Youth Prisons,'" Author, June 24, 2015, https://www.aecf.org/blog/annie-e-casey-foundation-ceo-calls-for-states-to-close-youth-prisons/

12 Pam Clark, "Types of Facilities," chapter 2 in *Desktop Guide to Quality Practice for Working with Youth in Confinement*, National Partnership for Juvenile Services, 2014, https://info.nicic.gov/dtg/node/4

13 Puzzanchera et al., "Juvenile Residential Facility Census Databook."

14 Charles Puzzanchera, Sarah Hockenberry, Anthony Sladky, and W. Kang, "Juvenile Residential Facility Census Databook," 2018, https://www.ojjdp.gov/ojstatbb/jrfcdb/asp/display_profile.asp

15 Sarah Hockenberry, Andrew Wachter, and Anthony Sladky, "Juvenile Residential Facility Census, 2014: Selected Findings," Washington, DC: OJJDP, September 2016.

16 Lacey Johnson, "JJDPA Reauthorization Passes Congress after 16 Years," Juvenile Justice Information Exchange, December 13, 2018.

17 Literature Review, "Status Offenders," Washington, DC: OJJDP, 2015.

18 Coalition for Juvenile Justice and the National Criminal Justice Association, "Summary of the Juvenile Justice Reform Act of 2018," 2019.

19 Sawyer, "Youth Confinement."

20 Zhen Zeng, "Jail Inmates in 2017," Washington, DC: Bureau of Justice Statistics, April 2019, NCJ 251774, appendix table 1.

21 Melissa Sickmund, W. Kang, and Charles Puzzanchera, "Glossary," (EZACJRP), National Center for Juvenile Justice, 2017, http://www.ojjdp.gov/ojstatbb/ezacjrp/asp/glossary.asp

22 Hockenberry, et al., "Juvenile Residential Facility Census, 2014."

23 Puzzanchera et al., "Juvenile Residential Facility Census Databook."; Sickmund, et al., "Easy Access to the Census of Juveniles in Residential Placement," National Center for Juvenile Justice, 2017, http://www.ojjdp.gov/ojstatbb/ezacjrp/

24 OJJDP Statistical Briefing Book, "Time in Placement," June 2017, https://www.ojjdp.gov/ojstatbb/corrections/qa08401.asp?qaDate=2015

25 Elizabeth Clarke, Elizabeth Kooy, Sara Balgoyen, "Detention of Juveniles in Illinois," Evanston, IL: Juvenile Justice Initiative, May 4, 2018.

26 Daniel Macallair and Mike Males, "A Failure of Good Intentions: An Analysis of Juvenile Justice Reform in San Francisco during the 1990s," *Review of Policy Research*, 2004, 21(1): 63–78.

27 National Juvenile Defender Center, "Confined without Cause: The Constitutional Right to Prompt Probable Cause Determinations for Youth," Washington, DC: Author, May 2018.

28 Karen Abram, Nicole Azores-Gococo, Kristin Emanuel, David Aaby, Leah Welty, Jennifer Hershfield, Melinda Rosenbaum, and Linda Teplin, "Sex and Racial/Ethnic Differences in Positive Outcomes in Delinquent Youth after Detention," *JAMA Pediatrics*, 2017, 171(2): 123–132.

29 National Juvenile Defender Center, "Confined without Cause."

30 Lee Underwood and Aryssa Washington, "Mental Illness and Juvenile Offenders, *International Journal of Environmental Research and Public Health*, 2016, 13(2): 228.

31 Marquita Stokes, Kathleen McCoy, Karen Abram, Gayle Byck, and Linda Teplin, "Suicidal Ideation and Behavior in Youth in the Juvenile Justice System: A Review of the Literature." *Journal of Correctional Health Care*, 2015, 21(3): 222–242; Matthew Aalsma, Laura White, Katherine Lau, Anthony Perkins, Patrick Monahan, and Thomas Grisso, "Behavioral Health Care Needs, Detention-Based Care, and Criminal Recidivism at Community Reentry from Juvenile Detention: A Multisite Survival Curve Analysis," *American Journal of Public Health*, 2015, 105(7): 1–7; Karen Abram, Naomi Zwecker, Leah Welty, Jennifer Hershfield, Mina Dulcan, and Linda Teplin, "Comorbidity and Continuity of Psychiatric Disorders in Youth After Detention: A Prospective Longitudinal Study," *JAMA Psychiatry*, 2014, 72: 84–93.

32 Development Services Group, Inc., "Intersection between Mental Health and the Juvenile Justice System," literature review, Washington, DC: OJJDP, 2017.

33 Annie E. Casey Foundation, "What Is Foster Care?" Baltimore, MD: Author, February 5, 2014.

34 Juvenile Law Center, "What Is the Foster Care-to-Prison Pipeline?" Philadelphia: Author, Mary 26, 2018.

35 Robert Woodson, "The Silent Scandal: Children behind Closed Doors," *The Hill*, July 3, 2018.

36 National Foster Youth Institute, "51 Useful Aging Out of Foster Care Statistics," Los Angeles: Author, May 2017.

37 Denis Theriault, "Foster Care Scandal: Oregon Releases Years of Shocking Abuse Complaints." *The Oregonian/Oregon Live*, January 12, 2016.

38 United States Senate Committee on Finance, "Chairman's News," Washington, DC: Author, October 17, 2017, https://www.finance.senate.gov/chairmans-news/hatch-wyden-respond-to-significant-need-to-improve-government-oversight-following-foster-care-investigation

39 Ryan Grim and Aida Chavez, "Children Are Dying at Alarming Rates in Foster Care, and Nobody is Bothering to Investigate," *The Intercept*, October 18, 2017, https://theintercept.com/2017/10/18/foster-care-children-deaths-mentor-network/

40 Ibid.

41 Rene Denfeld, "The Other Missing Children Scandal: Thousands of Lost American Foster Kids," *The Washington Post*, June 18, 2018.

42 Nick Juliano, "Child Welfare and Juvenile Justice Leaders," Boys Town, n.d.

43 National Institute of Justice, "Program Profile: Boys Town Family Home Program (Boys Town), Washington, DC: Office of Justice Programs, January 28, 2015.

44 Juliano, "Child Welfare and Juvenile Justice Leaders."

[45] OJJDP Statistical Briefing Book, "Facilities Evaluating Youth for Mental Health Needs, by Facility Operation and Facility Type, 2016, https://www.ojjdp.gov/ojstatbb/corrections/qa08540.asp?qaDate=2016&text=yes&maplink=link1

[46] Sawyer, "Youth Confinement."

[47] Sickmund et al., "Easy Access to the Census of Juveniles in Residential Placement."

[48] Puzzanchera et al., "Juvenile Residential Facility Census Databook."

[49] Office of Juvenile Justice and Delinquency Prevention, Easy Access to the Census of Juveniles in Residential Placement: 1997–2015, "Glossary," n.d.

[50] U.S. Government Accountability Office, "Residential Treatment Programs: Concerns Regarding Abuse and Death in Certain Programs for Troubled Youth," Washington, DC: Author, October 10, 2007, GAO-08-146T.

[51] Sickmund et al., "Easy Access to the Census of Juveniles in Residential Placement."

[52] Puzzanchera et al., "Juvenile Residential Facility Census Databook."

[53] Hockenberry, et al., "Juvenile Residential Facility Census, 2014."

[54] Development Services Group, Inc., "Wilderness Camp," Literature Review, Washington, DC: OJJDP, 2011.

[55] Daniel Macallair, "Boot Camp Blunder," August 5, 2002, http://articles.sfgate.com/2002-08-05/opinion/17557013_1_military-training-youth-programs-military-boot-camp

[56] Sarah Manchak and Frank Cullen "Intervening Effectively with Juvenile Offenders: Answers from Meta-Analysis," in J. Morizot and L. Kazemian (eds.), *The Development of Criminal and Antisocial Behavior* (New York: Springer, 2015), 477–490; see also Bitna Kim, Alida Merlo, and Peter Benekos, "Effective Correctional Intervention Programmes for Juveniles: Review and Synthesis of Meta-analytic Evidence. *International Journal of Police Science &Management*, 2013, 15(3): 169–189.

[57] Samuel Walker, *Sense and Nonsense about Crime, Drugs, and Communities*, 8th ed. (Stamford, CT: Cengage Learning, 2015).

[58] Ibid., 9.

[59] Mark Lipsey, James Howell, Marion Kelly, Gabrielle Chapman, Darin Carver, "Improving the Effectiveness of Juvenile Justice Programs: A New Perspective on Evidence-Based Practice," Center for Juvenile Justice Reform, 2010, 14.

[60] Sickmund et al., "Easy Access to the Census of Juveniles in Residential Placement."

[61] Ibid.

[62] Elizabeth Farmer, Maureen Murray, Kess Ballentine, Mary Elizabeth Rauktis, and Barbara Burns, "Would We Know It If We Saw It? Assessing Quality of Care in Group Homes for Youth," *Journal of Emotional and Behavioral Disorders*, 2017, 25(1): 28–36.

[63] Ibid.

[64] Ibid.

[65] Sawyer, "Youth Confinement."

[66] Hockenberry, et al., "Juvenile Residential Facility Census, 2014."

[67] Puzzanchera et al., "Juvenile Residential Facility Census Databook"; Sickmund et al., "Easy Access to the Census of Juveniles in Residential Placement."

[68] Hockenberry, et al., "Juvenile Residential Facility Census, 2014."

[69] Sickmund et al., "Easy Access to the Census of Juveniles in Residential Placement."

[70] Sickmund et al., "Easy Access to the Census of Juveniles in Residential Placement, 2017."

71 Bickel, "From Child to Captive," 38.

72 Maddy Troilo, "Locking Up Youth with Adults: An Update," Prison Policy Initiative, February 27, 2018.

73 Sourcebook on Criminal Justice Statistics (2011). "Prisoners under Age 18 held in State Prisons." Retrieved from: http://www.albany.edu/sourcebook/pdf/t6392011.pdf.

74 Ashley Nellis and Marc Mauer, "What We Can Learn from the Amazing Drop in Juvenile Incarceration," The Marshall Project, January 24, 2017.

75 Jeree Thomas, "Raising the Bar: State Trends in Keeping Youth out of Adult Courts (2015–2017)," Washington, DC: Campaign for Youth Justice, 2017.

76 The Campaign for the Fair Sentencing of Youth, "Tipping Point: A Majority of States Abandon Life-Without-Parole Sentences for Children," December 3, 2018.

77 Ian Lambie and Isabel Randell, "The Impact of Incarceration on Juvenile Offenders," *Clinical Psychology Review* 33(3): 448–459.

78 Karen Abram, Jeanne Choe, Jason Washburn, Linda Teplin, Devon King, Mina Dulcan, and Elena Bassett, "Suicidal Thoughts and Behaviors Among Detained Youth," Washington, DC: OJJDP, July 2014.

79 Anna Aizer and Joseph Doyle, "Juvenile Incarceration, Human Capital, and Future Crime: Evidence from Randomly Assigned Judges," *The Quarterly Journal of Economics*, 2015, 130(2): 759–803; James Sullivan, "From Monkey Bars to Behind Bars: Problems Associated with Placing Youth's in Adult Prisons," Seton Hall, *Law School Student Scholarship*, May 1, 2014.

80 Erving Goffman, *Asylums* (New York: Doubleday, 1961).

81 Bickel, "From Child to Captive," 38.

82 John Irwin, *The Felon* (Englewood Cliffs, NJ: Prentice-Hall, 1970), 74. See also James Austin and John Irwin, *It's About Time: America's Incarceration Binge*, 4th ed., Belmont, CA: Wadsworth, 2012.

83 Holly Nguyen, Thomas Loughran, Ray Paternoster, Jeffrey Fagan, and Alex Piquero, "Institutional Placement and Illegal Earnings: Examining the Crime School Hypothesis," *Journal of Quantitative Criminology*, 2017, 33(2): 207–235.

84 McCarthy, et al., "The Future of Youth Justice," 10.

85 Ibid., 12.

86 Allen Beck, David Cantor, John Hartge, and Tim Smith, Sexual Victimization in Juvenile Facilities Reported by Youth, 2012," National Survey of Youth in Custody, June 2013, NCJ 241708.

87 Allen Beck and Ramona Rantala, "Sexual Victimization Reported by Juvenile Correctional Authorities, 2007–2012.

88 Eileen Ahlin, "Risk Factors of Sexual Assault and Victimization among Youth in Custody," *Journal of Interpersonal Violence*, 2018, 1–24.

89 Thomas Loughran, Robert Brame, Jeffrey Fagan, Alex Piquero, Edward Mulvey, and Carol Schubert, "Studying Deterrence among High-Risk Adolescents," Washington, DC: OJJDP, August 2015.

90 Jerome G. Miller, *Last One Over the Wall: The Massachusetts Experiment in Closing Reform Schools*, 2nd ed., Columbus: Ohio State University Press, 1998, 18.

91 J. M. Lawrence, "Jerome Miller, 83, Altered Treatment of Juvenile Offenders," *Boston Globe*, August 26, 2015.

92 McCarthy, et al., "The Future of Youth Justice."

93 Ibid.

94 Ibid.

95 Molly Beck, "Lawmakers, Experts Eye Missouri as Model for Juvenile Justice Changes," *Wisconsin State Journal*, November 26, 2017.

96 Beth Huebner, "The Missouri Model: A Critical State of Knowledge," Appendix B in Committee on Assessing Juvenile Justice Reform, *Reforming Juvenile Justice: A Developmental Approach*, Washington, DC: The National Academies Press, 2013.

97 Beck, "Lawmakers, Experts Eye Missouri as Model for Juvenile Justice Changes."

98 McCarthy, et al., "The Future of Youth Justice."

99 Jake Horowitz, "States Take the Lead on Juvenile Justice Reform," Pew Public Safety Performance Project, May 11, 2017.

100 McCarthy, et al., "The Future of Youth Justice."

101 Annie E. Casey Foundation, "New Jersey Becomes First State to Implement JDAI Statewide," September 12, 2018.

102 Tony Fabelo, Nancy Arrigona, Michael Thompson, Austin Clemens, Miner Marchbanks, "Closer to Home: An Analysis of the State and Local Impact of the Texas Juvenile Justice Reforms," The Council on State Governments Justice Center and The Public Policy Research Institute, January 2015.

103 Pew Trusts, "State Juvenile Justice Work," March 29, 2018.

104 Maureen Washburn, "California's Local Juvenile Facilities Can Absorb the State Youth Correctional Population," Center on Juvenile and Criminal Justice, April 2018.

105 Jeremy Loudenback, "California Governor Signs Off on Sweeping Juvenile Justice Legislation," *The Chronicle of Social Change*, October 1, 2018.

106 Daniel Macallair, *After the Doors Were Locked: A History of Youth Corrections in California and the Origins of 21st Century Reform* (Lanham, MD: Rowman and Littlefield, 2015).

107 Ibid., 249.

108 Ibid.

109 Ibid., 254.

110 Ibid.

111 Macallair, *After the Doors Were Locked*, 255.

112 Maureen Washburn and Renee Menart. "Unmet Promises: Continued Violence and Neglect in California's Division of Juvenile Justice." San Francisco: Center on Juvenile and Criminal Justice, February 2019.

113 Alex Barrett-Shorter, "San Francisco Calls for Juvenile Hall Closure in Favor of Community-Based Alternatives." San Francisco: Center on Juvenile and Criminal Justice, April 18, 2019.

114 Center for Children's Law and Policy, "Implementation of New York's Close to Home Initiative: A New Model for Youth Justice," February 2018.

115 Jolie McCullough, "Following Sexual Abuse Scandals, Texas Juvenile Justice Department Submits Plan to Revamp Agency," *The Texas Tribune*, June 1, 2018.

116 Brandi Grissom and Sue Ambrose, "Fights, Sex, Drugs: Texas Juvenile Lockup on the Verge of Crisis, Reports Show," *Dallas News*, November 2017.

117 Nicolas Pollock, "The Last Kids Locked Up in Virginia," *The Atlantic*, March 16, 2018.

118 Virginia Department of Juvenile Justice, "Transformation Plan 2018 Update," 2018.

119 Horowitz, "States Take the Lead on Juvenile Justice Reform."

120 Jake Horowitz, "Kansas Reforms Improve Juvenile Justice," Pew Public Safety Performance Project, February 26, 2018.

121 Horowitz, "States Take the Lead on Juvenile Justice Reform."

122 McCarthy, et al., "The Future of Youth Justice," 22.

123 Ibid.

124 Ibid.

125 Ibid., 24,

126 Developmental Services Group, "Juvenile Rentry," Literature Review, Washington, DC: OJJDP, August 2017.

127 Laurence Steinberg, He Len Chung, and Michelle Little, "Reentry of Young Offenders from the Justice System: A Developmental Perspective," *Youth Violence and Juvenile Justice*, 2004, 2: 21–38.

128 David Altschuler and Rachel Brash, "Adolescent and Teenage Offenders Confronting the Challenges and Opportunities of Reentry," *Youth Violence and Juvenile Justice*, 2004, 2(1): 72–87.

129 This research includes the pioneering work of Joan McCord "A Forty Year Perspective on Effects of Child Abuse and Neglect," *Child Abuse and Neglect*, 1983, 7(3): 265–270) and the work of Robert Sampson and John Laub, *Crime in the Making: Pathways and Turning Points through Life*, Cambridge, MA: Harvard University Press, 1995; see also, Robert Sampson and John Laub, *A Life-Course Theory of Cumulative Disadvantage and the Stability of Delinquency*, New Brunswick, NJ: Transaction, 1997.

130 Developmental Services Group, "Juvenile Rentry.

131 Ibid.

132 Ibid.

133 Laura Abrams, Matthew Mizel, Viet Nguyen, and Aron Shlonsky, "Juvenile Reentry and Aftercare Interventions: Is Mentoring a Promising Direction?" *Journal of Evidence-Based Social Work*, 2014, 11(4): 404–422.

134 Developmental Services Group, "Juvenile Reentry."

135 Jessica Bouchard and Jennifer Wong, "Examining the Effects of Intensive Supervision and Aftercare Programs for At-Risk Youth: A Systematic Review and Meta-Analysis," 2018, *International Journal of Offender Therapy and Comparative Criminology*, 62(6): 1509–1534.

136 Ibid., 1530.

137 Developmental Services Group, "Juvenile Reentry."

138 Abrams et al, "Juvenile Reentry and Aftercare Interventions."

139 Developmental Services Group, "Juvenile Reentry."

140 Cox, *Trapped in a Vice*.

141 McCarthy, et al., "The Future of Youth Justice," 11.

142 Alexandra Cox, *Trapped in a Vice: The Consequences of Confinement for Young People*, New Brunswick: Rutgers University Press, 2018.

143 Macallair, *After the Doors Were Locked*.

Chapter 13

The Double Standard of Juvenile Justice

Women serve on the Supreme Court, in Congress, and on boards of directors of corporations. At first glance, it might appear that the twenty-first century has conquered gender inequality. Looking deeper, the reality is much less equitable. In 2019, Nevada became the first state legislature with a majority of female lawmakers. Women hold fewer than 30% of state legislative seats, and fewer than 25% of congressional seats.[1] In Mississippi, West Virginia, Alabama, and Louisisana, women make up about 15% of state lawmakers. Informal exclusion from public service is based on entrenched beliefs that women can't lead or balance their personal and professional lives.

More women than men have a high school education, university degrees, and graduate degrees, but women, especially women of color, are overrepresented in low-paying jobs.[2] Black women earn 63 cents for every dollar earned by white males; Latina women earn 54 cents; white women earn 87 cents. Census data compare the earnings of men and women who work full-time in one particular year.[3] Women frequently spend more time out of the labor force, so a multi-year analysis provides a more comprehensive picture of the gender wage gap. The Institute for Women's Policy Research found that women earned 19% of what men earned between 1968 and 1982; they earned 38% between 1983 and 1997; and they earned 49% between 2001 and 2015.

In 2016, 57% of women were employed in the labor force.[4] Participation in the labor force varies by marital status and differs for men and women. For example, divorced women had a higher labor force participation rate than married women (62.5% compared to 57.9%). By contrast, married men were more likely to participate in the labor force (73.1%) than divorced men (66%). Additionally, unmarried mothers have higher labor force participation rates than married mothers (75.9% compared to 68.6%). Women accounted for 52% of all workers employed in management, professional, and related occupations. For specific occupations, 38% of physicians and surgeons were women, 36% were lawyers, 27% of chief executives, 26% of architects, and 20% of software developers. Of registered nurses, 90% were women, as were 79% of elementary and middle school teachers, and 61% of of accountants and auditors. Asian (51%) and white (44%) women were more likely to work in high-paying management, professional, and related occupations than were Hispanic (32%) and African American (29%) women.

NORMATIVE BELIEFS ABOUT GENDER

In *Beyond the Double Bind*, Kathleen Hall Jamieson reveals the false choices women have been offered. A lineage of mixed messages women receive about who they are and what they should be is coined the "double bind"—either/or choices that trap and restrict women.

> Binds draw their power from their capacity to simplify complexity. Faced with a complicated situation or behavior, the human tendency is to split apart and dichotomize its elements. So we contrast good and bad, strong and weak, for and against, true and false, and in so doing assume that a person can't be both at once—or somewhere in between . . .
>
> In the history of humans, such choices have been constructed to deny women access to power and, where individuals manage to slip past their constraints, to undermine their exercise of whatever power they achieve. The strategy defines something "fundamental" to women as incompatible with something the woman seeks—be it education, the ballot, or access to the workplace.[5]

As Judith Lorber notes, gender is a social structure that originates in culture, not in biology. "Like any social institution, gender exhibits both universal features and chronological and cross-cultural variations that affect individual lives and social interaction in major ways."[6] Gender establishes expectations for behavior. These conceptions and stereotypes are woven through all social organizations of society, including the family, the economy, politics, and the criminal justice system.

Normative beliefs about femininity and masculinity are reinforced in the family.[7] Despite many advances for women, gender role socialization within some families continues to reflect stereotypic gender roles.[8] One meta-analysis found that the effects of child gender on the use of parental control were very small.[9] However, the study noted that differences within the studies did suggest that some parents do treat their sons and daughters differently—that gender stereotypes might explain the differences, although that has not been confirmed empirically. Higher socioeconomic status and more education are associated with less traditional views on gender roles. Some cultures have higher levels of gender inequality, which can mean that parents behave differently with sons and daughters.

Adolescent girls live in a world that has not changed much despite alterations to the adult female role. Modern girls, like girls in the past, are more closely watched than their brothers.[10] As girls approach puberty, parents begin to monitor them more closely—at the very stage of their lives when they desire more freedom and rely more on peer groups for approval. Clashes between daughters and parents may be more likely during late adolescence. Much of the family disharmony is an outgrowth of the long-standing sexual double standard (see discussion in chapter 5) that tacitly encourages male sexual exploration and punishes female sexuality. Despite recent cultural changes and the growth of the feminist movement, the double standard still persists.[11] The sexual double standard generally means that parents, concerned that too much freedom will result in poor behavior choices, try to exert more control to protect their daughters.

As discussed in chapter 5, some parents, who are not sure on how best to manage their children, turn to the juvenile court to enforce their authority. Parents whose communication with their children has broken down "look to the court for outside help and relief, yet find their children locked away as a result—sometimes repeatedly—without any resolution of the underlying problems."[12] One major reason for the presence of girls in juvenile courts is the insistence of their parents that they be arrested.[13] Some scholars suggest parents report daughters to juvenile courts as runaways when they become sexually active, while ignoring similar behavior by males.[14]

While parents, schools, social workers, or law enforcement can refer adolescents to court for status offenses, states decide when and how formal petitions can be made. For example, Wisconsin defines habitual truancy as missing five (or a portion of) days in a semester. A student can be sent to court for as little as being late to class five times.[15] In 2014, status offenses accounted for approximately one of every 11 juvenile court cases. Because of the different types of courts that handle cases in the various states (truancy, family, delinquency, municipal courts), the reported number of cases is probably low. Many courts do not report to a state or federal authority. The numbers also do not include cases in which justice-system involved youths are returned to court for misbehavior while on probation. Status offense laws vary greatly from state to state, as do the sanctions following the disposition of a case as well as diversion programs and practices.[16]

The history of the juvenile justice system was reviewed in some detail in chapter 1. In this chapter we will focus on how the system has historically responded to the behavior of girls. Historically, reformers have believed that girls are comparatively less harmed by the failures of the criminal justice system.[17] One reason is that girls make up 25% of justice-involved youth. As a result, girls have systematically been excluded from juvenile justice policy analysis and research. While we will focus on the double standard for girls, it is important to remember that gender is linked to justice involvement for all youth. The incarceration of boys of color is linked to racialized stereotypes of masculinity linking men of color with danger. Sexism and gender stereotypes based on normative views of masculinity and femininity affect law enforcement practices that drive youth into the system. The stereotypes harm boys, girls, and gender non-conforming youth who are overrepresented in the justice system.

THE CHILD-SAVING MOVEMENT AND THE JUVENILE COURT

Attitudes toward youths in U.S. society shifted during the Progressive Era (1890–1920). The stubborn-child law (see chapter 1) established the legal relationship

between children and parents. The Progressive Era extended that concept and ushered in unprecedented government involvement in family life, and more specifically in the lives of adolescents. The child-saving movement made much rhetorical
use of the value of such traditional institutions as the family and education: "The
child savers elevated the nuclear family, especially women as stalwarts of the family,
and defended the family's right to supervise the socialization of youth."[18] But while
the child savers were exalting the family, they were also crafting a governmental system that would have authority to intervene in familial areas and, more specifically,
in the lives of young people. The child savers regarded their cause as a moral one
and "viewed themselves as altruists and humanitarians dedicated to rescuing those
who were less fortunately placed in the social order."[19]

As discussed in chapter 1, the culmination of the child savers' efforts was the
juvenile court. The legislation that established the first juvenile court in Chicago
in 1899 became a prototype for legislation in other states. Juvenile courts soon
appeared in Colorado (1900), Wisconsin (1901), New York (1901), Ohio (1902),
and Maryland (1902). By 1928 all but two states had a juvenile court system.

Based on an assumption of the natural dependence of youth, the juvenile
court was charged with determining the guilt or innocence of accused underage persons and with acting for or in place of defendants' parents. The concern
of the child savers went far beyond removing the adolescent criminal from the
adult justice system. Many of their reforms were actually aimed at "imposing sanctions on conduct unbecoming youth and disqualifying youth from the benefit of
adult privileges."[20] One of the unique features of the new juvenile courts was that
they monitored and responded to youthful behaviors believed to indicate future
problems.

The Reformers

Lisa Pasko describes the changing boundaries of the court regarding girls.[21]

> Whereas the first juvenile court originally defined "delinquent" as those under
> sixteen who had violated a city ordinance or law, when the definition was applied
> to girls, the court included incorrigibility, associations with immoral persons, va-
> grancy, frequent attendance at pool halls or saloons, other debauched conduct,
> and use of profane language in its definition.[22]

Scientific and popular literature on female delinquency expanded enormously
during this period, as did institutions specifically devoted to the reformation
of girls.[23]

The child-saving movement was keenly concerned about prostitution and
other social evils such as white slavery.[24] [Today federal law prohibits sex trafficking, but girls who are commercially exploited end up in court for status offenses
and delinquency charges.[25] See chapter 5.] Just exactly how women, many of them
highly educated, became involved in patrolling the boundaries of working-class
girls' sexuality is a depressing but important story. Middle-class women reformers

initially focused on regulating and controlling male sexuality. They had a Victorian view of women's sexuality and saw girls as inherently chaste, sexually passive, and in need of protection. These women waged an aggressive social movement to raise the age of consent (which in many parts of the country ranged from 10 to 12 years of age) to 16 or above.

The pursuit of claims of statutory rape against men was another component of their efforts. Charges were brought in a number of cases. If a girl lost "the most precious jewel in the crown of her womanhood," it was the fault of men who had forced them into sexual activity.[26] Later research found that in almost 75% of the cases reviewed in Los Angeles, the girls entered into sexual relationships with the young men willingly. Led largely by upper- and upper-middle-class women volunteers, many of whom were prominent in the temperance movement (like Frances Willard), this campaign—not unlike the Mothers Against Drunk Driving campaign of later decades—drew an impressive and enthusiastic following, particularly among white citizens.

African-American women participated in other aspects of progressive reform, but they were less aggressive in pursuing statutory rape complaints. Mary Odem speculates that they rightly suspected that any aggressive enforcement of these statutes was likely to fall most heavily on young African-American men (while doing little to protect girls of color), which is precisely what occurred. Although the number of cases was small, African-American men were sent to prison to reform their "supposedly lax and immoral habits," while white men were either not prosecuted or were given probation.[27]

The statutory rape complaints met staunch judicial resistance, particularly when many (but not all) cases involved young, working-class women who had chosen to be sexually active. Reformers (many of them now professional social workers) began to shift the focus of their activities. The "delinquent girl" herself became the focus of reform. Moral campaigns to control teenage female sexuality began to appear. Reformers during this later period (1910–1925) assumed that they had the authority to define what "appropriate" conduct was for young working-class women and girls—based, of course, on middle-class ideals of female sexual propriety. Girls who did not conform to these ideals were considered "wayward and in need of control by the state."[28]

Alice Stebbins Wells was a social worker who became the first policewoman in the United States. She illustrates the ironies of child saving perfectly. In 1910 she was hired by Los Angeles because she argued that she could not serve her clients (young women) without police powers. Her work, and the work of five other female police officers hired during the next five years, was to monitor "dance halls, cafes, picture shows and other public amusement places" and to escort girls who were "in danger of becoming delinquent to their homes and to make reports to their parents with a proper warning."[29]

Women reformers played a key role in the founding of the juvenile court in Los Angeles in 1903 and vigorously advocated the appointment of women court workers to deal with the "special problems" of girls. This court was the first in the country to appoint women "referees," who were invested with nearly all the powers of judges in girls' cases. Women were also hired to run the juvenile detention facility in 1911. As Cora Lewis, chairman of the Probation Committee that established Juvenile Hall, declared, "In view of the number of girls and the type of girls detained there . . . it is utterly unfeasible to have a man at the head of the institution." The civic leaders and newly hired female court workers "advocated special measures to contain sexual behavior among working-class girls, to bring them to safety by placing them in custody, and to attend to their distinctive needs as young, vulnerable females."[30]

The Girl-Saving Movement

Girl-saving efforts evolved through a coalition between feminists and other Progressive Era movements. Concerned about female victimization and distrustful of male (and to some degree female) sexuality, prominent women leaders, including Susan B. Anthony, found common cause with the more conservative social purity movement around such issues as the regulation of prostitution and raising the age of consent. Once the focus had shifted to the delinquent girl, the solution became harsh, "maternal justice" meted out by professional women.[31]

Girls were the losers in this reform effort. Studies of early family court activity reveal that almost all of the girls who appeared in these courts were charged with immorality or waywardness.[32] For example, a detailed study of the Cook County Juvenile Court between 1906 and 1927 found that the two most common charges against girls were immorality and incorrigibility.[33] The third most common charge was larceny. The sanctions for such misbehavior were extremely severe. For example, the Chicago family court sent half the girl delinquents (but only a fifth of the boy delinquents) to reformatories between 1899 and 1909. In Milwaukee and Memphis, twice as many girls as boys were committed to training schools.[34] Identical findings have been reported in a study examining the juvenile court in St. Louis in the first years of the twentieth century.[35]

Large numbers of girls' reformatories and training schools were established during the Progressive Era, in addition to places of "rescue and reform." Twenty-three facilities for girls were opened during the decade from 1910 to 1920 (in the previous 60 years the average was 5 reformatories a decade), and they did much to set the tone of official response to female delinquency. These institutions were obsessed with precocious female sexuality and were determined to instruct girls to overcome their wayward behavior.[36]

There was a slight modification of the *parens patriae* doctrine during this period. The "training" of girls was shaped by the image of the ideal woman that had evolved during the early part of the nineteenth century. Women belonged in the private sphere, performing such tasks as rearing children, keeping house, caring for husbands, and serving as the moral guardians of the home. In this capacity, women needed qualities like obedience, modesty, and dependence. The domain of men was the public sphere: the workplace, politics, and the law. By virtue of this public power, men were the final arbiters of public morality and culture.[37] This white, middle-class "cult of domesticity" was, of course, very distant from the lives of many women in lower socioeconomic classes who were in the labor force by necessity. The Ladies Committee of the New York House of Refuge summed up their approval of the goals of institutions for girls.

> The Ladies wish to call attention to the great change which takes place in every girl who has spent one year in the Refuge; she enters a rude, careless, untrained child, caring nothing for cleanliness and order; when she leaves the House, she can sew, mend, darn, wash, iron, arrange a table neatly and cook a healthy meal.[38]

The institutions established for girls isolated them from all contact with males and trained them in stereotypical feminine skills (at the time), while housing them in bucolic settings. The intention was to hold the girls until marriageable age and to teach them domesticity during their sometimes-lengthy incarceration. The child savers had little hesitation about such extreme intervention in girls' lives. They believed delinquency to be the result of a variety of social, psychological, and biological factors, and they were optimistic about the juvenile court's ability to remove girls from influences that were producing delinquent behavior.

The juvenile court judge served as a benevolent yet stern father. The proceedings were informal, without the traditional judicial trappings. Initially no lawyers were required; constitutional safeguards were not in place; no provisions existed for jury trials; and so on. Consistent with the *parens patriae* doctrine, juvenile courts were not constrained by the legal requirements of criminal courts because of the rationale that they were acting in the best interests of the child. Nowhere has the confusion and irony of the juvenile court been more clearly demonstrated than in its treatment of girls labeled as delinquent. Many of these girls were incarcerated for noncriminal behavior during the early years of the court.

THE JUVENILE COURT AND THE DOUBLE STANDARD OF JUVENILE JUSTICE

The offenses that bring girls into the juvenile justice system reflect the system's dual concerns: adolescent criminality and moral conduct. Historically, they have also reflected a unique and intense preoccupation with girls' sexuality and their obedience to parental authority.[39]

Relatively early in the juvenile justice system's history, a few astute observers became concerned about the abandonment of minors' rights in the name of treatment, saving, and protection. One of the most insightful was Paul Tappan.[40] He evaluated several hundred cases in the Wayward Minor Court in New York City during the late 1930s and early 1940s and concluded that there were serious problems with a statute that brought young women into court simply for disobeying parental commands or because they were in danger of becoming depraved.

Tappan was particularly disturbed that the court was essentially legislating what is and is not morally acceptable. Noting that many young women were being charged with sexual activity, he asked, "What is sexual misbehavior—in a legal sense—of the nonprostitute of 16, or 18, or of 20 when fornication is no offense under criminal law?"[41]

When one group imposes their own definition of morality onto another group (a common method of social control), those efforts can be termed "moral imperialism." The major problem of such an imposition from a legal standpoint, as noted in chapter 1, is that it punishes someone for something they *might* do in the future. Tappan believed that the structure of the Wayward Minor Court invested the judge with judicial totalitarianism, and he cautioned that "the fate of the defendant, the interest of society, the social objectives themselves, must hang by the tenuous thread of the wisdom and personality of the particular administrator."[42]

Mary Odem and Steven Schlossman reviewed the characteristics of the girls who entered the Los Angeles Juvenile Court in 1920 and in 1950. In 1920, 93% of the girls accused of delinquency were charged with status offenses; of those, 65% were charged with immoral sexual activity (even though the majority had engaged in sex with only one partner, usually a boyfriend). The parents of the girls referred 51% of the cases to the court. Odem and Schlossman attributed these actions to parental fears about their daughters' exposure to the "omnipresent temptations to which working-class daughters in particular were exposed in the modern ecology of urban work and leisure."[43]

Women court officials attempted to instill a middle-class standard of respectability by "dispensing the maternal guidance and discipline supposedly lacking in the girls' own homes. Referees and probation officers scolded their charges for wearing too much makeup and dressing in a provocative manner."[44] Court officials were obsessed with the sexuality of these young women. Odem notes that after a girl was arrested, "probation officers questioned her relatives, neighbors, employers, and school officials to gather details about her sexual misconduct and, in the process, alerted them that she was a delinquent in trouble with the law."[45]

Between 1920 and 1950 the makeup of the court's female clientele changed very little: "the group was still predominantly white, working class, and from disrupted families. Girls were more likely to be in school and less likely to be working in 1950. Status offenses (78%) continued to be the most frequent charges, although somewhat different from those in 1920. Thirty-one percent of the girls were charged with running away from home, truancy, curfew, or "general unruliness at home." The percentage charged with sexual misconduct declined to less than 50% (once again usually with a single partner). Referrals from parents declined to 26% (referrals from police officers increased to 54% from 29% in 1920; referrals from schools decreased to 21% versus 27% in 1920). Although the rationale for detention had changed, concerns about female sexual conduct "remained determinative in shaping social policy" in the 1950s.[46]

As mentioned repeatedly throughout this book, contemporary status offense categories are extremely vague. They can serve as "buffer charges" for suspected sexuality. Researchers in the 1960s observed that although girls were incarcerated in training schools for what they called the "big five" (running away from home, incorrigibility, sexual offenses, probation violation, and truancy) "the underlying vein in many of these cases is sexual misconduct by the girl delinquent."[47]

A review of cases of ungovernability in New York in 1972 revealed that judges based their decisions on personal feelings. Consider this comment by one of the judges: "She thinks she's a pretty hot number; I'd be worried about leaving my kid with her in a room alone. She needs to get her mind off boys."[48] Another admonished a girl:

> I want you to promise me to obey your mother, to have perfect school attendance and not miss a day of school, to give up these people who are trying to lead you to do wrong, not to hang out in candy stores or tobacco shops or street corners where these people are, and to be in when your mother says.[49]

Empirical studies of the processing of girls' and boys' cases between 1950 and the early 1970s documented the impact of these sorts of judicial attitudes. Girls charged with status offenses were often more harshly treated than their male or female counterparts charged with crimes. A study of court dispositions in Washington State between 1953 and 1955 found that girls were far less likely than boys to be charged with criminal offenses—but more than twice as likely to be committed to institutions.[50] Some years later a study of a juvenile court in Delaware discovered that first-time female status offenders were more harshly sanctioned (as measured by institutionalization) than males charged with felonies. For repeat status offenders, the pattern was even starker: female status offenders were six times more likely than male status offenders to be institutionalized.

Despite the eventual changes detailed below, judicial discretion continues to impact girls in the twenty-first century.

> Studies indicate that judges continue to have sexist, paternalistic attitudes toward young girls. Courts believe that girls must be protected from the evils of the outside world. . . . Because of this view, judges continue to perceive a need to intervene in girls' lives to save the young females through the authority of the juvenile justice system. Moreover, as status offenders are not afforded procedural due process rights, they have no protections against the paternalistic attitudes of juvenile court judges.[51]

The nature of status offenses facilitates discretionary enforcement based on culturally fostered attitudes. Criminal cases have relatively clear guidelines; standards of evidence are delineated; elements of the crime are laid out in the statutes; and law, at least to some extent, protects civil rights. Judges have few legal guidelines in status offense cases. Many judges accepted one of the orientations built into the juvenile justice system: the puritan stance supportive of parental demands or the progressive stance where the court assumes parental roles. It was inevitable that such attitudes and the resulting actions would result in significant legal challenges. In the 1970s, critics mounted a major drive to deinstitutionalize status offenders and to divert them from formal court jurisdiction.

DEINSTITUTIONALIZATION AND JUDICIAL PATERNALISM

By the mid-1970s, correctional reformers had become concerned about juvenile courts' abuse of the status offense category. However, very little of the concern was based on the history of gender bias that characterized some, but not all, of these categories. Instead, the argument was that noncriminal youth should be treated and helped—not detained and institutionalized.

As discussed in previous chapters, the Juvenile Justice and Delinquency Prevention Act (JJDPA) of 1974 required that states receiving federal delinquency prevention money begin to divert and deinstitutionalize status offenders. "Despite inconsistent enforcement of this provision and some resistance from states to decriminalize status offenders, girls were the clear beneficiaries of the reform, as they no longer could be directly incarcerated for filial disobedience, running away, truancy, or immorality."[52] Incarceration of young women in training schools and detention centers across the country fell dramatically. Studies of court decision-making found less clear evidence of discrimination against girls in parts of the country where serious diversion efforts were occurring.[53]

The Conservative Backlash

There was resistance to deinstitutionalization. When the JJDPA was first being implemented, the director of the National Center of Juvenile Justice claimed that status offenses were offenses against the country's values. He said girls were "seemingly overrepresented as status offenders because we have had a strong heritage of being protective toward females in this country" and continued that it offended sensibilities when a fourteen-year-old girl engaged in sexually promiscuous activity.[54] He offered the opinion that the police, the church, or vigilante groups would probably act if their values were offended, and he preferred that action be taken in the court where the rights of the parties could be protected. In 1978, a General Accounting Office (GAO) report concluded that law enforcement had downplayed the act's importance and "to some extent discouraged states from carrying out the Federal requirement."[55] The GAO found that monitoring compliance with the law by the states was lax or nonexistent and that definitions of what constituted detention and correctional facilities were confusing.

Valid Court Order Exception

In 1980, an amendment to the JJDPA (see chapters 3 and 12) allowed judges discretion if a juvenile had violated a valid court order (VCO). The change, never publicly debated in either house, effectively gutted the act by permitting judges to reclassify a status offender who violated a court order as a delinquent. This meant that a young woman who ran away from a court-ordered placement (a halfway house, foster home, or the like) could be relabeled a delinquent and locked up.

Before the VCO exception, juvenile judges engaged in less public efforts to circumvent deinstitutionalization. These included "bootstrapping" status offenders into delinquents by issuing criminal contempt citations, referring or committing status offenders to secure mental health facilities, and referring them to "semisecure" facilities.[56] After the VCO exception, juvenile judges could confine status offenders in institutions. More than half the states use the VCO exception to confine status offenders in secure facilities. Status offenders are subjected to the most judicial discretion and usually have the least amount of formal protection.[57] Parents would normally have the responsibility of providing counsel, but most status offenders are referred to the court by parents. The juvenile judge's discretion is rarely questioned. If the VCO exception were eliminated, states would be driven to utilize diversion programs and to implement programs to strengthen families.[58]

Reauthorizations of JJDPA

In addition to making it a core requirement for states to address disproportionate minority contact (see chapter 11), the 1992 reauthorization established new programs to address gender bias.[59] States receiving federal funds were required to analyze gender-specific services for the prevention and treatment of juvenile delinquency. Funds were established for states to develop policies to prohibit gender bias in placement and treatment and to develop programs to assure girls equal access to services.[60] The 2002 reauthorization broadened the scope of disproportionate minority confinement to disproportionate minority contact (see chapter 11).

As discussed in chapter 12, Congress reauthorized JJDPA in December 2018. States must collect data and establish plans to address racial and ethnic disparities. Protections of youths held on juvenile court charges were extended to youth charged as adults. States must provide alternatives to detention, engage families in service delivery, use community-based services to serve at-risk youth, and promote trauma-informed programs and practices. By 2020, states must eliminate the use of restraints on pregnant girls housed in secure detention facilities.

> The juvenile justice system in the United States has gone through many changes in its history. From an initial goal of rehabilitation, to a realization of the punitive nature of the juvenile courts, the juvenile justice system has granted youth offenders greater autonomy by providing procedural due process rights and protections and a voice in their adjudications. These rights, however, have not been extended to status offenders. The denial of rights and the lack of a voice in their adjudications has left status offenders vulnerable to the discretion and paternalism of juvenile court judges. Because there are no procedural safeguards in place, many judges impose their own views in the adjudication and disposition of status

offenders which, in turn, leads to unequal and unpredictable results for many status offenders. To curb the broad discretion and paternalism demonstrated by some juvenile court judges, it is important that the rights and protections offered to juvenile delinquents be extended to status offenders, or alternatively, that status offenders be removed from the jurisdiction of the juvenile justice system.[61]

CONTINUING EVIDENCE OF GENDER BIAS

Reforms have reduced the number of girls in detention to less than 46,000; most states had fewer than 150 girls in placement in 2015 and many had fewer than 50.[62] Although gender bias is not as blatant as in earlier years, it is still visible. The legacy of sexual stereotypes and paternalism continues.

> With a focus on their physical appearance and sexuality, the characterizations of girls in their official court records and case files regularly deem them to be deceitful, manipulative, hysterical, wildly sexual, and verbally abusive. Under a paternalistic ideology, the current juvenile justice institutions—police, courts, and corrections—exercise the repeated need to protect their daughters, usually from sexual experimentation and other dangers on the streets. At the same time, the court frequently labels girls as sexually promiscuous, untrustworthy, and unruly, without connecting such behaviors to their life histories and social contexts.[63]

Punitive responses to misconduct such as running away or truancy too often ignore the reasons for the behaviors. Girls may run away from home after experiencing sexual abuse or because of conflicts with their families over sexual orientation. They may skip school to avoid harassment. When authorities ignore the social context in which behaviors occur, they reinforce the sexism that drives the treatment of girls. They endorse the stereotype that girls should be compliant and "ladylike."[64] The disparate treatment of girls for status and low-level offenses holds them to a different behavioral standard based on the gendered expectations that "boys will be boys" but girls must conform. When girls break rules by skipping school, violating curfew, or disobeying authority, they violate conventional expectations of compliant feminine behavior. They are perceived as rebellious; their behaviors conflict with the expectations that girls should be passive and submissive.

Nonconforming Identities

This chapter addresses the double bind faced by girls because of gendered stereotypes. It is important to emphasize that gender is not binary. Gender is a significant factor leading lesbian, gay, bisexual, transgender (LGBT), and gender nonconforming children into court and the juvenile justice system for status offenses.[65] Underage girls may be living on the street if parents do not accept them being lesbians. Transgender girls may become habitual truants because classmates bully and taunt them. A nonconforming child may avoid school because peer groups are segregated by traditional sex roles. Research has found that trauma, family conflict, and social isolation are a pathway to the juvenile justice system.[66] LGBT youth experience higher rates of neglect, abuse, and rejection by family members than straight counterparts. They are more likely to be removed from their homes for abuse or neglect, suspended or expelled from school, and to be homeless. Youths who identify as lesbian, gay, or bisexual are more likely to be stopped by the police, arrested, and convicted when engaging in the same behaviors as straight youth.

Gender affects expectations for behavior, relationships with family and peers, and how children see themselves and their roles in society. As mentioned earlier, masculine social norms affect the over-criminalization of boys. Feminine social norms lead to an overrepresentation of LGBT children in court and detention facilities for status offenses compared to gender-conforming peers. The experiences of girls have largely been overlooked by reforms that focus on boys. Sexism, racism, and misogyny have been exacerbated by justice involvement. One survey found that 40% of girls in detention identify as LGBT compared to 13% of boys.[67]

The experiences of juveniles whose identities are non-conforming are generally invisible.[68] Most juvenile justice systems operate facilities based on a child's biologically assigned sex. Non-binary children who do not identify with one gender are forced into categories based on how systems are organized.

Getting into the System

Many youths come to the attention of the juvenile court because of a complaint or referral from sources other than law enforcement agencies—particularly for status offenses. Girls, who are less than one quarter of the juvenile justice population, constitute 37–47% of children who cross over from the child welfare system into the juvenile justice system. For example, children who run away from foster care placement may be referred by child welfare.[69] Justice systems are frequently gendered institutions with traditional patriarchal norms. Paternalism is particularly prevalent for status offenses that are used to enforce school, parental, and civic authority. The adjudication of status offenders reflects judicial paternalism.[70]

Rates for petitioned cases involving truancy, runaway, and ungovernability were higher for juveniles 16 years old than for 17-year-old juveniles.[71] From 2005–2016, the number of petitioned truancy cases outnumbered all other status offense cases for both males and females and across all racial groups. Schools referred 93% of truancy cases; law enforcement referred 2%. Truancy cases were the least likely to involve detention (32%) and the least likely to be adjudicated (32% for males; 30% for females).

As discussed in chapters 3 and 5, the only status offense for which girls are the majority of the caseload is runaway. Law enforcement referred 46% of the petitioned runaway cases; relatives referred 24%.[72] The runaway case rate for black youth was more than 3 times the rate for white youth and more than 4 times the rate for Hispanic youth. Runaway cases were more likely to be detained than any other status offense type. The percentages of adjudicated runaway cases was 33% for males and 32% for females. Juvenile courts were most likely to order out-of-home placement following adjudication for runaway cases—23% of males and 18% of females.

Between 2005 and 2016, case rates for ungovernability declined 54% for males and 60% for females and decreased at least 55% for whites, blacks, and Hispanics, although the ungovernability case rate for black juveniles was more than twice the white rate.[73] Law enforcement referred 30% of ungovernability cases, schools referred 10%, and relatives referred about 50%. Adjudication was most likely in cases involving ungovernability (50%) and liquor law violations (53%).

Chapter 5 discussed arrests of girls in detail; a brief synopsis follows. In 2017, 29 of every 100 juvenile arrests was a girl.[74] Only 4 of every 100 arrests of a girl was for serious violent crime. Other assaults accounted for 20% of the arrests of girls and 15% of the arrests of boys. As explained in chapter 5, arrests for this offense are attributable to changes in formal responses to ordinary fights at school (i.e. increased use of law enforcement officers at schools) and in domestic violence legislation (i.e. changes in definitions of who can be charged with domestic violence including siblings, step-siblings, etc.).

Girls are most frequently arrested for status offenses—behaviors (running away, curfew violations, being incorrigible or ungovernable) that would not be subject to sanctions except for one's age. Female status offenders continue to be subjected to the historical perspective on gender roles that influenced juvenile courts.[75] Because the judiciary views their role toward status offenders as rehabilitative rather than punitive, courts provide few procedural protections to status offenders.[76] Status offenders can be deprived of their liberty, but they do not enjoy the same due process rights granted to delinquent individuals and adults. "It is a perversion of our justice system to punish juveniles who have not committed a crime, without allowing them due process rights."[77]

Girls on the Streets

In one of the first detailed studies of police contacts with girls, Christy Visher concluded that age was irrelevant in police interactions with males but relevant in interactions with females, with younger females receiving harsher treatment. Visher also noted that "police officers adopt a more paternalistic and harsher attitude toward young females to deter any further violation of appropriate sex-role behavior."[78] In addition, demeanor was an extremely important factor in the arrest decision: "female suspects who violated typical middle-class standards of traditional female characteristics and behaviors (i.e., white, older, and submissive) are not afforded any chivalrous treatment during arrest decisions."[79] Women suspected of property offenses were actually more harshly treated than their male counterparts.

There has been little research demonstrating overt police bias against girls in recent years. In fact, some studies suggest that police are far more likely to refer boys to court than girls, because their offenses are much more serious.[80]

Gender and Delinquency Referrals

What kinds of behavior result in referral to juvenile court? Are there significant differences between girls and boys in referrals? Juvenile court referrals include youths charged with both criminal violations and status offenses, such as incorrigibility (in some jurisdictions called unmanageability or ungovernability, and in others the child is labeled "in need of supervision") and truancy. In some parts of the country, youths who are abused or neglected are also handled in juvenile courts.

> When a child is brought before the court for behavior felt to be beyond the control of the parent/guardian, ideally there would be many alternatives to filing a petition in court, such as mental health services, family intervention and support, mediation or alternative dispute resolution, and other community-based services and supports aimed at helping these children in the context of their family and community life.[81]

As shown in table 13-1, 34% of males and 32% of females in 2016 were referred to court for a property offense—declining from 61% for boys in 1985 and 58% for girls. In 1985 only 16% of girls were referred for person offenses, compared to 32% in 2016. The bulk of these cases (as noted in earlier chapters) are for simple assault, stemming mostly from domestic violence cases and fighting at school (Juvenile Court Statistics source does not break down person offenses into simple and aggravated assaults). Public order offenses also increased for both boys and girls.

The nature of status offenses petitioned to court has also changed. Table 13-2 shows 24% of girl status offenders were runaways in 1995 versus 11% in 2016; the percentage decreased for boys as well. The proportion of girls and boys brought in for truancy and liquor law violations increased. As a reminder, these figures are for the cases petitioned to court; many status cases are handled informally by local social service organizations, making gender comparisons difficult. It has become increasingly difficult to obtain national data on status offenses, with the exception of arrest data (and these data only show arrests for runaways and curfew violations).

Table 13-1 Juvenile Court Referrals, by Offense and Gender

	Male			Female		
Offense	**1985**	**2005**	**2016**	**1985**	**2005**	**2016**
Person	16%	25%	28%	16%	28%	32%
Property	61	37	34	58	37	32
Drugs	7	12	13	6	8	11
Public Order	16	26	25	19	27	26

Source: Sarah Hockenberry and Charles Puzzanchera, *Juvenile Court Statistics 2016*, Pittsburgh: National Center for Juvenile Justice, August 2018; 13; Charles Puzzanchera, Benjamin Adams, and Melissa. Sickmund, *Juvenile Court Statistics 2006–2007*, 2010, 13.

Table 13-2 Petitioned Status Offense Cases and Gender

Offense	Male			Female		
	1995	2005	2016	1995	2005	2016
Runaway	12%	8%	7%	24%	16%	11%
Truancy	27	35	55	33	39	60
Curfew	12	11	7	7	7	4
Ungovernability	14	11	9	15	13	9
Liquor	28	23	13	17	18	11
Miscellaneous	7	12	9	5	8	5

Source: Sarah Hockenberry and Charles Puzzanchera, *Juvenile Court Statistics 2016*, Pittsburgh: National Center for Juvenile Justice, August 2018; 69; Charles Puzzanchera, Benjamin Adams, and Melissa. Sickmund, *Juvenile Court Statistics 2006–2007*, 2010, 77.

Table 13-3 shows that despite efforts to divert and deinstitutionalize status offenders, some juveniles continue to be confined for status offenses, particularly girls. While the percentage has declined from 21% in 1997, 12% of girls continued to be confined in 2015.[82] Technical violations and status offenses were more common reasons for confinement for girls than for boys.

Comparing Girls and Boys in Court

Not all research has confirmed the existence of judicial sexism. Several studies found that female status offenders were not more harshly sanctioned than their male counterparts after controlling for a variety of extralegal variables[83] Some of the findings could reflect actual changes attributable to the deinstitutionalization movement. However, it is also possible that bias against girls may be less overt.

Table 13-3 Offense Profiles of Juvenile Offenders in Residential Placement, 2015

Offense	All Facilities		Public Facilities		Private Facilities	
	Male	Female	Male	Female	Male	Female
Person	38%	34%	40%	38%	34%	26%
Property	22	17	23	17	22	16
Drug	5	6	5	6	7	7
Public Order	13	8	13	9	14	5
Technical Violation	17	24	18	26	15	20
Status Offense	4	12	1	5	8	25

Source: Sarah Hockenberry, *Juveniles in Residential Placement, 2015*, Office of Juvenile Justice and Delinquency Prevention, 2018, 11.

The most recent studies continue to find that girls are treated more harshly for status offenses— and that the variables of race and ethnicity impact decisions. For example, one study found that Native American boys are treated the most severely, followed by black girls and Hispanic girls.[84] Several other recent studies have documented the impact of race and ethnicity. A Florida study found that black girls received harsher dispositions than white girls. However, the dispositions for Hispanic girls were no harsher than for white girls.[85] Another study looked at the individual and joint effects of gender and race on the treatment of status offenders at two decision-making stages of the juvenile justice system and found that they impacted severity and leniency in case outcomes.[86]

Girls under Lock and Key

Barry Feld has researched the interaction of gender and geography. He cautions that despite statutes and court rules of procedure that apply throughout a state, the administration of juvenile justice differs depending on whether the context is urban, suburban, or rural, producing what he terms justice by geography.[87] He reviewed the few studies available that documented significant geographical differences in sentencing.[88] One study found that differential treatment of racial minorities was more pronounced in rural courts. Another found that rural juvenile courts treated female offenders more leniently but that gender differences declined with urbanization. Feld found that a court's social context has significant influence on the cases that are selected, heard, and disposed. Urban counties were more formal and were associated with greater severity in pre-trial detention and sentencing. In rural counties, juvenile justice was less formal and more lenient. However, the exercise of discretion by rural judges resulted in gender differences in the processing of female offenders. Rural female juveniles were more at risk for removal from their homes than males. Despite committing less serious offenses and having less extensive prior records, larger proportions of females were detained. One explanation was that rural juvenile courts could have been responding to parental preferences. Feld also noted that rural courts tended to deal with the smallest proportions of juveniles charged with serious criminal activity and the largest proportion charged with status offenses. Judicial paternalism was less marked in urban courts. Although urban courts tended to be more severe in sanctioning, that fact alone does not mean girls are better off in more informal circumstances.

Girls, Race, and the New Double Standard of Juvenile Justice

This chapter has reviewed numerous examples of how deinstitutionalization of status offenders has not yet been implemented in all jurisdictions. There is another problem—a *two-track* juvenile justice system in which girls of color are treated differently from white girls. The criminalization of responses of girls to adversity and trauma in their lives is more acute for girls of color. Sexism is magnified by racism and classism.[89] Racialized gender stereotypes label black girls as promiscuous, aggressive, and angry.

Jody Miller examined the impact of race and ethnicity on the processing of girls' cases from one area probation office in Los Angeles during 1992–1993. Latinas comprised the largest proportion of the population (45%), followed by white girls (34%), and African-American girls (23%).[90] Miller found that white girls were significantly more likely than either African-American or Latina girls to be recommended for treatment—75% of the white girls were recommended for a treatment facility compared to 35% of the Latinas and only 20% of the African-American girls.[91]

Examining a portion of the probation officer's reports in detail, Miller found key differences in the ways that girls' behaviors were described—reflecting what she called "racialized gender expectations." In particular, African-American girls were often framed as making "inappropriate 'lifestyle' choices," while white girls' behavior was described as resulting from low self-esteem, being easily influenced, and the result of "abandonment." Latina girls, Miller found, received "dichotomized" treatment, with some receiving the more paternalistic care white girls received, while others received the more punitive treatment (particularly if they committed "masculine" offenses like auto theft).[92]

Another study found that in one specific county white girls were more likely than black girls to receive out of home placement. The authors of the study attribute this to the belief among judges and probation officers that white girls were more likely to be in violation of "sex role expectations" and more likely to benefit from the treatment offered in out of home placements.[93]

Studies have shown that the effects of race on juvenile justice system contact may vary by the age and gender of youth as well as social and neighborhood contexts.[94] Black girls compared to white girls are more likely to be processed formally and to receive harsher dispositions. The intersection of gender and race may create a cumulative disadvantage.

A study focusing on the adjudication stage, found that white girls were treated more leniently than black girls, but overall girls were treated more leniently that males. The authors concluded that the gender gap was half as large as the racial gap. Gender disparities were relatively constant across offense types, perhaps because court officials view female youths as being less culpable or less deserving of formal punishment, regardless of the offense.[95]

The perception of black girls as less innocent and more adult than white girls of the same age may contribute to the exercise of punitive discretion by those in positions of authority and result in harsher penalties.[96] While black girls comprise 17% of the student population, they are 31% of girls referred to law enforcement by school officials and 43% of those arrested on school grounds. Research has shown that prosecutors dismiss 3 of every 10 cases for black girls but 7 of every 10 cases for white girls. Black girls are 3 times more likely to be removed from their homes and placed in a secure facility. After accounting for seriousness of the offense, prior records, and age, black girls consistently receive more severe dispositions.

Taken together, these studies suggest that deinstitutionalization pressures may have differentially affected girls depending on their race. For girls of color, particularly African-American girls, bootstrapping or upcharging status offenses into delinquency charges may be the response to their acting out while white girls face transinstitutionalization into the world of private institutions and placements. In either case, the true intent of the deinstitutionalization initiative is being subverted.

Pasko describes how we have arrived at a situation not all that different from earlier incarnations of the double standard in juvenile justice.

> Despite, and occasionally due to, transformations in juvenile justice processing and corrections (deinstitutionalization, demise of rehabilitation, increase in direct files and punitive sanctions, growth of private treatment centers, and re-characterization of juvenile sexual offense), the correctional focus—through one definition or another—continues to be on girls' sexual behavior as cause for legal response, detention, and commitment. . . . While girls are not directly arrested and adjudicated for sexual immorality, they are indirectly sanctioned: a higher risk assessment score and probation violations place them at a higher possibility of being incarcerated. Regardless of structural constraints and difficulties, the focus remains on girls' "bad" choices; they are still told to take responsibility for their decisions, as the context of such decisions remains recorded but rarely used as mitigation.[97]

SUMMARY

This chapter focused on encounters girls have with the police and the juvenile court. Boys are far more likely to experience contacts with the police. The police are more likely to release a girl than a boy suspected of committing a crime, but they are more likely to arrest girls suspected of sex offenses. Girls tend to be overrepresented in arrest statistics for status offenses, especially running away and incorrigibility. Much of this has to do with girls' alleged sexual behavior, which is so often associated (at least from the standpoint of adult authorities) with the two offenses. One critical variable in police decision-making on the streets is a young person's demeanor or attitude. In general, a boy or girl who is hostile or in any way aggressive is the most likely to be arrested. Especially important for girls is whether or not they follow middle-class standards of "proper" behavior for girls.

Juvenile court statistics show that girls are more likely than boys to be referred to court for the status offenses of running away and incorrigibility. Males, in contrast, are more likely to be referred for violent crimes. Property offenses bring large numbers of both girls and boys to court, but for girls the bulk of such offenses fall within the larceny-theft category (most are for shoplifting).

Evidence of changes in official responses to girls who appear in the juvenile courts is somewhat mixed. Some studies have found more evenhanded treatment in recent years; others have not. The types of status offenses that girls and boys commit seem to account for some of the courts' differential responses. Girls typically appear for running away and other offenses that signal that they are beyond parental control, and boys appear for curfew and liquor-law violations. Recent research has specifically identified the need to address an undue focus on race as well as gender in the handling of youths.

Notes

[1] Leila Fadel and Bente Birkeland, "A First: Women Take the Majority in Nevada Legislature and Colorado House," NPR, February 4, 2019.

[2] Courtney Connley, "Why the Gender Pay Gap Still Exists 55 Years after the Equal Pay Act Was Signed," cnbc.com, June 8, 2018.

[3] Emma Newburger, "A New Study Suggests Women Earn about Half what Men Earn," cnbc/com, November 28, 2018.

[4] Bureau of Labor Statistics, "Women in the Labor Force: A Databook," United States Department of Labor, November 2017.

[5] Kathleen Hall Jamieson, *Beyond the Double Bind* (New York: Oxford University Press, 1995), 5, 14.

[6] Judith Lorber, *Paradoxes of Gender* (New Haven, CT: Yale University Press, 1994), 1.

[7] For an extended discussion of the topic of this chapter, see chapters 7, 8, and 9 in Meda Chesney-Lind and Randall G. Shelden, *Girls, Delinquency, and Juvenile Justice*, 4th ed. (Malden, MA: John Wiley & Sons, Inc., 2014). The material has been revised and updated. Some portions were originally written by Meda Chesney-Lind, and some were written by Randall Shelden. Various editorial changes and the passage of time may have caused confusion as to who wrote what. I thank Meda for her collaboration on our successful book and for her gracious contributions to this chapter.

[8] Roberta M. Berns, *Child, Family, School, Community: Socialization and Support*, 10th ed. (Stamford, CT: Cengage Learning, 2016).

[9] Joyce Endendijk, Marleen Goreneveld, Maian Bakermans-Kranenburg and Judi Mesman, "Gender-Differentiated Parenting Revisited: Meta-Analysis Reveals Very Few Differences in Parental Control of Boys and Girls," PLOS ONE, 2016, 11(7).

[10] Barry Kuhle, et al., "The 'Birds and the Bees' Differ for Boys and Girls: Sex differences in the Nature of Sex Talks, *Evolutionary Behavioral Sciences*, 2014.

[11] Jessica Valenti, Full Frontal Feminism: A Young Woman's Guide to Why Feminism Matters, 2nd ed. (Berkeley, CA: Seal Press, 2014); Jessica Valenti, *He's a Stud, She's a Slut, and 49 Other Double Standards Every Woman Should Know* (Berkeley, CA: Seal Press, 2008); Deborah Siegel, Sisterhood, *Interrupted: From Radical Women to Grrls Gone Wild* (New York: Palgrave Macmillan, 2007); Carole McCann, C. and Seung-kyung Kim, eds., *Feminist Theory Reader: Local and Global Perspectives*, 4th ed. (New York: Routledge, 2017).

[12] Nancy Hornberger, "Improving Outcomes for Status Offenders in the JJDPA Reauthorization," *Juvenile and Family Justice Today*, Summer 2010, 19.

[13] Chesney-Lind and Shelden, *Girls, Delinquency, and Juvenile Justice*.

[14] Cheryl Dalby, "Gender Bias toward Status Offenders: A Paternalistic Agenda Carried Out through the JJDPA," *Law & Inequality: A Journal of Theory and Practice*, 2017, 12(2): 429–456.

[15] Mahsa Jafarian and Vidhya Ananthakrishnan, "How Status Offenses Lead Kids into the Justice System," Vera Institute of Justice, 2017.

[16] Naomi Smoot, "Status Offenses: A National Survey," Coalition for Juvenile Justice, 2015.

[17] Lindsay Rosenthal, "Juvenile Justice Reform Is Not about Boys vs. Girls," Vera Institute of Justice, September 15, 2015.

[18] Chesney-Lind and Shelden, *Girls, Delinquency, and Juvenile Justice*, 98.

[19] Anthony M. Platt, *The Child Savers: The Invention of Delinquency*, 40th anniversary edition (New Brunswick, NJ: Rutgers University Press, 2009).

[20] Ibid., 199.

[21] Lisa Pasko, "Damaged Daughters: The History of Girls' Sexuality and the Juvenile Justice System," *The Journal of Criminal Law & Criminology* 100(3): 1099–1130.

[22] Ibid., 1100.

[23] Mary Odem, *Delinquent Daughters: Protecting and Policing Adolescent Female Sexuality in the United States, 1885–1920* (Chapel Hill: University of North Carolina Press, 1996).

[24] Ibid.

[25] Rosenthal, "Girls Matter."

[26] Odem, *Delinquent Daughters*, 25.

[27] Ibid., 80.

[28] Ibid., 4.

[29] Mary Odem and Steven Schlossman, "Guardians of Virtue: The Juvenile Court and Female Delinquency in Early 20th Century Los Angeles," *Crime and Delinquency*, 1991, 37(2): 186–203; 190.

[30] Ibid., 190–92.

[31] Odem, *Delinquent Daughters*, 128.

[32] Steven Schlossman and Stephanie Wallach, "The Crime of Precocious Sexuality: Female Delinquency in the Progressive Era." *Harvard Educational Review*, 1978, 48(1): 65–94.

[33] Anne Knupfer, *Reform and Resistance: Gender, Delinquency, and America's First Juvenile Court* (New York: Routledge, 2001), 199.

[34] Schlossman and Wallach, "The Crime of Precocious Sexuality," 72; Randall Shelden, "Sex Discrimination in the Juvenile Justice System, Memphis, Tennessee, 1900–1917," in Margarite Warren (ed.), *Comparing Male and Female Offenders* (Newbury Park, CA: Sage, 1981), 55–72.

[35] Charlotte Bright, Scott Decker, and Andrea Burch, "Gender and Justice in the Progressive Era: An Investigation of Saint Louis Juvenile Court Cases, 1909–1912," *Justice Quarterly*, 2007, 24: 657–678.

[36] Schlossman and Wallach, "The Crime of Precocious Sexuality," 70.

[37] Kathleen Daly and Meda Chesney-Lind, "Feminism and Criminology," *Justice Quarterly*, 1988, 5(4): 497–538.

[38] Alexander Pisciotta, "Race, Sex, and Rehabilitation: A Study of Differential Treatment in the Juvenile Reformatory, 1825–1900," *Crime and Delinquency*, 1983, 29(2): 254–269; 265.

[39] Pasko, "Damaged Daughters."

[40] Paul Tappan, *Delinquent Girls in Court* (New York: Columbia University Press, 1947).

[41] Ibid., 33.

[42] Ibid.

[43] Odem and Schlossman, "Guardians of Virtue," 196.

[44] Odem, *Delinquent Daughters*, 142.

[45] Ibid., 143.

[46] Odem and Schlossman, "Guardians of Virtue," 200.

[47] Clyde Vedder and Dora Somerville, *The Delinquent Girl* (Springfield, IL: Charles C. Thomas, 1970); 147.

[48] R. Hale Andrews and Andrew Cohn, "Ungovernability: The Unjustifiable Jurisdiction," *Yale Law Journal*, 1974, 83(7): 1383–1409; 1403.

[49] Ibid., 1404.

[50] These and other studies are summarized in Chesney-Lind and Shelden, *Girls, Delinquency, and Juvenile Justice*, chapter 7.

[51] Julie Kim, "Left Behind: The Paternalistic Treatment of Status Offenders within the Juvenile Justice System, *Washington University Law Review*, 2010, 87(4): 843–867; 862.

52 Pasko, "Damaged Daughters," 1108.

53 Katherine Teilmann and Pierre Landry, "Gender Bias in Juvenile Justice," *Journal of Research in Crime and Delinquency*, 1981, 18(1): 47–80.

54 Quoted in Chesney-Lind and Shelden, *Girls, Delinquency, and Juvenile Justice*, 201. The reader can easily guess whose values were being challenged here and whose rights would be upheld.

55 Ibid.

56 Jan Costello and Nancy Worthington, "Incarcerating Status Offenders: Attempts to Circumvent the Juvenile Justice and Delinquency Prevention Act," *Harvard Civil Rights-Civil Liberties Law Review*, 1981, 16(1): 41–81, 42.

57 Dalby, "Gender Bias toward Status Offenders."

58 Zachary Auspitz, "Juvenile Status Offenses: The Prejudicial Underpinnings of the Juvenile Justice System," *University of Miami Race & Social Justice Law Review*, 2018, 8(1): 1–22.

59 OJJDP Statistical Briefing Book, "JJDPA Timeline, 2013."

60 Office of Juvenile Justice and Delinquency Prevention, "National Efforts to Address the Needs of the Adolescent Female Offender," in *Juvenile Female Offenders: A Status of the States Report*, 1998.

61 Kim, "Left Behind," 867.

62 Lindsay Rosenthal, "Girls Matter: Centering Gender in Status Offense Reform Efforts," Vera Institute of Justice, July 2018.

63 Pasko, "Damaged Daughters," 1112.

64 Rosenthal, "Girls Matter."

65 Ibid.

66 Angela Irvine and Aisha Canfield, "Reflections on New National Data on LGBQ/GNCT Youth in the Justice System," LGBTQ Policy Journal at the Harvard Kennedy School, January 29, 2018.

67 Ibid.

68 Rosenthal, "Girls Matter."

69 Ibid.

70 Andrew Spivak, Brooke Wagner, Jennifer Whitmer, and Courtney Charish, "Gender and Status Offending: Judicial Paternalism in Juvenile Justice Processing, *Feminist Criminology*, 2014, 9(3): 224–248.

71 Sarah Hockenberry and Charles Puzzanchera, *Juvenile Court Statistics 2016*, Pittsburgh: National Center for Juvenile Justice, August 2018.

72 Ibid.

73 Ibid.

74 Federal Bureau of Investigation, *Crime in the United States, 2017*, 2018, tables 39 and 40.

75 Spivak et al., "Gender and Status Offending."

76 Dalby, "Gender Bias toward Status Offenders."

77 Ibid., 450.

78 Christy Visher, "Gender, Police Arrest Decisions, and Notions of Chivalry," *Criminology*, 1983, 21(1): 5–28.

79 Ibid., 22–23.

80 David Farrington, Darrick Jollife, David Hawkins, Richard Catalono, Karl Hill, and Rick Kosterman, "Why Are Boys More Likely to Be Referred to Juvenile Court? Gender Differences in Official and Self-Reported Delinquency," *Victims and Offenders*, 2010, 5: 25–44.

81 Nancy Hornberger, "Improving Outcomes for Status Offenders in the JJDPA Reauthorization." *Juvenile and Family Justice Today*, 2010, 18.

82 Sarah Hockenberry, *Juveniles in Residential Placement, 2015, Office of Juvenile Justice and Delinquency Prevention*, 2018, 11.

83 See Chesney-Lind and Shelden, *Girls, Delinquency, and Juvenile Justice*, chapter 7, for a review of this research and relevant citations.

84 Tina Freiburger and Allison Burke, "Status Offenders in the Juvenile Court: The Effects of Gender, Race, and Ethnicity on the Adjudication Decision," *Youth Violence and Juvenile Justice*, 2011, 9(4): 352–365.

85 Lori Moore and Irene Padavic, "Racial and Ethnic Disparities in Girls' Sentencing in the Juvenile Justice System," *Feminist Criminology*, 2010, 5(3): 263–285. See also Michael Leiber, Sarah Brubaker, and Kristan Fox, "A Closer Look at the Individual and Joint Effects of Gender and Race on Juvenile Justice Decision Making," *Feminist Criminology*, 2009, 4(4): 333–358.

86 Jennifer Peck, Michael Leiber, and Sarah Brubaker, "Gender, Race, and Juvenile Court Outcomes: An Examination of Status Offenders," *Youth Violence and Juvenile Justice*, 2013, 12(3): 250–267.

87 Barry C. Feld, *The Evolution of the Juvenile Court: Race, Politics, and the Criminalizing of Juvenile Justice* (New York: NYU Press, 2017).

88 Barry Feld, "Justice by Geography: Urban, Suburban, and Rural Variations in Juvenile Justice Administration," *The Journal of Criminal Law and Criminology*, 1991, 82(1): 156–210.

89 Rosenthal, "Girls Matter."

90 Jody Miller, "Race, Gender and Juvenile Justice: An Examination of Disposition Decision-Making for Delinquent Girls," in Martin Schwartz and Dragan Milovanovic (eds.), *The Intersection of Race, Gender and Class in Criminology* (New York: Garland Press, 1996), 11.

91 Ibid, 18.

92 Ibid, 20.

93 Lori Guevara, Denise Herz and Cassia Spohn, "Gender and Juvenile Justice Decision Making: What Role Does Race Play," *Feminist Criminology*, 2006, 1(4): 258–282.

94 Ronald Claus, Sarah Vidal, and Michelle Harmon, "Racial and Ethnic Disparities in the Police Handling of Juvenile Arrests," National Criminal Justice Reference Service, June 2017.

95 Michael Evangelist, Joseph Ryan, Bryan Victor, Andrew Moore, and Brian Perron, "Disparities at Adjudication in the Juvenile Justice System: An Examination of Race, Gender, and Age," *Social Work Research*, 2017, 41(4): 199–212.

96 Rebecca Epstein, Jamilia Blake, and Thalia González, "Girlhood Interrupted: The Erasure of Black Girls' Childhood," Georgetown Law Center on Poverty and Inequality, 2018.

97 Pasko, "Damaged Daughters," 1129.

Chapter 14

Some Sensible Solutions

"We can't solve problems by using the same kind of thinking we used when we created them."

—Albert Einstein

It has become evident that many—if not most—traditional approaches to the prevention and treatment of delinquency have not fared well. It is time to "think outside the box." After years of studying and teaching the subject of crime and delinquency, we are convinced that some very fundamental changes need to be made in the way we live and think before we see any significant decrease in problems. Adults have referred to the "problems" with youths for centuries with such value-laden questions as "what's wrong with kids these days?"[1]

WE NEED A NEW PARADIGM

In 1962, Thomas Kuhn wrote *The Structure of Scientific Revolutions*, which presented his argument that scientific development is a succession of tradition-bound periods punctuated by revolutions that lead to replacing one conceptual view of the world with another. Those who are not "committed by prior practice to the traditional rules of normal science, are particularly likely to see that those rules no longer define a playable game and to conceive another set than can replace them."[2] He described how scientists move from disdain through doubt to acceptance of a new theory. The prevailing paradigm runs into a brick wall when it cannot answer the questions being asked or provide solutions for pressing problems. Einstein's quotation above identifies that type of crisis. The answers to difficult questions must come from a totally different way of thinking—from people who think outside the box.

The myopic view that youths are the only ones who need to change is usually accompanied with various labels that clearly describe the source of the problem. The labels keep changing, along with changing times. As Jerome Miller has noted, we began with *possessed* youths in the seventeenth century, moved to the *dangerous classes* in the eighteenth and late nineteenth centuries, and to the *constitutional psychopathic inferiors* of the early twentieth century. We continued in the twentieth century with the *psychopath* of the 1940s, the *sociopath* of the 1950s, the *compulsive* delinquent, the *unsocialized aggressive*, and finally the *bored* delinquent. "With the growth of professionalism, the number of labels has multiplied exponentially."[3]

Miller asserts that the problem with these labels is that they maintain the existing order, buffering it from threats that might arise from its own internal contradictions. They reassure

> that the fault lies in the warped offender and takes everyone else off the hook. Moreover, it enables the professional diagnostician to enter the scene or withdraw at will, wearing success like a halo and placing failure around the neck of the client like a noose.[4]

More importantly, the labels reinforce the belief that harsh punishment works, especially the kind of punishment that includes some form of incarceration, so that the offender is placed out of sight and, not coincidentally, out of mind.

A recurring problem in juvenile justice reform—and with other reforms—is that after all the political maneuvering, the end result is that nothing changes or the changes are cosmetic. Daniel Macallair and Mike Males reviewed reforms in San Francisco.

> There is no evidence of *system* change. Instead it appears that new services and programs were simply marginalized. Marginalization occurs when new programs are designed as simple *adjuncts to current operations*, rather than intended to replace core system elements.[5]

As noted in chapter 1, we continue to succumb to the "edifice complex." Perhaps it is because politicians like to point to a permanent structure as a legacy that they have done something about crime. Or perhaps these buildings—whether a new juvenile detention center, a new prison, a new correctional center, a new police station, a new courthouse, etc.—are a profitable part of the huge "crime control industry."

We believe that we need to quit looking solely at "troubled youth" or "criminals" as the problem. It is time that those of us among the more privileged sectors of society consider that we too contribute to the problem—perhaps we are the primary contributors. Forty years ago sociologist Edwin Schur suggested a change in paradigms. His views continue to have relevance today.

RADICAL NONINTERVENTION

Chapter 7 discussed the labeling perspective. One of the best illustrations of the labeling perspective as it applies to delinquency was Edwin Shur's *Radical Nonintervention: Rethinking the Delinquency Problem*.[6] He noted that the traditional response to delinquent behavior was that the system needed improvement. Thus, more facilities were built, accompanied by elaborate studies of cost-benefit and systems analyses. Schur outlined five general proposals.

1. *"There is a need for a thorough reassessment of the dominant ways of thinking about youth 'problems.'"*[7]

   Schur maintained that most behaviors in which youth engage (including many labeled as "delinquent") are "part and parcel of our social and cultural system" and that "misconduct" among youth is inevitable within any form of social order. We pay a huge price, he charged, for criminalizing much of this behavior.

2. *"Some of the most valuable policies for dealing with delinquency are not necessarily those designated as delinquency policies."*

   Addressing education needs, mental-health issues, and poverty/inequality could have a larger impact on delinquency than many of the legal sanctions currently enacted.

3. *"We must take young people more seriously if we are to eradicate injustice to juveniles."*

   Schur notes that many young people lack a sound attachment to conventional society (one of Hirschi's "social bonds"; see chapter 7). In conjunction with addressing the inequalities noted above, we need to build more respect for young people into our culture.

4. *"The juvenile justice system should concern itself less with the problems of so-called 'delinquents,' and more with dispensing justice."*

   Schur was talking specifically about narrowing the jurisdiction of the juvenile court, specifically over status offenses. Little did Schur realize the extent to which net widening would occur in subsequent years. While status offenders have been diverted from the juvenile justice system, many have also been returned through bootstrapping or VCO exceptions (see chapter 13).

5. *"As juvenile justice moves in new directions, a variety of approaches will continue to be useful."*

   Schur specifically suggested approaches such as prevention programs that have a community focus plus programs that are voluntary and non-institutional in nature. One such approach is the Detention Diversion Advocacy Program (DDAP) discussed below.

The juvenile justice system extends far too broadly into the lives of children and adolescents. Mike Males has made this point perhaps more forcefully than others when he accuses criminologists and public policy makers of blaming kids for most ills of society while ignoring the damage done by adults.[8]

One of the questions posed by the labeling perspective is: why are certain acts labeled criminal or delinquent while others are not? Another pertinent question is: how do we account for differential rates of arrest, referral to court, detention, adjudication, and commitment based on race and class? Also, why do we overburden juvenile court workers with dealing with behavior that would not be criminal if committed by an adult? Why criminalize adolescent behavior like disturbing the peace and minor altercations? (One may reasonably ask: Whose peace is being disturbed?) These are not merely academic questions; the lives of real people are impacted by policies that ignore such questions and focus only on punishment.

We continue to criminalize behavior that should be dealt with informally, outside of the formal juvenile justice system. Criminalizing truancy is a primary example. Why take formal police action because a child is not going to school? Certainly, children should stay in school, because an education is a prerequisite for a decent life. Ideally, children would comply with the reasonable demands of their parents, but families should be left alone to figure things out for themselves. There is no need for state involvement in private family matters, unless direct physical or other obvious harms are being committed. As noted several times throughout this book, zero-tolerance policies have labeled youths as delinquent or worse for behavior that would have been ignored or handled informally without the policies.

INTERVENTION TYPOLOGIES

Prevention and intervention strategies come in many different forms. In understanding where to go from here it may be helpful to distinguish among different types of interventions. Joy Dryfoos looked at four interrelated problems: delinquency, teen pregnancy, drug abuse, and school failure.[9] Her review of the research found that the majority of prevention programs fell into one of three broad categories: (1) early childhood and family interventions, (2) school-based interventions, and (3) community-based and/or multicomponent interventions.

Early Childhood and Family Interventions

Head Start is the primary federal preschool program for low-income children, which attempts to narrow inequalities in educational outcomes and to raise educational attainment levels.[10] In 2016, Head Start programs served over 900,000 children with a budget of almost $9 billion. Studies have confirmed the success of early intervention programs like Head Start and similar preschool programs.[11] Using data from the National Longitudinal Survey of Youth, researchers found that Head Start increases the probability that participants will graduate from high school and attend college. It also improves self-control, self-esteem, and positive parenting practices. A meta-analysis of 123 comparative studies of early childhood interventions found positive effects for children who attend a preschool program prior to entering kindergarten. The most significant impact was on the children's cognitive behaviors, social skills and school progress—all of which are correlated with reduced rates of delinquency.[12]

Evaluations of family-focused interventions have demonstrated that parenting practices affect the degree to which children and adolescents engage in substance use and delinquency.[13] The family is an important context for preventing antisocial behavior and for promoting healthy youth development.[14] Refining family-focused interventions to increase efficiency and effectiveness, as well as developing new interventions, can expand the number of families who will benefit from such services.

School-based Interventions

There are three primary types of school-based interventions: (1) curricula, (2) organization of school (teacher training, school team, and alternative schools), and (3) special services (counseling and mentoring programs, health services, and volunteer work). Schools incorporate prevention curriculum to reduce problem behaviors.[15] Developing student skills to manage impulses, to anticipate consequences, and to cope with peer influence reduces disruptive and aggressive behaviors. School-based programs targeting at-risk populations are effective. Programs staffed with well-trained, skilled individuals who have developed empathy and an understanding of youth subculture are more likely to be well received. Recreational programs and after-school events facilitate juveniles spending time on positive pursuits.

Community-based Interventions

Community-based interventions include three main types: (1) school-community collaboration programs, (2) community education, and (3) multicomponent, comprehensive interventions. Community-based interventions have increased as jurisdictions seek alternatives to costly residential commitment for juvenile offenders.[16] Programs should target medium- to high-risk youths with intensive, multifaceted approaches that focus on the development of social skills (for example, conflict resolution) and address the attitudes, values, and beliefs that reinforce antisocial behaviors. Ideally, the community should offer alternatives to activities and associations (such as gangs) that could lead to delinquent or criminal behavior. Programs should provide explicit reinforcement for positive choices. Linking programs with the world of work assists youths in developing job skills. Goals should be specific and culminate in some kind of award (for example, a diploma). It is important to recognize that relapse is normal (whether dealing with drug or alcohol abuse or any pattern of negative antisocial behavior) and that treatment is a continual process rather than a single episode.

Components of Successful Programs

In a meta-analysis of research on interventions with juveniles, Mark Lipsey found that the most successful programs had the following ingredients: a therapeutic intervention philosophy serving high-risk offenders with high quality implementation.[17] Lipsey grouped evaluations into seven categories: counseling, deterrence, discipline, multiple coordinated services, restorative programs, skill building, and surveillance. Comparing the effects, he found that interventions based on punishment and deterrence appeared to increase criminal recidivism, whereas therapeutic approaches based on counseling, skill building and multiple services had the greatest impact in reducing further criminal behavior. Cognitive behavioral skillbuilding approaches were more effective in reducing further criminal behavior than any other intervention. The Missouri Model, discussed below, has been highly successful and employs the elements Lipsey identified as most effective.

A Blueprint for Juvenile Justice Reform

The Youth Transition Funders Group (YTFG) consists of academics, practitioners, city/county agencies, nonprofits, and foundations working together to support the well-being of young people. In their series of recommendations for transforming youth justice, they refer to a sea change being underway in youth justice.[18] Decades of research and advances in neurobiology show that the human brain is not fully developed until one's mid-twenties. The Supreme Court since 2005 has repeatedly held that age, maturity, and circumstances should be primary considerations in sentencing because of developmental differences. In addition, fiscal reasons have moved states to reexamine their justice policies. Youth crime has declined to the lowest levels in 30 years, and public attitudes are shifting to favor rehabilitation over punishment.

Despite these encouraging changes,

> vulnerable young people, primarily youth of color, are funneled into the justice system, which is neither designed nor equipped to meet their needs or bolster their development. Overwhelmingly, evidence proves that reliance on punishment and incarceration, rather than restorative justice and rehabilitation, is harmful to young people and is associated with increased rates of reoffending, strained family relationships, lower educational and vocational attainment, and incarceration later in life.[19]

YTFG advises 10 tenets for youth justice reform.[20]

1. Divert Youth from the Justice System
2. Eliminate Racial and Ethnic Disparities
3. Engage Youth, Families and Community
4. Improve Cross-System Collaboration
5. Ensure Access to Quality Legal Counsel
6. Keep Youth Out of Adult Courts, Jails, and Prisons
7. Create a Range of Effective Community-Based Supports
8. Recognize and Serve Subpopulations of Youth
9. End Use of Detention and Confinement
10. Improve Aftercare and Reentry

The blueprint highlights the necessity of addressing disparate treatment and reducing arrests as significant factors keeping youth out of the justice system. Of the students arrested or referred by police at school, 70% are black or Hispanic. Half of school-based arrests are for disturbing the peace or disruptive conduct. Of incarcerated youth, 75% were charged with offenses that pose little or no threat to public safety—probation violations, status offenses, property, public order, and drug offenses. YTFG argues for improving cross-system collaboration, stating that 30% of justice-involved youth have a diagnosed learning disability; 65% have at least one mental health diagnosis, and 67% have been in the child welfare system.

The blueprint opens with a quotation from James Baldwin. "For these are all our children. We will all profit by, or pay for, whatever they become." The remainder of the chapter discusses some model programs and new paradigms to improve outcomes for youth—and society.

MISSOURI'S MODEL SYSTEM OF JUVENILE JUSTICE

Like most other states, Missouri had a history of confining young offenders in large institutions. As discussed in chapter 12, the state began experimenting with regionally based smaller, facilities in the 1980s. The Division of Youth Services (DYS) now has an agency-wide commitment to helping troubled youth change their antisocial, self-destructive behaviors and to prepare them to return to their communities and to continue their pathways to success.

The core DYS philosophy is that every young person wants to—and can—succeed. The hunger for approval, acceptance, and achievement is universal. "No matter how serious their past crimes, and no matter how destructive their current attitudes and behaviors, DYS considers every young person a work in progress. Each is redeemable and deserves help."[21] Three core DYS beliefs are:

> (1) that all people—including delinquent youth—desire to do well and succeed; (2) that with the right kinds of help, all youth can (and most will) make lasting behavioral changes and succeed; and (3) that the mission of youth corrections must be to provide the right kinds of help, consistent with public safety, so that young people make needed changes and move on to successful and law-abiding adult lives.[22]

Delinquent youth can't be reformed through military-style treatment, and few will be deterred from crime by fear of punishment. "Rather, change can only result from internal choices made by the young people themselves—choices to adopt more positive behaviors, seek out more positive peers, and embrace more positive goals."[23]

The Missouri approach emphasizes moving beyond symptoms to the root causes of juvenile delinquency.[24] DYS uses a therapeutic youth development approach that focuses on prevention and early intervention. The key tenets of Missouri's approach are:[25]

1. Continuous case management.
2. Decentralized residential facilities.
3. Small group, peer-led services.
4. Restorative rehabilitation-centered treatment environment.
5. Strong organizational leadership.
6. Organizational culture change.
7. Evaluation of treatment strategies and approaches to insure effectiveness; ineffective initiatives discarded.
8. Increased number of stakeholders.

Missouri has 45 juvenile or family courts.[26] DYS receives approximately 1,200 new commitments annually. More than 2,800 youth are in the system each year. The youths are primarily male (86% vs. 14% female); 37% are minority youth; 66% come from large metropolitan areas; 34% have a diagnosed educational disability prior to commitment; 20% have previously been in out-of-home placement for child abuse or neglect. More than half of all commitments are for a felony offense.

DYS operates residential facilities for offenders who require a more structured setting than the community.[27] The least restrictive residential environments are group homes, where about 10 youths live together in a home-like setting. Residents in some facilities go to public schools and participate in other activities on a regular basis. There are nine programs (three in state parks) that are moderately restrictive; they use the same treatment approach as group homes. Education is provided on-site. There are seven secure-care programs.

DYS uses the case-management approach to develop a unique treatment plan for each youth.[28] Everyone is assigned to a group of 10-12. The youths eat together, study together, exercise together, and attend daily treatment sessions together. The treatment process is enhanced by remaining with the same group—members learn to trust and feel responsible toward one another. The rooms are carpeted and resemble those in college dormitories.

The Missouri program emphasizes keeping youths safe physically and emotionally. It eliminates ridicule and emotional abuse through constant staff supervision and positive peer relationships.[29] Coercion and demeaning treatment are not part of the process. The youths spend 6 hours each day on education; each group has its own teacher. Staff members work to help youths develop self-awareness and communication skills, which are critical to future success. Missouri recruits family members as partners in the treatment process and for success after release—rather than treating them as the source of the delinquency. There is intensive aftercare planning before release and close monitoring and mentoring after release. Intensive support and supervision help youths transition to life outside the facility.

The ideas, strategies, and practices used in Missouri will not help other jurisdictions achieve improved outcomes unless those jurisdictions also embrace and value change. Cynthia Osborne, an expert on public systems reform, studied the Missouri approach intensively. She warns that importing new practices into an unchanged system will not yield good results. Rather, a jurisdiction "must relinquish the traditional correctional values of punishment and slowly grow a new system rooted in the values of treatment, compassion, and accountability. Practices cannot produce good results when used apart from the values."[30] Missouri has refined and revised its approach over four decades. Other states adopting the approach should concentrate on four areas: (1) everyone in the organization must embrace the core values and beliefs; (2) implementing the core values requires changes in facilities, staffing, treatment programs, and organizational structure; (3) administrators must hire educated personnel who believe in the core values and train them to be effective in working with youths; there must also be accountability proced-ures, and all procedures must be transparent; (4) the program must be supported by key constituencies in state government, courts, and communities; employees must work to cultivate and sustain that support.

The state of Missouri won a 2008 Harvard Kennedy School Innovations in Government award for its juvenile justice reforms. The Missouri Model is one of the most-replicated approaches in juvenile justice reform in the United States.[31] Other states (including California, Louisiana, New Mexico, New York, and Virginia) have followed Missouri's lead. The case management approach incorporated in the Missouri model is the foundation of the Detention Diversion Advocacy Program in San Francisco.

THE DETENTION DIVERSION ADVOCACY PROGRAM

The Center on Juvenile and Criminal Justice (CJCJ) in San Francisco, California, developed the Detention Diversion Advocacy Program (DDAP) in 1993 to reduce unnecessary youth detention and lengths of stay and to increase community engagement with youth offenders.[32] It was the first evidence-based pre-adjudication diversion program for high risk youth in the nation.

Youths selected for the program would likely have been detained pending their adjudication. This is a very important aspect of the program. By focusing on *detained* youth, the program ensures that it is a true diversion alternative; it is not an example of widening the net to ensnare lower-level offenders. Youths are screened by DDAP staff to determine if they are likely to be detained and whether they present an acceptable risk to the community. DDAP provides an intensive level of community-based monitoring and advocacy. The program has been repli-cated in numerous cities, including Philadelphia, Baltimore, Oakland, Boston, and the District of Columbia.

DDAP was designed to accomplish the following goals: (1) provide multilevel interventions to divert youth from secure detention facilities; (2) demonstrate that community-based interventions are an effective alternative to secure custody and that the needs of both the youths and the community can be met at a cost savings to the public; and (3) reduce disproportionate minority incarceration.[33]

Two primary components in DDAP are *disposition case advocacy* and *case man-agement.* Disposition case advocacy involves community members acting on behalf of youthful offenders at disposition hearings.[34] Case management is the collective process of coordinating community-based services to promote effective delivery of services to target populations.[35] The main focus of case management is to develop a network of human services that integrates the development of client skills and the involvement of different social networks and multiple service providers.[36]

Case advocates identify youth likely to be detained pending their adjudica-tion; DDAP case managers then present a release plan to the judge.[37] The plan includes a list of appropriate community services that will be accessed on the youth's behalf. Additionally, the plan includes specified objectives as a means to evaluate the youth's progress while in the program. Emphasis is placed on maintaining the youth at home. If the home is not a viable option, the program staff will identify and secure a suitable alternative. If the plan is deemed acceptable by a judge, the youth is released to DDAP's supervision.

The case management model provides frequent and consistent support and supervision to youth and their families. The purpose of case management is to link youths to community-based services and to closely monitor their progress. The case manager has *daily contact* with the youth, his or her family, and significant others. Contact includes a minimum of three in-person meetings a week. Additional services are provided to the youth's family members, particularly parents and guardians, in areas such as securing employment, day care, drug treatment services, and income support.

Clients are primarily identified through referrals from the public defender's office, the probation department, community agencies, and parents. As noted above, admission to DDAP is restricted to youths currently held, or likely to be held, in secure detention. The youths selected are those deemed to be "high risk" in terms of their chance of engaging in subsequent criminal activity. Qualification for participation in DDAP is based on whether youths can reside in the community under supervision without unreasonable risk and on their likelihood of attending court hearings. This is similar in principle to what occurs in the adult system when someone is released on bail pending his or her court hearings.

Client screening involves gathering background information from probation reports, psychological evaluations, police reports, school reports, and other pertinent documents. Interviews are conducted with youths, family members, and adult professionals to determine the types of services required. Once a potential client is evaluated, case managers design individualized community service plans that address a wide range of personal and social needs, including linguistic or medical needs. DDAP staff presents a comprehensive community service plan at the detention hearing and requests that the judge release the youth to DDAP custody.

DDAP staff monitors both the youth's participation and the quality of services provided. Using multiple service providers helps to insure that the program represents and addresses the needs of the various communities within San Francisco in the most culturally appropriate manner. Historically, youth services in San Francisco have been fragmented by ethnicity, race, and community. DDAP is trying a more unified approach. It has become a neutral site within the city, staffed by representatives from CJCJ and several other community-based service agencies.

In a three-year follow-up evaluation of a group of youths referred to DDAP compared with a similarly matched control group that remained within the juvenile justice system, the recidivism rate for the DDAP group was 34% and 60% for the control group.[38] Detailed comparisons holding several variables constant (e.g., prior record, race, age, gender, etc.) and examining several different measures of recidivism (e.g., subsequent commitments, referrals for violent offenses) showed that the DDAP youths still had a significantly lower recidivism rate. The recidivism rates for girls (about 20% of DDAP participants) essentially paralleled those for boys. Specifically, 30% of DDAP girls were recidivists compared to 48% of girls in the control group. Although this difference was not statistically significant, further analysis found that the control group was far more likely to have two or more subsequent referrals (43.5% vs. 11.6%).

There are several reasons for the success of this program. First, DDAP workers average about 10 cases each. Smaller caseloads mean more quality time with clients *in the field* (e.g., in their homes, on the street corners, at school), rather than visits to an office with interruptions of phone calls and other bureaucratic chores. Second, qualifications for being a caseworker with DDAP are not as restrictive as those of the juvenile justice system (e.g., age restrictions, educational requirements, arrest records, etc.). The backgrounds of some workers were similar to the backgrounds of some clients (e.g., neighborhood of origins, language, etc.). Third, the physical location of DDAP is user friendly, lacking the forbidding appearance of the formal system. There are no bars, no concrete buildings, no devices for screening for weapons, no cells for lockdown, etc. Further, the DDAP workers are not officers of the court with powers of arrest; they do not display visible symbols of authority (e.g., badges, guns).

San Francisco was established as a Second Chance Act National Demonstration Project Site in 2008.[39] Incorporating some of the basic principles of DDAP, the Juvenile Collaborative Reentry Team (JCRT) was designed to address historically high recidivism rates of youth exiting out-of-home placements in San Francisco through a partnership of key stakeholders including the youth and their family. In 2008, the majority of San Francisco's placement failures were low-income youth of color—reflecting the disproportionate concentration of crime and violence in San Francisco's most disadvantaged and underserved communities.[40] In 2011, youth living in San Francisco's poorest neighborhoods accounted for 76% of referrals. JCRT continued through 2012 and served 150 youth per year. By 2012, there was a 29% improvement in recidivism rates for participating youth compared to prior years. Because of the success of the program, the San Francisco Probation Department formalized JCRT as a unit of the department in October 2012.

In 2013, the program's name was changed to The Juvenile Collaborative Reentry Unit (JCRU). It works with a dedicated reentry court and attorneys to develop reentry plans for youth returning from out-of home placement.[41] The reentry plan is developed and approved by the reentry court up to 90 days prior to the youth's return. Components of the plan include family relationships, housing, education, mental health and substance abuse treatment, social recreation, and employment.

JCRU replaces the adversarial dynamic of the courtroom with one that is unified behind the child and family. Family members and youths are all involved in every decision about the services, education, and vocational opportunities that will be included in their comprehensive reentry plan.[42] After youths are released, they and their families meet with all the groups involved in the implementation and delivery of services. The JCRU consists of members from the San Francisco Juvenile Probation Department, the San Francisco Superior Court, the San Francisco Public Defenders Office and representatives from the Center on Juvenile and Criminal Justice.

The team works with a judge to ensure that they assist the youth in a reintegration process that addresses their needs. The average length of enrollment in JCRU is 6–24 months.[43] The Council for a Strong America included JCRU in its toolkit for practitioners in California as one of five case studies in probation partnerships connecting justice-involved youth to comprehensive services.[44] The grants that formed JCRU have ended, but it continues to be funded through each partner agency's operating budget. Part of the program's success is that it operates from the premise that giving needed resources to youth on the verge of serious criminality can change the direction of their lives. The National Conference of State Legislatures referred to JCRU as a pioneering reentry model.[45]

MODELS FOR CHANGE

The John D. and Catherine T. MacArthur Foundation began making grants to the juvenile justice field in 1996 when policymakers implemented punitive responses over fears of rising violent crime rates among juveniles.[46] By 2000, a record number of youths were held in detention facilities or other out-of-home placements. MacArthur lunched the Models for Change initiative to promote more effective and developmentally appropriate juvenile justice systems. It funded the Research Network on Adolescence Development and Juvenile Justice from 1996 to 2005. Studies from the network presented evidence that adolescents are less culpable and have greater capacity for rehabilitation than adults. The studies were cited in the Supreme Court decisions that ruled the death penalty and life without parole for juveniles unconstitutional. From 2011 to 2015, Models for Change operated in 37 states.[47] Its legacy phase was 2012 to 2016—a transition from a grant-based initiative to a more decentralized, self-sustaining movement. The exit strategy worked to sustain previous reforms and to create momentum for a broader national reform movement.

The program supported comprehensive systems change in four core states: Illinois, Louisiana, Pennsylvania, and Washington. Models for Change created a resource bank of experts in key areas of juvenile justice reform to assist state teams. The core states plus 12 others and many local jurisdictions created *action networks* to collaborate on reform strategies. During the legacy face, there was collaboration with federal agencies to expand the reach of the program.

Illinois Models for Change

Illinois was chosen as a core state for its strong juvenile justice leadership, potential for collaboration, community and civic engagement, ongoing reform efforts, and receptivity for change at many points throughout the juvenile justice system.[48] The state used Models for Change to reorient its system to treating youth offenders as juveniles and to provide support and services in their communities. The program in Illinois used research to demonstrate the cost benefit of extending eligibility for the juvenile court to committed felons younger than 18, which influenced changing the laws governing age limits for juvenile status.

Redeploy Illinois began in 2005 as a pilot project in 4 sites and 15 counties; it expanded to 13 sites and 46 counties.[49] The program provides financial assistance to counties that reduce by 25% the number of juveniles they commit to state facilities. State funds are used to provide counseling, substance abuse and mental health treatment, life skills education, cognitive therapies, and other direct services to young offenders in their communities. Any juvenile facing a possible commitment for a charge other than murder or a class X forcible felony is eligible for the program. The program has provided individualized intensive services to more than 2,500 youth. Counties have reduced commitments 58%, saving taxpayers $88 million. The average annual cost to serve a youth in the Redeploy Illinois program in 2015 was $5,502 compared to $111,000 to house a youth in a juvenile facility.

Pennsylvania Models for Change

Pennsylvania was selected as a core state because of its favorable reform climate, strong public-private partnerships, and demonstrated success in reforms. Efforts centered on aftercare to secure successful reentry and to reduce recidivism. It also improved the collection of data to test interventions involving large numbers of youth of color. Efforts to reduce disproportionate minority contact are ongoing and involve multiple strategies to address the complex problem, including strategies to counter unconscious biases by implementing value-neutral assessment tools. The establishment of a graduated response court improved responses to probation violations. When a jurisdiction in Pennsylvania saw data about increased arrests during the day, it determined the arrests involved youth suspended from school. The community developed a resource center to offer youth a structured program during suspension. The Juvenile Justice System Enhancement Strategy laid the foundation for sustained success after the end of funding from Models for Change.[50]

Pennsylvania Models for Change reform efforts concentrated on the need to link residential placement and the community. They published a toolkit that informed probation officers about the legal responsibilities of school districts.[51] They also developed a template for placement staff and probation officers to use to determine the educational and therapeutic services that would be provided during placement and after discharge. They also fostered the development of the Pennsylvania Academic and Career/Technical Training Alliance (PACTT) that improved the academic and/or technical training that youth receive during and after placement.

Models for Change found that reforms spread and were sustained when state and local stakeholders interacted frequently to share information. Philadelphia and

Allegheny, the two most populous counties in Pennsylvania, recognized a common problem and sought an effective solution for both counties. The common problem was that youth who returned to school after incarceration soon dropped out. The counties realized that Pennsylvania lacked a standard curriculum that would help residential programs and school districts reintegrate youth to school. State-county discussions eventually led to the creation of PACCT.

Successful reintegration was linked inextricably with core problems: academic failure, disconnection from school, and lack of job preparation and marketable skills. PACTT concentrates on improving education programs for committed youths. Teaching staff in the institutions are trained in literacy strategies and techniques for remedial education. The goal is to standardize instruction in the skills every young person needs to succeed in the job market—skills needed to find a job, to understand and meet employer expectations, and to handle typical workplace issues and conflicts. PACTT facilities have excelled in the area of career/technical education, offering programs in high-demand areas—culinary arts, indoor/outdoor maintenance, auto body, welding, and office support.[52] In 2018, there were 33 private residential PACTT affiliates, 6 state-operated residential affiliates, and 17 community-based, nonresidential affiliates.[53]

Louisiana Models for Change

In the 1990s, Louisiana had the highest juvenile incarceration rate in the United States; it was one of 12 states that housed juvenile detention facilities within the state's adult corrections system.[54] A federal lawsuit charged the state with chronic abuse and mistreatment of its incarcerated juvenile population. Louisiana entered into settlement agreements, which concluded in 2006 after improvements. As it worked to create a less punitive culture for its juvenile justice system, Models for Change helped Louisiana establish comprehensive stakeholder engagement to improve state decision making about policy and the use of resources.

One of the reforms was the Families in Need of Services (FINSS) program. One-third of the arrests of juveniles in Jefferson Parish, Louisiana, occurred in schools. The overwhelming majority of the school arrests were for nonviolent misdemeanor offenses—primarily "interference with an education facility" or "disturbing the peace." While disruptive, the status offenses did not threaten public safety. The problem was the culture. Roy Juncker, Director of the Jefferson Parish Department of Juvenile Services, commented: "It's built into the way the school system operates. Kids get arrested, suspended, expelled, and that's how you get rid of the problem. As opposed to focusing on the problems causing the misbehavior and dealing with that."[55] In 2008, the Jefferson Parish Public School System held a special training session to help school staff intervene more effectively. Carol Mancuso, the Director of School Safety, said: "It's learning what not to call the police for. You don't pick up the phone because a kid is running down the hall. You can't pick up the phone just because you don't know what else to do."[56]

The Department of Juvenile Services is working to minimize unnecessary formal processing and confinement—which disproportionately affect minorities—when youths are arrested.[57] It instituted a "Graduated Sanctions Ladder" policy to respond to probation violations without resorting to secure detention. Detention alternatives have expanded, and overall detention usage is 40% below 2004 levels.

Washington Models for Change

Washington was selected for its commitment to systems improvement through evidence-based interventions, the use of evaluation findings, and cost-benefit analysis techniques. The state planned to use its data system as a platform for juvenile justice reforms, to reduce reliance on formal processing and secure confinement, and to improve juvenile public defense.[58] It developed a truancy process and resources survey to determine the consistency and effectiveness of interventions. It used mental health screening to reduce unnecessary referrals to juvenile court.

The primary tool for addressing truancy in Washington was formal court processing, often resulting in secure confinement.[59] The state worked with pilot counties and with school districts to develop or expand alternative programs to keep youth out of the justice system. It established more consistency across schools in truancy petition filing practices, increased the number of truants who re-enrolled, decreased the number who dropped out, and demonstrated the cost effectiveness of truancy reforms. The Washington Assessment of the Risks and Needs of Students (WARNS) was developed to identify youth at risk of problematic behaviors and to facilitate appropriate interventions. The tool covers 12 domains: student demographics, school performance, school engagement, family environment, peer deviance, aggression, defiance, depression, anxiety, trauma experiences, and other student characteristics. To address disproportionate minority contact, Washington analyzes data on delinquency case processing. It engages stakeholders in plans for targeted interventions at key decision points that contribute to juvenile justice system involvement.

Washington implemented mental health screening and assessment to divert juveniles with mental health issues into community-based services versus deeper penetration into the juvenile justice system.[60] It provided training for service providers on youth and family engagement strategies and developed culturally appropriate mental health services for youth in the justice system. Its specialized Functional Family Therapy with an African American provider increased engagement rates from 45% to 83%.[61]

Washington worked to coordinate system responses for youth involved in multiple systems, particularly youth involved in the juvenile justice and child welfare systems. King County Juvenile Court and the Children's Administration of the Washington Department of Social and Health Services embarked on a collaboration with other local agencies serving multisystem youth—Uniting for Youth. The impetus for collaboration was a study that found that two-thirds of the youth referred to the juvenile court for offenses had a history of contact with the state's child welfare agency. More than a third (37%) had family issues serious enough to merit agency action. Youth with agency histories offended at earlier ages, spent longer periods in detention, penetrated deeper into the juvenile justice system, and recidivated at higher rates than those with no child welfare history. The jurisdiction began an extensive program of multisystem cross training. Each agency details and shares its goals and responsibilities, resources and programs, methods, and services. Participants form teams to develop case plans for crossover cases. People learn "how the systems can and should work together. They talk through the issues and understand what resources are available from each of them, how they all fit into that puzzle."[62] They become accountable as a group for the outcomes.

Working with the Models for Change Initiative, TeamChild created a Special Counsel position to improve access to quality juvenile public defense. Work included the development of a comprehensive training curriculum for juvenile defense attorneys and the creation of a network of juvenile indigent defense counsel proactive in juvenile justice reform.

The Legacy of Models for Change

Models for Change had a positive impact on juvenile justice policy in more than 35 states and 100 jurisdictions, partnering with multiple organizations to reform the juvenile justice system. Among the policy innovations it helped implement are mental health screening and risk/needs assessment, mental health training for the juvenile justice workforce, reducing racial and ethnic disparities, and improving the coordination of the juvenile justice and child welfare systems.

The legacy of Models for Change is a network of practitioners and advocates working to reform the juvenile justice system.[63] The Models for Change initiative was instrumental in key legislative reforms. All but four states set the age of criminal responsibility at 18. The research on brain science that mitigated the culpability of juveniles prompted courts, lawmakers, and defense attorneys to consider whether individuals between the ages of 18 and 21 should also be exempt from capital punishment and mandatory life without parole.[64] In 2017, a Kentucky state court ruled that capital punishment for individuals younger than 21 violated the state's constitution. A federal district court ruled that the *Miller* decision applied to people 19 years of age.

The momentum established by the Models for Change initiative can be leveraged to change policy "in five areas where current practice is fundamentally incompatible with healthy adolescent development: prosecution of youth in the adult criminal system; solitary confinement; confidentiality of juvenile records, registries for youth who commit sex offenses, and courtroom shackling."[65]

> Models for Change has helped to identify and spread practices that have already gone a long way toward creating a developmentally appropriate juvenile justice system. Its work is part of the reason that more and more policymakers, state

and local officials, practitioners, judges, prosecutors, defense attorneys, and advocates acknowledge that a developmental approach advances public safety, and should infuse the juvenile justice system and the programs devised to intervene with youth in trouble with the law.[66]

WHAT ABOUT GIRLS?

The majority of delinquency prevention programs were designed for boys; the specific needs of girls have been shortchanged or ignored because the population of delinquent boys greatly outnumbers the population of delinquent girls. Gender-responsive programming was developed to address issues uniquely experienced by girls.[67]

PACE Center for Girls

Professionals working in the juvenile court system in Jacksonville, Florida, in the early 1980s recognized that girls involved in delinquent activities were either: not being held accountable, were placed further into the system for their protection, or they were placed in programs designed for boys.[68] Founder Vicki Burke created a research-based alternative to institutionalization in 1985—The *PACE* (Practical, Academic, Cultural, and Educational) *Center for Girls, Inc.* The basement of a downtown Jacksonville church was the first location, which served 10 girls. PACE now has 19 centers throughout Florida and has served over 37,000 Florida girls.

PACE is recognized as a national model for reducing recidivism and for improving school success, employment and self-sufficiency.[69] It offers services tailored to how girls learn and develop. The nonresidential, year-round, voluntary program features a balanced emphasis on academics and social services. PACE serves girls between the ages of 11 and 18 with specific characteristics that put them at risk of becoming involved with the juvenile justice system.[70] An evaluation study found that girls in the program were struggling academically (40% had been expelled or suspended; more than 50% had been held back at least once); about 30% had been arrested previously and two-thirds had a family member with a criminal history; many had mental health issues (often as a result of experiencing trauma; 40% reported being abused or neglected). PACE works to reduce negative outcomes by fostering academic engagement, positive youth development, and healthy relationships.

Girls attend PACE daily during regular school hours.[71] They receive comprehensive assessment and care planning, a life skills curriculum, individual and group counseling, volunteer service and work readiness opportunities, and follow-up services. The emphasis is on strengths rather than deficits combined with an understanding of the effects of trauma when dealing with girls' risky behaviors. Typically, girls attend PACE for one year and then return to schools in their communities. PACE helps girls be more engaged in school and on track toward high school graduation. PACE services are less costly than residential programs, similar in cost to other comprehensive programs but more expensive than public school—about $23,500 per girl. The average size of PACE centers is 50 girls, and the staff-to-student ratio is much lower than in traditional schools. In addition, the intensive social service support is rare in public schools, which adds to the cost differential.

Girls Incorporated

Girls Inc. has local roots dating to 1864 and national status as a nonprofit organization in the United States since 1945.[72] Formerly known as Girls Clubs of America, the movement began in New England during the Industrial Revolution in response to the needs of young women who had migrated from rural communities for job opportunities in textile mills and factories. Today there are 83 local Girls Inc. organizations serving more than 150,000 girls between the ages of 5 and 18 in 32 states. Girls Inc strives to serve girls of color and girls from low-income communities; 62% of girls live in households earning $30,000 or less, and 10% come from households earning $10,000 or less. The ethnic composition is 39% African American and 24% Hispanic.

Throughout its history, the program has been guided by a fundamental belief in the inherent potential of each girl. The core values today include creating a safe gathering place for girls to learn, to share in a sisterhood, and a strong belief that each girl can develop her capacities and self-confidence to grow up healthy, educated, and independent.[73] Positive outcomes are achieved through three core elements: (1) *people*—trained staff and volunteers who build lasting relationships; (2) *environment*—girls only, physically and emotionally safe, and a sisterhood of support, high expectations, and mutual respect; (3) *programming*—research based, age appropriate, and hands-on.[74] Girls Inc. emphasizes that girls have the right to be themselves, to resist gender stereotypes, and to prepare for interesting work and economic independence.

Building on 30 years of mentoring experience and success supporting at-risk girls, the organization launched its *Bold Futures Mentoring Program* with a two-year grant of $2 million from OJJDP in 2016 and a second grant of $1.5 million in 2017.[75] Bold Futures serves girls at risk of juvenile delinquency and victimization; it helps girls navigate gender, economic, and social barriers by providing long-lasting mentoring relationships. The weekly small group mentoring programs feature a ratio of one staff person for every 4 girls at 20 Girls Inc. locations in high-need communities in 15 states. Each year, Bold Futures serves about 1,000 girls between the ages of 9 to 14, helping them strengthen their coping skills and increasing family engagement.

Girls Inc. implemented *Friendly PEERsuasion* to help girls ages 11 to 14 acquire knowledge, skills, and support systems to avoid substance use. The program consists of 15 hour-long sessions with a trained adult leader.[76] PEERsuasion uses a combination of adult leadership and peer reinforcement to teach girls how to recognize media and peer pressures and to acquire the skills for making responsible decisions about substance abuse. Participants learn decision-making, assertiveness, and communication skills to resist peer pressure and to develop healthy ways to manage stress. They also learn the short- and long-term effects of substance abuse. They practice how to leave situations where they feel pressured to use alcohol or drugs. After successfully learning these skills, the girls conduct substance-abuse prevention activities for children aged 6 through 10. Their status as leaders reinforces their commitment to resist using drugs and alcohol.

Another Girls Inc program is *Preventing Adolescent Pregnancy*. Despite a recent decrease in teen pregnancy, the United States continues to have the highest teen pregnancy among industrialized countries (more than twice the rate of Canada).[77] This program, which teaches skills, insights, and peer support, consists of three age-appropriate components. The first stage, "Growing Together," consists of two-way conversations between young girls (ages 9–11) and a trusted adult about sexuality to facilitate future communication. "Will Power/Won't Power" is the next stage. Throughout the sessions, girls (ages 12–14) learn to resist pressure and to avoid risky situations. Girls learn medically accurate information along with assertiveness and communication skills. The positive aspects of abstinence and the value of a positive sister-support system are stressed. The third stage is "Taking Care of Business" (for girls 15–18). Sessions stress smart choices, provide facts on contraception, focus on recognizing and moving beyond limiting sex-role stereotypes for women, and thinking about life goals. There is also an ancillary component, Growing Up! Body Basics. The 3-hour workshop is for girls ages 7 to 8. Girls receive accurate, age-appropriate information on why and how their bodies are changing.

OJJDP Model Programs for Girls

As discussed in chapter 2, OJJDP convened the Girls Study Group in 2004 to respond to a perceived increase in delinquency among girls. The Study Group found that official responses had changed rather than delinquency behaviors— and that policies disproportionately affected girls. In 2008, the Girls Study group examined the available literature and identified factors that may predict or prevent delinquency. In 2016 OJJDP funded research on trauma and justice-involved youths to develop evidence-based, trauma-informed practices.[78]

On its Model Programs Guide website, OJJDP lists evidence-based juvenile justice and youth prevention, intervention, and reentry programs.[79] Viewers can sort the programs by populations. In 2019, there were 14 programs listed for girls, including *Movimiento Ascendencia (Upward Movement)*. The culturally focused, gender-specific program located in Pueblo, Colorado, provides girls with positive alternatives to substance use and gang involvement. Activities are designed around three main components: cultural awareness, mediation or conflict resolution, and self-esteem or social support. The program includes mentoring, recreational activities, tutoring, cultural enhancement, and close involvement with parents. It also provides a safe haven for girls. Another program listed was SNAP®Girls. It is a multi-component intervention for girls with disruptive behaviors and their families. It focuses on self-control, emotion regulation, and problem solving.

In 2016, the National Crittenton Foundation became director of OJJDP's *National Girls Initiative*. Charles Crittenton opened a mission in New York City in 1883 to serve girls. For 135 years, through various iterations and mergers, the foundation has used a social justice approach to work for social and systems change for girls impacted by chronic adversity, violence, and injustice.[80] Many of the girls in the Initiative grew up in homes marked by domestic violence, substance abuse and poverty.[81] They are disproportionately girls of color, and many are single mothers. Others are in foster care, juvenile justice, or homeless. The initiative helps girls living at the margins who are largely invisible to families, communities, and the systems responsible for supporting them.

One of the projects undertaken by the National Girls Initiative is an evaluation of girls' courts.[82] Approximately 20 specialty girls' courts have been created; one of the first was established in Honolulu in 2004. There is no uniform definition of gender-specific courts. The Honolulu court focuses on girls charged with status offenses. Other girls' courts link female defendants with social services; some hear only sex trafficking cases. One aspect of the evaluation is to determine whether the courts bring more girls into the system or whether they offer an alternative to incarceration.

There are 26 independent nonprofit organizations in 31 states and the District of Columbia affiliated with National Crittenton. All the agencies share a belief in the potential of girls and young women impacted by violence and trauma. The agencies provide comprehensive, strength-based, developmentally-appropriate, trauma-informed gender services grounded in research. Services are provided in a range of settings—in the home, in school early learning centers, in foster care placements, in community-based programs, and in residential centers.

Children of the Night

Lois Lee, an expert in rescuing child sex trafficking victims, founded the nonprofit Children of the Night program in 1979 while she was a graduate student in sociology at UCLA.[83] In 1975, she had seen growing numbers of throwaway children on the streets of Hollywood prostituting themselves for food and shelter. Most were from abusive homes and had nowhere to turn. She offered them shelter in her apartment, helping more than 250 children.

The program consists of: (1) a 24-hour hot line; (2) a walk-in center that provides medical aid, clothing, crisis intervention, and referrals for housing, drug counseling, schools, jobs, and foster home placement; (3) professional counseling by volunteer psychologists and psychiatrists; (4) an outreach component whose trained volunteers walk the streets distributing informational materials to potential clients and engaging in on-the-spot counseling; and (5) a "turn-in-a-pimp" component that entails cooperation among the youths, the agency, the police, and the court system (the aim here is to obtain court testimony against pimps to assist in the prosecution of individuals who otherwise might go free because of lack of evidence). When built in 1992, the 24-bed home was the largest and most comprehensive residential program for child sex trafficking victims. Until 2017, it provided shelter, an accredited on-site school, and individual case management for girls 11 to 17 years of age.

OTHER MODEL PROGRAMS

As discussed throughout the text, research on adolescent development underscores the differences between adults and adolescents. A system that relies on control, punishment, and confinement affects development. Removing youth from their families, peers, and communities at a critical time in their lives can have devastating consequences. Early contact with the justice system can have social, economic, and health consequences. Many states and jurisdictions have started developing and implementing diversion programs as more developmentally appropriate ways of handling youth.[84] Specialized courts are one popular diversion model.

Youth Courts

There are more than a thousand youth court programs (also called teen, peer, and student courts) in the United States.[85] The number of youth courts increased exponentially from 1994 when there were less than 80. First-time offenders can choose to avoid juvenile court in favor of being sentenced by their peers.[86] Advocates believe that being held accountable by peers carries more weight than discipline by an adult authority figure. The courts are designed to empower youth.

Youth Court offers an alternative solution for relatively minor offenses. Perhaps most importantly, youth courts increase awareness in the community about issues that affect juveniles. It engages other youths and community members in finding workable resolutions to problem behavior. Youthful offenders learn to confront the consequences of their actions. Offenders and volunteers learn citizenship and the law as well as developing skills in public speaking, mediation, and pro-social leadership. Communities recover losses from crime and regain confidence and pride in local youths.[87]

Like other problem-solving courts, youth courts generally include two primary components: a court hearing and a period of supervision.[88] Teen courts vary in the agencies involved in administration, the training of jurors, and the criteria for participation for offenders, but the goal is to determine a fair and restorative disposition. Typically, peers determine the verdict and sentences. Teen courts are grounded in peer justice, procedural justice, specific deterrence, labeling, restorative justice, law-related education, and skill building. Restorative sentencing can include community service, apology letters, family/individual counseling, academic tutoring, and substance abuse services.

There are four types of youth courts: adult judge, peer jury, youth judge, and youth tribunal. In the latter two forms, youths perform all courtroom roles, including that of judge.[89] Youth tribunals involve a panel of (usually three) judges that hears cases presented by youth attorneys. The youth judge model replicates traditional hearings with opposing counsel and a jury. In adult judge programs (about half of all teen courts), youths perform all court functions except the role of judge. The peer jury model resembles a grand jury. An adult or youth volunteer presents each case to a jury of teens, who then question the defendant directly. Jury members choose the sentence, sometimes guided by the adult judge.

Despite the expansion in the number of teen courts, relatively few rigorous studies have examined their effectiveness.[90] The studies available have shown mixed results about the impact of teen courts on juvenile offender outcomes. The studies varied widely in research design, making comparison results difficult. Some studies show modest support for the positive impact of teen courts, but additional research is needed.

Juvenile Drug Treatment Courts

There are approximately 460 juvenile drug treatment courts (JDTC).[91] These courts began in the mid-1990s to divert young people from incarceration through a regimen of treatment, court supervision, drug testing, and family/community participation.[92] About 17% of youth entering the juvenile justice system have a substance use disorder—rising to 39% of youth who are detained and 47% of adjudicated youth in secure placements.

While JDTCs are moving away from traditional juvenile justice case processing to a more therapeutic model, implementation, impact, quality of practice and treatment provided varies widely from court to court.[93] The focus is on providing treatment to drug-involved juvenile offenders with the goal of reducing recidivism and substance abuse. Intensive judicial supervision is common. Juvenile drug court programs vary in length and often last for 12 to 18 months. There are frequent judicial hearings where judges review progress and work with program staff and/or families to develop individualized treatment and rehabilitation plans. There are frequent drug tests combined with incentives to abstain from drugs and sanctions for substance use. A review of 46 studies about the effectiveness of juvenile drug courts found no evidence that the courts reduced recidivism but also found that the methodological quality of most of the studies was low.[94]

Mental Health Assessment and Screening

At least two-thirds of the youth in the juvenile justice system have diagnosable mental health disorders, and there are critical intervention points within the juvenile justice process where interventions should occur. These include: initial contact with law enforcement, intake, detention, judicial processing, secure placement, probation supervisor, and re-entry.

There are research-based mental-health screening and assessment tools for use with youth in the juvenile justice system—as well as evidence-based intervention and treatment programs that produce positive results and are cost effective.[95] Through Models for Change, states (including Colorado, Connecticut, Illinois, Louisiana, Ohio, Pennsylvania, Texas, and Washington) have changed their policies and practices to meet the mental health needs of youth in the juvenile justice system. Important factors include: (1) mental health screening in juvenile justice settings; (2) diversion strategies for youth with mental health needs; (3) mental health training for juvenile justice staff and police; (4) implementation of evidence-based practices; (5) training and resources to support family involvement.

Cognitive-behavioral therapy (CBT) has been effective for justice-involved youths.[96] It helps youths adjust their thinking and their behaviors related to delinquency and violence. Functional family therapy (FFT) is a family-based prevention and intervention program for high-risk youth. Sessions typically occur over a 3-month period and can be held in clinical settings (outpatient therapy model) or in the home. Multisystemic therapy (MST) assesses the origins of behavioral problems and works to increase pro-social behavior. It includes intense family involvement and generally uses a home-based model of service delivery. The average treatment occurs over 4 months.

Chapter 12 discussed other programs working to establish effective reforms. The Juvenile Detention Alternatives Initiative (JDAI) has been working with states to close residential facilities and to decrease detention. After 25 years, 300 jurisdictions in 39 states have seen decreases in their detention populations.[97] The PEW Public Safety Performance program has helped 7 states reduce their residential commitments.

BROAD-BASED NATIONAL STRATEGIES

Addressing the delinquency problem will require a national strategy; the problem is not just local in nature. More than 30 years ago, criminologist Elliot Currie suggested five general categories for a national strategy to address the general problem of crime that are equally relevant today (the ten tenets of the blueprint detailed above urge similar reform).[98]

1. *Early educational interventions.* Delinquency is related to poor school performance and dropping out.
2. *Expanded health and mental health services.* Most violent youths suffer from childhood traumas of the central nervous system, exhibit multiple psychotic symptoms, and have also experienced severe physical and/or sexual abuse.
3. *Family support programs.* Research indicates that the majority of prison inmates, especially violent ones, experienced severe physical, emotional, or sexual abuse or some combination of all three as children.
4. *Reentry programs.* The key ingredient in virtually all successful rehabilitation programs is improving skills—work skills, reading and verbal skills, problem-solving skills, and so on.
5. *Drug and alcohol abuse treatment programs.* The treatment of addictions would reduce criminal behavior to support the habit.

At about the same time, sociologist Mark Colvin also wrote about the need for national strategies.[99] He focused on the concept of social reproduction—the process through which institutions (primarily families and schools) prepare children for productive roles in society. His main thesis was that institutions have largely failed to establish the necessary social bonds to link young people to legitimate avenues to adulthood. The result is that many become marginal to the country's economic institutions because of failure to invest in human development and human capital.

There is a need for a "national comprehensive program aimed at spurring economic growth, human development, and grass-roots, democratic participation in the major institutions affecting our lives and those of our children."[100]

Crime may be less likely to occur in communities with stronger social capital. Higher levels of community participation create social networks, consensus, and an environment of mutual support and trust.

> Improving social capital through volunteerism and political activism could alter the social norms surrounding crime and a community's reaction to crime. Civic engagement seems to mitigate those cultural norms that allow violence and crime to take root. Increasing youth participation in community activities could be an important tool in stemming the adverse effects of crime, as well as keeping individual youth more bonded to conventional social norms.[101]

A comprehensive approach must aim at broader economic and human-development programs that affect large segments of the population (for example, the social security system versus welfare for the poor). The country must do what other industrialized nations do and consider seriously the need to develop human capital for the continued overall well-being of society. In the United States, the system is so privatized that public or social needs are often undermined by private investment decisions that result in moving capital all over the world but eliminating jobs at home. Education is the key here. However, as Colvin notes, education must be more than what the term has traditionally meant (formalized public schooling leading to a diploma). Education should be a comprehensive policy that includes families, schools, workplaces and communities working to reduce the marginalization of young people. "For youth, who often feel the effects of social exclusion, social capital can be as simple as a positive relationship or affiliation with neighborhood and community associations. Thus, collective as well as personal efficacy can be achieved through volunteerism and political participation."[102]

Positive Youth Development

The science of adolescent development has influenced intervention approaches. Positive Youth Development (PYD) is a program that focuses on the ability of young people to thrive when they experience positive relationships and meaningful activities in supportive and safe environments.[103] Interventions based on PYD principles were not a natural fit for justice systems that focused on controlling misbehavior and measured effectiveness only by recidivism. Implementing punitive controls and watching for any recidivism is not compatible with developmental science. PYD measures success by tracking positive youth outcomes—academic engagement, readiness for the labor market, improved socio-emotional skills, and the formation of supportive relationships.

For most of the twentieth century, adolescence was viewed as a period of turmoil. The deficit-based approach to adolescence focused on what could go wrong in a young person's development.[104] The individual treatment philosophy of the original juvenile court movement was based on this approach. Prior to the newest research on adolescent development, researchers focused on negative outcome measures, such as delinquency, antisocial behavior, substance use, and risky sexual behaviors. "This widespread reliance on negative outcomes reinforced the public's perception that youth involved in the justice system were destined to follow a negative path."[105]

Other studies, however, noted that most youth succeed even in the presence of multiple risk factors and applied the label "resilience" to describe qualities that promote healthy development in the face of adversity. Youth advocates began to see adolescence as a process of positive opportunities for youth to learn, serve, and benefit from interactions with pro-social adults and communities.

> The basic premise of PYD is that even the most disadvantaged young person can develop positively when connected to the right mix of opportunities, supports, positive roles, and relationships. Having a wide range of pro-social experiences during adolescence allows a young person to practice and demonstrate competency and to embrace his or her responsibilities and value to the larger community. The central purpose of PYD is action. Communities are encouraged to break down barriers to opportunity, and provide positive roles and relationships for all youth, including the most disadvantaged and disconnected.[106]

Changing the Frame

	PRIMARY LENS		
ASSUMPTIONS	**Youth as Victim**	**Youth as Villain**	**Youth as Resource**
Origins of Most Delinquent Behavior	Symptom of underlying disturbance	Anti-social impulses, lack of restraint due to permissiveness and the absence of punishment	Normative response to adolescent needs for status, belonging, power & excitement, lack of empathy
How Delinquent Youth Compare with Other Adolescents	Fundamentally different in psychological and emotional makeup	Fundamentally different motivations and impulses toward different behavior	Largely similar to other adolescents but with fewer social assets
Delinquent Youth Capacity for Behavior Change	Incapable of conventional behavior without therapeutic interventions	Incapable of conventional behavior without strict discipline and the threat of punishment	Inherently capable of conventional behavior with sufficient access to supports and pro-social opportunities
Primary Intervention Strategy	Individual or family-based therapeutic treatment	Deterrence and retributive punishment	Skill development, attachment and engagement
Role of Treatment	Primary	Secondary	Secondary
Risks of Treatment	Could fail to address underlying cause(s)	Could delay or impede deterrence	Could introduce stigma or harm—i.e., iatrogenic effects

PYD involves building connections, valuing community and emphasizing learning/doing and attaching/belonging. A key concept involves changing the frame—looking at youth as resources rather than as victims or villains. People are beginning to question the rationale for interventions based solely on the punishment or individual treatment model.

- If delinquent behavior stems from a lack of integration and habilitation, why do correctional strategies focus on isolation of offenders?[107]
- If the goal is to make offenders more responsible and accountable, why do we place them in positions (e.g., in most treatment programs) where others assume responsibility for their activities and behaviors?
- If many sources of delinquency are to be found in communities, families, and schools, why do probation strategies often target only the individual offender?
- If youth justice professionals are experts in delinquent behavior, why are youth justice agencies so often viewed by policymakers as an all-purpose "dumping ground" for troubled youth rather than a resource for resolving problems in schools and communities?

The transition from adolescence to adulthood involves biological, psychological, and social change.[108] Juveniles have varying access to the resources and supportive environments that aid in navigating the changes. The most effective interventions to promote desistance from offending focus on positive opportunities and outcomes.

> Monitoring youths' acquisition of these positive assets shifts the focus of justice intervention from deficits to strengths and highlights the innate ability of all youth to navigate the challenging transitions of adolescence. Focusing on positive outcomes is also compatible with the other foundational purposes of justice intervention—accountability and safety.[109]

Restorative Justice

Seeking to find alternatives to a punitive response to crime, restorative justice emphasizes the needs of the victims, the offender, and the community. The movement began in Canada in 1974 when a probation officer arranged a direct meeting between two teenagers and the victims of their vandalism spree to determine restitution.[110] Since that time efforts to seek peaceful and nonpunitive solutions have evolved all over the world.[111] Dennis Sullivan and Larry Tifft explain the growing interest in restorative justice as an indication of people rejecting the conventional response of retribution. "An increasing number of people are coming to see that any method of correction that is based in punishment—whatever the conditions and justifications for its use—is just another form of violence."[112]

The Navajo call on the relatives of the person responsible for a harm to help the offender reconnect with the community. The offender has become disconnected and disengaged. The Navajo call the process of reconnection *peacemaking*. Community members work together to restore harmony to fractured relationships. Longstanding indigenous customs are based on the belief that if a wrong is not righted by accounting for the needs of those who have been harmed, the community will suffer. "All are responsible for making things right in such situations because all are in some way responsible for that harm occurring in the first place."[113] This ethic may seem strange to people who embrace individualism over collectivism. Proponents of restorative justice recognize the difficulty of convincing a capitalistic culture to reject power and control over others.

The underlying aim of the restorative justice process is to cease further objectification of those who have been involved in the offense—victims, offenders, families connected to both parties, and the community at large. Everyone engages in a healing process using traditional mediation and conflict resolution techniques to dissolve fears and resentments and to restore severed relationships[114]

The Mural Arts Program in Philadelphia, Pennsylvania, is one of many programs based on restorative justice principles. It offers a constructive, creative outlet for chronically truant/delinquent youth.[115] It began in 1984 as a program for youths who had been adjudicated for engaging in graffiti. The mural-painting component was designed to help adolescents learn more positive ways to express their creativity and to provide positive role models, structured activities, and opportunities to develop job skills. Over 3,000 murals have been created and are a tourist attraction in Philadelphia.[116] The program works with adjudicated youth at the city's detention center, a correctional center for young adults, a residential program for boys, and with adjudicated youths in supervised independent-living homes around the city. In 2017, it received one of the inaugural grants from the Art for Justice Fund, an initiative launched by Agnes Gund, a philanthropist and art collector who donates the proceeds from the sale of art in her collection to support efforts to reform the criminal justice system.

The peacemaking practices of Native Americans reflect each tribe's unique culture, religion, and collective experiences. The most widely-recognized model is that of the Navajo Nation discussed above. The formats and names vary, but all focus on problem solving and emphasize future relations rather than assigning guilt and punishment.[117] All forms of peacemaking are designed to help participants accept responsibility for their actions. Peacemaking circles are a structured process for organizing group communication, relationship building, decision making, and conflict resolution.[118] They are used in families, schools, communities, workplaces, and justice systems.

The city of Peoria (Illinois) was concerned about disproportionate detention. Analyses of juvenile arrest and detention data pointed to aggravated battery referrals from Manual High School as the largest contributor to the detention of minorities. Surveys and focus group interviews with Manual students and teachers revealed substantial anxiety about gangs and violence and a reliance on force to resolve problems. The fears and reactions created a culture of insecurity, broken relationships, and lack of trust. The effort to shift responsibility for responding to juvenile offending away from police, courts, and correctional systems began with an experiment in school-based peacemaking circles.

The circles were introduced on a voluntary basis in Manual classrooms in 2006. They allowed participants to raise issues, explain their feelings, work out misunderstandings, resolve differences, and support one another in a protected setting. Students participating in the programs reported better attendance, improved relationships with classmates and teachers, successful avoidance of trouble, and better schoolwork. Lori Brown, the coordinator for Peoria Models for Change, praised the program for its extraordinary ability to open lines of communication and understanding. Like other restorative justice practices, peacemaking circles emphasize "changing relationships by engaging people: doing things with them, rather than to them or for them. It's the relationships, not specific strategies, that bring about meaningful change."[119]

The program was so successful that Manual introduced MANYO (Motivating and Nurturing Youth Opportunity), a peer jury program that provides an alternative approach to school discipline. It emphasizes consensus-based conflict resolution by youths, with active efforts to repair harm and make peace. Holly Snyder, the local Restorative Justice Coordinator, describes the program as: "Holding youth responsible for their decisions and giving them a chance to repair the harm they've caused. It's easy to suspend them—no one talks to them, no one holds them accountable. And then they come back to school, and again no one deals with them."[120] Two other schools in Peoria introduced peer juries. In two years, school administrators referred 119 cases involving fighting, intimidation, classroom insubordination, or other disruptive misconduct to the peer juries. Only 6 of the cases (5%) had to be referred back to school administration for further disciplinary action.

Restorative alternatives are expanding out of the schools and into the Peoria community. In the summer of 2010, the Covenant with Black America and the Peoria Police Department with help from Models for Change coordinators launched Community Peace Conferencing—a diversion program for nonviolent, first- and second-time juvenile offenders. Police refer the young offenders to community volunteers trained in restorative justice techniques. As Brown comments, "If we want peace in our community, the community itself must take an active role in obtaining it. This program is about ordinary citizens partnering with the police to fight crime and improve the lives of youth."[121]

Researchers systematically reviewed the available research that compared participants in a restorative justice program to participants processed traditionally through juvenile courts. They found a moderate reduction in future delinquent behavior when compared to traditional juvenile court processing.[122] There was also evidence that victim-offender conferencing, family group conferencing, arbitration/mediation programs, and circle sentencing programs produced promising results in terms of delinquency outcomes for offenders. Studies with stronger research designs (i.e. random assignment studies) showed smaller results. Youths participating in restorative justice programs had a greater perception of fairness, were more satisfied with the outcomes, and had less supportive attitudes toward delinquency. Victims reported improved perceptions of fairness, greater satisfaction with the outcome, improved attitudes toward and willingness to forgive the offender.

Within the school setting, restorative justice encompasses many different types of programs. It can involve training all staff and students in restorative justice principles, or it can be used as an approach to specific incidents.[123] A restorative approach in schools shifts the emphasis from managing behavior to nurturing/repairing relationships. Research on restorative practices is still in the infancy stage. Several exploratory studies have indicated promising impact on school climate, student behavior, and relationships among students and staff. Researchers at the Rand Corporation conducted one of the first randomized controlled trials of the impact of restorative practices on classroom, school climate, and suspension rates.[124] The study found that schools using restorative justice practices reduced the number of days students were suspended and teachers reported their school environments felt safer.

SOME CLOSING WORDS

Saul Alinsky, the social reformer and agitator of the early twentieth century, offered a parable that is highly informative for readers who need a perspective to guide their own individual efforts to seek change. Imagine a large river with a high waterfall. At the bottom of this waterfall, hundreds of people are working frantically to rescue those who have fallen into the river. One individual looks up and sees a seemingly never-ending stream of people cascading down the waterfall, and he begins to run upstream. One of his fellow rescuers hollers, "Where are you going? There are so many people that need help here." The man replied, "I'm going upstream to find out why so many people are falling into the river." Some people choose to respond to problems related to crime and delinquency by working downstream. This is certainly a noble goal, and good people are always needed. We picture ourselves running upstream, asking "why?"

Alex Kotlowitz has been writing about the struggles and resilience of youths living in urban poverty for 40 years. His most recent work, *An American Summer*, explores the impact of 172 deaths and 793 people wounded over 3 months on the spirit of individuals and communities.[125] Little has changed since he wrote *There Are No Children Here* in 1991. Kotlowitz acknowledges that he alternates between despair and encouragement, but he writes about people who are fighting against hopelessness.[126] He provides insight into lives that have been reduced to stereotypes, allowing readers to understand adversity without reducing people to their hardships.

It's in these, the most ravaged of our communities, among the most desperate and forlorn, that we can come to understand the makings of who we are as a nation, a country marked by the paradox of holding such generosity beside such neglect. . . .

Then there's the rest of us, who, reading the morning newspaper or watching the evening news, hear of youngsters gunned down while riding their bike or walking down an alley or coming from a party, and think to ourselves, *They must have done something to deserve it, they must have been up to no good.* Virtually every teen and young man shot, the police tell us, belonged to a gang, as if that somehow suggests that what goes around comes around. But life in these communities is more tangled than that. It's knottier and more lasting than readings of a daily newspaper or viewings of the evening news would suggest.[127]

SUMMARY

This chapter reviewed some promising approaches in dealing with juvenile delinquency, but it merely scratched the surface of the vast literature that is available. Interested readers should consult the sources cited for additional information.

Two critical points were emphasized. First, it is mandatory that we begin to think "outside the box." Before we attempt to change youthful behaviors we don't like or fear, we need to change ourselves—especially the way we perceive youths and their potential. The second point is that we need to change the surrounding culture and social structure. In the richest society in world history, we fail miserably in providing good opportunities to all our citizens.

As discussed earlier in the chapter, the Youth Transition Founders Group believes that a sea change is underway in youth justice. Policymakers and the public now support alternative—and more cost effective— sanctions. The formal juvenile justice system is no substitute for strong families, schools, and communities. Diverse and effective interventions in the community are far more effective for most youths than confinement in an institution. If we want a smaller, more effective juvenile justice system, we need improved diversion programs, probation, and alternatives to incarceration.

Human behavior, both delinquent and nondelinquent, is shaped by outside forces. Our culture and our social institutions teach certain values, but the avenues for reaching those goals are often closed to some members of society. We need to work hard at providing the services that youth in trouble desperately need. Even if we succeed in teaching the necessary skills, the effort will be wasted if they return to the same environment that had so much to do with their original delinquent activities. We urge readers to remember the upstream/downstream parable and to use their unique talents to blaze new trails in how we deal with delinquency.

Notes

1   For an excellent discussion of this subject see Karen Sternheimer, *Kids These Days: Facts and Fictions About Today's Youth* (Lanham, MD: Rowman & Littlefield, 2006).

2   Thomas Kuhn, *The Structure of Scientific Revolutions: 50th Anniversary Edition* (Chicago: University of Chicago Press, 2012), 90.

3   Jerome G. Miller, *Last One Over the Wall: The Massachusetts Experiment in Closing Reform Schools*, 2nd ed. (Columbus: Ohio State University Press, 1998), 234.

4   Ibid.

5   Daniel Macallair and Mike Males, "A Failure of Good Intentions: An Analysis of Juvenile Justice Reform in San Francisco During the 1990s," *Review of Policy Research*, 21(1): 63–78. Emphasis added.

6   Edwin Schur, *Radical Nonintervention: Rethinking the Delinquency Problem* (Englewood Cliffs, NJ: Prentice-Hall, 1973).

7   Ibid., 166–70.

8   Mike Males, *Framing Youth: Ten Myths about the Coming Generation* (Monroe, ME: Common Courage Press, 2002); Mike Males, *The Scapegoat Generation: America's War on Adolescents* (Monroe, ME: Common Courage Press, 1996).

9   Joy Dryfoos, *Adolescents at Risk* (New York: Oxford University Press, 1991).

10 Marianne Bitler, Hilary Hoynes, and Thurston Domina, "Head Start Programs Have Significant Benefits for Children at the Bottom of the Skill Distribution," Policy Brief Center for Poverty Research, 2017, 6(1): 1–2.

11 Diane Schanzenback and Lauren Bauer, "The Long-term Impact of the Head Start Program," The Brookings Institution, August 19, 2016.

12 Gregory Camilli, Sadako Vargas, Sharon Ryan and William Barnett, "Meta-Analysis of the Effects of Early Education Interventions on Cognitive and Social Development," *Teachers College Record*, 2010, 112(3): 579–620.

13 Abigail Fagan, "Family-focused Interventions to Prevent Juvenile Delinquency," *Criminology & Public Policy*, 2013, 12(4): 617–650.

14 Abigail Fagan and Kristen Benedini, "How Do Family-Focused Prevention Programs Work? A Review of Mediating Mechanisms Associated with Reductions in Youth Antisocial Behaviors," *Clinical Child and Family Psychology Review*, 2016, 19(4): 285–309.

15 Denise Gottfredson, Philip Cook, and Chongmin Na, "Schools and Prevention," in Brandon Welsh and David Farrington (eds.), *The Oxford Handbook of Crime Prevention* (New York: Oxford University Press, 2012), 269–290.

16 Stephanie Ryon, Kristin Early, and Anna Kosloski, "Community-based and Family-focused Alternatives to Incarceration: A Quasi-experimental Evaluation of Interventions for Delinquent Youth, *Journal of Criminal Justice*, 2017, 51: 59–66.

17 Mark Lipsey, "The Primary Factors that Characterize Effective Interventions with Juvenile Offenders: A Meta-Analytic Overview." *Victims and Offenders*, 2009, 4: 124–147.

18 Youth Transition Funders Group, "A Blueprint for Youth Justice Reform,", 2016, http://www.ytfg.org/2015/12/a-blueprint-for-youth-justice-reform/

19 Ibid., 3.

20 Ibid.

21 Richard Mendel, "The Missouri Model: Reinventing the Practice of Rehabilitating Youthful Offenders," The Annie E. Casey Foundation, 2010, 37.

22 Ibid., 36.

23 Ibid., 37.

24 Missouri Division of Youth Services, "About the Missouri Approach," 2018, http://missouriapproach.org/approach/

25 Patrick McCarthy, Vincent Schiraldi, and Miriam Shark, "The Future of Youth Justice: A Community-Based Alternative to the Youth Prison Model," National Institute of Justice, October 2016, NCJ 250142.

26 Missouri Division of Youth Services, "About the Missouri Approach."

27 Division of Youth Services, "Residential Care," https://dss.mo.gov/dys/res.htm

28 Mendel, "The Missouri Model."

29 Ibid.

30 Quoted in Ibid., 50–51.

31 Jason Szanyi and Mark Soler, "Implementation of New York's Close to Home Initiative: A New Model for Youth Justice," Center for Children's Law and Policy, February 2018.

32 Denky Manek, "Detention Diversion Advocacy Program," Center on Juvenile and Criminal Justice, 2019.

33 Randall Shelden, "Detention Diversion Advocacy: An Evaluation," OJJDP *Juvenile Justice Bulletin*, September 1999, NCJ 171155.

34 Daniel Macallair, "Disposition Case Advocacy in San Francisco's Juvenile Justice System: A New Approach to Deinstitutionalization," *Crime and Delinquency*, 1994, 40: 84. Macallair, the director of the Center on Juvenile and Criminal Justice in San Francisco, was instrumental in developing DDAP. He can be reached at: dmacallair@cjcj.org.

35 Michael Bush, "Detention Diversion Advocacy Project," Wiley Online Library, November 20, 2017.

36 The ability of case advocacy and case management to promote detention alternatives was demonstrated by the National Center on Institutions and Alternatives (NCIA). Under contract with New York City's Spofford Detention Center, NCIA significantly augmented the efforts of that city's Department of Juvenile Justice to reduce the number of youth in detention and to expand the range of alternative options. Additional evidence in support of the use of case advocacy comes from a study by the Rand Corporation. This study compared two groups of randomly selected youths: a control group for whom probation officers recommended incarceration and an experimental group for whom case advocates prepared disposition reports. Only 49% of the control group were diverted from institutional care compared to 72% of the experimental group. The Rand study also found tremendous resistance from juvenile justice officials (especially probation officers) to alternative dispositions, particularly those coming from case advocates. It appeared that the probation staff resented the intrusion into what had heretofore been considered their "turf." (Peter Greenwood and Susan Turner, *Implementing and Managing Innovative Correctional Programs: Lessons from OJJDP's Private Sector Initiative*, Rand Corporation, 1991, 92).

37 Shelden, "Detention Diversion Advocacy."

38 Ibid.

39 Center on Juvenile and Criminal Justice, "The San Francisco Juvenile Collaborative Reentry Team," Program Brief, February 2012, http://www.cjcj.org/Direct-services/Juvenile-Collaborative-Reentry-Unit.html

40 Dinky Manek Enty, "Juvenile Collaborative Reentry Unit," Center on Juvenile and Criminal Justice, 2019.

41 David Altschuler and Shay Bilchik, "Critical Elements of Juvenile Reentry in Research and Practice," The Council of State Governments Justice Center, April 21, 2014.

42 Enty, "Juvenile Collaborative Reentry Unit."

43 Ibid.

44 Council for a Strong America, "Local Spotlights," in California Juvenile Justice Practitioners' Toolkit, February 1, 2018.

45 National Conference of State Legislatures, "Juvenile Collaborative Reentry Unit," September 20, 2015.

46 Beth Stevens, Samina Sattar, Michaella Morzuch, Douglas Young, Laura Ruttner, Jillian Stein, Meg Hargreaves, Leslie Foster, "Final Report from the Models for Change Evaluation," Mathematica Policy Research, June 24, 2016.

47 MacArthur Foundation, "Evaluation of the Models for Change Initiative," October 18, 2018, https://www.macfound.org/press/grantee-publications/evaluation-models-change-initiative/

48 Stevens et al., "Final Report from the Models for Change Evaluation."

49 Illinois Department of Human Services, "Redeploy Illinois Annual Report," March 2016, DHS 8250 (N-02-16).

50 Stevens et al., "Final Report from the Models for Change Evaluation."

51 Ibid.

52 Patrick Griffin, "Models for Change: Innovations in Practice," National Center for Juvenile Justice, November 2010.

53 PACTT, "What Is PACTT?" 2018, http://www.pactt-alliance.org/Pages/FAQs.aspx

54 Stevens et al., "Final Report from the Models for Change Evaluation."

55 Griffin, "Models for Change," 7–8.

56 Ibid., 8.

57 Ibid.

58 Stevens et al., "Final Report from the Models for Change Evaluation."

59 Andrew Wachter, Gene Siegel, and Hunter Hurts, "2013 Washington State Targeted Areas of Improvement & Strategic Opportunity for Technical Assistance Data Inventory," National Center for Juvenile Justice, February 2014.

60 Ibid.

61 Stevens et al., "Final Report from the Models for Change Evaluation."

62 Griffin, "Models for Change," 11.

63 Marsha Levick, "Momentum for Juvenile Justice Reform," MacArthur Foundation, December 14, 2018.

64 Laurence Steinberg, "Understanding Adolescent Development, Reforming Juvenile Justice," MacArthur Foundation, October 2, 2018.

65 Benjamin Chambers and Annie Balck, "Because Kids Are Different: Five Opportunities for Reforming the Juvenile Justice System," Models for Change Resource Partnership, December 2014, 4.

66 Ibid., 17.

67 Megan Millenky, Louisa Reskon, Lily Freedman, Caroline Mage, "Focusing on Girls' Futures: Results from the Evaluation of PACE Center for Girls," MDRC, January 2019.

68 PACE Center for Girls, "Pace History," https://www.pacecenter.org/about-us/pace-history

69 Ibid., "Why PACE?"

70 Millenky et al., "Focusing on Girls."

71 Ibid.

72 National Mentoring Resource Center, "Girls Inc. Mentoring Program Steers Girls towards Bold Futures," Office of Juvenile Justice and Delinquency Protection, 2018.

73 Girls Inc., "Our History," https://girlsinc.org/about-us/our-history/

74 Girls Inc., "Girls Inc. Receives $2 million to Reduce Girls' Risk of Involvement in Juvenile Justice System," January 13, 2017.

75 National Mentoring Resource Center, "Girls Inc. Mentoring Program."

76 Lisa Lunghofer and Weston Williams, "Evaluation of Friendly PEERsuasion: Final Technical Report," Maila Consulting Group, Inc., June 2016.

77 Girls Inc., "Preventing Adolescent Pregnancy," 2014.

78 Development Services Group, Inc., "Specialized Responses for Girls in the Juvenile Justice System," Literature Review, OJJDP, 2018.

79 OJJDP, Model Programs Guide: Delinquency Prevention, https://www.ojjdp.gov/mpg/Topic/Details/79

80 National Crittenton, "Our History," https://nationalcrittenton.org/who-we-are/our-history/

81 Ibid., "Who We Are," https://nationalcrittenton.org/who-we-are/

82 Julianne Hill, "Girls' Courts under Scrutiny," *ABA Journal*, November 2017.

83 Children of the Night, "Who We Are," https://childrenofthenight.org/who-we-are/

84 Lauren Gase, Tony Kuo, Elaine Lai, Michael Stoll, and Ninez Ponce, "The Impact of Two Los Angeles County Teen Courts on Youth Recidivism: Comparing Two Informal Probation Programs, Journal of Experimental Criminology, 2016, 12(1): 105–126.

85 National Association of Youth Courts. 2017, https://youthcourt.net

86 Merrill Balassone, "In Teen Courts, A Second Chance," California Courts Newsroom, June 9, 2017.

87 J. M. Schneider, "Youth Courts: An Empirical Update and Analysis of Future Organizational and Research Needs. *Hamilton Fish Institute Reports and Essays Serial*, The George Washington University, 2007, 11.

88 Gase et al., "The Impact of Two Los Angeles County Teen Courts on Youth Recidivism."

89 Jeffrey Butts and Janeen Buck, "The Sudden Popularity of Teen Courts." *The Judges' Journal*, American Bar Association, (41)1, Winter 2002.

90 Gase et al., "The Impact of Two Los Angeles County Teen Courts on Youth Recidivism."

91 Sophia Gatowski, Nancy Miller, Stephen Rubin, William Thorne, and Elizabeth Barnes, "Juvenile Drug Treatment Court Listening Sessions," OJJDP Juvenile Drug Treatment Court Guidelines Project, November 2016.

92 Katherine Volk, "What Are Juvenile Drug Courts," Substance Abuse and Mental Health Services Administration, October 12, 2018.

93 Gatowski, et al., "Juvenile Drug Treatment Court."

94 Emily Tanner-Smith, Mark Lipsey, and David Wilson, "Meta-Analysis of Research on the Effectiveness of Juvenile Drug Courts," National Criminal Justice Reference Service, December 2016.

95 National Center for Mental Health and Juvenile Justice, "Better Solutions for Youth with Mental Health Needs in the Juvenile Justice System," 2014.

96 Development Services Group, Inc., "Intersection between Mental Health and the Juvenile Justice System," Literature Review, OJJDP, 2017.

97 McCarthy et al., The Future of Youth Justice."

98 Elliott Currie, "Confronting Crime: Looking toward the Twenty-First Century." *Justice Quarterly*, 1989, 6: 5–25.

99 Mark Colvin, "Crime and Social Reproduction: A Response to the Call for 'Outrageous' Proposals," *Crime and Delinquency*, 1991, 37: 436–48.

100 Ibid., 437.

101 Jeffrey Butts, Gordon Bazemore, and Aundra Meroe, "Positive Youth Justice: Framing Justice Interventions Using the Concepts of Positive Youth Development," Coalition for Juvenile Justice, 2010, 27.

102 Ibid., 26.

103 Jeffrey Butts, Emily Pelletier, and Lila Kazemian, "Positive Outcomes: Strategies for Assessing the Progress of Youth Involved in the Justice System," Research and Evaluation Center, John Jay College of Criminal Justice, 2018.

104 Butts et al., "Positive Youth Justice."

105 Butts et al., "Positive Youth Outcomes," 2.

106 Butts et al., "Positive Youth Justice," 9.

107 Ibid., 15.

108 Butts et al., "Positive Youth Outcomes."

109 Ibid., 15.

110 Ted Wachtel, "Defining Restorative," International Institute for Restorative Practices, 2016.

111 John Braithwaite, *Restorative Justice and Responsive Regulation* (New York: Oxford University Press, 2002). See also: "Two Stories on Restorative Justice" posted on http://www.sheldensays.com/two_stories_on_restorative_justi.htm

112 Dennis Sullivan and Larry Tifft, *Restorative Justice: Healing the Foundations* (Monsey, NY: Willow Tree Press, 2001).

113 Dennis Sullivan and Larry Tifft, *Handbook of Restorative Justice* (New York: Routledge, 2008), 2.

114 Sullivan and Tifft, *Restorative Justice*.

115 Butts et al., "Positive Youth Justice," 14.

116 Mural Arts Philadelphia: About, Restorative Justice, Art for Justice at muralarts.org

117 Suvi Lambson, "Peacemaking Circles: Evaluating a Native American Restorative Justice Practice in a State Criminal Court Setting in Brooklyn," Center for Court Innovation, 2015.

118 Evelyn Zellerer, "Realizing the Potential of Restorative Justice," in Theo Gavrielides and Vasso Artinopoulou (eds.), *Reconstructing Restorative Justice Philosophy* (New York: Routledge, 2016), 260–290.

119 Griffin, Models for Change, 5.

120 Ibid., 6.

121 Ibid., 7.

122 David Wilson, Ajima Olaghere, and Catherine Kimbrell, "Effectiveness of Restorative Justice Principles in Juvenile Justice: A Meta-Analysis," National Criminal Justice Reference Service, June 2017, 25082.

123 Trevor Fronius, Hannah Persson, Sarah Guckenburg, Nancy Hurley, and Anthony Petrosino, "Restorative Justice in U.S. Schools: A Research Review," WestEd, Justice & Prevention Research Center, 2016.

124 Catherine Agustine, John Engberg, Geoffrey Grimm, Emma Lee, Elaine Wang, Karen Christianson, and Andrea Joseph, "Can Restorative Practices Improve School Climate and Curb Suspensions?", Rand Corporation, 2018.

125 Alex Kotlowitz, *An American Summer: Love and Death in Chicago* (New York: Doubleday, 2019).

126 Christopher Borrelli, "Fighting against Hopelessness," *Chicago Tribune*, Section 4, March 17, 2019.

127 Kotlowitz, *An American Summer*, 7, 8.

Glossary of Juvenile Justice Terms

Abuse: See **Child Abuse**

Adjudication: An adjudicatory hearing is a court proceeding in which it is determined whether the allegations of the petition are supported by evidence (also called a "jurisdictional" or an "evidentiary" hearing).

Adoption: A legal proceeding in which an adult takes, as his or her lawful child, a minor who is not the adoptive parent's natural offspring. The adopted minor loses all legal connection to the previous parent(s), and the adoptive parent undertakes permanently the responsibility of providing for the child. See also **Guardianship**.

Aftercare: Supervision of a juvenile who has been returned to the community from training school.

Allegation: A charge or claim set forth in a petition, which must be proven true or false at a hearing.

Bootstrapping: The tendency within the juvenile justice system to relabel a status offense or a violation of a court order (i.e. a violation of probation rules) as a more serious delinquent offense. The JJDPA prohibits juvenile courts from locking up status offenders, but if the charge is for a delinquent offense, the prohibition does not apply.

CASA: Court Appointed Special Advocate; a trained volunteer appointed by a family/juvenile court judge to represent the best interests of abused, neglected, or dependent children who are the subject of court proceedings.

Child Abuse: Traditionally, any physical mistreatment of a child, as opposed to child neglect or negligent care. However, the term is increasingly used to cover any physical or mental harm, sexual abuse, negligent treatment or maltreatment of a child by a person responsible for the child's welfare.

Child Neglect: Failure by a parent or custodian to render appropriate care to a child; an act of omission by the person legally responsible for a child's care which threatens the child's well-being. Failure to provide a child with suitable food, shelter, clothing, hygiene, medical care or parental supervision.

Child Protection Action: The filing of legal papers by a child welfare agency when its investigation has turned up evidence of child abuse. A civil rather than criminal charge designed to take preventive action (like appointment of a guardian ad litem) for at-risk children before abuse occurs.

Civil Protection Order: A form of protective custody in which a child welfare or police agency orders an adult suspected of abuse to leave the home.

Cognitive Behavior Therapy (CBT): Intervention program that focuses on how beliefs and attitudes affect behaviors; involves learning more beneficial ways of thinking.

Commitment: A court order sentencing a person to confinement in a penal institution or mental health facility.

Complainant: The person who applies to the court for legal redress by filing a complaint.

Complaint: A sworn statement filed in Court alleging that an individual has harmed or violated the rights of a person or has committed a crime. Forms include: 1) An oral statement, usually made to police, by a complainant charging criminal, abusive or neglectful conduct; 2) District Attorney's document that starts a criminal prosecution (also known in many states as an "information"); and 3) a filing in a criminal or civil case setting out the cause of action. In family court, the complaint is usually called a "petition."

Consent: An agreement of the parties resolving pending matters before the court.

Contempt: The action of a person who willfully disobeys a court order or fails to comply with a court decision.

Continuance: The adjournment or postponement of a session, hearing, trial or other proceeding to a subsequent day or time.

Counsel: Advice or assistance given by one person to another in regard to a legal matter often provided by an attorney.

Custody: The care, possession, and control of a person. Custody includes the responsibility of providing food, shelter, medical care, education and discipline. Custody can be joint or sole.

Deep End: Jerome Miller first used the term while he was the commissioner of youth corrections for the state of Massachusetts in the 1970s. It refers to those youth who are deemed the worst offenders housed in juvenile detention centers and other correctional facilities. They occupy the deepest end of the juvenile justice system. The theory behind Miller's approach was that if you could demonstrate that these offenders could be treated through alternative methods, then the rationale for locking up less serious offenders would be weakened. Miller and others who followed proved that most deep-end youths could be successfully treated in alternative locations.

Deinstitutionalization of Status Offenders DSO: Requirement of JJDPA to divert status offenders from being held in secure detention or confinement.

Delinquency: The commission of an illegal act by a juvenile.

Delinquency Proceeding: Court action to declare someone a juvenile delinquent. A "delinquent" is under the age of jurisdiction determined by the state who has been convicted in juvenile court of something that would be classified as a crime in adult court.

Delinquent Child: A child who commits an act that if committed by an adult would constitute a crime.

Dependent Child: A child under the age of maturity who relies on an adult for care and protection.

Detention: The confinement of a juvenile by a legally authorized person.

Detention Diversion Advocacy Project (DDAP): Program developed in San Francisco in 1993 to reduce the number of youth in court-ordered detention and to provide them with culturally relevant community-based services and supervision.

Detention Hearing: Court hearing to determine whether a minor who is alleged to be delinquent should be kept away from his parents until a full trial can be held. Detention hearings must usually be held within 24 hours of the filing of a detention request.

Dismiss: To dispose of an action or suit without any further consideration or hearing.

Disposition: Phase of delinquency proceeding similar to "sentencing" phase of adult trial. The judge must consider alternative and individualized sentences rather than imposing standard sentences. The judge (1) considers evidence about the juvenile's needs, available resources, and other relevant factors and (2) designs a plan to meet the juvenile's needs and the interests of the state. Case dispositions include: waived to criminal court; placement; probation; dismissed; and other (fines, restitution, community service, referrals outside the court for services with minimal or no further court involvement anticipated).

Disproportionate Minority Contact (DMC): At every stage of contact with the juvenile justice system, minorities are overrepresented compared to their representation in the general population. With each decision—to arrest, to refer, to commit—the differences are amplified.

Diversion: An alternative to trial decided at intake to refer the child to counseling or other social services.

Due Process: The constitutionally guaranteed right of persons to be treated by the law with fundamental fairness. In criminal proceedings, due process means the right to adequate notice in advance of hearings, the right to counsel, the right to confront and cross examine witnesses, the right to refuse to give self-incriminating testimony, the right to notification of allegations of misconduct in advance of the hearing, and the right to have allegations proven beyond a reasonable doubt.

Evidence: Any sort of proof submitted to a court for the purpose of influencing the court's decision.

Ex Parte: A judicial proceeding (motion, hearing, or order) granted on the request of and for the benefit of one party.

Felony: Differs legally from a misdemeanor because of the punishment imposed if found guilty—imprisonment for longer than a year and/or a fine greater than $1,000.00. Felonies include murder, rape, kidnapping, assault, robbery, burglary, and arson.

Fifth Amendment: The Fifth Amendment to the United States Constitution guarantees the right of a defendant not to self-incriminate. A defendant can refuse to answer a question (by "taking the Fifth") on the basis that the answer might incriminate him or her.

Foster Care: A form of substitute care, usually in a home licensed by a public agency, for children whose welfare requires that they be removed from their own homes.

Fourteenth Amendment: The Fourteenth Amendment to the U.S. Constitution secures to every person due process rights to life, liberty, and property.

Fourth Amendment: The Fourth Amendment to the U.S. Constitution protects every person against unlawful search and seizure.

Functional Family Therapy (FFT): Family-based prevention and intervention program for high-risk youth.

Guardian: An adult appointed by a probate or family court to serve as custodian of a minor until the minor's parent proves renewed ability to provide proper care to the child. A guardian has almost all the rights and powers of a natural parent, but the relationship is subject to termination or change.

Guardian Ad Litem: An adult who is appointed by a court to act in the minor's behalf *ad litem* (in a lawsuit), because minors lack the legal capacity to sue or defend against a legal claim. The guardian is considered an officer of the court.

Guardianship: The power and duty of taking care of and/or managing the property and rights of a child or an individual who is considered incapable of taking care of him/herself.

Habeas Corpus: See **Writ of Habeas Corpus**.

In Loco Parentis: The role of a custodian, guardian or other person acting in the parent's place and stead.

Incarceration: Confinement of a juvenile or adult in a secured correctional institution.

Intake: Procedure prior to preliminary hearing in which a group of people (intake officer, police, probation, social worker, parent, and child) meet to decide to approve a complaint for filing as a petition or divert the matter from court.

Judge: A lawyer (in some states an elected official and in others one who is appointed by the governor and confirmed by the senate) who presides over court hearings and has the power to enter orders affecting the parties.

Judgment: A final decision of the Court resolving the dispute and determining the rights of the parties involved in the case.

Jurisdiction: The power of a particular court to hear and dispose of cases involving certain categories of persons or allegations. Family/Juvenile Court has jurisdiction over most juvenile delinquency cases, adult misdemeanor domestic violent crimes, and family civil actions, such as divorce and custody.

Juvenile: States establish the age of juvenile court jurisdiction; in most states, juvenile jurisdiction applies to those under the age of 18.

Juvenile Collaborative Reentry Unit (JCRU): Program designed to address historically high recidivism rates of youth exiting out-of-home placements in San Francisco.

Juvenile Court: Court that has jurisdiction (legal power) over minors only, usually handling cases of suspected delinquency as well as cases of suspected abuse or neglect. In many states, terminations of parental rights occur in juvenile court proceedings, but that is generally the limit of juvenile court's power over adults.

Juvenile Delinquency: When a juvenile is found guilty of committing an act that would be a crime if the juvenile were an adult.

Juvenile Detention Alternatives Initiative (JDAI): Program established by the Annie E. Casey Foundation to reduce reliance on confinement of court-involved youth; JDAI works with states to close residential facilities and to decrease detention.

Juvenile Drug Treatment Courts (JDTC): Beginning in the mid-1990s, courts were established to divert young people from incarceration through a regimen of treatment, court supervision, drug testing, and family/community participation.

Juvenile Justice and Delinquency Prevention Act (JJDPA): The 1974 federal legislation, last reauthorized in 2018, provides funds to states that follow federal protections on the care and treatment of youth in the justice system.

Master: A person appointed by the juvenile or family court judge to hear cases. Masters' orders may be reviewed before a judge of family court.

Mediation: The process by which court mediators assist parties in reaching voluntary agreement in domestic relation matters (e.g., support, custody, visitation) without a formal court hearing before a judge. Mediation is an informal dispute resolution process in which a neutral third party (mediation officer) helps litigants reach an agreement. The mediator has no power to impose a decision on the parties.

Miranda Rule: In *Miranda v. Arizona,* the U.S. Supreme Court ruled in 1966 that confessions are inadmissible at trial if the police do not advise the subject of certain rights before questioning him or her: 1) the right to remain silent and to refuse to answer any questions; 2) the right to know that anything he or she says can and will be used against him or her in a court of law; 3) the right to consult with an attorney and to have an attorney present during questioning; 4) the right to have counsel appointed at public expense prior to any questioning if the subject cannot afford counsel. The *Miranda* ruling applied only to people in the custody of police; it was rarely used for juveniles under the theory that they were not under police custody and were free to leave any interview. Some states did require that a minor be advised of the right to have a parent, relative, or other advisor present during questioning. In *J. D. B. v. North Carolina,* the Supreme Court ruled in 2011 that police officers who remove students from a class to question them about a crime must inform them of their right to remain silent. The justices ruled that age is a critical factor in determining whether someone would understand the freedom to walk away from an interview.

Misdemeanor: A category of crime for which the punishment can be no more than one year of imprisonment (usually in a county jail rather than state prison) and/or fine of $1,000.00. Distinguished from a felony, which is more serious, and from an infraction, which is less serious (e.g., loitering).

Multisystemic Therapy (MST): A home and community-based intervention program that assesses the origins of behavioral problems and works to increase pro-social behavior.

Nonsecure Custody: The physical placement of a juvenile in a licensed foster home or other home or facility before disposition and pursuant to a written court order.

Order: The decision of a court or judge directing the disposition of a case.

Parens Patriae: From English law, the legal doctrine under which the Crown assumed the protection of certain minors, orphans, and other persons. It is a concept used by courts when acting on behalf of the states to protect and control the property and custody of minors and incompetent persons. Translated literally, it means "the father of his country."

Petition: A formal written application to a court requesting judicial action and describing the grounds for the court exercising authority and the relief requested.

Petitioner: The person initiating a legal action, usually in a civil case.

Placement: The residential and/or custodial arrangements determined for a child by the court, which involve removing a child from his or her natural home. Placement may be in a foster home, group home, relative's home, or an institution.

Positive Youth Development (PYD): A program focusing on the ability of young people to thrive when they experience positive relationships and meaningful activities in supportive and safe environments.

Pre-Disposition Report (PDR): A report to the court on the youth's offense, family history, community involvement, and recommendations for disposition.

Probable Cause: A reasonable ground for belief in the existence of facts warranting some action on the court's part.

Probation: Allowing a juvenile found to be delinquent to remain at liberty under a suspended sentence, generally under the supervision of a probation officer and usually under certain conditions.

Probation Officer: One who supervises a person placed on probation by a court in a criminal proceeding.

Prosecution: In a criminal action, a proceeding instituted for the purpose of determining guilt or innocence of a person charged with a crime.

Protective Custody: In child abuse and neglect cases, the removal of a child from his or her home when the child would be in imminent danger if allowed to remain with the parent(s) or custodian(s).

Public Defender: An attorney appointed by a court to defend indigent defendants.

Referral: When a youth is directed to the court based on an allegation of a criminal law or status violation.

Recidivism Rate: The rate at which juveniles reoffend, are rearrested or are readmitted to correctional facilities.

Restitution: A process by which a juvenile reimburses the victim for any loss or damage to person or property.

Revocation: Rescinding a conditional release—returning a juvenile conditionally released from an institution after a violation of the terms of the release

Risk Assessment: A method of estimating the chances that a juvenile will commit a future offense. Factors considered include: the juvenile's age, the most serious prior conviction, any prior assaults, runaway history, substance use, school behavior, positive or negative peer relationships, and parental supervision. The assessment, along with the current offense and delinquency history, are considered by the court counselor in making a recommendation during the intake process and by judges in determining a sentence.

Sealing: The closing of records to inspection by anyone except the parties involved.

Secure Custody: The placement of a juvenile in an approved detention facility pursuant to a court order.

Sentence (Disposition): The hearing officer's written order as to how a case was decided. In a criminal case, it is the punishment to be inflicted for the offense.

Social Report: The document prepared by a probation officer or social worker for the family court hearing officer's consideration at the time of disposition of a case. The report addresses the minor's history and environment.

Standard of Proof: The level of proof required in a particular legal proceeding. In criminal and delinquency cases, the offense must be proven beyond a reasonable doubt. In neglect and dependency proceedings, and in civil cases generally, the standard of proof is by a preponderance of the evidence, a significantly lower standard. The standard is met if the judge believes it is more likely than not that neglect occurred. In some cases, the standard of proof is by clear and convincing evidence, a standard more stringent than preponderance of the evidence and less demanding than beyond a reasonable doubt.

Stare Decisis: The doctrine of precedent—adhering to the rulings made by other courts. The literal meaning is to stand by a decision.

Status Offense: An activity illegal when engaged in by a minor but behavior that would not be illegal for an adult. Examples include truancy, curfew, running away, or habitually disobeying parents.

Taken into Custody: The physical control of a youth who is detained by a law enforcement officer due to a violation of law or a court order.

Termination of Parental Rights (TPRs): A legal proceeding to free a child from his or her parents so that the child can be adopted by others without the parents' written consent.

Temporary Custody: The physical taking and holding of a juvenile under personal supervision before a petition is filed and without a court order.

Training Schools: Residential facilities for delinquent juveniles who are a danger to persons or property in the community and for whom no less restrictive placement is appropriate.

Transfer: Changing the jurisdiction of a case from one court to another. See also **Waiver**.

Valid Court Order (VCO): An exception to JJDPA requirements that allows courts to hold status offenders in secure juvenile facilities if they violate conditions that were established by the court for their initial release.

Waive: To transfer a case to criminal court by a waiver hearing in juvenile court.

Waiver: The understanding and voluntary relinquishment of a known right, such as the right to counsel or the right to remain silent during police questioning.

Ward: As used in some states (e.g., California), a minor who is under the jurisdiction of the juvenile court for a delinquent act or an allegation/finding of abuse, neglect, or dependency. Also, a person who has a legally appointed guardian is the ward of that guardian.

Writ: An order issued by a court commanding that a certain act or acts be done or not done.

Writ of Habeas Corpus: A legal paper issued by the court ordering a person holding another in confinement to bring the person before the court for a hearing on whether the custody is legal. It is sometimes used in custody cases where one parent refuses to comply with court-ordered custody or to return the child at the end of a visitation period.

Youth Transition Funders Group (YTFG): A group of academics, practitioners, city/county agencies, nonprofits, and foundations working together to support the well-being of young people.

Index